The Okinawa Way

The Okinawa Way

BRADLEY J. WILLCOX
D. CRAIG WILLCOX
MAKOTO SUZUKI

MICHAEL JOSEPH
an imprint of
PENGUIN BOOKS

MICHAEL JOSEPH

UK | USA | Canada | Ireland | Australia
India | New Zealand | South Africa

Michael Joseph is part of the Penguin Random House group of companies
whose addresses can be found at global.penguinrandomhouse.com.

First published in the United States of America by Clarkson Potter as The Okinawa Program 2001
First published in Great Britain by Michael Joseph as The Okinawa Way 2001
Reissued in this edition 2018

004

Text copyright © Bradley J. Willcox, D. Craig Willcox and Makoto Suzuki, 2001
Grateful acknowledgement is made to the following for permission to reprint previously published material:
AMERICAN MEDICAL ASSOCIATION: Partial reproduction of Flavonoid Intake Table (Table 2) from the *Archives of
Internal Medicine*, 1995, volume 155, pp. 381–6. Copyright © 1995 by American Medical Association. Used by
permission. CELESTIAL ARTS: Excerpt from On *Life After Death* by Elisabeth Kübler-Ross. Copyright © 1991 by
Elisabeth Kübler-Ross. Used by permission of Celestial Arts, P.O. Box 7123, Berkeley, CA 94707. THE LANCET
LTD.: Partial reproduction of figure, "Plasma homocysteine and cardiovascular disease mortality" by G. Althan,
A. Aro, and K. F. Gay, 1997: 349:397. Copyright by The Lancet Ltd. 1997. Used by permission. LIPPINCOTT
WILLIAMS & WILKINS: "The Tecumseh Step Test: A Valid Alternative," text and table 10.3 from *Nutrition, Weight
Control and Exercise* by Frank I. Katch and William D. McArdle; and partial reproduction of Table 7.4 from
Modern Nutrition in Health and Disease (1999), Part 1, B-7, C. M. Weaver and
R. P. Heaney, "Calcium," p. 147. Used by permission of Lippincott Williams & Wilkins. MARLOWE & COMPANY:
Excerpt from *The Couple's Tao Te Ching* by William Martin. Copyright © 2000 by William Martin; and "The
Glycemic Index of Some Popular Foods" from *The Glucose Revolution*, copyright © 1996, 1998, 1999 by Jennie
Brand Miller, Ph.D., Thomas M. S. Wolever, M. D., Ph.D., Stephen Colagiuri, M. D., Anthony Leeds, M. D.,
and Kaye Foster-Powell, M. Nutr. & Diet. Appears by permission of the publisher, Marlowe & Company, a
division of the Avalon Publishing Group Incorporated. MAYO FOUNDATION: Illustrations from the pamphlet:
Relaxed Breathing Exercises. Rochester, MN: Mayo Foundation for Medical Education and Research, 1991;
material from "Move It or Lose It: Three Ways Exercise Can Make You Younger," Mayo Clinic HealthQuest,
February 2000. Rochester, MN: Mayo Foundation for Medical Education and Research; material from "Social
Support Assessment," Mayo Clinic Health Oasis. Rochester, MN: Mayo Foundation for Medical Education and
Research; tai chi drawings originally created by Mayo Clinic, 2000, Rochester, MN: Mayo Foundation for
Medical Education and Research; and partial reproduction of Figure 5 from *Epidemiology of Dementia* by
E. Kokmen, C. M. Beard, P. C. O'Brien, and L. T. Kurland from Mayo Clinic Proceedings, 1996, volume 71,
pp. 275–82. Reproduced by permission of Mayo Foundation for Medical Education and Research.

Set in 13.5/16 pt Garamond MT Std
Typeset by Jouve (UK), Milton Keynes
Printed and bound in Great Britain by Clays Ltd, Elcograf S.p.A.

A CIP catalogue record for this book is available from the British Library

ISBN: 978–0–241–34560–3

www.greenpenguin.co.uk

Contents

Authors' Note

It is with great care that we, the authors, present our scientific data. Throughout this work we strive to bring to you, the reader, the latest in scientific information. While we make every attempt to bring you information from your own country, much of what we present is new and has never been measured before in non-American populations. Moreover, there are reasons why the terms "Western populations" and "Western diets" are used, and other generalizations about Westerners are made, namely because despite the fact that we are separated by oceans and borders, we Westerners tend to eat similar things and practise similar health habits. Bacon and eggs is still a more familiar breakfast in the USA, Canada, Britain, Australia, New Zealand, Holland and other Western countries than is miso soup, fish and rice. And Western diseases such as breast cancer and prostate cancer are still much more common in all Western countries than in Okinawa, Japan and Hong Kong, and there are real and powerful lifestyle reasons for this. Thus, when we read "American diet" or "American horomone" levels, these, in general, can also be applied to Canadians, Britons, Australians, New Zealanders, and many Europeans, especially in the north of Europe. So bear with us when you read the terms "Western" or "American", since the lifestyle differences between Westerners tend to be small when compared to "Easterners", such as Japanese and Okinawans. And let's try to learn something from each other so that one day we can refer to healthy diets and healthy lifestyles as just "healthy", which we believe will ultimately be a blend of both East and West, similar to what the Okinawans have achieved. If we can help to bring this about by our work then our task will be complete. *Nuchi gusui* – may your food (and lifestyle) heal.

Preface

The desire to live a long and healthy life, free of disease and disability and surrounded by family and friends may well be universal. In Okinawa, where the occurrence of heart disease and most cancers is a fraction of what we see in most Western societies, and the number of centenarians among the highest in the world, many have been able to make this desire a reality. When we first wrote this book at the start of the new millennium, we had a vision of *The Okinawa Way* as a wellness model for the world. In many ways this vision has since been realized.

At the time of our book's first publication in 2001, Okinawa was little known to the outside world. It was undifferentiated from the other forty-six Japanese prefectures (administrative jurisdictions) and mostly known, ignominiously, as the only place in Japan where a Second World War battle was fought, and since as an ongoing contentious site for American military bases. To our pleasant surprise (and great satisfaction) our book became a *New York Times* bestseller in the United States, was translated into multiple other languages, and helped millions around the world get on the path to healthy aging and longevity. Accolades followed from our readers as well as from the literary world. A nomination from *Books for a Better Life*, an awards program that honors excellence in self-improvement books, as well as recognition as one of the "Top Fifty Books of the Year" by both Amazon and Barnes & Noble, among other notable honors, were bestowed upon us.

The popularity of *The Okinawa Way* also had another side benefit. That is, it allowed our readers to visualize another side of Okinawa. A side that had heretofore been hidden to all but a few who happened to have the good fortune to see and experience the islands for themselves. Those who were able to delve deeper into Okinawan nature, history and culture discovered an archipelago of enchanting subtropical islands home to a myriad of unique plant and animal species, surrounded by white sandy beaches and ringed by beautiful coral reefs that rested just beneath pristine cobalt blue and emerald green seas. No wonder Okinawa was also known by some as the "Galapagos of the East"! The islands were also home to a vibrant, optimistic and resilient people, with a special health-promoting culture and unsurpassable *joie de vivre*. Unique art forms that included dances for the ancestors (called *eisa*) and unusual musical scales intertwined with ancient rituals and matriarchal shamanistic spiritual traditions. Still others were drawn to *The Okinawa Way* as they knew that this former island kingdom was the birthplace of one of the world's most famous martial arts: karate.

As gerontologists and health professionals, what fascinated us most about Okinawa was the health-promoting lifestyle and culture. Moreover, the further we delved into the general principles of the Okinawa Way, the more we realized that they were not really all that foreign to us but actually quite consistent with the latest medical research on healthy lifestyles and healthy aging. Other experts familiar with traditional Eastern medical approaches generally had similar opinions. Integrative medicine expert, Dr. Andrew Weil, who had visited Okinawa, agreed to write the Foreword to our book, and stated that the general principles of living the Okinawa Way are "highly accessible to everyone" and include: regular physical activity, a healthy plant-based diet, strong social support and a sense of self-responsibility for health, among others.

As we look back after the passage of time and the gaining of perspective almost two decades later, we feel a certain sense of irony as well as a tinge of nostalgia. It seems that just as so many seekers around the world are discovering the health-promoting traditions of Okinawa, the Okinawans themselves seem to be giving them up. Therefore, despite our continuing enthusiasm for the healthy Okinawan culture and lifestyle, we are also very concerned that Okinawa is in danger of losing the way. Increasingly we are finding that in its drive to develop, modernize and adopt the latest technology, many of the old ways have been rapidly fading and replaced by a lifestyle that is fast paced, busy and stressful. The culture of convenience has gradually crept into daily life on the islands and brought with it fast food, video games and inactivity. We are already witnessing the consequences in terms of soaring rates of obesity, diabetes and metabolic syndrome among the younger generations. This generation of elders may very well be the last to have known and truly lived the Okinawa Way, and therefore their wellness message is now more vitally important than ever. We hope that by reading this book you may find your own way to healthy aging and longevity, just as the Okinawan elders have. We wish you the best of health and happiness on your journey.

The Authors   October 27 2017

Foreword by Andrew Weil, M.D.

Everyone wants to know how to live as long as possible and how to have the good health to enjoy it. Whenever we meet especially long-lived individuals, we always ask about their secrets of longevity and healthy aging. Unfortunately, the answers they give are totally inconsistent, from daily walks to daily cigars.

We are also fascinated by reports of societies in remote parts of the earth that boast of unusual numbers of healthy old people. Most of the reports turn out to be groundless. One that may not concerns the islands of Okinawa, formerly the Kingdom of the Ryukyus, now a prefecture of Japan. In the West, Okinawa is known as the only Japanese home territory on which the Second World War was fought—the battle of Okinawa was one of the longest and bloodiest of the war—and as the site of American military bases. Okinawans, particularly older Okinawans, have experienced unusual social turmoil in their lives. Nonetheless there are more centenarians there than anywhere else in the world, and the Okinawan population enjoys much greater health and longevity than other Japanese. And the Japanese have the best health and greatest longevity on the planet. Moreover, thanks to meticulous keeping of birth and health records in the islands, there is no doubt about the veracity of claims to longevity, as there is in other regions that have been promoted as conducive to long life.

The fundamental question to be asked about this population is how much of the good health and longevity is genetic and how much is environmental. It is impossible to answer it definitively, but I am inclined to think genetic factors are not the major cause. I say that because research on aging is generally demonstrating the overwhelming influence of such lifestyle factors as regular physical activity and social connectedness. Also younger Okinawans, who are abandoning traditional ways in favor of those of contemporary Japan and America, are beginning to show the expected declines in health and growing incidence of Western disease.

I have made many trips to Japan over the past forty years, but I have been to Okinawa only once, in November of 1999, when I went to the main island to lecture, meet local shamans and healthy oldsters, and get a little sense of cultural, especially dietary, differences from the rest of Japan. On that occasion I met the authors of this book and first learned about their research project on successful aging. My experiences during that brief visit left me eager to return, to see more of the islands and its remarkable people, and to learn more about what Drs. Willcox and Suzuki call "the Okinawa way to everlasting health."

At first meeting Okinawans seem different—both from Westerners and from other Japanese. They look different, have quite different customs, and eat very different foods, including a great deal of bitter melon and turmeric tea, for example. But, as you will learn in this scientifically factual and highly readable book, the general principles of living the Okinawa way are not foreign. Indeed, they are highly accessible to everyone and quite consistent with the latest medical research on healthy lifestyles and healthy aging. They include getting lifelong, regular physical activity, eating a mostly plant-based diet that includes fish and soy foods with a great variety of vegetables and moderate amounts of the right kinds of fat, and enjoying strong social and community support as well as a sense of independence and self-responsibility for health.

This book is not about magic potions or age-erasing supplements. It is a realistic, very thorough look at a remarkable society that has mostly escaped notice by Western medical researchers. I congratulate the authors on doing such an excellent job of introducing the health-promoting culture of Okinawa to Western readers. I look forward to learning about more of the findings of their ongoing research. In reading the book, I was happy to discover that I already practice many of the Okinawans' "secrets" of health and longevity. I am highly motivated to include more of them in my own life.

Tucson, Arizona
January 2001

1. Okinawa—The Real Shangri-la

At seventy you are but a child, at eighty you are merely a youth, and at ninety if the ancestors invite you into heaven, ask them to wait until you are one hundred . . . and then you might consider it.

In Ogimi, a pleasant small village typical of northern Okinawa, a stone welcome marker stands near the beach. The marker displays the ancient Okinawan proverb given above. The phrase could easily be the state motto of Okinawa, a Japanese prefecture (or state) where energetic great-grandparents live in their own homes, tend their own gardens, and on weekends might be visited by grandchildren who, in the West, would qualify for senior citizen pensions. People are healthy, active, and appear youthful beyond their years. The word *retirement* does not even exist in the traditional Okinawan dialect.[1]

If it sounds a bit like Shangri-la,[2] that's because, in a way, it is. Okinawa consists of 161 islands, in a beautiful palm-tree-laden archipelago that stretches for 800 miles between the Japanese main islands and Taiwan. It has been called the Galápagos of the East because of its abundance of fauna, flora, and pristine rain forest. Okinawa also happens to be the home of the longest-lived people in the world.[3] People there seem to have beaten the aging process and the debilitating diseases that accompany the "golden years" in the West. Heart disease is minimal, breast cancer so rare that screening mammography is not needed, and most aging men have never heard of prostate cancer. In fact, as a group, the three leading killers in the West—coronary heart disease (CHD), stroke, and cancer—occur in Okinawa with the lowest frequency in the world (see following table).

RANK	LOCATION	LE*	EATING PATTERN	DEATH RATES (per 100,000 people)			
				CHD[†]	CANCER	STROKE	ALL CAUSES
1	Okinawa	81.2	East-West fusion	18	97	35	335
2	Japan	79.9	Asian	22	106	45	364
3	Hong Kong	79.1	Asian	40	126	40	393
4	Sweden	79.0	Nordic	102	108	38	435
8	Italy	78.3	Mediterranean	55	135	49	459
10	Greece	78.1	Mediterranean	55	109	70	449
18	United States	76.8	American	100	132	28	520

*Average life expectancy world rank.

[†]Coronary heart disease.

Sources: World Health Organization 1996, Japan Ministry of Health and Welfare 1996.[4,5]

To understand the magnitude of this health phenomenon, imagine a typical town of 100,000 inhabitants. If the town were located in Okinawa, only eighteen people would die from coronary heart disease in a typical year. If the town were in the United States, 100 people would die. Simply put, if Americans lived more like the Okinawans we would have to close down 80 percent of the coronary care units and one-third of the cancer wards in the United States, and a lot of nursing homes would also be out of business.

By 1990, Okinawan life expectancy figures had even *surpassed* the absolute limits of population life expectancy assumed by the Japan Population Research Institute. Limits had to be revised *upwards* simply to account for the phenomenal longevity of the Okinawans.[6] Perhaps it's no coincidence that Okinawa is located in the same geographical area of the East China Sea as where ancient Chinese historical texts described "the land of happy immortals" ... a "Shangri-la."[7]

Immortality in the form of everlasting youth and health is such a powerful concept that most cultures have stories and myths surrounding it. In the West, none can match the original fictional Shangri-la of James Hilton's best-selling book *Lost Horizon*.[8] In the thirties the book was turned into a movie starring Ronald Colman and became an instant classic. Hilton's Shangri-la is a wondrous, peaceful paradise accessible only through a portal in the snowy Tibetan Mountains. It's a land where average life expectancy is measured in centuries, not decades, unless the inhabitants leave—in which case they age and wither in a matter of minutes. The hapless brother of the hero belatedly discovers this sad truth when he tries to take his gorgeous 100-year-old lover out of Shangri-la. Just minutes after they pass back through the portal into the real world, the glamorous centenarian collapses and dwindles to dust before his eyes.

While Hilton's Shangri-la centenarians are fiction, Okinawa's are not. And while they might not look quite as ravishing as their movie-star counterparts in *Lost Horizon*, they look pretty darn good—many are amazingly young for their age. They have slim, lithe bodies, sharp clear eyes, quick wits, passionate interests, and the kind of Shangri-la glow of youthfulness that we all covet.

This, of course, isn't the first time we've heard tales of real-life Shangri-las. In the 1970s three big stories hit the media like a cyclone and captivated the American imagination. They were centered on the alleged discovery of super-centenarians—some claiming to be as old as 168—in the Caucasus Mountain region of the former Soviet Union, the Hunza Valley in Pakistan, and the village of Vilcabamba in the Ecuadorian Andes. They were lovely fantasies, but in the end the facts and figures just didn't tally.[9]

Let's look at the Caucasus Mountains claim first. The Caucasus region covers the former Soviet republics of Georgia, Azerbaijan, and Armenia, and supercentenarians were alleged to be abundant in the area—about 5,000 centenarians or about 50 per hundred thousand, one of the highest concentrations of hundred-year-olds ever reported.[9] The problem was that few of them possessed birth certificates. And although ages were verified and documented by gerontologist Professor G. Pitzkhelauri, head of the gerontology center in Tbilisi, Georgia, no central birth registration system existed until after the Soviet Union was formed in 1917.[9,10] Church or baptismal records were the most valued documents for confirming actual ages, but unfortunately, most churches in the region were destroyed in the early days of the Soviet Union. That left age at marriage, memories of outstanding events, or sometimes carvings on doors and walls to document ages—not the most reliable sources.

Nonetheless, an investigative report of these supercentenarians in *National Geographic* in 1973 generated huge media interest, and journalists scrambled for flights to the republics to see this incredible phenomenon for themselves.[10] This was a public relations bonanza for the Soviets, who were eager to promote the benefits of the Communist workers' Shangri-la. It was also a dream come true for manufacturers of American yogurt, since yogurt was one of the principal foods consumed in the Caucasus. One enterprising company filmed a television commercial of a centenarian mom pinching her eighty-year-old son's cheek and urging him to eat his yogurt.

The commercial was such a success that the company decided to go one step further and film a centenarian mom with her centenarian child; finding such a pair shouldn't have been difficult in a land of 5,000 centenarians. This is when the Soviet version of Shangri-la began to unravel. Despite a scouring of the region, no centenarian mom and child could be found. By this time, demographers, who study population trends, as well as anthropologists and gerontologists from the West, had begun to publish their own interpretations of the Soviet data. And it was quite different from the homegrown version.

The conclusion from the Western research was that no longevity phenomenon existed.[9] Indeed, age exaggeration was rampant. With no birth certificates, and with plenty to gain from age inflation, both for the Soviet propaganda machine and for the individuals themselves, the conditions were right to dupe even the most skeptical of scientists. The hoax was perpetrated on all levels, from the alleged supercentenarians themselves to respected Soviet gerontologists who provided a veil of scientific legitimacy to the claims.

There were many reasons for this. First, the locals love to spin a yarn, especially to strangers. This isn't meant to be malicious, but is rather a kind of game. Khfaf Lasuria, a tiny, spry, white-haired woman who swilled vodka and smoked like a chimney, was an expert player. On one visit she'd claim to be 130 years old, a year later she would be 140 years old, and the next year she might be 150. She tended to age rather quickly in her last few years. Some men had exaggerated their age to escape military service by assuming the

4

identity of an older, deceased relative; others did so to gain the respect that came with being the most senior elder in the village— Shirali Mislimov, after all, claimed to be 168 and he got his picture on a postage stamp. Perhaps some exaggerated their ages simply to please their former dictator. Longevity stories grew exponentially around the time of Stalin, a Georgian himself, and everyone knew he loved hearing stories of his comrades living to ripe old ages.

Whatever the reasons, while some robust and healthy elderly were found in the Caucasus Mountain region, none of the extreme longevity claims was ever substantiated. Indeed, overall life expectancy there has not been found to differ significantly from that of the country as a whole, which is *lower* than in the West.[4]

The Hunzakuts of Pakistan's Hunza Valley didn't fare much better. While the area has definite Shangri-la overtones with its breathtaking scenery, temperate climate, fresh local produce, and respect for the wisdom of its elders, age validation was even more problematic here than in the Caucasus region. There were simply no birth or death certificates, no health records, no census data—alas, no written language. The best documentation was people's estimates of their age at the 1892 British invasion or simply asking the *Mir* (king), who had to keep several thousand birthdays in his head. It was pretty flimsy data, not what a gerontologist would want to hang his or her hat on. Validation of claims was impossible; all that was left was observation and opinions—the weakest form of evidence.[9,10]

It was essentially the same story with the Vilcabambans of the Ecuadorian Andes. The reports of their longevity sounded plausible at first, and were even supported by Ecuador's census data, but they were shattered with an in-depth analysis of the village. In contrast to initial reports of nine centenarians in their population of 819— which translates into a centenarian ratio of 1,100 per hundred thousand, a virtual gerontological miracle—not a single centenarian could be found.[11] True, there were high numbers of elderly, but this is common in rural villages where young people leave for the city to seek employment. Calling Vilcabamba an area of exceptional longevity because of its elderly population would be akin to calling Florida a longevity center because of its high concentration of retirees.

And that brings us back to Okinawa, a very different kind of

Shangri-la. In this case, claims are based on undeniable scientific documentation. Okinawa's record of remarkable health and longevity is backed by twenty-five years of scientific evidence that we have gathered, evaluated, and compiled in the Okinawa Centenarian Study. We've medically analyzed, carefully examined, and methodically screened the island's elderly population, and meticulously documented our findings every step of the way. It's real science and real data, *not* wishful thinking.

In Okinawa there are none of the age-guessing games that inevitably proved to be the downfall of other Shangri-la contenders. Every city, town, and village has a family register system *(koseki)* that has been recording reliable birth, marriage, and death statistics since 1879.[12] And those records definitively show one of the world's highest concentrations of centenarians.

There are more than 400 centenarians in a population of 1.3 million—about 34 per hundred thousand—many of them still healthy, active, and living independently.[5,13] In the United States there are only five to ten centenarians per hundred thousand—a huge difference—and most older Americans are in far less robust health.[14] When Okinawans do pass on—at the impressive *average* age of almost eighty-six years for women and seventy-eight for men (another world record)—it's often classified as old age because no discernible cause can be found, despite autopsy examination.

The Okinawans have obviously discovered something quite wonderful. They seem to have found many of the keys to everlasting health that have been the quest of various cultures from the ancient Chinese to Spain's Ponce de León, to North America's aging baby boomers. They are living right in sync with the findings of evolutionary biology that tell us we were built to last about 120 years. In the West, on the other hand, we're way out of step. Most of us hit our peak between twenty and thirty, and then start to decline yearly so that by seventy we have lost 60 percent of our maximal breathing capacity, 40 percent of our kidney and liver function, 15 to 30 percent of our bone mass, and 30 percent of our strength.

If we had a pill that could change that—a pill that could lower heart disease, breast cancer, and prostate cancer by 80 percent; cut many other chronic diseases by half; and give us another good five to ten years—it would be one of the biggest medical advances of the century. And that's exactly what the Okinawan lifestyle does. Okinawans may not live forever, but they are able to *stack the odds* in favor of lifelong health.

And so can we. While there is not yet a way to reverse the aging process, it *can* be slowed. And the decline often attributed to "normal aging" is not inevitable. We can get those extra five to ten good years—and look younger, be healthier, and feel more vital while we're doing it. We can think about celebrating our inevitable aging instead of fearing it. We can have everlasting health—if we do what the Okinawans do, if we follow *the Okinawa Program*.[15]

The Okinawa Program is a unique approach to health and life based on centuries of Eastern tradition and wisdom. It encompasses the Okinawans' diet, their approach to exercise, their stress-reducing psycho-spiritual outlook and supportive practices, and their successful integration of Eastern and Western health care. And it is truly a formula for Shangri-la. In fact, just their diet alone is a powerful prescription for lifelong health. Their low-calorie, plant-based diet high in unrefined carbohydrates not only meets the dietary recommendations of the U.S. National Cancer Institute (NCI) but exceeds them, and more than fulfills the criteria recommended by most other scientific and medical authorities. It affords protection against most diseases associated with premature aging, including coronary heart disease, cancer, and stroke, and gives people the best shot at remaining slim and healthy for life.[16] This has been clearly supported by the scientific literature, including our research, and debunks the popular low-carbohydrate diet craze.[17] As you'll see in Chapter Three, most carbohydrates are quite good for you—and will not make you fat. Complex carbohydrates constitute most of the Okinawan diet, and the Okinawans are not only hale and hearty well into old age but maintain lifelong healthy weight as well. Plus, their diet is incredibly delicious and readily adaptable to Western palates—as you'll find out when you try some of our recipes in Chapter Twelve. So much for fad diets!

Okinawans are also ahead of the game when it comes to exercise. Most of us are aware of the health benefits of exercise, yet fewer than 40 percent of North Americans actually do it. Not so in Okinawa. There, exercise is a way of life, and the ultimate goal is to cultivate lifelong health through maximizing healing energy—a very Eastern perspective. Okinawans keep fit in all three components of fitness—anaerobic, flexibility, and aerobic—mainly through the martial arts, which they have been practicing for centuries; traditional dance, which many Okinawan men and women learn from a very young age and continue to perform; and gardening and walking. Their exercise connects organically with their spiritual beliefs. They believe that health and longevity can be obtained by nurturing your *ki (chi)*, or "life energy," and living a balanced lifestyle that is in tune with nature's way. So while exercise tones their bodies it also reinforces their belief system, which may just give them an extra shot of healing power. Like their healing diet, many of the Okinawan exercise techniques are easily adaptable to the West. In Chapter Six we give you some solid tips on how to get started, including some basic tai chi exercises that are easy to do but amazingly empowering.

Whether expressed through exercise or living patterns, spirituality permeates all facets of the Okinawan lifestyle. The Okinawa Program reveals a unique blend of Taoism and its profound reverence for nature, Confucianism and its deep respect for others, and native spirituality, where women are the keepers of the spiritual bonds between modern society and all things past, and elders are revered. Successful aging is actually celebrated with healing rituals. For example, in one wonderful custom called *ayakaru* it's said that by touching an elder, you can share in that person's good fortune, health, and long life.

The Okinawan philosophy affirms a faith in humanity, a sincere belief that deep down all people are good, and it emphasizes both personal *and* group responsibilities. Okinawans believe that if someone fails, whether through bad luck or for any other reason, there is an obligation on the part of others to help. This is implicit in the Okinawan concept of *yuimaru,* or reciprocity, a philosophy that is rooted in old work-sharing practices where all villagers cooperated to help plant and harvest crops and were dependent on each other for survival. In a sense, *yuimaru* is similar to the "help thy neighbor" ethic of the farmers of the American Midwest and the Canadian prairies. These kinds of personal relationships are powerful stuff. Our studies and other significant research show that they not only help to extend our lives but also seem to offer protection from illness. Fortunately, they are concepts that can also be integrated into our daily lives here in the West.

Another great strength of the Okinawa Program lies in its integration of ancient Eastern and modern Western healing traditions. It uses modern Western strategies for disease control and risk reduction while incorporating ancient healing traditions of the East, including herbal remedies and spiritual practices. It emphasizes personal responsibility for health, yet shows how to gain strength from others. It focuses not just on the absence of disease but also on optimum health, both physical and psychospiritual, cultivated through a lifestyle conducive to wellness. Essentially, the program gives you the tools to health, a road map for healing.

The chief argument against using lifestyle factors such as diet, exercise, spiritual practices, and other elements of the program as preventive health measures is that genes rule. It's all in the DNA anyway, the argument goes, so why bother? That contention is now totally passé despite the fanfare surrounding the human genome project. Scientists may have believed it at one point, but no one who has read recent scientific literature could legitimately argue this case. Over the past fifty years there has been a flood of scientific studies that show that how we live our lives—what we eat, do, think, and believe—helps determine our health and longevity.[18]

Our choice of lifestyle gives us the power to alter our life course no matter how poor the cards Mother Nature has dealt us. It's not the cards we get but how we play them that determines the final outcome. Case in point again is the Okinawans. When they follow the Okinawan lifestyle they break health and longevity records, but according to migration studies, when Okinawans are raised abroad or relocate and adopt the habits of their host countries—when they lose the traditional ways—they also lose the protection of their Shangri-la.[19] They get the same diseases and die at the same rates as the people whose customs they embrace. It's living the Okinawa way—regardless of where they actually live—that provides the safeguard against ill health and grants longevity. And there is plenty of medical and scientific evidence to back that up.

Our research indicates that the Okinawa Program greatly minimizes some of the biochemical and physiological mechanisms that can lead to disease, such as free-radical-induced cellular damage, glycosylation of cellular proteins, and hormonal stimulation of cancer growth. We'll discuss these points more at length later, but suffice it to mention here that the detrimental results of those mechanisms are significantly less common in Okinawan elders. Their way of life stacks the odds in their favor.[15] Our study found the elders to have incredibly young arteries, low risk for heart disease and stroke, low risk for hormone-dependent cancers (healthy breasts, ovaries, prostates, and colons), strong bones, sharp minds, slim bodies, natural menopause, healthy levels of sex hormones, low stress levels, and excellent psychospiritual health. Okinawans who follow the traditional lifestyle are simply very healthy people. There is obviously a great deal to learn from them.

Although tales of Okinawan health and longevity have been around forever—Chinese legends about the islands date back as far as the third century B.C.—they have, until recently, been overlooked in modern times. Some Americans were aware of the phenomenon. Okinawa, after all, is home to the largest American military presence in the Far East. But optimum health is hardly a military concern. And scientific grants to study some "obscure island" in the Pacific are hard to come by, particularly when the subject is a controversial one, such as disease prevention or longevity. The Japanese knew about them, but Okinawa has always been a world apart from Japan, isolated in the East China Sea and separated by linguistic and cultural barriers. And, of course, Okinawans knew . . . but health and longevity are the natural order of things to them. "Just another day in paradise."

Today, fortunately, the Okinawa Program is finally getting the attention it richly deserves.[17] When my brother and I joined Dr. Makoto Suzuki's centenarian study seven years ago, we landed in Okinawa with little funding—a small grant from enlightened scientists at the Medical Research Council of Canada, and the rest scraped together from our own sources. We simply settled in and started looking for answers. Since that humble beginning the study has grown into an international collaboration with funding from multiple governmental and nongovernmental research funds. The story is still unfolding, but many of the answers are in, and we are happy to be able to share those answers with you here.

Our participation in the Okinawa Centenarian Study always had one major goal: to unlock the biological and psychospiritual connections responsible for the everlasting health of the Okinawan elders, preserve the old ways—the Okinawa way—and bring it to the West before it was lost forever. This book represents that goal fulfilled. We have written it for people like you who are looking to make positive changes in your health and life, whether it's trimming fat from your body, improving your fitness levels, increasing your energy levels, lowering your stress, decreasing your risk for heart disease or cancer, or adding a sense of meaning to your life. We offer you the common links in wellness and healing that work for thousands of Okinawans, and that we believe will work for you.

Our aim is to put you on the path to everlasting health—to help you find your own personal Shangri-la. Our Four-Week Turnaround Plan is a graduated healing prescription that addresses all facets of the Okinawa Program, from diet and exercise to spirituality, social relationships, and integrative health solutions, and gives you the tools, information, and strength you need to integrate each one successfully into your life—and to transform it. We are now into the new millennium and it's time for a shift in thinking, a new approach to life, a new paradigm for healing, fitness, and diet. We believe the time is right for the Okinawa Program.

2. A Twenty-Five-Year Study

In ancient times the people lived to be over one hundred
years, yet they remained active and did not become
decrepit in their activities.

Nei Ching Su Wen, *The Yellow Emperor's
Classic of Internal Medicine, circa 2600 B.C.*

Finding The Way: Our Journey

When my brother and I first arrived in Okinawa we came across an
ancient copper bell, hanging in a little-used corner of the old prefectural museum. It is known as the *Bankoku Shinryo No Kane,* or
the "Bridge Between Nations" bell, and it used to hang in front of the
state hall of Shuri Castle, the former residence of the king of the
Ryukyus. The bell was cast in 1458 and bears the following inscription
in ancient Chinese characters:

> Ryukyu [Okinawa] is located in a favorable position in the southern
> seas. This nation has gathered the wisdom of Korea and maintains
> close, mutually dependent relations with China and Japan. Situated
> between these two nations, it is the ideal land *where the immortals dwell
> (horai-jima).* With its ships, Ryukyu acts as a bridge between the
> nations, and thus abounds with exotic produce and great treasures.[1]

Upon reading the inscription we were struck by the similarity of the
words to the ancient Chinese writings about a "land of the immortals." The Chinese had searched for a Shangri-la in the East China
Sea for more than 800 years.[2] Was this a reference to that ancient
paradise? When we told Dr. Suzuki of our "great find," he smiled
and told us that our translation of the ancient words *horai-jima* was
more complex than just "land of the immortals." He deftly brought
out his handheld computer translator and punched in the Chinese

characters. The literal translation was "a peaceful paradise, a land of immortals, a Shangri-la."

Now it was our turn to smile. While we knew that a fifteenth-century inscription on a bell hardly constituted definitive proof that such a long-lived paradise ever existed, it was nonetheless a seminal moment. We had an inkling how nineteenth-century archaeologists must have felt when they opened an ancient Egyptian tomb or perhaps how Richard Burton and John Speke may have felt when they discovered a source of the Nile, for the words clearly indicated that more than 500 years ago the ancients already viewed Okinawa as a long-lived paradise, an isle of eternal youth.[3] And now we were about to discover why.

Although we had prepared for this work for months, obtaining the necessary government permissions, gathering research funds, and performing extensive background research, our study became real when we began our fieldwork and met our first Okinawan centenarian. It's hard to describe our feelings that day, but for us it was rather like meeting a living legend, a survivor from the past, someone with the cumulative wisdom of a century—an old soul, if you will. He was someone from whom we hoped to learn a great deal.

It was a typical Okinawa summer morning as we prepared for our quest. The sun was starting to bake the countryside, but the air was still fresh and the heat tolerable. In our khaki shorts and open-necked, short-sleeved shirts we looked like stereotypical anthropologists—save the stethoscopes hanging around our necks. Okinawans might be comfortable walking around in the stifling humidity in long sleeves and jeans, but it was out of the question for two Canadians just recently arrived in Okinawa—or as we liked to think of it, the ancient Kingdom of the Ryukyus.

We met our research team at 7 A.M. and started loading our equipment into a van: syringes for drawing blood for biochemical and genetic analyses, reflex hammers for assessing the health of the nervous system, an electrocardiograph for measuring the health of the heart, questionnaires for assessing mental status and memory, and a cutting-edge heel bone densiometer, a portable machine that measures the density of the calcaneus bone (heel bone) and provides valuable information in assessing risk for osteoporosis.[4] We were well equipped for our task.

Over the next few years everything in our arsenal proved to be essential for studying the health of Okinawan elders. Each year we collected vital information for complete geriatric assessments, including blood biochemistry, activity of daily living assessments (ADLs), dementia screens, and dietary and psychosocial data. And each year we probed deeper for explanations of the Okinawans' health and longevity—explanations that could not be readily accounted for by Western science. One year we might concentrate on their diets, the next year on their spiritual beliefs and practices.

It was what you might call an *integrative* approach. We integrated what was important from traditional Western science with the Eastern intuitive, holistic approach. This approach led to some startling but essential findings that forced us to reorganize and refine our methods to delve ever deeper into the very essence of the Okinawan spirit. Critical to our success was Craig's skill as an anthropologist. Trained in the technique of *participant observation,* he was able to enlist the trust of the elders, even live among them. It was the best way to gain access to information that would have otherwise remained hidden from Western eyes.

Our first Okinawan centenarian, Nakajimasan (*san* is an honorific suffix attached to surnames, similar to *Mr.* or *Mrs.*), was reported to be in particularly good health, completely independent, and still farming—a century after his birth! He had lived in the same house all his life, as had his ancestors and their ancestors before them.

We came to him bearing gifts, of course, to show our appreciation for his participation in our study. And we were fortunate enough to be accompanied by an Okinawan nurse who spoke the Okinawan dialect. This proved invaluable with Nakajimasan and countless other elders throughout our study, since Okinawan centenarians grew up at a time when few Okinawans spoke Japanese. (Okinawa was an independent kingdom until annexed by Japan in 1879.)[5]

After getting hopelessly lost on the twisting narrow roads, we finally approached Nakajimasan's small wooden cottage. There on the veranda, sorting through a variety of gardening tools, was a sprightly man of about seventy. He was casually attired in a white tee-shirt and long pants, and greeted us with a wave and a winning smile. We naturally figured he was Nakajimasan's son, and asked him in our broken Okinawan where we might find his father. We imagined that the old man was quietly resting in the house, safely protected from the now scorching sun, probably dressed in a *yukata* (the loose kimono worn by males). But in Okinawa things are not always what they seem. The energetic man, dressed in the kind of clothes we North Americans might wear on weekends to putter around the garden, was not seventy, he was one hundred—and gardening was exactly what he was preparing to do.

After recovering from our initial shock and getting to know each other, we completed a full geriatric assessment, including an electrocardiogram. Nakajimasan was in outstanding health, with the exception of a mild cardiac rhythm disturbance known as a first-degree heart block. It is a mild slowing of the conduction of electricity through the heart and considered harmless and very common—it's often seen in the elderly. When we informed him of our findings, he exclaimed, *"Chaganjuu,"* which in the Okinawan dialect means "I am in perfect health!" And he was right. Except for the mild conduction delay and a slight variance in arm size owing to a childhood snakebite, he was utterly healthy. After a hundred years of use, *there was basically nothing wrong with his body!* And this was a common finding during our field research of the Okinawans and their way of living.[6]

The Study

When Dr. Makoto Suzuki first began his studies of Okinawan elders in the mid-seventies, with the support of the Japan Ministry of Health, he found an unusual number of centenarians to be in the same extraordinary shape as Nakajimasan.[7] They were lean, youthful-looking, energetic, with low stress levels and remarkably low rates of heart disease and cancer—even stomach cancer, which claimed many mainland Japanese. And, of course, they enjoyed the longest life expectancy in the world.

You'd have thought such a momentous discovery would have been big news in the West, but it went largely unnoticed for a number of reasons. First, only a few small research reports made it into the English-language scientific literature. Most of the interesting findings (more than one hundred peer-reviewed studies) were published in the

Japanese scientific literature or in Japanese government publications—always, of course, in Japanese, making them fairly inaccessible to Western scientists.[8] Second, gerontology and preventive medicine research were relatively new in the 1970s, and baby boomers were not old enough to get the diseases of premature aging. Research dollars were only just beginning to flow into this area of investigation. Nutritional research was generally considered unscientific and unproductive, not much of a contribution to science or medicine. In fact, when we mentioned the low rate of heart disease among the Japanese to our medical and graduate teachers, we were told, "It's all just genetics. Nutrition has nothing to do with heart disease."

Today research suggests that while genes contribute to up to one-third of the diseases of premature aging, we are responsible for the other two-thirds.[9] An entire discipline is now devoted to the study of connections between nutrition and disease, called *nutritional epidemiology* and led by our colleagues at the Harvard School of Public Health.[10] At last, the significant links between nutrition, lifestyle, and health are receiving adequate research attention. But it was without much fanfare that our research group studied the ways of the healthiest and longest-lived people in the world for over twenty-five years. The walls of Dr. Suzuki's research center at the University of the Ryukyus are now lined with shelves containing medical files, comprehensive biochemical test results, dementia screens, ADL surveys, nutrition surveys, and age verification documents for over six hundred Okinawan centenarians. It is one of the most comprehensive studies of the "oldest-old" ever undertaken. And it has given us many of the answers as to why they are so healthy and long-lived.

One of the most important things about our study is the fact that it is based on a new paradigm shift in Western medicine called *evidence-based medicine.*[11] Evidence-based medicine allows us to study any therapeutic approach without the hindrance of preconceived ideas or biases because it relies on rules of statistics and epidemiology to gauge efficacy or healing potential. Evidence-based medicine uses a ranking system for data based on the quality of the evidence. Randomized placebo-controlled interventional studies are at the top of the evidence hierarchy and observations or "expert" opinion at the bottom. This approach gives everyone a fair shake, whether the expert is the head of the National Institutes of Health or an Okinawan shaman. And it creates a level playing field on which all treatments, regardless of origin, are given a chance to be evaluated by fair and impartial means, whether it's a new drug for osteoporosis prevention, an ancient Eastern martial art, or even an Okinawan herb.

Although the Japanese don't call it evidence-based medicine, a similar open-minded philosophy has existed for many years in Japan, the country with the largest number of patents in herbal medicines. It has also existed for over two decades in Germany, where there is a special government agency called Commission E to evaluate alternative therapies, such as herbs, for their healing efficacy.[12] This philosophy is finally taking root in the United States, where the National Institutes of Health have established the National Center for Complementary and Alternative Medicine to create evidence-based approaches for evaluating alternative medical practices.[13]

There's no question that the public is interested in what alternative medicine has to offer. A study that recently appeared in the *Journal of the American Medical Association* reported that almost 50 percent of patients had used some form of "alternative" medical therapy in the previous year.[14] Although the definition used by the researchers for "alternative" was quite liberal, including the use of vitamins and massage among other fairly common practices, the point was driven home to the mainstream medical community.

The main reason so many people are consulting practitioners of alternative medicine is that they are dissatisfied with what the mainstream has to offer. People are tired of going to their medical doctors, asking about alternatives to standard approaches to health, and either being scolded, laughed at, or simply told "it's not proven." Physicians are frustrated, too. We are told by insurance companies what tests we can order, how much time we can spend with patients (usually too little), and that none of the alternative treatments are covered. In medical school, few of us are taught about nutrition, alternative medicine, or Eastern medicine, and if we spend too much time studying these approaches we will fail our board examinations.

Some say the answer to these problems is to boycott the conservative medical establishment and consult only alternative practitioners. But there are real benefits to Western medicine, especially in times of crisis. If you were in a car accident and needed emergency surgery, who would you prefer to have operate on you—a Western surgeon from the Mayo Clinic or a psychic surgeon from the Philippines? So tossing the baby out with the bath-water is not the right approach. Some then argue that alternative practitioners should be allowed to practice their healing arts alongside conservative practitioners, in a complementary fashion. This is where the term *complementary medicine* comes from, but this approach implies that the primary system is Western medicine and that these other approaches are somehow inferior, used only to complement the main approach. A better phrase would be *integrative medicine*,[15] the type of medicine that merges the benefits of all approaches into one healing art. It offers the best of all worlds. This approach, as you'll see, is part of the Okinawa Program.

Our research network got started in 1975 when the Japan Ministry of Health and Welfare (Koseisho), fueled by the excitement generated by Dr. Suzuki's initial reports of everlasting health in Okinawa, decided to fund the Okinawa Centenarian Study. Dr. Suzuki was named principal investigator. The study became international in 1994, when my brother and I—whose research areas span preventive medicine, nutrition, aging, and traditional East-Asian medicinal systems—joined the team. We arrived armed with Western scientific training, medical and anthropological research tools, and a strong desire to construct a paradigm that could explain Dr. Suzuki's intriguing findings. If the Okinawan elders were doing something that was contributing to their health and longevity, we wanted to know about it. We wanted to study it, document it, preserve it, and bring the ideas back to the West before they were lost and forgotten. Thus began our work.

My brother and I have spent a good part of the last decade in Okinawa studying the Okinawan lifestyle and helping to compile the Okinawa Centenarian Study. We found the island to be an extraordinary research field. Indeed, for any scientist interested in healing, Okinawa is truly a paradise. Since the entire study would easily fill a number of books, we've concentrated here on the areas that we feel would be most relevant to you and your good health.

Everlasting Health
Key Findings of the Okinawa Centenarian Study

If I had known that I was going to live this long,
I would have taken better care of myself.
Eubie Blake

After examining over six hundred Okinawan centenarians and numerous "youngsters" in their seventies, eighties, and nineties, we saw certain patterns begin to emerge. It became clear that the Okinawan lifestyle was providing some real, scientifically verifiable reasons these people were so incredibly healthy so far into their senior years. And they were reasons that could have a profound impact on our health and well-being here in the West. Let's take a look at ten key findings and what they mean in terms of health and successful aging—for the Okinawans, and ourselves.

Young Arteries

Findings: Elderly Okinawans were found to have amazingly young, clean arteries, low cholesterol, and low homocysteine levels when compared to Westerners. These factors help reduce their risk for coronary heart disease by up to 80 percent and keep stroke levels low.

Lifestyle determinants: Diet, regular exercise, moderate alcohol use, avoidance of smoking, blood pressure control, and a stress-minimizing psycho-spiritual outlook.

Dr. William Osler, the father of modern medicine, once remarked that "a man is only as old as his arteries." Truer words were never spoken and they apply equally to women. Our arteries are our life-lines. Anytime blood circulation is compromised in any part of the body, we are at risk of injury or even death. Arteries deliver oxygen, glucose, amino acids, hormones, enzymes, and many other nutrients essential for cell function. Some cells, such as those from the brain, can survive only for a few minutes when their blood supply is interrupted. The heart cells and skeletal muscles last a while longer—up to several hours—but the bottom line is that *without good arteries the game is soon over.*

Usually the "pipes" get clogged gradually over years, they narrow, and finally they get blocked completely with what is called an *embolism*—a cholesterol, platelet, and fibrin-rich clot. Other times the pipes break in what is called a *hemorrhage.* High blood pressure (hypertension) is usually a major culprit here. Sometimes a clot causes a break or sometimes the reverse is true. When we have diseased arteries in one part of the body, chances are they are diseased in the rest of the body, too. That's why people with cardiovascular disease are also at higher risk for peripheral vascular disease, such as leg ulcers. It's also why when you go to the doctor complaining of chest pain, or *angina* (lack of blood flow to the heart), he or she often asks you about pain in your legs. Calf pain when walking is a sign of compromised blood circulation to the legs, or leg angina. Two of the three leading killers in the West—heart disease and stroke—are directly related to how well our arteries function. And there are many other diseases that may also be related to a compromised blood supply.

One of the more remarkable findings about Okinawans is that, even in old age, most have very healthy blood vessels, especially the arteries of the heart—the coronary arteries. It's their coronary artery health that enables them to have extremely low rates of coronary heart disease and heart attacks—among the lowest in the world. What has been even more fascinating is that Okinawans have been able to keep their stroke rates low as well. Many populations who have low coronary heart disease suffer higher stroke rates—not such a good tradeoff.[16]

It's a well-known fact that most men in North America die from arterial disease, usually from diseased coronary arteries that lead to heart attack death. What is less well known is that coronary heart disease (CHD) is also the leading killer of North American *women.*[17] Women have about a 50 percent chance of dying from heart disease, about ten times their risk of dying from breast cancer. The Okinawans seem to have found a way to defeat both of these scourges. (More on breast cancer later.) Okinawans have *80 percent fewer heart attacks* than

North Americans do. And if Okinawans do suffer a heart attack, they are more than twice as likely to survive.[18]

These are staggering statistics. And if you're thinking that genes explain it, you're wrong. Three important migration studies (the Ni-Hon-San Study, a study of Japanese including Okinawans living in Japan, Honolulu, and San Francisco;[19] the Honolulu Heart Program;[20] and migration studies of Okinawans in Okinawa and Brazil)[21] all point to the same conclusion: while genes play a part in Okinawa's low rate of arterial disease (coronary heart disease and stroke), lifestyle choices are vastly more important. These studies show that when Okinawans and other Japanese grow up in another country and abandon their traditional ways, they take on the same arterial disease risk as those in their adopted country. Their genetics haven't changed, but their lifestyles have undergone profound alterations.

Most diseases, including coronary heart disease, are the result of both genetic and lifestyle factors. Mix these factors and then roll the dice and your *probability* of getting heart disease will emerge. This is how we do risk factor analysis. If enough risk factors are known, we can make a pretty good guess as to what your chance is of dying prematurely from a particular disease. For instance, if you live in North America and have a typical North American lifestyle, your chances are excellent that coronary heart disease could rob you of up to 17 years of life.[22] Moreover, the arterial disease that is the forerunner of heart attacks also clogs up other vessels in your body, which leads to premature aging. If you've ever noticed the skin of a smoker you've seen clear signs of premature aging—and you were just looking at the outside.

On the inside, damage to the blood vessels that supply the skin and other organs is even more profound. Two of the main nutritional culprits in this poor arterial health scenario are high homocysteine and high cholesterol levels. Of course, other factors within your control include keeping your blood pressure under control, strict avoidance of smoking, regular exercise, maintenance of a healthy weight, and eating plenty of vegetables, fruit, whole grains, and legumes (e.g., soy). Fortunately the Okinawa Program supplies all of this and more. Here's how it works.

Key Factors for Maintaining Artery Health

Artery Protective Factor 1: Low Homocysteine Levels

In 1995, when medical researchers were just beginning to take notice of it, homocysteine was *conservatively* estimated to cause 10 percent of all coronary heart disease deaths in the West.[23] Recent studies suggest that it may be at least as important as, or even more important than, cholesterol in our arterial health.[24]

We all produce homocysteine. It's an amino acid that is a by-product of protein intake, mostly from meat sources. It is converted in the body into an essential amino acid called methionine, or harmless cysteine, if we have enough B vitamins in our diet—folate, vitamin B6 (pyridoxine), and vitamin B12 (cyanocobalamine). How we process this amino acid is also determined, to a certain extent, by our genes. Those who cannot effectively process this amino acid have a much higher risk of dying prematurely from coronary heart disease or stroke. They are also at higher risk for peripheral vascular disease (e.g., leg ulcers or blood clots called deep-vein thrombosis) and possibly dementia (including Alzheimer's). Think of any disease where arteries are important and homocysteine likely plays some role. There are people who do such a poor job processing homocysteine (secondary to a genetic condition called hyperhomocysteinuria) that they usually die before the age of thirty from complications of premature arterial disease, usually heart attack or stroke. These unfortunate victims usually have a defect in the vitamin B6–dependent pathway for processing homocysteine, and some are cured by supplementation with vitamin B6.

But such conditions are rare and there is much good news. Scientists have discovered several different genes for processing homocysteine, and most of them do a good job, so we need not fret that we might have bad genes for homocysteine. But we should fret if we are not getting enough folate or vitamins B6 and B12, which keep homocysteine levels in check. People who drink high amounts of alcohol or have a poor intake of folate-rich foods such as green leafy vegetables, orange juice, or whole grains may not be able to process homocysteine well, and therefore may be at a higher risk for heart disease and stroke.[24]

Fortunately, following the Okinawa Program gives you ample levels of folate. The *Lancet* reported in 1997 that Okinawans have among the lowest homocysteine levels in the world.[25] Sadly, this might soon change. Our research showed that young people, who are switching to a more Western-type diet and leaving the old ways behind, have homocysteine levels that are rising to those usually associated with older age and high-risk groups.[26] This is just one more piece of evidence that shows how lifestyle choices are at least as powerful as genetics in determining health. As you can see in the figure below (adapted from the *Lancet*), lower homocysteine levels are associated with lower risk for death from cardiovascular disease (heart disease and stroke)—the lower, the better.

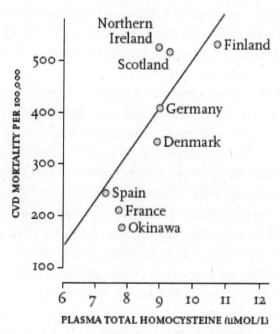

CARDIOVASCULAR DEATH AND HOMOCYSTEINE[25]

Artery Protective Factor 2: Low Cholesterol Ratio

Like homocysteine, cholesterol levels in Okinawa have traditionally been low—under 180 mg/dl. This is due to a life-saving blend of lifestyle habits,[27] including a low-fat diet spiced with powerful cholesterol-busting foods, regular exercise, avoidance of smoking, and a healthy, stress-minimizing psychospiritual outlook—all of which are part of our program. But this, too, could change, thanks to the same fast-food franchises and processed foods that are raising young Okinawans' homocysteine levels.

Compared to the Japanese norm, young Okinawans now have a higher than average risk for coronary heart disease, while older Okinawans have a lower than average risk.[28] We think of this as the *Okinawan paradox*. Dr. Hidemi Todoriki, a member of our research network and an epidemiologist with the Japan National Cancer Center, coined the term in the mid-nineties. Unlike the inexplicable *French paradox,* however, which involves a diet that should cause coronary heart disease but doesn't, the Okinawan paradox is easy to explain. The young Okinawans have begun to deviate from the traditional ways, while older Okinawans have maintained the East-West blend responsible for their long-lasting health. How long the older Okinawans can hang on depends upon how successful they are in preserving the old ways.

Like homocysteine, cholesterol depends somewhat on genetics. Some people can process it well and some cannot. Most do an average job. If you consume more saturated fat and dietary cholesterol, your blood cholesterol levels are generally higher. To compensate, the body makes more of the good cholesterol (HDL) to help take away the higher amounts of bad (LDL) cholesterol. (A good way to remember which cholesterol is good and which is bad is to think of the *H* in HDL as *healthy,* and the *L* in LDL as *lethal*—a bit of an overstatement perhaps, but it definitely makes the point.) The old saying in cholesterol research is "more garbage (LDL) needs more garbage trucks (HDL)." Some people have so many garbage trucks that no matter how much garbage comes their way they never get high cholesterol levels. This is why high HDL levels (more than 60) are considered a negative risk factor for heart disease. That is, it's a good thing! Of course, low levels (less than 35) are bad.

HDL is considered so important that the Framingham Study,[29] the study responsible for much of our knowledge about cholesterol and cardiovascular risk, suggests that your *total cholesterol to HDL cholesterol ratio* (or simply your cholesterol ratio) is more important than your total cholesterol level in predicting your risk for heart disease.

Obviously this is not as important to populations with very low cholesterol levels. With *no* garbage do you need *any* garbage trucks? Okinawan elders have low total cholesterol *and* moderate HDL cholesterol—the best combination—and, no surprise, they rarely die of coronary heart disease. Your best bet is to reduce your intake of foods that promote higher cholesterol levels and eat liberal quantities of cholesterol-busting foods such as soy foods, whole grains, and vegetables.

What's the right level of total cholesterol? There is another saying popular among doctors who study cholesterol: "No one with a cholesterol level of 150 ever died of a heart attack in the Framingham Study." In fact, heart disease rates rise steadily with total cholesterol levels from 150 to 200 and sharply above 200. Okinawan elders have levels generally under 180, and average around 170 in our experience, with a total to HDL ratio around 3.3—well under the 4.5 recommended by the National Cholesterol Education Program.[30] In the table below you can see that the lower your cholesterol ratio, the lower your risk for coronary heart disease. It's best to stay under 4—the lower the number the better. To calculate your ratio, take your total cholesterol and divide it by your HDL cholesterol (e.g., if your total cholesterol is 240 and your HDL cholesterol is 40, then divide 240 by 40 to get a ratio of 6.0; this gives you a moderate risk of dying from CHD).

CHOLESTEROL RATIOS AND RISK FOR DEATH FROM CHD

CHOLESTEROL RATIO	RISK FOR CHD DEATH
LESS THAN 4	LOW LIKELIHOOD
<3 Most vegetarians	
3–4 Most Okinawan centenarians and Boston Marathoners	
BETWEEN 4 AND 6	MODERATE LIKELIHOOD
4–5 Most American women	
5–6 Most American men	
GREATER THAN 6	HIGH LIKELIHOOD
6–9 Some American men and women	
9–25 Few Americans	

Sources: The Framingham Study and the Okinawa Centenarian Study.

One of the key factors in the rapid increase in life expectancy and better arterial health for the Japanese, the Okinawans, and indeed North Americans has been better blood pressure control.[31a] It's important to keep blood pressure in check, not only because it can break "the pipes" if too high but also because of a phenomenon called *shear pressure*. A few years ago this was a term more familiar to engineers than to cardiologists, but in the 1990s it became a vitally important piece of the arterial disease puzzle, especially in coronary heart disease. Shear pressure is pressure that forms at points in the blood vessels where blood flow is most turbulent. Think of a mighty river. In places where the flow is most turbulent, the river eats away at the bank. Eventually it will create meanders as deep and wide as the Colorado River did to form the Grand Canyon. The same process happens in your body's arteries. In areas of high pressure, small cracks appear in their walls.

Interestingly, your body uses *cholesterol* to repair the cracks—the same stuff that builds up on the walls and narrows the arteries. It's the body's plaster of paris. That's why some scientists believe that if your cholesterol levels are too low, then you are at higher risk for hemorrhagic stroke—the kind of stroke in which the brain artery bursts. They think some people may not have enough cholesterol to repair cracks. This is highly controversial because the body can make its own cholesterol if needed. The real problem occurs when you have too much cholesterol and your body liberally slaps it onto any small crack it finds; pretty soon the artery walls thicken and you are set up for a heart attack or embolic (cholesterol plug) stroke.[32]

So controlling blood pressure is a vital link in all diseases of the arteries. Luckily we know how to control it: maintain a healthy weight, a good diet, regular exercise, low sodium consumption, and use medications if lifestyle approaches fail. The power of dropping your salt intake can be seen from the Japanese experience. Government-mandated reduction of sodium (salt) in food products such as soy sauce and miso several decades ago had a huge impact on the blood pressure of the Japanese, and was one of the key reasons that stroke rates plummeted and life expectancy increased over the last few years. It was another triumph of diet over disease. Okinawans never developed the same taste for salt and consequently their coronary heart disease and stroke rates have traditionally been much lower—one of the reasons for their unparalleled health.

What Should Your Blood Pressure Be?

Until recently physicians were taught that it was normal to have blood pressure go up as we age, but now we know this is untrue. In fact, a recent study of blood pressure published in the *New England Journal of Medicine* tells us that for every ten points your systolic blood pressure (the top number) rises above 120, your risk for heart attack death increases by an astonishing 30 percent.[31a] The diastolic, or bottom, number only has to rise by five points over 80 to engender the same risk. Stroke risk rises dramatically as well. Follow the guide below and you should stay clear of the danger zone.

WHAT SHOULD YOUR BLOOD PRESSURE BE?[31b]

ARTERIAL DISEASE RISK	BLOOD PRESSURE
Optimal	Less than 120/80
Average	Less than 130/85
Above average	Between 130–139/85–89
High risk*	Greater than 139/89

*Based on average readings from at least three visits to your physician.

Other Important Factors in Arterial Health

This is not meant to be an exhaustive treatise on arterial disease, but after studying the Okinawans, it is clear to us that the elders avoid a number of other risk factors, including smoking, obesity, diabetes, and Type A personality (marked by habitual tension). Also present is a high rate of negative risk factors (factors that *decrease* your chance of getting the disease), such as high soy consumption and moderate fish intake.

The bottom line is that there is no special genetic protection for Okinawans. They have simply found the right recipe for combating coronary heart disease—and the formula will likely work for you, too.[33] The more research we do, the more obvious it becomes: a healthy lifestyle—adopting good eating habits, avoiding cigarettes, watching your blood pressure, getting regular exercise, and paying attention to your psychospiritual needs—sustains and improves heart health. This makes sense to most people, but it's the details that muddy the water, especially regarding diet. We are constantly bombarded with media messages that tell us a particular food will save us from one disease or another—oat bran for cardiovascular disease, tomatoes for prostate cancer, tofu for breast cancer, blueberries for every cancer. While there is good evidence for using these foods in a healthy risk-reduction strategy, there is much more to it than that. The truth is out there, as Fox Mulder of *The X-Files* might say, it just takes some deciphering.

The building blocks of a heart-healthy diet are vegetables, legumes (e.g., soybeans and other beans), fruits, and whole grains—high-fiber plant foods. But you don't need to be a vegetarian or fruitarian to be healthy; indeed, restricting your diet and lifestyle too much can also be unhealthy. Nor do you need to restrict your fat intake to less than 10 percent of your total calories. You can eat more fat—it just depends on what kind, as we'll discuss in the next chapter. The keys here are moderation and a healthy balance. It's important to find a good overall plan that's healthful, keeps you slim and fit, and ultimately makes sense. As you'll see as you read on, the Okinawa Program meets all those criteria. We have selected the most important lifestyle factors consistent with what we have observed in the Okinawans. These nonpharmacological factors are within your control and can increase or decrease your risk for arterial disease. Take a good look at the table below.

THE MOST MODIFIABLE LIFESTYLE FACTORS FOR ARTERIAL DISEASE[34]

EVIDENCE	PROTECTIVE FACTORS*	RISK FACTORS
EXCELLENT	Fish (omega-3 fat)	Diabetes
	Low body mass index	High blood pressure
	Low cholesterol ratio[†]	High cholesterol ratio
	Low homocysteine levels	High homocysteine levels
	Low saturated fat diet	High saturated fat diet
	Physical activity	Obesity (high body mass
	Soy intake	index)
		Smoking

GOOD	Flavonoids	Lack of social support
	Folate	Type A personality
	Moderate alcohol intake	Depression
	Monounsaturated fat	
	Vegetables	
	Vitamin E	
POSSIBLE	Vitamins B_3, B_6, B_{12}	

*Negative risk factors

†Levels of the different types of cholesterol (high HDL, low LDL) are also important, but the cholesterol ratio takes this into account.

Low Risk for Hormone-Dependent Cancers

Findings: Okinawans are at extremely low risk for hormone-dependent cancers, including cancers of the breast, prostate, ovaries, and colon. Compared to North Americans, they have 80 percent less breast cancer and prostate cancer, and less than half the ovarian cancer and colon cancer.

Lifestyle determinants: Mainly dietary—including low caloric intake, high consumption of soy, vegetables, fish, moderate alcohol; exercise habits—high levels of physical activity and low body-fat levels.

In medicine, we always look for connections. Is there, for example, a single disease process that can explain certain diseases such as cancer? Unfortunately, with cancer there isn't a single connection, but there are *common links* between certain cancers. Breast and prostate cancers, for example, are part of a group of cancers often referred to as *hormone-dependent cancers* because their growth is associated with certain hormones. This group also includes cancers of the endometrium (lining of the uterus), ovaries, and colon.

Theoretical models of how hormone-dependent cancers attack the human body have been developed; they follow a similar course: initiation, promotion, and progression. In other words, there is an event that initiates the growth of a malignant clone of cells, likely one of a number of "hits" to the cell's genetic machinery or DNA. A hit can come from many sources, including toxins from the diet, radiation, viruses, and bacteria. Scientists estimate that each cell in your body sustains approximately 127 hits per day. This damage can alter cellular machinery and might turn on a tumor-promoter gene and/or turn off a tumor-suppressor gene.

One of the first discovered genes that fulfilled this role was called *p53*, and it has been implicated in many different cancers as a tumor-suppressor gene: it protects against cancer.[35] If you are unlucky enough to sustain a hit to this gene early in life, you are at higher risk for developing one of the many cancers it protects you from. Not only can you turn off tumor-suppressor genes, you can turn on tumor-promoter genes—a deadly combination. The more DNA hits you get over your lifetime, the higher your susceptibility to cancer; it's like death from a thousand small cuts.

Once you develop a malignant clone of cells they may grow slowly or grow quickly, depending on their cell type and whether they get an adequate supply of growth factors. Prostate cancer, for example, generally grows rather slowly. Autopsy studies on men from different countries show that over 50 percent of men will have prostate cancer by the time they reach eighty years of age.[36] No matter what country you come from, you will eventually get prostate cancer. If you live to one hundred, your chances increase to about 80 percent. In most men, prostate cancer is microscopic in size. You have to dissect the prostate and look at cells under a microscope to see the cancer cells, but the cancer is there.

The key is finding what controls the *rate of growth*. Why do some malignancies grow to a clinically detectable size, spread beyond the prostate, and kill about 40,000 men every year in America, while in Okinawa prostate cancer is so rare that most men have never even heard of it? Cells will not grow unless you feed them, and hormone-dependent cancer cells feed on hormones. Starve them and they die like anything else in nature. Okinawans get 80 percent fewer hormone-dependent cancers (breast, prostate) than North Americans do because they don't feed the cancer cells.

There are undoubtedly a number of different genes involved with different hormone-dependent cancers, but the common link is that hormones are responsible for the growth of these cancers—and the good news is you *can* reduce your risk for dying from one of them. Hormones implicated include testosterone, estrogen, insulin, and insulinlike growth hormones. Let's look at common factors one by one, with an emphasis on prevention—the Okinawa way. The following table shows the profound difference in hormone-dependent cancer death rates among Okinawans, Americans, and people in several countries whose people are noted for their longevity.

HORMONE-DEPENDENT CANCER RISK[37]

RANK*	LOCATION	LE†	YEARLY CANCER DEATHS (per 100,000 people)			
			BREAST	OVARIAN	PROSTATE	COLON
1	Okinawa	81.2	6	3	4	8
2	Japan	79.9	11	3	8	16
3	Hong Kong	79.1	11	3	4	11
4	Sweden	79.0	34	10	52	19
8	Italy	78.3	37	4	23	17
10	Greece	78.1	29	3	20	13
18	U.S.	76.8	33	7	28	19

* Life expectancy world rank.

†Life expectancy.

Factors That Protect Against Hormone-Dependent Cancers

Cancer Protective Factor 1: Low Calories

No intervention has been found to be as important in overall cancer risk reduction as cutting back on calories. Whether it's cancer of the breast, prostate, or colon, or a host of other diseases, low intake of calories seems to be protective. It is also one of the few ways to extend life span in all species tested, almost certainly including primates. Early results from the ongoing National Institute on Aging's low-calorie studies show that primates on the low-calorie diet demonstrate the same health improvements seen in other species, including improved blood sugar control, younger-appearing, leaner bodies, and increased mental sharpness. Our research group has measured caloric intake in Okinawan elders and found that it is about 10 to 20 percent less than for the Japanese, who consume about 20 percent less than North Americans. That means that Okinawans eating the traditional way take in as much as 40 percent fewer calories than we do! Their low caloric intake has been noted by Dr. Richard Weindruch and Dr. Rajinder Sohal, world leaders in caloric restriction studies, whose report in the *New England Journal of Medicine* suggests that it is one of the possible reasons for Okinawa's incredible life expectancy.[38]

Low-calorie diets result in the lowered production of cell-damaging free radicals. When your body produces energy from food, it creates unstable molecules (free radicals, also called oxidants) that can damage cells. Your body has natural defenses, including its own antioxidants, and other defenses come from the antioxidants in your food. (More on free radicals later.)

This does not mean that we all need to become anorexic lest we be overcome by free radicals. Westerners are larger than Asians and need more calories. And nobody wants to go through life perpetually hungry. Eating is one of life's true pleasures and we should absolutely enjoy it. The trick is to eat well and be fully satisfied while still keeping the calories low. We'll show you how to do that in the next chapter. One of the keys, as you'll see, is to eat a high-complex-carbohydrate, high-fiber diet. Get full on low-calorie, antioxidant-rich, minimally processed ("whole") food. Eat more, weigh less. You can measure your success by how well you stay lean. And you can double-check that by calculating your body mass index with the formula in Appendix A (page 477). Try it. It's the Okinawa way.

Cancer Protective Factor 2: Vegetables and Fruits

A consistent message from the U.S. National Cancer Institute (NCI), the American Institute for Cancer Research, and many other world experts is to eat your veggies and fruits to decrease your cancer risk. More than 200 studies support this recommendation. The NCI has for years recommended "Five-a-Day" (eat five vegetables and fruits a day) for cancer risk reduction.[39] The active components for cancer prevention include vitamins, minerals, fiber, plant sterols (e.g., flavonoids), and other hormonal compounds and antioxidants. There is no better example of the success of these recommendations than the

Okinawans who in our nutrition studies get "Seven-a-Day" despite their low calorie intake and who, of course, have very low cancer rates. The take-home message? Eat more vegetables and fruits!

Cancer Protective Factor 3: Good Fats

Dietary fat was the original bogeyman when it came to hormone-dependent cancer. High-fat diets were the norm in high-risk populations. Again, like most of the original observations about diet and hormone-dependent cancer, this hypothesis came from comparing the high-fat American diet to the low-fat Japanese diet. Now we know it's more complicated than just the quantity of fat in your diet. It's not *how much* fat you eat, but what *kind* of fat.

High Intake of Monounsaturated Fat

Mediterranean countries have lower rates of hormone-dependent cancer than North America. Interestingly, the Mediterranean diet has been found to be *high-fat* but low-risk—a rather unexpected combination but one that makes sense when analyzed. The fat in the Mediterranean diet is one of the good guys—monounsaturated fat. Monounsaturated fat comes largely from olive or canola oil, and olive oil, as we know, is a staple in the Mediterranean countries. Remarkably, these oils are thought to be a protective rather than a risk factor, possibly owing to their relative resistance to oxidation, which is thought to damage blood vessel walls. Canola oil appears to be more protective than olive oil in this regard, as recent studies have shown.[40a] Oxidation turns oil rancid and makes it a potent source of cell-damaging free radicals—those solitary out-of-control electrons that attack other cells and are thought to contribute to human aging, as well as play a role in virtually every chronic disease including cancer. (Antioxidants counteract free radicals.)

The Mediterranean diet findings fit nicely with ours. We found that the most common fat in the Okinawan diet is also monounsaturated fat, mostly from the canola oil that they use for stir-fry cooking. The potential protective effect for monounsaturated fat against breast cancer was investigated in a study reported in the *Journal of the National Cancer Institute*. The results showed that one serving of olive oil per day was associated with a 25 percent lower breast cancer risk in Greek women. At least four other case-control studies now support these observations.[40b] The high intake of monounsaturated fat may play a similar role in the low breast cancer found in Okinawan women.

High Intake of Omega-3 Polyunsaturated Fat

It's fascinating to note that three populations—Okinawans, Japanese, and Inuit—that consume fish at least three times per week have a much lower breast cancer risk. This fact has been confirmed in a range of studies. The connecting thread here may be fish oil, which is rich in omega-3 fatty acids and seems to be the active component for breast cancer prevention.[41]

Most breast cancer arises in the breast duct tissue. These cells turn over faster than other breast tissue, and any cell that has a faster reproduction rate is at higher risk of producing a daughter cell that has gone awry, a cancer cell. If not detected and killed by the body, the cell can grow into a full-blown tumor. The reason that omega-3 fat seems to prevent breast cancer is that it changes the breast microenvironment into a less cancer-friendly state, perhaps more resistant to cellular damage. Scientists at UCLA are now testing fish oil capsules in prospective breast cancer prevention trials.

Okinawan women consume at least three servings of fish per week, which according to a study of ours results in three times more omega-3 fatty acids in their blood than is found in North Americans.[41] Cold-water fish, such as salmon, tuna, or mackerel—all extremely popular in Okinawa—have the highest content of omega-3 fats.

Cancer Protective Factor 4: Low Glycemic Index and High-Fiber Foods

A high glucose load—essentially high levels of blood sugar—has been linked to diabetes, and now there's evidence that there *may* also be a connection with hormone-dependent cancers. The connection lies with the insulin hormones. It basically works like this: When you eat high Glycemic Index (GI) foods (quick-release carbohydrates) and little fiber in your diet, such as cookies and white bread, the body immediately turns them into blood sugar (glucose) and shoots it into the bloodstream. Insulin's job is to take the glucose from the bloodstream and pack it into cells. If you habitually eat too many high-GI foods and not enough fiber (high glucose load), the body is forced to produce a lot of excess insulin to get rid of the extra glucose. This is usually compounded by our tendency to get fatter and less muscular as we age. Fat cannot take up glucose from the blood as efficiently as muscle tissue, so the glucose stays around longer, causing extra insulin secretion.

Your cells may then become resistant to the constant high levels of insulin and need more and more of it before they will accept any more glucose. This is called *insulin resistance*. Before long, the pancreas, the organ that has been producing all this insulin, gets overtaxed, burns out, and cannot produce enough insulin to meet the body's needs. Now you're really in trouble, because you lack insulin just when you need it most. This is called adult-onset diabetes (Type II), and is the reason serious Type II diabetics need to take insulin shots.

The link was made with cancer when several researchers noticed that diabetics seemed to have higher hormone-dependent cancer rates, and wondered if insulin might be the culprit. And there is a connection. Insulin and its cousins—the "insulin-like growth factors"—are growth hormones and they are linked to faster growth of most cells, including cancer cells. When your body is forced to produce excess amounts of these hormones, your risk for cancer increases. In essence you are feeding the cancer cells. The most strongly implicated cancers include cancers of the breast, prostate, and colon.[42]

Your glucose load and subsequent insulin response depends on the Glycemic Index *and* your fiber intake, so don't give up all carbs— just minimize refined ones by eating plenty of vegetables, fruits, and whole grains. Although most of them are high on the GI scale as well, when their fiber is intact they will not cause the problems associated with high glucose load or present a cancer risk. High fiber intake (at least 30 grams per day) has been shown to be protective against breast and colon cancer in several good research trials. Low-GI carbohydrates also are protective against colon cancer; this is an important direction for future cancer prevention studies.[43]

Remember, it's not carbohydrates that are causing hormone-dependent cancer. If they were, Okinawans would have the highest cancer rates in the world, not the lowest. Their main food for years was the sweet potato—about as high in carbohydrate as you can get, but balanced by its high fiber content—so the sweet potato ranks at a healthy low number on the Glycemic Index chart (see pages 114–18).

Cancer Protective Factor 5: Flavonoids

One of the most encouraging developments regarding nutrition and hormone-dependent cancer is that there may actually be foods that can cut your risk as much as drugs. Our study of the Okinawans provides provocative evidence for the benefits of an antioxidant and powerful hormone blocker called the *flavonoid*. The flavonoid family consists of many compounds with similar health properties. They all share the *flav* part of their name—*flav*onols, *flav*ones, iso*flav*ones, bio*flav*onoids—and they all seem to protect your health.

Okinawans may have the highest flavonoid load in the world. What we mean by *flavonoid load* is the amount of flavonoids in the blood. This is important because hormonal compounds that appear in high concentration in the blood usually have significant biological effects. The Japanese have a flavonoid load up to *fifty* times that of Caucasians, and the lowest rates of hormone-dependent cancers next to the Okinawans, who consume even more, as our studies have shown.[44] So the flavonoids they eat clearly get into their bloodstream where they can work their magic.

This has been supported by findings from the Japan Public Health Center Study, which found lower breast cancer levels in prefectures where women ate more soy products.[45] A recent case-control study of Australian women, published in the *Lancet*,[46] showed that women who ate the most flavonoids (mostly from soy products) were at significantly lower risk for breast cancer than those who had minimal flavonoid intake. This offers an intriguing biological explanation as to why the Okinawans have such amazingly low rates of hormone-dependent cancers. The evidence is rapidly accumulating especially for breast, prostate, and colon cancer, in that order. (More on flavonoids in Chapter Three.)

FLAVONOID INTAKE AND CANCER IN OKINAWANS, JAPANESE, AND AMERICANS

POPULATION	FLAVONOID INTAKE (mg/day)	CANCER MORTALITY (per 100,000/year)
U.S.	12.9	132
Japan	64.5	106
Okinawa	100.9	97

Sources: Hertog, M., et al. 1995. *Arch Intern Med* 155:381–86; Okinawa Centenarian Study; and World Health Organization, 1996.

Cancer Protective Factor 6: Moderate Alcohol Consumption

A consistent link is found between high alcohol consumption and increased risk for certain hormone-dependent cancers. Breast cancer is one the best studied. Over twenty case-control studies and more than eight prospective studies have shown that alcohol increases the risk for breast cancer.[47] The link is not in doubt. The risk is estimated to be as much as three times higher for heavy drinkers (more than two drinks per day) and increases with the amount consumed. Increased alcohol consumption causes increased production of estrogens, whether you are a man or a woman. And estrogen is the connection for breast cancer.

Even males who consume heavy amounts of alcohol increase their risk for breast cancer. Alcoholics have many telltale signs of increased estrogen, including broken capillaries called spider angiomata, palmar erythema (red hands), and gynecomastia (growth of breast tissue, which happens to both men and women). Men's breasts actually enlarge as their testicles shrink. For premenopausal women it's a double whammy, since they are already producing large amounts of endogenous estrogen (the body's own estrogen).

The link with colon cancer may be through folate, which is thought to protect against colon cancer and is destroyed by alcohol. Our studies of Okinawan women show that they are not big drinkers. Their average alcohol consumption amounts to less than an ounce of hard liquor per day (about one drink per day), whereas Okinawan men consume about twice that and suffer higher colon cancer rates. Moderation is the key.

Cancer Protective Factor 7: Low Body Fat Level

Like most risk factors for hormone-dependent cancer, high body fat is linked to increased production of hormones such as estrogen and insulin. Postmenopausal obesity is one of the strongest predictors of breast cancer risk.[48] The reason for this is simple. Estrogen is manufactured in excess body fat, especially the fat around the hips and waist. More fat means more estrogen (and more insulin). The production of too much estrogen from excess body fat can be a problem in premenopausal women as well. If a young woman is too obese, estrogen production can be so high that it even *prevents* ovulation.

The link with the insulin hormones is even more fascinating. We touched on one aspect of it already with insulin resistance. But there is another side to this story that involves a complex interplay between body fat, the insulin hormones, and estrogen, and it goes like this. One of the principal signals for the beginning of menstruation (menarche) is body fat, which signals the growth hormones, including the insulin hormones, to induce maturation. Higher body fat levels in young Japanese girls over the past few decades have led to earlier onset of menstruation, and consequently to earlier exposure to estrogen. This has been cited as a possible reason for increasing breast cancer rates in Japanese women.[49]

Our studies reveal that Okinawan elders have very low body fat. We will explore this in more detail in the "Lean and Fit Bodies" section on pages 54–8. All this boils down to the same message: stay lean like the Okinawan elders so that you can minimize your exposure to cancer-causing hormones.

Cancer Protective Factor 8: High Level of Physical Activity

We can never say enough about exercise. Exercise is considered so important in risk reduction for many diseases, including cancers of the colon and breast, that if you could package it in a pill it would outsell Viagra. Exactly why exercise is such a powerful prevention factor is not yet well understood. It may act through multiple means, including lowering body fat levels, which lowers postmenopausal estrogen production and decreases circulating insulin levels. Exercise helps the muscles take up insulin so that there is less around to stimulate cancer growth in breast or colon cells. Whatever the mechanism, several prospective trials strongly support its preventive ability. It may decrease your risk by as much as half, so our advice is to "move it"—practice your favorite martial art, take dancing lessons, plant your garden, and walk, walk, walk!

Specific Hormone-Dependent Cancers

Breast Cancer

Most breast tumors are not cancerous but consist of benign lumps that don't spread outside of the breast. The breast is made up of lobes, where milk is produced, ducts that deliver the milk to the nipple, and the rest is fat. The lobes and ducts are the most hormone-sensitive tissues and give rise to invasive "lobar" and "ductal" cancer—the two main forms of the disease.

Your risk as a North American woman is approximately one in ten of getting breast cancer in your lifetime. We can argue whether it's one in eight to one in twelve, depending upon whether you are white or black and how long you live. So let's say it's *approximately* one in ten. If you have other risk factors, such as a first-degree relative who had breast cancer, or you are overweight, or you are taking estrogen, your odds are substantially higher (find the NCI Website in Appendix B to calculate your risk). Breast cancer is so common in North America that if one of your sisters doesn't develop it, one of your cousins will. Everyone knows someone who has it or will get it.

In contrast, if you are an Okinawan woman, the chances are that *no one you know has it or will develop it.* You may have heard of it but never seen it—it is that rare. There is no need for screening mammography. You have to put 100,000 Okinawan women in a room to find six who will die from it. This improves an Okinawan's odds of living life without fear of breast cancer by more than 80 percent versus a North American woman. Even if you get breast cancer in

Okinawa, your chances of dying from it are less than half as much as among North Americans.

Some scientists may make the point that it's comforting to know that most North American women who get breast cancer do not die from it. This is not meant to give breast cancer short shrift, but to correct a widely believed misconception that breast cancer is the leading cause of death among women. It isn't; heart disease is. But breast cancer can be physically debilitating and psychologically devastating. And it causes approximately 5 percent of all deaths in North American women, about 50,000 per year—a significant number by any measure.

Most diseases have some genetic component, and scientists used that fact for years to explain away the great variances in Japanese and North American breast cancer rates. The same argument was made regarding heart disease, prostate cancer, colon cancer, and many other diseases that we do not completely understand. If we didn't know what caused it then, it all had to be "in the genes." Now we think that there may be common lifestyle links among people who get the same disease, especially through what we eat and how we live. There has been tremendous progress in understanding both the nonmodifiable or genetic basis of illnesses like breast cancer and the modifiable factors such as lifestyle choices.

In the genetic arena, scientists have identified several genes that have been implicated in breast cancer. Two of the best-studied genes are called BRCA-1 and BRCA-2. These two genes are thought to account for up to 15 percent of breast cancer in North American women. There are likely others, yet undiscovered, that play a part at different stages of the cancer process, including tumor-promoter genes and tumor-suppressor genes. Still, the simple fact is that *bad genes appear to account for only a small percentage of breast cancer cases.*

The initial evidence against genetics as the main cause of breast cancer was migration studies of Japanese immigrants to the United States. It was the same story as for heart disease. Move from Japan to the West, adopt Western habits, and you increase your risk for breast cancer. A Japanese woman, as she becomes acculturated to the West, loses her protective habits, especially her traditional diet, and within one or two generations her risk for breast cancer equals that of a Caucasian woman. This should serve as a huge incentive to follow the lifestyle plan we suggest here. We have touched on many of the lifestyle factors that affect your risk for breast cancer in the previous pages. Below is a table that illustrates some of the most relevant nonpharmacological lifestyle factors that affect breast cancer. These factors are consistent with what we have observed in the Okinawans and are largely within your control.

THE MOST MODIFIABLE LIFESTYLE FACTORS FOR BREAST CANCER[50]

EVIDENCE	PROTECTIVE FACTORS	RISK FACTORS
PROBABLE	Breast-feeding	Adult obesity
	Carotenoids	Alcohol
	Fiber	Late age at first pregnancy
	Flavonoids	Late menopause/early
	Fruit	menarche
	Low BMI	Nulliparity (no pregnancy)
	Natural SERMs*	
	Physical activity	
	Vegetables	
	Vitamin A	
POSSIBLE	Fish (omega-3 fat)	Animal protein
	Lycopene	Meat
	Monounsaturated fat	Pesticides (e.g., DDT)
	Omega-3 fat	Saturated (animal) fat
	Vitamin C	

*Selective estrogen receptor modulators (e.g., soy).

Prostate Cancer

The prostate gland, a walnut-sized organ located in front of the rectum and below the bladder, makes a high-energy fluid that mixes with sperm from the testes during ejaculation and helps nourish the sperm cells on their long quest for the elusive egg. Because the prostate tends to grow much larger over the years, mostly through feeding on testosterone and its stronger cousin dihydrotestosterone (DHT), it causes elderly men numerous problems, since it surrounds the urethra and sits just below the bladder. This is called benign prostatic hypertrophy (BPH), a separate process from prostate cancer; these are normal prostate cells growing larger.

Prostate cancer begins when a prostate cell begins to grow out of control (promotion) into a malignant tumor, which progresses into a bigger and bigger clump of cells that eventually can be felt as a lump on the wall of the prostate. If it breaks through the capsule surrounding the prostate it can travel to the bones (metastasis) or other surrounding structures, such as the bladder. Testosterone and its more potent active form dihydrotestosterone are thought to be the biggest culprits in promoting growth of the prostate. The more the prostate is fed these hormones, the more the cells reproduce, and the more likely an aberrant cell will be produced and grow into a cancer.

Prostate cancer is the most common cancer among men in the United States and many Western countries. In many ways prostate cancer is the male equivalent of breast cancer. It occurs in clinically detectable form at roughly the same rate (about 180,000 cases per year) and causes almost as many deaths—about 40,000 men per year in the United States. And it's just as devastating psychologically. The prostate stores about 80 percent of the ejaculation fluid, and impotence is a common side effect of surgical or medical treatment. One of the treatments is castration, a frightening thought for most men.

While prostate cancer is epidemic in North America and Europe, it's extremely rare in Okinawa—about 80 percent less common than in North America. Colleagues of ours in the Department of Urology at Ryukyu University conducted a study to look for prostate cancer and found so few cases they never bothered to publish the results.[51] Most Okinawan men have never even heard of it—unless, of course, they move to North America and change their lifestyles. Then, similar to breast cancer, rates increase dramatically.

Many of the same risk factors that apply to breast cancer apply to prostate cancer. One growth factor that might link these two cancers (and possibly colon cancer as well) is insulinlike growth factor (IGF-1). It's a hormone that looks like insulin and is produced in higher than normal amounts in overweight people. In a Harvard study published in the journal *Science*,[52] men with a high IGF-1 level were found to be much more likely to get prostate cancer. The message: watch your body fat levels.

Vegetables are a great source of prostate protection and are eaten heartily in Okinawa. They contain several components that can inhibit the cancer process: flavonoids (plant hormone blockers), carotenoids (e.g., beta-carotene and lycopene, found in tomatoes, watermelon, and probably Okinawan sweet potatoes), vitamin E, and other unidentified antioxidants and hormone blockers. We conducted a study to look at Okinawan eating habits and PSA (prostate-specific antigen) levels—a marker for prostate cancer risk. Total fat, saturated fat, and alcohol stood out as risk factors while protective trends were seen for those who ate the most soy foods.[53] In the next chapter we'll talk more about exactly which foods are best for your health.

Dietary fat has been extensively studied in relation to prostate health, and the conclusion is that specific fatty acids may increase your risk of prostate cancer (as well as breast, pancreatic, and colon cancers) while some others may actually be protective. Most animal studies support a link between high polyunsaturated fat consumption and prostate cancer. The culprit fatty acid has been hard to identify, but there is growing evidence to support a link between animal fats[54]—especially from red meat, butter, and dairy products—and prostate cancer. In the next chapter we show you how to modify and measure your meat and dairy intake so that you can reduce your risk of prostate cancer. This is an integral part of following the Okinawa Program.

The fascinating observation that prostate cancer risk is lower in populations with higher exposure to sunshine (ultraviolet light) has led some researchers to hypothesize that vitamin D is a possible deterrent.[54] Vitamin D is a hormone, so it is not surprising that it may be involved in some manner with a hormone-dependent cancer such as prostate cancer. Vitamin D is one of the few vitamins that the body can manufacture on its own—if it's exposed to adequate amounts of sunshine. This hypothesis has been supported by the discovery of vitamin D receptors in the normal prostate, as well as other evidence that vitamin D can modify cancer cells in a beneficial way. The fact that Okinawans are exposed to regular sunshine may be a factor in their low rates of prostate cancer. This, of course, does not mean that we should run out to the beach, slather on the oil, and bake ourselves to a fine crisp. Most of us know by now that prolonged sun exposure can lead to skin cancer—one of the most insidious of all cancers. Once again, moderation is the name of the game.

Although further study is needed to confirm the prostate cancer–vitamin D connection, it is comforting to think that a pleasant stroll in the sunshine may possibly reduce the likelihood of prostate cancer. Of course, keeping your dietary intake of vitamin D high is important, too. The foods that contain significant natural vitamin D are certain fatty fish, such as salmon, tuna, herring, mackerel, and cod (yes, cod liver oil, too), oysters, and mushrooms, especially dried shiitakes. Luckily, regular fish consumption is part of following the Okinawa Program (see Chapter Three).

A diet high in flavonoids—the hormone-blocking, cancer-fighting phytoestrogens found in soy and other legumes—is associated with a low risk for prostate cancer, although the reasons are not yet fully understood.[54] We believe that ongoing interventional studies will support the results seen in other studies: flavonoids kill prostate cancer cells, tumors grow more slowly or don't develop in animals that eat high soy or flavonoid diets, and human populations who consume high amounts of flavonoids are at low risk for prostate cancer. The Okinawans, with their impressive soy consumption, are at the top of the flavonoid table and the bottom of the prostate cancer table. (See Chapter Three for more detailed information on flavonoids.)

Lycopene, a carotenoid that is in the same family as beta-carotene, has received a lot of attention since a Harvard study[53] showed that it might protect against prostate cancer. Again, the mechanism is unknown, but its ability to block testosterone and/or its antioxidant effect may be partially responsible. Lycopene is thought to be a more powerful antioxidant than vitamin E, which also appears to decrease prostate cancer risk and seems to penetrate the prostate well, as evidenced by its presence in tissue samples from autopsy studies of the prostate.

One of the best sources of lycopene in the North American diet was found to be cooked tomatoes and tomato sauce, prompting Jay Leno to jokingly advocate the "pizza diet" for prostate cancer prevention. Okinawans have been found to have the highest lycopene levels of all the Japanese. Its most probable source in their diet is the reddish-purple pigment found in the *imo* (the Okinawan sweet potato), a favorite Okinawan staple. We are currently investigating this strong possibility—and are hopeful that in the very near future Jay Leno will have good reason to advocate the *imo* diet. Below is a table that lists the most well studied nonpharmacological lifestyle factors within your control that can affect your risk for prostate cancer.

THE MOST MODIFIABLE LIFESTYLE FACTORS FOR PROSTATE CANCER [54]

EVIDENCE	PROTECTIVE FACTORS	RISK FACTORS
PROBABLE	Carotenoids	Meat
	Flavonoids	Milk and dairy products
	Lycopene	Saturated (animal) fat
	Soy products	Total fat
	Tomatoes	
	Vegetables	
	Vitamins D and E	
POSSIBLE	Low calorie intake	Alcohol
	PUFAs* from vegetables	High calorie intake
		PUFAs from animal foods
		Body fat

*Polyunsaturated fatty acids.

Colon Cancer

The colon (also called the large intestine) is a long, muscular tube that connects the small intestine to the anus. Colon cancer is arguably the best understood of the hormone-dependent cancers in terms of process. Initiation, promotion, and progression can be clearly illustrated in colon cancer. A normal colon cell can turn abnormal after a number of dietary and other environmental insults damage its genetic machinery (initiation); it begins to rapidly reproduce itself (promotion), given an adequate supply of growth factors (such as insulin); and its progeny grow together into a lump called a polyp, which can quickly grow through the colon wall (progression) and spread (metastasize) to other parts of the body.

Cancer of the colon is the second most common cancer in the United States, affecting approximately *130,000* people yearly, mostly people over the age of fifty. It is an insidious cancer that rarely causes symptoms until it's too late. These might include a change in bowel habits, such as constipation or diarrhea, bloody, darker, or thinner stools than usual, or frequent gas pains.

Colon cancer is another cancer that has been associated with diet and other modifiable factors. It's seen at less than half the U.S. frequency in Okinawa. Lately, there has been a plethora of studies on colon cancer, and the genetic basis for this cancer is becoming clearer. Some genes make colon cancer a certainty before the age of forty. Usually these are obvious, since most likely a first-degree relative (mother, father, sister, brother) has already had the cancer.

With the majority of us, it is again an interaction of genes and environment, and you can significantly alter your risk through lifestyle measures. More good news is that colon cancer is easy to detect in its early stages with regular screening tests, such as sigmoidoscopies and colonoscopies and now a new noninvasive test called a virtual colonoscopy (a type of CT scan), and is susceptible to protective measures such as those we list in the table on page 47.

Fiber has long held a good reputation as a colon protector. However, two recent interventional studies called into question the long-held belief that fiber protects against colon cancer. While these studies were important, differences in fiber intake between groups were not that large and the studies were only of relatively short duration, so they don't knock out the fiber theory. In fact, the benefits of fiber were reconfirmed recently when researchers at Harvard University discovered that a fiber-derived enzyme turns on a protein that blocks the colon cancer process.[55] There is also the possibility that other substances found in grains that are closely linked to fiber, such as lignans, may play a more important role than we think. Clearly, the jury is still out and we have a lot to learn. The take-home message is that high-fiber whole grains (low glucose load), vegetables, fruits, and soy are still the key to colon cancer prevention along with regular colon screens after age fifty. The following table lists the most important lifestyle factors within your control that can affect your risk for colon cancer.

THE MOST MODIFIABLE LIFESTYLE FACTORS FOR COLON CANCER[56]

EVIDENCE	PROTECTIVE FACTORS	RISK FACTORS
EXCELLENT	Physical activity	
	Vegetables	
PROBABLE	Carotenoids	Alcohol
	Fiber	Obesity
	Flavonoids and lignans	Overcooked or processed
	High folate intake	meat
	Low GI foods (starch)	Red meat
		Smoking
		Total or saturated (animal) fat
POSSIBLE	Cereals	High calorie intake
	Coffee	Insulin/IGF-1 (insulinlike growth factor)
	Vitamins C, D, E	Iron

Ovarian Cancer

The ovaries are two almond-sized glands located on either side of the uterus and connected to it by passageways called fallopian tubes. Each month one or the other produces an egg, which travels down the fallopian tube to the uterus for potential fertilization. The ovaries also produce the female sex hormones estrogen and progesterone. Ovarian cancer occurs when a normal ovarian cell turns abnormal and begins to reproduce and grow into a tumor, depending on how rich the local environment is in hormonal growth factors.

Ovarian cancer affects about 23,000 American women every year. It is an especially worrisome cancer for most women, not because it occurs with high frequency—it doesn't—but because by the time it's detected it's usually too late to do anything about it. It grows silently, with few, if any symptoms, and usually appears at an advanced stage with poor treatment options. Death can be as high as 80 percent after it's first discovered. Early detection is key, but even the tumor markers that we currently possess, such as the blood test CA-125, are not very good screening tools for early detection. The "sensitivity" or ability of the test to detect the cancer is just not that high and results are not always reliable.

We do know that ovarian cancer tends to occur more in women who are at higher risk for breast cancer, and thus may be triggered or prevented by similar factors. Thus, once again, by following a low-risk lifestyle, such as the Okinawa Program, you will at least stack the odds in favor of prevention. Listed in the table below are the lifestyle factors over which you actually have some control.

THE MOST MODIFIABLE LIFESTYLE FACTORS FOR OVARIAN CANCER[57]

EVIDENCE	PROTECTIVE FACTORS	RISK FACTORS
PROBABLE	Breast-feeding	Estrogen
	Oral contraceptives*	Nulliparity[†]
	Vegetables/fruits	Obesity
POSSIBLE	Carotenoids	Milk products
	Fish	Saturated (animal) fat
	Flavonoids	Total fat intake

*Warning: Smoking while taking oral contraceptives greatly increases your risk for heart disease and stroke.
[†]Not having children.

A Note On Screening

We concentrate here on lifestyle factors, particularly those seen in our studies of the Okinawans, but medical tests for cancer screening are very important for all of us and save lives. Particularly effective screening strategies have been developed for colon, breast, and cervical cancer (not thought to be hormone-dependent). Screening tests are also available for prostate cancer. (See Appendix A, page 473, for further details.)

A Note On Other Cancers

No study of Eastern health would be complete without looking at stomach cancer, which has been a major scourge and is responsible for most cancer deaths in Japan and many in Korea, China, and other parts of Asia. See the reference section for more details how the Okinawans minimized their risk for this and other important cancers.[58]

Strong Bones

Finding: Okinawans have strong bones and about half the risk for hip fractures of North Americans.

Lifestyle determinants: Diet—especially flavonoids—exercise habits, minimal alcohol and tobacco use.

Osteoporosis is the term applied to bones that have lost large amounts of calcium for a multitude of reasons, including low calcium intake, lack of weight-bearing exercise, and aging. Medically, osteopenia (literally, "poverty of bone") is the bottom 5 percent of the bone density scale (which is based on healthy, young bones at low fracture risk), and osteoporosis is the bottom 2.5 percent of the bone density scale.

Bone is living tissue constantly being remodeled by bone cells called osteoblasts (which build bone) and osteoclasts (which clear away bone). This process depends on the physical demands we place on our bodies and its supply of nutrients, such as calcium. It takes between thirty and eighty weeks to complete a bone cycle in which the majority of bone has been remodeled (for better or worse). When we are young we build enough bone to last decades, and, indeed, we can lose calcium in our bones and skeleton for many years before the bones weaken enough to cause fractures in weight-bearing areas, especially in the hip, spine, or wrist. But by age sixty-five almost 25 percent of all U.S. women (especially Caucasians) have one or more fractures of the spine or hips. Men suffer too, but at about half the rate as women.

A particularly impressive finding in our studies was the Okinawans' low hip fracture rate, an indirect measurement of the strength and overall health of their bones. Our bone health is partly determined by our peak bone density, which is usually reached by the early twenties. Most of us start losing bone calcium in our thirties and continue losing it until the end of our lives. In women, this occurs particularly fast after menopause, when the protective effects of the body's estrogen are lost. Bone density is usually measured in the spine, hips, or wrists by a special type of X ray called a DXA—dual scan energy X-ray absorptiometry. People with osteoporosis, or "thin bones," are at high risk for fracture. Hip fracture is one of the worst fears of the elderly because at advanced ages it means hospital convalescence at best, and at worst can result in death from complications.

An excellent cross-cultural study on hip fractures published by colleagues of ours showed that Okinawans have about 20 percent fewer hip fractures than do mainland Japanese, and Japanese have about 40 percent fewer hip fractures than Americans.[59] Our research on Okinawan elders showed that their bone density, when adjusted for body size, is similar to that of Americans, and like the rest of us they continue to lose bone mass as they get older, but possibly at a slower rate. And this may be the key, according to a study our group conducted in 1995.[60] Our research suggests that several protective factors likely play a role, including high calcium intake by Okinawans in both food and their natural drinking water, high vitamin D levels from exposure to sunlight, increased physical activity, especially at older ages; and again that ubiquitous compound, the flavonoid, is a strong contender for another Okinawan health benefit, this time bone health.

While still early, the evidence is mounting that natural estrogens, especially flavonoids, may increase bone density. And you don't have to eat buckets of soybeans to get an effect. A recent cohort study of forty-three women by Dr. Ken Setchell of the University of Cincinnati found that 60 to 70 mg of flavonoids per day—the amount in three glasses of soy milk or three handfuls of soy nuts—resulted in significant increases in osteocalcin, a blood marker of bone formation.[61] Bone protective effects were also reported by researchers at the University of Washington, who conducted a study of flavonoid intake in 267 older Japanese Americans. Those in the highest intake group had 8 percent higher bone density at the hip and 13 percent higher bone density at the lumbar spine than those who had the lowest flavonoid intake.[62] When you consider that a 2 to 3 percent higher bone density can shift you from a high- to a moderate-risk group, these numbers are all the more remarkable. Irrefutable evidence that flavonoids in soy are bone protectors came from an Iowa State University study.[63] The dietary plan we provide in Chapter Ten provides 100 mg per day of flavonoids in an Eastern or Western approach to following the Okinawa Program.

The most important determinant of bone density in women is thought to be the body's own estrogen (endogenous estrogen). While most researchers have generally accepted this, new research, much of it from the Mayo Clinic, strongly suggests that estrogen may be the major determinant of bone density in men as well—not testosterone, as previously thought. We have analyzed the reasons for the bone health of Okinawans and believe that the following factors are playing a role in staving off the ravages of osteoporosis in Okinawans. We think they will help improve your bone health as well.

THE MOST MODIFIABLE LIFESTYLE FACTORS FOR OSTEOPOROTIC FRACTURE [64]

EVIDENCE	PROTECTIVE FACTORS	RISK FACTORS
EXCELLENT	Calcium/vitamin D	Early menopause (age < 45)
	Estrogen	Low body weight
	Physical activity	Smoking
POSSIBLE	Green, leafy vegetables	High alcohol consumption
	High-calcium foods	High protein intake
	Magnesium	High sodium intake
	Natural SERMs	
	(e.g., flavonoids)	

Sharp Minds

Findings: Most Okinawans have remarkable mental clarity even over the age of one hundred.

Lifestyle determinants: Dietary habits, which lead to clean arteries and better blood circulation to the brain; high dietary antioxidant intake; active engagement with life (lifelong learning).

Although a certain amount of mental decline is inevitable with aging, we've found the brain to have amazing resilience. And science continues to shatter many myths of the aging brain. We no longer think, for instance, that the number of brain cells is fixed in adulthood with no possibility for them to divide or be replaced. This change in decades-old medical thinking occurred in the early 1990s because a graduate student at the University of Calgary added a healthy cocktail of nerve growth factors to a petri dish containing old mouse brain cells and the unthinkable happened. They began to grow and divide—like the brain cells of younger mice.[65] This caused a major shift in attitudes toward the aging brain and rekindled the hope that we will find a cure for Alzheimer's disease and other dementias (memory loss) seen in the elderly.

One of the main causes of memory loss is dementia of the Alzheimer's type, which is characterized by the loss of brain cells (neurons) from the parts of the brain that deal with memory. Other non-Alzheimer's dementias are thought to be caused by repeated small or large strokes, and are characterized by a dramatic step-by-step decline in mental function, as opposed to the more gradual decline of Alzheimer's. Interestingly, all forms of dementia—whether they are Alzheimer-related or not—may be linked to common risk factors such as those that cause arterial disease. This is a shift in thinking that would have been considered radical as recently as five years ago. We currently divide dementia into two separate classes—vascular and nonvascular (mostly Alzheimer's disease)—and research suggests that both may involve diseases of the blood vessels. And one of the principal artery-clogging villains in this scenario may just be homocysteine, the toxic amino acid that directly damages the walls of arteries and veins, and that we've previously discussed in relation to heart disease. Others may include cholesterol and high blood pressure.

Your risk for dementia varies widely, according to your genetics and your lifestyle, and according to whose data you believe. Studies show that by your mid-nineties it varies from a low of 40 percent to a high of 77 percent—unless you live in Okinawa.[66] Our regular dementia screens of Okinawan elders showed that many of them retained remarkable clarity even over the age of one hundred. Population surveys also suggest that the dementia rate is fairly low among the Okinawan elderly, compared to other elderly populations (see the figure on page 54). One study, published in the *International Journal of Epidemiology*, showed a lower overall prevalence of dementia in Okinawa (6.7 percent) versus Canada (7.8 percent) and Italy (8.4 percent), despite the fact that so much of the Okinawan population is elderly.[66] Our research group participated in the initial planning for this study, conducted by the Department of Psychiatry at the University of the Ryukyus. It found that even into their late nineties Okinawans suffered lower dementia rates than reported for comparable populations in the United States and elsewhere—about 80 percent of men and 60 percent of women were cognitively intact, compared to less than 40 percent reported for most American and European populations.[67] Two good cross-cultural studies of dementia also show a lower rate of Alzheimer-related dementia in subjects who are living a more traditional Japanese lifestyle and eating more Japanese food, even if they live in America.[68] On the whole, the evidence suggests that the Okinawan lifestyle is somehow protective against dementia, most probably through a diet more friendly to the brain's arteries—that is, one that keeps cholesterol low, homocysteine low, and antioxidants high.

One recent study showed that taking the antioxidant vitamin E was actually more powerful in delaying the onset of dementia than one of the new drugs developed to treat Alzheimer's disease. Following this lead, we studied vitamin E levels in the elders and found that their blood level of vitamin E was 30 percent higher than that of Americans.[69] The elders' diets are likely responsible, possibly owing to their passion for sweet potatoes, other foods which are high in vitamin E, and their use of vitamin E–rich cooking oils.

Most of us have also heard of the potential protective effect of the herb ginkgo biloba against dementia. It's thought to decrease free-radical damage to the brain and increase the flow of blood to vital areas responsible for memory. Scientists have found support in several randomized, protective studies and ginkgo is already on the German Commission E list as a safe treatment for dementia.

Interestingly, ginkgo nuts have been a common food in Japan for centuries and are a common find in the typical Japanese pantry.

Keep in mind, however, that current therapies including vitamin E, ginkgo, and the medication Aricept only delay the progression of dementia by about six to twelve months. The best potential for natural therapies is early on—for prevention—and to stick to the protective factors we outlined previously for arterial health, since your body's arteries are crucial for maintaining the health of your mind as well as your body. Take a look below at a summary of some of the best cross-cultural studies on the prevalence of dementia as people age in the United States and Japan to see just how much better the Okinawans are doing than Americans are in minimizing dementia.[70]

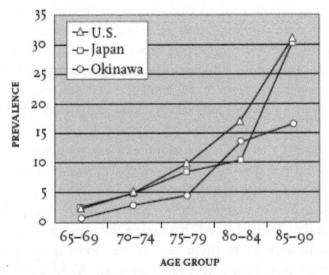

PREVALENCE OF DEMENTIA IN OKINAWA, JAPAN, AND THE UNITED STATES

Lean and Fit Bodies

Finding: Okinawan elders are lean, with average body mass index that ranges from 18 to 22 (lean is less than 23).

Lifestyle determinants: Diet—high carbohydrates, low calories; and exercise habits.

A lean body simply means healthy body fat levels. While there is some disagreement in the scientific community about what exactly the numbers should be, there is no disagreement that higher body fat levels increase your risk for cardiovascular disease (heart disease and stroke), many cancers, diabetes, and multiple other medical problems.

Body fat is difficult to measure, but, relying on body weight to assess our level of fatness can be very misleading. Fortunately, technology has progressed to the point where we can now measure our body fat fairly reliably by using a low-level electrical signal called bio-electrical impedance, or BIA. BIA allows you to really measure your fat, not merely your weight. Accurate and reasonably priced scales can be bought to measure body fat using the BIA method. For those interested in a simpler but less accurate method for assessing whether they are at a healthy weight, body mass index (BMI) can act as a rough estimate (see Appendix A, page 477).

Healthy body fat levels, according to our research in Okinawa and our extensive review of the latest scientific literature, should be 10 to 20 percent for men and 15 to 30 percent for women.[71] Highly trained athletes may be below these levels; few of us should be above, even as we age. Health risks climb steadily as our body fat rises—it's that simple. Scientists used to think low body weight at older ages was a health risk, but we now know if you exclude smokers (low body weight) and those who are malnourished or have cancer, leaner is healthier.[71] Scientists also used to believe it was normal and acceptable to gain weight (fat) as we age. This is also now known to be false. Even as little as ten additional pounds of weight (fat) can increase your risk for numerous diseases, including CHD, diabetes, and certain cancers.

The Okinawans stay lean by eating a low-calorie, unrefined complex carbohydrate diet, practicing *hara hachi bu* (only eating till they are 80 percent full), and keeping active the natural way—no Atkins Diet, no Zone, no Protein Power for them. Note that we say unrefined complex carbohydrates. These are very different from the high-calorie refined carbohydrates that push the pancreas into overdrive with insulin production. Unrefined complex carbohydrates are "whole" carbs and include fruit, vegetables, and whole grains with their natural fiber intact. They enter the bloodstream slowly, raise the blood sugar slowly, offer solid nutrition, and keep us healthy.

The health effects of recent dietary changes in the Okinawan population can be seen most clearly in Okinawans aged less than 50 years, who eat a much more Western diet—much higher fat and lower in carbohydrates—than the elders. They eat too many calories and engage in too little activity. The result has been the highest level of obesity in Japan, the worst cardiovascular risk factor profile, and the highest risk for premature death—a stark contrast to older Okinawans who have maintained a more traditional lifestyle and are by far the healthiest and longest-lived of the Japanese.[72]

When Dr. David Jenkins, our associate and the inventor of the Glycemic Index, pointed out that all carbohydrates are not created equal and that some carbohydrates increase blood sugar more than others, his comments launched a flurry of popular nutrition books that made the simple but false link that carbs make you fat because they increase your insulin levels too much. Millions of North Americans went on low-carb diets and miraculously experienced weight loss. Well, the weight loss was really no miracle—it was mostly water and lean muscle tissue, exactly what you don't want to lose. Carbohydrates really are nature's perfect fuel. Carbohydrates burn clean—they turn into glucose, water, and CO_2, which you breathe out with every breath. If the body doesn't get enough of them, it will kick and scream and make you feel miserable. And deprived of carbohydrate, the body will break down fat reserves and muscle protein reserves to make glucose because glucose is the preferred fuel for the brain. Unfortunately, fat and protein don't burn cleanly.

Toxic by-products of fat metabolism called ketones and aldehydes will make your breath bad, your skin smell, and your thinking cloudy, as your brain breaks down all nonessential tissue to make glucose. To the body low carbohydrate equals starvation. Like a drug addict needing heroin, it will do anything to get that glucose. It feels its very survival is at stake—it's going through glucose withdrawal. This seems like a fair trade at first. "Sure, I feel miserable, but look at all the weight I've lost!" Unfortunately, that weight only partially consists of fat stores. The rest is water and lean muscle tissue, the last thing you want to lose.

The critical point at which the body goes into ketosis and begins to feed on itself occurs when a person eats less than about 150 grams (5 ounces) of carbohydrate—roughly 600 calories a day. Then you begin to lose water in a big way. As you can see in the table below, when you compare our recommended moderate to high carbohydrate eating style with low-carbohydrate, high-protein, high-fat Atkins-type diets, the fat loss is actually greater on the higher carbohydrate plan.[73]

The study below was conducted in the 1970s when the Atkins Diet was undergoing its first "revolution." Two groups of people were fed the same number of calories but the groups were fed either a moderate amount of carbohydrates or a minimal amount. The table below illustrates a critical point: as you decrease the amount of carbohydrate you eat, the amount of weight lost from water and protein increases.

TYPE AND AMOUNT OF WEIGHT LOST WITH DIFFERENT DIETS—MODERATE CARB VS LOW CARB/HIGH FAT (ATKINS-TYPE DIET)[73]

DIET	DAILY WEIGHT LOSS	TYPE OF WEIGHT LOSS (g/day)		
		WATER	FAT	PROTEIN
MODERATE CARBOHYDRATE (45% carb)*	0.61 lb. (278 g)	103	164	11
LOW CARBOHYDRATE (5% carb; e.g., low-carb Atkins Diet)	1.03 lb. (467 g)	285	162	19

*The Okinawan diet is about 55 percent carbohydrate.

If you are on the Atkins Diet you will certainly lose weight—almost twice as much as you would following the Okinawa Program—but the difference is mostly *body water*, which you will quickly regain when you eat carbs again after your carbohydrate-starved body replaces lost reserves. You may even take on a swollen and puffy appearance as the water returns. For people with problems dealing with excess body water because of a weak heart, this can put them at serious risk for heart failure. That's why if you are dieting it's important for you to buy a scale that calculates body fat percentage, or calculate it based on the methods in Appendix A (page 477), so that you can make sure that the fat pounds melt away, not the water pounds. (See Appendix B for where to get a body fat scale.) There are other problems too. Long-term use of the Atkins Diet might increase your cardiovascular risk factors (e.g., cholesterol levels) by as much as 50 percent, according to a recent study.[74]

You also don't want to lose muscle because a higher resting muscle content means a higher resting metabolism, which means you burn more energy at rest with a muscular body than you would if your body consisted of fat. When you do resume eating carbohydrates your body wants them so badly that you put the weight back on in short order—this time as fat. The real tragedy is that you end up with a progressively higher body fat percentage each time you restrict carbohydrates. This is due to a protective mechanism that evolved in the days when we were roaming the plains: famine conditions (like a low-carb diet) encourage the body to create as much body fat as possible whenever food is available.

The best way to keep the body fat percentage down is to keep your activity level high in combination with a moderate to high complex-carb diet. Your body is happy, you feel good, and you will stay lean. In fact, the average BMI of the Okinawan elders is only 21 (lean is <23), which is a major factor in their lifelong health—and can be in yours, too. In the next chapter you'll find a positive, pro-complex-carbohydrate eating plan that will help balance your metabolism, make you healthier, and give you more energy for the rest of your life.

Natural Menopause

Finding: There are virtually no women in Okinawa using estrogen replacement therapy—they don't need it. They experience menopause naturally and nonpharmacologically with fewer complications such as hot flashes, hip fractures, or coronary heart disease.

Lifestyle determinants: Mainly diet—especially flavonoids derived from soy products; avoidance of smoking; and exercise in the form of dance, soft martial arts, walking, and gardening.

"Natural menopause" is simply menopause not caused by any medical intervention, as opposed to "induced menopause," which is usually due to removal of both ovaries (surgical menopause), but can also be secondary to drugs (such as chemotherapy) or radiation treatment. Natural menopause can also refer to the experience of menopause without the use of replacement hormones, such as estrogen or progesterone. Almost all Okinawan women experience menopause naturally, by both definitions.[75]

Hormone replacement therapy (HRT) is one of the most volatile issues in women's health care. Every day we have patients in our primary care clinic asking us about its pros and cons. Should I take estrogen or should I experience menopause naturally? Will HRT protect my bones? My memory? My heart?

These are all good questions. As of this writing, the heart benefits remain unproven. In fact, preliminary evidence from the largest placebo-controlled interventional study (the best evidence) ever done on hormone replacement therapy suggests that it may actually *increase* risk for heart disease.[76] The same is true for breast cancer. On the other hand, there is considerable evidence that hormone replacement therapy is good for your bones—in fact, it is the best available treatment for women with osteoporosis or at high risk for it.[77] But HRT should be based on your particular risk factors and your doctor's advice and not be a blanket prescription for all women.

What we do know is that the healthiest women in the world, the Okinawans, have little use for it. There are virtually no women in Okinawa using hormone replacement therapy. They simply don't need it. When your risk for heart disease and osteoporosis is low, the decision becomes much easier: there's very little to gain from hormone replacement therapy. So why would an Okinawan woman want to risk breast cancer or potentially life-threatening blood clots?

One of the most important known causes of breast cancer is the hormone estrogen, and one of the leading sources of postmenopausal estrogen in North American women is estrogen replacement therapy or hormone replacement therapy. The evidence that breast cancer risk increases with HRT is no longer in question—it does.[77,78] Physicians used to believe that adding progestin to the estrogen mitigated this risk. Unfortunately, recent studies suggest that the risk may be even higher with the estrogen-progestin combination than with estrogen alone. This may be due to the type of progestin used in HRT pills.

One of the best long-term studies, the Nurse's Health Study from the Harvard School of Public Health, looked at 65,000 women and found that after twenty years of hormone replacement therapy any long-term benefits gained through reduced risk for heart disease and osteoporosis were canceled out by increased deaths from breast cancer.[77,78] There seems to be two main reasons for this: (1) hormone therapy offers less protection from cardiovascular disease than previously thought; and (2) hormone therapy presents much more of a risk for breast cancer than expected, an average of 8 percent per year increased risk. Hormone replacement therapy never caught on with Okinawan women because they are already at very low risk for heart disease, hip fractures from osteoporosis, and other ailments and diseases that replacement hormones are supposed to help prevent or treat.

While we know hormone replacement therapy increases breast cancer risk, there is *some* good news on the horizon. There is a medication in development for high-risk women that might cut their risk by half—a selective estrogen receptor modulator (SERM). Many women are aware of it; it's called tamoxifen, and has been around for years for the treatment of breast cancer.[79] Unfortunately, while tamoxifen might reduce your risk for breast cancer, it increases your risk for blood clots and stroke, and it still gives you less than half the protection that you would get if you lived according to the Okinawa Program.

Raloxifene is another SERM that shows great promise. It's currently being tested in a prospective, randomized trial for its effectiveness in reducing the risk for women considered high breast cancer risks. Preliminary results are very promising: up to 77 percent risk reduction[80]—almost what you might expect to get if you adopted the lifestyle of an Okinawan woman and did it naturally!

Okinawan women get natural estrogens (natural SERMs)

through their diet, mainly from the large quantities of soy they consume.[81] Soy contains phytoestrogens, or plant estrogens, called *flavonoids*. The other important major phytoestrogens are *lignans*, which are derived from flax and other grains. All plants, especially legumes (beans, peas), onions, and broccoli, contain these natural SERMs, but not nearly in the same quantity as soy and flax.[82] Soy and flax are the undisputed king and queen of natural SERMs. (See the table on pages 146–7 for the most complete list of phytoestrogen-rich foods available.) The good thing about flavonoids and lignans is that they offer you protection from the damaging effects of estrogen while allowing you all the beneficial effects.[82] Here's how it works.

All estrogens, whether they are produced in your body or by plants, have one thing in common: they must connect with a cell receptor to work, to promote cell growth. If the estrogen receptor is blocked, the estrogen can't connect. You can think of it as the estrogen trying to get through the cell door with a key. The receptor is the keyhole. When the keyhole is blocked by SERMs the estrogen can't get in, and therefore can't promote growth. That's part of what flavonoids and lignans do: they're estrogen blockers—but they're *selective* blockers; remember, SERM means *selective* estrogen receptor modulator. That's the real beauty of these phytoestrogens. They allow estrogen to connect and promote growth at certain selected areas of the body where it is beneficial—that is, the bones—and block it from promoting growth at sensitive sites, such as the endometrium and breast, where it can do damage. With no extra cell growth there is much less risk of cancer.

This is important information for women in North America, where even the definition of high risk for breast cancer is scary. A high-risk woman is someone over the age of twenty-five who has at least a 1.7 percent projected risk of breast cancer in the subsequent five years—about double the average risk. This includes most women with a first-degree relative (sister, mother, or daughter) who had breast cancer and all women over sixty years of age—about 29 million American women, or roughly 20 percent of all women in the United States. In 1999, the American Society of Clinical Oncology (ASCO) met and debated the idea of endorsing tamoxifen use for all women over the age of sixty! According to their report, tamoxifen may be offered to this group depending on actual risk of breast cancer versus the potential side effects of the drug (hot flashes, uterine cancer, fatal blood clots).[83]

Our concern is that despite the best efforts of many dedicated health professionals menopause has become far too medicalized. Imagine—first, all women are put on estrogen, supposedly to prevent coronary heart disease and osteoporosis. But the estrogen increases risk for breast cancer. The solution? Put them all on tamoxifen, an antiestrogen. It's beyond insane. We need to rediscover the beauty of this stage of a woman's life cycle and celebrate this transition naturally rather than treat it as a disease. This is not to say we totally oppose hormone treatment. Clearly there are women who would benefit from hormone treatment, but it's time to search for alternatives that also might work. The best idea is to do as Dr. Susan Love, an oncologist, suggests in her excellent book *Dr. Susan Love's Hormone Book:* make your decision whether to take estrogen based on your own particular risk factors.[84] If you are at high risk for heart disease and osteoporosis and are unable to try lifestyle approaches that *might* substantially cut your risk, then you might try hormone replacement therapy, which also *might* cut your risk. There are unfortunately no guarantees for either approach.

Doctors, at the very least, should offer lifestyle alternatives first before putting patients on powerful hormonal drugs that clearly carry significant risks along with the benefits, just as we do with other diseases. We usually try six months of lifestyle therapy before we suggest drugs for high cholesterol, high blood pressure, or adult-onset diabetes. Hormone drugs should be no different. In the end, it should always be an *individual* decision between a woman and her doctor, based on her risk profile for heart disease, osteoporosis, breast cancer, and endometrial cancer.

Unfortunately, we don't yet have good intermediate predictors for who will get breast cancer as we do with other diseases, such as cholesterol for heart disease. This may change soon, however, with some fascinating work being carried on by our research colleagues at the University of Toronto.[85] Their current studies indicate that breasts at high risk for cancer may actually have denser tissue than low-risk breasts. If so, this could be picked up by mammography and may be amenable to dietary treatment. A recent study showed that Japanese woman had less dense breasts than Caucasian women—more evidence for the power of a healthy lifestyle.[86] These words of wisdom came from an editorial in a leading medical journal and drive home the importance of lifestyle over pharmacotherapy.

> The first issue is whether hormone use is needed at all; reducing risks of fractures and coronary heart disease rarely will provide sufficient justification because avoidance of smoking, performance of regular exercise, and consuming a good diet are effective preventive measures ... The commonly held belief that aging routinely requires pharmacological management has unfortunately led to the neglect of diet and lifestyle as the primary means to achieve healthy aging.[87]

For those who would rather experience a natural menopause free of hormone drugs, the Okinawan diet and lifestyle present a healthy plan of action. While there are many supposed natural remedies for the hot flashes that plague some perimenopausal women, there is little or no evidence to support most of these claims. The best evidence is for soy-derived flavonoids and their hormonal cousins, the lignans, present mostly in grain products,[88] and black cohosh, contained in the German nonprescription product Remifemin.[89]

As we discussed earlier, flavonoids and lignans are natural SERMs, and while the evidence is only preliminary, we find it promising. These weak plant estrogens seem to form a buffer of sorts for Okinawan and Japanese women. They provide a mild estrogenlike effect *postmenopausally*, at sites where we want them to work (e.g., blood vessels), so that strong estrogen withdrawal effects such as hot flashes are reduced. This has been supported by at least two randomized, placebo-controlled interventional trials—the best evidence.[88,90]

Natural SERMs also act as a block against the effects of powerful estrogens premenopausally, which eases wild pre- and post-menopausal estrogen swings. And the benefits may extend much further than to hot flashes and PMS. There is growing evidence to support their use in reducing risk for coronary heart disease, osteoporosis, and breast cancer.

Note that the Okinawans have a lot of flavonoids (natural SERMs) circulating in their blood, but Americans have very little.

Despite a much higher use of hormone replacement therapy, American women are *not* getting better overall results than Okinawan women are through natural means. Flavonoids may be providing some of the benefits of natural estrogen in the Okinawans, in conjunction with a healthy diet and regular exercise.

NATURE'S SERMS AND THEIR POSSIBLE EFFECTS [91]

	FLAVONOIDS (mg/day)*	MENOPAUSAL SYMPTOMS† (%)	HIP FRACTURES‡	HEART DISEASE MORTALITY§
Okinawans	100	16.1	4,414	18
Americans	13	46.2	8,206	100

*Amount in diet.

†Percentage of perimenopausal women who reported hot flashes, night sweats, or other menopausal symptoms in Japan and the United States.

‡Cases per 100,000 person-years per year.

§Average number of deaths in 100,000 people per year.

Does this mean that we can take the active components out of soy or grains and take them in pill form? Possibly, but this can lead to extremely high levels of one or two particular flavonoids, the health effects of which are unknown. The safest bet is to consume flavonoids in food itself rather than in pill form. It's best that you get your flavonoids naturally. Luckily, it's easy—and tasty. Just check the recipes in the back of the book.

Youthful Sex Hormones

Finding: Okinawan elders have higher levels of sex hormones, including natural DHEA, estrogen, and testosterone, than similarly aged Americans, suggesting that the Okinawans are physiologically younger.

Lifestyle determinants: Diet, low caloric intake, and exercise.

In the early 1990s the gerontology research community began to get excited about several hormones that seemed to hold great promise for slowing down the clock. Our research network in Okinawa was no exception. We studied several of the major hormonal players, including thyroid hormones, cortisol, and the sex steroids—DHEA, estrogen, and testosterone—in the Okinawan elders to see if nature or their lifestyles had conferred some hormonal protection upon them.

We found that most of these hormones declined as the Okinawans aged, just as was seen in other populations. What was interesting, though, was that sex hormones in the Okinawans seemed to decline more slowly. They may be *preserved* at higher levels than in their North American counterparts, suggesting that the Okinawans were actually physiologically younger than seniors of similar age in the United States[94]—and some say even more active in the bedroom. Following the Okinawa Program, it seems, might also help you realize a fuller and more satisfying sex life. Of course, assessing the evidence for these claims is a bit more delicate!

We should make one point very clear here. Higher levels of sex hormones at older ages do not place Okinawans at higher risk for hormone-dependent cancers, as one might expect from our previous discussion. Why is this? We are currently studying the reasons, but we believe that at least two factors may be playing a role. First, Okinawans may start out with lower sex hormone levels but may decline more slowly than Americans, so that by the time both groups reach their elder years American levels have fallen *below* those of Okinawans. This is exactly what we would expect with a slower aging process and a lengthening of the "health span." In fact, a similar phenomenon has been reported in the New England Centenarian Study, where researchers observed a lengthening of the reproductive years in their centenarian subjects.[92] More research is needed to confirm these fascinating observations.[93]

Second, Okinawans' overall balance of risk and protective factors, such as low insulin levels, and high levels of hormonal blockers, such as flavonoids, may negate any untoward effects of higher sex hormone levels at older ages.[93] Either way, it certainly has its advantages for the Okinawans and it's a balance that we should all strive for, naturally. The table on page 66 illustrates the major sex hormones and compares levels that we found in Okinawans with the levels other researchers found in Americans of similar age.

SEX HORMONES IN OKINAWANS AND AMERICANS[94]

AGE GROUP	DHEA (ng/ml)	TESTOSTERONE (ng/dl)	ESTROGEN (pg/ml)
Okinawan men 70	2.6	439	35.7
American men 70	2.0*	314	20.6
Okinawan men 100	0.8	298[‡]	12.1[||]
Okinawan women 70	3.0	13	15.5
American women 70	1.1[†]	17	5.5
Okinawan women 100	0.6	39[§]	4.2[#]
NORMAL RANGES FOR THESE AGE GROUPS	M 0.5–5.5 F 0.3–4.5	M 240–950 F < 90	M 0–50 F 0–35

*Okinawan men have higher DHEA levels than Americans; possibly reflecting a younger physiological age.

[†]Okinawan women have higher DHEA than reported for American women. This may reflect a much younger physiological age.

[‡]Okinawan men seem to preserve their testosterone levels for longer than Americans.

[§]Testosterone in women is normal and natural. These levels are not statistically different from each other.

[||] Natural estrogen is produced in men from testosterone and may help keep them younger longer, with better heart and bone health.

[#]Okinawan women may preserve their natural estrogen longer, suggesting a younger physiological age. This may contribute to better heart and bone health.

DHEA

DHEA is under active study by the U.S. National Institute on Aging as an anti-aging hormone. It's a steroid produced in the human adrenal gland, and some studies suggest that it may help ameliorate the ravages of aging. It has been reported to be protective against heart disease, memory loss, depression, osteoporosis, certain cancers, and diabetes. Not all the news is favorable, and there is also concern that taking DHEA supplements could increase breast cancer risk.[95] Yet, what may be even more interesting is that DHEA levels decline in direct ratio to age, so it may be the best marker of biological age we have. Measuring DHEA levels in people may be akin to counting rings for trees. The fact that Okinawans seem to have higher DHEA levels than similarly aged Americans may be the best proof yet for the ability of the Okinawa Program to slow the aging process. We are actively studying this possibility. Nevertheless, although this is a promising area of investigation, at this point most claims are still only speculation, and we do not recommend taking DHEA—yet.[96]

Estrogen Replacement

As we've mentioned before, estrogen is a double-edged sword. Several large-scale observational studies have supported the use of estrogen replacement as a means to reduce heart disease and osteoporosis, and even to extend life.[77] Recently, this has been called into question because the only two double-blind *interventional* studies performed to date have shown that hormone replacement therapy can actually lead to an *increased* risk for heart disease.[76-78] When interventional studies (these look at the effects of drug versus placebo in two different groups) and observational studies (these look at population differences between users and nonusers) disagree, there is cause for great concern, especially when a therapy has been touted as having the potential to prevent disease and increase life expectancy but may, in fact, do the opposite.

Now the principal investigators of the Women's Health Initiative, the best interventional study to date, are simply not sure whether hormone therapy protects or promotes heart disease. In a front-page article in the *New York Times,* Dr. Jacques Rossouw, acting director of the HRT trials at the Women's Health Initiative, was quoted as saying: "If my women friends ask me . . . I would say there never was proof that hormones help heart disease and there still isn't."[76] This, of course, is not an issue in Okinawa, since Okinawans already are very successful at using lifestyle means to substantially decrease risk for heart disease and osteoporosis.

While taking estrogen in pill form has not been proven to be the panacea that Western medicine had hoped for, our studies of natural estrogen levels in Okinawans showed that as Okinawans age, both sexes maintain remarkably high levels of estrogen.[97] Our preliminary studies suggest that for Okinawan women, estrogen levels may be as much as three times higher than the levels of estrogen in their seventy-year-old American counterparts.[94]

It's interesting to speculate that the higher levels of natural estrogen might be preserved because Okinawans are physiologically younger, which helps with their blood vessels and bones, while the bad effects of natural estrogen are reduced by strikingly high levels of flavonoids. It's certainly consistent with what we have observed thus far in the Okinawans. Meanwhile, as the evidence mounts, it would make sense to employ the risk-reduction techniques of the Okinawans for maximizing postmenopausal health: diet, including plenty of soy products (a health claim for the reduction of heart disease is now officially sanctioned by the U.S. Food and Drug Administration),[98] which will help supply your body with a natural-source estrogen it needs for ultimate health. Of course, exercise and avoidance of smoking are important, too, as well as regular self-exams and mammograms.

Testosterone

Testosterone is the male equivalent of estrogen. Higher endogenous levels increase our muscle mass and our body hair, deepen our voices, and control our libidos, among other functions. Testosterone has been marketed to aging baby boomer men as the answer to the male menopause, or "andropause," as endocrinologists know it. However, at this point testosterone replacement has not been employed on a wide scale, partly for fear of increasing prostate cancer risk. Limited research trials are under way.[99]

Interestingly, Okinawan men seem to have higher testosterone levels than similarly aged American men. Indeed, the level of testosterone of centenarian men in Okinawa is scarcely different from that of seventy-year-old Americans,[94] and some of our centenarian subjects report still being sexually active. Although no formal study has been conducted, these centenarians are likely in the minority.[100]

Testosterone is also important for the female sex drive, and some physicians prescribe it for low-testosterone states in women who have abnormally low sex drives, although this is controversial.

Growth Hormone

Growth hormone is another one of the highly touted "miracle" anti-aging hormones. It's released from the pituitary gland in a series of pulses over the day and night, mostly as we sleep. It was *the* hot anti-aging treatment in the 1990s, when researchers at the Medical College of Wisconsin injected the hormone into aging men with seemingly miraculous results. Twenty-one men, aged sixty-one to eighty-one, who had low growth-hormone levels, were injected with the drug three times weekly for six months. The men reported a 9 percent increase in muscle mass, 14 percent decrease in body fat, and a 2 percent increase in bone density. They also reported increased well-being and that they felt more alert. The fountain of youth was at hand. Or was it? When the men stopped the injections they reverted back to their former selves and had nothing but pleasant memories to show for their experience.[101]

When the research trials were repeated in men with normal growth-hormone levels, the results were less than spectacular. Two subsequent studies, including one at the prestigious Washington University School of Medicine, failed to show increases in strength in the men tested, although improvements were seen in muscle mass and fat reduction. Unfortunately, there were severe side effects, including diabetes, water retention, elevated blood pressure, and high cholesterol levels. And in animal studies long-term use is associated with cancer and possibly a shortened life expectancy. So much for that fountain of youth.[101]

What may be more promising are new research trials that are assessing the use of much smaller doses of growth hormone in combination with other hormonal agents.[101] Other trials are assessing the use of growth-hormone releasing hormone (GHRH). This hormone acts on the brain to cause greater production of the body's natural growth hormone. Results should be available in several years. In the meantime, there are natural ways to preserve your growth-hormone levels, and they include a low-calorie diet, regular exercise, and adequate sleep. The Okinawa Program helps to maintain high levels of growth hormone the natural way. We do not recommend that you take growth hormone itself unless better evidence supports its use, with regimens that produce far fewer side effects, especially with regard to cancer risk.

Reduced Free-Radical Damage

Finding: Okinawan elders have a lower level of free radicals in their blood than younger Okinawans.

Lifestyle determinants: Low calorie intake; high antioxidant intake from vegetables, legumes (especially soy), and herbs; and regular physical activity.

As we described earlier, free radicals are highly reactive compounds produced during normal metabolism that damage other cells in the body. They are thought to be one of the main causes of aging. Decrease their production and/or neutralize them, and you may unleash a powerful tool to help slow your body's own aging, including decreasing your risk for a multitude of chronic diseases linked to free-radical damage, such as coronary heart disease, cancer, stroke, and dementia.[102]

One of the most important findings in free-radical research has been that eating fewer calories increases life span.[103] The only evidence that this works in humans has been indirect and based on observation of the low caloric intake of the Okinawans and their long life expectancy.[104] Now we have real direct evidence that the Okinawans following the traditional ways have low blood levels of free radicals. We actually measured the amount of one of the main free radicals, called *lipid peroxide,* in centenarians and compared their levels to those of younger seventy-year-old "average" subjects.[105] The elders had significantly lower levels of lipid peroxide, compelling evidence that they suffer less free-radical-induced damage. This table shows that the elders in our study produced significantly fewer free radicals than younger Okinawans.[105]

GROUP	PLASMA LIPID PEROXIDE (FREE-RADICAL BY-PRODUCT
100-year-old elders	1.59 ┐ *
70-year-old normal population	2.96 ┘

*Statistically significant difference.

The elders' low caloric intake, their high intake of antioxidant foods and herbs, their regular physical activity, and, possibly for some, good genes all play a role in maximizing their protection against free-radical damage and keeping them young and healthy.

Excellent Psychospiritual Health

Finding: Personality testing found that centenarians, when in their prime of life, scored low when it came to feelings of "time urgency" and "tension" and high in "self-confidence" and "unyieldingness." Interviews revealed optimistic attitudes, adaptability, and an easy-going approach to life. Moderation was found to be a key cultural value. Strong social integration and a deep spirituality were particularly evident among older women.

Lifestyle determinants: Positive attitudes, strong social networks, and strong spiritual beliefs, which lead to a sense of well-being and life satisfaction.

Strong Spiritual Beliefs and Positive Health Outcomes

Just as we have separated religion and state in our political affairs, we have done so in the area of scientific inquiry. At one time this split was a necessity. Religious dogma threatened not only the objectivity of researchers but their very lives—just ask Galileo or Copernicus. Unfortunately, in our zeal to purge religion from science we overlooked a very important fact: the influence of the mind and spirit on health. When we found that the mind actually seemed to profoundly affect our health, we couched the phenomenon in scientific terms and summarily dismissed it as the *placebo effect*.

Recently, the pendulum has begun to swing back to a more balanced view. Western science has begun to investigate the nature of the placebo effect, the relaxation response, and other physiological, psychological, social, and behavioral mechanisms, to find out exactly why spirituality can have such positive effects on our health.

This is also a recent and active area of investigation in our studies of the Okinawan elders. We've found that Okinawans firmly believe that they and their villages are naturally healthy. Health and longevity are celebrated, and health is the theme of most prayers. Traditional shamanistic healing practices are an integral aspect of many of their lives. Religion and spirituality are particularly important to women, who take an active role in worship and prayer and are the religious leaders of society. Our surveys of elderly Okinawan women have revealed links between their traditional spiritual beliefs and their subjective sense of well-being or life satisfaction.[106] This is complemented by the lowest suicide rate for elderly women in East Asia, an area notorious for high suicide rates among older women.[107] Research firmly supports the positive effects of religion and spirituality in aging and health: they help people stay healthy and young.[108]

Low Stress Levels

One particularly important aspect of psychospiritual health is how we deal with stress. Numerous studies have shown that health is affected to a great extent by how we react to life's stressful events, including emotional losses such as the death of a loved one or divorce, conflicts with others at home or work, and just simple daily hassles like sitting in traffic.

The pathway by which the mind connects to the body in order to deal with stress is the neuroendocrine system. The neurochemicals typically produced as a response to stress have been associated with over a dozen serious degenerative diseases. Overexposure to these neurochemicals (such as cortisol, epinephrine, and norepinephrine) can also wear down the immune system, leading to lowered resistance to bacterial or viral infections, or more serious degenerative diseases such as cardiovascular disease, hypertension, and cancer— diseases that have been traditionally associated with aging.

Stressors come from many sources, including the physical,

psychological, social, and environmental. Noise pollution, information overload, fast-paced technological change, and ever-increasing demands on our time are just a few of the environmental stressors that we face every day. But it's more than just the stressors themselves; it's our reaction to them that makes the difference to our health. Our reactions are influenced by our beliefs, values, attitudes, prior experiences, and personality. Characteristic ways of reacting to stressors can be healthy or unhealthy—even stress-induced illness can be fought with healthy attitudes and improved coping skills.

Researchers have found something akin to a *stress-resistant personality*—that is, certain habitual attitudes and patterns of behavior that allow some individuals to withstand stress better than others.[109] These hardy individuals have an optimistic outlook on life, an internal sense of control, emotional stability, adaptability, and low levels of negative emotionality (including depression, anxiety, hostility, self-consciousness or social unease, impulsiveness, and vulnerability). Active coping with stress, or quickly getting over life's emotional setbacks, has therefore been proposed as extremely important for successful aging. Not surprisingly, many Okinawan elders fit this profile.

This doesn't mean that the elders led stress-free lives. On the contrary, we found that for the most part they had bounced back from significant emotional ordeals and losses including poverty, war, oppression, and other hardships with an amazing resilience. We also found low levels of negative emotions and depression and high levels of social contact—a known stress-reducing mechanism.

Personality testing revealed that centenarians, when in their prime of life, scored low when it came to feelings of "time urgency" and "tension."[110] This means that on a day-to-day basis they didn't feel rushed, hassled, and pressed for time, so they retained healthy low levels of stress. And they scored high in self-confidence and "unyieldingness," qualities that helped them cope with major stressful life events such as war and death in the family.[110]

Perhaps most interesting, however, was our finding that many centenarians had quite dominating personalities despite a cultural value system that emphasizes the qualities of *yasashii* (gentle, mild mannered, soft) and *taygay* (easy-going, relaxed, nonrigid). The centenarians we interviewed, for the most part, were strong-willed characters with youthful, can-do attitudes, who regarded themselves as the pillars of their families. Cultural attitudes that place the elderly in an exalted or respected position may be contributing even more to their sense of well-being.

Lastly, we found that the whole social structure seems to march to the beat of a slower rhythm known locally as *Okinawa time*. This unique sense of time seems to result in health benefits for the population as a whole. And it certainly wouldn't hurt us here in North America. A dose of Okinawa time might be just what the doctor ordered to help bring down the unnaturally high stress levels of our fast-paced society. We discuss this and other Okinawa stress-reducing techniques at length in Chapter Eight. Just because we don't live in Okinawa doesn't mean we can't live on Okinawa time!

Strong Social Networks

In the past thirty years, numerous studies have confirmed the importance of social connections for both physical and psychospiritual well-being.[111] Study after study has shown that social ties can actually affect the strength and resiliency of the immune system, which, of course, affects a person's resistance to disease, including cancer. Strong social networks and close family ties protect against illness and premature death. Japan has frequently been cited as a "socially cohesive society" with a traditional culture that puts a high value on social relationships. Our research on Okinawan society supports this thesis but with an interesting twist. Although social contact seems to be high in Okinawa, elders also retained a fair amount of independence. Attitudes toward independent living and self-realization were particularly important for elderly women.[112] Many of them live alone, especially in rural areas, yet at the same time have very active and strong social networks that support their independent living.[113] A traditional support system known as *yuimaru* and mutual support organizations known as *moai* may be part of the reason the oldest old can remain active and independent in the community until such extreme old ages. (See Chapter Nine for guidelines for setting up healing social networks in your life.)

Findings: The Okinawans incorporate both Eastern and Western healing methods into their health care system. Their use of natural or herbal tonics far exceeds that of North Americans.

Lifestyle determinants: Traditional diet, herbs, and an open-minded approach to Eastern and Western healing methods.

Research suggests that good health care is one of the main determinants of population health. Certainly places with the highest life expectancies all have good health care coverage for their citizens. Hong Kong ascended to the number two position in terms of world life expectancy among countries only when health care became more widely available and more integrated with Western medicine.[114] The same was true in Okinawa, at least in this century. When Western medicine became available in a system that offered health care to all citizens, health improved and life expectancy rates soared.

Okinawa, Japan, and Hong Kong are the top three areas of the world in life expectancy, and what is interesting in their health care systems is that they have all incorporated both Eastern and Western approaches to healing. The use of natural or herbal tonics in these populations far exceeds that of North America.[115] In many situations, though not always, the negative side effects of a natural or herbal preparation are less than those of a drug, sometimes with comparable clinical benefits. To help you integrate these methods into your own life, we have identified a number of herbs, foods, and therapeutic techniques that contribute to the Okinawans' impressive health. We present these in Chapters Three to Eleven.

Living the Okinawa Program

The evidence presented in this chapter clearly shows that what we do, how we live, what we eat, think, and believe, has a huge impact on our health and life expectancy. We have the power to alter our life course no matter how poor the set of cards Mother Nature has dealt us. It's not the cards we get, but how we play them that determines our final outcome. The bottom line is that lifestyle choices are critical—and the Okinawans, indisputably, have made all the right ones for staying youthful, disease free, and slim. Maybe they've known for centuries how to stack the odds in favor of lifelong health.

We'll never know for sure, but what we do know for certain is that with their traditional eating patterns, their penchant for exercise, and their psycho-spiritual practices—combined with integrative health care—Okinawans present an unparalleled picture of everlasting health and youthfulness. That's the Okinawa way. It works for them and it can work for you. In the coming chapters we'll show you how to integrate this amazing healthy lifestyle into your own life, starting with the healthiest diet. Let's get cooking.

3. The Healthiest Diet in the World

Nuchi gusui.
Food should nourish life. This is the best medicine.

Okinawan proverb

A Healing Story: It's Never Too Late To Change

We first spotted Yukin Tome on the cover of an Okinawan tourist magazine. He was decked out in a chic floral print aloha shirt, sporty sunglasses, and a Panama hat and looked like he was about to swing into a mambo routine. The picture of youth and vitality—at ninety-five years old! If there was anybody we had to interview for our centenarian study, it was Yukinsan, even if he was still a few years "under age." When we met him he didn't disappoint. Yukinsan perfectly captures the spirit that draws so many people to Okinawa. Footloose and fancy-free, laid-back and colorful—you can almost see the island's breezy palm trees, crystal-clear water, and white sandy beaches in the brightness of his brown eyes. When we tracked him down, though, he wasn't at the beach as we had expected—he was in his office.

Yes, even at ninety-five Yukinsan still works. He is a consultant in a company that publishes educational materials. He walks three-quarters of a mile to the office every morning, then after some desk work hits the streets again on business calls, making the rounds of the five or six bookstores in town. Walking, he says, "stimulates my brain and my body."

Yukinsan's father died at eighty-eight, relatively young by Okinawan standards and his last few years were not good ones. Yukinsan says that this taught him an important lesson: "My father loved eating pork and died young," he explains.[1] "My mother didn't like meat and was youthful and energetic until one hundred and two. I figured that she was stronger than my father because of her good eating habits, so thirty years ago I

77

started eating more fish and vegetables and less meat. I haven't spent a day in the hospital since then!" Yukinsan says he also gets energized from his social life; sitting at home is definitely not for him, and he's happy to share his formula for a long healthy life: "Eat good food, walk everywhere, and enjoy your work!"

Sage advice from a man who exemplifies what healthy living habits can do for you. For Yukinsan, switching at age sixty-five from a meat-heavy diet (by Okinawan standards) to one that emphasized vegetables, whole grains, soy foods, and fish was the key to his successful aging, even though he switched at a relatively late age.

Our research on Okinawan longevity suggests that good dietary habits are essential for maintaining health and a youthful appearance, as well as for optimizing one's healing potential. While nutrition is still a controversial area of research in the West, the Okinawan elders seem to be doing everything right. By following the old ways while judiciously incorporating some of the new, they have found the perfect dietary balance for lifelong health. The Okinawa diet completely fulfills the criteria recommended by most North American scientific and medical authorities, and actually *exceeds* the recommendations of the U.S. National Cancer Institute, which advises a minimum of five servings of vegetables and fruits a day. (The NCI had originally recommended even more servings, but felt it was unrealistic in light of the huge change in eating habits most Americans would have had to face.)

Okinawan elders eat an average of seven servings of vegetables and fruit a day, seven servings of grains per day, two servings of flavonoid-rich soy products per day; omega-3 rich fish several times a week; and minimal dairy products and meat. This is *exactly* the type of diet that affords protection against most diseases associated with premature aging, including heart disease, cancer, and stroke, and gives the best shot at remaining slim, healthy, and attractive for life.

Yet, there still seems to be general public confusion about just what kinds of foods we should eat to promote health. This is due partially to information issued by specific disease-oriented groups. Each group offers slightly different advice and diet plans geared to its particular disease, and everything can get rather muddled. The truth is that eating habits recommended by most experts for specific diseases have many more similarities than differences.

To resolve the confusion, scientific authorities including the American Cancer Society, the American Heart Association, the American Dietetic Association, and the National Institutes of Health have recently issued a set of *unified* dietary guidelines.[2] Together they suggest six simple rules that make for healthy and enjoyable eating. These rules are, in fact, remarkably similar to the Okinawan dietary principles *(nuchi gusui)*. Compare the Okinawa Program to what the authorities recommend and see for yourself how the Okinawan elders are doing. They may be the first population in the world that actually comes close to meeting all the guidelines!

How the Diet of the Okinawan Elders Compares to the U.S. Unified Guidelines

Guideline 1: *Eat a variety of foods, mainly from plant sources.* Varying the diet to include a wide selection of foods is one of the keys to healthy eating. The more variety the better. In the diet surveys, our sample of fifty-three centenarians ate 206 different foods in all, including herbs.[3] Thirty-eight different foods were eaten regularly. Each elder ate an average of eighteen different foods in a day. Seventy-eight percent of the foods in the elders' diets were plant foods. That's a lot of plant food and a lot of variety.

Guideline 2: *Eat at least five or more servings of vegetables and fruits daily.* The elders pass this one with flying colors. At least seven vegetables and fruits are eaten daily (generally six servings of vegetables and one serving of fruit) and at least two legumes (soy foods). Vegetables, potatoes, and legumes were among the most common foods in their diet.

Guideline 3: *Eat six or more servings of grain-based foods daily.* The elders have no problem meeting this one, either. They eat at least three servings of Japanese white (sticky) rice, supplemented by whole grains such as buckwheat noodles (soba) and wheat noodles (udon). Rice is the most commonly eaten single food in Okinawa. The only room for improvement here is eating more brown rice rather than white, since it contains more nutrients and more fiber and is lower on the Glycemic Index (more on this later).

Guideline 4: *Make complex carbohydrates the basis of the diet (more than 55 percent of total calories) and limit simple sugars (table sugars).* The elders hit this one almost right on the nose. Carbohydrates form 54 percent of total calories in their current East-West blend of cooking. In the old days they ate more than 80 percent of calories as carbohydrates, mostly from sweet potatoes *(imo)*. Few simple sugars are eaten. When table sugar is used it is usually raw cane sugar.

Guideline 5: *Limit fat intake to 30 percent or less of total calories.* Mono-unsaturates should comprise about 15 percent or less, polyunsaturates about 10 percent or less, and the remainder saturates. The elders do well here since about 24 percent of their total calories are from fat. Monounsaturates are about 12 percent, polyunsaturates are about 5 percent, and saturates are about 7 percent of total calories.

Guideline 6: *Limit total salt intake to less than 6 grams per day (3 teaspoons).* The elders eat a little too much salt, at about 7 grams per day, but much less than the mainland Japanese, who eat more than 12 grams (6 teaspoons) per day.

From the chart above you can see that Okinawan elders meet or exceed the U.S. unified guidelines for a healthy diet. The only place where they have room for improvement is their salt intake, which admittedly could be a little lower. But that could be easily remedied simply by using low-sodium products, especially low-sodium soy sauce or miso, the source of most of the salt in the Okinawan diet. Indeed, all of us who use soy products should go the low-sodium route. Low-sodium soy sauce, often labeled "Lite," is sold in most North American markets, and low-sodium miso can be found in most good health food stores and Asian markets.

One of the keys to the success of the Okinawan diet is their satisfying blend of Eastern and Western cooking, called *chample* (pronounced *champuru*), or East-West fusion. Their dishes are delicious and extremely easy to prepare, a winning combination. In fact, some of the hottest restaurants in the country serve California fusion, a mixture of American and Asian cuisines that is remarkably similar to Okinawan cookery.

The Okinawan's main method of cooking is low-temperature

WHAT DOES THE OKINAWAN ELDERS' DIET LOOK LIKE COMPARED TO THE AMERICAN DIET?[5]

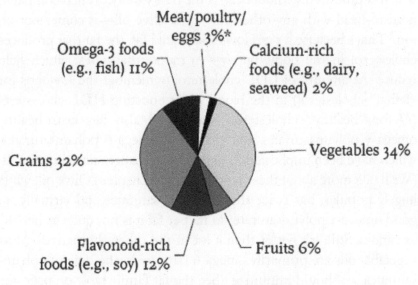

Meat/poultry/eggs 3%*
Omega-3 foods (e.g., fish) 11%
Calcium-rich foods (e.g., dairy, seaweed) 2%
Vegetables 34%
Grains 32%
Flavonoid-rich foods (e.g., soy) 12%
Fruits 6%

OKINAWAN ELDERS

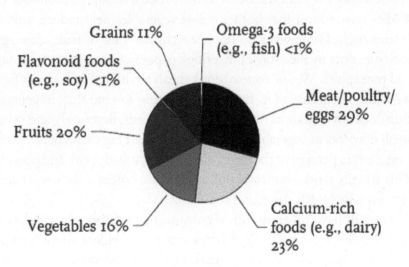

Grains 11%
Omega-3 foods (e.g., fish) <1%
Flavonoid foods (e.g., soy) <1%
Meat/poultry/eggs 29%
Fruits 20%
Vegetables 16%
Calcium-rich foods (e.g., dairy) 23%

AMERICANS

* Percentages are by weight of particular foods.

stir-fry (not deep-frying). Canola oil is the main cooking oil, and is one of the healthiest oils on the market. (Cold-pressed canola oil, which is produced without heat, is the best variety.) When compared head-to-head with any other oil—even olive oil—it comes out on top.[4] That's because it's *very* low in saturated fat, the fat that produces cholesterol in the body, but *high* in monounsaturates, which help reduce the amount of LDL cholesterol (remember the *L* stands for "lethal" cholesterol) in the blood while boosting HDL cholesterol (*H* for "healthy" cholesterol). Canola oil also has heart-healthy omega-3 polyunsaturates and very little omega-6 polyunsaturates, which have been implicated in higher breast cancer rates in animals. (We'll talk more about these fats later in this chapter.) Olive oil, while hugely popular, has twice the unhealthy saturates and virtually no good omega-3 polyunsaturate, so fat per fat it is not quite as healthy as canola. Still, it's better than a lot of the other alternatives. Most vegetable oils are primarily omega-6 fatty acids, the type of polyunsaturates we should minimize. (See the fat family table on page 127 for a snapshot of good and bad fats.)

The high vegetable and soy food content of the Okinawan diet is undoubtedly a significant factor in their robust health. A multitude of studies have found that both soy and vegetables help reduce cancer. Interestingly, Okinawans do not generally eat a lot of fruit, although their diet does include some tangerines, papayas, watermelon, bananas, and pineapples. We, of course, don't mean to discredit fruit—in fact, we highly recommend it. But it is interesting to note that, in general, fruit does not contain as many vitamins, minerals, flavonoids, and other small nutrients as vegetables. Okinawans are not big carnivores, either. Less than 10 percent of the elders' diet is meat, mostly pork and poultry. This usually works out to about an ounce of meat a day—certainly very little by North American standards.

The Okinawans' tradition of consuming pork on religious occasions has led to some lively debates among the elders about pork as a "longevity food." When Okinawan life expectancy skyrocketed after the Second World War, so coincidentally did the people's standard of living and thus they began to eat more pork. Only limited amounts had been consumed before the war, mostly on religious occasions. So Okinawan elders had very little of it over the course of their lives. Their prewar diet, like that of the mainland

Japanese, consisted of little more than sweet potatoes, minimal rice, soy, occasional fish, and too much salt. The high salt content predisposed both populations to high blood pressure and subsequent higher stroke rates than we see in the West. When they began to eat a more balanced diet—less salt, a wider variety of vegetables, fruit, grains, fish, and limited dairy and meat products—the stroke rate dropped and their life expectancy increased. Many elders concluded that eating more pork, their traditional holiday food, had saved their lives. In reality, they were saved by getting the right balance as outlined in the unified dietary guidelines: high in plant-based carbs, low in fat and protein, and low in salt. And the right balance could help protect your health, too.

Our Four-Week Turnaround Plan for everlasting health is based on our extensive studies of Okinawan eating habits, as well as an extensive evidence-based review of over two thousand scientific studies. As a dietary strategy it's a triple winner: delicious, evidence-based, and 100 percent healthy.

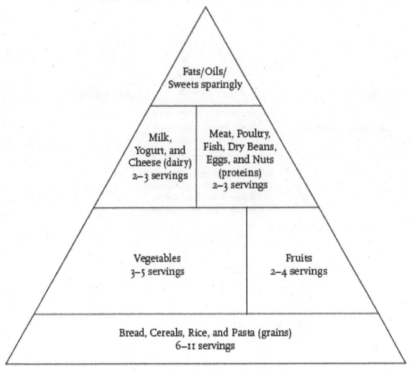

THE USDA FOOD PYRAMID
A Guide to Daily Food Choices

Okinawan Dietary Principles (Nuchi Gusui)

Never in the history of nutrition research has the evidence been more clear and consistent: a high-carbohydrate, low-calorie, plant-based diet is the best for long-term health.[6,7] There's no doubt about it anymore, despite what you might have read in books advocating low-carb–high-protein diets. A well-balanced high-carbohydrate–low-calorie diet helps you stay slim, look youthful, and minimize your risk for heart disease, stroke, and cancer. It's interesting to compare the U.S. Department of Agriculture Food Pyramid and the Okinawan Food Pyramid (see below and page 83). While there are definite similarities, the Okinawan Food Pyramid shows more clearly how to divide foods into daily and weekly categories so that you can easily judge whether you are eating certain foods too often or not often enough. It gives you a guide for healthy eating without having to worry about every meal or food choice—*all foods are allowed in moderation. It is the overall balance that counts.* (Starting on page 134 we show you how to follow the pyramid step-by-step.)

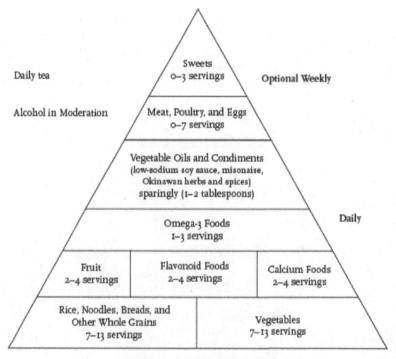

THE OKINAWA FOOD PYRAMID
A Guide to Daily Food Choices

Consider the current guidelines from the U.S. Department of Agriculture (see page 83). We believe that several improvements could be made to accommodate the weight of recent evidence concerning healthy eating habits, especially in light of the Okinawa findings.

Many of the problems that we see with this USDA Pyramid were outlined recently by Dr. Walter Willett, chair of the Department of Nutrition at the Harvard School of Public Health, in a review in the leading medical journal *Science*.[7] These are hugely important factors that must be fully recognized if we're to have a truly healthy diet.

1. The top of the pyramid ignores important differences among types of fats.
2. The dairy section should emphasize low-fat choices, and two to three servings a day may be too much.
3. Potentially health-promoting fish and beans are lumped in the same group with red meat. This gives the false impression that two to three servings a day of red meat might be healthy—it would not.
4. Vegetables and fruits should receive stronger emphasis.
5. The grain section should emphasize whole grains.

In light of these observations and data compiled in our Okinawa study, we created our own pyramid based on the East-West *chample,* or fusion diet, of the Okinawans to make up for the shortcomings in the USDA Food Pyramid.

Choosing your daily servings based on the Okinawa Food Pyramid gives you a general guide for healthy eating. If you combine this with the exercises and lifestyle changes that we recommend in subsequent chapters, you will have chosen a way of life that will put you on the path to everlasting health. You will see and feel the difference, physically and mentally. Your skin will take on a glow as your cleaner arteries allow more nutrients to enter your bloodstream, your energy levels rise, and your body feels lighter and younger as your body fat percentage drops. Changes can be measured in weeks, not years. Of course, the longer you follow the Okinawa Program, the slower the clock will tick.

We've designed the Okinawa Food Pyramid so that if you make proper food choices you do not have to count calories. If you are concerned about more precise estimates of your caloric intake, then estimate your caloric needs based on your activity level and age, using the Okinawa Program Nutrition Tracker in Appendix A (see table, page 486). A guide to serving quantities follows.

What Is a Serving?

The most common reaction to food pyramids is, "How can I eat that many servings?" The answer is simple: servings are really not all that large. A large carrot, for instance, is considered one vegetable serving. A piece of beef the size of a deck of cards is also considered one serving. That means some of those gigantic slabs of meat you get at steakhouses can be up to four servings! One meal could fulfill—or even put you over—your entire meat/poultry/eggs quotient for an entire week. With that in mind, check the following table to gauge your serving sizes.

SERVING SIZES

½ cup = a closed fist
1 cup = a softball
3 ounces = a deck of cards
1 cup = 8 fluid ounces

The following equals one serving:

VEGETABLES
1 cup of raw leafy vegetables
½ cup of other vegetables, cooked or chopped raw
¾ cup of vegetable juice

WHOLE GRAINS
½ cup of cooked cereal, rice, or pasta
1 ounce of ready-to-eat cereal
1 slice of bread or half of a bagel

FRUITS

½ cup of chopped, cooked, or canned fruit

1 medium apple, banana, orange, or half of a grapefruit

¾ cup of fruit juice

CALCIUM FOODS

Dairy

1½ ounces of reduced-fat cheese

1 cup of low-fat or fat-free milk

1 cup of low-fat or fat-free yogurt

Vegetarian

3 ounces of calcium-fortified tofu

⅓ cup of prepared seaweed

½ cup of watercress

FLAVONOID FOODS

1 tablespoon of ground flaxseed

½ cup of cooked beans, legumes

3 ounces of tofu

2 tablespoons of soy nuts

¾ cup of miso soup

¾ cup of cranberry juice

1 teaspoon of miso paste

1 tablespoon of arrowroot powder

¼ cup of soybean sprouts

¼ cup of chopped onion

OMEGA-3 FOODS

1 tablespoon of ground flaxseed

2 tablespoons of chopped walnuts

3 ounces of cooked fish

1 omega-3 egg

3 ounces of tofu

1 teaspoon of canola oil

1 teaspoon of flaxseed oil

MEAT/POULTRY/EGGS

2–3 ounces of cooked poultry

2–3 ounces of cooked lean meat

1 non-omega-3 egg

Nutrient Conversions

1 gram = 1,000 mg = 1,000,000 micrograms

5 grams ~ 1 teaspoon

14 grams ~ ½ ounce ~ 1 tablespoon = 3 teaspoons

28 grams ~ 1 ounce ~ 2 tablespoons

Guidelines for Healthy Eating Okinawa-Style

The thing we all have to remember is that the food we choose today is fundamental to our health tomorrow. Most of us know that "we are what we eat," but with so much going on around us on a daily basis, it's all too easy to forget and become disconnected from the food-mind-body link. We need to remain conscious of the benefits of good, healthy food and to care enough about ourselves to consider everything we put in our bodies. And we need to remember that it's quality, not quantity, that counts—a concept of which the Okinawan elders are astutely aware. At the same time, though, we should not feel guilty about every dubious food choice we make. Eating should be enjoyable—indeed, even an adventure. The following simple guidelines make it easy to take pleasure in our food, while simultaneously laying the groundwork for a long and healthy life.

Eat Consciously To Fully Enjoy Your Food

Eating is one of life's true pleasures and the experience should be savored. All too often we hardly taste the food we eat. We munch half consciously while reading, watching television, talking business, or even driving. "Grab it, gobble it, and run" seems to be the name of the game—some of us barely take time to even chew our food. Need we say, this is not a good thing. Aside from totally devaluing the whole eating experience, eating fast and on the run is not particularly healthy, nor slimming. Food needs to be properly chewed before it can be digested well. And without proper digestion you don't get the food's full nutritional benefits.

Variety From the Food Groups

Eating a wide variety of foods is important for lifelong health. In Japan, variety is considered so important that government guidelines spell out a minimum number of different foods you should eat in a day for optimum health. For most adults this should be at least fifteen different foods. Note that some foods exist in more than one food group. For example, flaxseed is both an omega-3 food and a flavonoid food. When you calculate your daily food consumption, a food that is in more than one group can be listed in either category, but not in both at the same time (unless you had two servings).

Vegetables

Dark Green Leafy

Beet greens	Endive
Broccoli	Escarole
Carrot tops	Kale
Chard	Mustard greens
Chicory	Romaine lettuce
Chrysanthemum greens	Spinach
Collard greens	Turnip greens
Dandelion greens	Watercress

Deep Yellow

Carrots	Sweet potato
Pumpkin	Winter squash

Starchy

Breadfruit
Corn
Green peas
Hominy

Potato
Rutabaga
Taro

Other Vegetables

Artichoke
Asparagus
Beets
Brussels sprouts
Cabbage
Cauliflower
Celery
Chinese cabbage
Cucumber
Daikon radish (Japanese
    white radish)
Eggplant (aubergine)
Green beans

Green pepper
Lettuce
Mushrooms
Okra
Onions
Radishes
Shiitake mushrooms
Snow peas (mangetouts)
Summer squash
Tomato
Turnip
Vegetable juices
Zucchini (courgettes)

Grains

Whole-Grain (maximize)

Brown rice
Buckwheat groats
Buckwheat noodles (soba)
Bulgur
Corn tortillas
Granola
Oatmeal
Popcorn

Pumpernickel bread
Ready-to-eat cereals
Rye bread and crackers
Whole-grain pasta
Whole wheat bagels
Whole wheat bread
Whole wheat cereals
Whole wheat crackers

Whole wheat English muffins · Whole wheat pita bread
Whole wheat pasta · Whole wheat rolls

Enriched (minimize)

Bagels · Hot dog rolls
Cornmeal · Italian bread
Crackers · Noodles
English muffins · Pancakes
Farina · Pasta
Flour noodles (udon) · Pretzels
Flour tortillas · Ready-to-eat cereals
French bread · Waffles
Grits · White rice
Hamburger buns · White bread

Grain Products with Too Much Fat and Sugar*

Biscuits (most) · Danish
Cake · Doughnut
Cookies · Muffin
Corn Bread · Piecrust (pastry)
Croissant · Tortilla chips

Fruits

Apple · Dates
Apricot · Figs
Asian pear · Fruit juices
Banana · Grapefruit
Blueberries · Grapes
Cantaloupe · Guava
Cherries · Honeydew melon
Citrus juices · Kiwifruit
Cranberries · Lemon

Mango
Nectarine
Orange
Papaya
Passion fruit
Peach
Pear
Persimmons
Pineapple
Plantain

Plum
Prickly pear
Prunes
Raisins
Raspberries
Rhubarb
Star fruit (carambola)
Strawberries
Tangerine
Watermelon

Calcium Foods

Low-Fat Dairy Products

Fat-free cheese
Fat-free sour cream
Fat-free yogurt
Low-fat cheese

Low-fat sour cream
Low-fat yogurt
Reduced-fat milk (1%)
Skim milk

Other Dairy with More Fat or Sugar

Cheddar cheese
Cheese spreads
Chocolate milk
Creams
Flavored yogurt
Frozen yogurt
Ice cream

Ice milk
Processed cheeses
Puddings made with milk
Sour cream
Swiss cheese Whole milk
Yogurt

Vegetarian

Agar-agar
Broccoli
Calcium-fortified orange juice

Calcium-fortified tofu
Canned table beans
Collard greens

Kale
Mustard greens
Rhubarb

Seaweed
Spinach
Turnip greens

Seafood

Canned salmon

Canned sardines

Flavonoid Foods

Soy Products

Meat substitutes
Miso
Soybeans
Soybean chips
Soybean sprouts
Soy concentrate
Soy cream cheese
Soy flakes, defatted

Soy flat noodles
Soy flour
Soy nuts
Tempeh
Texturized vegetable protein
Tofu
Tofu frozen yogurt

Other Beans, Legumes

Kidney beans
Lentils

Low-fat peanut butter
Red clover

Vegetables

Bok choy
Carrot tops
Celery

Kale
Lettuce
Onions

Fruits

Applesauce
Avocado
Cherries

Cranberries
Plums

Whole Grains

Flaxseed

Other Sources

Arrowroot (kudzu)

Tea (jasmine, green, oolong, or black)

Omega-3 Foods

Fish

Bonito
Eel (unagi or anago)
Flounder
Halibut
"Horse" mackerel
Mackerel
Pacific saury

Salmon
Sardines
Sea bream
Shrimp
Tuna
Yellowtail

Other Sources

Black currant oil
Evening primrose oil
Flaxseeds/oils
Fish oil capsules
Omega-3 eggs

Omega-3 margarine
Pumpkin seeds
Soy products or soybean oil
Walnuts

Beans

Great Northern (cannellini)	Navy (haricot)
Kidney	Soybeans

*Fats**

Good Fats (maximize)

Canola oil (M; O-3)	Olive oil (M)
Fish oil (O-3)	Peanut oil (M)
Flaxseed oil (O-3)	Trans-free margarine (M)

Good Fats (minimize)

Corn oil (O-6)	Sesame oil (O-6)
Cottonseed oil (O-6)	Soybean oil (O-6)
Grapeseed oil (O-6)	Sunflower oil (O-6)
Safflower oil (O-6)	

Bad Fats

Animal fat (S)	Hydrogenated oils (T)
Butter (S)	Margarine (T)
Coconut oil (S)	Palm oil (S)
Dairy fat (S)	

*M = monounsaturated fat,

O-3 = Omega-3 polyunsaturated fat,

O-6 = Omega-6 polyunsaturated fat,

S = saturated fat,

T = trans fat

* Note: low-fat or low-sugar varieties are acceptable.

So it's time to pause and consider your food, before you eat it—to think about the nutrition it has to offer your body and savor the taste before you swallow. Food that can bring you health should be respected and, when time allows, presented in a loving and beautiful manner. This is what we mean by conscious eating. It's about bringing true pleasure and joy to the eating experience, whether you're eating quietly on your own, dining with family or friends, or feasting at a joyous celebration.

In Okinawa, food is so important that it is offered regularly to the ancestors after their passing to the next world. The last time we joined the Obon celebration in Okinawa, a celebration of Ancestor Day, we did the appropriate thing: we brought a bean cake for one of the ancestors, a friend's uncle who had passed on several years back. Later, the family's ninety-year-old matriarch, whose role it is to communicate with the ancestors, told us that the uncle had enjoyed it immensely, and gave us many thanks and blessings in return for our conscious act of caring. Everyone felt good. Even the ancestors, it seems, practice conscious eating in Okinawa! Food is sacred.

One of the things most Westerners remark on when visiting Japan is the great care taken in the preparation and presentation of food. In Okinawa and, indeed, all over Japan, food is meticulously prepared and great attention is paid to detail. Ceremonies such as *Cha-no-yuu* (the Way of Tea), the famous Japanese tea ceremony that dates back to the fifteenth century, require years of training to perfect. We don't suggest that you take a multi-year sabbatical to learn how to present tea, but the concept behind the tea ceremony could be of use to us in the West: *visuals count*. Perhaps family members might be more inclined to eat vegetables and soy foods if they were presented aesthetically. Rather than serving instant mashed potatoes and gravy, or opening a can of beans and dumping them in a bowl, perhaps we should consider a more respectful, artistic approach. In Japan there is a saying: not dressing up the meal with color is like sending someone out of the house without clothes. They feel that food should look as good as it smells and tastes. We agree, and offer some suggestions here from the Japanese, who have perfected the art of food presentation.

Think Five Colors

Make your dinner beautiful with color. There is a philosophy in Japan best exemplified by the *Shojin Ryori*, the rituals of preparing and eating vegetarian Buddhist temple fare. The goal is to "get five colors on your table." The colors are red, yellow, blue-green, white, and black. It turns out that this may not just be visually appealing but healthy as well. It adds a variety of nutrients that are more concentrated in one food or another. Red could be red cabbage, red pepper, paprika sprinkled on fish, red onion, or tomato—the possibilities are many. Yellow could be egg, corn, polenta, squash, or mushrooms. Green choices are endless— any of the green vegetables or herbs, salad, avocado, cooked zucchini, basil leaves on thick-sliced tomatoes. For white you could use onions, tofu, or a staple carbohydrate food such as rice, bread, noodles, potato. And black beans, black-eyed peas in a soup or a salad, or sliced black olives can represent black; or if you are interested in Japanese and Okinawan dishes, you could try nori seaweed sheets (available in most health food stores and Asian markets). You can put crushed nori in miso soup, sprinkle it on salad, or roll rice with some cooked fish and avocado. It looks beautiful and is quite delicious.

This five-color concept doesn't mean you have to spend hours preparing fancy gourmet meals. The idea can be applied to something as simple as a veggie burger or tuna salad. With tuna salad, for instance, you could put a scoop on a bed of lettuce, sprinkle finely chopped black olive pieces on top, and surround it with sliced red pepper, tomatoes, and diced carrots. Not that much extra work, but so much more pleasing to the eye than a scoop of white tuna on a white plate. You get the idea. Try it. It gives you a chance to express yourself artistically while at the same time adding more nutrition to your meal—one of those win-win situations we love. If you have children, you could even make it a game the whole family can play. They might be inspired to think of some creations of their own.

Invest in Some Japanese Tableware

Japanese tableware, of course, is not a necessity for following the Okinawa Program. The guideline will work perfectly well with whatever dishes you already own. We only mention this because we've found that a few exotic new bowls and dishes can be added incentive to follow a new way of eating. New tableware can help to get you in the mood and add to your overall aesthetic experience. Most commercial Japanese tableware is very reasonably priced and readily available. Check online for Asian or global markets, or the next time you're in a Japanese restaurant ask them if they know any local sources. Also, we've found it's great fun to look for Asian-inspired pottery when visiting craft fairs—there are generally some wonderful pieces offered. (See Appendix B for online resources.) At the very least, you might want to think about buying some chopsticks and learning how to use them.

Here, then, are the basics of Japanese tableware—pieces to consider if you're ready to go all out and try a totally new dining experience. And, of course, these pieces can be used for serving Western dishes as well.

- Small round lacquer bowls with lids for soup
- Oval bamboo-woven basket for bread
- Assorted Japanese pottery: small and big plates, 2-inch diameter small plates for condiments, short cups without handles for tea, teapot, chop-stick rests, lacquer rice bowls, large round pot for "one-pot" dishes
- Bamboo, wooden, or lacquered chopsticks
- Bamboo skewers for barbecued fish and vegetables
- Small pottery pots for soy sauce, vinegar, chili pepper, and other condiments
- Lacquered round tray to hold teacups, teapot, snacks

There's no doubt that Japanese tableware can be beautiful and soothing to the mind and the eye, but so can good Western tableware—if it's actually used. Many people keep their most wonderful tableware locked away in drawers and cupboards, or stored in attics. So take a few minutes to rummage through the treasures you may already own. Bring out your beautiful serving bowls and dishes and add an extra dose of visual enjoyment to your meals.

Use Healthy and Aesthetic Garnishes

Herb or leaf garnishes add more than just beauty—they can offer a quick herbal tonic that you may have missed earlier in the day. A more in-depth description of some of the health-promoting qualities of Okinawan and Japanese herbs is provided later in this chapter and in

Chapter Five, but here are a few quick tips to beautify a meal and add nutrients at the same time.

- **Green mint leaves**—perilla (called *shiso* in Okinawa), peppermint, spearmint, or flat-leaf parsley are excellent garnishes.
- **Yellow turmeric (ucchin) flakes**—sprinkle on white miso soup or combine with rice to make turmeric rice.
- **Red chili peppers**—give you vivid red color. Sprinkle on baked potato, Japanese noodles, or tuna salads. Dried red pepper flakes can be substituted and have an indefinite shelf life.
- **White sesame seeds**—have a savory taste and never hinder the taste of other ingredients. Good color contrast with something green; add to spinach, green salad, spinach fettuccine, et cetera. These are commonly available in most grocery stores.
- **Black dried seaweed**—Nori or wakame seaweed can add an interesting black accent to your food. Sprinkle on fish, potatoes, and salads, or put dried wakame in your miso soup with diced tofu. Seaweed is now available in the Asian section of most good supermarkets (be sure to get the kind you don't have to soak).

Cut Excess Calories

Hara Hachi Bu—Eat Only Until You Are 80 Percent Full

If there were a simple way to increase your life span, virtually eliminate cancer, decrease all forms of chronic disease, and age at half the rate you are currently aging, would you want to know what it is? Well, there seems to be a way to do just that. An astute scientist from Cornell University, Dr. C. M. McKay,[8] detected it in the 1930s. He made the remarkable discovery that *calorie restriction* is a consistent and reproducible method of prolonging life and vitality in animals, and it's been shown to be effective in every species tested, from aquatic organisms to primates.

Interestingly, only one human population that we know of has a self-imposed habit of calorie restriction—the Okinawans, the longest-lived population in the world. Okinawans eat a lot and certainly do not go hungry. But they tend to stop eating before they are bursting at the seams. They call their secret *hara hachi bu,* which loosely translates to "eat until you are eight parts full (out of ten)." Simply put, leave a little room at the end of each meal. Here's why: It takes the stretch receptors in the stomach about twenty minutes to tell the brain how full you really are. You will actually feel fuller twenty minutes *after* you put down your fork. If you eat until you are 100 percent full, you will go about 20 percent overcapacity with *every* meal. Your stomach will stretch a little bit each time to accommodate the extra food. Then you have to eat more next time to get the same feeling of fullness. It's a vicious cycle. It served a good purpose in the days when we had to forage for our calories, but with a mini-mart around every corner it's a dangerous mechanism. Think *hara hachi bu*—in fact, make it your new mantra—and you'll have a better chance of winning the battle of the bulge.

Studies show that this kind of simple calorie restriction also has remarkable health consequences. The straightforward explanation boils down to mastering the notorious free radical. Free radicals damage the tissue of your body and are generated mostly as by-products of the food (calories) we eat. *Calor* in Latin means "heat." When we eat calories we burn them for energy and release heat, creating free radicals in the process. It's the burning of calories that creates the free radicals. The more calories we eat, the more calories we burn, and the more free radicals we create. The fewer calories we consume, the fewer free radicals we produce—it's that simple. Does that mean we should eat less food? Not necessarily. We just have to eat less "calorie-dense" food, such as foods high in fat and sugar.

The Okinawans are able to eat a lot of food while still keeping their calorie count low because they consume foods that are high in unrefined carbohydrate and fiber. They fill up on hearty, low-calorie food and therefore don't get exposed to all of those damaging free radicals that are the by-products of high-calorie fare. In fact, they actually eat more food by weight than North Americans, but because they eat less fat, they eat fewer calories overall—a very healthy trade-off. All in all, there is strong support for the idea that fewer calories means better health. The Okinawa Program shows you how to reduce your calories while still getting plenty of delicious food to eat.

Tips For Minimizing Your Calories

- *Make wise choices when dining out.* Choose lean fish instead of steak. Stress the vegetables. Watch out for fatty sauces. One good ploy is to ask for dressings and sauces on the side. That way you have control over quantity. Some restaurants bring you entrees swimming in sauce and salad soaked in dressing when all you really need is a smidgen to get the taste. A little bit usually goes a long way.

  You can also have your waiter ask the chef to prepare food a certain way for you. You could, for instance, request that your fish be poached or broiled (grilled) dry (without butter). If a dish is served with mashed potatoes, you could ask them to substitute broccoli. Or you can ask what vegetables are available and request a mélange—even if it's not on the menu. Remember, restaurants are a service business—they are there to make you happy. You're the customer and hence always right. A very nice position to be in.

  Also check menus for a vegetarian or a heart-healthy section; many restaurants offer them these days. If you're dining out as a couple, order salads for both (dressing on the side, please), but *share* the main dish. And share desserts, too. This is not only romantic but saves calories and money as well. Not many of us can eat an appetizer, a main dish, and a dessert—it's simply too much. If we're served big portions, we feel obligated to eat everything on our plates, just like Mom taught us—especially if it's tasty. Then we end up feeling bloated and sluggish. Not a good way to end a meal. It's always better to take home the extras in a restaurant container rather than in your stomach. So break bad restaurant habits: bond with your mate, save money, save calories, and have a lovely lunch of last night's meal—a quadruple-win situation.

- *Follow the Okinawa Food Pyramid.* Smart food choices are, of course, essential for cutting excess calories. Choose wisely and follow the Okinawa Food Pyramid on page 84 to approximate your required number of servings per day. A more precise guide to serving number and size requirements is offered in the tables that follow the pyramid. If you find yourself gaining weight, it could be a result of muscle enhancement owing to your exercise program. But if you are gaining fat—which you can tell by looking at your body fat scale (see Chapter Two), then you should cut back on your number of food servings or increase your activity levels. Our four-week program in Chapter Ten will guide you in your overall plan.

- *Keep a record of what you eat.* One of the quickest ways to get a handle on how many and what type of calories you are consuming is to keep a tally of what and how many servings you eat for three days. It's only three days, so it shouldn't be too painful. The goal is to consume, on a weekly basis, the number of calories that fits with your caloric needs based on the Okinawa Food Pyramid. If your three-day record suggests that you are deviating from the Okinawa Food Pyramid in a major way, then try to correct yourself by eating more of the groups you are underemphasizing, and eating less of the groups that you are overemphasizing. After a few attempts it will become second nature. Using the Okinawa Program Nutrition Tracker in Appendix A (page 486), you would only have to fill in three days to get a general idea, although the longer you keep your record the more conscious of your eating habits you will be. See Appendix A for this simple but powerful means of tracking your progress or Chapter Ten for a healthy weight-loss plan.

Sixteen Secrets for Eliminating Excess Calories

1. *Spice up your meals.* Using hot chili peppers or other hot spices can add flavor and zip to your meal. We tend to eat less when our food is a bit hot.

2. *Bulk up your salads.* Chop up celery, carrots, broccoli, onions, or other vegetables instead of shredding or slicing. Chewing bigger pieces takes more time and effort so you will be chewing more and eating less during the main course.

3. *Drink water before your meal.* This decreases your appetite, helps mix up the digestive juices, and keeps you from eating too much.

4. *Try a juice spritzer, instead of juice.* Mix half of your favorite juice with water or sparkling water. You can cut up to 100 calories per glass. Over a year this could mean 7 pounds.

5. *Have a cup of green or jasmine tea before you walk.* Caffeine liberates fatty acids from muscles so that you can burn fat faster. And the flavonoids in tea are good for your general health. If you have high blood pressure, go easy on the caffeine.

6. *Spray, don't pour the oil.* When cooking with oils—we, of course, recommend canola oil—use a sprayer for grilling, baking, or to add flavor to salads and cut calories at the same time. Two seconds of spraying gives you about ½ teaspoon of oil, compared with four to six times that amount you would get if you poured. That can save a lot of calories. Spray bottles are available at many stores.

7. *Have chunky soup.* One study reported that people who ate soup full of large vegetable pieces felt fuller and ate one-fifth less for lunch than those who ate pureed soup made of the same ingredients.

8. *Read labels.* When you see a bag of chips or a candy bar, they appear to contain a set number of calories per bag or bar. A closer inspection can uncover the not-so-sweet facts: one bag or bar may equal two or more servings, so it is actually double what you thought you could get away with.

9. *Get a lunchbox.* Dining out can make you fat, especially if you're tempted by the pre-meal bread. Some studies suggest you get as many as 300 extra calories in a day if you eat lunch out. Instead, once or twice a week pack some whole-grain bread with fat-free cream cheese or soy butter and salad in your lunchbox, then take it to work with a bottle of water. It'll save you money, too.

10. *Measure before cooking pasta.* Everybody tends to cook too much pasta and this can lead to overeating. But you can avoid this pitfall if you measure the pasta and cook the proper amount. Keep a pasta measurer near your pasta; its diameter tells you how much pasta you should serve per person. For smaller pastas such as penne, macaroni, or rotini, use a measuring cup. One cup equals approximately 150 calories. And use spoons to measure oils, salt, sugar, or anything you should not overeat.

11. *Savor your snack.* When you are ready to gobble down a half dozen of your favorite cookies, just hold off for 10 seconds. Take in the aroma for another 10 seconds, place a bite on your tongue, hold for another 10 seconds, and then eat slowly, enjoying every bite. This strategy can help you stop at one.

12. *Earn your calories.* Sometimes we just open the fridge and get a piece of cake or a cup of ice cream without thinking. Before you grab your fork or spoon to start eating, do ten sit-ups or push-ups. This way you earn your indulgences and you are less likely to take them for granted or feel guilty.

13. *Satisfy your cravings in other ways.* Chewing sugarless gum or popping a menthol mint can help cut your cravings in an instant.

14. *Friendly reminders.* Even when we decide not to eat extra sweets, the decision sometimes becomes like a distant tune—we simply can't hear it after a while. For these occasions, you might need to be inspired by quotations in strategic spots, such as on the fridge, freezer, mirror, or computer. Suggestions: "Do I really need that cookie now?" "How will my new pants feel and fit if I eat that ice cream?" This might sound a little ridiculous, but written reminders will help you stay on the right track.

15. *Think small.* The smaller the package of food, the less is available for you to eat. Obvious but worth remembering.

16. *Get inspired.* Seek inspiration in someone you admire—someone who looks the way you would like to look and does things you would like to do. It helps to clearly see the possibilities. But don't beat yourself up for not

instantly attaining the ideal of the role model. Just use the role model as a way to help you visualize your goals.

Graze, Don't Gorge

Eating several small meals a day is much better for your body than eating the same number of calories in three large meals. One study that our Toronto group published in the *New England Journal of Medicine* showed that simply spreading the calories out over eight small meals instead of eating three large meals led to 13 percent lower LDL (lethal) cholesterol levels, 4 percent lower blood sugar levels, an impressive 28 percent lower level of insulin in the blood (over-production of insulin can lead to diabetes and possibly cancer), and a host of other health benefits.[9] Starving yourself all day and then gorging at night, incidentally, is definitely not the way to achieve health or fat loss—imagine what that does to your insulin levels! Here are the right ways to approach the grazing method.

Portion Size

In Okinawa, serving sizes are about two-thirds to one-half the size seen in North America. If you find yourself craving unhealthy "indulgence food," such as potato chips or chocolate chip cookies, buy the smallest bag available (think sample-size airplane packaging). That way you'll lessen the damage but won't feel deprived—and you'll be more likely to stick with an overall healthy eating plan. Better yet, try a helping of these healthy snacks when hunger strikes during the day.

Ten Quick and Healthy Snacks

- One piece of whole-grain bread with 1 tablespoon of hummus.
- One whole-grain English muffin with 1 tablespoon fat-free cream cheese.
- Half a cantaloupe filled with low-fat yogurt.
- A baked potato with fat-free sour cream.

- A microwavable veggie burger with misonaise, lettuce, and tomato.
- A handful of soy nuts (no salt or lightly salted).
- Celery sticks with hummus, almond butter, or peanut butter (nonhydrogenated—check labels; best to buy freshly ground).
- A piece of fruit.
- A low-fat muffin.
- A brown rice cake with a dab of nonfat cottage cheese topped with a slice of tomato.

Emergency Survival Techniques

We can't always control where we'll be at mealtimes or when hunger strikes. If you end up in a restaurant where special orders aren't taken or in a fast-food joint, here's what to do.

At a Diner

- Order pasta or a baked potato. If you like sour cream on potatoes, get it on the side and use very little. Order the pasta with the sauce on the side, then just use a few teaspoons for taste.
- Order fish or chicken for the entree, baked or grilled.
- Avoid the margarine, butter, and fried foods.
- Eat a few crackers, and avoid the doughy white bread.
- If you get a sandwich, request no mayo. Try a little mustard instead.
- Split the dessert with your partner or, better yet, have a sugarless mint.

At a Fast-Food Outlet

- Fill up at the salad bar first. Go easy on the dressing.
- Order the grilled chicken sandwich instead of the burger. Take off the top piece of bread.
- Order a baked potato and load up on the veggies instead of fries.
- Drink water instead of soda pop.

- Steal just a few fries from your partner if you must.
- Try a veggie burrito (ask for half the sour cream and cheese, please).
- Go for the veggie wrap.

Eat Mostly Complex Carbohydrates (50 Percent or More of Total Calories)

There's been a lot of talk recently about carbohydrates, so let's set the record straight on exactly what they are. Carbohydrates derive their name from their chemical components: molecular chains of carbon *(carb)*, oxygen *(o)*, and hydrogen *(hydr)*. Vary the structure and you get the different forms of carbohydrates, including simple carbs such as refined sugars—ordinary table sugar, for example—and complex carbs (digestible starches, such as potatoes, and indigestible fibers, such as bran). Complex carbs can be refined (fiber absent, such as in bleached white flour) or unrefined (fiber present, such as in stone-ground wheat flour and other whole-grain flours). We advocate unrefined complex carbohydrates made from whole grains, since the fiber is the healthiest part of the carbohydrate, containing most of the vitamins and minerals and other disease-fighting antioxidants.

Carbohydrates form the preferred fuel for the body and are clean burning, like propane, in contrast to fats and proteins, which are much dirtier and much less efficient fuels, more like burning coal. Carbs provide direct fuel—for the brain, the central nervous system, and the muscles—in the form of glucose, also called blood sugar. Here are some examples of refined and unrefined carbohydrates.

REFINED AND UNREFINED CARBOHYDRATES

REFINED (LESS HEALTHY)	UNREFINED (MORE HEALTHY)
White flour*	Whole-grain flour
Table sugar	Raw (cane) sugar
White rice (polished)	Whole-grain rice (brown)
Jam	Fruit
Packaged mashed potatoes, chips	Whole potatoes
	Beans and other legumes

* Prime ingredient of cakes, piecrusts (pastry), bread, and buns.

Carbohydrates have—undeservedly—received a lot of bad press lately and have even been fingered, wrongly, as the root of obesity and heart disease. The widespread phobia with regard to carbs can be linked in part to popularization and misinterpretation of the Glycemic Index (GI).[10]

The Glycemic Index is, in simplest terms, a research tool that tells us how much our blood sugar rises after we eat a particular carbohydrate. The type of carbohydrate may be quick-release, slow-release, or a combination of the two. Carbohydrates that are quick-release convert into glucose (or blood sugar) quickly so that after these carbs have been eaten, glucose enters our bloodstream fairly rapidly. Carbohydrates that are slow-release convert more slowly into glucose, which then enters our bloodstream more slowly.

Here's how the Glycemic Index works. The Glycemic Index of pure glucose is set at 100, and every other food is ranked on a scale of zero to 100 according to its actual effect on blood sugar levels. Carbohydrates that break down the fastest raise blood sugar the most and rank the highest on the scale. For example, a food with a GI of 90 would have 90 percent of the effect of pure glucose, a food with a GI of 70 would cause 70 percent of the rise attributable to pure glucose, and so on. Some carbohydrates belong in a high-GI group, some in a mid-GI group, and others in a low-GI group. Remember that most foods are usually a mixture of carbohydrate, protein, and fat. Any food high in fat, protein, fiber, or slow-release carbohydrate ranks low on the scale. A GI of 55 or less is considered low, 56 to 70 intermediate, and greater than 70 high.

As you learned in Chapter Two, the amount of blood sugar in our bloodstreams is regulated by insulin; the pancreas releases insulin to take glucose from the bloodstream and pack it into cells. If you eat a lot of quick-release, high-GI food—like cookies and white bread—your body experiences a rapid and high increase in glucose and is forced to produce a lot of extra insulin to get rid of the excess glucose.[10] After the rush of insulin gets rid of the excess blood sugar, your blood sugar level will dip low. So with high-GI meals, you experience a rapid spike in your blood sugar level followed by a flood of insulin that brings on a quick drop in your blood sugar level.

If you eat slow-release, low-GI food—pasta, whole-grain bread, high-fiber fruits and vegetables—your bloodstream receives a lower and slower dose of glucose and your pancreas only has to produce moderate amounts of insulin to take care of the smaller amounts of glucose in your blood. Less work for your pancreas, and you won't experience severe blood sugar highs and lows. Over the years, keeping your blood sugar levels moderate without extreme highs and lows means less wear and tear on your pancreas. Wearing out the insulin-producing pancreas can lead to adult-onset diabetes in genetically susceptible individuals. Moreover, a low-GI meal will keep your blood sugar levels moderate over a longer period of time, so you feel less hungry less often. Smaller meals also have a similar effect and actually allow us to nibble more often without gaining fat[9–11]—good news for those of us watching our weight. The figure below displays the concept of the glycemic index in an easily understandable form.

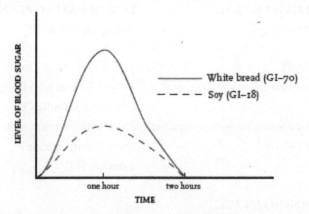

AVERAGE BLOOD SUGAR LEVEL AFTER CONSUMPTION OF
HIGH– AND LOW–GLYCEMIC INDEX FOODS

So what's the bottom line? There are healthy carbs and not-so-healthy carbs. The latter are quick-release high-Glycemic Index carbs, which most often fall into the camp of simple sugars and refined (fiber stripped away) grains, such as anything made with white flour or white sugar. *If it's white, it's probably refined and less healthy.* The good carbs are slow-release, low-Glycemic Index carbs, such as fruit, vegetables, and whole grains that are high in fiber, filling, and nutrient dense—perfect fuels for our bodies. That said, it's important not to get hung up on counting the GI of every food you eat; *it's the overall balance of high- and low-GI foods that counts.* High-GI foods may have deleterious consequences if eaten in large quantities over many years, but these "bad carbs" aren't terrible if eaten sparingly. For example, it's okay now and then to eat a high-GI carbohydrate like a white-flour bagel (GI 72), especially if you eat low-GI carbohydrates in the same meal, such as peanuts or peanut butter (GI 14). The combination of high-GI and low-GI foods produces a moderate GI meal. (Better yet, eat a stone-ground whole wheat bagel—GI 53—and you will already start with a low-GI food.) One particular food or single meal will not make or break your health. It's how well you balance all the foods you eat, creating a healthy lifetime eating pattern that will decrease your risk of cancer, heart disease, and diabetes. Look at the table below to see how easily you can decrease the GI of your meal.

HIGH-GI EATING PLAN	LOW-GI EATING PLAN
(Glycemic Index: 73)	(Glycemic Index: 47)
BREAKFAST	
1 cup Rice Chex cereal (89) and regular milk (34)	1 cup All-Bran with Extra Fiber (51) and skim milk (32)
2 slices white toast (70) with margarine and honey (87)	2 slices whole-grain toast (64) with trans-free margarine
	1 orange (44)
MIDMORNING SNACK	
2 vanilla wafers (77)	2 trans-free oatmeal cookies (54)
LUNCH	
1 white-flour bagel (72) with regular cream cheese	1 pumpernickel bagel (51) with nonfat cream cheese
1 doughnut (76)	1 apple (39)
MIDAFTERNOON SNACK	
1 Mars bar (68)	1 ounce peanuts (14)

DINNER	
Lamb chops (N/A)	Fish steak (N/A)
Instant potato (85)	Boiled new potatoes (54)
Carrots (71)	Sweet corn (59)
Parsnips (97)	Peas (47)
Low-fat ice cream (61) with banana (60)	1 container (6 ounces) yogurt (36) with peaches (52)

AFTER-DINNER SNACK	
1 ounce (small bag) nachos (74)	⅔ cup fruit cocktail (55)

ENERGY VALUE	
2,070 calories	1,300 calories

FAT CONTENT	
75 grams (33% of calories)	25 grams (17% of calories)

The Glycemic Index is a very useful concept in terms of helping you to create a moderate lifetime eating pattern.[12] But unfortunately, it has been misinterpreted by many, resulting in an irrational fear of carbohydrates. This has helped popularize a number of nutrition books that advocate unhealthy low-carbohydrate diets. Some books even claim that carbohydrates are the root of obesity and heart disease.[10,11] The virtual absence of obesity and heart disease in the high-carbohydrate-eating Okinawan elders and the rapid increase of obesity, diabetes, and heart disease in the low-carbohydrate, high-fat, protein-eating young Okinawans nips this fallacy in the bud. It's the same unfortunate story for Hawaiians, Australian Aborigines, and North American natives who adopted a high-fat and protein Western diet after doing well on high-carbohydrate traditional diets for thousands of years. The Okinawa Program is also consistent with the core recommendations of the USDA Food Pyramid, Health Canada's Food Groups, and most other governmental groups. It's the sensible way to eat and it's based on real evidence from our group and leading-edge research in the field of nutritional science, not pop nutrition. Some pop nutrition writers claim that after you eat enough carbohydrates to replenish your liver's glycogen stores, all the rest is turned to fat so you should, paradoxically, eat fat to lose fat. In reality, any calories you consume in excess of your body's needs turn to fat whether they are from carbohydrates, protein, or fat—except it's a little easier to turn fat into fat.[11]

Take a look at the table. Do you see anything amiss?

WHERE NORTH AMERICANS GET THEIR CARBS[13]

TYPE	CARB FOODS	PERCENT
Simple	Sugar (mostly sucrose or table sugar)	40
Complex	Grains (mostly refined)	36
	Fruits	7
	Dairy (minimal carb as milk sugar)	6
	Potatoes	5
	Vegetables	4
	Legumes (beans) and nuts	2

What is clearly amiss is that we are eating *way too much refined sugar.* We need to cut back drastically on refined sugars and replace them with unrefined, complex carbs. Even though we eat a lot of grains in North America, they are usually in the form of white flour, a refined grain with its fiber stripped away. The two most important beneficial carbohydrate foods—legumes (beans) and vegetables, with their impressive content of cancer-fighting antioxidants—amount to an abysmal 6 percent of our carbohydrate intake! This must change. Eating healthy unrefined whole carbs helps us increase our fiber, which also has important consequences for blood sugar.

Your Glucose Load

The glucose load is another very useful concept. It's a research tool that considers the blood sugar effect of dietary fiber and the Glycemic Index (slow- or quick-release carb). Glucose load is lowered by taking in less refined carbohydrates (fiber stripped away), such as sugar candy, cakes, soft drinks, and white bread; and eating more unrefined (fiber present) carbs like whole grains, stone-ground whole wheat bread, pasta, and vegetables such as peas, sweet potatoes, and onions. It can also be lowered simply by adding fiber to your diet in the form of fiber supplements. Researchers at the Harvard School of Public Health and the University of Toronto found it a particularly good research tool for predicting who would develop Type II (adult-onset) diabetes over the next few years. (The group with the highest glucose load, also called "glycemic load," was at two to three times the risk of those with the lowest glucose load.)[14] Recently, the same Harvard researchers reported that glucose load is also an important risk factor for coronary heart disease.[14]

Keeping your glucose load low is good, since it produces a lower insulin response. This is because foods high in fiber enter the bloodstream slowly (remember slow release) and raise blood sugar levels at a very slow rate. Most refined carbohydrates, on the other hand, increase your glucose load because their fiber is stripped away, so there's nothing to slow down the absorption of glucose. They zip through the bloodstream at an accelerated pace, quickly raise the blood sugar, and produce an exaggerated insulin response. This is not good. You get an instant rush and minutes later an instant drop as insulin comes flooding in to clean up the extra glucose. This can cause energy swings that affect your mood, make you feel listless, and possibly increase your risk for adult-onset diabetes. There is some evidence that a high glucose load is also associated with increased risk for hormone-dependent cancers and coronary heart disease (see Chapter Two).[14] Too much glucose in the blood can be bad for other reasons, as well. It literally sticks to other cells and interferes with their function in a process called glycosylation ("making sugar").

This is especially true in diabetics who have high blood glucose levels. They experience accelerated heart disease, neurologic disease, kidney disease, and blindness, since each of these body systems is particularly susceptible to glucose-induced damage.[15] The same mechanisms are thought to operate at a much slower level in the rest of us, depending on how many and what kind of calories we consume, our activity levels, and our genetics. The key is to lower your average blood glucose levels by eating unrefined, high-fiber, whole carbohydrates.

Does this mean we have to avoid all simple refined carbohydrates or check every food's Glycemic Index before we eat it? No, it just means we must minimize the foods that have a very high GI (80 or above) and eat plenty of whole grains, fruits, and vegetables. If you absolutely must have a high-GI fix on a regular basis, then use some of the tips below to lower the overall glucose load of your meal. In the big picture, you need not worry about the GI of a particular food if you eat largely from the Okinawa Food Pyramid. But just to keep you as informed as possible we have provided the Glycemic Index of different foods in the table below.

To sum it up, carbohydrates are, by and large, nature's perfect clean-burning fuel, which is why we strongly suggest you avoid all the low-carbohydrate fad diets currently all the rage (low is 40 percent or less of total calories). A healthy diet is high in unrefined, complex carbohydrate, high in fiber, and relatively low in fat, protein, and calories. If you eat this way you will automatically lower your glucose load. Okinawan elders have, for most of their lives, consumed a diet that is 70 to 80 percent carbohydrate owing to their high consumption of *imo,* or sweet potato.[3] This is the same type of sweet potato that, according to the anti-carb fear mongers, is a forbidden food because it's a carbohydrate! So break out the bagels (whole-grain, please) and bring on the sweet potatoes, because carbohydrates are back in! (See one of our favorite recipes, Sweet Potatoes with Orange, page 419.)

The Glycemic Index of Common Foods

Low—up to 55
Medium—56 to 70
High—over 70

BAKED GOODS

Cake		Croissant	67
Angel food	67	Crumpet	69
Pound	54	Doughnut	76
Sponge	46	Flan	65
Muffins		Pastry	59
Bran	60	Pizza, with cheese	60
Blueberry	59	Waffles, Aunt Jemima	76

Carrot	62
Oatmeal (Quaker mix)	62

BEVERAGES

Apple juice, unsweetened	41	Orange juice	46
Grapefruit juice, unsweetened	48	Pineapple juice, unsweetened	46
Lucozade	95		

BREADS

Bagel, white	72	Kaiser roll, white	73
Bagel, pumpernickel	51	Melba toast	70
Bagel, whole wheat, stone-ground	53	Pita bread, white	57
		Pumpernickel, whole-grain	46
Barley bread (75% kernels)	27	Rye bread	62
Barley bread (100% flour)	67	Rye kernel bread (80% kernel)	55
Bread stuffing, Paxo	74	Wheat bread, white	70
Bulgur bread	53	Wheat bread, whole-grain	64
Hamburger bun, white	61		

BREAKFAST CEREALS

All-Bran	51	Grape-Nuts Flakes	80
Bran Buds	58	Muesli	63
Bran Buds with Psyllium	47	Multi-Bran Chex	58
Cheerios	74	Oat bran, porridge	59
Corn Bran	75	Oat bran, raw	55
Corn Chex	83	Oats, one-minute	66
Corn Flakes	83	Puffed Wheat	67
Corn Flakes, high-fiber	74	Quaker Quick Oats	65
Cream of Wheat	70	Shredded Wheat	75
Golden Grahams	71	Wheetabix	75
Grape-Nuts	67		

CEREAL GRAINS

Barley	25	Rice, Cajun style	51
Barley, cracked	50	Rice, garden style	55
Barley, pearled	25	Rice, instant	80
Buckwheat	54	Rice, Mexican Fast and Fancy	58

Bulgur	46	Rice, parboiled	48
Cornmeal	68	Rice, wild	57
Corn, sweet, fresh	59	Rice, wild, long-grain	54
Corn, sweet, frozen	47	Rice, white, long-grain	57
Corn, taco shells	68	Rice vermicelli	58
Couscous	65	Rye, whole kernel	34
Millet	71	Tapioca, boiled with milk	81
Rice, brown	55	Wheat, whole kernel	45

COOKIES

Arrowroot	63	Oatmeal	54
Digestives	59	Rich Tea biscuits	55
Highland oatcakes	57	Vanilla wafers	77

CRACKERS

Breton Wheat Crackers	67	Stoned Wheat Thins	67
Premium Soda Crackers	74	Water crackers	63
Rye crispbread, high-fiber	64		

DAIRY FOODS

Ice cream	58	Milk, whole	34
Milk, skim	32	Yogurt	36

FRUIT AND FRUIT PRODUCTS

Apple	39	Orange	44
Apricots, canned, light syrup	64	Peach, canned, light syrup	52
Apricots, dried	32	Pear	41
Banana	60	Pear, canned in pear juice	44
Fruit cocktail, canned	55	Plum	37
Grapes	46	Raisins	64

LEGUMES

Baked beans, canned	48	Lentils	25
Black-eyed beans	42	Lentils, canned	52
Broad beans	79	Lima beans, baby, frozen	32
Butter beans	36	Mungbeans	26
Chickpeas	33	Pinto beans	39

Chickpeas, canned	42	Pinto beans, canned	45
Haricot (navy) beans	33	Romano beans	46
Haricot beans, cooked	44	Soybeans	15
Kidney beans	39	Soybeans, canned	14
Kidney beans, canned	52	Split peas, yellow, boiled	32

PASTA

Capellini	45	Spaghetti, protein	27
Macaroni, boiled 5 minutes	45	Spaghetti, white	42
Macaroni cheese, boxed	64	Spaghetti, whole-wheat	37
Mr. Noodle instant noodles	47	Tortellini, cheese	50

SNACK FOODS

Mars bar	68	Peanuts	14
Nachos	74	Potato crisps	51

SOUPS

Black bean	64	Split pea	60
Green pea, canned	66	Tomato	38
Lentil, canned	44		

SUGARS

Fructose	23	Lactose	48
Glucose	100	Maltose	105
Honey	87	Sucrose	62

VEGETABLES

Beetroot	64	Peas, green, frozen, boiled	51
Carrots	71	Potatoes, French fried	75
Parsnips	97	Potatoes, instant	85
Potatoes, new	54	Rutabaga (swede)	72
Potato, russet, baked	56	Sweet corn, fresh	59
Potato, white, baked	60	Sweet corn, frozen	47
Potato, white, boiled	56	Sweet potato	54
Potato, white, mashed	70	Yam	51

Tips to Decrease your Glucose Load

- *Eat soy.* Soy foods are extremely low on the GI scale and this will help to keep your glucose load low.
- *Add a twist of lemon.* Lemon juice will significantly lower the Glycemic Index for a food. The reasons are not entirely clear, but it may have something to do with the acidic qualities of lemon juice.
- *Add a splash of good fat.* Use a bit of olive or canola oil with your meal—adding just a dash of beneficial fat will slow the absorption of carbohydrate and result in a lower post-meal rise in blood sugar.
- *Cut back on refined carbs and sugar.* These include white flour, white rice, and concentrated sweets. Read labels and try to purchase products that are made with whole grains, not refined ones. Look for items made from whole-grain flour (whether it is wheat or rye or any other grain.) In general, white is less healthy, and brown or dark is healthier. Whole-grain fiber, especially soluble fiber, which forms a viscous gel when digested, will slow the absorption of the carb.
- *Save sweets for special times.*

Tips To Add Healthy Carbohydrates

Breakfast

- Eat high-fiber whole grains for your cereals, breads, pancakes, or waffles.
- Top cereal with sliced bananas and/or strawberries instead of sugar.
- Drink 100% fruit juice, not juice-sugar combos.
- Eat miso soup with vegetables and steamed rice at least once a week.
- Top pancakes with blueberries or strawberries instead of syrup.

- Make fruit salad with cantaloupe, strawberries, kiwis, and bananas. Sprinkle on lemon juice.
- Have crepes with fruit (such as strawberries, blueberries, and apples). Add low-fat sour cream or low-fat yogurt.

Lunch

- Add some vegetables to your Caesar salad (e.g., tomato, onion, broccoli, celery).
- Steam or boil several kinds of vegetables even if you make salad. (You can eat more kinds of vegetables that way.)
- Use hummus as your bread spread instead of trans-fat margarine or saturated-fat butter.
- Fill pita bread with romaine lettuce, cucumber, onion, and hummus.
- Top prepared pizza crust with tomato sauce, onion, zucchini (courgette), tomato, mushroom, fat-free cheese, and crumbled tofu.
- Choose a tuna and veggie sandwich instead of a beef sandwich or burger.
- Pack cut-up vegetables or salad in your sandwich bag.
- Try a veggie, whole-grain wrap sandwich.

Dinner

- Make vegetable soup with various kinds of vegetables, such as onion, zucchini (courgette), carrot, carrot leaves. Make enough for the whole week and store it in the fridge.
- Garnish your entree with something green: for example, herbs, water-cress, steamed zucchini (courgette).
- Add herbs such as cilantro (coriander), dill, fennel, parsley, rosemary, or Italian parsley to your fish. Sprinkle on lemon juice before serving.
- Add vegetables to instant dishes when you are in a hurry. (Celery or spinach for canned soup; mushrooms, tomatoes, and zucchini (courgette) for prepared pizza; canned beans for tuna helper, etc.)

- Have miso-simmered zucchini (courgette), mushroom, spinach, or broccoli with tofu once in a week.
- Select tomato sauce with celery, broccoli florets, mushrooms, or green peppers for your pasta instead of meat sauce or plain tomato sauce.
- Have vegetable stir-fry once or twice in a week, with at least three kinds of vegetables (e.g., onion, cabbage, soybean sprouts, carrots, broccoli, mushrooms, and tofu). When you need meat flavor, add one small can of water-packed tuna fish.
- Have a small amount of the entree and eat a large amount of salad or steamed vegetables.
- Have stir-fried rice with a variety of greens and vegetables such as carrot leaves, spinach, etc. Cook with canola oil or olive oil.
- For a quick salad, use pre-cut lettuce or spinach and mix with shredded carrots and broccoli florets. Dress with olive oil and balsamic vinegar.
- Eat tofu and vegetables three times or more in a week (see Chapter Twelve for various tofu recipes).

Other

- Stock your refrigerator with at least two kinds of fruits, such as berries, grapes, cantaloupe, oranges, or apples.
- Spinach is a useful vegetable not only for Western cuisine (like lasagna) but also for Japanese/Okinawan cuisine. Add to miso soup or cook with noodles.
- Choose fat-free microwave-popped and low-sodium popcorn instead of oil-popped, when watching home videos. You can spray on some canola or olive oil for taste.
- Squeeze in lemon or lime juice when you drink water or tea.

High-Fiber Carbohydrates

Remember that complex carbs are composed of two main types of carbohydrate: starch and fiber. The indigestible fiber slows the absorption of the carb. When fiber is stripped away, as it is in foods made from white flour and white sugar, carbs get absorbed quicker. Slow absorption, of course, as we've discussed, is better. Aim for a minimum of 30 grams (one ounce) of fiber per day. If you eat that much fiber your blood sugar will be rock stable! Try high-fiber breakfast cereals or beans; they are chock full of fiber. One can of beans alone can give you 30 grams of fiber and makes for a simple meal when served with whole-grain bread, corn bread, or other side dishes. Beans also tend to be high in flavonoids—an added bonus. Fiber supplements such as psyllium are a good choice. Psyllium is an ancient Indian grain that has been found to be extremely high in fiber. It's the active ingredient in Metamucil. One large scoop in a glass of freshly squeezed orange juice gives you about 5 grams of fiber. *Watch out for gas and intestinal cramps.* Increased intestinal gas is a common but temporary side effect of adding more fiber to your diet. It can be avoided by upping your fiber intake slowly, and largely resolves in a few weeks. You can also buy gas-aid supplements such as Beano. Don't forget to drink plenty of water, as extra water is needed to move fiber through your digestive tract.

Fiber Helps Keeps off the Pounds!

Wheat bran, whole-grain bread, baked beans, and other high-fiber foods may be keys to a trim figure. Over a period of ten years, young men and women who ate at least 21 grams of fiber a day gained 8 pounds less than people who ate the same number of calories but 40 percent less fiber.[16]

How To Increase Your Fiber

- Get breakfast cereals with at least 7 grams of fiber in one serving. (See the recipe for Flaxseed and Berries Granola, page 406.)
- Eat high-fiber vegetables, such as celery, cabbage, radish, fennel, and sweet potato.
- Konnyaku—glucomannan (see next chapter)—is a good source of dietary fiber, about 13 grams of fiber per 100

grams (3.5 ounces) of konnyaku. Konnyaku jelly (strawberry, apple, plum-flavored) tastes great; and because it may help keep off the pounds, it's a big hit with Japanese youth. It is usually available in Asian food stores. The next time you visit your local Asian market, also ask for white konnyaku. It's delicious when sliced thinly and dipped in a lemon-miso-sugar (just a pinch) mixture.

Eat Less Protein
(Aim for 10 to 20 Percent of Total Calories)

Most of us in the West eat too much protein. Metabolic studies have shown that the human body requires only 0.25 gram (healthy adult women) to 2.0 grams (infants) of protein per pound of body weight per day, depending upon stage of life, muscle mass, and activity level.[17] To figure out your minimum daily needs in grams (the way it is listed on all food labels), simply multiply your recommended body weight in pounds by 0.36. The resulting number is your minimum daily protein requirement. An adult woman of 120 pounds, for instance, would multiply 120 × 0.36, which equals 43 grams per day of protein. That's the amount present in two servings of meat and all she would need to stave off protein malnutrition. How much is this? About the size of two decks of cards—that's it!

When you look at it that way it's easy to see that most of us eat way too much protein. The average person eats 60 to 100 grams (women—65 g; men—90 g) of protein in a day.[17] Follow some of the high-protein diets currently all the rage and you will get about double or triple that amount! Eating significantly more or less than your minimum daily need of protein over a long period of time will produce problems. Less than the minimum can lead to protein malnutrition (kwashiorkor), but this condition is seldom seen in Western society, except among people suffering from rare illnesses or anorexia nervosa. On the other hand, eating too much protein—the problem most of us have—can lead to a number of common health concerns, such as high blood pressure, osteoporosis (through the calcium-leaching effects of protein on the bones), kidney stones, and arterial aging. And too much protein from animal sources (e.g., red meat) can lead to high levels of artery-clogging homocysteine, especially if you ingest too little folate (found in green, leafy vegetables), which is needed to get rid of this toxic amino acid. Protein by-products—such as ammonia and urea, which happen to be highly toxic to the body—are produced when protein is broken down into amino acids for reuse in muscles and organs. Should the kidneys fail to clear them in sufficient time—which is a possibility if the liver is not functioning well—the results can be catastrophic. High urea or ammonia levels cloud the consciousness, cause inflammation of various body organs, and can lead to coma and death.

The popular 1971 classic *Diet for a Small Planet* by Frances Moore Lappe does a nice job of presenting the case for vegetarianism, and it is a good read if you're considering going that route.[18] Let's just say here that scientific thinking has shifted on just how much protein we need to eat at each meal to make "complete" proteins (proteins with all eight essential amino acids). The amino acids that we get from proteins and that are necessary for the body to build and repair tissue stay in our bodies for a *minimum* of four hours, and in some cases up to forty-eight hours. So there is simply no need to keep replenishing the supply at every meal. One complete protein source (e.g., soy, fish, dairy products, nuts) in a day is enough. When combined with other foods over the day you will have no problems meeting your daily protein needs. And the benefits of eating less protein may be more than long term. On a day-to-day basis, many people report having increased energy, clarity of mind, and overall an improved sense of well-being.

Tips For Healthy Protein Balance

Eat According to the Okinawa Food Pyramid

This will keep your protein intake in the desired range. Some recommendations below will help you get healthier proteins.

- *Try these substitutions:*
  Red meat: Substitute fish or extra-firm tofu.
  Beefsteak: Try grilled salmon with pepper and rosemary.

Hamburger: Try a tofu burger (mashed firm tofu with same seasonings, but low salt).

Pizza toppings: Try crushed and seasoned tofu, water-packed tuna, vegetarian sausages, or soy bacon bits.

Beef/chicken sandwiches: Try water-packed tuna fish with tofunaise.

Barbecue: Try trout, salmon, or tuna steaks, seasoned with your favorite herbs and canola or olive oil.

Have only one to two servings of dairy products in a day. Be conscious of what dairy you eat throughout the day, then think balance. If, for instance, you have a half cup of yogurt in the morning and a small amount—say, 3 tablespoons—of low-fat ice cream for dessert at night, you will still have only had one serving of total dairy for the day, and will probably have satisfied your sweet tooth at the same time.

- *Don't eat eggs for breakfast every morning.* Although recent evidence suggests that dietary cholesterol is not as bad as once thought in raising blood cholesterol levels,[19] seven eggs a week are more than enough for most people. If you have cholesterol problems or are diabetic, limit yourself to no more than four until further evidence supports using eggs freely. Or try Egg Beaters or other egg substitutes. Omega-3 eggs are also a good option and can be eaten more often, since the omega-3 fatty acids help counteract any negative effects of the cholesterol from the egg yolks. In fact, they may even change your cholesterol profile for the better.[20]
- *Make vegetables the centerpiece of most meals.* And try to always have two or three times as many vegetables as meat.
- *Watch your serving sizes.* If a piece of meat is bigger than the palm of your hand or a deck of cards, it's more than one serving.
- *Remember: the less meat you eat, the less you will miss it.* Wean yourself slowly. Soon, only a couple of bites will satisfy you.

Eat More Soy Products

Replacing animal protein with vegetable protein will not only lower the overall protein content of a meal but also keep the protein quality high and give you the bonus of extra flavonoids, antioxidants, and vitamins and minerals. (Check out the recipes for East-West Tofu Croquettes, page 425, and Baked Tofu Mediterranean Style, page 422.) Consider vegetarian meat substitutes such as veggie burgers, veggie hot dogs, soy cheese, and vegetarian chili. All these products are made with soy protein and are excellent sources of healthy protein and flavonoids. The highest quality vegetable proteins are soy, other legumes (beans), peanuts, peas, whole-grain rice, and whole-grain flour.

Eat Unsalted or Lightly Salted Raw Nuts and Seeds

All nuts are good sources of protein. They also deliver healthy fats and are thought to provide significant antioxidant benefits. Studies of "nut eaters" suggest that they get less heart disease and less illness in general than those who forgo nuts.[21] Nuts are high in calories, though, so it's best not to eat more than 2 to 3 tablespoons at a time. Almonds and soy nuts are particularly healthy choices because of their heart-healthy monounsaturated fat content and flavonoid content, respectively, and walnuts can give you a hefty dose of omega-3s. Your best bets: nuts that are fresh, raw, or roasted, and minimally salted. Pumpkin and sunflower seeds are also tasty nutritious snacks.

Eat Good Fats And Avoid Bad Fats
(Keep Fat Less Than 30 Percent of Total Calories)

One thing is clear from all the research on dietary fat: not all fats are created equal. Some cannot be made by the body and hence are considered *essential;* others seem to be beneficial in limited quantities; while still others seem to have nothing to offer but increased risk for chronic disease. These distinctions are something of a revelation in the nutrition world. It wasn't that long ago that fat—all fat—was considered the pariah of nutrients. It was thought to cause heart disease and cancer, and make us fat. Some fats, of course, will do exactly that, but not all of them.

There are fats that are essential to our existence, without which we would die. Fat is an essential component of the walls of our body's cells, and is vital for the healing and repair of cells and tissues. It provides the backbone of all our body's hormones, and the essential raw material needed for a child's developing nervous system, including the infant brain.[22] Without it we could not absorb vitamins A, E, D, and K. So it's clearly not fat per se that's the problem, *it's too much of the wrong kind* that we have to worry about.

Good Fat versus Bad Fat

Fats are made up of four different types of fatty acids, which come in various mixtures depending on what kind of food they're in.[23] They are composed of a carbon backbone and a bunch of hydrogen atoms, and they derive their names and their health properties from the number of hydrogen atoms, and where those atoms are placed. There are two bad fats—*saturated* fats (also called SFA for saturated fatty acid) with all their carbon sites filled with hydrogens; and *trans fatty* acids (TFA), which is unsaturated fat *trans*formed into saturated fat by the chemical process of hydrogenation. Trans is really a saturated fat in disguise, and is hidden in cookies, pastry, pie, french fries, deep-fried fast food, and most margarines. Remember the word *hydrogenation* because it's something you should look for on labels and avoid, mostly because it's a potent artery clogger. The other two fats are the good ones. They're both *un*saturated fats. One is called *polyunsaturated,* or PUFA, which stands for polyunsaturated fatty acid; it has many sites for hydrogen. The other is *monounsaturated,* also known as monounsaturated fatty acid, or MUFA, which has one site for hydrogen.

Polyunsaturated fats can be further subdivided into *omega-3 fatty acids* (mostly found in flax, canola oil, and fish oils) and *omega-6 fatty acids* (mostly vegetable oils), according to which carbon atom has the unsaturated site (omega-3 = 3rd carbon, omega-6 = 6th carbon). This confers different properties on each of these fats, which will become clear in our discussion of omega-3 and omega-6 fat. All foods that contain fat have a mixture of fatty acids. Even olive oil, which is mostly monounsaturated, has some saturated fatty acids. If you try to avoid all saturates and all trans fats you will be fighting a losing battle; it's the balance of fats that counts. The table below gives you an overall look at the fat family and some of its members' most common sources.

THE FAT FAMILY—THE GOOD, THE BAD, AND THE UGLY

MONO	POLY (OMEGA-3)	POLY (OMEGA-6)	SATURATED	TRANS
Flaxseeds/oil	Flaxseeds/oil	Poultry	Animal fat	Hydrogenated
Almonds	Soy*/oil	Margarine[†]	Red meat	oils
Margarine[†]	Margarine[†]	Corn oil	Butter	Cookies, pastries,
Avocados	Walnuts	Cottonseed oil	Cocoa butters[§]	pies
Olives/oil	Fish oil	Grapeseed oil	Margarine[†]	Margarine[†]
Peanuts/oil	Canola oil	Safflower oil	Dairy fat	Fried food
Canola oil	Mackerel	Sesame oil	Coconut oil	(e.g., french fries)
	Salmon	Soybean oil*	Palm oil	
	Sardines	Sunflower oil		
	Tuna			
	Other fish[‡]			
GOOD			BAD	UGLY

* More omega-6 than omega-3.
[†] Varies widely; read the labels.
[‡] Most cold-water fish.
[§] The best of the bad fats, doesnt raise cholesterol much.

Now let's take a look at the major fats individually and see what they have to offer, both good and bad, starting with the unhealthiest ones.

The Bad Fats

Saturated Fat (SFA)

Saturated fat has been the traditional bogeyman of fats. These fats are derived mostly from animal sources and are found in red meat, poultry to a lesser degree, whole dairy products, and palm and coconut oils (major ingredients in some cakes and candies). They are solid at room temperature, like lard. Even the latest findings on fats have not improved the image of saturated fats, except that their place in the pecking order of unhealthy fats has been supplanted by trans fatty acids, the undisputed champion of bad fat.

The major problem with saturated fat is that it raises your bad (or lethal) cholesterol levels—the LDL—and clogs your arteries. The high death rate from heart attacks among the Nordic peoples (Danes, Swedes, Norwegians, and Icelanders) is consistent with their high intake of saturated fat from dairy products.[7] The same is true in North America with our high intake of meat and dairy products. There is also a fear that too much cholesterol causes the body to make too many hormones, which can increase risk for hormone-dependent cancers. So keep your saturated fat at a minimum; we'll show you just how to do that in the following pages.

Trans Fatty Acids or Trans Fat (TFA)

Trans fat, the reigning king of bad fats, is a relatively new arrival in the food supply. It rarely occurs in nature except for trace amounts in dairy products, and was virtually unknown before 1900. Today trans fat forms greater than 6 percent of total fat intake in North America.[24] It is formed from the partial hydrogenation of vegetable oils and can be a significant component of margarine, nondairy creamers, and other vegetable oil products. It is also frequently used in packaged foods like crackers and chips to ensure greater shelf life. Seeking to overcome the dangers of butter's saturated fat, food chemists developed margarine, unknowingly loading it up with lethal trans fat. Recently, a couple of margarines have been developed that have very little trans fat and consist mainly of monounsaturated fat and cholesterol-lowering plant stanols (they block cholesterol absorption from the gut) or sterols (cholesterol-lowering flavonoids). Examples include Benechol and Take Control, respectively. This new generation of margarines beats butter hands down and may actually lower your cholesterol levels. Read labels carefully.

Trans fats are often compared to saturated fats in terms of their harmful effects on the heart, but in fact, they're even worse. Not only do they raise bad cholesterol but they also simultaneously lower HDL (healthy cholesterol), a double whammy. As the amount of trans fat has increased in Western diets, so has heart disease. In fact, some scientists feel that trans fats are the most heavily implicated of all fats in the worldwide heart disease epidemic.

Since manufacturers, as of this writing, are under no obligation to list trans fatty acids on their food labels, products can be labeled fat-free when in reality they are loaded with trans fat. One popular margarine even goes so far as to advertise that it has 0 grams of trans fat when it actually has 0.5 gram per serving—not a lot, but certainly more than advertised. Fast-food restaurants are notorious for cooking foods in hydrogenated oils, loading them with trans fat. The best idea is to avoid all deep-fried foods and the foods listed in the trans table on page 130–31.

Tips For Balancing Healthy Fat Intake

- *Watch the 30 percent limit.* Most experts currently recommend reducing the amount of total fat in our diets to less than 30 percent of total calories, keeping saturated fat to less than 10 percent and restricting cholesterol intake to less than 300 mg per day. But in fact, fat intake varies greatly among populations. Some, such as the Greeks, eat up to 40 percent of their calories as fat, and the prewar Okinawan and Japanese diets were as low as 10 percent fat.[7] The current diet of the elders, the *chample* or East-West fusion diet, is about 24 percent fat. You could even go a little higher (up to 40 percent) if it is of the *good* fat category, but since fat provides over twice the calories of protein or carbohydrate the calories tend to add up in a hurry. Reducing the bad fat helps reduce heart disease, and likely reduces prostate and colon cancer, which are associated with a high intake of dietary fat and may possibly lower your risk for breast cancer. But as we've discussed with carbs, it's as much a matter of quality as quantity. Avoid the bad fats and stick with the good fats, which have additional age-busting benefits and are good for the cells that make up your brain, your arteries, and your skin.

- *Watch out for saturated fat.* Avoid fats that are solid at room temperature. Don't use lard. Cut the marbled fat off beef and peel the skin off chicken.

- *Keep tabs on your trans fat intake.* Read labels and minimize the use of hydrogenated or partially hydrogenated oils. Use cold-pressed oils instead. Limit trans fat to 2 grams a day (on a 2,000-calorie diet) or 1 percent of total calories. See the Appendix for calculating the trans fat content of foods—this is important because, as of this writing, manufacturers are allowed to list foods as "fat-free" when in reality they are loaded with trans fat.[25] If your mind is already too filled with facts and figures, simply avoid anything that says hydrogenated or partially hydrogenated! It doesn't get easier than that.

TRANS-HEAVY FOODS TO AVOID[26]
TRANS FAT CONTENTS

food	(g/100 g)	(g/serving)	1 serving
Biscuits, plain	3.6	1.8	1 medium
Cake, pound, cholesterol free	5.4	1.6	1 piece
Cake, with chocolate frosting	3.2	2.0	1 piece
Candies, chocolate-coated cookie bar	6.9	4.0	1 bar
Chicken bouillon cubes	3.9	0.2	1 cube
Cookie bar, chocolate-coated, with caramel	6.9	4.0	1 bar
Cookies, chocolate chip	6.5	0.7	1 cookie
Cookies, vanilla sandwich	7.1	0.7	1 cookie
Cookies, chocolate sandwich with cream filling	5.6	0.6	1 cookie
Crackers, cheese	7.4	2.0	1 serv. bag
Crackers, cheese sandwich with peanut butter filling	3.0	0.4	½ ounce
Crackers, regular, snack-type	7.2	0.6	2 crackers
Crackers, saltine, regular	2.3	0.2	2 crackers

	food	(g/100 g) (g/serving)	1 serving
Doughnuts, glazed or sugared	5.7	2.7	1 medium
Frostings, chocolate, ready-to-eat	3.5	1.3	1/12 pack
Frostings, marble, ready-to-eat	3.6	1.4	1/12 pack
Frostings, vanilla, ready-to-eat	3.9	1.5	1/12 pack
Margarine, stick	19.0	1.0	1 tsp.
Margarine, tub	11.3	0.5	1 tsp.
Muffins, corn	3.6	2.1	1 muffin
Popcorn, microwave-popped (buttered)	7.5	1.2	2 cups
Popcorn, microwave-popped, low-fat (buttered)	3.2	0.5	2 cups
Popcorn, oil-popped	9.2	1.5	2 cups
Potato chips	7.1	2.0	1 ounce
Potatoes, french-fried	3.0	4.0	10 strips
Taco shells	8.0	1.0	1 medium
Tortilla chips	4.1	1.2	1 ounce
Vanilla wafers, lower fat (12 to 17%)	4.3	0.5	2 wafers

g = grams

The Good Fats

Polyunsaturated Fats (PUFA)—Omega-3 and Omega-6

There is no doubt in the scientific community that we should eat more polyunsaturated fat than saturated—and that it should constitute about 10 percent of our diet. The goal is to reduce heart disease by replacing harmful saturated fat with fats that have beneficial or at least neutral effects on total cholesterol—that is, fats that lower LDL (lethal cholesterol) but maintain high HDL (healthy cholesterol). While this might seem like an intelligent strategy for lowering the risk of heart disease, recent studies suggest a more sinister side to omega-6 polyunsaturates (found in vegetable oils and animal products). When we have too much polyunsaturated fat in our diet, it can promote inflammation, blood clotting, and possibly cancer cell growth.[27] At the same time, these fats are necessary for health, since they form part of the essential fatty acid group. When the ratio of omega-6 fat to omega-3 fat is too high, we may be at increased risk for the previously mentioned problems. When it's too low or reversed, we may be at increased risk for bleeding and its complications such as hemorrhagic stroke. *Ideally we should consume between three and ten times more omega-6 fats than omega-3.* The typical American consumes an average of ten to twenty times more omega-6 than omega-3. Our studies of Okinawans reveal that the elders have a ratio (omega 6 to omega 3) between 3:1 and 4:1, which is likely another factor in their outstanding health.

Obviously we need to achieve a more healthy balance. Since it's rather difficult to consume higher levels of healthy omega-3 than omega-6—unless you're on a traditional Inuit diet of mostly fish and other marine animals—the smartest thing is to lower your omega-6 intake. A healthy ratio of omega-6 to omega-3 (in the range of 3:1) may be especially relevant for heart health, the health of the developing infant brain, and possibly for cancer prevention.[22,27]

Certain omega-6 fatty acids, such as alpha-linolenic acid from meat, have been a prime suspect in prostate cancer. Interestingly, this doesn't hold true for the same fat from plants. It may be that there are other protective compounds in plants that reduce this effect.[28] Indeed, diets high in soy oil, which consists of omega-6, that are counterbalanced by high levels of omega-3 and monounsaturated fat seem to have a *cancer-inhibiting* effect. The bottom line is that getting your omega-6:omega-3 ratio closer to 4:1 is easier than it sounds, and if you eat at least one food per day that is high in omega-3 fat you will be on your way.

Monounsaturated Fatty Acids (MUFA)

Interest in monounsaturated fats rose in the 1960s after the Seven Countries Study reported low heart disease rates in countries that followed the high-fat Mediterranean diet.[4,5] Monounsaturated fat is more resistant to attack from free radicals than most other fats. Fat that has been attacked and made toxic by free radicals tends to stick to arterial walls, like the walls of your heart arteries—not a particularly desirable outcome if you want to keep your arteries young. Monounsaturated fat may also help to protect against diabetes and cancer—quite a comeback for the former pariah of nutrients. Olive oil, canola oil, and flaxseed oil are high in monounsaturated fat. Avocados and almonds are also good sources.

Fat Fact

Fats can be liquid or solid. When they are in liquid form at room temperature they are called oils. Solid fat, such as lard or marbled fat in meat, is just known as fat. When fat circulates in the blood it's called cholesterol.

Now that we know the basics of healthy nutrition, let's get to the practical aspects and take nine steps to everlasting health.

4. Eating the Okinawa Way

Aramun jouguu ya duu ganjuu.
One who eats whole food will be strong and healthy.
Okinawan proverb

Nuchi Gusui: *The Nine-Step Approach to Everlasting Health*

Eating as if your food is a source of healing power is called *nuchi gusui* in the Okinawan dialect.[1] It's a powerful concept that has had impressive health benefits for the Okinawans and can for you, too. We've developed the guidelines in this chapter based on our twenty-five-year study of Okinawan dietary habits[2] and the Okinawa Food Pyramid. But as you read through them, keep in mind that our guidelines are simply that—guidelines. They are not meant to be engraved in stone. Stick as close as you can to them, but fine-tune and readjust them to suit your personal tastes. The first guideline, for example, suggests that you eat ten servings a day of fruit and vegetables, but it also provides a healthy target range of servings (nine to seventeen) based on how many calories you eat in a day. Simply vary the number of servings according to your appetite and activity levels.[3]

Here we go, then, starting at the bottom of the pyramid.

Sweets
0–3 servings

Optional Weekly

Alcohol in Moderation

Meat, Poultry, and Eggs
0–7 servings

Vegetable Oils and Condiments
(low-sodium soy sauce, misonaise,
Okinawan herbs and spices)
sparingly (1–2 tablespoons)

Omega-3 Foods
1–3 servings

Daily

Fruit
2–4 servings

Flavonoid Foods
2–4 servings

Calcium Foods
2–4 servings

Rice, Noodles, Breads, and
Other Whole Grains
7–13 servings

Vegetables
7–13 servings

THE OKINAWA FOOD PYRAMID
A Guide to Daily Food Choices

Step 1: Eat Ten Vegetables and Fruits Daily
(Nine to Seventeen Servings)

There's no longer any doubt about the fact that vegetables and fruit are good for you. They are full of nutrients, yet contain few calories. Although the Okinawans flourish on about seven servings a day, Westerners are generally bigger and would do better on ten or more servings per day. A diet full of vegetables and fruit will not only decrease your long-term risk for heart disease, cancer, stroke, hypertension, and obesity but also keep you looking younger. Vegetables are one of the main sources of dietary antioxidants, and as we discussed in Chapter Two, more antioxidants means less cell damage from free radicals.[4] Less damage to collagen in the skin means fewer wrinkles; less damage to the internal organs means they wear out slower.

It is estimated that your DNA and other important cellular constituents all together take a few billion damaging hits a day from free radicals. Free-radical-induced damage is thought to be the major basic biochemical mechanism implicated in the aging process.[5] While our bodies do have their own built-in defenses, our foods supply much of the ammunition. It is wise to load up on antioxidant-rich food rather than stocking up on empty calories or, worse, foods that are high in *pro-oxidants,* such as deep-fried food and hydrogenated oils. Most antioxidants consist of a closely related group of healthy enzymes and phytochemicals widely distributed in plant foods.

The most antioxidant-rich foods are legumes (beans), vegetables, grains, and fruits, probably in that order. If you stick to a largely plant-based diet (the Okinawan elders eat about 80 percent plant food), you will be in good shape. The antioxidant concentration in your blood-stream at any one time forms a major component of your overall free-radical defense system. Despite the fact that the majority of plants contain antioxidants in abundance, some plant foods do seem to contain almost pharmacological levels of biochemically active compounds that put them head and shoulders above other plants.

The following list contains fifteen foods that contribute to the lifelong vitality of the Okinawans. These Okinawan power foods are frequently consumed, are high in known protective phytochemicals, and seem to be particularly rich sources of antioxidants, including flavonoids. Most of them are available in North America and, if not, we recommend choosing foods in the same family. We discuss some of them in more detail in the next chapter.[6]

THE TOP FIFTEEN OKINAWAN HEALING FOODS	MAIN ACTIVE COMPONENTS	WESTERN EQUIVALENT
1. Okinawan tofu	saponins, flavonoids (mostly isoflavones)	Extra-firm tofu
2. Miso	saponins, flavonoids (mostly isoflavones)	White miso (low-sodium)
3. Dried bonito	omega-3 fat	Bonito broth powder
4. Carrots and carrot tops	carotenoids, flavonoids	Carrots and carrot leaves
5. Sanpin tea	catechin (a flavonoid)	Jasmine tea
6. Goya (bitter melon)	mormordin protein	Bitter melon or zucchini (courgette)
7. Konbu (dried kelp)	lignans	Dried kelp
8. Cabbage	indoles	Cabbage
9. Nori (dry seaweed)	lignans	Seaweed sheets

10. Onions	flavonoids, allylic sulfides	Onions
11. Bean sprouts	flavonoids	Bean sprouts
12. Hechima	lutein	Zucchini (courgette)
13. Raw soybeans	flavonoids (mostly isoflavones)	Frozen soybeans or soy nuts
14. Imo (purple sweet potato)	saponins, lignans, carotenoids, lycopene, vitamin E	Sweet potatoes, purple potatoes
15. Sweet peppers	flavonoids, vitamin C	Green peppers

Step 2: Eat Ten Whole Grains Daily
(Seven to Thirteen Servings)

Diets high in whole grains decrease risk for heart disease, stroke, diabetes, and cancer. We spoke at length about whole grains earlier in the previous chapter. If you have been eating lots of white bread, white bagels, white buns and rolls, and other bakery goods made from bleached flour, you are getting little fiber and setting yourself up for lots of problems, including hemorrhoids and diverticulosis (small outpouchings of the colon from a low-fiber diet). These latter two are diseases of modern civilization that are rarely seen in traditional societies eating a high-fiber diet, and are thought to come from the pressure the colon has to generate to push through small-volume stools. Your body will thank you if you make the switch to whole grains.

Guide to Whole Grains

Most whole grains are oval-shaped and range in color from light brown to dark brown. If a grain is white or has fewer than 2 grams of fiber per ounce serving, the chances are that the grain is refined and no longer a "whole" grain. The oval-shaped grains are versatile and can be exchanged in recipes. Use your imagination and experiment. A few whole grains consist of small round seeds. They need to cook a bit longer and have a distinctive texture, like tiny pasta. Grocery products derived from broken or ground grains may not contain the entire fiber or the nutrient-packed inner part called the germ, but are usually close enough to whole to be healthy.

- *Barley.* A staple in the Middle East, it is familiar to most Americans in soup. Its mildly sweet taste makes it a good choice in salads and casseroles.
- *Kamut* (a type of wheat). This is also known as "Egyptian wheat," for it was found sealed in the pyramids. It's a close relative of wheat, but some people who are wheat-intolerant can nonetheless eat kamut. Kamut is a better nutrition choice than wheat and most think it has a better taste. Kamut contains gluten, so those with celiac disease (gluten intolerance) should avoid it.
- *Oats or oat groats.* Oats are often used in breakfast cereals and baked goods. Oat bran is high in soluble fiber, which can help lower blood cholesterol levels, so it's a heart-healthy choice. Rolled oats (groats) can be used in many dishes like fish cakes and can also be used to thicken soups and sauces.
- *Rice—basmati.* Native to Pakistan and India, this aromatic, usually white rice has a flavor and aroma similar to that of roasted popcorn or nuts but a sweet taste. When cooked, the grain swells only lengthwise, resulting in long, thin grains. It is good for curry dishes, but hard to find in whole-grain form.
- *Rice—generic brown.* Only the hull is removed from these kernels of rice. Cooked, it has a slightly chewy texture and a nutlike flavor. Its color is caused by the presence of germ layers rich in minerals and vitamin E.
- *Rice—japonica short-grain.* This short-grain rice has a short, plump, roundish kernel. The shorter the grain, the more tender and sticky it cooks. Most often found in "sticky" white form, it is the main type of rice eaten by Japanese and Okinawans. Easy to find in whole form.
- *Rice—jasmine.* This is an aromatic rice grown in the United States and Thailand. It has a flavor and aroma similar to that of roasted popcorn or nuts, a soft, moist texture, and clings together. Hard to find in whole (brown) form.

- *Rice—wild.* This is not true rice but a wild grass endemic to the lakes and marshes of the Great Lakes area. Previously gathered by hand by Chippewa and other Native Americans, wild rice is now cultivated commercially and harvested by machine, a far cry from the old days but just as tasty. It is dark brown and has a nutty flavor.
- *Rye.* Often used for bread and fodder, especially in Europe, rye contains some gluten, but less than wheat flour. This is why rye and pumpernickel breads are heavier and moister than wheat breads. Rye is popular in crackers and crisp breads.
- *Spelt.* An ancient variety of wheat, spelt has been a hit in health-food stores for years. Its Italian name is *farro,* and it can be found as a crunchy grain in gourmet stores and Italian restaurants. Easier to digest than most other types of grain, it's a good grain source for making pasta or bread.
- *Triticale.* This is a hybrid of wheat and rye. It is also very high in protein; its flour is often mixed with wheat flour to increase its nutrition content.
- *Wheat.* Wheat is among the most widely eaten grains in the world. Whole wheat grain has twenty-two vitamins and minerals in the bran and germ (the fiber). Okinawans make delicious udon noodles and very fine somen noodles from wheat flour. Try our somen chample recipe on page 416.

Small, Round Whole Grains

- *Amaranth.* Amaranth was thought to have spiritual power by the ancient Aztecs. They used it to make beautiful figures of various gods, which were then eaten in religious festivities. Amaranth has a high protein content and also has all eight essential amino acids. It doesn't have gluten, so can be eaten by people with celiac disease or other wheat-intolerant people. Baking it in wheat bread adds a nutty flavor and a delicious aroma.
- *Buckwheat.* Americans are probably most familiar with buckwheat in breads and pancakes, which are made from the flour of the plant's seeds. Okinawans make delicious gray-colored soba noodles with this grain's flour.

- *Millet.* An ancient grain of Asia, it is still eaten in Okinawa and North Africa. Millet is gluten free. Made into tasty flat breads, it can also be used in pilaf or as a stuffing for vegetables. Browning millet in a dry skillet for a few minutes before cooking helps it retain its shape and adds a nutty flavor.
- *Quinoa.* An ancient grain of the Americas, quinoa has been eaten in the Andes for more than 5,000 years, and was used to sustain Incan armies during long war campaigns. It's known today as "little rice" in South America. Most of the 160 calories in 1 cup of cooked quinoa (made from ¼ cup dry quinoa) come from complex carbohydrates. It also provides healthy amounts of iron, magnesium, phosphorus, potassium, and zinc, as well as numerous B vitamins. It can be used as a replacement for rice, potatoes, and other starchy foods or combined with vegetables or seafood to make a pilaf. Try adding it to soups and stews. It is easy to cook in the microwave.
- *Whole kasha.* These hulled and roasted buckwheat seeds can be boiled to make cereal, pudding, or a side dish similar to bulgur wheat. Kasha porridge is a popular staple in Russia and the Middle East. When cooked, it has a nutty flavor that goes well with strong-tasting vegetables like cabbage or Brussels sprouts. A half-cup serving of kasha contains about 90 calories, 3 g of protein, and 51 mg of magnesium, a mineral needed for proper energy metabolism.

Broken or Ground Grains

- *Bulgur.* Bulgur is cracked and roasted whole wheat kernels. It's especially common in Turkey. It has a nutty flavor and can be used to make pilaf or stuffing, or it can be combined with chickpeas, raisins, or nuts to make a delicious high-protein salad.
- *Cracked wheat.* Uncooked, broken wheat berries. Delicious and nutritious. Often available in breads.

Of course, it helps to know how to cook whole grains as well. Below is a guide to cooking whole grains in a steamer or on the stovetop. Remember also that if you purchase an electric rice cooker, it can double as a whole-grain cooker and you save yourself the trouble of having to stand near the whole grains, checking their consistency. It's as easy as a flip of a switch.

Cooking Whole Grains

When you are using an electric steamer, fill your steamer base with water all the way to the top level. Take the steamer basket and place it on the base. Fill the steamer bowl with grains and add water or broth of your choice. Place the bowl in the steamer basket and cover, plug in, and set the timer for the recommended time (see Appendix A, page 478). After cooking, let the grains cool off so that you can drain them in a colander if there is any leftover liquid. Remember that you can cook enough grain for multiple uses throughout the week and reheat it in a microwave or even chill it for later use in salads.

The first time you cook a new grain, check it five to ten minutes before the end of the cooking time to make sure the grains are not getting mushy. If they aren't tender enough to suit you at the end of the recommended time, cook them a little longer.

When you are cooking whole grains on the stovetop, use a medium-size pot with a tight-fitting lid. Bring fat-free, low-sodium broth (or water) to a boil in the pot, stir in the grains, and return to a boil. Reduce the heat to low, cover the pot, and simmer until the grains are tender and most of the water is absorbed (see Appendix A, page 479, for cooking times).

The same proportions of liquid to grains should be used when cooking in a rice cooker.

What to Look for in a Breakfast Cereal

The healthiest breakfast is based on whole foods, especially whole grains. To add sweetness or taste without compromising health, try adding cinnamon, raisins, vanilla, or a touch of "raw" (turbinado) sugar. Packaged hot whole-grain cereals work well, too.

For cold cereal, there is a vast variety available. Mom's favorites, such as shredded wheat, are precooked and are nicely formed bite-size whole grains. Check out the list of ingredients: it should lead with a whole grain or combination thereof. Ditch the cereals that have sugar as the first or second ingredient or contain any partially hydrogenated oils. Also avoid cereals based on milled corn, white rice, or any refined grains.

Oat cereals are a little fat-heavy with 3 grams of fat per serving, but since this is "good" fat it's okay by us. Cereals with raisins can fool you, as they have as much sugar as a frosted cereal, but this is fructose—low on the Glycemic Index—so it fits right in with a healthy eating pattern.

Remember, the key word is *fiber*. Whole-grain cereals will have 2 grams or more of fiber per ounce. All-bran or high-bran cereals have even more fiber. Experiment with several varieties and enjoy.

Step 3: Eat Three Calcium Foods Daily
(Two to Four Servings)

There seems to be nothing but good news about calcium. It strengthens the bones, prevents osteoporosis, and may even help prevent colon cancer, high blood pressure, and premenstrual syndrome.[7] Where should you get your calcium? Good vegetarian sources are green leafy vegetables, soy (especially calcium-fortified), seaweed such as nori or wakame (see recipes on pages 415 and 459), and calcium-fortified orange juice. Dairy products are also excellent sources of calcium, but they are best consumed in moderation—there is little support from interventional studies that they actually help reduce risk for osteoporosis.[8] In fact, osteoporosis rates are lower in societies where people eat few, if any, dairy products. This may be because they are high-protein foods, and *too much protein tends to leach calcium out of bones.* For every gram of protein that you eat, you lose 1 to 2 mg of calcium in your urine.[9] For postmenopausal women your protein:calcium ratio (how much protein you eat versus how much calcium) is actually a stronger predictor of your risk for bone fracture than your calcium intake alone.[10] If you maintain a high-protein diet for an extended period with marginal calcium intake, you could be increasing your risk for osteoporitic fracture.

The type of saturated fat in dairy products is also the worst offender for making cholesterol in the body. Perhaps it's no surprise that the Scandinavians have an epidemic of heart disease with their high dairy product consumption. Dairy products are also more difficult to digest as we get older. Many of us tend to become lactose intolerant as we age—nature's way, perhaps, of telling us that milk is for babies (but we still love our yogurt!). Worldwide it is estimated that 70 percent of people cannot digest dairy products. Finally, the protein in cow's milk has been fingered as a potential cause of juvenile diabetes and allergies in infants.[11] This finding is controversial and still under investigation.

If you do eat dairy, go for the nonfat or low-fat varieties. They're available in most dairy products from milk to ice cream to yogurt. If you eat yogurt, incidentally, check the label to make sure it contains live acidophilus cultures, which keep intestinal flora healthy and aid digestion.[12] The bottom line with dairy is: no more than two servings per day for adults. And try the healthy vegetarian alternatives, such as calcium-fortified orange juice, calcium-fortified soy milk, firm tofu, and seaweed. Look for foods that provide 15 to 30 percent of the daily requirement for calcium per serving. Taking a daily calcium supplement will also ensure that you meet your daily requirements (1,000 to 1,500 mg per day).[13]

Tips for Getting Your Calcium

- *Learn about calcium in foods.* Calcium-fortified foods and some green, leafy vegetables provide an excellent vegetarian source of calcium. Compare the vegetables below with dairy products and see for yourself: many are actually absorbed better and on a per-gram basis provide better sources of calcium than dairy products.

FOOD	ABSORPTION (%)	1 CUP SERVING	TOTAL CALCIUM	USABLE CALCIUM
Tofu, calcium-fortified	31.0	252 g	516 mg	160 mg
Orange juice, calcium-fortified	31.0	240 g	350 mg	109 mg

FOOD	ABSORPTION (%)	1 CUP SERVING	TOTAL CALCIUM	USABLE CALCIUM
Soy milk, calcium-fortified	31.0	240 g	300 mg	93 mg
Milk (or 8 oz. yogurt or 1½ oz. cheddar cheese)	32.1	244 g	291 mg	93 mg
Beans, soy, dried	15.6	186 g	515 mg	80 mg
Kale	58.8	67 g	90 mg	53 mg
Broccoli	61.3	88 g	42 mg	26 mg
Cabbage	52.7	89 g	42 mg	22 mg
Spinach	5.1	180 g	245 mg	12 mg

- *Use calcium-fortified soy milk.* It can go on your breakfast cereal, in your tea or coffee, or in any recipe that calls for milk. You will get all the calcium of milk and the added benefit of soy—a combination that can't be beat.[13]

Step 4: Eat Three Flavonoid Foods Daily
(Two to Four Servings)

Flavonoids—ubiquitous plant compounds found in large quantities in soy products and some other legumes (beans), and to a lesser extent in tea, onions, and apples—are powerful antioxidants. They provide a weak form of estrogen where the body needs it and block the body's own estrogen in locations where estrogen may induce cancer. (See Chapter Two for more details.) They are present in almost all plant foods, but two plants—soybeans and flaxseed—have pharmacological levels of these compounds, levels that exceed those in other plants by as much as 1,000 times.[14] Since most of us in North America don't eat either of these foods, we rely on tea, onions, apples, and broccoli as our best sources. Unfortunately, this leaves us with only a few milligrams of flavonoids a day in our diets, which is not enough for much disease protection unless we are big tea drinkers or onion eaters (and we all know what eating too many onions can do to our social life).[15]

Europeans who have a high intake of flavonoids from drinking black tea have been shown to gain protection against heart disease, and of course, the Japanese are far ahead of everyone else.[16] Indeed, the first study that measured *blood levels* of flavonoids in Japanese showed that they had up to fifty times the levels of Caucasians.[17] No one has measured blood levels of flavonoids in the Okinawans, but our research group has calculated their flavonoid dietary intake, and it is impressive—significantly higher than other Japanese.[18] We think this is one of the reasons they have such a low rate of hormone-dependent cancers such as breast and prostate cancer. It could also be a factor in their low heart disease rates.

The importance of flavonoids is only beginning to take hold in the medical research community—twenty years, incidentally, after our colleague Dr. Ken Setchell and his collaborator Dr. Herman Adlercreutz first isolated them in the lab.[19] And it could be years before your doctor recommends them, but we hope not too many. Soy has just been allowed the unprecedented honor of an official U.S. Food and Drug Administration (FDA) health claim.[20] The evidence is so overwhelming for soy's role in cardiovascular disease reduction that food manufacturers are now allowed to talk about the benefits of heart-healthy soy in their products. It is thought that the flavonoids play a major role in soy's cardioprotective effects.[21] Our prediction is that as the evidence mounts for soy consumption reducing the risks for breast cancer, prostate cancer, and possibly other cancers, such as colon cancer, other USDA-approved health claims will follow.[22] This will likely take a few more years and a lot more research.

You, however, don't have to wait to take advantage of their anti-cancer and heart-healthy properties. Eat soy or other flavonoid foods daily and you will maintain a high blood level of flavonoids. After a high-flavonoid meal they appear in measurable levels in blood or urine for up to thirty-six hours. Studies have shown that once-a-day consumption, usually of about 30 grams of soy (one ounce), is adequate for physiological effects.[23] Twice a day would be even better, as proved by the Okinawans, who are at least twice-a-day soy consumers. Study the table below. It provides you with our most up-to-date understanding of all major high-flavonoid foods. While researchers have been touting the benefits of soy (including us), how many people realize that some of the most flavonoid-rich foods are just around the corner at the local grocer? Check out the flavonoids per serving of cranberry juice, applesauce, and celery sticks. Note that we include all known flavonoids and closely related compounds. The lignans and boron are not flavonoids but are closely related in terms of structure and function, and we have included them in our analysis for this reason. The recipes in this book will show you how to incorporate these foods easily into your daily routine, so that you can get at least a daily dose of your favorite nutraceutical!

FLAVONOIDS AND RELATED COMPOUNDS (PHYTOESTROGENS): THE TOP 50[24]

FOOD	PHYTOES-TROGENS* (mg/100g)	PHYTOESTRO-GENS* (mg/serving)	SERVING SIZE
Soy flakes, defatted	311.7	87.3	1 cup (28 g)
Flaxseed	240.6	28.9	1 tbs. (12 g)
Arrowroot (kudzu)	207.7	16.6	1 tbs. (8 g)
Soy concentrate	167.1	47.4	1 oz. (28 g)
Soy flour	164.8	164.8	1 cup (100 g)
Carrot leaves	153.4	5.8	1 tbs. (3.8 g)
Soy nuts	135.1	58.1	¼ cup (43 g)
Soy bacon pieces	126.6	12.7	2 strips (10 g)
Texturized vegetable protein	113.9	66.1	¼ cup (58 g)
Miso	89.0	5.3	1 tsp. (6 g)
Tofu, dry spiced	67.4	11.5	1 piece (17 g)
Red clover	59.0	9.4	½ cup (16 g)
Soybean chips	54.2	30.1	2 oz. (57 g)
Tempeh	47.9	79.5	1 cup (166 g)
Onions	44.8	35.8	½ cup (80 g)
Soybeans, cooked	44.4	38.2	½ cup (86 g)
Soybean sprouts	37.5	13.1	½ cup (35 g)
Cranberry juice	24.9	44.3	¾ cup (178 g)
Tofu	20.6	17.5	3 oz. (85 g)

FOOD	PHYTOES-TROGENS* (mg/100g)	PHYTOESTRO-GENS* (mg/serving)	SERVING SIZE
Meat substitutes	18.8	16.9	1 patty (90 g)
Soy cream cheese	17.8	25.8	1 tbs. (15 g)
Soy diet shakes	17.6	29.2	1 cup (166 g)
Kale	16.7	11.2	1 cup (67 g)
Celery	11.2	6.7	½ cup (60 g)
Snow peas (mangetouts)	9.4	4.6	½ cup (49 g)
Soy salad dressing	7.8	1.4	1 tbs. (18 g)
Broccoli	7.7	3.4	½ cup (44 g)
Jasmine tea (sanpin tea)	6.7	16.8	1 cup (250 g)
Cornbread, multigrain mix	6.6	2.2	¼ cup (34 g)
Japanese green tea	5.8	14.5	1 cup (250 g)
Turnip greens	5.5	3.0	1 cup (55 g)
Alfalfa sprouts	5.0	0.1	½ cup (17 g)
Black tea	4.7	11.8	1 cup (250 g)
Broad beans	4.9	2.7	½ cup (55 g)
Soy flat noodle	4.6	7.4	1 cup (160 g)
Soy milk	4.2	10.8	1 cup (240 g)
Soy cheese	4.1	1.7	1½ oz. (43 g)
Chickpeas (garbanzos)	3.6	3.6	½ cup (100 g)
Chili, vegetarian	3.2	8.2	1 cup (256 g)
Green beans	3.2	1.8	½ cup (55 g)
Soy sour cream	3.2	0.5	1 tbs. (16 g)
Apricots	3.0	0.2	½ cup (83 g)
Applesauce	2.5	3.0	½ cup (122 g)
Strawberry	2.2	1.8	½ cup (83 g)
Grapes	2.2	1.0	½ cup (46 g)
Tofu frozen yogurt	2.1	3.6	6 oz. (170 g)
Green peppers	2.0	0.1	½ cup (75 g)
Pasta with tomato sauce	2.0	0.5	1½ cups (260 g)
Pinto beans	1.9	1.9	½ cup (100 g)
Lentils	1.8	1.8	½ cup (100 g)

* Total of flavonoids (excluding catechins), lignans, and boron.

- *Learn about soy products.* Picking the right soy product is important. It needs to fit the texture and flavor of your meal. This guide will help you sort out any confusion.

Tofu is manufactured by coagulating soy milk with mineral salts, usually magnesium chloride (nigari), calcium chloride, or calcium sulfate (gypsum). Therefore, it provides a good source of calcium, complete protein, and good fats including omega-3 fat, not just flavonoids. Three main methods are used to make tofu, which produce three separate textures—soft, firm, and extra-firm. Firmer tofu has less moisture and more protein. Since flavonoids are most concentrated in the protein, the firmer the tofu (less moisture), the more concentrated the flavonoids.

Silken tofu is very soft and creamy. It's made like yogurt by adding the coagulant to hot soy milk, which is then drained into containers to set. A company called Mori-Nu sells it in vacuum-packed boxes that do not require refrigeration. Silken tofu makes a satiny smooth puree, desirable for desserts, dressings, dips, sauces, and soy shakes.

Tempeh, pronounced *TEM-pay,* is a tasty and health-promoting Indonesian food. It is made by combining cooked soybeans with grains in a fermenting enzyme culture and incubating it for twenty-four hours. A chewy bean cake with a rich, smoky taste, it makes a great meat substitute and is quite versatile. Tempeh's smoky flavor works well with spicy dishes like tacos and chili. It's an excellent choice for the grill and goes well with barbecue sauce or sweet and sour sauces. Tempeh is widely available: you will find it in natural foods stores, specialty markets, and even regular supermarkets. Check the freezer or refrigerator sections. Tempeh, if frozen, will keep for months. Defrosted tempeh will last a week in your fridge.

Miso is a salty paste with a deep, earthy appeal. It is used as a soup base or flavoring for multiple dishes. Miso comes from soybeans fermented with a grain—usually rice, though often wheat or barley—combined with salt and a friendly bacterial culture. Miso can be aged for more than a year, depending on the type. The end result is a paste that resembles peanut butter. Regular sodium miso can replace salt or soy sauce in recipes and will add a flavonoid punch. Choose low-sodium brands for regular soup use. Just dissolve ¼ cup of miso in a quart of water and you will have a nice broth. Pile on vegetables, chunks of tofu, a few strips of nori or wakame seaweed, and a teaspoon of fish stock (dashi) to produce a soup with a zesty flavor. In Okinawa, as in Japan, miso soup is a regular breakfast and evening meal soup. Look for miso in natural foods stores, Asian markets, or regular supermarkets. It can be stored for months if tightly covered and kept in the refrigerator.

Soy milk is a rich, creamy liquid made from cooked and soaked soybeans. It's a nutritious, lactose-free beverage that can be used as a dairy milk replacement. Try replacing half or all of the dairy milk in pancakes, waffles, muffins, and other baked items with soy milk. Try using it to make cream soups, frosty shakes, or creamy puddings. You can have soy milk with cereal, in your coffee or tea, or even as a drink by itself. Okinawans occasionally sweeten and use it as a hot or cold beverage, or they use it with soy sauce, onions, and other vegetables and spices in a tasty soup. Soy milk is usually sold in aseptic cartons similar to milk cartons. After opening, soy milk should be treated like dairy milk, refrigerated and used within several days. Soy milk can be found in a variety of flavors including plain, vanilla, chocolate, carob, and almond.

Soy flour is just that—flour made from soybeans. It's an incredibly rich source of flavonoids, the richest on a per-serving basis (see table, page 146). Try substituting it for one-quarter to one-half the flour in quick breads, muffins, cookies, cakes, and pancakes. For yeast-raised breads, try one-quarter soy flour. They will be slightly denser if made with soy flour, but it adds a delicious nutty flavor and a moist texture. Soy flour can be used in gluten-free diets. Quite versatile, it can even be used to replace eggs in baking. Try replacing each egg with one tablespoon of soy flour and two tablespoons of water—it's a great way to lower your cholesterol.

Texturized soy protein (TSP), or **texturized vegetable protein (TVP)**, is a dehydrated soy product that is protein- and flavonoid-rich and has a long shelf life. It needs to be rehydrated before cooking with ⅞ cup boiling water to 1 cup TVP. When rehydrated, TVP has a texture like ground beef. Rehydrate and add to meat loaf, tacos, chili, spaghetti sauce, pizza, or anywhere else you might use ground beef or ground turkey. TVP can be exchanged for half the meat in a recipe or used alone. TVP is fat-free, so it will cut down the fat content wherever you use it. TVP can be stored in an airtight container for up to several months. When rehydrated, it must be refrigerated and used within four days or it will spoil.

- *Eat raw or roasted soybeans.* Farmers in Minnesota and other soybean-producing states will attest to the appeal of eating them raw as a healthy snack. In Okinawa, raw soybeans (called *edamame,* which literally means "beans still on the branch") are often served as a snack in bars. In North America, you can usually find them frozen in supermarkets and in health food stores, where they are also roasted and referred to as "soy nuts." Reach for them the next time you want a quick, healthy snack. Who knows? If their health reputation continues to grow, someday they may replace peanuts as America's most popular nut.
- *Have a morning soy smoothie.* Throw a package of silken tofu into a blender with some fresh fruit (or frozen fruit) for a super healthy breakfast. The taste is outstanding and your smoothie can act as a low-calorie meal replacement if you are trying to lose weight. (See recipe on page 405.)
- *Try soy alternatives.* There is a vast array of soy products available today, and fortunately you can find most of them in good supermarkets, as well as in health food stores. Try soy milk, soy ice cream, soy hot dogs, soy bacon, soy bacon bits, soy cheese, soy yogurt, soy burgers, and even soy turkey. There are many recipes in this book that will help you to incorporate them into delicious meals.
- *Add a scoop of flaxseed.* Try flaxseed on your breakfast cereal, salads—in fact, you can sprinkle it on just about anything.

Flaxseed has a terrific, slightly nutty taste, especially if you grind it into a powder. (We use a small electric coffee grinder.) It can be found in bulk in many stores or in health food stores. There are also many commercial breakfast cereals now available with flaxseed, such as Red River Cereal (in Canada) or Nature's Path Flax Breakfast Cereal. Also try incorporating it into your recipes for muffins or bread.

- *Drink tea.* Tea is a major source of flavonoids. It is *the* major source for Europeans.[25] Green, black, sanpin (jasmine), or oolong teas all supply 12 to 16 mg of flavonoids per cup (250 cc) and will help to max your flavonoid load. If you need caffeine to get through the day, then let the tea steep longer. In general, a cup of tea contains about half the caffeine of coffee, but if you let it steep for 5 minutes the caffeine dose approaches that of regular drip coffee. On the other hand, you can get decaffeinated green or black tea in bags in almost every grocery store. All the popular tea manufacturers are now also supplying loose green tea or jasmine (sanpin) tea, now that their health benefits are becoming more widely known. Try it—the tea will almost certainly be cheaper and likely fresher.

- *Remember, veggies provide flavonoids, too.* Soy is not the only kid on the flavonoid block. Broccoli, kale, celery, onions, snow peas (mangetouts), turnip greens, and alfalfa sprouts are terrific sources of flavonoids. Eat them often.

- *Eat flavonoid-rich fruits.* Apples, cranberries, strawberries, grapes, and apricots all score high on the flavonoid chart. Mix them for use in fruit salads. Buy them fresh and freeze them for fruit smoothies or for use as desserts later. Try drinking them in pure fruit juice as well. Flavonoids are very hardy and will not be lost in the freezing or cooking process.

- *Use arrowroot (kudzu) as a starch or thickener for soups or other baked goods.* This little-known vine plant is one of the top three flavonoid foods in terms of its concentration of flavonoids. It will not adversely affect flavor in your recipes, and can be a powerful addition to your Okinawa-style pantry. It is available as a powder at any food store and is a good way to sneak flavonoids unnoticed into any recipe that requires thickening.

Step 5: Eat Two Omega-3 Foods Daily
(One to Three Servings)

Unless you are eating fish or flax several times per week, you're probably not getting enough long-chain omega-3 fatty acids. These fatty acids are critical for maintaining optimal performance of your brain,[26] cardiovascular system,[27] and immune system.[28] Without realizing it, your grandmother recognized the importance of these fatty acids when she made your parents take cod liver oil. Cod liver oil is without a doubt one of the world's worst-tasting supplements, but it contains high levels of long-chain omega-3 fatty acids.

One type of omega-3 fatty acid is called docosahexaenoic acid (DHA). DHA is found throughout the fatty tissue in our brains, and it appears to play a role in how our brain functions. A growing body of research has confirmed that infants who are deficient in levels of this fatty acid have less than optimal neurological function, especially intelligence.[29] Furthermore, a great number of neurological conditions, such as depression, attention deficit disorder, and schizophrenia, also have a high correlation with deficient levels of DHA in the bloodstream. Researchers have found that patients with bipolar depression (the most difficult form of depression to treat) often respond dramatically to very high dose supplementation with oils rich in DHA.

You can get adequate amounts of DHA by eating one serving of fish rich in omega-3 fatty acids several times per week. These are generally the darker-fleshed fish like salmon, tuna, and mackerel. You can also take fish oil supplements to ensure that you are getting enough. If you're a vegetarian, you could try a new alternative. Scientists have developed certain algae that produce a large amount of DHA-containing oils. Supplements using these DHA-rich oils solve the problem of getting enough DHA for optimal brain function for the vegetarian.[30] These are found in most supermarkets and health food stores.

As mentioned earlier, the type of polyunsaturated fat in your diet may be the most critical factor in reducing mortality, especially from heart disease. There has been a wealth of evidence to support eating omega-3 foods, including fatty fish like salmon, tuna, and mackerel. The initial observations of very low death from heart attacks in Inuit (Eskimo) populations—despite a diet high in total fat consumption—led to research that demonstrated the blood-thinning qualities of omega-3 fatty acids. These fatty acids were obtained mostly from saltwater fish. The fish themselves get them from sea vegetables such as algae, and we can, too.

The Asian diet, especially that of the Okinawans and Japanese, also contains a good deal of saltwater fish. Of the Nordic peoples, Icelanders and Swedes are the longest lived—and also the greatest fish eaters. The balance of the research suggests that omega-3 fatty acids have a multitude of actions, including the ability to lower bad cholesterol.[27]

Evidence suggests that omega-3 fat inhibits the production of immune cell signalers (interleukin-1, tumor necrosis factor, and prostaglandins) that tell the immune system to rev up for attack.[28,31] A consistently high level of these factors in the blood causes the swelling, stiffness, pain, and appetite loss seen in rheumatoid arthritis and many cancers.

This is all to say that if you're a meat eater, make the switch to fish and keep your arteries clean. Fish is one of the most heart-healthy foods you can eat. The omega-3 fat in fish acts as a platelet inhibitor and keeps them from forming clots in the coronary arteries and elsewhere. That's actually why omega-3 fats are present in higher quantities in cold-water or saltwater fish. They keep the blood thin and flowing freely, like antifreeze for your car in the winter. (See our recipes for Simple Simmered Mackerel with Miso, page 450, or Barbecued Mahi-Mahi with Lime-Soy Sauce, pages 450–51.)

Step 6: Drink Fresh Water and Tea Daily

The first cup of tea moistens my lips and throat,
the second cup breaks my loneliness,
the third cup searches my barren mind

but to find volumes of wandering thoughts.
The fourth cup raises a slight perspiration—
all the wrongs of life pass away through my pores.
At the fifth cup I am purified.
The sixth cup, and I can hear the immortals call.
The seventh cup—ah, but I could take no more—let me ride
on this sweet breeze to the land of the immortals.

Lotung, a Chinese poet from the T'ang dynasty

All of your body's cells live in water, so you must replace water regularly. We recommend that you drink enough water so that your urine is clear. Whether it takes three glasses a day or twelve, that's the right amount for you. It's best to drink spring water from a known source or to filter your own water, since many chemical contaminants or pathogens, such as bacteria or viruses, are not eliminated by conventional treatment of tap water. A randomized, controlled study published in the *American Journal of Public Health* reported that as many as 35 percent of gastrointestinal illnesses among tap-water drinkers were tap-water-related and preventable if micro-filters were used.[32] Water filters are available everywhere, and you can install them on your kitchen tap or purchase them as part of a filter-water jug set (see Appendix B).

Because tea is a mild diuretic (which causes you to lose water), you can consider a glass of tea equivalent to half a glass of water. Tea will provide you with 12 to 16 mg of flavonoids per cup and is a very healthy beverage. Tea drinkers get less colon, bladder, and lung cancer, and less heart disease as well.[33]

Guidelines for Enjoying Tea the Okinawa Way

The health implications of drinking tea include helping to metabolize fat, easing digestion, and adding healthy flavonoids. Enjoying tea involves far more than just boiling water, adding tea, and gulping it down. To truly enjoy tea you must feel its effect on the sensations: the visual appeal of the tea; the pleasant aroma; the stimulatory taste on the tongue; the smooth touch of the cup; and most important, the healing power of communicating and sharing time with friends and family.

Rules for Brewing and Drinking Tea

1. Fully fermented tea (black) steeps best in 212° F (100° C) water; semi-fermented tea (jasmine or oolong) requires water between 194 and 212° F (90–100° C); unfermented tea (green) needs water between 158 and 176° F (70–80° C), to bring out the full bouquet.
2. Tea leaves can be brewed from four to seven times, depending on leaf quality.
3. Drain every drop of tea from the teapot after each use.
4. Avoid tea that has been standing for more than one hour. Tannins from the leaves make the tea taste bitter. Okinawans also consider this unhealthy.
5. Use a different teapot for each distinct type of tea—for example, do not make jasmine tea in your black tea teapot.
6. Avoid washing your teapot with detergent. Merely rinse it with warm or cold water.

Step 7: Weigh Your Options Carefully

The Okinawa Food Pyramid offers you limitless food options. The only thing that's limited is *quantity,* so that you don't overdo certain foods. Up to seven servings per week of high-protein meats, poultry, and eggs are acceptable.[34] That's really all you need. Sweets are fine, if you keep them to three servings or less a week. Weigh your options carefully and choose what you really want. Here are some guidelines to help you make the right choices.

Minimize Your Animal Food Consumption

The more we learn about food and health, the clearer it becomes that we should try to eat as low on the food chain as possible. Contrary to popular images of "man the hunter," our remote ancestors did not evolve by gorging on huge quantities of meat. Rather, the archeological record shows that throughout most of human evolutionary history, the major part of the diet came in the form of wild plants, which were supplemented by mostly smaller game or the scavenged remains of larger carnivore kills.[35]

Anthropological studies of hunter-gatherer societies have also contributed to a shattering of the myth that pre-modern human societies ate mainly animal products, even though the myth occasionally resurfaces in the high-protein–low-carb fad diets supposedly based on the Stone Age or "evolutionary diet."[36] Although the Paleolithic diet of our remote ancestors contained higher amounts of animal protein than is currently consumed today, it also contained considerably lower levels of saturated fat and consisted mostly of the unrefined, complex carbohydrates found in foods such as wild fruits and vegetables. In fact, as medical anthropologists S. Boyd Eaton and Melvin Konner revealed in their oft-misquoted *New England Journal of Medicine* article "Paleolithic Nutrition," "The percentage of daily calories derived from carbohydrates in the late Paleolithic period amounts to about the same as it does today."[37] The key difference, as we stressed in the previous chapter, was that Paleolithic humans had a low intake of sugars and other simple carbohydrates and no refined foods, which are the bane of the modern North American diet.

Moreover, as anthropologist Dr. Richard Lee, perhaps the world's foremost expert on hunter-gatherer societies, points out, *women* are responsible for supplying the majority of calories in most modern hunter-gatherer societies, and those calories come mainly from *gathered* plants—grasses, nuts, seeds, roots, and tubers—not hunted meat.[38] So much for the "man as carnivore" myth. In anthropology circles, the concept of meat-eating cavemen has been largely dismissed—now it just has to filter down to the pop nutrition scene.

Cut Back on Red Meat

At the risk of running afoul of the meat lobby, it is becoming increasingly evident that something in red meat must be increasing the risk for colon cancer and prostate cancer, among other diseases.[39] We used to think the villain was saturated fat, but now we think it may have more to do with certain fatty acids. Other research suggests that carcinogens formed in cooking meat, especially when the meat is charred, might be an important factor for prostate and colon cancers.[40]

On the other hand, undercooking presents hazards, too. Outbreaks of toxic bacterial infections, including the killer bacteria *E. coli 0157*, have been linked to undercooked animal meats, especially beef.[41] So when it comes to cooking meat well, we are damned if we do and damned if we don't. Add to this the fear of Creutzfeldt-Jacob disease (aka mad cow disease), an unremitting dementia caused by a "slow virus" that kills within six months, and you see why many people are making the switch to a more vegetarian diet.[42] The upshot is that it's best to minimize red meat.

That doesn't mean you have to avoid all meat. The Sunday barbecue can still be a good steak occasion, if that's what you want. Just don't eat red meat every day of the week; three times a week is plenty. And choose lean cuts.

Tips for Healthy Meat Consumption

- *Use the ¾ rule.* Fill your plate with three-fourths plant foods and no more than one-fourth animal food. This way you will automatically keep your consumption of animal products closer to the 20 percent intake of the Okinawans.
- *Cut the burnt parts off grilled meats.* The black parts are carcinogenic.[40] And don't feed them to the dog, either. They're not any better for Fido than they are for you.
- *Boil it.* When Okinawans eat meat they often stew it for hours (sometimes up to twelve hours), scooping away the fat so that by the time it's ready to eat, the fat content is much lower. We could learn a lesson here: try stewing instead of frying or grilling.

Watch Your Egg Consumption

Seven eggs or fewer a week is plenty for most people, and those with cholesterol problems should limit themselves to no more than four. The problem with eggs lies in the yolk, which is high in fat and packed with cholesterol. Recent studies suggest that dietary cholesterol does not raise your blood cholesterol as much as dietary fat. So eggs have been removed from the danger list (except for diabetics) of many dieticians.[43] We feel that the jury is still out on this one, so use caution.

The Okinawan elders use eggs on a regular basis but their portions are small. Be judicious. The whites, though, are relatively benign and a good source of protein. So if you're feeling like eggs, try egg whites or egg substitutes. Get the protein, avoid the fat. Check out a wonderful recipe for Wild West Omelet on page 412. Another option is to eat omega-3 eggs, which are eggs from chickens fed high omega-3 diets. You can count these as an omega-3 food and therefore be more liberal in your use of eggs. Free-range eggs, from chickens allowed to roam and eat a wider selection of grains, are also a healthier alternative than the usual white eggs. Both free-range and omega-3 eggs can be found at supermarkets and health food stores.

Sweets

We all want something sweet occasionally, and this is perfectly compatible with the Okinawa Program. Just keep your indulgences within the pyramid minimums. Here are some low-cal ideas that may satisfy your sweet tooth and help keep you within healthy bounds.

Soy Smoothie (see recipe, page 405)

A piece of fruit

Low-fat cookies—make sure they're trans free, such as the Health Valley variety

Angel food cake (small piece please), with fresh fruit and 2 table spoons low-fat yogurt

Low-fat ice cream and strawberries

Low-fat fruit yogurt

Fresh or unsweetened canned peaches or pears topped with low-fat ice cream or sugar-free Jell-O

Fruit crumble—top cooked fruit with a crumbled mixture of toasted muesli, wheat flakes, a little bit of honey

Baked strudel—wrap chopped apples, raisins, currants, and cinnamon spice in filo pastry and bake

A firm banana sliced into some low-fat pudding

Fruit salad with low-fat yogurt

A baked whole apple with cinnamon

Step 8: Drink Alcohol in Moderation or Not at All

Drinking low to moderate amounts of alcohol, especially with meals, actually seems to be good for you. Studies show that having one or two glasses of wine may reduce the risk of cardiovascular disease and possibly strokes.[44] Red wine has received much attention for its health benefits, and has been offered as a possible explanation for the "French paradox"—why the French have low mortality from heart disease despite a relatively high-fat consumption.[45] And there might be something to that. Red wine is a potent source of iso-flavone phytoestrogens, a type of flavonoid which has both weak estrogenic effects and powerful antioxidant ability, and may help protect against heart disease and osteoporosis. Okinawan, Japanese, and Nordic diets also contain moderate amounts of alcohol with no apparent ill effect on overall mortality. The bottom line is moderation, yet again. A good basic rule—no more than one glass of red wine or other alcoholic beverage per day for women and two glasses for men.

Tips for Healthy Drinking

- *Don't forget your folate.* Alcohol destroys folate, and low folate levels may put you at higher risk for heart disease and certain cancers, including breast cancer and colon cancer. Women in one important study who had a drink a day but also consumed 600 micrograms a day of folate cut their risk for breast cancer by half.[46] If you wish to drink alcohol, make sure you get adequate levels of folate. The Okinawa Program should provide you with plenty, but a supplement of at least 400 micrograms per day will ensure you are meeting your needs.
- *Try a nonalcoholic cocktail, beer, or wine.* There are plenty of them on the market and we are told they are not bad.
- *Alternate between alcoholic and nonalcoholic drinks at social events.* If you do want to drink alcohol at parties, follow every alcoholic drink with a tall glass of water, seltzer, or a weak wine spritzer. You'll find yourself drinking half as much alcohol and feeling much better in the morning.

Step 9: Consider a Nutritional Insurance Policy With Vitamins and Minerals

The best way to get medical experts arguing is to ask their opinion about vitamin and mineral supplements. There used to be two camps—for and against—and there was almost a religious fervor to the debate. Now there is grudging acceptance throughout the medical profession that some vitamins and minerals taken in amounts difficult or impossible to achieve through dietary means alone may help prevent certain diseases and promote your general well-being.

The fear doctors have of recommending vitamins is that the public will start popping dangerous quantities of them. Fat-soluble vitamins (vitamins A, D, E, and K) are stored in the body and can accumulate to toxic levels if consumed in extremely high doses (megadoses) for extended periods of time. They can also interfere with the action of other nutrients needed by the body in minute quantities for health. And until recently, there has been limited evidence that megadoses of any vitamins do much for you. Studies of people already taking vitamins can lead to misleading conclusions because such people are generally more health conscious to start, so it is difficult to attribute a particular health outcome to a particular vitamin or mineral. Any of their healthy behaviors—for example, exercise, frequent medical checkups, or meditation—could be responsible for their overall good health.

Doctors also fear that some people believe more is always better. This is a close cousin to the "if it's natural it can't be harmful" school of thought. Both are risky attitudes when it comes to vitamins and minerals. If 200 international units of vitamin E helps prevent heart disease, the thinking goes, I'll take 2,000 units and get even more protection. It doesn't work that way. Vitamin E, like anything else in nature, has a mechanism of action. One action is its significant anti-oxidant capacity. However, another is to inhibit platelets (i.e., clotting), so that blood becomes thinner—good for preventing heart attacks because thin blood flows through arteries better. Too much vitamin E, on the other hand, may increase your risk of hemorrhagic stroke because the blood may not be able to form a "platelet plug" when small leaks appear in fragile vessels.[47]

Another case in point is the former superstar vitamin beta-carotene, which has now been shown, in two well-conducted studies, to increase lung cancer rates in smokers.[48] Even drinking too much water can be toxic to the body: your blood sodium can drop, which can lead to swelling of the brain cells and a seizure, although it would take an enormous amount of water to bring that about, so we need not worry too much about it.

Nonetheless, there is good evidence to suggest that levels beyond those that easily can be supplied by diet for vitamins C, E, and folate (folic acid) may help lower your risk for certain diseases.[49] Calcium also has clear indications, along with vitamin D, for the prevention of osteoporosis, and both could possibly reduce your risk for cancer.[50] Other vitamins and minerals have received much less support in the scientific literature and you are taking your chances with megadoses. If you follow the Okinawa Food Pyramid you will get more than adequate doses of all vitamins and minerals. A little extra of the following vitamins and minerals *may* lead to better overall health for you and your family, but as evidenced by the Okinawan elders, you can still live healthily without them. Let's look at the vitamins and minerals that have the best evidence to support their use in disease prevention.

Vitamin C

Vitamin C is known as ascorbic acid to the scientific community and is famous for its role in preventing scurvy, whose characteristic bleeding gums, swollen joints, and muscle weakness were described as far back as the days of the Egyptians. Its cure—found in 1747 by Scottish surgeon James Lind—by supplementing the diet of the British Navy with vitamin C–rich limes, earned the British seamen the nickname "limeys." Now it's more known for its role as an antioxidant and is taken by 35 percent of the U.S. population as a dietary supplement.[51]

What it does. Vitamin C helps make collagen, the body's natural cement, and is key to the health of the body's connective tissue (tendons, cartilage, etc.) and bones. It aids wound healing, increases iron absorption, and protects vitamin E from oxidation. It also maintains the health of blood vessels; protects the tissues of the eyes against free-radical damage that can cause cataracts and macular degeneration, an irreversible loss of vision found in many elderly; and helps protect against effects of heavy metal toxicity. As a water-soluble antioxidant, it prevents free-radical-induced cell damage and can cut down the production of cancer-causing nitrosamines in the stomach.

Top food sources (in descending order of vitamin C content). Black currants, broccoli, Brussels sprouts, cauliflower, strawberries, lemons, cabbage, oranges, spinach (fresh and frozen), grapefruit, pineapple, turnips, potatoes, tomatoes, peaches, beans, bananas, and peas.[52]

Average intake. The average adult gets about 100 mg/day of vitamin C in the diet, 90 percent of it from fruits and vegetables. If you follow the Okinawa Program (ten fruits and vegetables per day), you will get over 400 mg/day.[53]

Optimum intake. Plenty of circumstantial evidence supports the use of higher doses of vitamin C for optimizing immune health, protecting against cardiovascular disease, and reducing cancer risk, but further study is needed. The Okinawan elders have a higher dietary intake of vitamin C than other Japanese and Americans, but don't take supplements. Eating a diet high in vegetables and fruits is the best initial course of action, but for optimal levels, take 500 mg once a day.[54]

Cautions. As a water-soluble vitamin it is safe even in large doses (several grams per day). Some people, however, report nausea and diarrhea with doses as low as 2,000 mg/day, since vitamin C can have an osmotic effect (draws out water) in the gut.[51] Rare cases of kidney stones in people with kidney disease have been reported with large doses, so these people should use special caution.[51]

Best Evidence

1. A review of twenty-one interventional studies of high-dose vitamin C showed no consistent effect on reducing the incidence of colds, but the duration and severity were reduced an average of 23 percent.[55]
2. Multiple studies have supported a role for reduction of stomach cancer, possibly through reduction of cancer-causing nitrosamines.[56] Human epidemiological studies also suggest strong support for reduced risk for cancers of the oral cavity, esophagus, and pancreas and moderate support for protection against cancer of the lung, breast,

cervix, and rectum.[56] A large review of the cardiovascular evidence suggests a possible protective association for cardiovascular disease.[57]

Vitamin D

Vitamin D has been around for a long time. Ocean-dwelling phytoplankton began producing it over 500 million years ago, after exposure to sunlight. Vertebrates during evolution became dependent on it for the health of their skeletons, the health of their nervous systems, and cellular functions (in close conjunction with calcium and phosphorus). Vitamin D deficiency (rickets) has plagued humans for millennia, causing deformation of long bones and the rib cage, bowed legs, bent spines, and weak muscles in those affected (e.g., up to 90 percent of children in autopsy studies in nineteenth-century Holland).[58] Since it rarely occurs with adequate sunlight exposure, it did not become a major public health concern until the industrial revolution, when smog-filled crowded cities arose in northern Europe and America, and people (including small children) spent extended periods indoors. This led to a 270-year search for a cure, and eventual isolation of vitamin D in the early 1900s. Supplementation of dairy products with vitamin D since the 1930s has virtually eliminated the problem in children.[58]

Getting the right amount of vitamin D can be tricky for adults. Dermatologists tell us to use sunscreen at all times, since the sun causes premature aging of the skin and skin cancer. Yet, this virtually eliminates vitamin D production in the skin; an SPF of 8 cuts vitamin D production by 95 percent.[59] Moreover, if you live much north of Los Angeles (e.g., in New York, Boston, or Toronto) you will have a tough time making vitamin D from November to March because the sun is too weak.[60,61] To further complicate matters, healthy elderly produce only 30 percent of the vitamin D that younger subjects do with the same sun exposure.[62] You can see the problem here.

What it does. Vitamin D is a hormone. It is essential for packing calcium into your bones. Without it you cannot absorb adequate calcium for bone health. It also helps with the function of your heart and recent evidence has shown a potential role in reduction of cancers of the breast,[58] prostate,[63] and colon.[64]

Top sources. Seafood—cod liver oil, tuna, salmon, and sardines—dairy products (fortified), margarine (fortified), mushrooms, and sunshine.[65]

Average intake. Top vitamin D researchers believe 9 to 40 percent of the U.S. population is vitamin D deficient, depending on age, ethnicity, and locale.[58,61,66]

Optimum intake. If you wear sunscreen outdoors and eschew fish or dairy products, you had better take a supplement, especially if you have darker skin. Adults up to age fifty require a minimum of 200 IU a day, fifty-one- to seventy-year-olds need 400 IU a day, and those over seventy require a minimum of 600 IU a day *with* minimal sun exposure.[58,66]

Some researchers believe those with darker skin (brown or black) who are sunlight deprived require at least 1,000 IU a day, despite a diet that contains vitamin D foods.[61] A prudent recommendation is for five to fifteen minutes of sun exposure of hands, forearms, and face two to three times per week (not to the point of sunburn) and application of sunscreen (SPF at least 8) thereafter. Then take a daily supplement of 200 to 600 IU according to your age. With no sun exposure and little dietary intake, a supplement of 800 IU is advisable.[58,66]

Cautions. Toxicity can result from prolonged high doses because of overabsorption of calcium.[67] Signs and symptoms include headaches, high blood pressure, nausea, constipation, growth retardation, seizures, and calcium deposits in the blood vessels, kidneys, or heart.

Best Evidence
1. A one-year, double-blind, placebo-controlled interventional study of 249 healthy postmenopausal women found those who received a 400 IU supplement of vitamin D

significantly reduced wintertime bone loss and improved net bone density versus the placebo group.[68]

2. In a study of sunscreen users, almost 50 percent of subjects in Springfield, Illinois, who always wore a sunscreen before going outdoors and did not take vitamin D supplements were vitamin D deficient, some of them severely so.[69]

Vitamin E

What it does. Despite its current fame as a free-radical warrior, vitamin E was for years a vitamin searching for a disease. All other vitamins had special roles as enzymes (speed up or slow down chemical reactions) or in a particular body function. But after seventy-five years of research, vitamin E is still waiting.[70] It may have to be happy with its unique position as the main dietary guardian of cells and vessel walls against free-radical damage. To the body, this function is considered so important that a variety of other antioxidants (e.g., vitamin C) protect vitamin E from oxidation. If a free radical comes near a cell wall rich in vitamin E, it would be 1,000 times more likely to be snuffed out by vitamin E than it would be to damage the cell wall.[71] In this way vitamin E may also decrease heart attack risk (less damage to heart artery walls),[72] improve immunity[73] (less damage to immune cells), decrease cancer risk (less damage to cell DNA),[74] and reduce the risk for dementia.[75]

Top food sources. Almonds, canola oil, hazelnuts, margarine, mayonnaise, olive oil, peanut butter, rice bran oil, safflower oil, shrimp, sweet potatoes, sunflower seeds and oil, wheat germ and oil, whole grains, and cereals.[76]

Average intake. Even if you have a high dietary intake, it's difficult to get more than 50 IU vitamin E in a day, far below the level found protective in most studies against heart disease.[72]

Optimum intake. Try to get as much vitamin E from your diet as possible. Our study of Okinawan elders shows that blood levels of vitamin E (alpha-tocopherol) in Okinawan elders are approximately

30 percent higher than those of similarly aged Americans, possibly through their use of canola oil and sweet potato.[77] If you are not on blood thinners, we suggest that an additional 200 IU per day may provide additional antioxidant protection against heart disease, cancer, or stroke, but the evidence is not definitive. If you already have coronary heart disease, then 400 IU per day would be a more appropriate dose.

Cautions. Seek your physician's advice before taking vitamin E with medicines that are prescribed to prevent blood clotting (e.g., warfarin, ticlopidine).

Best Evidence

1. In a Cambridge University study of men with preexisting heart disease, 2,002 subjects took 400 to 800 IU of vitamin E daily for a year and a half, and they reduced their risk of nonfatal heart attack by 77 percent.[78]
2. A double-blind, placebo-controlled interventional study of 29,133 male smokers showed the group who took 50 mg of vitamin E daily for 5 to 8 years had 41 percent fewer deaths from prostate cancer.[79]

Folate (folic acid)

What it does. The term *folic acid* was created in 1941 by Mitchell et al., who found folate in the green "foliage" or leaves of spinach.[80] Folate is critical for repairing breaks in genetic material (DNA or RNA), helping form new genetic material, protecting the health of red blood cells, and encouraging amino acid formation.[81] Folate is also thought to help protect against breast cancer and colon cancer.[81] Since 1998, U.S. grain manufacturers have been required to fortify their processed grain products with folic acid (another problem that could be avoided by eating whole grains).[82]

Preliminary evidence suggests that this has already improved blood folate levels in the elderly, who are at higher risk of deficiency because of lower folate absorption with age. It is destroyed by alcohol and up to 80 percent of alcoholics are folate deficient.[83] Low folate intake (<100 mcg/day) in pregnant women causes birth defects (neural tube defects) and also leads to high blood levels of homocysteine, an amino acid toxic to arteries and nerve cells.[81] People who eat less than one fruit and one green leafy vegetable per day or drink more than two alcoholic drinks per day are at much higher risk for folate deficiency.[84]

Top food sources. Spinach, black-eyed peas, kidney beans, pinto beans, lentils, oatmeal, asparagus, orange juice, and legumes (including soy).[85]

Average intake. Up to one third of Americans don't meet their minimal recommended intake of 200 mcg per day.[86] A recent study since folate fortification began estimated 68 to 87 percent of women of childbearing age took in less than their recommended intake.[86] Folate deficiency is among the most common vitamin deficiencies in the world.[84]

Optimum intake. If you eat less than two fruits and vegetables per day or drink more than two alcoholic drinks per day, you should be supplementing with 400 to 800 mcg per day. If you plan on getting pregnant you should be taking a multivitamin with 400 mcg of folate per day. If you follow the Okinawa Program you will be doing well but might benefit from an extra 200 to 400 mcg/day (the amount present in a typical multivitamin), especially if you are over seventy years of age.

Cautions. Greater than 1,000 mcg (1 mg) daily for extended periods (weeks to months) may mask a vitamin B12 deficiency, decrease zinc absorption, and produce damaging folacin crystals in the kidneys.[84]

Best Evidence

1. A meta-analysis of twelve interventional studies of folate's effect on blood homocysteine levels found that dietary supplements reduced blood homocysteine concentrations in those with elevated levels by 25 percent.[87]

2. A study of 5,000 Canadians found that those who had the highest folate intakes had lower risk for heart disease over the next fifteen years.[88]

Calcium

Calcium is the fifth most common element in the biosphere. It was likely abundant in the watery soup in which life first appeared, and without it we would all soon cease to exist. Calcium has deservedly received significant attention in the public health arena and few of us are unconvinced of its importance to health. The problem with calcium is that our needs tend to increase just as our intakes begin to decline (as we age). In women, 99 percent of peak bone mass is achieved by age twenty-two and then it's a battle to slow the rate of bone loss.[89] Calcium intake is one of the key defenses.

What it does. Calcium helps build and maintain bones and teeth; it is required for proper function of most of the body's cells, including the muscles, the heart, and the brain. High dietary calcium intake has also been associated with better blood pressure, reduced risk for colon cancer, and protection against kidney stones and lead poisoning.[90] Calcium intake and osteoporosis prevention go hand in hand, so much so that the FDA has allowed food labels to advertise the connection. Individual calcium tablets are used for people who need significant extra calcium, since a typical multi-vitamin contains only limited amounts.

Top food sources. Beans, milk, cheese, yogurt, calcium-fortified orange juice, calcium-fortified soy milk, and tofu.[91]

Average intake. If you eat according to the Okinawa Program, your average intake will be about 1,200 mg per day based on a 2,000-calorie intake. If you eat a typical American diet, it will be around 800 mg per day.[90]

Optimum intake. In line with the National Osteoporosis Foundation we recommend 1,200 to 1,500 mg of calcium per day for women ages eleven to twenty-four; 1,000 mg per day for women age twenty-five and over; 1,500 mg daily for postmenopausal women; and 1,200 to 1,500 mg of calcium daily for pregnant or lactating women. Men should aim for 1,200 to 1,500 mg calcium per day.[92] You have to be diligent in your food choices to get your daily quota. A simple solution (and what we do) is to calculate your approximate intake and to supplement with the difference.

Cautions. Too much calcium in the blood (hypercalcemia) causes severe problems, including lax muscle tone, constipation, large urine volumes, nausea, and ultimately confusion, coma, and death. But this almost never occurs from ingestion of natural food sources.[90] A good example of the safety of food calcium sources is illustrated by the Masai tribe of Africa.[93] Their calcium intakes are above 5,000 mg/day or about ten times what we ingest, but they don't suffer from a higher incidence of hypercalcemia or kidney stones. High calcium intakes from supplements may contribute to kidney stones in certain susceptible individuals, but in most individuals calcium helps reduce their stone formation.[90] A high-calcium diet binds oxalate (stones are made from calcium oxalate) in the gut and takes it out of the body in the stool.

Best Evidence

1. A meta-analysis of fourteen studies found that adding a 300 mg daily calcium supplement (equivalent to one glass of fortified orange juice) decreased bone fractures in high-risk groups up to 70 percent.[94]
2. Our nutritional studies of Okinawan elders show that centenarian men and women get about 625 mg and 400 mg per day of calcium from food, respectively. This would be the equivalent of 900 mg and 730 mg for men and women, respectively, when standardized to a 2,000-kcal diet. However, they are also thought to get a significant amount of unmeasured calcium from their drinking water (Okinawa is surrounded by coral reefs and thus the drinking water has high calcium levels), which may help to keep their hip fractures low.[95]

Tips for Supplementing Your Vitamin and Mineral Intake Wisely

- Discuss any vitamin/mineral use with your doctor.
- Choose a multivitamin and mineral supplement that provides 50 to 100 percent of the recommended daily value for a broad range of micronutrients.
- Consider optimizing your vitamin and mineral levels with additional daily vitamin C (500–1000 mg), D (200–1000 IU), E (100–400 IU), folate (200–800 IU), and calcium (300–1500 mg elemental calcium) depending upon your dietary intake, age, gender, ethnicity, and other health factors. Taking other supplements is either unproven, unhealthy, or a waste of money until more evidence is in.
- Don't take extra beta-carotene in pill form because of its uncertain health effects and its potential role for increasing lung cancer (especially in smokers).[96]
- Men and postmenopausal women should avoid iron supplements because iron can act as a pro-oxidant and may increase your risk for heart disease (currently an active area of study).[97]
- Avoid vitamin K supplements, which can increase blood clotting. Instead get K naturally through a wide range of vegetables, especially greens, broccoli, radishes, cabbages, beans, canola and soybean oils, and green tea. Anyone taking the drug Coumadin (warfarin) should strictly avoid supplementing with vitamin K because of micronutrient-drug interactions.
- Avoid extra enzymes, time-release preparations, or chelated preparations, since they add little value. They are unproven and generally ineffective.
- If you are on blood thinners (e.g., Coumadin), use caution with vitamin E and check with your physician before use.
- Avoid "stress-tabs" or taking large doses of B-vitamins. Despite the fact that B-vitamins are water soluble and eliminated in the urine, supplementing with greater than 100 mg of vitamin B6 (pyridoxine) for extended periods

can cause nerve damage (peripheral neuropathy) in susceptible individuals.[98]

For further information on vitamin and mineral intakes, see Appendix A (pages 479–81).

5. Okinawa's Healing Herbs and Foods

A flower of hibiscus, its crimson petals, like your beautiful
lips, are nourishment for my soul.

Okinawan poem

"Let food be your medicine." The Greek physician Hippocrates said
it more than 2,000 years ago, and the Okinawans are still living by the
principle today, nobody more so than Fumiko Ota. This ninety-five-
year-old dynamo not only lives the Okinawa way but also probably
knows more about Okinawa's healing foods and herbal medicines
than anyone else on the island. Fifteen years ago (when she was a
mere eighty), Otasan wrote a book called *Okinawa no Yakuso Hyakka
(Herbal Medicines of Okinawa),*[1] in which she shared the vast knowledge
that had been passed down to her from her mother-in-law and had
been part of the Ota family lore for generations.

Although she enjoyed learning about healing plants in those pre-
World War II days, Otasan admits that she had some reservations
about their usefulness. Store-bought medicine was starting to
replace home remedies in the early part of the twentieth century,
and traditional herbal medicines seemed a bit old-fashioned and
impractical to her. Then World War II came along and gave her a
very different perspective. During the war and its aftermath, modern medicines were scarce, almost impossible to come by. The only
remedies available to treat the ravages of wartime injuries and the
inevitable diseases were medicinal plants and herbs from the
Okinawa rain forest. Many lives—including Otasan's own—came
to depend upon them and her knowledge of their healing powers. It
was from her hands-on healing experience with these amazing
plants that Otasan developed a new respect for herbal medicines
and fully realized the value—the necessity—of passing them on to
future generations. This continues to be her lifelong work.

As evidence-based scientists, we don't have all the answers concerning how the Okinawans' natural herbs and medicines have contributed to their outstanding health, youthfulness, and longevity. But we feel certain that there's a beneficial effect. Our research group is actively investigating this area and our findings are very promising—indeed, tantalizing. There is certainly strong evidence that some of the compounds in the herbs and medicinal plants regularly consumed by Okinawans have powerful antioxidant and positive hormonal effects, and few ill effects have been associated with using them as foods, condiments, spices, teas, or home remedies.[2]

Not that this is particularly surprising. Herbs and plants have always been a major medicinal source for traditional cultures. The World Health Organization estimates that 85 percent of the world's inhabitants depend directly on plants as medicines.[3] And many countries have adopted traditional medicines as part of their primary health care systems, including China, Thailand, Mexico, Nigeria, Japan, Germany, and France. The Germans have a government agency called Commission E that assesses herbal products and licenses them for use for specific ailments.[4] In the United States, more than 60 million people use some form of alternative medicinal product, many of them herbs.[5] Indeed, most of the world's people use herbs in one form or another in their medical systems.

The National Center for the Study of Complementary and Alternative Medicine (NCCAM), at the National Institutes of Health, was set up to study herbal products, a clear demonstration that there is significant interest in the United States. The Canadian government has also launched a multimillion-dollar initiative to investigate "nutraceuticals," foods that have pharmaceutical-like properties when eaten whole, such as soy foods, flax, and various herbs.

Research into plants found in rain forests (such as those found in Okinawa), which yield an incredibly vast diversity of species, is also a substantial area of activity for many pharmaceutical companies or government agencies, such as the National Cancer Institute.[6] They have come up with some interesting findings. A team of botanists from Harvard University, for example, brought back leaves, bark, and branches from the tree *Calophyllum lanigerum,* which they collected while trekking through a swampy rain forest in Sarawak, a Malaysian state on the island of Borneo in East Asia. The tree turned out to contain a substance called calanolide A, which has subsequently been synthesized as a potential weapon against AIDS by MediChem Pharmaceuticals in partnership with the government of Sarawak. Trials with AIDS patients are currently under way.[7]

This kind of discovery comes as no surprise to Seikichi Shimoji, an herbalist who grew up in the rain forests of Miyako Island in southern Okinawa and has spent the last fifty-five years of his life studying and cultivating herbs. His interest in herbs and plants was fostered by his grandmother, who taught him about traditional medicines derived from locally grown herbs, such as aloe, guava, huchiba (mugwort), kandaba, and unjana. His grandmother knew exactly which herb healed a wound, brought down a fever, lowered high blood pressure, or cured an ailing stomach. Although Shimojisan's parents wanted him to become a medical doctor, he preferred to skip classes and spend his time trudging through the rain forest on magical quests for new medicinal plants. Over the years he discovered a vast array of herbs and plants, many of which were at first deemed worthless, only to turn out later to be of great nutritional and medicinal value. Shimojisan now cultivates over a thousand varieties of herbs commercially, and runs a healthy herb restaurant located in the town of Sashiki on the main island of Okinawa.

Shimojisan's work is made easier by the fact that Okinawa's 160 islands are home to forty-five times more plant species per unit of land than the Japanese mainland. These islands have been called the "Galápagos of the East" because of their amazing array of unique flora and fauna, which flourish in their humid subtropical climate.[8] The islands' combination of mild temperature (about 70° F on average) and abundant precipitation seems to create the perfect habitat for both plants and animals. Okinawa is home to many species that cannot be found anywhere else in the world, including the Iriomote mountain cat (a wild prehistoric cat) and a flightless bird called the Yambaru quina (a type of rail).

Okinawa's herbs and traditional foods are less rare than the flightless quina, but just as precious. They have actually been enjoying a sales boom lately in mainland Japan, as people have become more aware of their healing properties. Still, they're not panaceas and shouldn't be taken indiscriminately. Everything we put into our bodies has health consequences, and herbs and medicinal foods are no exception. Some herbs cause allergic reactions, some increase blood pressure, others thin the blood—all these consequences and others should be considered seriously if you are on other medications.[9] If herbs are taken in pill form they should be judged by the same criteria as any other medication, each carrying its own risks and benefits, and your physician should be consulted prior to use. Many of our current drugs are purified and concentrated forms of former herbal medicines (e.g., aspirin from willow bark), which attests to the fact that plants can be powerful medicines.

With this caveat in mind, we present some of the potential neutraceutical foods and healing herbs that Okinawans have been using and that may be playing significant roles in their lifelong health.

Ten Healing Foods and Herbs

Our research in Okinawa has revealed that many healing herbs and foods have been used for decades to maximize the healing power of the traditional Okinawan lifestyle, and studies suggest that common phytochemical ingredients might be responsible for their beneficial effects. Two common factors that we have observed are high flavonoid content, which, as we've discussed, gives you powerful antioxidant and hormonal protection, and high vitamin and mineral content.[10]

Ucchin, or Turmeric
(*Curcuma longa*, Jiang Huang, Curcuma, Indian Saffron, Ukon, Valerian)

Ucchin, commonly known in North America as turmeric, is one of the Okinawans' favorite herbs (as it is in India), and claims a multitude of health benefits. It's known as *ukon* to the Japanese, *jiang huang* to the Chinese, and curcuma and Indian saffron in other areas of the world. In North America, turmeric can readily be found in regular supermarkets and in Asian and international markets. Now, as word spreads about its health benefits, turmeric is even available in some places in capsule form. Okinawans use it as a curry spice for certain dishes (soups, chicken, and fish), in tinctures (wound care), and in tea (adding turmeric powder to oolong tea), or take it in pill form. We use it to perk up our chicken and vegetable soups, tuna and bean salads, and even to add zip and color (a lovely orange-yellow) to salad dressings.

Folkloric claims. Turmeric is from the ginger family. The stalk of the plant is the part most commonly used in both herbal and traditional medicine, and is the part that provides the distinctive yellowish-orange powder that adds flavor and color to curry. It was probably brought to Okinawa centuries ago from India, which had active trade relations with the Ryukyu Kingdom (as Okinawa was formerly known). In Ayurvedic medicine, the traditional medicine of India that Dr. Deepak Chopra has popularized in America, turmeric is thought to strengthen the immune system, relieve inflammatory conditions such as arthritis, improve digestion, relieve gas, kill parasites and worms, alleviate menstrual problems, dissolve gallstones, and relieve other ailments.[11] The Okinawans are in full accord with these claims, and highly prize their turmeric.

The evidence. Perhaps both the Indians and the Okinawans are onto something. Turmeric has been well studied for its potential medicinal properties, especially by Indian researchers who discovered that it has anti-inflammatory actions.[12] While it's still too early to recommend it for specific medicinal uses, turmeric shows early promise for several medical conditions, mainly due to the powerful properties of its major active component, curcumin.[13] Curcumin consists mainly of the smaller bioactive components tumerone, atlantone, zingiberone, and heptanoids. Other compounds mainly consist of various proteins, sugars, resins, vitamins, and minerals.

If turmeric is proved to do even half of what it appears to do, it will be considered an important medicine. First, it seems to halt the cancer process at all three stages: initiation, promotion, and progression.[14] This occurs both in the test tube *and* in the body, a critical hurdle before a drug or herb can gain credibility as an anticancer agent. In the lab, rats pretreated with turmeric had far fewer tumors than their untreated counterparts when exposed to cancer-causing chemicals.[15] Turmeric possesses significant antioxidant properties, comparable to that of vitamins E or C, which is probably why it proves powerful against cancer.[16] The American Institute for

Cancer Research has reported some degree of inhibition for cancers of the GI tract, including oral, esophageal, stomach, and colon cancers.[17] And there is further evidence for its effectiveness against breast and skin cancers. The effects of turmeric still have to be confirmed in interventional, placebo-controlled trials before it can officially be placed alongside other proven anti-cancer treatments, but the preliminary evidence is promising and worthy of serious attention.

Cancer is not the only disease for which turmeric seems to hold such promise. It also looks like a good bet for prevention and treatment of gallstones. Turmeric significantly reduces cholesterol absorption, one of the building blocks of gallstones,[18] and it has the ability to interfere with the replication of bacteria associated with inflammation of the gallbladder.[19] This germ-busting effect extends from bacteria to viruses. Potent inhibition of the HIV virus was reported by scientists at Harvard's Dana-Farber Cancer Institute.[20] Remarkably, turmeric has been able to increase the CD4 count in AIDS patients. (Also called helper T cells, CD4 cells are white blood cells that are required to fight infection, but are killed by the HIV virus.)[21] The hepatitis virus also seems to fall victim to turmeric's power.[22]

Turmeric's bug-busting ability is one reason it has been used for centuries to treat wounds. It seems to have an impressive ability to reduce pain and inflammation.[12,17] Turmeric has been shown in some studies to be as effective as treatment with nonsteroidal anti-inflammatory drugs (NSAIDs), the usual treatment for pain associated with rheumatologic disorders such as rheumatoid arthritis, osteoarthritis, and postoperative pain.[17] Curcumin, an extract of turmeric, is thought to be able to stimulate the body's ability to release cortisol (a hormone that regulates metabolism and maintains blood pressure), and to sensitize the body's receptors for this hormone.[17] Cortisol release is thought to further decrease inflammation.

Furthermore, turmeric may be able to slow the elimination of cortisol from the body.[17] Turmeric even appears to be able to protect the stomach's mucosal layer against NSAIDs, which are notorious for promoting bleeding of the stomach, one of the leading causes of death in people who are on these medications.[23] Turmeric might be likened to a new type of medication for arthritis sufferers called

Cox-2 inhibitors. Celebrex and Vioxx are the two most popular of this class of medicines. They are considered "miracle drugs" for treatment of inflammatory conditions such as rheumatoid arthritis because they have virtually the same ability to reduce inflammation as nonsteroidal anti-inflammatory drugs, but with far fewer stomach complications, such as bleeding ulcers. Within weeks of their release in 1999 they became two of the leading prescribed medications in America. Turmeric is not about to replace Cox-2 inhibitors, but it seems to have a promising future as an herbal tonic and great-tasting spice.

Usage. If taken as a supplement in tablet form, the usual dose is 8 to 60 grams up to three times per day for turmeric, or 400 to 600 mg by mouth two or three times a day for curcumin.[17] Curcumin is not well absorbed by the body and is often sold in conjunction with bromelain (pineapple enzyme), supposedly to enhance absorption.[17,24] If used in supplement form, turmeric should be taken on an empty stomach and only after consultation with a health professional. It can be used liberally as a spice.

One of our favorite recipes using the spice is Okinawan Sautéed Chicken with Turmeric (see page 445). This dish brings the spicy bite of curry to chicken, leaving the palate eager for more. It's also good for you and takes less than a half-hour of simple preparation. Once reserved for the nobility, this dish creates a meal fit for a king.

Cautions. Side effects are rare and consist only of mild upset stomach if they do occur. Those taking nonsteroidal anti-inflammatory drugs or blood thinners should not take turmeric as a supplement because of possible additive effects, nor should pregnant or lactating women take supplements, since side effects are unknown. Those on immunosuppressants such as steroids should use caution and check first with their physicians. Long-term use in pill form is to be avoided, as long-term effects are unknown.

The bottom line. Turmeric seems to be living up to its health claims. It is on the GRAS (Generally Regarded as Safe) list of the U.S. Food and Drug Administration, and is approved by Germany's Commission E for use as an anti-inflammatory and for the treatment of gallstones.[4] The best way to consume turmeric would be to use it as a spice on already healthy food. If there's a choice, food is always the best medicine, not capsules or pills.

Goya, Bitter Melon

(*Momordica charantia,* African Cucumber, Balsam Pear, Bitter Apple, Bitter Gourd, Bitter Pear, Chin-li-chih, Goo-fa, Ku Gua, Wild Cucumber)

Goya is known to North Americans as bitter melon, and bitter it is. The first time we tried it, it was hard to fathom why the Okinawans have developed such a taste for this strange vegetable. Its Latin genus is *Momordica,* which means "bite"—an appropriate name in more ways than one. This vegetable curves like the shape of the mouth, giving it a bitelike appearance, and has a real bite when it's turned into *goya chample,* a favorite Okinawan dish.

A member of the melon family, goya was probably brought to Okinawa from ancient China during one of the many trade exchanges between the Ryukyu Kingdom and the Ming and Manchu dynasties. Reference to it first appeared in 1713, although it was probably used as a food source as early as 600 years before that.[25] It is widely available in North America in Chinese markets or Asian food stores, where it's referred to as chin-li-chih, goo-fa, or ku gua. In our experience, the Chinese version seems a little less bitter than its Okinawan counterpart. Okinawans like to hang goya from bamboo eaves on the roofs of traditional houses, which serves a dual purpose: it blocks the hot sun from entering the house, and it gives the melon the full sun exposure it needs for rapid growth.

Goya, like caviar, is an acquired taste. The more you eat it, the more often you want it. Goya is most often featured in a stir-fry of tofu, eggs, and canola oil, and these other ingredients tend to offset the bitter taste. Throw in a dash of pepper and a few other goodies and you have a great-tasting meal that may indeed help you achieve everlasting health.

Folkloric claims. Much of goya's claim to fame rests with its folkloric abilities to treat or prevent diabetes, cancer, and various infections, especially gastrointestinal infections and, more recently, the HIV virus that causes AIDS.[26] In India and Sri Lanka, goya has been used as a tonic, emetic, and laxative, as well as a treatment for rheumatic pains and diabetes. In Central and South America, the fruit or tea has been used to treat colds, fevers, stomach aches, constipation, and diabetes.

The Chinese and Okinawans have used the fruit, seeds, vines, stems, and leaves for gastrointestinal maladies, including chronic stomach ulcers and dysentery. Other uses include the treatment of fever, viral infections, and toothaches. Chronic diseases such as diabetes, cancer, rheumatism, gout, and spleen and liver disorders have also been treated with goya. It has even been claimed to act as a male aphrodisiac!

The evidence. After that impressive list of folkloric claims, should we all be stampeding to the Asian food market to fill our shopping bags with goya? Well, yes and no. We confess to eating a lot of it when we are in Okinawa, and we are not alone in our fondness of this amazing vegetable. But despite the host of anecdotal evidence, we are still waiting for stronger evidence from actual studies before we take a full leap onto the goya bandwagon and begin treating actual diseases with goya or its extracts. The good news is that Western science is finding that some of the claims made for goya are bearing fruit, if you will.

It turns out that the bitter taste of goya is due to the presence of curcurbitacins from the triterpine family, one of the phytochemicals that is thought to play a role in cancer prevention.[27] Several well-conducted clinical trials support goya's ability to lower blood sugar in diabetics.[28] (So check with your doctor before drinking goya in liquid form because you may experience a drop in your own blood sugar.) Goya juice may also be able to lower a diabetic's need for large doses of insulin, an effect likened to that of Avandia (rosiglita-zone) and some of the other new "insulin sensitizers" on the market.[29]

Plus, numerous other benefits have been reported. Test-tube studies have shown beneficial activity against the AIDS virus.[30] A protein in goya seeds was found to inhibit the growth of the herpes and polio viruses.[31] An extract of the roots and leaves has been shown to inhibit the growth of *E. coli*, one of the most common causes of urinary tract infections in women.[32] Antitumor activity has been shown in animal studies and linked to a specific anticancer protein found in goya.[27] Two small studies suggested benefit for treatment of glaucoma and hemorrhoids.[32] And some case studies suggest that it can stimulate the appetite.[32]

Goya is also very high in vitamin C, as are many of the green vegetables. But goya seems to be able to retain its rich quantities of vitamin C even when cooked at high temperatures, which is a rarity.[33] Interestingly, our research revealed that Okinawans have a higher intake of vitamin C than other Japanese.[34] Part of this is almost certainly related to their love of goya and other green vegetables. Okinawans believe that goya helps keep their skin and bones young, which again might possibly be related to its vitamin C content and its ability to help synthesize collagen, an essential protein for bone and connective tissue health. Goya is sounding better by the minute.

Usage. For medicinal purposes, fresh goya juice has been used in doses of 50 to 100 ml per day ($^1/_5$ cup to $^2/_5$ cup).[32] Concentrated extract, available in some health food stores, has been used at a dose of 50 ml two times per day. It is also available as goya tea, which is drunk hot or cold.

Our favorite goya recipe is the delicious Goya Chample (see page 443). It's extremely easy to prepare and is a great fast meal, full of vitamin C and flavonoids. If you cannot get goya in your area, substitute a large peeled zucchini (courgette).

Caution. Goya is a widely eaten food in Asia and is considered safe. Eating cooked goya in a meal is highly unlikely to cause any adverse effects. Diarrhea and stomach ache have been reported when consumed in excess, but then again, eating anything in excess can be problematic. Diabetics should watch their blood sugar when eating goya. Goya has been reported to increase the effectiveness of the diabetic medication Diabenese (chlorpromamide), a sulfonurea.[35] Caution should also be exercised when using other medications in the sulfonurea class, such as Amaryl (glimepiride), Glucotrol (glipizide), and Micronase or DiaBeta (glyburide). Safety has not been established in pregnancy or lactation, and it should be avoided during these times.[32,35,36] Those with kidney and liver disease should use caution, as momordin protein, along with some of the lesser-known active ingredients in goya, is eliminated from the body by these organs.

The bottom line. The American Herbal Products Association has not classified goya, nor has Germany's Commission E studied it. But eating goya is definitely part of the overall dietary approach that has worked for the Okinawans. Westerners who shy away from goya or have difficulties finding it may wish to eat more vegetables from the gourd (squash) family, where goya finds its home: zucchini (courgette), wax gourd, pumpkins, and squash. This would be in keeping with the National Cancer Institute's recommendation for five servings of veggies and fruit a day, and our ten-a-day recommendation. But on your next visit to an Asian market, go for the goya.

Hechima, or Vegetable Sponge
(*Luffa cylindrica*, Nabera)

No discussion of Okinawan foods would be complete without hechima, which is another one of those Okinawan vegetables that defies description. Unlike goya, hechima is not bitter. Indeed, it looks and tastes like a sweet zucchini (courgette) and has an amazing texture that just melts in your mouth. It is one of those foods that everyone loves at first bite, and Okinawans cannot seem to get enough of it. It is usually served with Okinawan tofu in a miso-sake sauce, in a combination that can only be described as delicious— pure heaven. You should be able to find hechima in your local Asian market, but if not, substitute zucchini or yellow squash or experiment with other members of the gourd family. Zucchini is a vegetable that looks a lot like hechima and is also loaded with nutrition. It's a very low-calorie vegetable, since it's 94 percent water. One cup of raw, shredded hechima or zucchini provides only 20 calories and at least 12 mg of vitamin C (20 percent of the recommended daily amount), 28 mcg of folate (16 percent of the recommend daily amount), plenty of carotenoids, and some very interesting proteins that could have important health consequences.

Hechima was introduced to Okinawa some 350 years ago and is closely related to *Luffa actangulla,* which is consumed in Hawaii and parts of Southeast Asia. People in mainland Japan don't eat much hechima, but they do use its dried outer core as a body or dish scrubber, which is most likely why it is also known as dishcloth gourd. Quite a versatile little vegetable.

Folkloric claims. The health claims for hechima center on cancer prevention and its reputation as an immune booster.

Evidence. Extracts from members of the gourd family (cucurbitaceae plants, including green and yellow squash) may contain one or more of eight distinct but related proteins that have anticancer, antiviral, anti-AIDS, and immune-enhancing properties.[37] There are more than twenty studies on hechima's special proteins alone.[38]

Usage. Hechima is best used as a healthy adjunct to your Okinawa pantry. Try our recipe for Simmered Hechima with Miso Gravy (page 441).

Cautions. No adverse effects have been reported with eating hechima. Its safety has not been established in pregnancy or lactation, but it has been eaten for generations in Okinawa, southeast Asia, and the Polynesian islands, and several members of the gourd (squash) family possess the cucurbitaceae proteins.[39]

The bottom line. Loading your plate with hechima, its cousin zucchini (courgette), or yellow squash makes good nutrition sense. It may reduce your risk for cancer and tastes fantastic—it's a no-brainer. Add it to your weekly shopping list.

Huchiba, or Mugwort

(*Artemisia vulgaris,* Ai Ye, Carline Thistle, *Carlina vulgaris,* Felon Herb, *Radix cardopatiae*)

Everyone at one point develops an upset stomach, and in Okinawa huchiba has always been there to provide relief. In fact, the elders tell us that in the old days huchiba was the only readily available treatment for stomach ailments in Okinawa.[1] Now it's often blended with other treatments, including Western medicines. Huchiba, known in the West as mugwort (*wort* simply means "plant" in Old English), is usually available in liquid or tea form; the dried herb is used for cooking. Its leaves are dark green and it smells a little bit like rosemary. Some say that aside from curing upset stomachs, mugwort also strengthens the liver.[1] Both claims need to be scientifically tested, but in Okinawa mugwort is becoming more and more popular as people are rediscovering traditional herbal medicines.

Folkloric claims. Mugwort's medicinal actions go well beyond stomach ailments. Folkloric claims include efficacy in treating asthma, bronchitis, the common cold, fever, headache, dysmenorrhea (painful menstruation), gout, epilepsy, gallstones, kidney stones, gastritis, tuberculosis, skin cancer, and wounds.[1] Roots from mugwort are used in traditional Chinese medicine to treat neuroses, depression, irritability and restlessness, insomnia, and anxiety.

The evidence. More than 100 studies have been done on mugwort, many of them supporting its folk uses. One recent study supported mugwort's traditional role as a stomach protector, showing that it and similar plants reduced alcohol-induced stomach damage in rats by 47 to 76 percent.[40] There are a few small studies to support mugwort's use in treating pruritus (itch) and atopic dermatitis, a type of psoriasis.[41] Another study supported its use for decreasing postoperative blood loss, bacterial infections, and inflammation when used as part of an herbal preparation in postoperative bladder irrigation.[42] The best evidence for the *Artemisia* class of plants, of which mugwort is a member, is for the treatment of infectious disease. Approval is pending in Europe for it as a new and effective treatment for malaria.[43] Chemically active compounds in its seeds, fresh roots, and leaves are in the same class of compounds—terpenes and flavonoids—as those found in ginkgo biloba, green tea, soy, and soy products.[44] These compounds, of course, are extremely beneficial to your health. Much more research needs to be done, especially in humans, before mugwort can be recommended for other medical treatments, but its future looks very promising.

Usage. Mugwort is most commonly prescribed by alternative practitioners for two conditions: stress (take 5 ml, or 1 teaspoon, tincture by mouth before bed or 15 mg, ½ ounce, of dried herb added to a half-cup of water) and poor appetite (1 to 2 teaspoons dried herb steeped for 5 to 10 minutes in 150 ml, or 3/5 cup, boiling water, then strained; 2 to 3 cups before meals).

Mugwort is frequently used in Okinawan cooking in vegetable pilaf dishes and as a soup spice. Because it eliminates strong odors, mugwort is a natural in fish soups, and gives a fresh spring scent to almost any other recipe. It's also great as a tea (see recipe, page 404).

Cautions. Allergic reactions have been reported, especially in those with hay fever or allergies to hazelnuts. Those taking anticoagulants (blood thinners) should use caution. Mugwort is not on the German Commission E list for approved herbs because it may stimulate uterine contractions during pregnancy, so avoid it during this time.

The bottom line. Mugwort shows great promise. Use it in your cooking or drink it as a tea. Mugwort tea is available at Asian food stores in loose leaves or in bags.

Okinawa Tofu, or Firm or Extra-Firm Tofu

What is so special about Okinawan tofu? Well, where do we start? Okinawans love their tofu, no doubt about it. They probably eat more tofu than any other group in the world. Our studies confirm that they consume, on average, an impressive 3 ounces of soy products a day, mostly as tofu and miso (soy paste), but also in a few intriguing creations of their own.[45] These include a tofu-peanut combination and a cheeselike sweet tofu that was considered so special that in the days of the Ryukyu Kingdom it was reserved for the royal family's plates alone. Fortunately, the descendants of the royal family, from the Sho lineage, have provided us with a few recipes (one of them is in Chapter Twelve) that might tickle the taste buds of Westerners and help jump-start the journey toward everlasting health.

Folkloric claims. Tofu has always been considered good for the digestion and overall health. It's been a staple food for centuries in the East, and Okinawans believe it is partly responsible for their outstanding health. In fact, during the *tokachi* celebration, a special party for one's eighty-eighth birthday, guests are served savory tofu that has been carved into numbers that run from 1 to 60. The number 60 is used to represent the poem that many elders like to repeat at their party. It goes: "sixty on top of sixty equals one hundred and twenty . . . may you live until then."

The evidence. Western science is finding that tofu does a lot more than aid digestion and help keep the body fit. Okinawan tofu in particular has a higher protein and fat content (good fat) than even its Japanese or Chinese counterparts.[46] This probably accounts for its richer taste and firmer texture, and likely a higher flavonoid content, since flavonoids are closely associated with the protein part of soy.[47] Soy, as we've discussed, has shown great ability in fighting heart disease and is strongly implicated as a weapon against hormone-dependent cancers, such as those of the breast and prostate.[48] A recent study at the University of Texas showed that women who ate a soy-fortified diet for one month reduced their blood estrogen (a risk factor for breast cancer) by 25 percent.[49]

Okinawan tofu is difficult to find in North America, although we are certain that as more people are exposed to it, it will become more popular and more readily available. Meanwhile, firm or extra-firm tofu is an excellent substitute. It is also extremely high in cancer-fighting flavonoids and the closest in texture to its Okinawan cousin. You can find firm or extra-firm tofu in most supermarkets.

Usage. Use tofu freely as a meat substitute, in stir-fries, salads, or any dish which calls for meat, chicken, or cheese.

We thank the ex–vice governor of Okinawa and professor of nutrition Hiroko Sho for one of our favorite tofu recipes—East-West Tofu Croquettes (see page 425). It takes less than thirty minutes to prepare and it is delicious.

Cautions. There is some concern about children in early puberty and post-menopausal women consuming a lot of soy products because of the high concentration of flavonoids and their weak estrogenic actions.[50] While this is a legitimate concern, there is little evidence to support adverse health claims for soy other than for the limited number of people who report soy allergies.[50] Soy has been used for thousands of years in Asia, and Okinawan children and women are among the healthiest in the world. Indeed, the drugs used to prevent and treat breast cancer are in the same class of compounds as flavonoids (i.e., selective estrogen receptor modulators). There is no known upper limit with regard to safety for soy consumption.

The bottom line. Eat two servings a day of soy or other flavonoid foods, as per the Okinawa Food Pyramid's guide to healthy food choices. Firm tofu, which can be enjoyed either in the Okinawan way (e.g., stir-fried with vegetables or in miso soup) or in the Western way, as a meat substitute (e.g., soy burgers), should be right at the top of your Okinawa pantry shopping list.

Imo, or Sweet Potato
(*Ipomoea batatas,* numu)

Historical records indicate that in 1605 an Okinawan man named Sokan Noguni brought a sweet potato seedling back from Fujian, a neighboring Chinese province with close cultural ties to Okinawa, and began growing it in his garden.[51] Over the years he shared seeds with neighbors and taught his friend, Gima Shinjo, how to raise this amazing new plant. Before long Mr. Shinjo was enthusiastically spreading it among other people on the Okinawa islands.

In those days, there were about four strong typhoons every year, and rice paddies were often completely destroyed, exposing the people to potential famine. But the hardy imo, buried deeper in the ground and better protected, held on and prospered despite the fierce storms and floods that hit the islands of Okinawa in the summertime. (Okinawa is smack in the middle of what is known as "hurricane alley.") This strange and wonderful sweet potato proved to be a literal lifesaver to Okinawans. It was largely due to the imo, and the stable source of calories it provided, that the population of Okinawa grew from 120,000 to 200,000 in the first decades of the 1600s.[51] Since that time imo has been one of the main carbohydrates consumed in Okinawa. Mr. Noguni became known as "Lord Sokan," or "the Imo King," and is still remembered and widely respected by all Okinawans. In the town of Kadena, near one of the American bases, there is a statue dedicated to his achievement. And there is an old greeting in Okinawa that perhaps honors him and his work even more: *Nmu kamatooin,* which means "Are you getting enough imo?" In Okinawa, well-being and the imo go hand in hand.

While Okinawans have traditionally eaten imo, it was the expansion of the Okinawan diet to include many other plant foods, soy, fish, and a limited quantity of meat and dairy products that was associated with their rapid post-World War II increase in life expectancy. They still retain their love for the sweet potato, however. You can even get imo french fries at Okinawan fast-food restaurants, probably a healthier choice than the usual variety, but like all deep-fried foods, they are best consumed in limited quantities. If you visit Okinawa or Japan, try the stone-baked imo (*ishi-yaki imo*) from the imo truck that is a fixture on many local street corners in Okinawa, much like the hot dog stand is in America. We recommend it!

The imo comes in two main forms in Okinawa—light yellow inside and brown-purple skin (satsuma-imo) or purple inside and light brown skin (beni-imo). Until imo starts being imported regularly to North America, simply substitute American sweet potatoes or purple potatoes, which we see in supermarkets occasionally. We have tried both in all our imo recipes and they are equally delicious and nutritious.

Folkloric claims. There are some health claims attributed to sweet potatoes and wild yams that surface repeatedly in the popular nutrition press. These include treatment of HIV, diverticulosis, stomach and muscle cramps, asthma, vascular disease, menopausal symptoms, and gallstones. Sweet potatoes and yams have also been touted for arthritis and other rheumatic disorders.[52]

The evidence. Yams and sweet potatoes are in different families, but do share some similarities. Both have a high carotenoid content and are rich in saponins, flavonoids such as beta-sitosterol, alkaloids, tannins (healthy compounds found in tea), and vitamin E. Originally, the wild yam was the sole raw material for manufacturing contraceptive hormones, cortisone, and anabolic steroids.[52] It is also believed to contain significant quantities of dioscin, a hormonelike compound with anti-inflammatory ability, but there is little evidence that dioscin gets into the human body when either yams or sweet potatoes are ingested.[52] Nevertheless, sweet potatoes are extremely high in vitamin C, fiber, and carotenoids, especially alpha-carotene, one of the healthiest carotenoids.[53] In addition, there's a good chance that it accounts for the high lycopene content found in Okinawan blood. Lycopene is a powerful antioxidant and carotenoid (same family as beta-carotene) that has been found in tomato products, and has been strongly associated with reduced risk for prostate cancer.[54] We are betting that the imo, with its reddish-purple pigmentation, may, like the tomato, be a potent source of lycopene, and our research group is currently investigating this possibility.

Usage. Use imo or sweet potatoes as a frequent side dish or mix them into other dishes. Purple potatoes have a similar pigment to imo and provide a good substitute in many dishes. Try our Sweet Potato Waffles recipe (page 408); it is one of our favorites and it takes only about fifteen minutes to prepare.

Caution. No adverse effects have been reported with imo consumption. Okinawans have eaten all parts of the imo, including the leaves, for centuries. Claims by some pop nutrition writers that the sweet potato is too high on the Glycemic Index to be a healthy carb are totally unfounded.

The bottom line. Imo, as well as our regular North American varieties of sweet potato, certainly merits a place in our Okinawan approach to healthy eating. They contain flavonoids, carotenoids, saponins, vitamin E, and other healthy nutrients, and they taste great. Eat them liberally.

Jasmine Tea, or Sanpin Tea

One of the more surprising findings from our studies of the Okinawan diet was the high consumption of jasmine tea, especially among the centenarian population.[55] Jasmine tea is the most popular beverage of the elders, who rarely drink plain Japanese green tea.

Jasmine tea, though, contains all the goodness of green tea and more. It is made from green tea leaves (and occasionally oolong or black tea) and mixed with fresh jasmine flowers, which gives it a wonderful, distinctive aroma. The Chinese name for this unique fragrant tea is *shan-pien,* which translates to "tea with a bit of scent." Jasmine tea is produced in July and August, when jasmine flowers are in full bloom in Okinawa and south China.

Folkloric claims. Tea has been used for centuries and multiple health claims surround its usage. These claims range from the ability to induce relaxation to slowing the aging process and curing cancer and cardiovascular disease. Buddhist and Shinto priests used tea to help stay awake through long bouts of meditation.

The evidence. These folkloric claims may actually have some basis in science. Once again it harkens back to the free-radical connection. The antioxidant EGCG (a catechin of the flavonoid class) is thought to be the most active component of tea's free-radical defense system. The question, then, is whether the health benefits of different teas vary according to their antioxidant capacities. Scientists from Rutgers University recently tested this hypothesis and found that the teas that underwent less oxidation in the natural fermentation process yielded higher levels of EGCG.[56] The teas most closely resembling green tea acted as the most powerful antioxidants in the body, in line with the free-radical theory that less fermented (less oxidized) teas should be more powerful antioxidants because more of the original antioxidants are present.

The health benefits of jasmine tea may actually surpass those of green or black teas. Its flavonoid content is roughly equivalent to that of green tea, since it is minimally fermented, but it has a higher lignan content, giving it more antioxidant bang for the buck.[57] Most tea studies have concentrated on plain Japanese green tea or black tea. One animal study that did focus exclusively on jasmine tea, conducted by Dr. Hiroko Sho at the University of the Ryukyus, found it could lower cholesterol levels.[58] This has been seen in several studies of jasmine tea.[59] Other studies found that fruit flies lived twenty percent longer when jasmine tea was added to their drinking water.[60] Japanese researchers at Nagasaki University School of Medicine reported similar findings with laboratory rats that ingested tannins.[61] More study is needed, but these findings are exciting nonetheless.

Green and black teas as a group (which, of course, includes jasmine tea and oolong tea) were found to be excellent health boosters in a multitude of studies.[62] The winning components, once again, are artery-cleansing flavonoids (those of the catechin class), which have been the subject of several hundred studies since their discovery in 1979. Tea is one of four main sources of flavonoids in Europe, and has been found to be effective against the development of heart disease and stroke in the European population, possibly owing to its antioxidant capacity.[68,71] Multiple studies have also supported the potential role of tea flavonoids in cancer prevention, including cancers of the skin, lung, breast, prostate, bladder, stomach, and colon.[62] There is also evidence that it may help reduce tooth decay through antibacterial action.[63]

The chief difference among green tea, jasmine tea, oolong tea, and good old English tea (black tea) is oxidation. The teas all come from the *Camellia sinensis* plant, but black tea is black because the original green leaves are oxidized—essentially dried and heated—in a natural fermentation process. This somewhat diminishes the quantity of flavonoids, but leaves sufficient quantities for us to reap health benefits.[64] Benefits do seem dose-dependent: the more tea you drink, the more benefits.[65] Jasmine tea is available in Asian markets, where it is usually found as tea leaves, often in a pretty yellow-gold can (like the flower). Most supermarkets in North America carry it as loose tea and in tea bags as well. Look for it as jasmine tea, since it is rarely referred to as sanpin on this side of the Pacific.

Usage. Since the benefits of tea appear to be dose-dependent—that is, the more you drink, the lower your risk for heart disease, cancer, and possibly premature aging—the motto should be the more the better. Each cup of tea contains between 12 and 16 mg of flavonoids (and lignans), so even one cup a day theoretically should bring you some health benefits. The consumption among Okinawans is about three cups per day.[55,66]

Caution. Drinking extremely hot tea has been associated with cancer of the oropharynx and esophagus, likely due to recurrent heat injury.[67] Tea does contain caffeine, so if you are caffeine sensitive you may wish to limit your intake or use decaffeinated versions. Those with heart arrhythmias should carefully watch their caffeine intake or stick to decaffeinated versions. Late-night consumption of caffeinated beverages may also keep you awake, so you may wish to curtail your consumption after 6 P.M.

Despite early worries about a possible link between bladder cancer and caffeine, there has been little proof that caffeine itself causes any harm to health.[68] Nevertheless, moderation is wise when it comes to caffeine, especially during pregnancy.

The bottom line. Your best bet is to think tea the next time you reach for an extra cup of coffee. Tea generally contains about half as much caffeine as a cup of coffee (by volume), so if you're really looking for a pick-me-up, you may need two cups instead of one, but then you get more health benefits, a nice trade-off. Don't confuse green, black, or jasmine tea with herbal teas such as mint, lemongrass, or chamomile. The latter teas are from entirely different plants, and while they can be delicious, they contain far fewer cancer-fighting flavonoids than true teas.

Kudzu, or Arrowroot
(*Pueraria lobata*, ge-gen)

Kudzu is used as a food in China, Japan, and Okinawa, and as a thickening starch in other Asian cooking. It can be generally substituted for flour, tapioca, gelatin, and other starches. It is also used as an herb in traditional Chinese and Okinawan medicine. Interestingly, it was imported to the United States early in the twentieth century to control soil erosion and for use as animal feed. It was such a prolific plant that it spread like a weed through the southeastern United States. Kudzu can grow a foot a day during the summer heat and about sixty feet per year. This has earned kudzu the nickname " mile-a-minute vine." Thank goodness we now have a use for it!

Folkloric claims. Kudzu has been used for centuries in the Far East for treatment of inflammation, especially injuries of the skin including burns, cuts, and infections. It has also been used to treat fever, colds, influenza, and "alcohol cravings." The Chinese brew tea from the root to "sober up the drunk." Other uses include treatment of chest pain from heart disease (angina) and high blood pressure.

The evidence. Analysis of kudzu has revealed strikingly high levels of the flavonoid called daidzin (of the isoflavone class).[69] This is also one of the flavonoids found in high concentration in soy protein. Kudzu ranks as number three in the flavonoid table found in Chapter Three, a pretty impressive accomplishment for a former weed. The antialcohol claim for kudzu in Eastern medicine was chalked up to the high daidzin content by one researcher, who published his findings in the journal of the prestigious U.S. National Academy of Sciences.[69] This finding has not found support in other studies, so we're not sure if it will help a hangover or not.[70] We figure it's best to just cut down on the drinking.

Claims for the treatment of colds, heart disease, and high blood pressure may have more basis in science as artery-cleansing flavonoids are able to dilate blood vessels in animal experiments, and have been associated with reduced incidence of heart disease in several studies.[71] The recent FDA approval for soy protein's health claim of reducing risk for heart disease may similarly be due to its high flavonoid content.

Usage. Kudzu is available in two different forms: as a powder, which is available at Asian food stores; and as a tablet, which is available at most health food stores in North America. Usual doses range from 9 to 15 grams (1 to 1½ tablespoons) daily in powder form. Tablet doses vary according to manufacturer. To make tea, purchase kudzu powder at an Asian food store and dissolve the powder in a cup of hot water. We have a nice pâté recipe (see Immortal Pâté, page 419) that includes kudzu powder.

Caution. Kudzu is generally regarded as safe owing to its extensive use in Asian cooking. Its safety, though, has not yet been established with young children, pregnant or lactating women, and those with liver or kidney disease, so caution is advised in these groups.

The bottom line. Kudzu has been used for centuries in Okinawan and Asian cooking. It is extremely high in flavonoids. Keep it on hand and use it in cooking any time a recipe calls for a thickening starch, or drink it in tea form.

Konnyaku
(*Amorphophallus konjac,* Devil's Root, Glucomannan, Konjac Mannan)

Okinawans say konnyaku "cleans your stomach." It is made from a type of yam and is valued more for its texture than flavor. Typically, the tubers of the plant are collected and treated to yield a powdered extract or a jelly. This popular root has been used in the Far East, including China, Japan, and Okinawa, for centuries. It generally comes as a dense, gelatinous cake, dark brown to hazy gray in color, about the size of a deck of cards. It also comes in thick or thin noodle form. Its flavor is neutral, and it is not porous enough to easily absorb flavors from foods that it is cooked with. For this reason, konnyaku is always simmered for a long time or enjoyed in raw cake form with a special sauce—a delicious combination of white miso, vinegar, and sugar that makes the cakes a tasty snack. It is sold in the refrigerated goods area of most Asian food sections of grocery stores or at Asian food stores. Konnyaku noodles are often found in sukiyaki or other one-pot meals. Fruit-flavored konnyaku jelly, very similar to our breakfast jellies, is popular in Japan as a fiber supplement. In North America, konnyaku powder is also available at many health food stores.

Folkloric claims. Both konnyaku powder and cake have been used to treat gastrointestinal complaints such as stomach ache, indigestion, and constipation. Other claims include an ability to treat obesity, diabetes, heart disease, and cancer.

The evidence. Konnyaku's major component is glucomannan, which is similar to bran, methylcellulose, pectin, and other dietary fiber, in both composition and action.[72] Glucomannan has been shown in numerous studies to be effective in the treatment of constipation and high cholesterol, which may be due to its ability to help balance the natural bacteria of the colon.[73] It also may help reduce cholesterol levels[74] and possibly help lower the risk for lung cancer,[75] although further study is needed. Glucomannan has also been found to be an effective adjunct for treatment of Type II adult-onset diabetes[76] and has been studied as a potential weight-loss agent,[77] partly because it absorbs up to sixty times its weight in water, forming a bulky gel that helps create a feeling of fullness and suppresses appetite.

Usage. As a fiber supplement and for treatment of high cholesterol and diabetes, take ¼ to ½ tablespoon of powder with meals. Eat the prepackaged raw cubes (one to six a day) anytime, or substitute the noodles in any dish where noodles are required. For weight loss, take 500 mg of powder supplement two to three times per day thirty minutes before meals. Also try our delicious Okinawan White Miso Soup with Vegetables (page 459) to sample the goodness of konnyaku. It's easy to prepare and takes about fifteen minutes.

Caution. Konnyaku and glucomannan are generally regarded as safe because of their use for many years in the Far East. As with most dietary fiber, excessive consumption of konnyaku may produce diarrhea, loose stools, bloating, or intestinal gas.[73] Those on cholesterol-lowering or diabetes medications may have to take a lower dose because of additive effects. And you should always drink six to eight glasses of water per day when taking it, since intestinal obstruction has been reported in patients who ingest excessive amounts of plant fiber without adequate liquid.[78] Diabetics should discuss the use of any agent that may affect their blood sugar with their physician prior to use.

The bottom line. Several human and animal studies support the use of glucomannan as a natural cholesterol-lowering and diabetic agent. It may prove a valuable addition to conventional treatment. Use konnyaku powder in cooking as a starch replacement or eat konnyaku noodles as part of the Okinawan approach to healthy eating. If you are reluctant to try konnyaku now, try vegetarian sukiyaki or mizutaki (chicken in a pot), or autumn chestnut rice in a Japanese restaurant. You will find fine konnyaku noodles in the sukiyaki and mizutaki, and chopped konnyaku cake in the autumn chestnut rice. We think you will discover that you like this interesting root.

Seaweed
(*Laminaria japonicum*—Kombu or Kubu; Nori; Hijiki; *Undaria pinna*—Wakame)

Seaweed comes in more than 2,500 varieties, including algae that appear on freshwater ponds and ocean kelp that sprouts stems and leaves.[80] In general, seaweed is classified according to its color—brown, red, green, and blue-green, which some seaweed more closely matches than others.

Kombu is a kelp, a brown seaweed that comes largely from the northern Japanese island of Hokkaido, where it thrives in the cool sea waters. It's been very popular in Okinawa since the early nineteenth century, when it was first gathered and imported to southern China. Okinawans still love their kelp and they currently eat about three times the Japanese average.[79] It has a consistency similar to pasta but with the characteristic flavor of the ocean.

Nori is classified as red seaweed, but when it is dried, it appears black. This seaweed is used to wrap sushi and rice balls and to season salads, soups, and noodles. It is often eaten at breakfast in small flat strips that taste delicious when wrapped around rice. The Irish and Welsh call it laver and use it to make flat cakes.

Hijiki is a black, slightly bitter-tasting seaweed that comes in short strips about the size of a match. Okinawans like to eat it simmered with vegetables and soybeans.

Wakame, our personal favorite, is another kelp, which has a taste and appearance that somewhat reminds Westerners of spinach lasagna. It is used in soups and cold salads. Don't miss wakame soba—a delightful mix of wakame and buckwheat noodles—on your next visit to a Japanese restaurant.

Folkloric claims. Kelp's main claim to fame is as a folk treatment for gray hair, the Grecian Formula of vegetables. It also has been used to treat baldness. As such, it has found its way into shampoos and conditioners all over Japan. Other claims for seaweed include the ability to help cure obesity, high blood pressure, tumors, rheumatism, and as an energy or immune booster.

The evidence. Most seaweed provides a rich supply of many essential nutrients, including protein, calcium, and iodine.[80] Iodine is essential to the function of the thyroid gland, which needs it to make hormones that regulate your body's metabolism. Many areas of the world have soils that are deficient in iodine and as a result goiter (enlarged thyroid) is endemic in these areas. Table salt has iodine added for this reason in North America.

Seaweed is also low in calories (a ½ cup serving of kelp contains only 50 calories). But it's nutrient dense, as the same serving provides 2 grams of protein, 200 mcg of folate (half of the adult requirement), 120 mg of magnesium (almost one third of the adult requirement), and iron and calcium. A ½ cup serving of nori (laver) contains only 40 calories, and it provides 6 grams of protein as well as 5,200 IU of vitamin A (greater than 100 percent of the minimum adult requirement), 2 mg of iron (greater than 10 percent of the adult requirement), and slightly less magnesium and calcium than kelp.

Lignans, the cancer-fighting phytoestrogens that you read about in Chapter Two, have been found in high quantity in seaweed (mostly kelp), which could conceivably provide some protection against certain cancers. Two studies of female mice showed a protective effect of kelp against chemically induced cancers.[81] Lower rates of breast cancer were reported in Japanese patients eating a diet high in kelp.[82] Kelp has also been shown to reduce DNA damage induced by several known carcinogens.[83] Other health claims await more extensive investigation, and currently seaweed supplements, including kelp tablets, are commonly sold as energy boosters. There is no evidence that seaweed boosts energy, except in those who are iodine deficient and have underactive thyroids, an extremely rare condition in locales that use iodized salt. A few practitioners claim that these supplements can boost the immune system as well. There is no good evidence for this claim and, in fact, the supplements can cause harm (see Caution, page 198).

Usage. Seaweed is best used in combination with other foods. Kelp comes packaged in three-foot-long dried strips and is prepared by cutting the long strips into smaller two- to three-inch strips and boiling them for about ten minutes. Remove the kelp, and then use the broth in soups, salads, and other dishes. Kelp simmered with vegetables or tofu, and served in miso soup, is an Okinawan favorite. This versatile sea vegetable is also soaked in water and then wrapped around fish and vegetables that have been seasoned with soy sauce, sake, and sugar. This dish is an integral part of the annual New Year feast and is called *kombumaki* or *osechi*.

Nori is sold in crisp, dried sheets, usually ten or forty sheets to a package. Store it in your pantry for later use. It doesn't tolerate moisture, so after you open the package, store it wrapped in the fridge. You can enjoy it for about three weeks. Nori is best used as a rice wrapper. Not only used for sushi, nori is used for wrapping fist-size rice balls for picnics. (See Picnic Rice Balls with Salmon, page 414.) Just cut the nori sheet into strips, and then wrap up a bite-size morsel from your rice bowl. This is one of the easiest and most delicious ways of eating nori. Drop a few small nori sheets into miso soup for added flavor and health benefits.

Hijiki is best used in dishes that require simmering. Soak hijiki and dried soybeans about two hours or until tender (Okinawans prepare them the night before), then simmer in a bit of water with carrots and konnyaku, and season with soy sauce, sugar, and sake. A half cup of dried hijiki will do for four people.

Wakame is best used uncooked. Soak dried wakame, 1 tablespoon per person, in water for a minute. It will expand about ten times in size. After draining, use it in your salad, drop it into miso soup, or use it as a topping for noodle dishes. A recipe we particularly like is Wakame and Soba Noodles with Broth (page 415).

Caution. Those on sodium-restricted diets should use caution. A half-cup serving of raw wakame contains approximately 900 mg of sodium. The Unified Guidelines stress that daily sodium intake should not exceed 6 grams. Kelp and laver have less sodium, containing 250 mg and 60 mg, respectively, in half a cup.[80]

Avoid seaweed supplements, as they can cause significant health problems. High doses of kelp tablets can cause outbreaks of pimples and acne, which most of us were happy to leave behind in our teen years. The high iodine content can cause thyroid problems, including overactive thyroid glands, sometimes requiring surgery. Some pills containing iron can cause hemochromatosis (iron overload), and others may be contaminated with arsenic.[84]

The bottom line. Seaweed is an excellent source of calcium, zinc, and iodine, and it also supplies a hearty dose of lignans. It tastes great and, if used wisely, should not tip you into sodium overload. Avoid the use of supplements because of possible iron overload, heavy metal toxicity, and thyroid toxicity.

Spice your Food with Healing Herbs

The use of herbal tonics is a topic that is sure to generate controversy among nutritionists and doctors. While there are definite benefits to certain herbs, there are some risks involved as well. Consuming herbs in pill form is equivalent to taking a drug—a weaker drug perhaps, but a drug nonetheless. Moderate use of herbs in cooking, however, is a relatively safe way to incorporate them into your diet. A number of flavorings, herbs, and spices are favorites of the Okinawans, and very likely have health benefits as well. Most of them contain specific anti-oxidants and phytochemicals that may help combat the ravages of time and give your system an extra boost of healing power. Although some of the Okinawan health claims are folkloric at this point, others have been borne out in clinical trials. But the point here is to enjoy them, and if they make you feel better and look younger, all the better! All we can say is that they seem to work wonders for the Okinawans.

Nine Flavorings, Spices, and Herbs

Bonito

Benefit: Bonito is a relative of tuna, and dried bonito strips are very popular in Okinawa and Japan. This omega-3 and zinc-rich food forms the basis of Japanese soup stock, called dashi, which is one of the most distinctive and delicious flavors of Japanese cooking.

How to use: Bonito can be used to make a soup base or a sauce and to add texture. The most frequent use of bonito strips is to make a soup stock called dashi. Dashi is usually used to make noodle sauce, miso soup, Japanese omelets, and so on.

Availability: Dried bonito strips are available in most Asian food stores. Bonito powder is easily found in most supermarkets; Ajinomoto is the leading brand.

Hippazu, or Okinawan Pepper
(Piper retrofractum)

Benefit: This vinelike plant bears fruit that can be dried and ground for use as a pepper. Okinawans believe it helps with stomach ailments. Indeed, pepper increases gastric secretions and stimulates water loss. Pepper has been shown to have an anti-infective activity against several microbial agents.[85] Five phenolic amides have been identified in piperine and all have higher antioxidant activity than vitamin E.[85]

How to use: The hippazu powder adds a uniquely stimulating taste and a fresh scent to most foods, including rice, pasta, soups, or vegetables. Sprinkle the powder on noodles or soups. Salads, rice, vegetables, and soups all can benefit from a pinch of hippazu, or when cooking, simply use it as a type of healthy pepper.

Availability: Hippazu can be found in some Asian food stores or on-line (see Appendix B). Hippazu shares many characteristics with fresh ground black pepper, which makes a nice substitute.

Kandaba, or Sweet Potato Leaf
(Ipomoea batatas)

Benefit: Kandaba used to be a famine-survival food, since sweet potato grows well and quickly even under harsh environmental conditions. Now we know that it's highly nutritious as well. Okinawans eat not only the root but also the leaf, which is very high in vitamin A and is a good source of vitamin C.[80] Okinawans claim that it helps prevent and treat various intestinal diseases. It is thought to contain flavonoids but no analysis is available.

How to use: Kandaba is often used for flavoring in miso soup or rice. Boil it and eat it with bonito strips and soy sauce. Or stir-fry it with tofu and season with miso.

Availability: Kandaba can be found in some Asian food stores, or substitute with spinach, which shares many characteristics.

Koregusu, or Chili Pepper in Awamori Liquor

Benefit: You cannot miss this unique-tasting seasoning when you eat Okinawan soba, a famous variation on Japanese soba (thick wheat noodles). In any Okinawan soba shop you can see a tiny bottle full of small, colorful hot chili peppers and strong Awamori liquor (Okinawan sake). This chili pepper charges up the taste buds and nicely complements low-sodium dishes. It contains capsaicinoids (an antioxidant), high levels of carotenoids, and vitamins A and C.[86]

How to use: When you need to spice up a meal, add a dash of this seasoning to the recipe. It goes well with seafood, in barbecue sauce, or in dressings.

Availability: Available at some Asian food stores and on-line (see Appendix B). Red-hot chili peppers are a close relative and make a good substitute.

Ndjana or Nigana or Bitter Leaf
(Crepidiastrum lanceolatum)

Benefit: Okinawans eat this bitter leaf raw. They say it "freshens" the stomach after one has indulged in something too greasy. Okinawans also use this leaf in traditional medicine to treat fever, stomach ulcers, and heart disease. Ndjana contains significant amounts of vitamin C and carotenoids,[80] and helps to stimulate digestion.

How to use: Slice the leaves and top with any sauce such as white miso, tofunaise, or peanut butter. Works well as a garnish for grilled fish.

Availability: Available at some Asian food stores or on-line (see Appendix B). Turnip greens can make a nice substitute.

Sakuna or Long Life Grass
(*Peucedanum japonicum*)

Benefit: "If you eat one leaf, you can make your life one day longer," claims Okinawan folk medicine. Sakuna leaf has been used to treat asthma, high blood pressure, neuralgia, rheumatism, pleurisy, and bronchitis in Okinawa. It has a nice aroma and is also used on ritual occasions. More research is needed to support these health claims, but it does add a nice minty taste to your meal.

How to use: It goes well with salads and soups, especially miso soup.

Availability: Sakuna is available at some Asian food stores or on-line (see Appendix B). A good substitute is spinach or turnip greens.

Shichimi or Seven Spice Powder

Benefit: Shichimi is a mixture of chili pepper, hemp seeds, dried orange peel, nori seaweed flakes, white sesame seeds, *sansho* leaf, and white poppy seeds. Since one of chili's phytonutrients, capsaicin, is widely believed in Japan to be a fat burner, young Japanese use this powder with everything they eat. Folk tales about "fat burning" aside, the hemp seeds provide omega-3 fatty acids, the seaweed is very high in calcium, and there are a host of other phytonutrients, from carotenoids to flavonoids, in seven spice powder.[80] Highly recommended.

How to use: This powder can be used for any food that needs a bit of flavor. Just sprinkle onto soup, grilled fish, noodles, or simmered vegetables. It even makes a nice addition to plain rice or potatoes.

Availability: Seven spice powder is readily available at grocery stores with Asian food sections or at Asian food stores.

Dried Shiitake Mushroom
(*Lentinus edodes*)

Benefit: This mushroom is full of vitamin D (840 IU per 100 g),[80] and in Okinawan folk medicine it is used to treat coughs and heart disease and to prevent cancer.

How to use: Soak a few pinches of dried shiitakes in a bowl of water at least fifteen minutes before adding to a dish. You should never throw the soaking water away, because it adds great flavor to any recipe. Adding a few pinches of reconstituted shiitakes to rice before cooking also provides a nice taste. (See the recipe for Warm Mushroom Salad with Garlic Dressing, page 455.)

Availability: Dried shiitake mushrooms are available in most grocery stores.

Shiso, or Perilla
(*Perilla frutescens*)

Benefit: Shiso is very high in vitamin A; at about 8,700 IU per 100 grams, it surpasses the widely acclaimed herb parsley at 7,500 IU per 100 grams.[80] With a refreshing flavor somewhere between mint and basil, it is used in traditional medicine to treat fever, headache, and hair loss.

How to use: This leaf complements any dish that uses basil, such as grilled fish, casseroles, soups, and pastas.

Availability: Shiso is commonly available at Asian food stores. If not, you can substitute basil leaves.

Remember, virtually all of these herbs and spices are available online (see Appendix B).

The Okinawans, of course, don't have a monopoly on all healing herbs and foods. Westerners have quite a few of their own, most as close as the local corner store. Here are some of our favorites.

Apples. Apples have always gotten good press and it's totally justified. They are a wonderful snack. Aside from being tasty, apples are filling, low-calorie, and terrifically handy—easy to tote, no silverware necessary. Most apples have about 90 calories and contain plenty of fiber, especially pectin, which helps drop blood cholesterol levels. They are also a storehouse of cancer-fighting flavonoids, and their natural sugar is mostly fructose, which is absorbed into the bloodstream more slowly than table sugar and thus presents no hazard for diabetics. Dried apples provide a more concentrated source of fiber, making them a super snack (about 70 calories for 1 ounce of dried apples).

Chamomile. Chamomile is a wonderfully healing herb. It can help alleviate heartburn, indigestion, and insomnia.[87] And its mild sedative effect on mucous membranes makes it a very gentle and reliable "stomach-settling" herb. You can't go wrong having a cup or two of chamomile tea before going to bed. You can find chamomile tea bags or loose tea in most supermarkets. If you use loose tea, add one tablespoon of the whole dried flowers to one cup of hot water, steep for ten minutes, then strain. Its gentle flowery scent is pleasant and soothing. Chamomile, however, does contain a compound called coumarin that can act as a blood thinner, so we don't recommend drinking more than six cups a day, especially if you are already on a blood thinner.

Cranberries. Their main claim to fame has been as a treatment for cystitis and kidney and bladder stones. Cranberry juice has long been used as a home remedy—and it works.[87] At least one good study has shown that it keeps bacteria from attacking the wall of the urinary tract.[88] However, commercial cranberry juice is often too diluted with sugar or water to be effective. The solution is to buy 100 percent cranberry juice (available at health food stores) or to make your own cranberry juice with a juicer. If you feel that you need to add sugar to make it palatable, use a healthy sugar or dilute the concentrated juice with two or three times its volume of apple juice.

Echinacea. This purple cornflower root has moved beyond its former status of a simple home remedy for flus and colds. Scientific evidence shows that it actually may work.[87,89] People who take echinacea recover from colds and flus more quickly. And if it is taken at the first sign of a cold, it might prevent it altogether. More research is needed, but echinacea looks very promising. Nevertheless, taking handfuls of echinacea to "strengthen your immune system" is definitely not advisable. Research suggests that if you take echinacea year-round it may *increase* your susceptibility to colds. So the best bet is to keep it as part of your emergency herbal arsenal. Try taking 300 mg three times per day when you first feel a cold coming on. See for yourself if it works—you may be pleasantly surprised.

Garlic. Garlic is an age-old healer. The Romans used garlic poultices to prevent wound infections, and this practice was continued up until World War I. Studies have found that garlic can inhibit bacterial growth and have supported its role for the treatment of asthma, candida, colds, diabetes, high cholesterol, and high blood pressure.[90] It may even help prevent heart attacks and cancer. Add it liberally to your recipes.

Ginger. Ginger has been used for centuries as a folk medicine treatment for motion sickness and nausea, and it appears to be effective.[91] Fresh ginger is also used extensively in Okinawan and Japanese cooking as a flavoring, and as a side dish with sushi and sashimi. It is available in whole root, candy, powder, and capsule forms. If you take ginger for medicinal purposes, the powder form is the best because of its high concentration of nutrients. Take 4 grams (about 1 teaspoon) of powder divided in two to four doses over the course of the day. Ginger tea is a good herbal tonic for influenza because of its soothing qualities and its antiviral abilities.[87] To make fresh ginger tea, cut a 1-inch slice of fresh gingerroot into small slivers. Place the ginger in a pot and simmer at a near boil for about 15 minutes, then strain into a cup. Add a little honey to taste.

Hot peppers. Hot peppers provide an excellent source of vitamin A and vitamin C. A mere quarter-ounce (about 1 tablespoon) of chili peppers has 18 mg of vitamin C—about a third of the recommended daily allowance. Hot chilies are more nutritious than sweet peppers, and red ones are more nutrient-dense than green ones.[80] Try Japanese seven spice powder, which is a mixture of 80 percent ground hot chili and 20 percent hemp seeds, dried orange peel, nori seaweed flakes, sansho (Japanese pepper), white sesame seeds, and white poppy seeds. Just sprinkle it over your meal when you feel the need for spice. Its fruity scent and stimulating taste are guaranteed to perk up any meal. It's available at most Asian food markets.

Lemon. Lemon is also another great source of vitamin C, and it can't be beat in terms of versatility. From juices to sweets, from fish to salad dressing, it adds a pleasant tart bite to whatever it touches. The grated peel is also used in many recipes, but make sure you wash lemons thoroughly before grating, since they are often sprayed with fungicides and pesticides. Avoid lemons with wax—the coating seals in those nasty chemical sprays. While controversies about vitamin C never seem to go away, there is some evidence to suggest that vitamin C from sources such as lemons helps to decrease symptoms of colds and flus.[92] This is best seen in those not consuming enough of the vitamin. The next time you have a cold, try mixing one tablespoon of lemon juice and one tablespoon of honey in a cup of hot water. It's a healing and comforting brew.

Onions. Onions are an Okinawan favorite. As you can see from the flavonoid table in Chapter Four, the onion is the top flavonoid-rich vegetable. Almost 45 mg of cancer-fighting flavonoids are contained in 100 grams (about ⅔ cup) of chopped onion, a veritable storehouse. Science is looking at the many other benefits that may be offered by the humble onion, from reducing cholesterol levels and inhibiting blood clots, to lowering blood pressure and preventing superficial infections.[93] Since it is already highly valued for its tangy flavor, we don't have any difficulties advising liberal use of this amazingly healthy veggie.

Papayas. Another prized Okinawan fruit, the papaya is readily available in North America. Like most yellow-orange fruits, papayas are high in vitamin C and natural beta-carotene (the plant form of vita-min A), and are thought to be an excellent digestive aid.[80] This delicious fruit can be eaten raw, dried, or cooked. Add it to chicken or fish and the food will take on a sweet tropical flavor. Medicinally, topical ointments rich in papain (an enzyme contained in papaya) are often used to promote the shedding of dead skin, such as wrinkled skin around the eyes. The jury is out as to whether this works or not, but it certainly can't hurt. We consider papaya an overall winner.

Parsley. This common herb can be used as a garnish for a multitude of dishes and is a great breath freshener. Parsley contains significant amounts of B vitamins and vitamin C.[80] It may stimulate smooth muscle contraction in the bladder and uterus and act as a diuretic. There are several forms of parsley available other than fresh leaves, including capsules, extract liquid, oils, and teas, but we don't recom-mend them, since their efficacy still lacks support from human clinical trials. Women who are pregnant or breast-feeding should not take parsley oil capsules because it can increase the levels of some plasma proteins, blood calcium, and water loss.[94]

Peppermint. Peppermint tea has a long history as a folk treatment for aiding digestion and for the symptomatic treatment of cough, colds, and fever. We love it as an after-dinner beverage. Some studies support use of peppermint oil for gallstones and the treatment of can-dida fungal infections.[95] Enteric-coated capsules have been used for this purpose but should not be taken without a doctor's supervision.

Rhubarb. This vegetable is rich in vitamin C, potassium, and calcium. Its tart flavor ensures that most people consume it only when cooked with a large quantity of sugar, which increases the calorie count but still makes a healthy snack. One cup of cooked sweetened rhubarb provides about 280 calories.[96] To minimize the extra calories but maintain a sweet flavor, cook it with sweet fruits, such as berries, apples, and bananas. It still tastes great and you will have increased your fruit intake and lowered the calories. A triple win!

Tomatoes. A recent study by Harvard researchers showed that eat-ing tomatoes regularly might decrease the risk for prostate cancer.[97]

The reason seems to be their lycopene content. Lycopene is a carotenoid, like beta-carotene but much more potent. Cooked tomatoes appear to be more cancer-protective than fresh, especially if cooked in oil (lycopene is fat-soluble so it needs oil for absorption). Definitely add tomatoes to your shopping list.

There was a time—not long ago—when doctors were reluctant to acknowledge that herbs or foods might offer specific health benefits. That time is over because we now have scientific studies to support the use of specific foods and herbs in the healing process. Remember *nuchi gusui:* food really is medicine, and what you put into your body should foster healing rather than hinder it.

Almost a quarter-century has passed since our team first began the search for Okinawan herbal tonics and healing foods in the rain forests of this island archipelago. Since that time much of the rain forest on the main island has disappeared. Roads are being built through previously impassable terrain, large swaths of forest are being used as training grounds for the local military bases, and shells are lobbed into the forest for Navy target practice. Unique plant and animal species are disappearing at an alarming rate. The herbal knowledge held by Okinawa's elders and its dwindling number of traditional healers is fast disappearing, and the rain forest itself is retreating to outlying smaller islands. Fortunately, efforts to preserve the forest and its inhabitants are meeting with some success as Okinawans rediscover the value of their ancient forests, their traditional medical system, and its healing herbs. There is now a National Park in Yanbaru and the northern forests may be declared a UNESCO World Heritage Site. We hope that the pressures to develop and modernize can be balanced successfully with preservation of the old ways so that the "Galápagos of the East" can continue to thrive for generations to come. The ancestors and their offspring— indeed, all of us—deserve nothing less.

Living in harmony with nature and one's community rather than trying to dominate or destroy is key to a healthy life. This philosophy is implicit in the Okinawa Program and is exemplified not only by the Okinawans' beliefs regarding food but also by their approach to physical activity, as we'll explore in the next chapter.

6. Lean and Fit

Yield and overcome;
Bend and be straight;
Empty the self and be full;
Wear out and be new.
Therefore the ancients say,
"Yield and overcome."
Be whole,
And all things will come to you.

Tao Te Ching

These words from the *Tao Te Ching* capture the essence of the Eastern approach to physical fitness, and the spirit of the Okinawans. For the elders, physical activity is part of the natural rhythm of life. Most older Okinawans are active in some way that not only helps keep them physically fit but also connects with their spiritual belief system. The activity might be as simple as gardening, where plants and herbs are considered imbued with spiritual energy. It may be a more structured activity such as traditional Okinawan dance, which is meditative and celebrates myths and stories of the old kingdom. Or it may be an invigorating martial art like karate, which demands a harmonious blend of mind and body. All these activities and most others that the elders choose help connect their physical selves with their psychological and spiritual selves. And this makes them feel whole.

For ninety-six-year-old Seikichi Uehara, the feeling of completeness comes from *mutubu-udundi*, a rare karatelike martial art that for centuries had been known only to masters with blood lineage to the king of the Ryukyus (as Okinawa was formerly known). Every Sunday morning you can find this lithe martial arts master on a beach in the middle of the main island of Okinawa, leading a class of eager pupils through the rigors of this special karate form. Shortly before the death of the last King Sho early in the twentieth century, Seiki-chisensei (*sensei* is an honorific term meaning "teacher" or "doctor"), then in his early thirties, was chosen to receive the sacred knowledge and preserve it for the future. Now, at close to one hundred years old, he not only still teaches but also is a formidable opponent.

In fact, to usher in the new millennium, Seikichisensei was featured in a nationally televised New Year's Day match pitting his skills against those of Katsuo Tokashiki, a thirty-something former World Boxing Association Flyweight champion from Okinawa. The old master displayed amazing flexibility and agility from the minute the bout began. He deftly twisted and turned to avoid the lightning blows of the powerful ex-boxer (*mutubu-udundi* focuses on avoiding confrontation, and striking only after all other options are exhausted). This went on for more than twenty minutes. Finally when Tokashiki tired and momentarily dropped his guard, Seiki-chisensei landed one quick blow—and it was over. The young boxer, who was stunned but not seriously injured, left the ring in a daze, shaking his head in disbelief and muttering, *"Yarareta, yarareta!"*—"I can't believe it . . . he beat me . . . he beat me." When Seikichisensei later recounted the match to our research assistant, he laughed and said, "It was nothing. He was just too young and had not yet matured enough to defeat me." This man was ninety-six years old!

There is no doubt that martial arts, which concentrate on maintaining a high level of physical and mental fitness, can help keep us young and fit. But that doesn't mean we all have to become masters like Seikichisensei. Aside from the "hard" rough-and-tumble martial arts, there are "soft" martial arts that, while more gentle, can also help tone your body and mind and lead you toward a unity of body, mind, and spirit. And young and old alike can easily practice them.

Tai chi is probably the most well known soft martial art in North America. It is a calm, low-impact aerobic activity, often described as meditation in motion, which repeats slow, concentrated, graceful movements in different combinations. When practiced regularly, tai chi provides the health benefits of aerobic exercise, strength training, and flexibility, along with the psychospiritual fulfillment of meditation or prayer.[1] A little further on in the chapter we'll introduce you to some of the fundamental moves so that you can try it yourself at home.

Tai chi and other martial arts were originally developed in China between 2500 B.C. and A.D. 400 as a means of cultivating the Tao, or spiritual energy. According to *The Yellow Emperor's Classic of Internal Medicine,* written somewhere between 2500 and 1000 B.C., the martial arts were first designed to improve the longevity of the First Emperor Ch'in's subjects, who were living only half their expected life span.[2]

Today, in their various forms, they are still helping practitioners live longer. Because of their long history of cultural exchange with China, Okinawans were early pioneers of the martial arts. Indeed, some forms, such as karate, were developed by the Okinawans themselves.[3] Although karate is still the most frequently practiced martial art in Okinawa, tai chi is becoming increasingly popular, not only in Okinawa but throughout the world, as its health benefits are becoming better known.

In North America, while most of us are aware of the health benefits of exercise, fewer than 40 percent of us engage in a regular fitness program.[4] It is hard to pinpoint exactly why. Maybe too many of us think of exercise as an ordeal—something we have do in order to achieve some vague purported benefit down the road. Maybe we don't value it, or maybe we are just "too busy." Not so in Okinawa. In Okinawa, exercise is a way of life. Data from the Japan Public Health Center Study, which looks at lifestyle, diet, and health, show that middle-aged Okinawans are more active than the average Japanese—and, by extension, North Americans.[5] Okinawan elders are more fit as well, as evidenced by their lower average body mass index. Let's look at just what we mean by fitness.

The Three Components of Fitness

For us to look and feel our best we have to meet three fitness criteria: anaerobic, aerobic, and flexibility. It's not unusual to see people—even serious athletes—who train to extreme levels of fitness in one of these areas while totally neglecting the others. Weight lifters are a good example. Some (the minority) do little else but weight-train.[6]

They may be able to squat with 800 pounds on their back, but they get winded climbing a flight of stairs and are so inflexible they can hardly bend over to tie their sneakers. They are fit anaerobically but completely out of shape aerobically and in terms of flexibility. Our goal here is to get you fit on all three levels.

Aerobic Fitness

Aerobic fitness (requiring oxygen) is defined as the *body's energy efficiency*—that is, how efficiently the body gets oxygen to the muscles. The stronger and healthier the heart, the more efficient the oxygen transport and the more aerobically fit you are. Here's how it works: Like a fire, the body needs oxygen to burn fuel for energy. The oxygen has to be extracted from the blood. When we are aerobically fit, the heart pumps a lot of oxygen-carrying blood in one heartbeat. It gets the oxygen to the exercising muscles quickly and efficiently. When we are not aerobically fit, the heart has to pump much more often to get the same amount of oxygen to the muscles. This raises the heart rate, as well as produces more wear and tear on the body. The heart and lungs of an aerobically unfit person, in effect, have to work harder for the same amount of oxygen as an aerobically fit person's do. That's why we can use heart rate to test for aerobic fitness: if a person's heart rate increases a lot with minimal effort, he is not fit aerobically. His heart is out of shape and needs to be exercised, probably like the rest of his body.

People who are not fit aerobically are often out of breath with minimal exertion—even walking half a block can wear them out. There is elaborate equipment that measures aerobic fitness. Many of us have seen athletes running on a treadmill wearing a mask and breathing apparatus, which in turn is attached to a complex machine designed to measure the amount of oxygen used for a set level of exercise. This equipment definitely does the job, but you can roughly estimate your aerobic fitness on your own, without expensive machines. A simple "step test" can give you an excellent general idea of where you stand. Try the Tecumseh step test opposite. The beauty of this test is that the work level is manageable by most of us, and the stepping surface is roughly the same height as most stairs. You can do it alone, but it goes much smoother with a partner.

The Tecumseh Step Test for Aerobic Fitness

Start by finding a stair or a stool eight inches high. If you need to adjust the stepping surface or the floor to the surface height, try a board or another wide flat object. The correct stepping cadence is key, so practice briefly to make sure you get it down before you start timing yourself. The idea is to step up and down twice within a five-second time span, resulting in twenty-four complete step-ups each minute for three minutes. Your partner can cheer you on and give you the correct cadence by repeating "up, up; down, down; up, up; down, down" as one foot then the other is placed on the stair, then back on the floor, within a five-second time span. A metronome set at 96 beats per minute, giving one footstep per beat, is the most precise measure, but the second hand of a watch will do as well.

After mastering the cadence, either time yourself or have your partner signal you when to start and stop your three minutes of stepping. When finished, find your pulse. Exactly 30 seconds after stopping, measure your pulse for 30 seconds. The number of heartbeats, from 30 seconds after stopping to the 1-minute mark, is your aerobic fitness score. Check the table below to find out your fitness classification for your age and sex. As your circulatory system becomes more efficient in delivering blood and oxygen, it will require fewer heartbeats for the same amount of work. The most important point is that the procedure must be identical each time the test is taken.

STEP TEST FITNESS CLASSIFICATION BASED ON 30-SECOND RECOVERY HEART RATE[7]

AGE CLASSIFICATION	20–29	30–39	40–49	50 AND OLDER
MEN	NUMBER OF HEARTBEATS			
Outstanding	34–36	35–38	37–39	37–40
Very good	37–40	39–41	40–42	41–43
Good	41–42	42–43	43–44	44–45
Fair	43–47	44–47	45–49	46–49
Low	48–51	48–51	50–53	50–53
Poor	52–59	52–59	54–60	54–62

WOMEN

Outstanding	39–42	39–42	41–43	41–44
Very good	43–44	43–45	44–45	45–47
Good	45–46	46–47	46–47	48–49
Fair	47–52	48–53	48–54	50–55
Low	53–56	54–56	55–57	56–58
Poor	57–66	57–66	58–67	59–66

Anaerobic Fitness

Anaerobic fitness (nonoxygen requiring) is well illustrated in the weight-lifting example. It's all about the ability to do work. In Newtonian physics, work equals the ability to generate force and move it through a certain distance—moving a weight during a bench press, for example. For our purposes we can just think of it as *muscular strength*. To maintain your muscular strength you have to exercise your muscles—it is as simple as that. Most gyms are equipped with machines and free weights especially for this purpose, but later in this chapter we will also show you how to build up your strength with some simple and enjoyable soft martial arts exercises.

Flexibility

Most people are familiar with the concept of flexibility: the ability to move joints through their full range of motion. But because most of us do not equate it with fitness, we all too often neglect it. This is a big mistake. Flexibility is one of the great secrets of looking and feeling young. It brings a spring to our walk, improves our posture, and helps delay or eliminate the loss of function associated with old age.

By our late twenties or early thirties, if we have not been active, we will start to notice subtle changes in our muscles, joints, and connective tissue (e.g., tendons that connect muscles to bones). Our muscles begin to shrink and our joints are not as limber. We feel increasing stiffness after any physical exertion more strenuous than normal everyday activities. Poor flexibility puts us at higher risk for muscle strain, stiff joints, pain, falls, and associated injury.[8] In a sense, our muscles and connective tissue are like rubber bands. If stretched regularly, they maintain their shape. If left in a corner unused, they simply break when suddenly stretched. Not a pretty picture.

The Okinawan elders provide the best example of what a few simple stretches can do for you. Most Okinawans, even those in their hundreds, can sit cross-legged on the floor for extended periods of time.[9] They do not need or use chairs. How many elderly in North America can do that? In fact, how many *middle-aged* Americans can do that? Not that sitting around cross-legged is necessarily our goal. The message is simply that we need to stretch our bodies in certain ways or we will lose our range of motion. "Use it or lose it," as the saying goes.

The good news is that it's never too late to start stretching. Even at advanced ages we have the capacity to turn things around and retrieve much of our old selves. In studies done at Tufts University, ninety-year-olds were shown to have made vast improvement in strength and flexibility.[10] So now is the time to start, whether you are ninety or nineteen. Incorporate flexibility exercises into your five- to ten-minute warm-up and cool-down sessions before and after exercise. Also try stretching every night before bed, even if you stretch during the day. This helps relax your muscles before you sleep and ensures that you will have some type of flexibility training each day, even if you miss your regular exercise session. Here are some tips to keep in mind when you stretch:

- Stretch slowly and avoid bouncing.
- Do not stretch to the point of pain.
- Avoid holding your breath during stretching (or when doing any type of exercise, for that matter).

Slow, static stretches are especially beneficial after you exercise. They help to reduce muscle soreness and help muscles that tightened up during your workout to stretch back to their original position. It is always a good idea to stretch all muscle groups, even if your exercise concentrated on one particular group more than the others. Runners and walkers, for example, should stretch more than just quads; tennis players more than just shoulders, arms, and back. A full body stretch doesn't take that long and your whole body will definitely thank you.

Muscle groups that should always be stretched include shoulders, chest, arms, and stomach to back, hip flexors, quadriceps, hamstrings, and calves. After you stretch, tense muscles will relax, muscle flexibility will improve, and you will increase the range of motion in your joints. Soon you will notice that all activities, from climbing stairs to housework and sports, are easier to perform.

Some Quick and Easy Stretches

1. Stand straight with your feet shoulder-width apart and arms extended over your head. Reach as high as possible while keeping your heels on the floor. Hold for ten counts. Flex your knees slightly and bend slowly from your waist, touching the floor between your feet with your fingers. Hold for ten counts. If touching the floor is too difficult, just go as far as you can—try to touch tops of your shoes, ankles, or calves. Repeat three to five times. *Stretches upper/lower back and arms.*

2. Stand facing a wall, arms' length away. Place the palms of your hands flat against the wall, just below shoulder height. Keep your back straight, heels firmly planted on the floor, and slowly bend your elbows until your forehead touches the wall (or as close as you can get comfortably). Tilt your hips toward the wall and hold position for twenty seconds. Repeat exercise with your knees slightly flexed. *Stretches upper arms and lower back.*

3. Circle your arms together forward five times, and backward five times. *Stretches shoulders.*

4. Reach your arms high overhead, then slowly lower them and wrap them across the front of your body, one after the other, as if giving yourself a big bear hug. *Stretches upper back.*

5. Slowly turn your head to the left, return to the middle, then turn slowly the opposite way. Repeat three times. *Stretches neck.*

6. Keeping your torso pointed straight ahead, rotate your hips left, then right, then forward and back. Repeat series three times. *Stretches lower back and hips.*

7. Lift your right knee to your chest and hold for ten seconds, slowly release back to the floor, then lift left leg to chest and hold for ten seconds. *Stretches lower back and hamstrings.*

8. Place one leg behind the other in a long stride. Keep the back leg straight while pressing heel to the floor. Bend the front leg. Hold the lunge for ten seconds. Reverse leg positions to stretch other leg. *Stretches calves and hamstrings.*

9. Using a wall for balance, take the top of your right foot in your right hand and gently raise it toward the left buttock. Hold for ten to twenty seconds. Repeat with left leg. *Stretches thighs (quads).*

10. Place right hand behind neck between shoulders. Using your other hand, gently push against your elbow to feel a stretch in your upper arm. Hold for ten seconds. Do the same with the left arm. *Stretches back of the arms (triceps).*

11. Place right hand between your shoulders and the left across your lower back. Then behind your back, reach down with the right hand and up with the left until your hands meet. Hold for ten seconds. Reverse arm positions. If you find your hands are far from meeting, try holding a belt, necktie, or towel in your upper hand, and grabbing it with the lower hand. *Stretches upper back (lats).*

12. On a mat or padded surface, lie flat on your back with your legs extended in the air and arms at your sides. Bend your knees to your chest. Wrap your arms around your legs just below your knees and pull your knees to your chest, raising your buttocks slightly off the floor. Lower your buttocks and, holding your knees to your chest, slowly rock from side to side. *Stretches lower back and buttocks.*

These stretches can either prepare your muscles for impending physical activity or help cool you down after. Be gentle—overstretching before exercise can cause injury to cold muscles. After exercise, you can hold the stretch a little longer, since your muscles are warm and can take a little more—and it will increase flexibility.

If you have not been doing any kind of exercise, incorporating regular physical activity into your life can constitute a real change, mentally as well as physically. As we all know, it is always easier to talk about life changes than to actually make them. There are various stages that we all go through when contemplating change. Some of us are at a more advanced stage than others—that is, we are more ready to make the change. In this particular instance, some of you will have already gone through the initial stages of incorporating exercise into your life and are tying up your gym shoes as you read. Others will be starting from scratch, thinking "Hmmm, exercise sounds like a good idea, but do I really need to do it?"

For every major life choice, there are seven stages you need to go through in order to embrace change. It helps to know what stage of change you are in so that you can avoid common stumbling blocks and get yourself successfully to the next phase. The seven stages are explained for you here, with specific tips for successfully easing yourself through each one of them. See where you fit in. These tips are based on a very effective psychological model called "Stages of Change" that has been used successfully in overcoming addictive behaviors such as smoking or alcoholism.[11] We've found that it is equally effective for initiating and maintaining the Okinawa Program and creating a new level of fitness, self-confidence, and well-being—a new dimension of health.

The Seven Stages of Change

1. *Disbelief:* You are still unconvinced of the need to change.
   - Read about the health consequences of inactivity and obesity.
   - Read inspirational stories of those who have successfully changed their lives.
   - Speak to others who have changed successfully.
   - Talk to your doctor about the health consequences of inactivity and the benefits of exercise.

2. *Belief but uncommitted:* You believe that you should be more active but cannot get started.
   - Visualize yourself as a new person: what you look like, how much you weigh, the new clothes you fit into, how energetic you feel, how much younger you look. Contrast this with the old you.
   - Tally the health benefits—how exercise will reduce your chances of heart disease, diabetes, depression, osteoporosis, and more.
   - Visualize new social possibilities.
   - Be realistic about the alternatives—TV watching, more work, watching life pass you by, as opposed to active engagement, and meeting new challenges.

3. *Active planning:* You are actively planning the new you.
   - Set a start date.
   - Set small, achievable goals—even minutes a day, three to four days per week.
   - Make a detailed plan including scheduling your exercise time into your daily planner for at least the next three months.
   - Be specific: when, how long, and where will you exercise, what backup plan you have for uncooperative weather or unforeseen events, including heavier workload, illness, and vacations.
   - Enlist support. Let others know that you will be exercising. See if friends have advice or are interested in joining you.
   - Set goals. If you're a walker, think about training for short races or even a marathon through a combination of short jogs and fast walking.
   - Believe in yourself and let nothing stand in your way. It's your life!

4. *Active engagement:* You are currently engaged in a training routine.
   - Keep a training journal.
   - Reward yourself every week. It could be dinner at your favorite restaurant, a good movie, a concert, or another activity you especially like.

- Maintain a positive attitude toward your progress.
- Be consistent.
- Don't worry if you miss a session. Make it up the next day.

5. *Image creation:* You are not only training, you are creating a new image for yourself. You see yourself as a "walker" or a "swimmer."
   - Visualize this paradigm shift. You should be trying to define yourself by your actions—you are a "tai chi practitioner," you are a "marathoner."
   - Subscribe to magazines or journals that reinforce your new image.
   - Seek out others who are involved in similar activities.

6. *Image maintenance:* You have a new self-image and only severe setbacks such as illness or injury will deter you from keeping up your training.
   - Make a backup plan for setbacks.
   - Continue to refine your goals. Are you training for fitness only? Would you like to set a weight-loss goal? Would you like to enter a competition?

7. *The new you:* You are a new person.
   - Expand your horizons by seeking more knowledge about your fitness pursuits.
   - Help others to become whole by introducing them to your techniques.
   - Consider writing about your experiences.
   - Maintain your training diary.

Introduction to the Martial Arts

The martial arts embody the spirit of the Okinawan commitment to physical activity as a way of life, and as a means of attaining higher goals and centering oneself.[12] It is a spirit that is becoming increasingly popular in the West as a way to improve fitness while gaining a sense of control over one's life. We've included some of the more popular styles here for you as an introduction. Some are practiced in Okinawa, some elsewhere, but they all offer impressive health benefits. Perhaps one of them will appeal to you.

Aikido

Aikido means "the way of all harmony," and is a purely defensive art. A Japanese martial arts expert named Morihei Ueshiba developed it in 1942. It works like this: The defender (referred to as *tori*) avoids harm without causing injury to his opponent (known as *uke*). An elegant series of flowing or twisting circular movements, which may include locking, holding, twisting, and tumbling, are employed at arm's length. With a blend of arm and wrist holds and momentum drawn from the hips and legs, the *tori* attempts to throw the *uke* to the ground. The *tori* must try to "blend" with the *uke* to redirect momentum or steer away oncoming strikes from his opponent—a feat that is often compared to redirecting a runaway vehicle. In aikido, as in many martial arts, the ultimate goal is to cultivate *chi,* or universal energy. Aikido has most recently been popularized by the action movies of Hollywood tough guy Steven Seagal.

Jiujitsu

Jiujitsu was developed by the Japanese samurai (warrior class) as a system of unarmed self-defense. A combination of balance, strength, timing, leverage, and speed are used to overcome one's opponent. Using strength and leverage on an elbow or wrist joint, one can lock an opponent into a painful position and induce him to surrender.

Judo

Judo means "the gentle way," or "the way of flexibility," and was the first martial art to be accepted at the Olympic Games (in 1964). Japanese physical education instructor Jigoro Kano popularized it in 1882 as a sport based on various grappling and throwing techniques. It originated as an offshoot of jiujitsu and focuses on speed, timing, balance, and falling. In this sport, the object is to throw and pin one's opponent. Using a series of throws and chokeholds, the *judokas,* or judo opponents, attempt to pin the other on the mat for thirty seconds to win the match.

Karate-do

As self-defense, karate is meant to be weaponless. Indeed, the word itself means "empty hand" (*kara,* "empty"; *te,* "hand"). This often comes as a surprise, since many people associate karate with violence, weapons, and aggression. In fact, nothing could be further from the truth. While some may use karate aggressively, this is in direct contradiction to its philosophical ideals, known as *karate ni sente nashi,* or "there is no first attack in karate." These words, which the Okinawan grandmaster Gichin Funakoshi often repeated to his students, are inscribed on a monument dedicated to him in a Zen monastery near Tokyo.[12] The words speak to the hearts of Okinawans. They are part of a cultural tradition that extols the virtues of peaceful conflict resolution.

Karate-do (the way of the "empty" or "Chinese" hand) is Japan's most popular "hard" martial art and has millions of followers worldwide. It was originally developed in Okinawa as a means of self-defense after weapons were banned during the reign of King Sho Shin (1477–1526). It was likely adapted from similar Chinese techniques that were being practiced in the 1600s but dated back even earlier.

Karate is most recognized for its impressive array of hand and foot strikes; its demanding regimen of physical conditioning; its emphasis on breathing techniques; and its *kata,* or rehearsals of striking, blocking, and turning. The feet, legs, elbows, head, and fists are used for kicking, punching, defensive blocking, and other techniques. Intense concentration is used to focus as much strength as possible on the object of impact. To most of its followers, however, karate is much more than sport or a defense technique. It is deeply connected to a way of life that emphasizes self-discipline and spiritual awareness. Two types of contests are popular in sport karate: *kata,* where judges award points for technique and timing; and *kumite,* where points are awarded for well-timed attacking blows. In karate contests, opponents are not allowed to actually strike each other. They must stop just short of making contact.

Shoshin Nagamine, one of the grandmasters of Okinawan karate, who was still perfecting the art into his nineties, wrote the following about karate's physical and philosophical aspects:

> Karate is training in self-perfection, a means whereby ... there is not the thickness of a hair between a person and their deed. It is training in self-efficiency. It is training in self-reliance. Its rewards are here and now, for it enables a person to meet any situation with exactly the right expenditure of effort, neither too much or too little, and it gives you control of your otherwise wayward mind so that neither physical danger from without nor rampant passion from within can dislodge you.[12]

Kung Fu

Kung fu is the English name given to a range of Chinese fighting styles. The object of kung fu is to halt one's opponent using a variety of moves, including kicks and punches. Originally there were only five styles, which were based on observing natural movements of animals. Now there are hundreds of different styles. The five most popular styles are tiger, crane, leopard, snake, and dragon, which as a group are called "the five animals fist."

Tae Kwon Do

This is a modern Korean martial art characterized by fast, high, and spinning kicks. The name *tae kwon do,* "the art of kicking and punching," comes from *tae,* meaning "to kick," *k'won,* meaning "fist" or "strike with the hand," and *do,* meaning "the way." It has influences from shotokan karate as well as traditional Korean martial arts. The origin of tae kwon do goes back to before 50 B.C., when the martial art *tae kyon* was practiced. Tae kwon do became a demonstration sport at the 1988 Olympics.

Tae bo is a Western combination of tae kwon do and boxing performed to dance music. It incorporates the punching style of boxing and the kicking style of tae kwon do with the fast pace of aerobic hip-hop dance music. A typical one-hour class is a choreographed series of eight-count combinations of steps, kicks, punches, and jabs. It was created by martial arts expert Billy Blanks in 1975, and has become extremely popular in the last five years for the intense overall body workout that it provides in a relatively short time.

Tai Chi—A "Soft" Martial Art for All

Tai chi ch'uan (tai chi) emerged from relative obscurity a few years ago to become one of today's most popular martial arts. It shares some remarkable similarities with traditional Okinawan dance, from the hand movements to the slow, deliberate, and graceful twisting of the torso. Designed to enhance physical, emotional, and spiritual well-being, tai chi consists of a series of postures that flow into one another through connecting transition moves. These slow, graceful, precise body movements were originally modeled after the movements of animals and are said to improve body awareness and enhance strength and coordination while helping the practitioner achieve inner peace. They further work gradually to regulate the breathing cycle. Over 100 million people worldwide now practice it.

As a low-impact aerobic activity, tai chi uses up an average of 250 calories per hour for a 140-pound adult, and 350 calories per hour for a 200-pound adult. It improves strength, mostly of the lower body, and increases flexibility, especially of the upper and lower limbs and back.

Noting the range of health benefits that can be derived from tai chi, the Japanese government adapted some of its movements for a nationwide exercise program aimed at promoting fitness and successful aging among the Japanese elderly. It is part of the ongoing *Radio Taiso,* a hugely popular radio fitness program that helps keep the population fit and healthy. Every morning for over fifty years, millions of Japanese get up to *Radio Taiso* and do a version of calisthenics where flexibility and balance are emphasized.

The advantages of tai chi have been known for thousands of years in the East, but have only recently been demonstrated scientifically. Most of the research has targeted older populations. Some research comes from the cooperative effort known as the FICSIT studies (Frailty and Injuries: Cooperative Studies of Intervention Techniques). The studies are supported by the U.S. National Institute on Aging (NIA) in an effort to uncover the functional, physiological, psychosocial, and environmental factors most responsible for disability in older adults.

FICSIT studies have evaluated tai chi's ability to reduce frailty and falls in older persons and came up with some fascinating results. They found that tai chi helped reduce risk of falls, improved grip strength, lowered blood pressure, and offered improved confidence and mobility.[13-15] And all these benefits were realized in only a few weeks to months of regularly practicing tai chi. No wonder the Okinawans have been practicing the soft martial arts for centuries.

The National Institute on Aging reports that falls among the elderly are a serious public health problem. In a typical year in the United States, one of every three people over the age of sixty-five falls, resulting in thousands of deaths and costing $12 billion in health care.[14] The most effective preventive strategy is exercise that improves strength, mobility, and flexibility. Tai chi certainly fits the bill. In fact, tai chi was the most successful of all fall-prevention strategies tested by FICSIT thus far.[14] The improved balance and strength one gets from tai chi have also been found to keep people physiologically younger.[15]

Taiwanese scientists have found that as a moderate-intensity aerobic workout, tai chi offers yet another benefit: cardiorespiratory health.[16] The deep-breathing component of tai chi appears to retard the age-related decline in respiratory function.[17] In a different study, twenty men and women aged 58 to 70 who practiced tai chi three to six times per week for an average of 24 minutes gained on average 19 percent in their aerobic fitness, 10 degrees in spine flexibility, and 18 percent in lower extremity muscle strength.[18] Arthritis sufferers may also benefit from tai chi because the slow, deliberate movements can lessen joint stiffness and improve flexibility.[19]

Amazingly, all these studies point out that a simple, gentle exercise, practiced for fifteen minutes once or twice a day, can make a substantial improvement in fitness and the quality of our lives. No fancy equipment, no expensive clothes and shoes, no elaborate machinery is needed, just the desire to feel better and the discipline to do it. The fact that an enjoyable *inexpensive* fitness regimen has had better outcomes than many high-tech expensive ones has been of great interest to health care planners, who are always on the look-out for evidence-based but cost-effective means of reducing our growing health care expenses.

Kame Miyagi, 101, says, "I face the ocean every morning and do finger exercises. Then my brain starts working." As she showed us her exercises, which were simple flexion and extension movements of fists and fingers, we could not help but wonder if they were in part responsible for her continued remarkable clarity of mind despite her advanced age. They seemed simple enough but they also contained the power of belief. She believes they spark her mind every morning . . . and for her they probably do. See what similar exercises can do for you.

Getting Started

Anyone can learn tai chi, from toddlers to seniors; even wheelchair and walker users can join in, since many routines can be adapted to the sitting position. As we mentioned, there's no equipment needed. All you need is your body and some loose-fitting cotton clothes— comfortable tee-shirt or sweatshirt, shorts or lightweight pants, cotton socks, and comfortable walking shoes. Before enrolling in a tai chi class, or any exercise class for that matter, discuss your game plan with your primary physician, and talk about your goals and any physical limitations you might have with the instructor.

Tai chi is best learned from a teacher in a class situation, but videos or books can help. All are relatively inexpensive, and once you learn proper techniques, ten square feet of quiet space is all you need to practice at home, in a park, or even on the beach. The benefits of taking a class are that the instructor can correct your form and keep you from picking up bad habits, and you'll meet other students with whom you can practice between classes and share similar interests. Try to find a tai chi class tailored to your age group, and check to make sure that the master has had adequate training and experience. Avoid classes that stress passing tests imposed by tai chi masters, since there is no official belt system as in karate. To find tai chi classes, contact community hospitals, community recreation programs, college or university continuing education departments, or martial arts or tai chi schools in your area.

Some Basic Tai Chi Guidelines

Whether you practice at home via books and tapes or in a class, here are a few things to keep in mind.

- Before starting tai chi, warm up your muscles with a brisk walk or gentle calisthenics for five to ten minutes, and some stretches.
- Tai chi movements can be either stationary (chi kung) or continuous (tai chi ch'uan). The ultimate goal is to flow gracefully in a gentle series of movements for twenty to thirty minutes three to six times per week.
- The movements vary in range of motion depending on your flexibility. Don't exceed a comfortable range of motion—you will invite injury. Remember to "start low and go slow."
- Don't lock your knees or elbows.
- Always rotate your head in line with your trunk during any movements that emphasize rotation.
- Stop if you feel pain. "No pain, no gain" doesn't belong in the tai chi vocabulary.
- Stop if you feel too tired. Rest for a few moments and start again when you feel ready.
- After your tai chi session, do five to ten minutes of gentle stretching.

Tai Chi Series for Mind/Body Training

For a gradual approach to the soft martial arts, we recommend starting with a series of movements that will give you a solid base and put you well on the way to lifelong fitness. We have adapted some of the more popular tai chi movements into a user-friendly but powerful series that cultivates internal strength and nourishes mind and body. There are sixteen movements in all, which are broken into four one-week lessons. At the end of four weeks you should be able to perform them all together in a fluid meditative series. And we can guarantee that you will feel a real difference in your mental, physical, and spiritual energy.

A   B   C

Series 1: Gathering Healing Energy

First Week Goals

To familiarize yourself with the first three basic movements, learn the proper techniques of breathing, standing, and relaxation, and to get in touch with your inner source of energy.

First Week Benefits

The ancients say that these movements, when performed properly, allow you to cleanse your lines of energy (also called energy meridians) and renew your healing power. The initial standing position (position A) represents the birth of the universe, when it was whole, before separating into the polarities of yin and yang. The following two movements (positions B and C) have been described by modern practitioners as "smoothing your aura" (the energy field around you) or "massaging your chi" (your body's inner source of energy). We believe that this series of movements can help calm and refocus the mind, relax the body, and help you develop powerful techniques of deep stress-reducing breathing. Furthermore, the wrist and hand movements teach you how to relax these important areas of the body. For anyone who has experienced carpal tunnel syndrome or spends long hours at a computer keyboard, these movements may help provide welcome relief.

First Week Positions and Techniques

Position A. This is the basic standing position. Find a quiet place ideally near a tree or plants. It could be outdoors, in a sunroom, or in another quiet locale. Clear your mind of all thoughts. Try concentrating on a single object near you or repeating a word or phrase that makes you feel good. Repeat it over and over as you empty your mind of all thoughts. Stand in the illustrated position with your feet together, weight evenly distributed and centered in the middle of the soles. Imagine that you are suspended by an invisible thread that stretches from the heavens through your body to the earth. Concentrate on your breathing. Feel your belly moving in and out with each breath.

- Relax your entire body.
- Relax your head. Feel your facial muscles relax.
- Relax your shoulders. Shrug them a few times to shake out the tension.
- Relax your chest and the front part of your body. Feel the natural rhythm of your breathing.
- Relax your back. Feel your muscles loosening up.
- Relax your upper limbs from the upper arms to the fingertips. Shake out the tension and feel it drain from your fingertips.
- Relax your lower limbs from your hips down to your toes. Feel all your worries and tension running out the soles of your feet into the ground.
- After relaxing your entire body, relax your mind by focusing on something close to you or by repeating a phrase that makes you feel good about yourself, over and over. Feel your mind empty completely.

Breathe from your energy center. This requires practice. Your breathing should center on your abdomen as opposed to your chest. Breathing from the abdomen is said to refocus your chi in what Eastern medicine describes as the original center of the body—the umbilicus—which nourished us as we grew from a collection of cells to a full human being. Eastern mystics say that the body's energy gathers here before flowing to the rest of the body. They call this part of the body the *tan tien*. One old tai chi master of ours was known to vibrate at the center of his abdomen as he gathered his chi. We were never quite able to explain this in Western scientific terms.

Position B. Quietly and slowly breathe in through your nose as you draw your arms up from your sides. As you inhale, raise your arms slowly, with your wrists and fingers hanging loose, similar to floating in water, until your arms are approximately parallel with the ground. Use your abdomen so as to squeeze in the air. Breathe in gradually and fully, until you have completely filled your lungs. Pause for 2 seconds.

Position C. Now slowly begin to exhale as you simultaneously lower your arms slightly and bend your wrists back so that the hands (but not the arms) are now parallel to the ground. Stop short of pushing your palms too far forward. Think of the hands as floating on water and the wrists dropping rather than bending backward. This relaxes the wrists. Bring your elbows backward a little but avoid tensing the shoulders. Move only the arms and avoid moving the back. Continue until your arms are halfway to your sides (about 45 degrees of arm extension). Make sure you inhale through your nose and let your abdomen expand outward as if filling a balloon in your abdomen. Let this happen naturally—don't force your abdomen out. Just let the air filter in smoothly and steadily without tension. Practice this series, beginning at movement A and ending at movement C for 10 to 15 minutes, at least three times the first week. You will become more fluid each time. It's best to practice first thing in the morning or after the day's work.

Series 2: Getting Connected

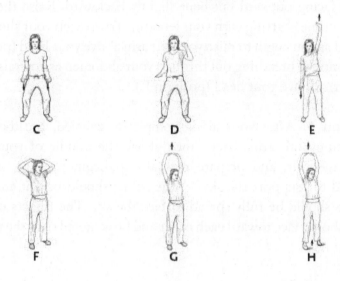

C   D   E

F   G   H

Second Week Goals

The goals this week are to improve your balance and flexibility, learn how to stretch the upper torso and make a fluid transition between last week's positions and this week's, and nurture a feeling of "connectedness" between the earth, your body, and the cosmos.

Second Week Benefits

The ancients call this series of movements "supporting the sky" and say that it "invigorates the internal organs." You will certainly feel invigorated after performing this series, as it stretches the muscles of the upper torso, including your upper back, chest, and neck and shoulders, and improves your balance.

Second Week Positions and Techniques

Position C. Start in the same position you finished at last week. Breathe in deeply as you place your feet shoulder-width apart, shoulders relaxed, arms parallel to the ground, wrists and knees slightly bent, face straight ahead.

Positions D and E. Slowly breathe out as you raise your arms, palms facing outward but bent slightly backward. Raise the arms one at a time, starting with your left arm. Try to keep your shoulders relaxed as you begin to raise your left arm above your head (position D). Continue breathing out through your abdomen as you raise your right arm above your head (position E).

Position F. After your air is completely exhaled, breathe in as you bring both arms back down above the middle of your head simultaneously, and prepare mentally to begin pressing straight upward to "support the sky." Your palms should be flat and your fingers should be fully spread to face the sky. The fingers of each hand should face toward each other and be centered over the middle of your head.

Position G. Now breathe out as you press both hands upward, straightening your arms as much as possible—your hands should not touch. Press your feet firmly down into the ground, connecting with the earth. Continue to breathe out as you stretch to meet the sky. Hold your arms in the extended position for one second.

Position H. Breathe in as you lower your arms so that the backs of your hands are just above your head, and breathe out as you rise on the balls of your feet. Straighten the arms once again. Pause for a second. Then repeat the cycle, moving your hands up and down over your head until you have done this ten times, each time increasing slightly the force with which you support the sky (position H).

Now try to complete the entire series in one fluid motion (positions C to H). Remember to try to do it slowly and deliberately, and to breathe in and out as you switch from one position to the next. Later in the week, practice series 1 and 2 together in one fluid series of movements.

Series 3: Renewing the World

Third Week Goals

This week you want to increase the movement of energy, or chi, through your body, work on balance, continue to smooth out the transitions from position to position, and integrate the third series of movements.

Third Week Benefits

The ancients say that this series of movements is akin to an energy exchange where you draw in healing energy from around you as you discharge negative energy and emotions from within. Indeed, as you'll see it's easy to imagine position J as throwing away the bad.

Third Week Positions and Techniques

Position H. Begin from the same position you ended with last week. Continue your slow in-breath as you lower your arms and shift to position I.

Position I. Continue your slow in-breath as you shift about two-thirds of your weight onto your left leg. Now lift your right foot, heel first and moving it in a slightly clockwise direction, step around toward your right side, and plant the right foot on the ground, heel first. The in-breath should be near completion as your heel makes contact with the ground and the out-breath begins. The hands should be rising simultaneously as the heel touches down and you begin position J.

Position J. Breathe out slowly as you bend your right knee to bring your weight forward and adjust your back heel to a comfortable position. Finish with your right and left arms slanting upward at a 45-degree angle and the fingers of the left and right hands facing each other.

Position K. Breathe in slowly as you rotate your palms into a pushing position and then shift about two-thirds of your weight slightly forward onto your right leg. Your hands should be in front of your body, with your thumbs almost pointing toward each other; this position will take the elbows away from your sides and enable your breath and your chi to flow freely in the chest. Keep your shoulders and arms relaxed and try not to move very far during this movement; the "push" comes from the legs—the bending of the knees, not the arms. Don't lean too far forward with the push and keep your back straight.

Position L. Breathe in as you shift backward onto the rear leg and straighten your arms. Avoid locking the elbows (which should never be done in tai chi). Your palms should face downward. Keep your arms relaxed and in the same position as they were at the end of the push, as if they were floating on water. Tai chi should be smooth and without effort.

Position M. Breathe out as you shift your weight slightly backward, letting your arms bend effortlessly and shifting your palms upward into the push position again.

Practice all three series in one smooth series of movements toward the end of the week.

Series 4: Building Healing Power

M   N   O   P

Fourth Week Goals

In this final week you are aiming to increase your speed and body strength, add grace to your transitions, and visualize your healing power growing stronger.

Fourth Week Benefits

The ancients say that this series of movements enhances the flow of healing energy from your feet to your head, and projects it through the fists. In our experience, it strengthens the upper body and improves coordination.

Fourth Week Positions and Techniques

Position M. Breathe in as you shift your weight back and draw your arms in from position M to position N.

Position N. As you shift your weight slightly backward, fold your thumbs inside your fists and hold them beside your hips, palms facing upward.

Position O. Breathe out as you extend your left arm slowly forward at chest height, turning your fist over to finish palm down. At the same time, pull your right elbow back beside you. Look straight ahead and hold the position for one second. Repeat the exercise ten times, alternately extending your left and right arms.

Position P. In the last position, the weight is shifted evenly to both feet and the arms are drawn together in a rounded fashion, as if embracing a tree. Imagine your vital energy flowing around the midline of your body, up the spine, and down along the inside of the arms.

Spend the beginning of the week practicing this series of movements and then toward the end of the week practice positions A to P in one fluid series. And now you're on your way to being a tai chi practitioner! If you've practiced these movements regularly over the last four weeks, you are feeling more vitality and energy. Keep it up. Share the secret with your friends!

Think about incorporating walking into your exercise regime. It is one of the most underrated and undervalued exercises around. It may not be quite as exotic as tai chi, but as you will see, walking has a lot to recommend it.

Walking For Aerobic Fitness

When Okinawans are not practicing martial arts or traditional dance, they are walking. At its highest level this simple activity is an Olympic sport called racewalking. In its less competitive mode it is a wonderful exercise readily available to us all. Walking provides an excellent aerobic adjunct to the more anaerobic and flexibility components of fitness provided by the soft martial arts. The two together are a powerful combination for lifelong health and fitness. Studies of walkers exceeding a pace of five miles per hour (10 km/h) estimate that they burn twice as many calories as runners traveling at the same pace. This is good news for those of us who wish not only to keep fit but also to shed excess pounds. You could walk after your tai chi exercises or do one routine in the morning when you wake up and the other in the evening after work. Or you could alternate the activities.

Beginning Your New Life as a Walker

Beginning is easy. It's important to remember that you are not in a hurry. Progress comes in weeks, not days, but again in four weeks you will begin to notice changes in your body and your well-being. The first few times, don't worry about measuring your heart rate, or your technique, or your speed—just get up and go. Aim for fifteen minutes at a pace slightly above a stroll. If you have never exercised before and you are over forty, now is the time to check with your doctor and get medical clearance.

Equipping Yourself

- Good walking shoes are key. You should be able to get good help in most sporting goods stores, but a professional athletic shoe fitter is best. Fit the shoes at the end of the day when your feet are at their largest. Keep a thumbnail's distance between the end of the shoe and your longest toe.
- Dress in layers with bright-colored, reflective loose-fitting clothes. Do not wear rubberized material, since it doesn't allow your body to breathe. Protect yourself from the sun by using a UV A/B sunscreen with an SPF (sun protection factor) of 15 or more, sunglasses, and a hat, if needed.

The Next Steps

After you have completed a week or two of regular walking and have gotten into the habit, it is time to get serious. Here are the next steps.

1. *Chart your course.* Measure out two miles. There are a couple of ways to do it. You can estimate the distance using city blocks—twenty blocks equals approximately one mile (2.2 km). Or drive your chosen course while tracking the distance on the car's odometer, or ride the course on a bike with an odometer. The truly serious can buy a pedometer from a sporting goods store and walk it out. Chart several different courses for variety.
2. *Test yourself.* Time how long it takes for you to walk one mile on level ground without getting short of breath. Most of us will be able to do this in about twenty minutes. This is your baseline, and as you get fit you will be able to walk a mile in less and less time. This would be a good time to

find out your general level of aerobic fitness. This can be accomplished by taking the step test on pages 213–14. It will give you an estimate, based on your heart rate after the test, of what your approximate aerobic fitness level is.

3. *Maintain your training zone.* Physiological studies over the last forty years have defined an aerobic training zone that maximizes your aerobic fitness and minimizes your risk for injury. Keep your heart rate within the training zone and you will improve your aerobic fitness. This is actually quite simple. Your training zone should be 60 to 90 percent of your maximum heart rate. Your maximum heart rate is measured roughly as 220 minus your age. If you multiply your maximum heart rate by 0.6 and 0.9, you will get minimal and maximal training zones, respectively. You should stay within this training zone during your walk. Halfway through your walk, measure your pulse for fifteen seconds (either on your neck near the carotid artery, on the wrist, or with a hand over the heart). Multiply by 4 to get your heart rate. If you are outside the zone, adjust your pace accordingly and remeasure after another half mile, so that you stay within your training zone.

4. *Maintain your exercise frequency.* Plan on walking a minimum of three times per week. Keep the heart rate in the training zone for a minimum of fifteen minutes and a maximum of two hours.

5. *Enjoy yourself.* Think of this not as work but as leisure. Think while you walk, work out the problems of the day, breathe deeply. This is your quiet time. You've earned it. If you prefer company, it can be quality time that you spend with a loved one or with a pet. Maybe now is the time to adopt that dog you have been thinking about. A dog can certainly keep you in your training zone.

Maximizing Your Performance

After a few weeks of walking, consider the following techniques to increase the intensity and quality of your training routine.

- *Add weight.* Wearing a weight belt, carrying light dumbbells, or wearing weighted wristbands or ankle bands will add to the resistance of your training routine and result in significant gains in your aerobic and anaerobic capacity. Use your heart rate as the guide to how much weight to use. Some muscle soreness is to be expected in the beginning as with any increase in training intensity. Don't let this deter you. If it persists more than three or four days, temporarily lighten your load.
- *Adjust your stride.* Smooth is more important than long when it comes to stride. Make it comfortable. The supporting leg should be straight as the hip rises and passes over it. Maintain ground contact for as long as possible before pushing off with the supporting leg and transferring your weight to the other leg.
- *Correct your posture.* A small forward tilt from the ankles, as if walking into the wind, is the best posture. Avoid leaning from the waist, as this will place undue stress on your lower back.
- *Maintain good arm swing.* A good arm swing can add a lot to your walk. Clench your fists, bend the elbows at about 90 degrees, and move from the deltoids (shoulder muscles). Forward swing should end with fists at shoulder height and backward swing with upper arms at a 90-degree angle to the trunk.
- *Stretch midway through your walk or afterward.* It's important to do some basic stretching of your muscles.
- *Have a great time!*

MOVE IT OR LOSE IT THREE WAYS EXERCISE CAN MAKE YOU YOUNGER[20]

SIGN OF AGING	WHAT HAPPENS	HOW EXERCISE HELPS
Loss of muscle strength	Inactive adults continually lose muscle mass. The rate of loss in men typically increases to 10 percent each decade after age 65.	Exercise increases the size and strength of your muscles, including your heart. Stronger arms and legs help you carry heavy things, like grocery bags.

SIGN OF AGING	WHAT HAPPENS	HOW EXERCISE HELPS
Loss of bone calcium	Women lose about 35 to 50 percent of bone calcium content by age 90, increasing the risk of bone fracture. Men also lose some calcium.	Weight-bearing exercise slows bone-strength loss, improves balance, and decreases the likelihood of slipping and breaking brittle hips or other bones.
Loss of aerobic capacity	Most people lose more than half their cardiovascular fitness between ages 20 and 80.	Exercise slows this loss. It also helps stave off heart disease and other chronic diseases and may even increase your life expectancy.

For further information on calories burned by types of aerobic activity, see Appendix A (page 483).

7. Healing Spirits

Isha-hanbun, Yuta-hanbun.
One should rely half on the doctor and half on the shaman.

Okinawan saying

In Okinawa we often hear the expression "Isha-hanbun, Yuta-hanbun." It literally translates to "half doctor, half shaman," and is commonly used to refer to the necessity of consulting both a shaman *(yuta)* and a modern physician *(isha)* in order to fully comprehend an affliction. Many Okinawans believe that while the medical doctor, with his powerful repertoire of modern drugs and technology, is essential for the treatment of physical symptoms, the shaman is also needed to address the spiritual imbalance that is often the root cause of illness.

This is not as exotic as it might sound. In North America and Europe, holistic doctors traditionally integrated spiritual concepts into their practices. And although modern scientific and medical communities largely discounted religion and spirituality in the past, many scientists and conventional medical practitioners are currently rethinking their positions. Today the consensus is that we may have acted prematurely in separating science and medicine from the spiritual realm, and that in doing so we may have overlooked an important aspect of health—our spiritual well-being.

Spiritual Health And Well-Being

Although spirituality and religion are once again being considered viable health factors, it is important to draw a distinction between the two. Spirituality and religiosity are not, by any means, one and

241

the same. You don't have to be religious to be spiritual—or the other way around. Dr. Kenneth R. Pelletier, director of the National Institutes of Health-funded Complementary and Alternative Medicine Program at Stanford University School of Medicine, does an excellent job of distinguishing the concepts in his book, *The Best Alternative Medicine*.[1] He broadly defines spirituality as "an inner sense of something greater than oneself, a recognition of a meaning to existence," and describes religion as "the outward expression of spiritual impulses, in the form of a specific religion or practice." Dr. Pelletier also notes that spirituality includes "a diminished focus on self; a feeling of love that leads to acts of compassion, empathy, gratitude; and the experience of inner peace." These characteristics, he writes, are not only "inherently enriching," but also "eminently conducive to health and well-being."

We agree wholeheartedly. Spirituality connects us to our deepest values, beliefs, and feelings. It also gives meaning and purpose to our lives, and affects the way we feel about aging, how we deal with illness and death, and what kind of lifestyle choices we make. And in the larger sense, spirituality reflects humankind's eternal quest for something greater than our limited selves.

It's ironic that spirituality has only recently been rediscovered as a potent healing tool. Shamans and other religious figures have delivered health care for as long as human societies have existed. Through invoking powerful religious symbols and imagery—often in the form of healing rituals—shamans have long used expectation, faith, and suggestion to bring about beneficial health effects. In fact, before the spread of Western medical practices, most traditional societies harbored a wide variety of health-care practitioners including magico-religious healers (shamans), herbalists, acupuncturists, midwives, and diviners. Often the functions of these healers overlapped. The shaman, for example, was often an herbal specialist as well as a spiritual adviser. Although Western medical thinking has now infiltrated almost every corner of the earth, people in most societies worldwide continue to rely upon such folk healers either exclusively or in tandem with Western-type health care. (This is definitely the case in Okinawa.) Although the idea that psychospiritual factors affect health is an ancient one, modern variations on this old theme are cropping up in the most unlikely places.

In a recent study at the California Pacific Medical Center in San Francisco, doctors examined the effects of prayer on patients being treated for AIDS in the advanced stages.[2] Forty patients were divided into two groups. One group was prayed for by a number of different healers from various traditions including those of the Christian, Jewish, Buddhist, Native American, and shamanistic faiths, while the control group received no prayers. Both groups were aware of the possibility that they might be prayed for, but neither knew for sure which group would be the recipient of the multifaith prayer effort. Analyzed over a six-month period, patients in the group that was prayed for visited their doctors less often and were hospitalized fewer times than those in the control group. Even more amazing is the fact that the patients who were prayed for described their mood as "much improved."

Although this may sound fanciful, this study was carried out according to strict scientific protocol. Similar studies are being undertaken throughout the scientific world, and they are coming up with similar surprising results.[3] Intrigued scientists have been gathering to discuss the significance of these findings. In December 1997, for example, approximately one hundred researchers from medical schools and universities around North America came together at Harvard University to discuss experiments that they had been performing at their respective institutions on various forms of "non-local healing."[4] Preliminary results from smaller research trials at other institutions suggest that energy transfer may actually work, although no one yet has been able to offer a viable explanation of exactly how, and methodological limitations of several studies make it difficult to draw firm conclusions. However, most scientists agree that from the evidence presented thus far, prayer, distant intentionality, and other phenomena collectively referred to as "nonlocal healing" definitely merit further study.[5]

The New Science of the Spirit

The idea that you can transfer healing energy through prayer, or heal through faith or ritual, might at first glance seem to lead us back to our pre-scientific past. Indeed, one of the major advances of Western science was to banish such so-called superstition from our cultural ethos and replace it with a scientific tradition based on observable and repeatable natural phenomena. Today scientists gather observations about nature, form a hypothesis, and attempt to *disprove* the hypothesis through experimentation. Note that it is extremely difficult to say that we can *prove* something by experimentation. So we try to *disprove* our hypothesis. We are not satisfied until we *cannot disprove* our hypothesis. Western science has developed criteria for proof. To prove something the results of our studies must be consistent, they must make biological and temporal sense, and they must be repeatable, among other criteria. If the hypothesis stands up under repeated scrutiny we have a theory. If the theory stands up under repeated testing, we begin to gather enough evidence for proof. Only then do we begin to believe.

In the old days this kind of scientific method was essential because anyone could claim that anything was caused by anything else. Any man, woman, or child could justify any natural occurrence simply by convincing others that one power or another was responsible. Kings or queens could abuse their subjects because they claimed that the will of God was on their side. Holy wars could be waged against alleged infidels who did not believe the official version of the "truth"—no proof required. If you didn't accept the officially sanctioned version of reality you could be tortured, burned at the stake, or beheaded. Unspeakable crimes were committed in the name of faith. This untenable situation, of course, reached its zenith in the so-called Dark Ages when scientific progress ground to a halt. The Spanish Inquisition, witch-hunts, and other atrocities were direct consequences of superstitious beliefs leading to abuses of power without the requirement of proof.

The Western scientific approach was a way out of this insane chaos. With the scientific method in place, if you made a claim you had to follow a set path to gather proof for it. This approach has served us well and has led to incredible scientific progress, from splitting the atom to the development of computers. Then the scientific method itself underwent a profound transformation. With the development of statistical probability theory, we now have a method of gauging our probability of being correct. We have even developed so-called confidence intervals, statistical methods that allow us to claim with 95 to 97.5 percent confidence that the result in a study is correct and not due to chance. To give up these methods leads us down a slippery slope, back to the Dark Ages.

So where are we going with this teleological outline of Western scientific progress? Back to the beginning. We now have the scientific and statistical tools to judge whether or not some of the age-old healing techniques—known to Westerners as healing prayer, to the Chinese as *qigong*, and to the Okinawans as *ugwan*—actually have any validity. This is not pop science. Once maligned, the study of religion and its effects on health has become mainstream, with treatises on the subject already published by such stalwarts of medical science as the World Health Organization[6] and the National Institute of Mental Health.[7] The growth of this field is mirrored in an explosive increase in funded research as well. There have been several National Institutes of Health research projects exploring the links between religion and health.[8] The National Institute on Aging has also been exploring the role of religion and spirituality in aging and health.[9] This all signals an increasing recognition of the importance of spiritual or religious practices and beliefs, and their positive effects on our health and psychological well-being.

The Evidence for the Positive Effects of Spirituality on Health

While the findings regarding the healthful effects of religion and spirituality are not unequivocal, incoming evidence continues to support the idea that spiritual or religious involvement can reduce the risk of disease, lower levels of depression and other forms of psychological distress, enhance our levels of well-being, and add years to our lives.[10] During a 1995 review of studies of the effect of religion on health, Dr. Dale Matthews of the Georgetown University School of Medicine found that scientific studies have shown religion to be beneficial to healing 81 percent of the time, neutral 15 percent of the time, and harmful 4 percent of the time.[11] Needless to say, any new drug or medical therapy with these kinds of benefits and with that little risk would almost certainly be an instant success! Thirty of the most recent well-designed and highest-quality studies on religion and health—all of which were reviewed by Dr. Matthews and Dr. David Larson of the National Institute for Healthcare Research—found religious participation to be protective against death from respiratory disease, cancer, heart disease, and suicide, among others.[12] Among these was a particularly well designed study by the National Institute on Aging (NIA) that followed 5,286 adults in Alameda County, California, over 28 years. The study found that frequent church attendance (at least once a week) was associated with lower death rates independent of age, gender, education, ethnicity, or baseline health.[13] In fact religion has been linked to longer life (through lower death rates) in 80 percent of studies that have examined this association.[14]

Nor are benefits restricted to just longer lives. More important, studies show that psychological distress is reduced and quality of life enhanced. Reviewing studies that measured the effects of religious commitment on mental health, Dr. Matthews and Dr. Larson found a beneficial effect of higher religious commitment in twelve of seventeen studies of depression (71 percent), fourteen of fifteen studies of coping (93 percent), sixteen of eighteen studies of alcoholism (89 percent), and twelve of twelve studies of drug use (100 percent).[15] Dr. Christopher Ellison of Duke University also reports in the *Journal of Health and Social Behavior* that individuals with strong religious faith claimed higher levels of satisfaction, greater personal happiness, and fewer negative consequences of traumatic life events.[16] The evidence for the role of spiritual and religious factors in the healing process not only continues to mount but can often be explained by known scientific mechanisms.

Why Spirituality Is Good for You

In March 1995, the National Institute on Aging and the Fetzler Institute brought together a panel of scholars with expertise in religion and health sciences at an interdisciplinary conference in Bethesda, Maryland. The purpose was to determine which areas of religiousness and spirituality are most likely to affect our health, both mental and physical, and to suggest how these variables might operate. The group divided the possible mechanisms into four areas—behavioral, social, psychological, and physiological—and came to some important conclusions that we'd like to share with you here.

1. *Behavioral.* The beliefs that most spiritual and religious traditions have about maintaining the purity of body, mind, and soul often lead to healthier lifestyle choices. Groups such as Seventh-Day Adventists or Mormons, for instance, actively promote the avoidance of drugs, alcohol, and tobacco, or excess meat in the diet, as part of their belief systems. Lower mortality from cancer, heart disease, and other diseases has been consistently found in research on these groups.[17] Organized religion also ties its followers into networks of supportive relationships that often provide improved information and access to health care resources, better compliance with health care regimens, and quicker response to acute health crises.[18]

2. *Social.* Social support, as measured by the number of ties to other people, has been linked to reduced mortality in dozens of studies (as we will see in Chapter Nine). Involvement in a religious or spiritual community enhances supportive relationships that, in turn, benefit health by providing a sense of belonging, giving a reason for living, and influencing people to practice better health behavior.[19]

3. *Psychological.* Organized religious or spiritual traditions offer members help in addressing life's most fundamental issues, such as the meaning of life and death, human relationships, ethical behavior, and a belief in a higher power. In research on subjective well-being, individuals who describe themselves as having a strong religious faith report themselves to be happier and more satisfied with their lives, and are found to have lower levels of depression, anxiety, and less suicidal behavior.[20] Religious involvement provides a ready-made means of coping with crisis situations. It is particularly effective in instances of bereavement, serious illness, and other situations where we have little direct control.

4. *Physiological.* Religious or spiritual practices such as prayer or meditation also promote a sense of relaxation and inner peace that helps to reduce stress. Physiologically, spirituality may provide a cushion against stress through

neurophysiological pathways. The neuroendocrine messengers (e.g., cortisol) that are released during the stress response have been associated with numerous stress-related diseases, including coronary heart disease, and can suppress the immune system response, leaving us more vulnerable to infections, cancer, and other invaders. (We'll explore this more in the next chapter.)

Maladaptive Uses of Religion

While religion and spirituality can have very positive effects on our health, they can be equally destructive and unhealthy when misused. Religious dogma can cause harm if it leads to excessive fear or guilt, lowered self-esteem, intolerance, obsessiveness, or perfectionistic expectations. Any religion used pathologically will inevitably have negative effects on our physical and mental health. While pathological misuse of religion or spirituality is not as widespread as it used to be in the Dark Ages, it does occur and includes cult groups and those with a political or economic axe to grind. It's usually precipitated by individuals with insecurities or other forms of psychological or emotional disturbances, or is used as a device to consolidate political or economic power. The abuse of religion for personal gain or to justify violence, war, or political or economic agendas is often a result of a selective use of religious doctrine, often taken out of context. Counterbalancing statements or teachings are simply ignored. The bad news is that maladaptive, intolerant, or overly rigid belief systems are still with us. The good news is that the *adaptive* use of spirituality or religion has none of these negative health effects. Flexibility and tolerance in spiritual and religious beliefs enable people to cope, accept loss, and adapt to an ever-changing world.

Are We Wired for God?

Why should religious or spiritual involvement be such an integral part of the human experience, with the potential for such healing benefits? A provocative theory has been put forth by Dr. Herbert Benson, the founder and president of the Mind/Body Medical Institute at Harvard Medical School.[21] He theorizes that we are somehow "wired for

God"—that the tendency of human beings to worship and believe may be "rooted in our physiology, written into our genes, and encoded into our very make-up." He suggests that we may be "custom-made to engage in and exercise beliefs," and notes that our spiritual beliefs may be the most powerful of all. Positive effects of faith or beliefs have been shown most convincingly by research on the so-called placebo effect. Dr. Benson's research, as well as that of others, reveals that positive thinking, expectations, or suggestions on the part of the patient, healer, or healing environment actually seem to help to mobilize the body's internal healing mechanisms to bring improved health.

At the forefront of placebo effect investigations, Dr. Benson, a pioneer in the field, went so far as to rename the phenomenon "remembered wellness."[22] Why the renaming? According to Dr. Benson, we all have the ability to "remember" the calm and confidence associated with health and happiness, and this memory has not only emotionally or psychologically soothing effects but physical ones as well. The positive health effects can be attributed to what has been called the *relaxation response,* a kind of bodily calm that we can all evoke and that is thought to have the opposite effect of the well-known fight-or-flight or stress response. During the relaxation response blood pressure, metabolic rate, heart rate, and breath rate all lower. Dr. Benson's research and clinical experience show that many long-term health benefits can be gained with simple meditation or mental focusing exercises that invoke the relaxation response.[23]

By using the term "remembered wellness," Dr. Benson hopes to not only more accurately describe the brain mechanics involved in eliciting the relaxation response but also to avoid the pejorative meaning generally associated with the term *placebo* by the medical community. He hypothesizes that the relaxation response is elicited in both secular and religious settings and "in everything from Lamaze breathing exercises to religious rituals around the world."[24]

Until recently, the healing benefits of the placebo effect have been mostly ignored or derided by scientists. In fact, the usual procedure in scientific experiments is to try to control the effects of the placebo by not telling subjects which experimental treatment they are receiving. Subjects are referred to as "blinded" or "masked," and ideally neither the participants nor the investigators know whether a particular participant has been assigned to the treatment group or the control group. This is the ideal experimental scientific procedure and is referred to as the "double-blind study."

However, in the past few years, forward-thinking researchers, including Dr. Benson, have been exploring how to harness the power of the placebo effect for therapeutic purposes. And it is powerful. In the past most researchers relied upon the 30 percent success rate for the placebo effect—that is to say, a bogus therapy will still work 30 percent of the time if the patient *believes* it will work. That gold standard, which was introduced by Dr. Henry K. Beecher in a landmark 1955 study,[25] however, now seems to be a conservative figure. According to more recent reports, in certain areas of application, the number may be closer to *twice* the earlier estimates. In 1994, the *Journal of the American Medical Association* reported on a study by Dr. Judith A. Turner of the University of Washington, in which she reviewed over seventy-five published studies and concluded that the placebo effect had "strikingly high" success rates—in some cases more than double the commonly attributed 30 percent success rate.[26] These new findings of 50 to 60 percent success rates do not surprise longtime placebo-effect researchers. To them the placebo effect is an incredibly effective therapeutic intervention just waiting to be discovered—or rather rediscovered.

Connecting Bodies, Minds, and Spirits

One of the most interesting mind-body stories we heard during our research in Okinawa was about a group of older women in a nursing home. We were told that some of the oldest residents would spontaneously burst out into religious songs and prayers on the first and fifteenth of each month. Why is this so unusual? Well, these women were nearing the end of the incredibly long, healthy part of their lives and were suffering from various physical and mental illnesses that rendered them usually quite unresponsive. They were expected to pass away within a few months. Yet as the first and fifteenth days of each month approached they would gradually become more lucid, active, and talkative. As it turns out, the first and fifteenth of the month are the days that hold the most important religious significance in Okinawa. In all likelihood, these women had been observing regular religious rituals on these days for more than fifty years, and the practices had become such a part of their regular body rhythms that twice a month their unconscious minds were simply instructing their bodies to perform the same songs and prayers that they had been consciously performing for decades. Although this was no more than an anecdotal story told to us by a nursing home staff, we have no doubt that the mind is capable of such powerful effects upon the body. Although we were trained in the scientific traditions of the West, our many experiences with Okinawan spirituality, ritual life, and religious belief systems have led us to believe that strong spiritual beliefs and practices may indeed produce serious health benefits. To us it's interesting that while Western medicine still struggles with a mind-body dualism, in Okinawa the body, mind, and spirit have been eternally linked in ancient healing rituals and traditions—and the results have been impressive to say the least.

A Place Of Healing

Although Japan is frequently described as a country where religion has very little to do with the daily lives of its inhabitants, this is a somewhat misleading picture, for it totally ignores the importance of ancestor veneration. In Okinawa, the ancestors and gods are never far away. During our field studies of the elders we have danced among ancestors in a ritual central to Okinawan identity called *esa* (wonderfully described in Christopher Thomas's dissertation, *Dancing with the Dead*)[27] and have fallen asleep to the rhythms of beating drums honoring the gods.

Okinawa has a long-standing attachment to spiritual activities. The entire society was once organized for religious as well as political purposes, and it still reflects a cultural cosmology where the female embodies and transmits sacred forces *(shiji)*. Most Okinawan villages still have "divine priestesses," called *noro* or *nuru*, whose job it is to commune with the gods and ancestors and serve as spiritual advisers. In fact, until the late nineteenth century, the king's wellbeing and success as ruler depended on the spiritual sustenance granted by the high priestess *(kikoe ogimi)*, who was of equivalent social standing. This is a unique cultural phenomenon. Although women act as religious functionaries in other societies, there is no other modern society in the world where women hold title as the main providers of religious services.[28] Although the *noro* priestess system at the state level died out when the Ryukyu Kingdom was annexed by Japan in the late nineteenth century, the system still operates in Okinawan villages, clans, and families, and a strong and active shamanistic complex—again led by women—supports the traditional priestess system.[29]

Ancient Ways

One of the most mysterious and exotic rituals that we have observed in Okinawa is called *Miyaku Zutsu,* which was part of a *matsuri,* or celebration to the gods. The ritual celebrates the oldest living member of the patrilineal descent group (something like a clan), and priestesses play a very important role. During this ritual, the health and longevity that was bestowed upon the elder is passed on to other members of the clan in a ceremony called *ayakaru.*[30] This is an important concept in Okinawan culture, for it embodies the belief that one can share in the prosperity, good health, and longevity of an older person who has been given these gifts by the gods. In this festival, the gods are asked to bless the newborn children of the clan so that they too will live long and healthy lives, and be imbued with the same upstanding moral character as the oldest living member of the clan. Finally, parents pray for the wisdom that will enable them not only to raise strong healthy children but also to become wise elders themselves someday.

At the festival that we observed, which took place on the lush green island of Irabu, about 285 kilometers southwest of Okinawa Island, the celebration began with the prayers of three divine priestesses who are considered both goddesses and normal women at once. Dressed in white kimonos, they sat regally in a row and, led by the senior priestess, made offerings of *awamori* (Okinawan sake). After the leading priestess lit packets of incense, all three clasped their hands in prayer to the gods and ancestors and sang sacred songs. The praying and singing was followed by *kuicha,* a special kind of dance where the villagers circulated in a clockwise direction to the beat of drums and rhythmic singing. A villager stood in the middle of the dancing circle and poured *awamori* from a large flask. There was much celebrating and toasting, in which we were delighted to participate. Lanterns lit the evening sky as we danced long into the night. We had never seen anything quite like it before.

Women, Spirituality, And Longevity

In Okinawa, as our story illustrates, it is mostly the women who are the shamans and spiritual leaders. It is also mostly the women who seek out and actively engage in these spiritual practices. And, perhaps not coincidentally, it is also mostly the women who have been responsible for Okinawa's achieving the world's longest average life expectancy. Women in Okinawa outlive men by eight years. Although, as we reported earlier, women almost everywhere outlive men, the average life expectancy gap between the men and women in Okinawa is particularly large. In India women outlive men by an average of only one year. In China it is about four years. In the United States the spread is about seven years. In Okinawa it is *eight* years. Why this unusually wide gap? Could Okinawan elderly women's strong spirituality be giving them an edge?

Part of the longer life expectancies for women in general seems to be based in biology, but differences between societies clearly point out that social and behavioral factors may play an even more important part.

Studies have shown consistently that as countries modernize, women tend to live longer than men.[31] WHO explains that women in modernized societies are generally more health-conscious than men in that they usually have better eating habits, smoke less, and drink less alcohol than men, and also that men exercise much less than did their grandfathers.[32] Men's aggressive behavior also seems to hurt their longevity. Of the twelve leading causes of death in America in the late 1990s, at least three were attributable to aggressive or risk-taking behaviors: accidents, suicide, and homicide. Men were three times as likely to die in accidents, more than five times as likely to die from suicide, and more than four times as likely to die from homicide than women were.

Exploring these gender-based behavioral differences in her

provocative book *Why Women Live Longer than Men,* Dr. Royda Crose, associate professor of psychology at Ball State University, argues that feminine patterns of cooperation, health awareness, family attachment, friendship, nurturance, and multiple social roles give women distinct health advantages over men—and help them live longer.[33] Many of these "feminine behavioral patterns" converge in women's spiritual and religious practices. Research shows that American women are more religious than men at all stages of life.[34] Women pray, attend church, and participate in religious activities more often than men. This is particularly true for older American women.[35]

Okinawan women, like their American sisters, are also clearly more religious than their male age-mates. Yet, unlike their American sisters, Okinawan women are also the leaders of the official mainstream religion and the acknowledged religious leaders within the home, clan, and village. This difference in social organization allows women not only the opportunity to make health-promoting social contacts but also to gain respected leadership roles as they grow older. Village women typically become more active with religious work in their fifties or sixties as their household responsibilities wane and they have more time for rituals and other religious activities.

While spirituality is important at all stages of life, it becomes increasingly important to health as we grow older and physical health becomes more tenuous. Old people who have outlived their significant relationships, including their spouses, siblings, friends, and even some of their children, have to rely more on internal resources for sustenance and meaning. Research shows that as we age we tend to develop greater *interiority*—that is, we spend more time reflecting on the past and seeking understanding, purpose, and meaning in life.[36] The well-known developmental psychologist Erik Erikson referred to this process as developing "ego integrity."[37] He believed that those who achieved this developmental transition were able to look back over their lives to find satisfaction and purpose in their existence. Those who could not, he felt, were prone to live out the remainder of their lives in despair.

Dr. Crose's studies support the idea that people who maintain spiritual health have greater ego integrity, positive interiority, and optimism for the future—all of which help them to live longer. And she suggests that those positive characteristics remain with them no matter how aged or disabled they become.

These findings also reflect our research regarding the role of spirituality in the lives of older Okinawan women. In a survey we conducted with 325 Okinawan women aged sixty-five years and older, we found that the women who had deep spiritual beliefs and regularly took part in religious practices also reported higher levels of life satisfaction or well-being.[38] Differences in overall health or health habits or other factors could not "explain away" these findings. We have observed spirituality in Okinawa to have the following benefits.

1. *Stress relief.* The most salient theme of Okinawan prayer is health. Okinawan people, particularly the women, pray to be healthy, and they pray for the health of others. We have already seen that what we believe can exert powerful influences on our health. Okinawan beliefs that the gods and ancestors are taking care of them and that their villages are naturally healthy places may be helpful in this regard.

2. *Social connection.* The gods and ancestors are thought to be always ready to intervene on behalf of the living in Okinawa. So sharing troubles and complaints with them, and asking them for help and guidance, is rather like tapping into an otherworldly support system. In addition, many elderly women look forward to worship because it can be a social occasion. Visiting the shaman in Okinawa is often an outing for friends or family. Even consultations can take the form of group therapy sessions with many participants present, sympathizing or lending support. Indeed, the shaman is like a "folk therapist" who often takes on the role of psychospiritual counselor.

3. *Enhanced self-esteem, life satisfaction, and ego integrity.* Sisters in Okinawan families were once commonly referred to as sister gods *(onari gami)* for their protective and benevolent spiritual power over their brothers.[39] In fact, many Okinawan men carried a lock of their sister's hair to

protect them from harm during the terrible destruction and loss of life in the war. Older Okinawan women's traditional beliefs that they can heal others through ritual prayer or ceremony may help give them a sense that their lives are meaningful, satisfying, and purposeful.

4. *Coping mechanism.* Life's crises are more easily handled if one has a set of beliefs about one's place in the universe in relation to gods, ancestors, ethical dilemmas, human relationships, and the meaning of life and death. Spiritual belief systems put life in perspective and lead to a greater sense of happiness, life satisfaction, and reduced risk for self-destructive behavior. This may help explain why Okinawan elderly women have the lowest suicide rate in East Asia.[40]

5. *Respected role in society.* Elderly women in Okinawa are typically described as *genki* (lively) and are objects of pride within their extended families. They tend to keep very busy with a variety of activities, including gardening, traditional dance, meeting their longtime friends at *moai* (mutual support group), and attending religious functions. For Okinawan women, the later years are often a time where they are freed from family responsibilities—a time to joyfully take on the roles as spiritual leaders and symbolic bridges between this world and the next.

Kame Miyagi: A Healing Spirit

When we met Kame Miyagi for our scheduled interview, it seemed she had been waiting for us with great anticipation. In her classy suit and perfectly groomed silver hair, it was clear that she had taken great care with her appearance. And her efforts had certainly paid off! It was hard to believe that Kamesan was 101 years old. Indeed, she looked great for any age and her mind was sharp as a tack. Kamesan told us she reads the newspaper every morning and that her daily schedule is always packed full. But even so, she emphasized, she never ignores her spiritual practices. The first thing she does upon rising is face the sea and say her prayers. While her prayers may differ slightly from day to day, she always asks the gods and her ancestors for guidance and protection.

Kamesan's granddaughter, Shizuko, was just as impressed with the strength of her grandmother's faith as we were, although she readily admits that at first she didn't know quite what to make of it. "When my husband and I began living with Grandma four years ago," explains Shizuko, "I thought that she was showing signs of dementia *(boke)* because her faith in the gods was so strong . . . now we pray together every morning." Kamesan and Shizuko make a nice pair as they present offerings to the sacred sites and the home altar where the ancestors dwell. When they're finished, Kamesan thanks the ancestors for her longevity.

If Kamesan has any regrets in life, it's that she couldn't realize her dream to become a doctor. Her parents were poor farmers "tilling their tiny field" and could not afford to send her to medical school in mainland Japan. While a medical career was an ambitious, if not impossible, dream for any woman in Japan some eighty or ninety years ago, Kamesan has never been deterred. "I am determined not to let this dream die," she says. This lively centenarian is certain that when she is reborn into this world again she will fulfill her dream to become a doctor. Could it be Kamesan's faith in the benevolence of her gods and ancestors, or her strong belief that this is just one journey that leads to the next, that helps keep her young and vibrant? There's no way of knowing for sure, but in view of the ever-accumulating evidence of the importance of spiritual well-being for everlasting health it's a very strong possibility.

Learning From Okinawan Healing Spirits

What's the point of exploring the health benefits of religion or spirituality in a modern society that is becoming increasingly secularized? Well, despite common notions that religion is losing influence in North America, it appears that the vast majority of Americans still believe in God or some kind of higher power. According to the results of a 1994 *U.S. News & World Report* poll, 94 percent of younger Americans (ages eighteen to twenty-nine) and 97 percent of older adults (age fifty and over) still have faith.[41] It's the character of their religion that appears to have changed. People are less committed to particular denominations, more eclectic in their religious views, more tolerant of other faiths, and more focused on their own spiritual journeys and on meeting their own personal needs. This bodes well for adapting psychospiritual insights from the Okinawan traditional beliefs to a Western lifestyle.

Dr. Larry Dossey, medical doctor and author of *Reinventing Medicine: Beyond Mind-Body to a New Era of Healing,* predicts that doctors of the future will actually use the power of the mind to heal. "As healers," he states, "we need to get smart and use prayer, for it's a tool that's essentially lying there for us, waiting to be used." A strong proponent of nonlocal healing (healing at a distance) by prayer and other spiritual practices, Dossey may well represent the wave of the future.[42]

While we remain a little bit more cautious in our claims with regard to the therapeutic efficacy of nonlocal prayer, we are convinced that spiritual practices have potent healing potential. We have certainly observed many benefits of spirituality in the daily lives of the world's longest-lived people. Indeed, after studying the Okinawan approach to healing spirits, we have developed seven powerful prescriptions that will maximize your own inner potential for self-healing and boost your immune system. Try them. We guarantee they will lift your spirits and give you a new and improved outlook on life. Still, don't forgo your Western medication without full consultation with your doctor. It's often the combination of the two—Western medicine and Eastern spirituality—that proves to be more powerful than one or the other. That's the Okinawa way.

Seven Healing Prescriptions For The Psyche And Spirit

With an open mind, you will be openhearted.
Being openhearted, you will act royally.
Being royal, you will attain the divine.
Being divine, you will be at one with the Way.
Being at one with the Way is eternal.
And though the body dies, the Way will never pass.
Tao Te Ching

Healing Prescription 1: Use Prayer to Enhance Your Innate Healing Power

Prayer has been recommended by many health professionals, as well as the Okinawan ancient ones, and has many health-promoting effects. It can reduce stress, promote healing, calm the mind, soothe the soul, and help elicit the relaxation response. As we begin to practice prayer regularly, it helps to bring about many other healing effects for the spirit and psyche. It provides us with inspiration, promotes a sense of hope, gives meaning to our lives, and helps us to transcend the mundane world. It also guides us to a higher awareness of a purposeful and intelligent pattern to the universe—a pattern of which we are all a part and can reconnect to at any time once we are aware of it. The greatest physicist of our time, Albert Einstein, once said, "God does not play dice with the universe." With these few words, Einstein was expressing his deep reverence for the innate meaningfulness of the universe, that it has an unfolding plan. Prayer deepens our awareness of this plan and helps to develop the spiritual dimension of our lives. It helps link us to what some spiritual traditions call God, others the Great Spirit or the Universal Mind, Brahman or Allah. Prayer also links us to one another and ultimately to our selves.

There are many types or styles of prayer depending upon one's particular religious or spiritual tradition. Some types of prayer do not seek a specific outcome but simply ask that "God's will be done." The Lord's Prayer of the Christian tradition is a good example of this type of prayer. A more directed style of prayer seeks to achieve a desired outcome—a prayer that asks for aid in healing, for instance. Okinawan prayers often focus on asking for blessing in the form of health and happiness for one's family. The Christian tradition seeks divine intervention in the form of forgiveness of one's transgressions against God or one's fellow human beings. In the Buddhist tradition, prayer usually takes the form of seeking enlightenment or a greater awareness. All prayer can be practiced either alone or with others—it can be wonderfully effective either way. To get in tune with the Okinawa Program, let's start with the *reflective prayer.*

Reflective prayer resembles the Okinawan traditional shamanistic practice of getting in touch with a higher source of spiritual energy. It combines the practices and benefits of both meditation and prayer. Reflective prayer is not difficult to do, nor is it restricted to any one tradition or faith. It's effective for relaxation, stress relief, and awareness expansion. Once you become accustomed to regular usage of reflective prayer you may want to try a healing prayer, which follows. We highly recommend healing prayer as an adjunct to any medical regimen.

First, choose a reflective prayer that conforms to your own beliefs, then set aside a quiet place and time to practice your prayer. The time should be convenient for you and fit easily into your schedule. Some find it easier to practice prayer at night before sleep, others upon rising in the morning. Still others prefer afternoon or early evening. Whatever feels right for you and encourages regular practice is your perfect time. Your place of prayer should be private, so that others will not disturb you, and it should be personally meaningful. Everyone has a favorite place where he or she naturally feels at home. For some this might be outdoors, on a patio, in the park, on a beach, or near a river. For others it might be indoors—a corner of the den, the bedroom, a special sanctuary. Do your best to find a peaceful spot that appeals to you and where you can fully relax.

Once you've decided on your special place, sit comfortably on a pillow, mat, bed, or chair, close your eyes, and concentrate on your breathing. Breath is vital to life and proper breathing is essential for achieving a state of relaxation. Your breathing should be as natural as possible; nothing should be forced. Take slow, long, and deep breaths. Observe your breath as it is coming in and out of your lungs. If you prefer, you can count your breaths as you begin. When you inhale, count "one." With the exhalation, count "two." With each exhalation allow your body to relax. By the time you count to ten your breathing should be deeper, more relaxed, and natural.

It's important to enter into a state of relaxation in order to receive maximum benefit from your prayer sessions. Remind yourself that there is no other place you need to be, and nothing else you need to be doing at this point in time. You are in your healing place where everything is peaceful and calm. Try to notice where you are holding tension in your body and relax that area. Begin with your toes and work upward until you have gone through your whole body and relaxed all areas of tension. This should take no more than a few minutes. (See the progressive muscle relaxation techniques in the next chapter.)

Now begin to say your prayer either quietly to yourself or in a soft voice out loud. Focus your mind on the words of your prayer, and reflect upon their deep significance. Inevitably, competing thoughts will creep into your consciousness, especially in the beginning. Don't be discouraged or upset. It's perfectly natural. Simply let all interfering thoughts flow through you. Acknowledge them, let them go, and gently redirect attention to your prayer. Gradually, with practice you will become better able to focus your mind, stay centered, and reflect upon the prayer. Repeat this process every day for fifteen to twenty minutes. If in the beginning you find this is too long for you to stay focused, start with less time—say, five minutes or so—and gradually work your way up.

After practicing reflective prayer a while, you may begin to experience what mystics refer to as transcendental states of consciousness or even see visions—although these kinds of altered states usually do not occur until one has been practicing regularly for many years. The purpose of reflective prayer, though, is not to seek out such experiences but rather to enable yourself to enter into a deeply relaxed healing state accompanied by a sense of being part of something larger than yourself. And this comes easily with time and practice. If you cannot at first find a prayer that means something special to you, try one of the following Okinawan prayers—or use them as a template on which to create your own.

Three Adaptations of Traditional Okinawan
Reflective Prayers

I

Heavenly Spirit, my body is made of thee
We are One
I am immortal
For thou art Life and I am thee

II

I am one with the ancestors
The ancestors are one with the gods
The gods are one with the universe
The universe is one with me

III

Wherever I am, God is
Watching over me, protecting me
Leading me back to the source of all life

Healing Prayer

Healing prayer essentially follows the same principles as reflective prayer. Once you choose the prayer and decide on a regular time and place, repeat the prayer either silently to yourself or aloud in a soft voice. Again, it is important to focus your mind upon the words of the prayer and not to get caught up in distracting thoughts. Just remember to re-center, return your mind to a place of peaceful calm, and concentrate again on the repeated words of your prayer. The goal of healing prayer sessions is to enter into a deeply relaxed healing state, to invoke the relaxation response, and to enhance your body's natural ability to heal itself.

Three Adaptations of Traditional Okinawan Healing Prayers

I

Blessed sister, holy mother
Spirit of the sacred grove
Spirit of the sea
Heal me with your nourishing love

II

I call upon those who have gone before,
The ancestors, to protect me with your benevolence
I call upon the presence and healing power of the Great Spirit
Let your children walk these lands in perfect health
In perfect love

III

Divine Creator, shine through me as I rejoice in your healing spirit
Soothe my wounded heart and soul
Help me to remember that I am already whole
That I am already perfect
That I was created in your image
That I am one

Healing Prescription 2: Create a Healing Space

In Okinawa, healing places abound. The main sites for worship are hundreds of sacred groves *(utaki)* scattered throughout the islands. Okinawan shamans regularly visit these sacred places to receive their divine energy, and local people visit them to worship and renew their spirits. Healing spots in Okinawa are called places of high spirit energy *(chiji ga takai tokoro)* and are most often places that are close to nature, generally found near the sea or in the forests. Traditional cultures have a deep rootedness in nature, a strong sense of interconnectedness to the land and all living things whether they be animate or inanimate. In Okinawa, for instance, trees are believed to have spirits called *kijimuna* that are thought to protect and guide humans. In the West, modernization and urban life have disconnected many of us from our roots in nature. Reconnecting can be a source of deep healing to the spirit and psyche.

Short of visiting Okinawa (which, of course, we wholeheartedly recommend if you get the chance!), how can you tap into this source of health? Simply by seeking out your own special healing places. Most of us have them already—places that bring us closer to nature and inspire a sense of the divine within our spirits. For many people such a place may be by the sea, in the mountains, or near a river, lake, or stream. For most of human history we lived in small bands subsisting upon what was available to us from our natural environment, so it's no wonder that a return to nature helps us heal. A stroll by the seaside or a walk in the forest helps to retune the spirit. If you live far from the ocean or woods, then locate your nearest park. Find your personal healing spot.

You can create a natural healing space within your home as well.

This is particularly important for those of you who live in urban centers far from the country or shore. Interior healing places can be easily created with inspirational art—objects that have personal meaning or are of spiritual significance to you, plants, flowers, or even the small meditation water sculptures that are sold in home decorating stores like Pier One. Most run on electricity and are designed so that a small amount of water continuously flows over and through small stones creating a sort of babbling brook effect. You can also use healing music or soothing sounds to help you relax. Most of us have at least passed by the "healing music" section in our local CD shop or come across some beautiful sounds online. The next time, stop and investigate. Natural sounds, such as waves breaking on the shore, wind chimes, birds, or the rush of a river over stones, are thought to be some of the most healing forces of all. Recent research from Japan in neuro-science (the science of the brain) has shown that the sound of flowing water or other organic sounds calms the mind and produces healing alpha waves in the brains of listeners.[43] Whichever way you set it up, your healing space should be a place where you feel secure and can practice your nurturing prayers and meditations undisturbed. Create your space and use it to take a spiritual time out.

Healing Prescription 3: Embrace Life, Accept Death

If religion or philosophy has already given you an answer to life's final mystery, then you can pass on this section. If not, then most likely, somewhere deep down inside of you, lurks a fear of death. You're not alone. In Western culture there has always been a fear of the dreaded grim reaper. But fear of death can actually interfere with our enjoyment of life, so it's worth taking a look at the way the Okinawans view death. They become familiar with it, allow it to become part of their daily lives, and view it as just a passage from this world into the next—and that helps them become much less fearful of it.

Familiarity is the first step to acceptance. When a person dies in Okinawa, the body is embalmed and taken home, where the family receives relatives, visitors, and friends. The deceased is then cremated and the ashes are taken to the family tomb to join dozens (sometimes hundreds) of ancestors, and a tablet with the deceased's name is created and kept on the altar in the family home. Visitors are received every week for seven weeks, and days of passing are ritually celebrated for thirty-three years. Eventually, it is believed, the deceased will be reborn. A few times a year celebrations with the ancestors, called *shimisai,* take place at the family tomb. Thus those that have passed on are ever present among the living.

When we had been in Okinawa for about five years, we were invited to our first *shimisai* and found it a thoroughly enjoyable experience. In Okinawa, tombs are not eerie places as they are in North America, but rather cheery gathering spots for the living and the ancestors to meet regularly, catch up, and picnic. Our *shimisai* began with an offering of food to the ancestors. One ancestor, we were told, was especially appreciative of the *mochi* (rice cakes) we offered, since it was one of his favorite treats. We were struck by the way the elderly women addressed deceased family members enshrined in the tomb as if they were still alive and sitting right next to us. And we were quite moved when one great-aunt remarked that many more ancestors than usual had come to this particular celebration because of the "special guests" (me and my brother)—"so many ancestors from so long ago," she said, "that I cannot even recognize some of their faces!"

Wherever we went in Okinawa we found ancestors to be present among the living. Tombs are almost always close to the living quarters and can be found just about anywhere—next door, in the fields, or in the backyard. They are never hidden away and are seldom seen in graveyards. This kind of everyday proximity to the deceased demystifies death for the Okinawans. They regard it as an intrinsic part of life, a natural conclusion to earthly existence, and the beginning of a pleasurable journey to becoming a benevolent and protecting ancestor.

Naturally, we don't suggest that you adopt Okinawan sepulchral customs, but we do advise you to familiarize yourself with the broad concept of death. It will definitely help you alleviate your fear of death, no matter how subconscious that fear may be. There are a number of excellent books on the subject, and courses on death and dying are offered at most universities—and they can be fascinating.

In the 1970s, we and many others in the scientific community were intrigued by Dr. Raymond Moody's *Life After Life*. In that best-selling book, Dr. Moody, a psychiatrist, wrote about the experiences of patients who were brought back to life after almost dying. When they came back they had memories of traveling through a tunnel of light, meeting benevolent spiritual beings in another dimension, and sometimes reliving the significant events of their lives. Dr. Moody named this phenomenon the "near-death experience."[44] Most people who have gone through a near-death experience have been spiritually transformed by it. Dr. Suzuki is among them.

Dr. Suzuki, who retells his experience in his book *Chronicle of a Stroke Victim* (in Japanese), was genetically predisposed to stroke and suffered one in his fifties.[45] He has since fully recovered—thanks in no small part to practicing what he preaches, the Okinawa Program!—but will never forget his experience. Dr. Suzuki saw bright lights, multiple soft colors, and a tunnel that led to a beautiful radiant light that he felt inexplicably drawn toward. But as he moved toward the source of the radiance, he says, he felt that it was not quite his time. A split second later he found himself in a hospital bed being examined by colleagues. He motioned with his right hand to the examining doctor and said, "Don't worry. I'm OK," but neither his hand nor his lips moved at all. He was unable to speak or move the right side of his body, and had to learn to walk and talk all over again.

Dr. Suzuki feels that through this brush with death he became calmer, more patient and easygoing. Most important, he says, he felt that there was a reason he had to come back. He believes that reason was to continue his work, to help others on their journey to a more healthy and fulfilling way of life.

Dr. Suzuki's personal experience is strikingly similar to the twenty thousand or more cases that Dr. Elisabeth Kübler-Ross and her colleagues have studied over the past thirty years. As the world's foremost research expert on death, dying, and the afterlife, Dr. Kübler-Ross was largely responsible for making the subject a legitimate field of inquiry for scientists. She has written a number of classics in the field. One, *On Death and Dying,* is even required reading in many American high schools.[46] Here's how Dr. Kübler-Ross describes the near-death experience, which she feels is part of what we will all experience at the moment of death.

After you have passed this tunnel, bridge or mountain pass, you are at its end embraced by light. This light is whiter than white. It is extremely bright, and the more you approach this light the more you are embraced by the greatest, indescribable, unconditional love you could ever imagine. There are no words for it. If someone is having a near-death experience, he is allowed to see this light for a short moment. After this he must return. But when you die, I mean really die, the connection between the cocoon and the butterfly (i.e., the body and soul) will be severed. After this, it is not possible to return to the earthly body. But you wouldn't want to return to it anyway, for after seeing the light nobody wants to go back. In this light you will experience for the first time what man could have been. Here there is understanding without judging, and here you experience unconditional love. In this presence, which many people compare with Christ or God, with love or light, you will come to know that all your life on earth was nothing but a school that you had to go through in order to pass certain tests and learn special lessons. As soon as you have finished this school and mastered your lessons, you are allowed to go home, to graduate. (*On Life After Death*, pp. 16–17)[47]

Dr. Kübler-Ross goes on to tell us that the dying experience is almost identical to the birth experience, only it is birth into a different existence. Our greatest wish resonates with Dr. Kübler-Ross's in that we all start looking at life differently. If we realize our lives are something that we were created for, that we are here for a very special purpose that is ours alone, then perhaps we can learn to embrace life and release our fear of dying.

Healing Prescription 4: Celebrate Aging through Rites of Passage

In Okinawa, age milestones and longevity have been traditionally celebrated with rites of passage. This refers to the symbolic use of ritual and ceremony to mark the passage from one stage of life to another (a good example is the bar mitzvah in the Jewish faith, which celebrates the passage from boyhood to manhood). Rituals are powerful social statements that help us to maintain order and continuity in the face of change and uncertainty in the life cycle. In Okinawa aging is seen as a progressive gain in wisdom and an achievement to be celebrated. In our youth-worshipping North American society, on the other hand, aging is often perceived as a loss or decline rather than an attainment of something valuable, and we have comparatively few celebrations that mark important stages in our life cycle.

The first time that we saw an older person in Okinawa dressed in red, carrying a pinwheel *(kazeguruma),* and being driven around in an open car with people lining the streets to cheer, we thought that we were witnessing a parade for some famous celebrity. But, in fact, what we were observing was a *kajimaya* celebration, which is arranged by the community to formally mark the transition of one of its citizens to the age of ninety-seven. There is a folk belief in Okinawa that a long-lived person has attained some kind of supernatural power through his or her health and longevity and that others can share in that power by participating in the ceremony. This is called *ayakaru* and it means to share in a person's good luck. People try to touch or shake hands with the long-lived celebrant or receive a cup of sake from him or her. Those unable to attend the ritual often stop by to see the person the next day. The most popular ritual celebrations for older persons take place at the ages of seventy-three, seventy-seven, eighty-five, eighty-eight, ninety-seven, and one hundred. The rituals are often associated with the Chinese zodiac, which consists of twelve animals (one for each year), thus completing a cycle every twelve years. The seventy-third, eighty-fifth, and ninety-seventh years begin new cycles and are therefore of particular ritual importance.

The most important lesson for us here is that passages that come with growing older should be celebrated. It doesn't matter if it's a birthday, an anniversary, or a long-awaited retirement. Ritual celebrations provide a link with tradition, connect the present and the past, offer a sense of continuity to one's life course, and bestow a sense of identity and security. They can also be mysterious and awe-inspiring, and are, in and of themselves, very powerful mechanisms that can bring about the healing phenomenon of "remembered wellness," as we mentioned earlier. Lastly, the actual ritual event is much less important than the opportunity that it affords us to get together as families, friends, neighbors, and communities. The support that we show for each other on these occasions is without doubt a deep source of healing for all.

Healing Prescription 5: Make Use of Healing Imagery and Visualization

Research on mind-body medicine has made it clear that our beliefs, thoughts, and images can be powerful adjuncts to therapeutic regimens. There's no question that the Okinawan belief that the ancestors are always near and ready to intervene on one's behalf helps to soothe the mind and relax the body of those who hold to that faith. The fact is that dramatic changes in the neurochemical environment of the brain can be brought about through the thoughts and images that we hold in our heads. If there's any question in your mind that this is true, think on this: When we cut open a piece of our favorite fruit, its smell or taste can cause us to salivate. If we're skilled in visualization we can also salivate just picturing the knife cutting into the fruit. We can actually sense its smell, texture, taste, and flavor, and feel our mouth begin to water. Try it and see. Sit still, close your eyes, and conjure up the image. You'll find the experience quite amazing. The significance of this little exercise is that the internal mental environment that we create through our thoughts and images can help to enhance our health—or help to bring about its destruction.

Images are obviously highly personal. What elicits a physiological response for one of us may or may not elicit a similar response in someone else. Images that are personally emotionally charged have the strongest healing potential. Mental imagery is often used as an adjunct to other therapies, such as chemotherapy in the case of cancer. Here, for example, you would imagine the white blood cells as a strong well-armed battalion wreaking havoc on a puny force of cancer cells and knocking them out one by one. Athletes also frequently make use of visualization as a part of their training regimen. Visualizing successful completion of moves and peak performance helps to set up their bodies to execute these very same performances during competition.

Try visualization, relaxation, and guided imagery exercises to help your body access its natural ability to heal itself, or to enhance performance in other areas of your life. One of the most convenient and effective ways to practice these exercises is to listen to CDs in the privacy of your own healing place. There are some excellent relaxation and guided imagery CDs available through mail order, the Internet, or at your local record shop or bookstore.

Healing Prescription 6: Create Healing Affirmations

Healing affirmations are healing statements that we make to ourselves about ourselves. In Okinawa they are often mantras or healing words or phrases written on special paper and placed at the head of the bed where they can be seen every night before retiring. Healing affirmations may or may not be ritually repeated, but they are certainly reflected upon at bedtime. In the West, practitioners of mind-body medicine think of healing affirmations as a kind of positive self-talk or even something akin to autosuggestion. Talking to oneself may at first seem crazy, but the fact is that we all carry on a self-dialogue all of the time. We just don't give voice to our self-talk, unless we are alone. Unfortunately, much of our self-talk is an exercise in self-bashing. Negative thoughts become self-defeating statements like "I'm too fat," "My nose is too big," "I'll never pass that test," "People don't like me," and on and on.

Negative self-talk usually takes place on a subconscious level and is the result of ideas and attitudes that we picked up from our environments while growing up. We were all exposed to criticism, shame, and guilt during our childhood, and these early experiences leave lasting impressions, which manifest in negative self-talk—among other things. Healing affirmations in the form of positive self-talk can help you create a new inner reality, build confidence and self-esteem, and maximize your healing potential. Although healing affirmations can be practiced anytime and anywhere, they are particularly effective when done in a relaxed meditative state. Healing affirmations are also available on CDs just about everywhere. Or you can design your own affirmations to suit your own specific purposes. Some examples:

"I am a good person."
"I am a successful person."
"I trust in myself and in my potential to succeed in all endeavors."
"Every day in every way life is getting better and better."
"I am a loving and lovable person."
"I love and accept myself for who I am."
"I was not put on this earth to please others."

"I am getting stronger, healthier, and more energetic with each
   passing day."
"I deserve to be happy."
"My life is filled with joyful abundance."

Try some healing affirmations and choose the ones that work for you,
or personalize them to meet your individual needs.

Healing Prescription 7: Find a Guide

Although we are giving you the keys to the wisdom of the Okinawans
here, you may also benefit from the guidance of an experienced health
professional who is well versed in the principles of mind-body medicine and can give you feedback on your progress. Most beginners find
group guidance or instruction, where they're buoyed by the support
of others interested in spiritual growth, to be most comfortable.
Whether you are guided in reflective prayer, meditation, relaxation
techniques, or any other centering method, it is important that you
feel at ease with both the technique and the particular approach of
your guide. Always familiarize yourself with your guide's qualifica-
tions before undertaking any new program.

Finally, for similar reasons, we recommend that you cultivate your
relationship with your medical doctor. Health professionals and physicians familiar with mind-body medicine, such as Andrew Weil or
Herbert Benson, point out that the doctor-patient relationship is a cor-
nerstone of healing. Dr. Weil even recommends that you never stay in
treatment with a doctor who thinks that you cannot get better—and
with good reason, we might add. Studies show that patients recover
more quickly when their doctors are upbeat, kind, supportive, and most
important, express confidence in the patient's potential for recovery.[48]

Although researchers continue to explore the links among spirituality, health, and longevity, a good deal of the public is already
convinced of the many benefits of mind-body medicine. Currently
almost half of adult Americans visit an alternative medical practitioner yearly. More and more people are seeking medical care that is
grounded in spirituality—and as they do they are getting closer to
the Okinawa Program.

8. Okinawa Time: Life Rhythms, Stress, and Aging

In this world there are two times.
There is mechanical time and there is body time . . .
The first is unyielding, predetermined.
The second makes up its mind as it goes along . . .
Each time is true, but the truths are not the same.

Albert Einstein[1]

Japan is a country famous for its meticulous attention to detail, an aspect that reveals itself in a certain sense of orderliness. Everything has its proper place and time, and everything runs according to schedule. Buses, trains, planes, and events—all start and finish right on time. With that in mind, we were intrigued when we learned about the Okinawan way of viewing time. In these lush and temperate islands, life simply unfolds at its own pace. It seems to make up its mind as it goes along, like "body time" in the quotation above. This easygoing approach, known locally as "Okinawa time," is a fascinating contrast to Japan's precision and punctuality. In Okinawa people don't view the clock as the enemy—in Okinawa time is your friend.

Our first personal experience with Okinawa time was on a hot summer day about seven years ago. We were scheduled to visit a senior citizen center *(rojin fukushi senta)* where we were to conduct interviews and give health exams to a number of elders as part of our study. The plan was to collect dietary and lifestyle records, as well as blood and urine samples, then take them back to Canada for analysis and comparison with older Japanese Canadians.

Examinations were scheduled to begin at 9:00 A.M. We left for the center about 8:30, figuring that would give us more than enough time. An hour later we were still maneuvering through nameless winding alleyways that pass for streets, and getting all sorts of conflicting directional suggestions from wonderfully polite locals who felt that any advice was better than no advice at all. Needless to say, by the time we finally reached the center we were hopelessly late—or so we thought. By local standards we were right on time! Dr. Suzuki and the rest of the team were still setting up, while some of the village elders were chatting amicably—seemingly without a care in the world—and others were trickling in at a leisurely pace. No rush, no worries. Sensing our alarm and surprise, Dr. Suzuki laughed off our concerns and introduced us to the concept of Okinawa time, a concept we've since grown to know and cultivate.

Once we settled into the slower rhythms of Okinawan culture we, too, began to slough off the feeling that "time waits for no one"—the unchallenged creed of the harried modern city dweller. Interestingly, Okinawa time is not simply a *subjective* feeling, like the one we often sense in sunny, tropical island cultures. There is actually an *objective* reality to Okinawa time that shows up in delayed starting times for ceremonies, parties, lectures, and symposia, not to mention casual meetings of friends or family gatherings. To some degree time has been catching up with things in Okinawa in recent years as it adjusts to the frantic pace of modern society. A recent newspaper survey conducted in Naha, the bustling capital of Okinawa, showed that 40 percent of events held at local hotels actually started on time! Quite a record for Okinawa. The remaining 60 percent were still anywhere from fifteen to sixty minutes late.

The longer we stayed in Okinawa, the more we began to wonder if Okinawa time might actually help buffer some of the negative health effects of stress on its citizens. We also began to wonder if the fast-paced bustle of our lives back home in North America was in fact the best way to live, or simply another alternative lifestyle. We began to wonder if stress was really a "natural" part of life.

Stress: The Cultural Construction Of An Illness

Nan kuru nai sa.
Don't worry, it'll work out.
Popular Okinawan expression

A recent article in *Prevention*[2] magazine stated that 4 million Americans suffer from generalized anxiety disorder, with American women twice as likely to develop the disorder as men. Generalized anxiety disorder (GAD) is characterized by constant worry, insomnia, muscle tension, fatigue, inability to concentrate, and a feeling of edginess, and it has recently been associated with increased risk of heart disease. According to Dr. L. J. Miller, chief of the Women's Services Division of the University of Illinois, the fact that anxiety disorder rates among men and women are equal in some countries "tells us that GAD is culturally mediated." In other words, it's not genetic or hormonal vulnerabilities but social or cultural reasons that play the larger role in bringing about GAD. If so, it would not be the first time that social or cultural factors have influenced disease patterns. The last thirty years of research have shown that the effects of social and cultural factors on disease are quite pervasive. So much so, in fact, that whole disciplinary fields have developed to study them, including social epidemiology, health sociology, and medical anthropology.

Separating cultural factors from biological ones, however, is difficult. Take cardiovascular disease. The culture we were born and raised in will decide whether we pick up chopsticks to dig into our fish, rice, and vegetables at breakfast time or whether we grab a fork and knife to carve up our ham and eggs. Our hearts might benefit more from the former but our minds might lead us to the latter. It just depends on whether we were born in Okinawa or Oklahoma. The same idea could be applied to stress. Some cultures cultivate lifestyles that predispose people to behavioral patterns, attitudes, or values that lead to stressful lives, while others may inculcate values, attitudes, and behaviors that lead to relatively stress-free lifestyles.

In North America, we live in a culture that is constantly feeding us stress-producing messages. We are bombarded with ads, junk mail, and spam e-mail informing us how we can lose weight or install the latest ultimate locks on our doors. Ever-present billboards and television public service announcements advise us that our children are at risk for guns, drugs, and sexually transmitted disease. And subtle messages such as "you do not make the grade unless you purchase the latest gadget" are pervasive. With today's round-the-clock access to news we now can receive a twenty-four-hour-a-day parade of mostly negative information about random shootings, drug wars, environmental disasters, racially motivated hate crimes, rampaging serial killers, terrorism, and gruesome sex crimes. As they say in the world of television news production, "If it bleeds, it leads." The news, in fact, has become so stressful that some health experts such as Dr. Andrew Weil recommend periodic "news fasts" to improve psychological health.

New technology also creates new sources of stress, particularly with regard to information overload. Is it any wonder that stress has become a topic on everyone's lips in the last few years? Stress management is now a booming industry. Self-help books on the subject abound. Stress has become so endemic to our lives that it is hard to believe that the concept has only been with us since the 1930s.[3] But despite the nonstop discussions of stress, there is, interestingly, still considerable disagreement about stress and how to manage it.

One thing that most experts seem to agree on is that stress is particularly bound up with our conceptions of time. The Western preoccupation with doing more things in less time is the most formidable stressor of this era—and it is wreaking havoc on our health. Multitasking feverishly, we try to cram more and more into every waking moment. Our mantras are "time is money" and "this new technology will get the job done faster." A packed agenda is the new status symbol. Going faster is certainly an advantage if you are competing in track and field, but zipping through other facets of life at warp speed can be disastrous. Nurturing family and friendships, enjoying nature, cultivating the arts, and maintaining our cultures and traditions—all take time and cannot be rushed.

In Okinawa and in many traditional cultures, time is valued for its long-term processes; for notions of fertility, growth, and development; for agricultural cycles; for intergenerational relationships with ancestors and descendants. The old lunar calendar is still frequently used and is particularly important with regard to the scheduling of rituals and festive occasions. In this context, time cannot be encapsulated into small units such as hours and minutes, but must be grasped in notions that encompass seasons, years, generations, and epochs.

"Hurry Sickness": The Disease of Modernity

Psychologist and author Wayne Sotile has identified a behavioral pattern that seems to capture the spirit of our times. He calls it *hurry sickness*. Similar to the Type A behavioral pattern typical of highly stressed persons, the defining characteristic of "hurry sickness" is a prevailing sense of time urgency, a feeling that there is never enough time in the day to accomplish one's tasks. The result is impatience with oneself and others, as well as a tendency toward perfectionism, irritability, loss of temper, and getting caught up in trying to do too many things at one time. Those who suffer from this syndrome are said to be competitive, hostile, controlling, cynical, and most often, workaholics.[4]

Yet haven't we all experienced the effects of hurry sickness to one degree or another? Nobody can juggle the dozens of things most of us try to do every day, day after day, and remain unscathed. Our fast-paced lifestyles put enormous pressure on our family lives, affect our sleeping and eating patterns, and ultimately age us before our time. Our conception of time also plays a key role in the disease process. From an early age we are taught to look ahead, to be goal-oriented, and to plan for the future, but the fact is that too much emphasis on our tomorrows may actually be harmful to our health today. By focusing on what may potentially happen in the future, we not only fail to respond in a productive manner to our present challenges but also create anxiety by projecting our present difficulties into tomorrow, next week, and next year. Projecting ahead instead of living in the present keeps our worries alive by literally "programming" them into our future. Living only for the future limits our ability to see the eternal, the unchanging—the program. And worrying too much can be deadly.

Worried to Death

We have all heard the expression "worried to death," and most of us are well aware that too much worry is unhealthy. But did you know that it really is possible to worry yourself into an early grave? Worry increases our risk of cancer, heart disease, and stroke, and this is true regardless of gender. A couple of studies help to illustrate this point. The Framingham Study, which we mentioned earlier, followed 749 healthy women for twenty years and showed that homemakers who reported symptoms of anxiety were seven times more likely to develop heart disease.[5] Similar results were found for men by the Northwick Park Heart Study, which followed 1,457 healthy men for ten years. The results of this study revealed that those participants who reported the most anxiety had triple the risk of having a fatal heart attack![6]

Clearly, anxiety affects the health of hearts. How it works is still under investigation. Some scientists think that neurochemicals associated with negative emotions (such as worry) trigger electrical instabilities within the heart or initiate further chemical reactions that lead to clogged arteries, which accelerates development of heart disease. These chemicals are also thought to cause spasms in the blood vessels feeding the heart, and to rupture plaque from artery walls. Take your pick; none of these scenarios is particularly pleasant and all are associated with the negative effects of the stress response.

Note that we say negative effects of the stress response. Contrary to popular opinion, *stress* is not just another term for "pressure" or "tension." Nor is stress always bad for you. We actually need some stress in our daily lives to provide challenge and stimulation. This type of beneficial stress is called *eustress*. It turns out that, just as with cholesterol and fat, there is good stress and bad stress.

Good and Bad Stress

The term *stress* simply refers to any situation that requires a body response more active than equilibrium. Even a small change in room temperature, for example, is experienced by the body as stress. Why? Because it is an environmental event that requires the body to respond by mobilizing its resources in order to raise or lower body temperature. Playing baseball, watching an exciting movie, and planning an evening out with your lover are all sources of stress in that they demand a response from the body, even though these activities may be experienced as enjoyable.

We all differ quite markedly in how we react to stress. Many people thrive on challenges that for others cause a great deal of negative emotional reactions, such as fear, anxiety, or worry. Some of us are thrill seekers who revel in jumping out of airplanes or climbing the world's highest mountains. Others tremble at the mere idea. Some love the limelight. Others cringe at the thought of being center stage. So we can think of stress as being internally defined in a very personal way. It encompasses how you personally respond to a stressor. If you react positively to it, there's no problem. It's when stress is dealt with in a negative manner, or is prolonged, that health problems occur. People who do not respond well to stress not only are more susceptible to stress-related diseases but also live noticeably shorter lives.

The body's response to stress consists of three stages: alarm, resistance, and exhaustion. The alarm stage happens when the body releases the various neurochemicals that prepare it to deal with whatever is threatening equilibrium. The next stage, resistance, occurs when the body adjusts to counteract stress-induced physiological changes. If the stressor does not go away, the third stage, exhaustion, sets in. The body then enters a situation of negative stress, or *distress*. It can respond to this with anything from extreme fatigue to any number of different stress-related disorders.

Stress-related disorders can best be thought of as inappropriate or maladaptive bodily responses, according to Dr. Robert Sapolsky, professor of biological sciences and neuroscience at Stanford University and author of *Why Zebras Don't Get Ulcers*.[7] Professor Sapolsky points out that it is hardly a general mammalian trait to become anxious about mortgages, the Internal Revenue Service, public speaking, job interviews, or the inevitability of death. In other words, human beings get stressed about things that wouldn't make sense to wild animals (like zebras), and more important, don't make sense to the physiological systems of our bodies, which have evolved similarly to respond to the physical threats of life in the wild. Anthropologists tell us that for all but around 10,000 of the last 5 million years, evolving human beings lived a precarious existence roaming around in small bands as scavengers, hunters, and gatherers, competing with bigger, stronger, and more fearsome creatures. In modern society stress does not result so much from physical threats to our safety as from psychological stressors that activate our physiological response systems for weeks or months on end as we worry about the what-ifs of life. What if I don't get that promotion? What if my kid takes drugs? What if I can't pay my mortgage? As far as our bodies are concerned, these are all anxiety-producing responses that lead us down the road to increased susceptibility to disease, premature aging, and shorter life spans.

Finding Balance: The Yin and Yang of the Autonomic Nervous System

Physiological reactions to stress are modulated by the autonomic nervous system, which consists of a network of nerves that start in the brain, run down the spine, and go out to the smooth muscles and glands of our organs, skin, and blood vessels. The autonomic nervous system regulates body activities such as digestion, heartbeat, contraction or dilation of blood vessels, and operation of the glands. These functions were once thought to be involuntary, automatic, or beyond conscious control, hence the name "autonomic" nervous system.

The autonomic nervous system has two subdivisions: the *sympathetic* and the *parasympathetic*. The sympathetic nervous system responds to alarm messages relayed from higher centers of the brain by the brainstem (a short bundle of nerves connecting the brain to the spinal column) and helps mobilize the body for action. It was around the turn of the century that Harvard University physiologist W. B. Cannon first described the action of the sympathetic system as the "fight or flight" reaction. He named it that because it is the sympathetic nervous system that prepares the body for emergencies or life-and-death situations. Needless to say, it was an extremely important adaptation for the survival of early humans. Imagine the following scene: One million years ago, an early human out gathering roots and berries happens upon a predator such as a hungry lion. Survival depends upon the sympathetic nervous system initiating several events almost simultaneously. Sympathetic nerve signals speed to the adrenal glands, which begin pumping out powerful hormones such as epinephrine and norepinephrine. These chemical messengers get the body into a state ready for action—the heart beats faster, breathing speeds up to get more oxygen to the muscles, blood pressure increases, and the liver releases stored-up glucose to feed the muscles, which tense in anticipation of engaging in combat (fight) or running to safety (flight). With a little luck, quick thinking, and these bodily reactions brought about by the sympathetic nervous system, our early human ancestor survives to see another day.

The parasympathetic system, on the other hand, works to bring about and maintain a state of relaxation, calm, or tranquillity. Let's go back to our early human ancestor. She has luckily managed to escape from the clutches of the lion, returned to her base camp, and plopped down on a bed of leaves to rest and recover from her ordeal. She pops some berries into her mouth and savors the tangy taste. Her parasympathetic system now begins to take over. Her heart beats more slowly, her breathing slows and deepens, and her brain and endocrine glands no longer pump out stimulating hormones. She begins to daydream and enters a deep state of tranquillity and calm.

The sympathetic and parasympathetic nervous systems work together in a delicate balancing act much like the Taoist forces of yin and yang. The sympathetic system could be considered the active yang force and the parasympathetic system the passive yin. Each system works in tandem with the other, balancing and counterbalancing, matching the moves of the other in an intricate dance of opposites. When the systems are out of sync and not properly balanced, one can feel ill at ease and unwell. In Japan, in fact, autonomic nervous system disorder *(jiritsu shinkei shicho sho)* is recognized as a specific condition and is frequently diagnosed, as it is in Okinawa. Diagnosis consists of taking a careful patient history and then checking for signs of a habitually overactive sympathetic nervous system, such as irritability, insomnia, stiff shoulders, headaches, eye fatigue, digestive disturbances, and cold sweaty palms caused by reduced circulation and restricted blood flow to the extremities. In North America, interestingly, this disorder does not officially exist in the medical textbooks, but it does exist in real life. If you are on nonstop alert owing to habitual worry about finances or your tenuous position on the corporate ladder, you are experiencing negative stress. It is precisely this kind of negative stress that is particularly unhealthy and leads to exhaustion—and subsequently to an increased risk of hypertension, heart disease, migraines, ulcers, and other stress-related diseases. And it is also the kind of stress that can wreak havoc on the immune system.

Exciting new research in the field of psychoneuroimmunology, which studies the relationship among the mind, stress, and the immune system, reveals that stress has a powerful impact on immune system functions. Chronically stressed individuals have been shown to suffer from a variety of depressed immune responses that result in increased chances of becoming ill. Stress causes natural disease-killing cells to decrease in number and activity; it causes a drop in the production of cytokines, the chemical messengers of the immune system, and it causes immune responses to antigens, such as bacteria and toxins, to weaken.[8]

As mentioned earlier, chronic stress also has been shown to cause overproduction of various neurochemicals (epinephrine and norepinephrine, also known as adrenaline and noradrenaline), which can cause serious problems for the immune system. Under prolonged exposure to these neuro-chemicals, the body—including the immune system—begins to break down. Anabolic metabolism, which is responsible for tissue building, turns into catabolic metabolism and the body, in effect, begins to consume itself. This is a necessary phenomenon for responding to life-and-death situations, but disastrous on a day-to-day basis. Prolonged exposure to epinephrine and norepinephrine also interferes with communication between an immune cell's receptors and the cell's nucleus, which prevents immune cells from responding to toxic antigens. And to top it off, stress results in cortisol production from the adrenal glands. Cortisol works for us beneficially by regulating energy use in crisis situations, but too much of it in the system results in depressed immune function, as well as a depressed state of mind.

The bottom line is that too much stress weakens the immune system. And this raises the likelihood that you will suffer from any one of a long list of stress-related disorders, from bacterial or viral infections to more serious degenerative diseases, such as cardiovascular disease, hypertension, asthma, diabetes, inflammatory bowel disease, ulcers, and cancer. You may also be at increased risk for autoimmune disorders such as multiple sclerosis, rheumatoid arthritis, lupus, and more. Fortunately, by following the Okinawa

Program you can effectively neutralize these negative effects of stress, as you will see a little further on in the chapter.

Adaptability—A Key to Successful Aging

It is interesting to note that many of the stress-related diseases mentioned above are diseases commonly associated with aging. In fact, in Japan, heart disease, cancer, and stroke are called "adult diseases" *(seijin byo)* because they usually appear after the age of forty. All evidence considered, there is no doubt that *stress accelerates aging.* One pertinent example is the recent discovery that stress actually causes shrinkage of the hippocampus, the main area for memory function in the brain.[9] And memory loss, as we all know, is a hallmark of old age. Because maladaptive or negative responses to stress have been implicated in premature aging, some researchers are convinced that proper stress management—the ability to adapt to stressful life events through coping—is one of the most important factors for successful aging.

As we mentioned earlier, we all differ in the way we function under stress. Some people thrive in high-pressure jobs, deadline situations, or the heat of competition. But why is this? Is it possible that stress just does not get to these people? In a way, yes. Their stress responses are simply not being activated. Why? Because they don't *interpret* the events as stressful. Interpretation is an important middle stage. The way we appraise a stressful event is key to the way we react to it. Yes, modern life is full of potential stress producers— crowded trains, crime, excessive noise, air pollution, traffic jams, rude people, and time pressures. There is little we can do about that. But what we can do is control how we react and adapt to these stressors—and this, in the long run, will ultimately determine our levels of stress and consequently influence the rate at which we age.

Perhaps we could all learn a lesson from Jeanne Calment. She reached the ripe old age of 122—the oldest authenticated age of any human being in history—mainly owing to her "unflappability." Jean-Marie Robine, her biographer and a researcher on aging, reported that "biologically and constitutionally speaking," Calment was someone who was "immune to stress." Her motto seemed to be: "if you can't do anything about it, then don't worry about it."[10]

Others who have reached a healthy old age seem to live by the same philosophy. They simply handle stress better than the average person. They react less negatively and with less hostility, and seem to have learned to accept change as an inevitable part of life. This attitude allows them to avoid generating stress internally because they do not take the inevitable frustrations of life personally. The bottom line seems to be that if we want to live to a healthy old age we must learn to accept change—even if that change appears at first to be negative.

Most psychologists and gerontologists agree that centenarians are much better at managing stress than the general population—which, incidentally, does not mean that they have had stress-free lives. Some centenarians are Holocaust survivors, others grew up in extreme poverty or were orphaned or widowed at young ages. Most have had their share of loss, grief, and hardship. However, what many centenarians have in common are coping skills that help them get on with their lives. In fact, Dr. Margery Silver and Dr. Thomas Perls, directors of the New England Centenarian Study, were so impressed by the ability of these successful-agers to handle stress and cope with adversity that they referred to them as "stress-resistant personalities."[11]

Personality and Longevity

Personality, although commonly used when talking about people, is a difficult term to define. Most often the word is used to refer to a person's habitual patterns of behavior, attitudes, and ways of adapting to life's challenges. Personality has long been considered an important factor for healthy aging and has been studied extensively.[12] Most studies agree that there are a number of key personality characteristics that are important for healthy aging: easygoing, cheerful, self-confident, adaptable, active, independent, creative, happy, relaxed, satisfied, calm, open, agreeable, conscientious, sociable, and having a high tolerance for frustration being mentioned most often. The traits that lead to an unhealthy, shorter life? Being repressed, dogmatic, stubborn, hostile, neurotic, angry, guilty, sad, fearful, anxious, depressed, and aggressive.

One of the most important personality characteristics or attitudes that has been investigated as of late is optimism. A recent UCLA study on seventy-eight men with AIDS showed that those who indicated they had what they considered a "realistic view" of their disease died an average of nine months sooner than those who were more optimistic about living longer.[13] In other words, optimism about our health may actually influence our life expectancy.[14] Optimism has also been shown to have a positive effect on immune system response. Researchers from the Pittsburgh Cancer Institute have shown that cancer patients who underwent cognitive and relaxation therapy to boost optimism and overcome self-defeating beliefs had higher levels of natural cancer-killing cells in their system upon completion of the program compared to the control group who received only the standard medical treatment.[15] And Dr. Michael Scheier, a psychologist at Carnegie Mellon University, found that for men undergoing coronary bypass surgery, the optimists recover more quickly, begin to walk earlier, express greater life satisfaction, and are less likely to experience a subsequent heart attack.[16]

Optimism is a key component for feeling in control and successfully coping with stressful situations. Optimists almost always feel more in control of their circumstances than pessimists do. If things go bad for optimists they often just create a new approach or strategy, believing that if they persist eventually things will turn out for the best. Pessimists, on the other hand, tend to perceive themselves as helpless and therefore give up sooner. An internal sense of control or feeling of mastery not only is essential for interpreting otherwise stressful situations as exciting and challenging but lowers stress levels as well.[17]

The opposite of believing that we are in control is the belief that we are helpless to influence a situation. Psychologists have coined the term "learned helplessness" to describe the gradual loss of willpower that comes in dealing with an unchangeable situation over and over again. Animal experiments on mice first demonstrated the importance of a sense of control for reducing stress-induced illness many years ago. A mouse that hears a warning buzzer seconds before receiving a shock gets fewer ulcers than a mouse that is not provided with the warning. When a mouse is given a lever that terminates the shock when pushed, ulcers are reduced further still. Variations on the same theme have been reproduced numerous times across species and in humans as well.

To sum up, most personality and longevity experts agree that a positive outlook, as seen in optimistic, emotionally stable, and flexible personalities, is a definite advantage for coping with the inevitable stresses of life—and helps us to stay healthy far into our senior years. Studies on American centenarians have found them to be flexible, adaptive, emotionally stable, seldom depressed, and assertive when necessary. The oldest old tend to possess a certain strength or resiliency of character that is expressed by self-confidence, independence, and strength of will. They are definitely not wallflowers! These traits also typify many of the centenarians we have met in Okinawa. Their stories of survival attest not only to their resourcefulness in coping but also to the resilience of the human spirit in the face of great odds.

Toku Oyakawa: A Story of the Human Spirit

Fi-tu-ya chimu gukuru.
What counts most is heart.
Okinawan proverb

When we first called to set up an interview with centenarian Toku Oyakawa, a naturalized Canadian citizen living in a small town in the province of Ontario, we were told he was out fishing—a favorite pastime for more than eight decades. Oyakawasan was then 106 years old. He was living with his wife, Emi, eighty-nine, who had also emigrated to Canada from Okinawa over a half-century ago, and his extended family, which included his second son, daughter-in-law, and three grandchildren. This was back in 1994. Oyakawasan passed away four years later at the age of 110, but his legacy continues on—and it personifies the resilience of the human spirit.

Oyakawasan was born in Nago City, Okinawa, the third of eight children, and spent his youth gathering and selling firewood from the nearby mountains of Yanbaru to help support his family. In 1905, when he was seventeen, he was caught up in the emigration movement that was then sweeping Okinawa. Oyakawasan was one of tens of thousands who opted to leave the stifling poverty that engulfed Okinawa at that time for the promising shores of North and South America. (Overseas Okinawans now form an *Uchinanchuu* [Okinawan] network of hundreds of thousands linking many communities across the Americas.) Oyakawasan chose Canada.

Being a small, underage, Asian boy who knew only a few words of English, Oyakawasan immediately met with stiff resistance from immigration officers upon landing in Victoria on Vancouver Island. But with determination and a solid dose of chutzpah, he managed to convince a kindly immigration official that although his body was small he was much healthier than other candidates. And moreover, he assured them, his eyesight was particularly strong! He was passed through as an eighteen-year-old man and began his new life as an immigrant on the Canadian West Coast, laying ties for the railroad. It was back-breaking labor but his spirit helped to push his small body to its limits. He later worked as a lumberjack and a salmon packer—all the while learning the language of his new country and prudently saving money to buy land.

In 1935, at the age of forty-seven, after thirty years of hard work, he was able to purchase fifty acres of land in a suburb of Vancouver, British Columbia, and build his first house. One goal had finally been attained. At this point, a number of factors converged to bring him back to Okinawa. First, having at last the means to support a family, he was now ready to look for a wife; and second, his mother, whom he had not seen in three decades, was ailing. He headed back to Okinawa, soon met Emi, and fell in love. Unfortunately Emi was already promised to someone else. Her suitor had gone to the United States and she planned to follow. Fate, however, intervened to bring them together. War broke out in China, which prevented Emi from going to America and she remained in Okinawa, working as a textile weaver. Eventually her relationship ended, and with her father's blessing, she married Oyakawasan.

Oyakawasan went back to Canada first to get the paperwork started that would allow Emi to enter the country. The process took two years. When she finally arrived they started a farm on Oyakawasan's fifty acres, bought five thousand chickens, and began a family—Oyakawasan was fifty-one years old and Emi was thirty-four when their first son was born. Two daughters followed in the next two years. Life was good. The couple was happy together. The children were healthy. Their farm was going well. And they were beginning to save some money. Then war broke out between Japan and the allied nations of the West.

Oyakawasan and Emi were informed that they were no longer

welcome in Canada and instructed to go back to Japan. In 1941 they sold the chicken farm for a pittance, abandoned their belongings, and prepared to depart for Okinawa. But after soul-searching discussions they decided to stay and tough it out in Canada—and were put into a detention camp. Their fourth child (and second son) was born in a stable. When the war ended and they left the camp, Oyakawasan, then fifty-seven years old, had to start all over again. Everything he had worked so hard for was gone. They rented a house in a small town in Ontario, and raised potatoes and cabbages; Oyakawasan supplemented their income with woodcutting. A few years later they had enough money scraped together to build a new house. And life went on.

Over the years Oyakawasan's only real medical problem was the removal of his appendix at the age of ninety-two, and even then he left the hospital the next day because he considered the food inedible. (He had always eaten as close to a traditional Okinawan diet as possible even though living in Canada.) To celebrate his 105th birthday, Oyakawasan and Emi vacationed in California for three months. The huge fish they snagged on that holiday now hangs on the wall of their house.

During our interview, both Oyakawasan and Emi appeared happy and healthy. Oyakawasan sat with a straight back and glossed skin, and spoke in a deep clear voice. His eyes were still strong enough to read the newspaper without glasses, although he was a bit hard of hearing. Emi proudly told us that between the two of them they were 195 years old! She also let us know that Oyakawasan's excellent health was due, in no small part, to how well she cared for him. Later, Oyakawasan shared his secrets for health and longevity. "It is important," he said, "to enjoy life . . . and to get a good night's sleep. One should not be concerned with the little things, or worry about age or appearance, or complain about the body's natural aches and pains . . . one must focus on the good things in life . . . and remember to smile."

The words of advice struck us as very similar to what Jeanne Calment, the oldest woman in the world, had said to her biographer. As we left, Oyakawasan advised us "not to dwell on the past, but rather look forward and not backward," as he himself always did. Oyakawasan and Emi were already making plans for travel to Okinawa the next year and Hawaii after that.

In our experience with the oldest old we rarely find that their lives have been easy or without hardship. Elders do not reach a healthy old age because of having *avoided* stressful life circumstances. Rather, they have *responded* to challenges in an effective and healthy manner. When Toku Oyakawa came out of the internment camp at age fifty-seven, having lost everything, he made a conscious choice to look forward and start again, rather than dwell on the past and carry around bitterness, resentment, and other negative feelings. His personality may have helped to insulate him from the kind of emotional damage that often befalls those who have experienced similar devastating losses.

Most Okinawan elders have similar tales of loss and hardship. Okinawa was the site of the most destructive battle of World War II. One in four Okinawans lost their lives. The positive attitudes of most Okinawan centenarians and their strength and resilience in the face of adversity are no doubt important factors contributing to their incredible health and longevity.

The Taygay Personality

Okinawans like to use the term *taygay* to refer to people or their society in general. It is a word from the Okinawan dialect that can be translated as "easygoing" or "laid-back." Social relations in Okinawa tend to operate on this principle, in that they lean toward a flexible, nonhierarchical, loose style. Nothing seems to be set in stone. Okinawans often comment that "nothing ever starts on time in Okinawa," or that "things lack organization," or that "people around here are not very ambitious." But these descriptions are not meant to be critical; they are simply matter-of-fact statements. Combined with Okinawans' special sense of time, *taygay* has come to refer to the typical Okinawan character type—calm, easygoing, and relaxed.

We were intrigued at the possibility that Okinawan culture seems to place a high value on a behavioral pattern that may lead to a stress-reduced lifestyle. Science, however, demands proof. So we set about trying to identify the lifelong personality traits that might have been contributing to the Okinawans' exceptional health and longevity. We decided to test for the presence or absence of the hurry-sick Type A personality. It had been over forty years since M. Friedman and R. Rosenman first published their ground-breaking research on Type A personality syndrome in the *Journal of the American Medical Association*. Back then, the idea that habitual patterns of behavior or personality could be linked with coronary heart disease was a novel concept. Since that time, the significance of Type A personality as an important risk factor for heart disease has been well established.[18]

If indeed *taygay* was the most characteristic behavioral pattern among Okinawan elders, then theoretically they should show low levels, or even an absence, of the Type A personality traits—time-pressured, competitive, over-achieving, impatient, and hostile. This would help bolster our theory that Okinawa time and the *taygay* behavioral pattern were indeed health promoting. Therefore our group conducted personality testing on centenarians to measure lifelong personality traits—and bolster our theory it did.[19]

We found that Okinawan centenarians scored extremely low in "time urgency" and "tension," which explains how they kept stress levels low and maintained mental health. And they scored high in "self-confidence" and "unyieldingness" (or determination), which explains how they maintained their strength of will and resilience of character over a lifetime of one hundred years or more. Okinawan elders, interestingly, are often referred to as *gajuh,* which is an Okinawan word meaning a "self-willed character." They do not easily give in to others once their minds are made up, nor do they give up easily when faced with a challenge. Although more research is needed, we feel that these traits, combined with the low tension and lack of time urgency that typifies Okinawa time and *taygay* style, are important contributing factors leading to a long and healthy life.

Meditation, Aging, And Okinawa Time

Meditation helps slow us down—inside and out. It helps set our inner rhythms to Okinawa time. An enterprising UCLA student named R. Keith Wallace came up with the first scientific evidence to support this thesis when he decided to hook up some electrodes to various body parts to measure the body's physiological responses to transcendental meditation (TM).[20] TM, of course, is the form of meditation that was popularized by Maharishi Mahesh Yogi in the 1960s and came to world attention when the Beatles subsequently embraced it.

TM is based on the repetition of a specific word or mantra, which is alleged to cause internal vibrations that synchronize the mind and the nervous system. Physiologically, it places you in that internal void that the Indian mystics called "pure awareness." Western researchers of mind-body medicine refer to this state as the "relaxation response." The Okinawans call it "the Way." Keith Wallace called it "hypometabolic wakefulness" because even while physiological measures such as oxygen consumption and heart rate slowed, his subjects remained alert enough to push a button, signaling that they had "transcended" into this state.

After a decade more of study, Wallace, perhaps sensing his own pending rendezvous with middle age, began to probe the effects of meditation on human aging. He chose three well-accepted markers for physiological age: eyesight, hearing, and blood pressure. Remarkably, Wallace showed that all three of these factors could be improved with long-term meditation, suggesting that *meditation may actually slow the aging process*.[21] Those who had been meditating for five years or more measured, on average, five years younger than nonmeditators. Those meditating longer scored an impressive twelve years younger on average. Subsequent observational and case-control studies proved quite fascinating. Two thousand meditators were compared in overall health status to nonmeditators in a large insurance plan. Meditators used physicians and medical services almost 50 percent less than nonmeditators. More impressive, heart disease was 80 percent lower and cancer 50 percent lower in the meditation group. Similar numbers are seen in Okinawans as compared to North Americans.

While these were revolutionary findings for Western science, it was old hat in the East. At the heart of most great Eastern spiritual traditions are esoteric schools of meditation that offer practitioners guidelines for developing spiritual qualities such as compassion, love, and wisdom, and are said to lead to great longevity. Chinese monks were among the first mystics to engage in such meditation practices. *The Bubishi,* an ancient Chinese historical text brought to Okinawa several hundred years ago, alleges that the truly enlightened were able to extend their lives by decades, some by centuries, using meditation techniques. Okinawan contact with the Chinese in the ancient days was responsible for the spread and subsequent adaptation of *Bubishi* teachings by Okinawan masters.

Slowing yourself down to reduce stress and its negative effects—whether through meditation or the other techniques we suggest on the following pages—is learned behavior. That means all of us can learn to do it. We can learn how to *unlearn* Western time. This does not mean that we have to be half an hour late for that important business meeting. It simply gives us a choice between feeling *in control of time* or feeling *controlled by* it. The following techniques will show how you, too, can use the concept of Okinawa time to gain control over your own time and life. But first, answer the questionnaire below and see what time you are actually operating on right now.

What Time Are You Operating On?

Read the following questions and check off the ones that generally apply to you.

1. There is rarely enough time in the day to do all the things that I have to.
2. It's irritating for me to sit in traffic.
3. I sometimes finish other people's sentences for them in midconversation.
4. I prefer reading short stories, newspapers, or magazines to novels.
5. My job requires me to punch a time clock or to record my hours.
6. I can't seem to exercise on a regular basis.
7. I spend more time and attention on my career than on my family.
8. I often feel that I have too many things to do.
9. I often begin a new project without finishing the last one.
10. I don't always take the full allotment of vacation time due to me.
11. I sometimes have trouble concentrating on one thing at a time.

12. Life is rushing by at too fast a pace.
13. Passengers in my car sometimes ask me to slow down.
14. I often have trouble getting to sleep at night.
15. I often feel irritable.
16. I often feel competitive with others.
17. I periodically lose my temper.
18. People sometimes call me a cynic.
19. Coffee is good for keeping me awake.
20. People sometimes call me a workaholic.
21. I would describe myself as goal-oriented.
22. I don't like to finish a job until it is just right.
23. I have been called a "micro-manager" or "controlling" by others.
24. I have a nervous twitch or habit like biting my nails, gnashing my teeth, etc.
25. I have many deadlines at work that I must meet.
26. I have very few hobbies or interests.
27. I eat out a lot.
28. I often work on weekends.
29. People tell me that I talk fast.
30. I often use tobacco, alcohol, or other intoxicants to wind down.

Add up your score: Each check is worth one point.

5 or less points: You are operating pretty close to Okinawa time. Keep the rhythm!

6 to 10 points: You are not far off the mark, but still would benefit from making some lifestyle changes as detailed in the list that follows.

11 to 15 points: Your internal clock needs definite adjusting. Try out the suggestions below.

16 points and up: You may be suffering from a "time-sick behavioral pattern" and would benefit from seriously rethinking your relationship to time. Definitely try out the healing prescriptions below.

Many of our so-called new modern therapeutic techniques have really been around in one form or another for hundreds or even thousands of years. Many are part of daily life in Okinawa, which we adapt here to suit a Western culture. Try them—and manage time (and stress) with the Okinawa Program.

Resetting Your Internal Clock To Okinawa Time: Healing Prescriptions

> The ancients have stolen all our best ideas.
> *Mark Twain*

Stress Reliever 1: Meditate

Meditation may be the single most effective way of dealing with stress. There are literally thousands of meditation techniques from many different traditions. Transcendental meditation, which we discussed briefly, is but one of them. TM must be learned from a practitioner, but it is relatively inexpensive, and most cities have TM centers. Your community center or local college probably offers classes in meditative traditions as well. Seeking the advice of other meditators or finding a private teacher is also an option. Check out people advertising their services through your local YMCA/YWCA, community bulletin boards, local alternative newspapers, online, or even the yellow pages. Meanwhile, you can do very well practicing the meditations described in this book.

The concept of meditation is deceptively simple. In its most basic form, it is simply the process of quieting the mind. With a quiet mind comes a sense of peace and an absence of stressful feelings. When we meditate we empty our minds of all thoughts and problems and focus on "nothingness." This allows us to live more in the present moment, to exist in the here and now rather than being separated from it by our thoughts, feelings, plans, or analyses. Being wholly present puts us more in tune with our natural rhythms, more in sync with Okinawa time, and ultimately leads to a healing sense of relaxation, peace and harmony, and expanded awareness.

Although meditation is simple in theory, it can, in practice, be rather challenging. Anyone who has practiced meditation can attest to the fact that it is not easy to quiet the mind. Meditators are fond of referring to the undisciplined mind as an unruly child or restless drunken monkey—in other words, difficult to control. With regular practice, though, it gets easier, and eventually you'll find that you can quiet your mind almost effortlessly.

One thing that we've found very helpful when starting meditation is the following focused breathing exercise. It's the simplest and most direct method of developing your concentration skills. And it will also help prepare you for your meditation by relaxing your mind and body.

A Focused Breathing Exercise

1. Sit in a comfortable position with your spine straight.
2. Focus your attention on your abdomen as you inhale and exhale in a natural manner.
3. Take a few deep conscious breaths without straining.
4. Let the flow of your breath settle into its own natural rhythm while keeping focused and aware during the whole process.
5. Allow your attention to focus on the changing rhythms of your inhalations and exhalations. When your attention begins to wander, gently but firmly bring it back to your breathing.
6. Count your breaths. (Beginning meditators find this extremely helpful for keeping the mind from wandering.) Upon exhalation count "one." The next exhalation count "two" and so on until the count of ten, then start over again. If you lose count or your attention wanders, then begin at one again. Counting may be abandoned once you become better at concentrating and focusing your attention.

By regularly practicing this focused breathing exercise, you'll find that your skills of concentration and attention will improve and your mind will become clearer and more balanced. Although you can meditate anywhere at any time, it is important to find a time and a place that are comfortable for you. It would be ideal to have a special room or healing place to meditate in, but it is not necessary—anywhere quiet and calming will do. The amount of time you devote to your meditation again depends on your comfort zone. Twenty minutes a day seems to work well for most meditators, but anywhere from ten to forty minutes once or twice a day is sufficient. Here are a few more tips to help ease you into meditation.

- Talk to friends, do a little research and reading, and choose the meditation techniques that you intuitively feel most comfortable with.
- Try to set aside a specific time each day to meditate. It's not essential that you meditate at the same time every day, but in the beginning it makes it easier to get into the habit.
- Aim for twenty minutes, but if you find it too difficult to sit in one place that long, start with five or ten minutes, then gradually work yourself up to twenty by adding an extra minute or two every couple of days.
- Use the healing space you've created for yourself (as in Chapter Seven) for meditation whenever possible, but if it is not possible to get there, simply find a quiet comfortable spot wherever you are—even your car will do.
- Before sitting down to meditate, take a few minutes to stretch or to do one of the relaxation techniques described below.
- And finally, although it is absolutely possible to meditate on your own without professional guidance, it's always a good idea in the beginning to find a guide. A qualified meditation teacher not only will possess the right knowledge and skill but will be genuinely interested in your progress and be able to lend invaluable support if you get frustrated along the way. Look for a teacher who inspires confidence and trust and who has good communication skills. Learn to trust your intuition.

A Basic Meditation Technique

This wonderful basic technique was taught to us by an Okinawan *sensei* (master) years ago and has remained part of our healing apothecary ever since.

1. Start by getting into a comfortable position in a quiet place and closing your eyes. Use a posture that will allow your back to remain straight without straining it (sitting in a straight-backed chair, on a floor mat in a cross-legged position, or even lying flat on your back if you cannot sit comfortably).

2. Sit (or lie) as still as possible.

3. Focus your awareness on your own breathing and count your breaths (as in step 6 of the focused breathing exercise). Without changing how you breathe, simply observe how the air comes into your lungs as you inhale, and then goes out again as you exhale.

4. Another technique is to focus on a sound. Instead of counting, repeat a chosen word or sound upon exhalation. Most people find that words, sounds, or phrases that hold some spiritual significance for them are best. A Christian meditator may, for instance, choose the word *Amen*. Some prefer a humming sound that produces a soothing vibration, such as *Ommmm*. According to our Okinawan sensei, chanting mantras (simple but meaningful words or phrases that are repeated over and over) has the double effect of focusing your awareness while creating a peaceful healing state.

5. Allow all of your thoughts, feelings, or sensations to drift in and out of your mind without fixating upon them or trying to chase them away.

6. Avoid overanalyzing the meditation, forcing the process, placing too much emphasis on perfect technique, or trying to turn off your thoughts.

That is all there is to it. Sound simple? We can guarantee that your mind will have other plans at first. It will begin to wander and you will find yourself thinking about something other than your breathing or your chosen sound. You may even begin to question what you are doing sitting there when you have a million things you have to do. This is quite normal so don't get discouraged. When this happens just gently but firmly redirect your focus to your breathing or your sound.

Through the practice of meditation you will be able to develop your awareness and gain more control over your mind, and slowly but surely your mind will begin to quiet down. This will result in a greater sense of inner peace, happiness, and a feeling of oneness. When we pay attention to our thoughts it becomes clear just how much time we spend dwelling on the past or future. Meditation keeps us focused on the eternal present and allows us to fully experience the Okinawa Program.

As you become more adept at the basic technique, move on to the following healing meditations that we have collected from our travels around the world. Our studies have found them to be particularly powerful tools for self-transformation and psychospiritual growth.

Resetting Time

What is time and how do we relate to it? How does our metabolism of time affect the way we live? It seems simple at first. Time is a progression from past to future. Like a clock ticking away it seems to be always moving forward in a straight line, one minute following the next. Yet, as both Einstein and the mystics of the East tell us, space and time are dynamic qualities. Time is but a product of our imagination. It is illusionary. In the spiritual world there are no time divisions. Still, we tend to habitually think of time in concrete terms, as made up of the present, past, and future. The past seems real to us because we carry memories of it—some pleasant, others that cause regret. We remember past friends and lovers, former places we've lived, our triumphs and failures. The future holds promise of hopes, dreams, or fears. The present, for the most part, gets short shrift. Yet the present is where life unfolds. Once we take off our perceptual filters, we realize that the present is all that is real. For the following meditation, adapted from a traditional Okinawan ancestor prayer, we ask you to try to go beyond your usual perception of time. Shake it up. Reset your internal clock.

1. Begin your meditation by taking a moment to relax.
2. Practice your abdominal breathing technique and let go of any tension, worries, or stress.

3. Now, become aware of yourself at this very moment. Notice the experience of time passing. Second by second. Moment by moment. Like the flowing of ocean waves breaking against the side of a ship.

4. Again, take notice of yourself and appreciate that your previous state of awareness is now a memory. The past moment is gone. It has passed. Let it go. Do not hold on to it. Feel it wash away with the waves of the deep blue sea.

5. Imagine time passing as if your consciousness were the bow of a ship cutting through an open expanse of water and your memory is the wake. Follow the wake backward.

6. Imagine that you are following the wake backward in time further and further.

7. Think of yesterday. What did you do? Go back a week more. Can you remember what you did a week ago? A year ago?

8. Think of those who have come before you. Think of your parents, your grandparents, and your great-grandparents. Think of the hundreds of ancestors and events that have come before you to make you what you are.

9. Release yourself from any guilt or blame that may have come to you from their misdeeds. Forgive them for any pain or misfortune they may have brought upon you or your family. Be thankful to them for the blessings in your life.

10. Now, stop flowing backward. Your ship has slowed to a stop and the current of flowing water now extends in front of you to the future.

11. Follow the current forward. Within this current lie the potential decisions you could make, and actions you might take that will decide your future. Connections between events are hazy and undefined.

12. Reflect upon the infinite waves of possibility that will converge together to create the next moment and the one after that and the one after that.

13. At the convergence of these many influences, imagine that the current extending forward is a wave that you are now riding on. Your ship is cresting the wave of present events.

14. Past, present, and future now begin to merge into one. A sense of deep calm and tranquillity comes over you.

15. Take each moment as it comes. Continue to breathe as you get a sense of being in the here and now. Nothing else exists but the unfolding present that you are now creating. You hold your destiny in your hands. The possibilities are unlimited.

Refiguring Emotions—The Inner Smile

Emotions are not isolated entities. We experience them in response to what we perceive in our environments. They are triggered by our perceptions of external events. When someone we care about smiles at us we perceive the smile and interpret the smile as an expression of warmth toward us. Our perception in turn triggers our mind and body to respond by releasing chemicals that induce certain changes in our body that we interpret as a pleasant emotion. We may think to ourselves that we are feeling the love emanating from our loved one. What if the loved one frowns at us? We perceive the frown. We interpret the perception, and we experience an emotion. This time it is an unpleasant feeling. Does this mean that we are at the mercy of those around us? If our emotional well-being is entirely dependent upon our external circumstances, we are going to be in for a world of pain. Even people who love us are not going to smile and be nice all the time. The good news is that we store perceptions in our memories. We can remember a time when a person we loved smiled at us. If we can remember that, we can still conjure up the image as a fantasy. A mental image held vividly in the mind can create the same emotional response as the real experience. Just as we can call up a memory at will, we can direct the character of our thoughts. We can choose to think positive thoughts or negative thoughts, loving thoughts or hateful thoughts. Which we choose largely dictates the quality of our emotional experience. It may take practice to think more positively and more compassionately, but just as you must guide a child to behave the way you want him or her to, you must guide your mind to healthy thought patterns. Try this meditation and see if it doesn't make you feel better.

1. Sit comfortably in an upright position. If using a chair, sit with your feet flat on the floor. Put your hands on your thighs or fold them comfortably in your lap. Keep your head nicely balanced on your spine and relax your shoulders. Allow your eyes to close.

2. Take two or three slow relaxing breaths. Exhale slowly and completely, then wait for the inhaling to begin on its own.

3. Relax. Bring forth in your mind the energy of smiling. Use your powers of visualization to create an image that makes you feel like smiling. You might imagine before you the face of a loved one beaming love toward you. The image could be of your own smiling face, or a memory of a time when you felt love and peace. Perhaps you would like to imagine the beatific face of a divine being shining love upon you.

4. Hold the image in mind as you continue to breathe slowly and calmly. Feel the welling in your heart as the image stimulates your emotional response. Allow your heart to open to the smiling. Allow yourself to smile back at the image. The change in your facial muscles may be very slight, but let a peaceful, loving expression overtake you.

5. Become fully aware of the feeling of smiling energy in your mind and body. Register this as a state that is readily available to you. This pleasant emotional state can be summoned, just as you would summon a memory. You need only remember to smile inwardly.

6. Continue to feel the smiling energy. Let this pleasant thought and feeling course through your body. You can place your inner smile anywhere in your body. You may want to focus your inner smile at what have been called *chakras,* or energy centers, by ancient Indian sages, working from the crown of your head to the base of your spine, or from the root of your spine to the top of your head. The seven major *chakras* include the crown, forehead (third eye), throat, heart, solar plexus, abdomen, and base of the spine. Smile into each area and allow the loving energy to swirl.

7. You may also practice smiling into the various organs of your body. Send your inner smile to your heart, lungs,

stomach, liver, kidneys, glands, and so on. Direct your love to parts of your body that you don't think about much, or that you don't like about yourself. Be whole in your compassionate, smiling self.

8. Cultivate the loving feeling that arises with a smile. Awaken the love energy in your heart and mind. Move into the flow of love that fills the universe.

9. Fill yourself with loving kindness. Share your smile and your loving heart with people in your life.

10. Grow the circle of your compassion wider and wider, so that it includes yourself, and those you love. Include those you know that you didn't think you loved.

11. Grow it wider so that it includes people you don't know, and wider still to include people you don't want to know, and whom you didn't think you could love.

12. Send your smiling energy to the most pathetic and unlovable. Shine that smile into their hearts.

13. Wish them greater wisdom and wish them awakening awareness of love.

14. Expand the scope of caring to include all beings in the universe. Know that the force of love pervades the universe, seen and unseen. When you love, you attune yourself to that great force and come into accord with the divine unity.

The inner smile meditation should be used to open your heart, awakening love and compassion, releasing negative emotional states, forgiving others, and making peace with your world. (Our thanks to Mantak and Maneewanwan Chia for this wonderful meditation.)

The Sun God

The *Omoro Soshi* is the most important literary work in classical Okinawan literature. It is a twenty-two-volume collection of 1,533 ancient songs *(omoro)* from the villages of Okinawa. The word *omoro* means "feeling" or "thought." Thus *omoro* is a poetically expressed thought or feeling, often accompanied by simple dancing and sung to the clapping of hands or the beating of drums. Local priestesses intoned the *omoro* during religious rituals and villagers sang them at agricultural festivals. For

centuries the songs were transmitted orally from generation to generation. Often themes revolved around simple pastoral lives, festivals,
offshore fishing, and worship of gods and the sun. Every Okinawan
home still has an altar dedicated to the fire, hearth, or sun god *(hi nu
kan)* placed strategically in the kitchen. The following meditation is an
adaptation of a traditional song of sun worship from the *Omoro Soshi*. It
should be used for tapping the life-giving forces of nature, mastering
mental distress, and awakening love and compassion.

1. Sit comfortably in an upright position. Allow your eyes to
   close.
2. Take a couple of slow, relaxing breaths. Feel the tension
   dissipating into the atmosphere like the moist dew
   evaporating on a warm summer morning.
3. Imagine that you are lying on a moist green, grassy knoll
   listening to the chirping of the birds in the trees as your body
   melts peacefully into the soft carpet of grass beneath you.
4. Feel the sun shining brightly overhead, warming the air as
   it rises in the clear blue sky.
5. Feel your body soaking up those golden yellow rays of healing
   sunlight energy like the lush green life surrounding you.
6. Imagine now that you are riding one of those rays of
   sunlight where you merge into the very center of the sun.
   How safe and warm it feels!
7. You are now completely relaxed as you revel in the midst of
   the warm healing energy of the sun. Your breathing is deep
   and rhythmic.
8. The sun is replete with loving, healing energy. It is the very
   embodiment of love itself. Feel yourself as part of that
   loving healing energy. Be completely one with it. Stay with
   that feeling for a while.
9. Feel that loving healing energy of the sun flowing to every
   part of your body. To every part of your mind. To every
   part of your soul. Notice how warm and radiant you feel.
10. Feel that warm radiant loving energy as it flows throughout
    the rest of the world. To all living creatures. You are part of
    that warm healing energy as are all of God's creations. Be
    thankful and carry that feeling throughout the rest of the day.

Stress Reliever 2: Breathe Your Stress Away

In many cultures life is believed to begin with the first breath and end with the last. Breath, in these cultures, connects the mind, body, and spirit. Breath is often believed to animate the fetus with life-giving spirit. In fact, in many languages spirit and breath are both expressed by the same word, such as the Latin *spiritus,* the Hebrew *ruach,* or the Greek *pneuma.* It comes as little surprise, then, that conscious breath control is essential to many healing practices. The various systems of yoga in India, for example, teach many kinds of breathing exercises that are known as *Pranayama, prana* meaning both "spirit" and "breath" in the ancient Indian tongue of Sanskrit.

Breath is also an important component of the meditative techniques revealed in *The Bubishi,* the ancient Chinese philosophical text we talked about earlier. In fact, the Chinese character for chi, most often translated as "universal energy," can also mean "air" or "breath." The ancient masters believed that every being shares in and is a natural manifestation of this fundamental energy. As we saw in Chapter Six, tai chi stems from this philosophy and incorporates breathing exercises as part of its teachings.

In the West, science has taught us that breath influences nervous system response. Heart rate, blood pressure, and circulation can all be affected by changing the speed, rhythm, and depth of our breathing. When experiencing stress, we tend to breathe in short, shallow bursts that take place mainly in the chest. This kind of thoracic (chest) breathing is very inefficient, since it prevents the lungs from filling up and emptying completely. When we are under stress it is particularly important to breathe from the abdomen. Abdominal breathing allows more air into the lungs, helps to relax the muscles, and oxygenates the system. It's a very handy technique to have in your stress-reducing repertoire. A few deep abdominal breaths can bring almost instant relief in situations where you are feeling stressed, tense, or anxious.

The following simple abdominal breathing exercise is extremely effective in energizing the body, calming the mind, and releasing tension. It is a supine (lying down) variation of the breathing exercises that you learned in Chapter Six. Once you can breathe easily in this position, you can go on to practice in a sitting or standing position. This breathing exercise is remarkably similar to some of the breathing techniques that we came across in our studies in Okinawa. It is used at the prestigious Mayo Clinic and is another fine example of how modern science is increasingly coming face-to-face with ancient wisdom.

Relaxed Abdominal Breathing Exercise

1. Lie on your back in a comfortable position on a bed, a recliner chair, or a well-padded floor.
2. Loosen any tight clothing, especially around your abdomen or waist.
3. Place your feet slightly apart. Rest one hand comfortably on your abdomen near your navel. Place the other hand on your chest. Initially, you might be more comfortable with your eyes closed.
4. Inhale through your nose because this allows the air to be filtered and warmed. Exhale through your mouth. If you have nasal stuffiness or other nasal difficulty, inhale through your mouth.
5. Quietly concentrate on your breathing for a few minutes and become aware of which hand is rising and falling with each breath.
6. Gently exhale most of the air in your lungs.
7. Inhale while counting slowly to four, about one second per count. As you inhale gently, slightly extend your abdomen, causing it to rise about one inch. You should be able to feel the movement with your hand. Do not pull your shoulders up or move your chest.
8. As you breathe in, imagine the warmed and relaxing air flowing in. Imagine this warmth flowing to all parts of your body.

You may feel some dizziness at first, but as you become experienced with the technique you will be able to do it more comfortably and easily. Once mastered, you can use this abdominal breathing exercise anytime and anywhere stressful situations present themselves. By becoming aware of your breathing you help to relieve tight muscles and fight stress.

Stress Reliever 3: Shed Tension through Muscle Relaxation Exercises

Muscle relaxation techniques—basically the tensing and relaxing of muscles—are simple and effective tools for countering insomnia, as well as Type A behavior and other stress-related behavioral patterns. The best known of these techniques is called *progressive muscle relaxation* and was first developed by Edmund Jacobson in the 1930s. It has been used extensively in a variety of stress-management programs, sleep laboratories, and physical and occupational therapy programs across the country. This technique will give you a clear idea of just how much tension you are holding in your body. Don't be surprised if it is a lot. Most of us tend to carry an enormous amount of tension around with us throughout our normal waking hours. Here's what to do.

1. Find a quiet place to sit or lie down.
2. Tense your whole body as tightly as possible by clenching your fists, wrinkling your face, flexing your feet and toes. Squeeze and tense. Squeeze tightly but not so tightly that you feel pain.
3. Use a slow count to ten as you contract your muscles and hold this tension. Be conscious of how your muscles feel when they are so tensed up.
4. Now, relax gradually for about thirty seconds. Completely relax and let go of all tension. Focus on the relaxed feeling that you get when your muscles are released. Breathe in naturally and as you exhale let go of any remaining tension. Let the feeling of heaviness take over. Become one with gravity.
5. Now, once again, tense your whole body, but this time use only half as much strength as you did before. Tense and hold. Notice the difference in feeling between your current level of muscle tension and your previous level. Count to ten.
6. Now, let go of all tension. Breathe naturally and as you breathe let go of any remaining tension, as before. Consciously feel what it's like to have released all your tension. Let go and sink into gravity like a stone dropped

into the clear blue ocean. Allow the waves to wash away your tension with each breath for about thirty seconds.

7. Repeat the above process two or three more times. Each time use half the previous amount of strength when tensing your muscles.

8. When you are finished, take a few deep breaths. As you breathe, consciously take in a new flow of life energy, or chi, with each new breath. Carry this renewed sense of vitality and calm with you throughout the day.

Stress Reliever 4: Try Hypnosis

Hypnosis has been used in some form or another for centuries to treat a variety of medical and spiritual concerns. Today, migraines, stress-related illnesses, and chronic pain are the most common problems treated by hypnosis. Even warts have been found to respond to hypnotic suggestion! What we are most interested in, however, is the fact that hypnosis can induce a state of deep relaxation. This is usually done by providing the patient with a mental task or a repetitive suggestion. Through the task or suggestion, perception is altered and awareness is focused selectively. For this reason hypnosis is often called a *selective awareness technique*. Hypnosis should be learned from a trained professional who can teach you, with sufficient practice, how to enter a deeply relaxed state on your own.

Stress Reliever 5: Experience Healing Touch

We highly recommend touch as a stress-management technique. It is effortless and 100 percent enjoyable—truly one of the most pleasurable experiences around. While there are many forms of bodywork that utilize touch, most practices share a common belief in the unity of body and mind. Beliefs, thoughts, and emotions, as we have seen, all leave their imprint on the muscular, nervous, endocrine, and circulatory systems. Touch helps to release accumulated emotional and physical tension that builds up in the body.

Touch has been a part of East Asian healing traditions for

thousands of years. It is recognized as an important medium for transmitting life force (in Chinese *qi* or *chi,* in Japanese *ki*) from one person to another. Healing touch, as experienced through the laying on of hands, therapeutic touch, acupressure, shiatsu, or other kinds of massage therapy, can be thought of as a way of transferring healing energy from the healer to the patient. Acupressure and shiatsu (Japanese acupressure) are massage techniques for transmitting *ki* to specific acupuncture points and meridians along the human body. This is thought to stimulate and release blocked energy and thus restore the balanced flow of life force, which in turn restores health and vitality to organs and tissues. It's certainly great for releasing tension and stress from the body.

European forms of massage, including Swedish massage, which is the most widely practiced, make use of deep tissue massage techniques along with manipulation, rubbing, and gentle touch, based closely on principles of anatomy and physiology. European-style massage is often used to treat back pain, sleep disorders, and other stress-related disorders.

Shiatsu, acupressure, therapeutic touch, and other massage therapy techniques create a profound state of relaxation and sense of well-being that positively affects your body's biochemistry and immune system. We recommend a monthly—or even biweekly—massage utilizing any of these techniques. You might even want to think about taking a massage course with your partner. Many colleges, universities, community associations, and adult education centers offer them. That way you could alternate giving each other treatments—a special way to bond and, in the long run, very cost-effective. Whichever way you approach it, incorporate some bodywork into your life—it is a potent antistress device. Try two of our favorite self-massage techniques for one-minute stress relief.

Self-Shiatsu—Gokuku

Shiatsu is Japanese for finger *(shi)* pressure *(atsu).* It combines acupressure, (finger pressure) upon acupuncture points and other techniques, including pressing, hooking, sweeping, shaking, pinching, rolling, grasping, and in some schools, walking on the patient's back, legs, and feet. These techniques are employed to correct imbalances in *ki*, or energy flow in the body. Here's a quick stress reliever that you can perform on yourself.

The *gokuku* is a shiatsu technique that the elders say helps relieve headache, toothache, menstrual cramps, and stomach ache. We can't vouch for each one of these claims, but at the very least, this shiatsu technique provides a nice stress break during a busy day.

1. Grasp your nondominant hand between the thumb and first finger of your dominant hand. You will be touching one of the 108 different pressure points that are considered energy points in the Chinese and Japanese traditional healing systems. This particular point is called *gokuku*, or "meeting mountains," and corresponds to the large intestine.

2. Press at the base of the intersection of the thumb and the first (index) finger and hold this pressure for five seconds. Release for five seconds and then repeat. Continue this for up to a minute, then switch hands. If you use a computer frequently, this technique can help clear up some of the tension in your hands.

Reflexology—*Ashi Jitsu*

Reflexology maximizes the flow of chi (or *ki*), but it does so using the energy meridians that occur on the feet. These energy points correspond to specific organs. Pressing and massaging the energy points can provide a terrific stress break at the end of a hectic day, or make for a quick pick-me-up anytime. Try this self-massage, also called *ashi jitsu*, for instant stress relief.

1. Grasp the foot with one hand, so that the fingertips touch the sole near the base of the big toe, and the thumb is balanced on the top of the foot.

2. Press your fingers into the sole of your foot with a moderate amount of pressure for five seconds, then release.

3. Move along the sole of the foot, inch by inch from the base of the big toe to the outer side of the foot, pausing for five seconds of pressure and then releasing for five seconds.

4. Continue the movement along the outside of the foot, slowly inching up toward the heel.
5. When you reach the heel, grasp your Achilles tendon between the thumb and the first finger and move up in a similar fashion.
6. Repeat with the other foot.
7. Wash your hands in cold water afterward to break the energy cycle.

The ancients say that this massage helps to strengthen the flow of energy to your colon and reproductive organs, respectively. We can attest to the fact that it certainly feels good.

Stress Reliever 6: Consider Biofeedback

Biofeedback, as the name suggests, is a modern technique for learning to control biological or physical processes through feedback about bodily functions. It accomplishes this through monitoring equipment that tracks all functions on a moment-to-moment basis. By hooking up to a device that measures your body temperature, heart rate, pulse, or perspiration you can directly experience how your bodily processes can be affected by your thoughts. Through this positive feedback loop you can learn how to control stress and achieve a deep state of relaxation. Biofeedback has been used successfully for treating a variety of problems, including anxiety, chronic pain, epilepsy, migraine headaches, insomnia, hypertension, phobias, and intestinal disorders. Look for a professional counselor, psychologist, or other professional therapist who practices this technique, or contact the Biofeedback Association Network (see Appendix B).

Stress Reliever 7: Get Regular Exercise

We cannot overemphasize the importance of regular exercise for overall health: we have seen the positive effects it has on the Okinawans. Physical activity is wonderful for relieving stress and building resistance to new stressors. Not only does it help the body eliminate the metabolic by-products of stress that build up in our systems but it also helps fight the blues and depression through the release of endorphins (your brain's feel-good chemicals). Moreover, it helps build self-confidence, improves appearance, offers a feeling of control and sense of accomplishment, and keeps you looking and feeling younger. Even if you can't get to a gym, at least commit to twenty minutes a day of brisk walking, tai chi movements, or gardening, as the Okinawan elders do. As Saburosan tells us, "If you are involved in gardening work, you are involved in a relationship with living things in a spiritual sense as well as a physical sense. I take care of them and they take care of me." Choose an activity that fits organically into your life. Owning a dog, for instance, will most certainly help get you out for a morning walk. Or if you watch early morning talk shows, park a stationary bike in front of the TV and pedal from segment to segment.

Stress Reliever 8: Eat Right for Your Psychospiritual Health

In the previous chapters we discussed the many ways that the Okinawa diet—high in complex carbohydrates, rich in whole grains, legumes, fresh vegetables, and fruits—can benefit our physical health, but it's also extremely beneficial to our mental and emotional health. Carbohydrates found in whole grains stimulate the production of serotonin, which promotes feelings of relaxation and well-being, and helps to regulate sleep patterns. Whole grains are also rich in B vitamins, which are essential for dealing with stress. Pantothenic acid, often referred to as the "antistress" vitamin, plays an important part in the production of the adrenal hormones, which, as we have noted, are rapidly produced when we are under stress.

Aside from eating well, it's also important to drink plenty of fresh water, preferably filtered or spring water. It helps to rid the body of toxins and other by-products of stress. Avoid smoking and excessive caffeine and alcohol consumption; these popular vices only raise your stress levels. And it's never too late to change. Kotokusan, ninety-five, tells us that he quit smoking ten years ago and feels much better for it, although he still admits to the occasional puff of extra-light cigarettes every now and then. Moderation: it's the Okinawa way.

Stress Reliever 9: Maintain Your Healing Web

Social relationships are particularly important for health when we are under stress. If you don't have many social contacts, then think about how you can connect more with other people. Nothing is more stressful than going through a major life event alone. It is important to find people to talk to about your difficulties. Call on family and friends, and think about seeking support groups where you can find people who are more understanding of your situation. Social ties reduce stress. Keep your relationships healthy and they will keep you healthy by buffering the effects of stressful life events or the daily hassles of life. You will find plenty of specific advice on how to do this in the next chapter.

Stress Reliever 10: Discard Negative Attitudes and Beliefs

Attitudes and beliefs are the filters through which we appraise our life experiences, and as we have seen, they form our core personalities and contribute directly to how much stress we feel in our daily lives. We have witnessed the benefits of optimism and positive coping styles among centenarians in Okinawa and elsewhere. We have also seen the destructive effects of negative emotionality as expressed by Type A behavioral patterns, hurry sickness, and other unhealthy approaches to life. Often the attitudes and beliefs that we hold dear have been part of our personalities for a long time. But that doesn't mean they are carved in stone.

We are all capable of changing our mind-sets and ridding ourselves of negative and unhealthy attitudes, beliefs, and behavioral patterns. To do that we have to be willing to be truthful with ourselves, to open ourselves up, and to let go of the old stuff. This can be frightening at first, since it often means confronting past traumatic experiences. Often the best strategy is to work closely with a professional therapist, counselor, psychologist, minister, or psychiatrist. There is certainly much less stigma associated with seeking professional help these days than there used to be. The fact is that all of us have had life experiences that have left their scars on our emotional well-being. For some of us, these scars are like open wounds that refuse to heal. They are always lying below the surface and affecting our behavior and outlook on life. Although medication can help see us through emotional crises, it does little to change the psychological or emotional stressors that may still be plaguing us. Because these topics need more discussion than can be practically offered in this book, we advise you to seek out books that deal closely with your particular issue, and then if you feel it is warranted, seek professional help.

Aside from unresolved past traumatic life experiences, present stressful life circumstances such as bereavement or divorce can also be a cause of depression. Depression, in fact, is one of our society's most prevalent and physically crippling diseases. Because it can have both biological and psychological roots, it is of little use to tell a person suffering from clinical depression that he or she should "try and be more optimistic." Sometimes the best treatment for depression is antidepressant medication. Sometimes it is psychotherapy. Often it is a combination of the two. Depression becomes more common as we age and is diagnosed more often in women, especially after giving birth or during menopause. The bottom line here is that depressed people are two to three times more likely to die of heart disease than persons who do not suffer from this psychological disorder. They also suffer more immune dysfunction. If you suspect that you or someone you care about might be suffering from depression, we suggest you seek help from a professional immediately.

Perhaps the most common—and certainly one of the most destructive—habit of the mind is just plain worry. No matter where we are or what we are doing, it's always possible to find something to worry about. Yet when we think about it, how many times has what we were worrying about actually happened? What has our worrying accomplished, other than to disturb our peace of mind? If you find yourself starting to obsessively worry about something over which you have no control, stop mid-worry and remind yourself that there's simply no point to it. What will be, will be. When you think about it, you know that the only things that are within your control are your beliefs, attitudes, and responses.

Stress Reliever 11: Learn to Manage Hostility and Anger

Hostility and anger are two particularly dangerous emotions from the viewpoint of healthy longevity. People with hostile personalities have up to five times the death rate before the age of fifty than people who are less prone to these negative emotions. An analysis of fifty or so studies on the effect of hostility on physical health showed that hostility is equal to or greater than the usual risk factors for heart disease such as high cholesterol levels and high blood pressure.[18]

Like depression, hostile emotions may be dealt with through psychotherapy aimed at changing deep-seated attitudes. *Cognitive therapy* is one of the most effective short-term therapeutic interventions. It works on changing how a person interprets everyday encounters and experiences, as well as the behaviors and emotions that follow in their wake. Anger management classes are also an increasingly common means for dealing with this challenging emotion. Most professional counselors, including psychiatrists, psychologists, and social workers, are familiar with both cognitive therapy and anger management and can either help you themselves or suggest someone who can. Learning to express your anger positively and respectfully can actually help you turn your stress into strength.

Tips for Controlling Anger

- *Be a positive reactor.* If someone says something that might be construed as criticism, remember that you are a good person and the comment may just be a way of trying to help. Try to rethink it in a positive light.
- *Avoid accusations and escalations.* If you feel hurt, don't begin a verbal sparring match. Avoid accusations by rephrasing "you hurt me" into "I feel hurt by that statement." Telling people how you feel as opposed to what they did to you sets up the possibility for a positive dialogue instead of creating a negative dialogue that escalates.
- *Practice unconditional affection.* It's easy to be affectionate when someone does something you like. It's important to be affectionate even when someone disappoints you. Remember these words from *The Couple's Tao Te Ching* the next time someone close to you disappoints you.

> When your beloved delights you, you respond with affection—a smile, a hug, a touch of the hand gently on bare skin. But when your beloved disappoints you, can you still respond with affection? Can you still open your arms, hold tenderly, caress healingly, and talk lovingly? This affection is

genuine—it does not depend on the behavior of others. It lies within you at all times.[22]

- *Learn to laugh.* It's tough to stay angry if you laugh. Laughter is a profound physiological response that involves rhythmic motion of the diaphragm, contraction and relaxation of the abdomen and upper torso, even the flow of tears. It touches us at a deep emotional and physical level. It usually is invoked by a twist in our normal perceptions of some event or experience. By its very nature it changes our perception and invites us to look at things in a different light. It shows us that life can be silly, even crazy at times, but it still can be enjoyable.
- *Be empathetic.* Listen to others and try to truly feel what they are saying. If they are angry with you it is very useful to acknowledge what they are saying to you and repeat back a summary and apology. For example, "I understand that you are angry because . . . and I am sorry."

Stress Reliever 12: Be Optimistic

Optimistic people are more able to roll with life's punches and slough off stress—and they live longer. A fascinating study conducted by the Mayo Clinic over a thirty-year period found that subjects who were categorized as pessimistic had a 19 percent greater chance of early death than those who were categorized as optimists.[23] You don't have to be a Pollyanna, but we strongly suggest that you look at the glass as half full rather than half empty. Here are some tips that can help you cultivate this most advantageous trait.

Four Keys to Becoming and Staying Optimistic

1. *Find a role model.* Everyone knows a person who never seems to let things keep him or her down. Rest assured that these people get blue at times, too. They just have the ability to bounce back sooner than most. Seek their advice. Ask what their strategies are. Forget originality here. These are learned behaviors. Learn them.

2. *Create positive self-talk.* We all have a voice inside us that tells us how we are doing, that criticizes and praises. It's an internal friend or parent. Some call it the eternal parent. If you grew up under constant criticism you may have an eternal parent who is still criticizing you. This has definite negative implications for your health and is a self-perpetuating cycle. A recent study from Washington University used a brain scanner to show that the brain releases similar chemicals during negative self-talk and clinical depression, suggesting that you can talk yourself into depression.[24] You can reprogram yourself by speaking to yourself in a positive light. Try this exercise to diagnose and treat your negative self-talk.

- Sit in your healing spot or another quiet place.
- Listen to your internal dialogue. If the first thing you hear is "This is stupid" or "What the heck am I doing?" the chances are that you are a negative self-talker. What other thoughts and emotions drift into your head?
- Feel your body's reactions. Try to see if your body feels something when a particular feeling comes into your head. Does your self-talk calm or stress you?
- Watch for word triggers. Single words or phrases can trigger a chain of thoughts and negative or positive associations.
- Reroute the triggers. If a word triggers a negative association or negative self-talk, immediately think of something positive. Then repeat the word and practice linking it up to the positive association. You will find after several attempts that the positive thought will begin to replace the negative thought. For every negative association immediately repeat out loud "I am a good person" and remember something good you have done for someone. You will find this a powerful technique.

Remember that your thoughts have their biochemical counterparts. They are collections of neurotransmitters and nerve cell connections that can be triggered by electrical stimulation of the brain. In a famous experiment at Montreal's McGill University in the 1930s, stimulation of different brain areas brought back specific memories complete with the original sights, smells, and sounds. The brain is constantly making new connections, but it keeps many old subconscious ones that are not necessarily good for your health. Fill your brain with connections that lead to positive thoughts through positive self-talk. Try these positive statements.

- Things did not go well today, but I will do better tomorrow.
- I am a good person.
- I am an intelligent person.
- I am doing my best to help people.
- He (she) may have treated me badly, but in the long run he is only harming himself. I forgive him.

3. *Look for the positive.* If your initial impression of people is that they are good, then you will be looking for proof of that, rather than proof that they are bad. It's a much healthier starting point and puts you more at ease with people. Everybody has something good about them. Try to find it.
4. *Expect to be happy.* Optimistic people act self-confident and extroverted, expecting to be happy. This kind of behavior creates a positive feedback loop. The Okinawans expect to be happy and healthy—and for the most part they are. If you act happy and gregarious it causes others to perk up, increasing the chances that they will say or do something positive. It causes a chain reaction—pretty soon you have a room full of happy people.

Stress Reliever 13: Learn to Manage Your Time Wisely

Use of time-management techniques such as a daily planner or daily list of "things to do" can be very productive and can relieve stress. Listing what you need to get done, often in order of importance, can make tasks seem less overwhelming and more manageable. And there's a great sense of accomplishment that comes with crossing a completed task off the list. You also reduce your risk of burning yourself out by trying to do too many things at once, which more often than not just results in running around in circles. Finally, good time-management skills entail knowing your limits. Knowing when to say no—that you are just too busy to take on anything else—is a valuable and learned skill.

Stress Reliever 14: Cultivate a Healthy Sense of Humor

In our stress-fighting repertoire of strategies perhaps none is potentially more enjoyable than a good laugh. During laughter, muscles throughout your body tense and relax in a way that is strikingly similar to stress-reduction techniques such as Progressive Relaxation Therapy. Laughter keeps muscles supple as well as relaxed. It also has been shown to stimulate the immune system. Studies conducted at Loma Linda University School of Medicine found that students who watched comedy videos had a significant increase in T-cells and natural disease-killing cells, and lower blood levels of the stress hormone cortisol. Other studies have found that laughter helps release bottled-up feelings of frustration and anger, lessens pain through the release of endorphins, and alters the breathing cycle in a way that increases the amount of oxygen in the system.

Former *Saturday Review* editor Norman Cousins has written extensively on the healing effects of humor. In his best-selling book *Anatomy of an Illness,* he reported how he helped to cure his ankylosing spondylitus, a painful and potentially crippling arthritis, with a combination of mainstream medicine and large doses of laughter.[25] His doctors were amazed when within eight days of watching comedy videos such as *Candid Camera,* the Three Stooges, and the Marx Brothers, his pain began to subside. Eventually he returned to work completely healed, despite the fact that his doctors had given him little chance of recovery.

A sense of humor also contributes to healthy aging. It helps us to cope emotionally with life's inevitable stressors, as well as to deal with physical and psychological pain. In our research on Okinawa's elders we were constantly impressed with the bright and humorful people we encountered. A few standouts: Tabasan, 102 years old, an active Buddhist priest, who playfully lectured a group of age researchers at a conference on longevity science to listen to the real expert—himself! And Tonakisan, who passed away two years ago at the age of 113, and had had a running joke with the examining nurse to whom he always proposed marriage at our yearly visits. He joked that he was living so long only because he was waiting for her to accept his proposal! In research on America's oldest old, humor was referred to as one of centenarians' "most effective self-protective devices . . . a visible and consistent component of their repertoire."[11] We suggest that you make it one of yours, too.

Tips for Getting Laughter into Your Life

- When you read the newspaper, always check out the funnies.
- Buy comedy CDs or cassettes and listen to them on the way to work.
- Buy a joke book and memorize one new joke a day.
- Play with a kitten or puppy.
- Rent a humorous video.
- Find a comedy club in your town.
- Exchange an e-mail joke with a friend.

Stress Reliever 15: Practice Conscious Awareness in Your Daily Life

Finally, it's important to be aware of warning signs of stress by learning to recognize the conditions that cause you *personally* to feel stressed. Consciously note your reactions to various circumstances. Becoming aware of the problem is the first step in dealing with it. Then try the following tips.

- Strive for self-control and an internal center of control. Self-talk is helpful here. Tell yourself that you can handle any situation. Be confident.
- Try to reframe stressful situations in a more positive way. Is there another way of interpreting the problem? Look at that long commute to work as a chance to plan out your day, relax, listen to tapes, or meditate, rather than as a source of frustration.
- If possible, avoid situations that cause you stress. If unavoidable, then try to approach the situation in a different way. Plan it out. Change the context. Don't get caught in a rut.

- Choose nourishing rather than toxic friends. If certain individuals cause you stress, consider whether it is really necessary for them to be part of your life. If they are family members or workmates, try to understand what their motivations are for behaving the way they do. Be prepared to talk to them in a way that does not make them feel that they are being blamed. Work it out by becoming a better listener and communicator.
- Work on your coping skills: Take a time-out when pressure and stress begin to mount. Accept the things you cannot change. Have the courage to change what you can.

There is no better example to follow than that of Uto Naka. One hundred and one years young, she shared her story with us.

> You just never know what life will throw at you. The man I married seemed nice enough before we got married and my parents approved of him, but after we had a few children together he found himself a lover. I rarely saw him after that. I raised five children on my own. What could I do? I worked in the fields and made traditional Okinawan red roofing tiles. It was the family business, you know. Then the war came; I lost both my parents so I had to raise my younger sisters, too. Those days were so tough. I didn't even have time to think that I was having a tough life, though. I just did what I had to. You've got to look on the bright side of things. What's the point of carrying around bitterness and resentment all your life? You pick up and go on. Now I have forty-eight grandchildren, six great-grandchildren, and five great-great-grandchildren. I live with my eldest son and his wife. Life's good! I garden, walk, visit my grandchildren, and go to day care to see my friends. Last year I flew to the mainland to see my great-great-grandchild. It was my first time on an airplane!

We asked her if she had any motto that she lived by. Uto revealed that she had always tried to live by her father's words of wisdom. "My father was a wise man. He told me something that I have tried to follow all my life. He said that you have to learn how and when to let go by picking and choosing your battles carefully. He used to say, 'In the face of typhoon winds, be a swaying palm tree. In the face of castle walls, be a typhoon wind.'"

9. The Healing Web

Shikinoo, chui shiijii, shiru, kurasu.
One cannot live in this world without the support of others.
Okinawan proverb

One day after we had been in Okinawa for a few years, we were walking down a street near the university in Naha with a colleague, Professor Yamaguchi, when we came upon an elderly white-haired woman pushing a wooden cart covered with a tattered blanket. We guessed her to be about eighty-five years old. She was no taller than 4 feet 10 inches and slightly stooped, but she still looked wiry and sprite. She called to us and pulled back the blanket to reveal a number of packages of *mochi* (rice with sweet beans inside). "Won't you buy some?" she asked us. "Three hundred and fifty yen. Special price today." Our companion, Professor Yamaguchi, pulled out a 500-yen coin, bought one of the packets from the old lady, and said, "Grandmother, keep the change." Her eyes sparkled as she grinned and thanked us. As we walked on, Professor Yamaguchi handed us the package. "Here you go, guys. Have some *mochi.*" We expressed our thanks and commented that the package didn't appear too fresh. He chuckled and said, "I often see that old woman pushing her cart up and down the street. I don't imagine that her goods are ever very fresh!" *Yuimaru?* we conjectured. Professor Yamaguchi laughed heartily, turned to us and said, "So, you are finally beginning to understand our Okinawan culture!"

Yuimaru *In Okinawa*

Yuimaru is a typically Okinawan concept that exemplifies the spirit behind the kind of social networks that nourish and heal us—the kind that we call *healing webs. Yuimaru* is the practice of sharing and helping others that was developed long ago in Okinawa's farm communities and rural villages, and is still part of the fabric of the Okinawan culture today. The word itself literally means "connecting circle" and originally referred to the reciprocal work arrangements among Okinawan villagers in times when a group effort was needed—when building homes, harvesting crops, and the like. The whole village would work together to accomplish whatever task happened to be at hand. In farming communities, when one family's fields were harvested, that family would help harvest the next neighbor's fields, and so on down the line until everyone's crops were in and the job was done. In essence, it was a joining of fellow villagers, friends, and neighbors who circled or rotated their reciprocal exchanges of favors and obligations to one another. *Yuimaru* was the glue that held these villages together.

Today in Okinawa, *yuimaru* is manifested in more subtle ways. People, especially older people in villages, simply look out for one another and offer help almost by instinct. It's an important contributing factor to their healthy (disability-free) longevity. It enables the elderly to go about their daily lives while still living in the community, even if they are slowing down a little. One story told to us by a northern Okinawan villager paints a very clear picture of the way this can work. An older woman and her husband had been running a little mom-and-pop store in the village for years. The husband passed on and the woman got old. The stock was low in her store and the goods a little stale, but people still bought from her anyway. Sometimes they didn't even eat what they bought. But they would stop by to chat with her, buy a little something, check up on her. In that way she continued with her work and her life, and still felt like a necessary part of the community. "That's the way," explained the villager, "that *yuimaru* lives on in our hearts today."

Stories like this abound in Okinawa. The *yuimaru* spirit is still alive and well as a kind of "help thy neighbor" attitude. When we got back to the university with Professor Yamaguchi's generous gift of the old woman's *mochi*, we opened up the package and sure enough it was not all that fresh. We peeled off the top parts of the rice that had been hardened through exposure to the air and ate the part with the sweet beans. It was actually rather tasty. We have no doubt that part of the reason for its good taste was that little bit of *yuimaru* spirit contained within.

After all is said and done, we need each other. The friends, loved ones, relatives, and acquaintances who make up our social network and community are essential to our well-being. A sense of belonging and connection to other people helps keep us healthy, increases our longevity, and makes us feel happier and more fulfilled. This is not especially revelatory news. We've always felt it in our hearts. The difference today is that there is plenty of scientific evidence to back it up.

A huge body of research has accumulated since the father of modern sociology, Emile Durkheim, carried out the first major scientific research linking social relationships and health in 1897 and subsequently discovered that less socially integrated individuals were more likely to commit suicide.[1] Study after study has shown how strong social relationships contribute to our peace of mind, counteract some of the ill effects of stress, ward off isolation—a major risk factor for mortality—and help speed recovery from psychological and physical illness.

In fact, there's strong evidence that social ties actually help protect us from a wide range of illnesses, including heart disease, depression, alcoholism, tuberculosis, arthritis, schizophrenia—maybe even the common cold. In one study that was reported in the *Journal of the American Medical Association,* researchers exposed 276 healthy volunteers to a cold virus and found that the volunteers with the most diverse social networks were the most disease resistant. Only 35 percent of those with six or more close relationships actually caught the cold, compared with 62 percent of those with three social relationships or fewer. And differences in the overall health or health habits of the volunteers could not explain away the findings.[2]

Conversely, we suffer significant negative physical effects when we are suddenly cut off from close social ties. Studies consistently show higher death rates for recently widowed spouses, especially men. Research also reveals that married people in general suffer fewer health problems than single people, and that divorce and other relationship problems can compromise immune system function.[3]

The Miraculous Power of Companionship

In the course of our research we visited a nursing home which was the residence of a blind centenarian woman named Ushisan. She had lost her eyesight a few years earlier, and because she had no family to take care of her she had moved into the elderly care facility. Dr. Suzuki had checked her and found her to be healthy despite the fact that she was blind. Yet she was nervous and easily upset because of her lack of sight and could hardly be examined. About a year after our visit, Dr. Suzuki heard from a local journalist that Ushisan had miraculously regained her eyesight, and immediately scheduled another visit to reexamine her.

Upon meeting her again—she was then 101—Dr. Suzuki found that she indeed could see! According to the medical record of our previous exam the year before, only a small reaction to light was observed in her left eye. But this time, even though there was a cataract on her right eye, both of her eyes reacted to light normally. We went over all the possibilities for this seemingly miraculous recovery, which, not surprisingly, was creating quite a stir in the local press. Could the cataract on her left eye have somehow become naturally detached? Not likely, since cataracts do not naturally dislodge, and neither the nursing staff nor Ushisan could recall a sudden return of her eyesight. It had happened more gradually. Moreover, she had put on weight and the color of her complexion was better than it had been on our last visit.

We were all mystified by this vast improvement in Ushisan's eyesight—indeed, in her entire physical condition. Then Dr. Suzuki asked whether there had been any change in her environment, and at last we had the lead we were looking for. It turned out she had changed rooms about two months previously and had acquired a new roommate. Since that time, the nurses told us, "she has been like a completely different person, eating more, socializing more, and then her eyesight returned!" They attributed "the miracle" to the joy of making this new friend. As scientists we are skeptical of so-called miracles but certainly good relationships seem to have miraculous effects at times. And there can be no better example of the power of the healing web.

While Ushisan's story is one of the most dramatic we've heard, it's by no means the only one. Several high-quality epidemiological studies have come to be considered classics in the field. Let's outline a few of them.

- In 1965, Harvard epidemiologist Dr. Lisa Berkman began a study of close to seven thousand men and women living in Alameda County, California. What this groundbreaking study found was that those who lacked social and community ties (as defined by contact with friends and relatives, marriage status, or membership in church or other social groups) were two to three times more likely to die in the nine-year follow-up period (1965–1974) than those who were more socially connected, regardless of their age, gender, health practices, or physical health status. Most surprising of all was the finding that those with close social ties and unhealthful lifestyles actually lived longer than those with poor social ties but more healthful living habits. Of course, those persons who had both healthful lifestyles and close social ties lived the longest.[4]
- In Evans County, Georgia, over two thousand people were followed in a study using a questionnaire similar to the one used in the Alameda Study. Scientists found that men who were married, had close contacts with extended family and friends, and had strong group affiliations such as church membership had lower mortality rates in the follow-up period eleven to thirteen years later.[5]
- In the Tecumseh Community Health Study, almost three thousand men and women were studied for nine to twelve years. Men with fewer social connections as measured by number of friends, closeness of feelings toward relatives, participation in group activities, and so on were found to suffer from two to three times the disease rates of men with stronger social ties in the ten- to twelve-year follow-up period. Higher levels of heart disease, stroke, cancer, and lung disease were reported that were unrelated to age, occupation, or prior health status.[6]
- In a study of elderly men and women from three community-based groups in East Boston, New Haven,

and rural Iowa over a five-year period, those with no social ties had two to three times the risk of mortality found among those with at least four social ties.[7]

- In Sweden, more than 17,000 men and women between the ages of twenty-nine and seventy-four were studied for six years. Those persons who were most socially isolated were almost four times more likely to die prematurely during this period. Controlling for other factors such as age and health behavior or prior health status did not change the results.[8]

And other major studies have reported similar findings. The message is clear: we need social relationships to truly thrive. In fact, in 1988 the esteemed journal *Science* published a paper by House, Landis, and Umberson that reviewed the evidence tying social relationships to health; the researchers concluded that it is even stronger than the evidence that relates Type A behavior to coronary heart disease, and at least equal to the evidence that led the surgeon general to issue his warning that cigarette smoking can cause cancer.[9] That's enough evidence to make anybody a believer.

Other Benefits of Social Support

The most obvious benefit of social relationships is companionship. Isolation is as hazardous to our health as it was for Ushisan's. But social support also promotes health in a number of other ways. For one, it can help us obtain faster or better medical services.[10] Spouses, for instance, often prod us to seek medical attention sooner than we might otherwise. And most of us, at one time or another, have received doctor referrals from a friend and know how valuable this can be. Trying to track down a good specialist—especially when you really need one—can be incredibly time-consuming and frustrating. A recommendation from a friend who knows, trusts, and has a good relationship with a particular medical professional can be worth its weight in gold.

People in our social networks can also introduce us to disease-specific support groups and mentoring programs that can be invaluable to our psychological well-being as well as our physical health. Moreover, if we are ever in an emergency situation where we are incapacitated and incapable of being our own best medical advocate, it can be life-saving to have a friend or loved one stand in and speak up for us when dealing with hospital and medical red tape. Facing an illness without social support is, at the very least, difficult.

Social networks can also be a great support in health-promoting behavior such as quitting smoking or drinking, or joining a regular exercise group. Biking, running, hiking, and other healthy activities are usually more enjoyable when done with comrades. One of the main attractions of twelve-step programs, such as Alcoholics Anonymous or Alanon, is group support. In fact, it's an incredibly important factor in the success of the programs. People who have tried to stop self-destructive behavior on their own and failed often succeed when buoyed by their fellows.

Biologically, social support seems to buffer the effect of stress by lowering the production of epinephrine, norepinephrine, and cortisol, the hormones that are produced in our bodies when we feel threatened or scared. As we have mentioned, the overproduction of these hormones can weaken our immune systems over time and leave us more susceptible to disease. By keeping the production of these bodily chemicals in check, social support actually helps us stay physiologically healthier. Stress studies, in fact, have shown that people who perform stressful tasks with a friend have lower heart rates and blood pressure than people who go it alone.[11]

The Moai And Health

Moai is another Okinawan cultural institution that could be of great inspiration to us in the West. Moai can be translated to mean "meeting for a common purpose." Essentially, a moai is a group of friends, relatives, workmates, or cohorts that get together regularly for purposes of reciprocal support. The support is at once financial, emotional, and social. When a moai is first formed, everyone agrees on a certain amount of money to be brought to each meeting by each member—say, twenty dollars. If there were ten members of the group, then the collected total for any particular meeting would be $200. At each meeting, one of the members (whoever needs it most) receives that $200. When each member has had his or her turn as recipient, the process starts anew. *Moai,* which have been referred to as "the people's banks," are not formed indiscriminately. The members always have something in common. They might work in the same occupation, or be old school chums, childhood friends, relatives, or from the same hometown.

But handy as they are monetarily, *moai* are much more than just mutual financial aid co-ops. The average person enters into a *moai* more for the social aspects than the financial ones. Okinawans like them for the camaraderie and contact they provide for people who have gone through similar experiences at similar stages of life. *Moai* are like natural "social support convoys" that follow one throughout one's life. Although some members may drop out and others may be added, a *moai* member always has a convoy of support to help in times of need, offer guidance, and share life experiences. When we were in Miyako, a small island in the Ryukyu archipelago, we interviewed the members of a *moai* that had been meeting regularly for over eighty years. They were a group of former elementary school pals, now all eighty-eight years old. After more than eighty years they were still keeping in contact with one another through their *moai!*

The Wisdom of the Elders: The Origins of Yuimaru and Moai

Moai, like *yuimaru,* came out of the village mentality steeped in social obligation and group responsibility. Originally, *moai* were formed to pool the material resources of the village for particular projects or occasions such as preparing a funeral ceremony, paying taxes, or constructing housing. For hundreds of years in Okinawa, the village was the social space where one was born, lived, and died. The average person rarely ventured beyond the confines of the village. The village was also the tax unit. Cultivated land was held as common property. If a household was unable to produce its full share of the village tax assessment, the other villagers made up the difference. The community as a whole accepted the obligation to meet the shortcomings of individual members. This system of mutual obligations fostered a deep sense of social obligation and group responsibility in maintaining the welfare of community members suffering hardship. Interdependence and cooperation were necessary for one's very survival. The system of accepted mutual obligations has left its historical stamp on modern Okinawan society in the form of *moai* as well as *yuimaru*. These are cultural institutions that have adapted and survived. In fact, *moai* are thriving. Over 50 percent of all Okinawans—young and old—participate in a *moai*. Most are in more than one. Being a member of five, six, seven, or eight *moai* is not uncommon.

In North America the *moai* spirit can be seen in co-ops, church groups, charities, Rotary clubs, and other organizations that operate on principles of mutual support. Wedding and baby showers, where women gather together to offer practical gifts that are meant to help a friend glide easily into the next cycle of her life, may feel like a party, but in essence they are subtle and winning forms of social support.

Can We Have Too Much Social Support?

In a word, yes—if it's the wrong kind. For any kind of social support to be beneficial it has to be appropriate and needed. Unwanted or unneeded support is, in fact, sometimes more detrimental than no support at all. It can alienate the person you are trying to aid and leave that person helpless to take care of himself or herself—even when your help is offered with the best of intentions. Unwanted assistance causes people to lose faith in themselves and their abilities, and the less faith they have in themselves, the less they can do for themselves. This holds true for people of all ages and for all endeavors, from sports to basic thinking and reasoning.

Social support from questionable groups can also be a problem. Certainly the reason many teens join gangs or people join cults is the desire to belong—to be a part of a social group. The instinct is natural and healthy, but the choice of the particular group is faulty. There's also a danger of over-reliance on group support, which can diminish feelings of autonomy or self-respect. The lesson here is that social support is incredibly important, but we have to be both discriminating and compassionate to make it work for ourselves and for others. All support must be properly suited to the person to whom it is being offered.

Taira Hiro's Story

Taira Hiro's story is a good example of too much support being offered. If not for her strong will and determination, she might have been negatively affected by well-intentioned but misdirected support. At the age of ninety-seven, Hirosan fell and broke her hip, and was hospitalized. "Everyone was telling me to take it easy. Just lie back and rest," she recalls. "They told me that I was old and that my bones would take a long time to heal, and that I would probably never walk again. I guess they meant well but after a while I couldn't take it anymore. Once you give up in one of those places [the hospital] you're done for. I made sure that I dragged myself around the ward every day and visited with the ladies a few floors up from me. People scolded me at first, but they eventually relented and let me carry on. When I walked home with just a walking stick, everyone in the hospital was amazed, but I just did what I had to do . . . In the end, it was they who all came to receive *ayakaru* [good fortune] from me!"

Maintaining Independence in the Healing Web

When we interviewed Hirosan she was 102 and still going strong. She was well known in her community, still went for her daily walks, and was fond of saying "to rest is to rust." Kame Nakasone, another strong-willed woman, is nine years her junior. Kamesan has farmed sugarcane for most of her life. Recently, at ninety-three, she has begun to think about switching to chrysanthemums. "Easier to grow and more of a market for them," she explains. Small in stature, she wouldn't quite reach five feet even if she wore heels, which, of course, she doesn't. She prefers rubber boots. "They keep the *habu* [poisonous snakes] away," she says with conviction.

Kamesan lives by herself in her own home. Her husband passed away four years ago, but even so, she has resisted moving in with any of her children who live in the city. "If I left who would take care of the farm?" she asks. "And what would I do there? All of my friends are here. We have fun together, eating, drinking, and dancing. And we look out for each other. I also have a granddaughter who lives close by and twelve grandchildren and sixteen great-grandchildren who live throughout Okinawa and the mainland, so there's always someone coming to visit." Kamesan allows that she is way too busy to ever be lonely.

Kamesan is typical of rural elderly Okinawan women. Even when their husbands pass away first (the usual pattern) and they are living alone, it is hard to get them to pack up and move in with their children, even when their children insist upon it. This is due to the fact that rural Okinawan women are deeply embedded in community life, and despite not living with their families, they still maintain close ties with family and friends. They just like to stay put and prefer to have their children and grandchildren (or great-grandchildren) come to them. A sense of belonging and being necessary to the community, as well as the support they receive from their families, neighbors, and friendship networks, keeps them independent—or "aging in place," as gerontologists call it. And as we discovered, many of these older women are quite an autonomous bunch.

When polled in social surveys, older women in Okinawa score particularly high in "attitudes toward autonomous living" when compared with their counterparts in mainland Japan.[12] These women almost always participate in activities that lead to a sense of self-accomplishment—a trend, incidentally, that is catching on among older women throughout Japan as a whole. Elderly Okinawan women, though, are leading the way. They manage their own households, control their own finances, and interact daily with friends or kin. Most of them live close to female relatives of similar ages, such as sisters or cousins, whom they visit on a daily basis. They are active, prefer to be outside rather than indoors, and are always on the go.

For most Okinawan elderly women, widowhood is not perceived as a time of misery; rather, it is a time for independence. It is a life stage that most women go through in their late seventies or early eighties. Since women outlive men in Okinawa by an average of eight years—and usually marry men a few years older than themselves to start—the average Okinawan woman has approximately fifteen or more years of widowhood. Their strong social connectedness helps to buffer them from the adverse effects of stressful life events, such as the loss of a husband and the accompanying sense of loneliness or isolation. The freedom enjoyed by elderly Okinawan women comes not only from their autonomous living patterns but also from the social safety net provided by the Japanese social welfare system. They're offered excellent medical care and welfare benefits at little cost. Elder day care involves such services as baths, physical rehabilitation, recreational activities, a nice lunch, and a lot of opportunity for socializing—all for little or no charge. Strong women's social networks, and the sense of belonging that comes with being the main repositories of ritual knowledge of both community and kin, are a winning combination for keeping them tightly integrated into community life.

In the Okinawan language there is no equivalent word for "retirement," nor has there traditionally been an *inkyo* (retirement) system such as seen in mainland Japan. Although they may gradually decrease their workloads, older villagers mostly just keep doing what they have been doing all their lives—working in their gardens, meeting their lifelong friends or relatives at *moai,* or participating in community, family, and household rituals. And these days, they might also go to a senior citizens' center, where they can play croquet, socialize, or practice singing, dancing, and other traditional arts.

Social Support Networks And The Oldest-Old

When Dr. Suzuki first began the Okinawa Centenarian Study some twenty-five years ago, there were few centenarians anywhere in the world, including Okinawa. At that time there were only a couple of dozen people in Okinawa over a hundred years old. Most of them lived with their families, were in robust health, and were regarded as the pride of their families and "living treasures." Today while there are more centenarians—over 400—many of them no longer live with their families. Urbanization and the exodus of younger people to the cities have strained familial support networks and left many of Okinawa's oldest-old living in communities that are older, rural, and depopulated. It is here especially that the social institutions of *yui-maru* and *moai* have helped fill in the support gap for the oldest-old.

Our studies show that many have lifelong friends, are quite active and gregarious, and bask in the warmth of their active social lives. The majority of the oldest-old report the presence of at least one very close friend, and most of those who live in communities have maintained their friendships over the length of their lives. They have surprisingly active friendship networks considering their extreme ages. And many centenarians have a passion or purpose that brings them regularly in contact with others—one raises bulls for traditional Okinawan bullfights, another teaches folk music, and another is a full-time Buddhist priest. It is friends and networks, and interests and passions, that help us reach a healthy old age. If you don't have these ingredients in your life at this time, first take comfort in the fact that you're not alone—the Mayo Clinic tells us that nearly half of all Americans report that they don't have enough close relationships.[13] Then make some changes. It is never too late— or too early—to find new interests and gather and cultivate new friendships. Wherever you are in your life, now is the right time to create a healing web.

Answer the following questionnaire to see where you stand in terms of your support network. The questionnaire, from the Mayo Clinic, is designed to give you a good idea of the strength of your social support system based on three important categories: confidants, social and special interest friends, and material supporters. Once you ascertain how you stand, read on for advice on how to improve your healing web.

Assessing Your Social Support

Check off each statement that applies to you.

1. If I wanted to go on a day trip to the country or mountains I could easily find someone to go with me.
2. There is someone with whom I can share my most private worries and fears.
3. If I were sick, I could easily find someone to help me with my daily chores.
4. There is someone I can turn to for advice about handling family problems.

5. If I decide one afternoon that I would like to go to a movie that evening, I could easily find someone to go with me.
6. When I need suggestions on how to deal with a personal problem, I know someone I can turn to.
7. I often get invited to do things with others.
8. If I had to go out of town for a few weeks, it would not be difficult to find someone to look after my house or apartment.
9. If I wanted to have lunch with someone, I could easily find someone to join me.
10. If I were stranded ten miles from home, there is someone I could call who would come and get me.
11. If a family crisis arose, it would be easy for me to find someone who could give me good advice how to handle it.
12. If I needed some help moving to a new location, it would be easy to find someone to help me.

Add up your totals: Each check equals one point. (For a more in-depth analysis, go to *www.mayohealth.org* and type in the search term *social support*.)

11–12 points: You have high levels of social support.

9–10 points: You have moderate levels of social support.

8 points or lower: Your healing web could use some patching.

Even if you checked off each statement, think about how you can improve your healing web. We all can stand to strengthen our social relationships and make them more satisfying—our health depends on it!

Strategies For Strengthening Your Healing Web

Start with Your Immediate Family

If you want to live a long, healthy life, "looking out for number one" can no longer be the creed of the day. That sort of sentiment went out with the last century. This is a new millennium and with it should come a full awareness of family support as a factor for enhancing longevity. As reported earlier, research consistently shows that those who are married live longer and report higher levels of well-being and life satisfaction than their single counterparts. A happy marriage is associated with decreased stress levels, less psychological difficulties, lower suicide rates, and less alcoholism, as well as decreased risk of early death. Of course, it is not the institution of marriage itself that results in these health benefits, but the mutual support that is found within the bounds of the marriage relationship. The same type of support can be found in other caring relationships.

With this in mind it only makes sense to make family (or your special close relationship) the first priority. The Okinawans highly value marriage, family life, and children—and they live extraordinarily long, healthy lives. Establish your own family and nurture it. Make it a priority. Sound simple? It's not. Both North America and Japan are seeing increasingly higher divorce rates. Even young Okinawans have high divorce rates despite the value placed on family life by the elders. Part of the reason for increasing divorce rates around the globe is that for many people family time is what is left over after everything else has been taken care of. This needs to change. Pencil family time into your schedule, make it a priority, and stick to it. There are many ways to strengthen family bonds. Here are some that we have found to be particularly helpful.

- *Establish a family assembly.* Set up a regular time, once or twice a week, for family members to get together to discuss conflicts, problems, or other matters that concern the family. Be open to discussion about any issue that might affect the family members—school problems, relocation problems if you've recently moved, or kudos for a job well done.
- *Develop family traditions.* Make it a special point to celebrate holidays, birthdays, and anniversaries together. Engage in family sports, prayers before mealtime, bedtime stories, a regular chat time, or after-dinner strolls. These kinds of activities when performed regularly can develop into

family traditions that have a special meaning for all family members.

- *Eat together.* Often mealtimes are the only time the whole family gets together in a day. Try to minimize distractions and promote conversation by shutting off the television during meals. Instead, put on some soothing music and talk about the day's events and future plans.
- *Give your child a pet.* This not only offers a valuable lesson for children in responsibility, but pets are also a powerful source of social connectedness through the emotional bonding that takes place between humans and animals.

Join (or Establish) a Self-Help Group

Not everyone has a family to turn to in times of need. Occasionally family relations are the most painful source of conflict in a person's life. If that's true for you, you can supplement what may be lacking in your regular social support network with a self-help group composed of other people in similar stressful situations. Outside support groups are especially helpful during difficult life transitions. Alcoholics Anonymous is one model, but there are literally thousands of self-help support groups in North America that meet practically any need you may have. If you or someone you love needs support, consider contacting the National Self-Help Clearinghouse, an American nonprofit organization founded in 1976 to facilitate access to self-help groups. The clearinghouse provides referrals to regional self-help groups and information about how to form your own self-help group if there isn't one in your area. They can advise you on whom to get in touch with for concerns about almost any situation, including medical treatment, dealing with addictions and other mental-health issues, elder care, infant care, human rights issues, and so on. They can be contacted at *www.selfhelpweb.org.* Or for a small fee you can purchase their *Self-Help Sourcebook,* which includes a listing of all national groups and clearinghouses. Similar organization exist in many countries throughout the world.

Also, try checking the telephone directory of your city or town or search online. Your local community center should have information on social support groups and services as well. You will be surprised at the number and variety of programs and groups available. If you are feeling a certain need, then most likely someone else somewhere close by is feeling the same way, too. Seek them out. If still not sure where to start, then talk to a caring professional such as your local priest, minister, rabbi, or doctor for advice about supportive groups.

Be a Joiner—Get the Moai Spirit

Reach out and connect to other people by joining a club, a choir, a political group, or a social cause. Think about what it really is that interests you and then get involved. It's a wonderfully freeing feeling to know that you can meet new friends with similar interests whenever you want to. If you are into the environment, then join your local chapter of the Sierra Club or the Audubon Society, or any of the numerous other eco-groups. Interested in chess, finance, antique cars, or coin collecting? There is a club for you. Does your passion lie in the arts? Join a theater club, a writers' workshop, a photography club, a painting or a film class. Whatever your interests, there are groups out there with other like-minded people just waiting to meet you. Getting active and involved in areas that spark your imagination is a wonderful way to get out of your house, meet new people, and grow and expand your horizons. Information or advice on clubs can be obtained from family, friends, or workmates, the phone book, the Internet, your community association bulletin board, church, university or community college, local board of education, and newspapers.

Take Up a Sport

Taking up sports is one of the healthiest things you can do for yourself. It not only widens your social network but improves your physical and mental health at the same time. There are, of course, a vast variety of sports to choose from. There are organized team sports such as baseball, ice hockey, soccer, and basketball, as well as individual social sports such as tennis, racquet ball, squash, and golf, most of which have a local club where you can drop in and participate. And then there are sports clubs for biking, skiing, running, hiking, mountain climbing, kayaking, and just about any other sport you can think of. There are also classes in everything from modern dance and Pilates to tae bo and karate. No matter what sport or physical activity you choose to get involved in, there will be plenty of people exactly at your level—whether you are a rank beginner or a seasoned pro. You can't go wrong taking this route. At the very least, join a gym or sports club near you and take a tai chi, martial arts, exercise, or aerobics class.

Become a Volunteer

Volunteering is one of the most gratifying experiences there is. It simply feels good to help other people—to be of service. There are countless organizations that need your help: animal pounds, homeless shelters, crisis centers, low-income education projects. The list is endless. But there's another side to helping those less fortunate than yourself besides pure altruism. You just might be making yourself healthier in the process. Studies show that people who help other people are consistently in better health and are more able to overcome life-threatening crises and diseases.[14] It's a win-win situation. So choose a cause that is close to your heart and volunteer. Participate in Meals on Wheels, become a Big Brother/Big Sister, or help with forest conservation. The rewards to your spirit will far outweigh the time you invest. To make contact with an appropriate volunteer organization search online or look in the yellow pages under "volunteer organizations." On the Internet, *www.volunteermatch.org* is devoted to helping individuals find volunteer opportunities posted by local nonprofit and public sector organizations.

Join Your Local Community Association

The old maxim "Think globally—act locally" still rings true. Community associations are nothing more than your fellow community members working together for the good of your community. Sure, things can get political or factional at times. That is the nature of human groups. Nevertheless, communities cannot operate without the input of people of the community. They are the contexts where successful aging takes place.

Get Involved in Your Spiritual Community

Your religious denomination most likely has a chapter located near you. Get involved with their study groups, classes, and clubs. If not a follower of traditional religious faiths, seek out other groups that are more along the lines of your philosophical belief system. You may want to read a few books on spirituality, such as *The Art of Happiness* by the Dalai Lama, for inspiration.[15] Classes or workshops in the area of personal growth, meditation, or other avenues to greater spiritual growth should also be available in or near your community. Check out your local community college or board of continuing education or your local health food store bulletin board for further information.

Reach Out to Someone Today

Extend yourself. Expand your social network by reaching out and inviting an acquaintance or neighbor for a cup of coffee or a drink—the person may end up being your next best friend. Reconcile with an estranged friend or family member. Be the first to apologize and tell that person how much you need him or her in your life. You might be pleasantly surprised to hear the reaction.

A Final Story Of The Healing Web

When we went to interview Nakasan, he was hard at work in the fields. At almost ninety years old, he still makes raw sugar from sugarcane the traditional Okinawan way. As we stood talking, his wife and a younger man fed long stalks of cane into a machine that crushed it and squeezed the juice out. When we asked the age of their son, Nakasan told us he had no idea. The young man was in no way related to them. He was simply a helpful stranger. Can there be a better example of the *yuimaru* spirit? The younger man's selfless assistance and the older couple's relaxed attitude toward accepting it is human interaction at its best. People helping people. It's at the core of human existence, and it's something we all need to practice in our daily lives—for our health, and the health of society.

10. Four Weeks to Everlasting Health

The Way does not strive, and yet it overcomes.
It does not speak, and yet it is answered.
It does not ask, yet it is supplied with all its needs.
It seems at ease, and yet it follows a plan.

Tao Te Ching

You now have the tools, essence, and spirit of the Okinawa Program, and you're ready to put them all together into a simple, practical, workable plan. Our Turnaround Plan, a four-week integrative program, is a holistic interpretation of the program. We've interpreted the wisdom of the elders and adapted it into an easy-to-follow lifestyle plan geared to help you maintain a healthy body weight, slow down the ravages of time, and increase your energy. With this plan, we'll guide you step-by-step to everlasting health and a new feeling of vitality and wellness.

It's important to note that this is a graduated healing prescription and is meant to be flexible, so stick as close as you can to the plan, but don't be hard on yourself if there's any part that you cannot do "on time." Remember that it is not about accomplishing more in less time, but rather about focusing on your journey. Simply adopt as much as you can at the pace that is comfortable for you. You'll find that each week integrates a few more simple, healthy lifestyle changes into your eating and fitness habits, and spiritual and health practices. By week four you will be well on your way to a new life. So why wait any longer—let's get started!

The Okinawa Program Pantry

Essential Staples

Condiments, Oils

Nonstick canola oil spray
Olive oil spray
Cold-pressed extra-virgin olive and canola oils
Sea salt
Brown sugar
Balsamic vinegar
Sake rice wine
Arrowroot (kudzu) powder, available at most health food stores, to use as thickener
Turmeric and/or curry powder
Green tea
Jasmine tea
Black tea
Oolong tea
Bonito broth powder *(hon-dashi),* available at most health food stores, Asian food stores and websites (see Appendix B)
Shichimi seven-spice chili powder, such as S&B's Shichimi Togarashi, available at most Asian food stores and websites (see Appendix B)
Nori dried seaweed sheets and wakame dried seaweed flakes, available at most health food stores, Asian food stores and websites (see Appendix B)

Grains, Beans, and Nuts

Brown rice
Short- or long-grain white rice
Whole-grain flour
Soy flour
All-purpose (plain), unbleached wheat flour
Whole wheat dried pasta
Walnuts and almonds (unsalted or low-sodium)
Low-sodium soy nuts

Various dried or canned beans, such as soybeans, broad beans, garbanzo beans (chickpeas), pinto beans, kidney beans

Japanese dried udon wheat noodles (white, thick), available at most health food stores, Asian food stores, or Japanese food websites (see Appendix B)

Japanese somen noodles (white, thin), available at most health food stores, Asian food stores, or Japanese food websites (see Appendix B)

Japanese dried soba buckwheat noodles (gray, thin), available at most health food stores, Asian food stores, or Japanese food websites (see Appendix B)

Prepared, Ready-to-Eat Healthy Foods

Various fat-free bean soup-in-cups, such as Health Valley's fat-free Black Bean Soup, Lentil Soup, Split Pea Soup

Various fat-free soup-in-cans, such as Health Valley's fat-free 14 Garden Vegetable Soup, Tomato Soup, Chicken Broth, Beef Flavored Broth, Vegetable Broth, Vegetarian Chili Beans

Instant miso soup in small bags

Healthy cereals, such as flax cereals, soy cereals, oat bran flakes, fat-free granola

Buy as Needed

Firm, extra-firm, or silken lite tofu in tab container

Lite soy milk, nonflavored or vanilla

Low-sodium miso, preferably white

Lite soy sauce, such as Kikkoman's Lite Soy Sauce

Low-trans margarine

Hummus

Onions

Garlic

Calcium-fortified orange juice

Eggs, omega-3 or free-range

Useful Kitchenware

A rice cooker

A wok

Chopsticks

Coffee grinder for grinding flaxseed

Note: We hesitated to provide brand names in this book because we do not endorse any particular product or brand, but we have found that it can be very difficult to choose health-promoting foods when many companies are using the words "low-fat," "light," "healthy choice," or other terms when their products may not be particularly wholesome. Certain companies provide excellent and consistently "wellness-promoting" products. We have therefore included some prepared foods, a limited number of the more widely available brand-name products that we consider compatible with the Okinawa Program. We have also included a number of websites in Appendix B that are evidence-based resources for bettering your health and also can help guide you on your journey toward everlasting health.

The Four-Week Turnaround Plan

Making dietary changes can be difficult, especially if the changes consist of entirely unfamiliar foods, spices, or eating styles. Miso soup, rice, vegetables, and fish, for instance, is common breakfast fare in Okinawa, but most Westerners would balk at the idea of eating that combination as the first meal of the day—if, indeed, at all.

So with that in mind, we've created two specific dietary tracks for you here.[1] The first one is more in keeping with traditional Western cuisine, though we do incorporate a few Asian elements over the four-week plan to gently nudge you toward the Okinawan way of eating. (Personal growth, after all, is about being open-minded and willing to consider alternatives.) The second track is very close to the East-West fusion cooking of Okinawa. It's designed for those of you who are already fans of Asian cooking, or are culinary adventurers who want to try something new, different—and, need we say, delicious.

Whichever track you follow will put you on the right path. Simply follow the one that most suits your tastes and sensibilities. You can also choose foods or meals from either track on a daily basis, or alternate the tracks weekly, following the East-West one week and the Western the next. Any way you do it will work as long as you follow the general guidelines. We also provide the Okinawa Program Nutrition Tracker in Appendix A (page 486) to help you calculate your nutritional requirements, examine your eating habits, and watch your progress.

First, congratulate yourself for taking this first step toward everlasting health. It takes courage to try new approaches. No spiritual growth or physical improvement is possible without effort. But know that this is a challenge that can absolutely be met. If you commit yourself, there is nothing that can hold you back. We guarantee the feeling of satisfaction, good health, and positive energy will be worth all your efforts.

Sundays are a good time to study this weekly guide, formulate a schedule based on the suggestions, and pencil it into your daily planner. If you don't have a daily planner, this is the perfect time to get one. It can double as a journal in which you track your thoughts and feelings as you progress through the program. It might help to make a copy of each new week's prescriptions, and place it in a visible location as a reminder of your commitment to a better and healthier life. Next step—preparations. You'll need to get your kitchen stocked, and your cooking, fitness, and spiritual accoutrements ready for their debut. Here's what to do.

- Clean up the kitchen. Eliminate all cooking oils except cold-pressed, extra-virgin olive oil and canola oil. Toss out all butter, margarines, and vegetable shortenings, except margarines that are *extremely* low in trans fatty acids, such as Benecol and Take Control. (Low levels of trans are 0.5 gram per serving or less.)
- Check to see if your local grocery has a good Asian section. Also try to locate a good health or Asian food store in your area. Refer to the yellow pages, or ask friends or the managers of your local Asian restaurants. (Also see Appendix B for a list of websites.)
- Check to make sure you have a wok or deep skillet. If not, buy a stainless-steel wok. Look for nonstick varieties, which allow for less oil use, and try to avoid aluminum, since there are still some questions about its health implications.

- Buy or borrow a blender (or food processor) and an electric rice cooker, which makes hassle-free, perfectly cooked rice. Just put in the rice and water, close the lid, and turn it on. Electric cookers have autosensors that detect when the rice is ready and switch the temperature to warm mode automatically. Look for styles with a simple cook/warm switch and avoid the fancy computerized timers. Good brands include National and Zojirushi. Microwave rice cookers are also good.
- Make sure you have a good pair of walking shoes.
- Buy a weight scale that also calculates body fat. (The Tanita body fat scale is excellent and available in most sporting goods stores or online.) Remember to weigh yourself naked (or in the same clothes) at the same time of day no more than twice a week. Measurements on these scales can vary as much as 10 percent during the day and depend on many factors. Don't get hung up on too frequent weigh-ins or taking too many body fat measurements. Look for long-term trends (weekly or monthly) and be consistent.
- Buy a notebook for a fitness/wellness diary to record your thoughts, feelings, and accomplishments daily. Write down your goals. If your goal is healthy weight loss, follow the calorie guide for your activity level on page 488, and aim for 500 calories a day less than you need. Over seven days you will drop a pound of fat (not water). If you lose more than two pounds per week, it's likely water and muscle loss, both of which your body needs.
- Go over the Okinawa Program Pantry list, and start stocking up on the basic herbs, spices, and condiments. Also select some low-calorie snacks (see Appendix A, page 483) and buy enough for one week.
- When following the menus for the Four-Week Turn-around Plan, remember to add liberal amounts of vegetables to pastas, sandwiches, and wraps; use low-calorie or fat-free tomato-based sauces; and use omega-3 eggs whenever possible.

WESTERN TRACK

MONDAY

Breakfast

2 toaster waffles (preferably whole-grain, Flax-plus, or Soy-plus)
1 tbs. trans-free margarine
1 tbs. maple syrup
¾ cup calcium-fortified orange juice
1 cup jasmine tea

Mid-A.M. Snack

1 low-calorie snack[t]
1 cup tea or coffee

Lunch

1 whole-grain bagel with smoked salmon, nonfat cream cheese, and tomato slice
Organic salad green mix with low-fat dressing
¾ cup sugar-free cranberry juice or iced tea

Mid-P.M. Snack

1 low-calorie snack[t]
1 cup tea or coffee

Dinner

1 serving Tropical Papaya Salad*
1 serving Beef Teriyaki with Cabernet Sauce*
1 cup brown rice, cooked with fat-free vegetable broth
¼ cup low-fat vanilla ice cream with ½ cup strawberries
1 cup decaf black or green tea

TUESDAY

Breakfast
2 pieces Corn Bread*
1 wedge cantaloupe
1 cup jasmine tea

Mid-A.M. Snack
1 low-calorie snack†
1 cup tea or coffee

Lunch
1 tuna sandwich on whole-grain bread with lite mayo and 1 slice each
of onion, tomato, and lettuce
1 cup low-fat yogurt
1 cup jasmine tea

Mid-P.M. Snack
1 low-calorie snack†
1 cup tea or coffee

Dinner
1 serving Chicken and Vegetables with Mustard Sauce*
1 serving Simple Peperoncini Spaghetti*
1 cup strawberries with 3 tbs. low-fat plain yogurt
1 cup decaf black or green tea

WEDNESDAY

Breakfast
2 slices whole-grain toast
2 eggs any style except fried
¾ cup calcium-fortified orange juice
1 cup jasmine tea

Mid-A.M. Snack
1 low-calorie snack†
1 cup tea or coffee

Lunch

1 cup baked beans with 1 whole-grain roll
Cole slaw with low-fat dressing
¾ cup sugar-free cranberry juice or iced tea

Mid-P.M. Snack

1 low-calorie snack[†]
1 cup tea or coffee

Dinner

1 serving Shangri-la Spinach Lasagna*
Garden Salad*
1 cup unsweetened fruit salad
1 cup decaf black or green tea

THURSDAY

Breakfast

1 cup oat bran cereal
½ cup skim milk
Strawberries
1 cup jasmine tea

Mid-A.M. Snack

1 low-calorie snack[†]
1 cup tea or coffee

Lunch

1 cup Manhattan clam chowder with
1 whole-grain roll
1 orange
¾ cup sugar-free cranberry juice or iced tea

Mid-P.M. Snack

1 low-calorie snack[†]
1 cup tea or coffee

Dinner

1 serving Atlantic Caesar Salad*

1 baked sweet potato or 1 cup new potatoes

1 tbs. fat-free sour cream

½ cup cantaloupe cubes in a bowl, sprinkled with 1 tsp. lime juice
and topped with ½ cup low-fat plain yogurt

1 cup decaf black or green tea

FRIDAY

Breakfast

1 cup flax cereal or bran flakes with ground flaxseed

½ cup skim milk

1 banana

Strawberries

¾ cup calcium-fortified orange juice

1 cup jasmine tea

Mid-A.M. Snack

1 low-calorie snack†

1 cup tea or coffee

Lunch

1 turkey sub on whole-grain bread with lite mayo

Caesar salad with low-fat dressing and 1 tbs. soy bacon bits

1 cup jasmine tea

Mid-P.M. Snack

1 low-calorie snack†

1 cup tea or coffee

Dinner

1 serving Stir-Fried Rice with Watercress and Tuna*

1 serving Mediterranean Minestrone*

½ cup steamed spinach and ½ cup steamed winter squash, seasoned
with 1 tsp. canola oil and a pinch of sea salt

½ small papaya, cut lengthwise, seeded, and filled with ¼ cup low-fat
vanilla ice cream

1 cup decaf black or green tea

SATURDAY

Breakfast
2 slices whole-grain toast
2 slices lean Canadian bacon
2 eggs any style except fried
¾ cup calcium-fortified orange juice
1 cup jasmine tea

Mid-A.M. Snack
1 low-calorie snack[†]
1 cup tea or coffee

Lunch
1 bean burrito
Celery sticks
1 apple
1 cup jasmine tea

Mid-P.M. Snack
1 low-calorie snack[†]
1 cup tea or coffee

Dinner
1 serving Creamy Carrot Soup*
1 serving Spicy Tomato Pasta*
½ cup mashed sweet potatoes
1 banana, halved lengthwise and sprinkled with 1 tbs. lime juice,
1 tsp. brown sugar, and ½ tbs. sesame seeds
1 cup decaf black or green tea

SUNDAY

Breakfast
1 serving Blueberry Pancakes*
1 tbs. trans-free margarine
¾ cup calcium-fortified orange juice

1 wedge cantaloupe
1 cup jasmine tea

Mid-A.M. Snack
1 low-calorie snack†
1 cup tea or coffee

Lunch
1 chicken wrap
½ grapefruit
¾ cup sugar-free cranberry juice or iced tea

Mid-P.M. Snack
1 low-calorie snack†
1 cup tea or coffee

Dinner
1 serving Summer Field Gazpacho Soup*
1 serving Greek Barbecue*
1 serving Easy Creamed Peach*
1 cup decaf black or green tea

* See recipes, Chapter Twelve.
† See Low-Calorie Snacks, Appendix A (page 483).
Note: If you cannot eat fish, any recipe with fish may also be
prepared with skinless chicken, lean beef, or pork.

Menus for Week One[1]

EAST-WEST TRACK

MONDAY

Breakfast
1 Soy Smoothie*
2 slices pumpernickel bread
1 cup jasmine tea

Mid-A.M. Snack

1 low-calorie snack[†]

1 cup tea or coffee

Lunch

1 whole-grain bagel with 1 tbs. nonfat cream cheese and 1 slice each of tomato, onion, and smoked salmon

Caesar salad with low-fat dressing and 1 tbs. soy bacon bits

1 tbs. walnuts

¾ cup sugar-free cranberry juice or iced tea

Mid-P.M. Snack

1 low-calorie snack[†]

1 cup tea or coffee

Dinner

1 serving Simple Wakame and Tofu Miso Soup*

1 serving Easy Okinawan Vegetable Chample*

1 cup cooked brown rice

1 serving Green Tea Ice Cream*

1 cup decaf black or green tea

TUESDAY

Breakfast

1 serving Flaxseed and Berries Granola*

¾ cup calcium-fortified orange juice

Mid-A.M. Snack

1 low-calorie snack[†]

1 cup tea or coffee

Lunch

1 tuna sandwich on whole-grain bread with lite mayo and 1 slice each of onion, tomato, and lettuce

Baby carrots

1 apple

1 cup jasmine tea

Mid-P.M. Snack

1 low-calorie snack[†]

1 cup tea or coffee

Dinner

1 serving Stuffed Portobello Mushrooms*

1 serving Spinach Chicken Soup

2 whole-grain rolls

½ cup steamed broccoli, seasoned with olive oil spray

½ cup stewed tomatoes

1 cup strawberries with 3 tbs. low-fat plain yogurt

1 cup decaf black or green tea

WEDNESDAY

Breakfast

1 serving Ryukyu Scrambled Eggs*

2 slices whole-grain toast with 1 slice of cheese

1 tbs. trans-free margarine

1 cup jasmine tea

Mid-A.M. Snack

1 low-calorie snack[†]

1 cup tea or coffee

Lunch

1 cup baked beans with 2 whole-grain rolls

Celery sticks with 2 tbs. hummus

¾ cup calcium-fortified orange juice

Mid-P.M. Snack

1 low-calorie snack[†]

1 cup tea or coffee

Dinner

1 serving Creamy Carrot Soup*

1 serving British Columbia Poached Salmon*

1 cup steamed spinach and ½ cup steamed winter squash, seasoned with 1 tsp. canola oil and a pinch of sea salt
1 cup brown rice, cooked with low-sodium, fat-free vegetable broth
1 cup unsweetened fruit salad
1 cup decaf black or green tea

THURSDAY

Breakfast
2 Carrot and Flax Muffins*
¾ cup calcium-fortified orange juice
1 cup jasmine tea

Mid-A.M. Snack
1 low-calorie snack[†]
1 cup tea or coffee

Lunch
1 turkey sub on whole-grain bread with lite mayo
Baby spinach and walnuts with low-fat dressing
1 orange
¾ cup sugar-free cranberry juice or iced tea

Mid-P.M. Snack
1 low-calorie snack[†]
1 cup tea or coffee

Dinner
1 serving Simmered Hechima with Miso Gravy*
Garden Salad*
1 cup cooked brown rice
½ cup cantaloupe cubes sprinkled with 1 tsp. lime juice and topped with ½ cup low-fat plain yogurt
1 cup decaf black or green tea

FRIDAY

Breakfast
1 Banana Smoothie*
1 whole-grain English muffin
¾ cup vegetable juice

Mid-A.M. Snack
1 low-calorie snack[†]
1 cup tea or coffee

Lunch
1 cup prepared nonfat vegetable soup with 2 whole-grain rolls
1 pear
1 cup jasmine tea

Mid-P.M. Snack
1 low-calorie snack[†]
1 cup tea or coffee

Dinner
1 serving Mexican Herbed Tofu with Chapati Wraps*
½ cup steamed winter squash and ½ cup steamed potato cubes,
seasoned with olive oil spray
½ small papaya cut lengthwise, seeded, and filled with ¼ cup low-fat
vanilla ice cream
1 cup decaf black or green tea

SATURDAY

Breakfast
2 servings Sweet Potato Waffles*
¾ cup calcium-fortified orange juice
1 cup jasmine tea

Mid-A.M. Snack
1 low-calorie snack[†]
1 cup tea or coffee

Lunch

1 serving Tofu Tortillas*
1 cup prepared nonfat lentil soup
1 cup jasmine tea

Mid-P.M. Snack

1 low-calorie snack[†]
1 cup tea or coffee

Dinner

1 serving Italian Baked Fish*
1 serving Simple Peperoncini Spaghetti*
Garden salad*
1 banana, halved lengthwise and sprinkled with 1 tbs. lime juice,
1 tsp. brown sugar, and ½ tbs. sesame seeds
1 cup decaf black or green tea

SUNDAY

Breakfast

1 cup cooked brown rice
1 serving Simple Wakame and Tofu Miso Soup*
½ cup steamed spinach with ½ tsp. lite soy sauce
¾ cup calcium-fortified orange juice

Mid-A.M. Snack

1 low-calorie snack[†]
1 cup tea or coffee

Lunch

1 serving Picnic Rice Balls with Salmon*
Cucumber sticks with 1 tsp. white miso or 2 tbs. hummus
¾ cup sugar-free cranberry juice or iced tea

Mid-P.M. Snack

1 low-calorie snack[†]
1 cup tea or coffee

Dinner

1 serving Kimchee Okinawa Style*

1 cup cooked brown rice

1 serving Super Vanilla Tofu Cheese Cake* with strawberries

1 cup decaf black or green tea

* **See recipes, Chapter Twelve.**
† **See Low-Calorie Snacks, Appendix A (page 483).**

Week One Lifestyle Projects

Fitness

- Practice the first tai chi series from Chapter Six at least three times during the week.
- Chart your walking course and begin walking at a leisurely pace two to three times this week.
- Take the step test to measure your aerobic fitness (see page 212). Record your score in your journal.
- Check your weight and body fat percentage on the body fat scale, and record it in your fitness notebook with date and goal weight noted. See Appendix A (page 477) for healthy weights and body fat percentage.

Psychospiritual

- Identify and briefly list areas of your psychospiritual life that you feel need improvement. Measure your approach to time with the questionnaire on page 291, and assess your social support network with the questionnaire on page 332.
- Prepare your own healing spot in or near your home.
- Practice the breathing exercises in Chapter Eight (see pages 294 and 302).
- Make it a point to listen to some of your favorite relaxing music, or try some new music such as folk music, native drumming, nature sounds, or other meditative pieces.

- Investigate what screening tests are covered by your health plan.
- Plan your screening based on your age, family history, and the recommendations in Appendix A (page 473).
- Consider supplementing your diet with vitamins (see Chapter Four).

Week Two

Pat yourself on the back. You stuck to the plan (well, mostly) for a week. After this week you will be well into the healing rhythm. This week provides more healthful food choices, introduces a powerful new tai chi series that you can integrate with the first series, helps you to nurture further your meditation techniques, and gives you helpful resources to strengthen your healing web.

Menus for Week Two

WESTERN TRACK

MONDAY

Breakfast
   1 whole-grain English muffin
   1 Soy Smoothie*
   1 cup jasmine tea

Mid-A.M. Snack
   1 low-calorie snack†
   1 cup tea or coffee

Lunch
   Pasta with tomato sauce

1 cup organic salad green mix with low-fat dressing
¾ cup calcium-fortified orange juice

Mid-P.M. Snack

1 low-calorie snack[†]
1 cup tea or coffee

Dinner

1 serving Spinach Chicken Soup*
1 serving Italian Baked Fish*
2 whole-grain rolls
¼ cup low-fat vanilla ice cream with ½ cup strawberries
1 cup decaf black or green tea

TUESDAY

Breakfast

1 cup hot porridge with brown sugar to taste
½ cup skim milk
1 chopped apple
¾ cup calcium-fortified orange juice

Mid-A.M. Snack

1 low-calorie snack[†]
1 cup tea or coffee

Lunch

1 tuna fish sandwich on whole-grain bread with vegetables and a slice
of cheese
1 pear
1 cup jasmine tea

Mid-P.M. Snack

1 low-calorie snack[†]
1 cup tea or coffee

Dinner

1 serving Creamy Carrot Soup*

1 serving Okinawan Sautéed Chicken with Turmeric*

2 whole-grain rolls

1 cup strawberries, served with 3 tbs. low-fat plain yogurt

1 cup decaf black or green tea

WEDNESDAY

Breakfast

2 slices whole-grain toast

1 tbs. trans-free margarine

3 strips turkey bacon

Strawberries

1 cup jasmine tea

Mid-A.M. Snack

1 low-calorie snack[†]

1 cup tea or coffee

Lunch

1 cup vegetarian chili with 2 whole-grain rolls

Caesar salad with low-fat dressing and 1 tbs. walnuts

¾ cup calcium-fortified orange juice

Mid-P.M. Snack

1 low-calorie snack[†]

1 cup tea or coffee

Dinner

1 serving Chicken and Vegetables with Mustard Sauce*

2 whole-grain rolls

½ cup sliced tomato with 2 tbs. chopped fresh basil leaves

1 cup unsweetened fruit salad

1 cup decaf black or green tea

THURSDAY

Breakfast

1 Carrot and Flax Muffin*

½ grapefruit
1 cup jasmine tea

Mid-A.M. Snack
1 low-calorie snack[†]
1 cup tea or coffee

Lunch
1 cup Boston clam chowder with 2 whole-grain rolls
1 orange
¾ cup sugar-free cranberry juice or iced tea

Mid-P.M. Snack
1 low-calorie snack[†]
1 cup tea or coffee

Dinner
1 serving Sunshine Spinach Pasta*
Garden Salad*
½ cup cantaloupe cubes sprinkled with 1 tsp. lime juice and topped
with ½ cup low-fat plain yogurt
1 cup decaf black or green tea

FRIDAY

Breakfast
2 slices whole rye bread
½ cup low-fat plain yogurt
Strawberries
¾ cup calcium-fortified orange juice

Mid-A.M. Snack
1 low-calorie snack[†]
1 cup tea or coffee

Lunch
1 turkey sub on whole-grain bread with lite mayo and 1 slice each of
onion, tomato, and lettuce

½ grapefruit

1 cup jasmine tea

Mid-P.M. Snack

1 low-calorie snack[†]

1 cup tea or coffee

Dinner

1 cup spinach stir-fried in canola oil

1 serving Chicken Kabobs*

½ small papaya cut lengthwise, seeded, filled with ¼ cup low-fat vanilla ice cream, and sprinkled with 1 tbs. walnuts

1 cup decaf black or green tea

SATURDAY

Breakfast

2 slices whole-grain toast

1 serving Wild West Omelet*

¾ cup calcium-fortified orange juice

Mid-A.M. Snack

1 low-calorie snack[†]

1 cup tea or coffee

Lunch

1 chicken wrap

Cucumber sticks with 2 tbs. hummus

1 cup jasmine tea

Mid-P.M. Snack

1 low-calorie snack[†]

1 cup tea or coffee

Dinner

1 serving Summer Field Gazpacho Soup*

1 serving Quick Paella*

1 banana, halved lengthwise and sprinkled with 1 tbs. lime juice,
1 tsp. brown sugar, and ½ tbs. sesame seeds
1 cup decaf black or green tea

SUNDAY

Breakfast
2 servings Raspberry Pudding*
1 wedge cantaloupe
1 cup jasmine tea

Mid-A.M. Snack
1 low-calorie snack†
1 cup tea or coffee

Lunch
1 serving Tofu Tortillas*
Baby carrots
1 apple
¾ cup sugar-free cranberry juice or iced tea

Mid-P.M. Snack
1 low-calorie snack†
1 cup tea or coffee

Dinner
1 serving Lentil Stroganoff*
½ cup steamed winter squash and ½ cup steamed broccoli, seasoned
with 1 tsp. canola oil and a pinch of sea salt
1 serving Chocolate Kahlúa Mousse*
1 cup decaf black or green tea

* See recipes, Chapter Twelve.
† See Low-Calorie Snacks, Appendix A (page 483).
Note: If you cannot eat fish, any recipe with fish may also be prepared
with skinless chicken, lean beef, or pork.

Menus for Week Two

EAST-WEST TRACK

MONDAY

Breakfast
2 toaster waffles (preferably whole grain, Flax-plus, or Soy-plus)
1 tbs. trans-free margarine
1 tbs. maple syrup Blueberries
1 cup jasmine tea

Mid-A.M. Snack
1 low-calorie snack[†]
1 cup tea or coffee

Lunch
1 bean burrito
1 cup prepared fat-free vegetable soup
¾ cup sugar-free cranberry juice or iced tea

Mid-P.M. Snack
1 low-calorie snack[†]
1 cup tea or coffee

Dinner
1 serving Grilled Tofu with Mushrooms*
1 serving Simple Wakame and Tofu Miso Soup*
1 cup cooked brown rice
1 serving Tropical Papaya Salad*
1 serving Green Tea Ice Cream*
1 cup decaf black or green tea

TUESDAY

Breakfast
2 slices whole rye bread

1 Soy Smoothie*
1 cup jasmine tea

Mid-A.M. Snack

1 low-calorie snack[†]
1 cup tea or coffee

Lunch

1 chicken wrap
1 cup baby spinach, seasoned with 1 tsp. canola oil, a few drops of
lemon juice, and a pinch of salt
1 cup jasmine tea

Mid-P.M. Snack

1 low-calorie snack[†]
1 cup tea or coffee

Dinner

1 serving Gado-Gado Salad*
1 serving Okinawan Sautéed Chicken with Turmeric*
2 whole-grain rolls
1 cup strawberries with 3 tbs. low-fat plain yogurt
1 cup decaf black or green tea

WEDNESDAY

Breakfast

1 serving Flaxseed and Berries Granola*
¾ cup calcium-fortified orange juice
1 cup jasmine tea

Mid-A.M. Snack

1 low-calorie snack[†]
1 cup tea or coffee

Lunch

1 serving Spicy Tomato Pasta*

1 pear
1 cup jasmine tea

Mid-P.M. Snack
1 low-calorie snack[†]
1 cup tea or coffee

Dinner
1 serving Creamy Carrot Soup*
1 serving Tuna Caesar Salad*
2 whole-grain rolls
1 cup unsweetened fruit salad
1 cup decaf black or green tea

THURSDAY

Breakfast
1 cup hot porridge with brown sugar to taste
1 chopped apple
1 cup jasmine tea

Mid-A.M. Snack
1 low-calorie snack[†]
1 cup tea or coffee

Lunch
1 tuna or salmon sandwich
Caesar salad with low-fat dressing and 1 tbs. soy bacon bits
¾ cup sugar-free cranberry juice or iced tea

Mid-P.M. Snack
1 low-calorie snack[†]
1 cup tea or coffee

Dinner
1 serving Warm Mushroom Salad with Garlic Dressing*
2 whole-grain rolls
½ cup steamed broccoli, seasoned with olive oil spray

½ cup stewed tomato

½ cup cantaloupe cubes sprinkled with 1 tsp. lime juice and topped
with ½ cup low-fat plain yogurt

1 cup decaf black or green tea

FRIDAY

Breakfast
1 Carrot and Flax Muffin*
½ grapefruit
1 cup jasmine tea

Mid-A.M. Snack
1 low-calorie snack[†]
1 cup tea or coffee

Lunch
1 cup prepared vegetarian chili with 2 whole wheat rolls
1 apple
1 cup organic salad mix with low-fat dressing
¾ cup calcium-fortified orange juice

Mid-P.M. Snack
1 low-calorie snack[†]
1 cup tea or coffee

Dinner
1 serving Simple Wakame and Tofu Miso Soup*
1 serving Goya Chample*
1 cup cooked brown rice with ½ sheet nori seaweed
½ small papaya cut lengthwise, seeded, and filled with ¼ cup low-fat
vanilla ice cream
1 cup decaf black or green tea

SATURDAY

Breakfast
1 serving Okinawan Chinbin Crepes*

1 wedge honeydew melon
1 cup jasmine tea

Mid-A.M. Snack
1 low-calorie snack[†]
1 cup tea or coffee

Lunch
1 prepared veggie burger with whole-grain bun, ½
cup romaine lettuce, 2 onion slices, and lite mayo
¾ cup calcium-fortified orange juice

Mid-P.M. Snack
1 low-calorie snack[†]
1 cup tea or coffee

Dinner
1 serving Beer Crepes*
1 serving Spinach Chicken Soup*
1 banana, halved lengthwise and sprinkled with 1 tbs. lime juice,
1 tsp. brown sugar, and 1 tbs. walnuts
1 cup decaf black or green tea

SUNDAY

Breakfast
1 cup cooked brown rice
1 serving Simple
Wakame and Tofu Miso Soup*
½ cup steamed spinach
½ sheet nori seaweed
½ tsp. lite soy sauce (for spinach and nori)
1 cup jasmine tea

Mid-A.M. Snack
1 low-calorie snack[†]
1 cup tea or coffee

Lunch

1 serving Wakame Seaweed Soba Noodle with Broth*

¾ cup sugar-free cranberry juice or iced tea

Mid-P.M. Snack

1 low-calorie snack†

1 cup tea or coffee

Dinner

1 serving Summer Field Gazpacho Soup*

1 serving Baked Tofu with Cheese*

1 serving Sunshine Spinach Pasta*

1 serving Chocolate-Kahlúa Mousse*

1 cup decaf black or green tea

* **See recipes, Chapter Twelve.**

† **See Low-Calorie Snacks, Appendix A (page 483).**

Week Two Lifestyle Projects

Fitness

- Practice the second tai chi series in Chapter Six. Try at least one day of the first two series as an integrated series.
- Continue walking two or three times this week.

Psychospiritual

- Work on an area of your healing web that you identified last week by practicing one of the healing prescriptions on pages 258–71.
- Reach out to someone with whom you have lost contact. You may be estranged from them or you may just have gotten too busy. Either way, reestablish communication.

- Try practicing the basic meditation technique on page 295 for ten to twenty minutes a day. Gradually build up to twenty minutes by aiming for ten minutes on Monday, Tuesday, and Wednesday, fifteen minutes on Thursday, Friday, and Saturday, and then twenty minutes on Sunday.
- For a good, short, and inspiring read on the subjects of life, death, and the afterlife, we recommend Elisabeth Kübler-Ross's book *On Life After Death*. For a good synthesis of Eastern spirituality and Western psychology, try the Dalai Lama's *The Art of Happiness: A Handbook for Living* (coauthored with a Western psychiatrist). And for a thought-provoking look at how it might be possible to gain a deeper understanding and awareness of God or a higher power, we recommend Deepak Chopra's *How to Know God: The Soul's Journey into the Mystery of Mysteries*.

Integrative Health

- Read more about herbal tonics and the specific roles of vitamins and minerals from a reputable source such as *The Compendium of Alternative Medicine* or the *Natural Health Bible*.

Week Three

You are now halfway through the Turnaround Plan. You should be starting to feel the effects of the Okinawa Program's wellness prescription. You should be thinking clearer, feeling stronger, losing fat, and feeling better about yourself and your life's direction. You are on the right path. Stick to it. This week you will further refine your meditation technique, explore reflective prayer, improve your walking technique, and learn a useful shiatsu method for soothing the stresses of the day. Make your home more nature-friendly by adding some plants. Ending the week with a massage will be a perfect way to cap a week of learning.

Menus for Week Three

WESTERN TRACK

MONDAY

Breakfast
2 slices whole-grain toast
2 eggs, any style except fried
½ grapefruit
1 cup jasmine tea

Mid-A.M. Snack
1 low-calorie snack†
1 cup tea or coffee

Lunch
whole-grain bagel with 1 tbsp. nonfat cream cheese and a slice of smoked salmon
1 cup organic salad green mix with low-fat dressing
¾ cup sugar-free cranberry juice or iced tea

Mid-P.M. Snack
1 low-calorie snack†
1 cup tea or coffee

Dinner
1 serving Zucchini Lasagna*
¼ cup low-fat vanilla ice cream with ½ cup strawberries
1 cup decaf black or green tea

TUESDAY

Breakfast
1 cup flax cereal (or bran flakes with ground flaxseed)
½ cup skim milk

Strawberries
1 cup jasmine tea

Mid-A.M. Snack
1 low-calorie snack[†]
1 cup tea or coffee

Lunch
1 cup prepared fat-free vegetable soup
1 bean burrito
1 cup jasmine tea

Mid-P.M. Snack
1 low-calorie snack[†]
1 cup tea or coffee

Dinner
1 serving Stuffed Portobello Mushrooms*
1 serving Simple Peperoncini Spaghetti*
Garden Salad*
1 cup strawberries, served with 3 tbs. low-fat plain yogurt
1 cup decaf black or green tea

WEDNESDAY

Breakfast
2 slices pumpernickel bread
1 Banana Smoothie*
1 orange
1 cup jasmine tea

Mid-A.M. Snack
1 low-calorie snack[†]
1 cup tea or coffee

Lunch
Pasta with tomato sauce

Celery sticks with 2 tbs. hummus
1 cup jasmine tea

Mid-P.M. Snack

1 low-calorie snack[†]
1 cup tea or coffee

Dinner

1 serving British Columbia Poached Salmon*
½ cup steamed winter squash and ½ cup steamed broccoli, seasoned
with 1 tsp. canola oil and a pinch of sea salt
2 whole-grain rolls
1 cup unsweetened fruit salad
1 cup decaf black or green tea

THURSDAY

Breakfast

2 slices whole-grain toast
2 slices lean bacon
¾ cup calcium-fortified orange juice
Strawberries

Mid-A.M. Snack

1 low-calorie snack[†]
1 cup tea or coffee

Lunch

1 cup chili beans
2 whole-grain rolls
1 cup baby spinach, seasoned with 1 tsp. canola oil and a pinch of sea
salt
1 orange
¾ cup sugar-free cranberry juice or iced tea

Mid-P.M. Snack

1 low-calorie snack[†]
1 cup tea or coffee

Dinner

1 serving Beef Teriyaki with Cabernet Sauce*
Garden Salad*
1 cup brown rice, cooked with fat-free vegetable broth
½ cup cantaloupe cubes sprinkled with 1 tsp. lime juice and topped
with ½ cup low-fat plain yogurt
1 cup decaf black or green tea

FRIDAY

Breakfast

1 cup kamut cereal
½ cup skim milk
Strawberries
1 cup jasmine tea

Mid-A.M. Snack

1 low-calorie snack[†]
1 cup tea or coffee

Lunch

1 tuna sandwich on whole-grain bread with lite mayo
Cole slaw with low-fat dressing
1 cup jasmine tea

Mid-P.M. Snack

1 low-calorie snack[†]
1 cup tea or coffee

Dinner

1 serving Creamy Carrot Soup*
1 serving Shuri Shrimp Salad*
1 whole-grain roll
½ small papaya cut lengthwise, seeded, and filled with ¼ cup low-fat
vanilla ice cream
1 cup decaf black or green tea

SATURDAY

Breakfast
2 pieces Corn Bread*
½ papaya
1 cup jasmine tea

Mid-A.M. Snack
1 low-calorie snack†
1 cup tea or coffee

Lunch
1 serving Somen Chample*
1 apple
1 cup jasmine tea

Mid-P.M. Snack
1 low-calorie snack†
1 cup tea or coffee

Dinner
1 serving Summer Field Gazpacho Soup*
1 serving Sunshine Spinach Pasta*
1 banana, halved lengthwise, sprinkled with 1 tbs. lime juice, 1 tsp.
brown sugar, and ½ tbs. sesame seeds
1 cup decaf black or green tea

SUNDAY

Breakfast
1 Carrot and Flax Muffin*
1 kiwi
1 cup jasmine tea

Mid-A.M. Snack
1 low-calorie snack†
1 cup tea or coffee

Lunch

1 bean burrito
1 pear
¾ cup calcium-fortified orange juice

Mid-P.M. Snack

1 low-calorie snack†
1 cup tea or coffee

Dinner

1 serving Carrot Leaf Pilaf*
1 serving Tuna Caesar Salad*
1 serving Mediterranean Minestrone*
1 serving Okinawan Orange Brûlée*
1 cup decaf black or green tea

* **See recipes, Chapter Twelve.**
† **See Low-Calorie Snacks, Appendix A (page 483).**
Note: **If you cannot eat fish, any recipe with fish may also be prepared with skinless chicken, lean beef, or pork.**

Menus for Week Three

EAST-WEST TRACK

MONDAY

Breakfast

1 Soy Smoothie*
2 slices pumpernickel bread
1 cup jasmine tea

Mid-A.M. Snack

1 low-calorie snack†
1 cup tea or coffee

Lunch

1 whole-grain bagel with 1 tbs. nonfat cream cheese and a slice of smoked salmon

Caesar salad with low-fat dressing and 1 tbs. soy bacon bits

¾ cup cranberry juice

Mid-P.M. Snack

1 low-calorie snack[†]

1 cup tea or coffee

Dinner

1 serving Shuri Shrimp Salad*

1 serving Easy Okinawa Chample*

1 serving Green Tea Ice Cream*

1 cup decaf black or green tea

TUESDAY

Breakfast

1 serving Flaxseed and Berries Granola*

¾ cup calcium-fortified orange juice

1 cup jasmine tea

Mid-A.M. Snack

1 low-calorie snack[†]

1 cup tea or coffee

Lunch

1 tuna sandwich on whole-grain bread with lite mayo and 1 slice each of onion, tomato, green bell pepper, and lettuce

½ grapefruit

1 cup jasmine tea

Mid-P.M. Snack

1 low-calorie snack[†]

1 cup tea or coffee

Dinner
- 1 serving Mediterranean Minestrone*
- 1 serving Atlantic Caesar Salad*
- 1 serving Simple Peperoncini Spaghetti*
- 1 cup strawberries with 3 tbs. low-fat plain yogurt
- 1 cup decaf black or green tea

WEDNESDAY

Breakfast
- 1 Carrot and Flax Muffin*
- 1 apple
- 1 cup jasmine tea

Mid-A.M. Snack
- 1 low-calorie snack†
- 1 cup tea or coffee

Lunch
- 1 cup prepared fat-free vegetable soup
- 1 whole-grain roll
- Cole slaw with low-fat dressing
- ¾ cup calcium-fortified orange juice

Mid-P.M. Snack
- 1 low-calorie snack†
- 1 cup tea or coffee

Dinner
- 1 serving Simple Wakame and Tofu Miso Soup*
- 1 serving Okinawan Eggplants with Miso*
- 1 cup cooked brown rice
- 1 cup unsweetened fruit salad
- 1 cup decaf black or green tea

THURSDAY

Breakfast
1 cup kamut cereal
½ cup skim milk
Strawberries

Mid-A.M. Snack
1 low-calorie snack[†]
1 cup tea or coffee

Lunch
1 cup prepared fat-free black bean soup
1 turkey sub on whole-grain bread with lite mayo and a slice each of
onion, tomato, and lettuce
1 apple
1 tbs. walnuts
¾ cup sugar-free cranberry juice or iced tea

Mid-P.M. Snack
1 low-calorie snack[†]
1 cup tea or coffee

Dinner
1 serving Spinach Chicken Soup*
1 serving Baked Tofu Mediterranean Style*
2 whole-grain rolls
½ cup cantaloupe cubes sprinkled with 1 tsp. lime juice and topped
with ½ cup low-fat plain yogurt
1 cup decaf black or green tea

FRIDAY

Breakfast
1 Banana Smoothie*
1 whole-grain English muffin
1 cup jasmine tea

Mid-A.M. Snack
1 low-calorie snack[†]
1 cup tea or coffee

Lunch
1 bean burrito
1 cup organic salad green mix with 1 tsp. canola oil, a few drops of lemon juice, and a pinch of sea salt
¾ cup calcium-fortified orange juice

Mid-P.M. Snack
1 low-calorie snack[†]
1 cup tea or coffee

Dinner
1 serving Carrot Leaf Pilaf*
1 serving Okinawan White Miso Soup with Vegetables*
½ small papaya cut lengthwise, seeded, and filled with ¼ cup low-fat vanilla ice cream
1 cup decaf black or green tea

SATURDAY

Breakfast
2 pieces Corn Bread*
1 pear
¾ cup calcium-fortified orange juice

Mid-A.M. Snack
1 low-calorie snack[†]
1 cup tea or coffee

Lunch
1 cup fat-free lentil soup
1 prepared veggie burger on whole-grain bun with lite mayo, ½ cup romaine lettuce, and 2 onion slices
1 cup jasmine tea

Mid-P.M. Snack

1 low-calorie snack[†]

1 cup tea or coffee

Dinner

1 cup prepared fat-free vegetable soup

1 serving Stuffed Green Peppers*

2 whole-grain rolls

1 banana, halved lengthwise and sprinkled with 1 tbs. lime juice,

1 tsp. brown sugar, and 1 tbs. walnuts

1 cup decaf black or green tea

SUNDAY

Breakfast

1 serving Okinawan Blueberry Pancakes*

1 tbs. trans-free margarine

1 peach

1 cup jasmine tea

Mid-A.M. Snack

1 low-calorie snack[†]

1 cup tea or coffee

Lunch

1 serving Simple Wakame and Tofu Miso Soup*

1 serving Somen Chample*

¾ cup sugar-free cranberry juice or iced tea

Mid-P.M. Snack

1 low-calorie snack[†]

1 cup tea or coffee

Dinner

1 serving Tofu, Salmon, and Vegetables with Creamy Miso Sauce*

1 cup brown rice, cooked with fat-free vegetable broth

½ cup sliced tomato with 1 tbs. chopped basil leaves

1 serving Okinawan Orange Brûlée*
1 cup decaf black or green tea

* See recipes, Chapter Twelve.
† See Low-Calorie Snacks, Appendix A (page 481).

Week Three Lifestyle Projects

Fitness

- Practice the third tai chi series in Chapter Six at least twice this week.
- Practice the first, second, and third series at least once this week as an integrated series.
- Start timing your walks.
- Check to see whether there are any tai chi or other martial arts classes in your area.

Psychospiritual

- Practice the basic meditation technique for a minimum of twenty minutes on meditation days (about three times per week).
- Try substituting a reflective prayer for one or two of your meditation sessions.
- Visit a nature spot such as a park, the sea, the woods, or the mountains.

Integrative Health

- Practice a shiatsu technique from pages 308–9 on yourself or a loved one.
- Get a massage or other bodywork this week.

Week Four

Fantastic—you made it to week four. You have now entered a space where you truly can build on what you have learned. You should be feeling great about yourself. You are in better shape, closer to a healthy weight, and feeling renewed inner strength. This week is meant to consolidate the gains you have made over the previous three weeks. You will learn one more tai chi series and integrate the entire series as one, and recheck your aerobic fitness and assess the gains that you have made. This week you will also be able to make some decisions about what has worked for you and what hasn't, what you would like to incorporate into your life, and what more you can do to enhance your wellness. If you started out on the Western eating track, try to incorporate some more of the East-West fusion foods and recipes into your eating habits. Now is the time to expand your wellness efforts. Let's take the next step.

Menus for Week Four

WESTERN TRACK

MONDAY

Breakfast
    1 cup hot porridge with brown sugar to taste
    ¼ cup skim milk
    Strawberries
    1 cup jasmine tea

Mid-A.M. Snack
    1 low-calorie snack[†]
    1 cup tea or coffee

Lunch
    1 tuna sandwich on whole-grain bread with lite mayo
    Caesar salad with low-fat dressing and 1 tbs. soy bacon bits
    ¾ cup calcium-fortified orange juice

Mid-P.M. Snack
1 low-calorie snack[†]
1 cup tea or coffee

Dinner
1 serving Spinach Chicken Soup*
1 serving Greek Barbecue*
¼ cup low-fat vanilla ice cream with ½ cup strawberries
1 cup decaf black or green tea

TUESDAY

Breakfast
2 toaster waffles (preferably whole-grain, Flax-plus, or Soy-plus)
1 tbs. trans-free margarine
1 tbs. maple syrup
¾ cup calcium-fortified orange juice

Mid-A.M. Snack
1 low-calorie snack[†]
1 cup tea or coffee

Lunch
1 chicken wrap with vegetables
1 pear
1 cup jasmine tea

Mid-P.M. Snack
1 low-calorie snack[†]
1 cup tea or coffee

Dinner
1 serving Chicken and Vegetables with Mustard Sauce*
1 cup baby spinach with 2 tbs. walnuts seasoned with canola oil 2 whole-grain rolls
1 cup strawberries with 3 tbs. low-fat plain yogurt
1 cup decaf black or green tea

WEDNESDAY

Breakfast
1 Carrot and Flax Muffin*
1 wedge cantaloupe
1 cup jasmine tea

Mid-A.M. Snack
1 low-calorie snack[†]
1 cup tea or coffee

Lunch
1 cup Boston clam chowder
2 whole-grain rolls
Cucumber sticks with tuna and lite mayo dip
1 orange
1 cup jasmine tea

Mid-P.M. Snack
1 low-calorie snack[†]
1 cup tea or coffee

Dinner
1 serving Simple Wakame and Tofu Miso Soup*
1 serving Goya Chample*
1 cup cooked brown rice
1 cup unsweetened fruit salad
1 cup decaf black or green tea

THURSDAY

Breakfast
1 slice rye bread
1 Soy Smoothie*
½ grapefruit
1 cup jasmine tea

Mid-A.M. Snack

   1 low-calorie snack[†]
   1 cup tea or coffee

Lunch

   1 whole-grain bagel with 1 tbs. nonfat cream cheese
   1 cup organic salad green mix with low-fat dressing
   ¾ cup sugar-free cranberry juice or iced tea

Mid-P.M. Snack

   1 low-calorie snack[†]
   1 cup tea or coffee

Dinner

   1 serving Stuffed Green Peppers*
   1 serving Mediterranean Minestrone*
   1 serving Tomato Bruschetta*
   ½ cup cantaloupe cubes sprinkled with 1 tsp. lime juice and topped
   with ½ cup low-fat plain yogurt
   1 cup decaf black or green tea

FRIDAY

Breakfast

   1 cup flax cereal (or bran flakes with ground flaxseed)
   ½ cup skim milk
   1 banana
   Strawberries
   1 cup jasmine tea

Mid-A.M. Snack

   1 low-calorie snack[†]
   1 cup tea or coffee

Lunch

   Pasta with tomato sauce
   1 apple
   1 cup jasmine tea

Mid-P.M. Snack
1 low-calorie snack†
1 cup tea or coffee

Dinner
½ cup steamed squash and ½ cup steamed broccoli, seasoned with
1 tsp. canola oil and a pinch of sea salt
1 serving British Columbia Poached Salmon*
2 whole-grain rolls
1 cup prepared fat-free vegetable soup
½ small papaya cut lengthwise, seeded, and filled with ¼ cup low-fat
vanilla ice cream
1 cup decaf black or green tea

SATURDAY

Breakfast
1 serving Ryukyu Scrambled Eggs*
2 slices whole-grain bread, toasted
1 wedge honeydew melon
1 cup jasmine tea

Mid-A.M. Snack
1 low-calorie snack†
1 cup tea or coffee

Lunch
1 cup baked beans
2 whole-grain rolls
Cole slaw with low-fat dressing
¾ cup calcium-fortified orange juice

Mid-P.M. Snack
1 low-calorie snack†
1 cup tea or coffee

Dinner
1 serving Summer Field Gazpacho Soup*

1 serving Barbecued Mahi-Mahi with Lime-Soy Sauce*
1 cup brown rice, cooked with fat-free vegetable broth
1 banana, halved lengthwise and sprinkled with 1 tbs. lime juice,
1 tsp. brown sugar, and ½ tbs. sesame seeds
1 cup decaf black or green tea

SUNDAY

Breakfast
1 serving Sweet Potato Waffles*
½ tbs. trans-free margarine
1 tbs. maple syrup
¾ cup calcium-fortified orange juice

Mid-A.M. Snack
1 low-calorie snack†
1 cup tea or coffee

Lunch
1 turkey sub on whole-grain bread with lite mayo
½ grapefruit
¾ cup sugar-free cranberry juice or iced tea

Mid-P.M. Snack
1 low-calorie snack†
1 cup tea or coffee

Dinner
1 serving Tofu, Salmon, and Vegetables with Creamy Miso Sauce*
1 serving Simple Peperoncini Spaghetti*
½ cup sliced tomato with 1 tbs. chopped basil leaves
1 serving Delectable Strawberry Mousse*
1 cup decaf black or green tea

* See recipes, Chapter Twelve.
† See Low-Calorie Snacks, Appendix A (page 483).
Note: If you cannot eat fish, any recipe with fish may also be prepared
with skinless chicken, lean beef, or pork.

EAST-WEST TRACK

MONDAY

Breakfast
  1 cup hot porridge with brown sugar to taste
  ½ cup skim milk
  1 apple
  1 cup jasmine tea

Mid-A.M. Snack
  1 low-calorie snack[†]
  1 cup tea or coffee

Lunch
  1 chicken wrap
  Caesar salad with low-fat dressing and 1 tbs. soy bacon bits
  ¾ cup sugar-free cranberry juice or iced tea

Mid-P.M. Snack
  1 low-calorie snack[†]
  1 cup tea or coffee

Dinner
  1 serving Quick Paella*
  Garden Salad*
  1 serving Green Tea Ice Cream*
  1 cup decaf black or green tea

TUESDAY

Breakfast
  2 toaster waffles (preferably whole-grain, Flax-plus, or Soy-plus)
  1 tbs. trans-free margarine

1 tbs. maple syrup Strawberries

1 cup jasmine tea

Mid-A.M. Snack

1 low-calorie snack[†]

1 cup tea or coffee

Lunch

Pasta with tomato sauce

1 pear

1 cup jasmine tea

Mid-P.M. Snack

1 low-calorie snack[†]

1 cup tea or coffee

Dinner

1 serving Okinawan White Miso Soup with Vegetables*

1 serving Simple Simmered Mackerel with Miso*

1 cup brown rice

½ cup steamed spinach

1 cup strawberries with 3 tbs. low-fat plain yogurt

1 cup decaf black or green tea

WEDNESDAY

Breakfast

1 serving Ryukyu Scrambled Eggs*

2 slices whole-grain toast

1 tbs. trans-free margarine

1 cup jasmine tea

Mid-A.M. Snack

1 low-calorie snack[†]

1 cup tea or coffee

Lunch

1 cup baked beans

2 whole-grain rolls
1 cup organic salad green mix with low-fat dressing
¾ cup calcium-fortified orange juice

Mid-P.M. Snack
1 low-calorie snack[†]
1 cup tea or coffee

Dinner
1 serving Tuna Caesar Salad*
1 serving Creamy Carrot Soup*
1 serving Simple Peperoncini Spaghetti*
1 cup unsweetened fruit salad
1 cup decaf black or green tea

THURSDAY

Breakfast
1 serving Flaxseed and Berries Granola*
¾ cup calcium-fortified orange juice

Mid-A.M. Snack
1 low-calorie snack[†]
1 cup tea or coffee

Lunch
1 cup Manhattan clam chowder
2 whole-grain rolls
Celery sticks
1 apple
¾ cup sugar-free cranberry juice or iced tea

Mid-P.M. Snack
1 low-calorie snack[†]
1 cup tea or coffee

Dinner
1 serving Spinach Chicken Soup*

1 serving Stir-Fried Rice with Watercress and Tuna*
½ cup cantaloupe cubes sprinkled with 1 tsp. lime juice and topped
with ½ cup low-fat plain yogurt
1 cup decaf black or green tea

FRIDAY

Breakfast
1 Carrot and Flax Muffin*
1 pear
1 cup jasmine tea

Mid-A.M. Snack
1 low-calorie snack†
1 cup tea or coffee

Lunch
1 baked potato with nonfat sour cream
Coleslaw with low-fat dressing
1 cup jasmine tea

Mid-P.M. Snack
1 low-calorie snack†
1 cup tea or coffee

Dinner
1 serving Simple Wakame and Tofu Miso Soup*
1 serving British Columbia Poached Salmon*
1 cup cooked brown rice
1 cup steamed spinach
½ cup stewed tomato
½ small papaya cut lengthwise, seeded, and filled with ¼ cup low-fat
vanilla ice cream
1 cup decaf black or green tea

SATURDAY

Breakfast
   1 serving Raspberry Pudding*
   ½ cup low-fat yogurt
   1 cup jasmine tea

Mid-A.M. Snack
   1 low-calorie snack†
   1 cup tea or coffee

Lunch
   1 serving Okinawan White Miso Soup with Vegetables*
   1 cup brown rice
   1 cup jasmine tea

Mid-P.M. Snack
   1 low-calorie snack†
   1 cup tea or coffee

Dinner
   1 serving Mediterranean Minestrone*
   1 serving Okinawan Sautéed Chicken with Turmeric*
   2 whole-grain rolls
   1 banana, halved lengthwise and sprinkled with 1 tbs. lime juice,
   1 tsp. brown sugar, and ½ tbs. sesame seeds
   1 cup decaf black or green tea

SUNDAY

Breakfast
   1 serving Simple Wakame and Tofu Miso Soup*
   1 cup brown rice
   ½ cup steamed spinach
   ½ sheet nori seaweed
   ½ tsp. light soy sauce (for spinach and nori)
   1 cup jasmine tea

Mid-A.M. Snack

1 low-calorie snack[†]

1 cup tea or coffee

Lunch

1 cup prepared fat-free vegetable soup

1 serving Cilantro-Scented Tofu Rice Salad*

¾ cup calcium-fortified orange juice

Mid-P.M. Snack

1 low-calorie snack[†]

1 cup tea or coffee

Dinner

1 serving Summer Field Gazpacho Soup*

1 serving Barbecued Mahi-Mahi with Lime-Soy Sauce*

2 whole-grain rolls

1 serving Delectable Strawberry Mousse*

1 cup decaf black or green tea

* See recipes, Chapter Twelve.
† See Low-Calorie Snacks, Appendix A (page 483).

Week Four Lifestyle Projects

Fitness

- Practice the first, second, third, and fourth tai chi movements as a fluid series at least three times.
- Consider incorporating some of the more advanced walking techniques from Chapter Six into your walking routine.
- Continue timing your walks, picking up the pace if possible.
- Retake the step test for aerobic fitness (page 213).
- Recheck your weight and body fat percentage on the body fat scale or use the body mass measurement technique in Appendix A (page 477).

Psychospiritual

- Volunteer for one or two hours or help a friend in need.
- Continue practicing your basic meditation technique for at least twenty minutes daily, but substitute a healing meditation for one or two of your sessions.
- Make time for music or art this week.

Integrative Health

- Schedule a repeat of your cholesterol panel for six weeks from now if your initial cholesterol ratio was more than four (total divided by HDL).
- Continue your dietary supplements daily.
- Consider investigating an alternative healing technique such as acupuncture.

You did it! Four weeks have passed and you have learned much. You have several powerful new tools at your disposal to help prepare you for a lifelong journey toward everlasting health (including the Okinawa Program Nutrition Tracker in Appendix A, page 486). Use them wisely, keep an open mind, and continue your quest for wellness. We truly wish you a healthy and happy journey.

11. Everlasting Health Is Within Your Grasp

Nuchi du takara.
Life is a sacred treasure.

Okinawan saying

Now is clearly the time for a shift in thinking, a new approach to life, a new paradigm for healing, one that provides us with the tools to learn from the past, navigate the future, and seek health and fulfillment in the present. With this book we've provided the tools, but the journey is uniquely yours. The Okinawan lifestyle has resulted in unparalleled health for thousands of people in Okinawa who are living as the elders do, and it will be equally beneficial to you. One of the most appealing qualities of the program is its timeless adaptability. It allows us to take personal responsibility for our health, and expects us to have healthy bodies and minds—indeed, it is the natural order of things.

Life holds no guarantees except the inevitability of change, and it's our responsibility to ensure that change is positive. Change involves exposing ourselves to risk, and the road is sometimes rocky—all of us will experience some failure, it's inevitable—but we will also experience success. We need to focus on our successes and learn from our mistakes. All the parts of our essence—the physical, the psychological, the social, and the spiritual—require attention if we are to view changes positively and live life to its fullest—if we are to be whole. The key to integrating these disparate parts of ourselves is to nurture them all. And that's what we hope you have learned here. We think of this book as a road map to the full integration of body and soul—a guide to optimum health and life satisfaction.

Following the Okinawa Program will also help you steer clear of dubious quick fixes. There are plenty out there—high-protein weight-loss diets that cause us to lose water and muscle; herbs that supposedly rev up our metabolism, but are in reality laced with caffeine or amphetamines; bizarre rules for food combining; and more. Inevitably they fail because they try to circumvent the laws of nature and distort scientific evidence. Fortunately, the truth about well-being is becoming ever more clear—and much of it is coming from the East.

Leading scholars of integrative medicine have already begun to spread the word about some of the benefits of the Eastern approach to healing: these include Dr. Andrew Weil, with his impressive knowledge of Eastern medicine;[1] Dr. Dean Ornish, with his low-fat heart-disease-reversal diet, which includes yoga and Eastern meditations;[2] and top researchers in the field of evidence-based medicine. They are looking eastward for answers to chronic health problems that have not responded well to the Western approach. These range from heart disease and certain cancers to chronic fatigue syndrome and chronic pain syndromes. We need to look no further than Okinawa. The answers are there—and have been there for centuries. Over the coming years you will hear more and more about the Okinawans and their way, and we are proud to be in the forefront of this paradigm shift.

Health Expectancy Versus Life Expectancy

At the start of the new millennium, the World Health Organization states that at least 120 countries (total population about 5 billion) have a life expectancy at birth of more than sixty years. The global average life expectancy has increased to sixty-six years, compared with only forty-eight years in 1955. Life expectancy worldwide is projected to reach seventy-three years in 2025. Seniors over eighty-five years of age are the fastest-growing segment of the population in most Western countries.[3]

Yet, as WHO reports have recognized, "increased longevity without quality of life is an empty prize." *Health expectancy*—that is, the number of years expected to be lived in good health—is more important than *life expectancy*. Very few of us want to live an extra twenty or more years if those years are spent in decrepitude or dementia. Unfortunately, unless we live more like the Okinawans, many of us will realize our worst fears, and society may be over-burdened with long-lived but unhealthy seniors.

In the year 2000, the United States was ranked a dismal twenty-fourth by the World Health Organization in terms of health expectancy.[4] This was by far the lowest ranking among the developed countries. Japan ranked number one, and the Okinawans are perched right on top of the Japanese tables. This is definitely telling us something.

And what it's saying is this: Americans not only die earlier, but also spend more time disabled before they die. This is a country that spends an incredible 15 percent of its gross domestic product on health care, and yet still leaves a third of the population without health coverage. The Okinawans, on the other hand, have found the right recipe for everlasting health. While they too possess the latest technology for diagnosis and treatment, they don't use this equip-ment as often as Americans do, because of their integrative approach to overall health, which includes low-tech approaches to wellness based on diet and a healthy lifestyle that includes attention to their psychospiritual needs. This has not only extended the length of the lives of the elders, but has added *quality* years. Okinawans look and feel younger, because most *are* physiologically younger than their chronological ages. They are more active and enjoy life to the "healthy end"—the way it's meant to be lived.

Okinawa has already received kudos from WHO's former secre-tary general, Dr. Hiroshi Nakajima, as a "world longevity region" that far exceeds the Japanese average (the world's highest).[5] Seem-ingly miraculous, this triumph of successful aging is no miracle; it is the result of profound differences in Eastern and Western philo-sophical approaches to health.

In the East there is a stronger orientation toward preventive medicine and natural healing. Eastern medicine concentrates on increasing the body's own internal forces of resistance because dis-ease is thought to be brought on by internal imbalance. In old Chinese medical practice, people paid their doctors a small fee as long as they stayed well, but stopped payment when they got sick. That would certainly have provided incentive for the doctor to prac-tice preventive medicine!

In the West, disease has generally been thought to be caused by something outside of ourselves, such as invading bacteria or a virus. So Western doctors concentrate their treatments on eliminating the invader instead of strengthening the body's own healing defenses. While this model has had some definite advantages, such as spurring the development of life-saving antibiotics and other high-tech medical interventions, it leaves little room for the idea of prevention and wellness. Moreover, modern "wonder drugs" can backfire by causing unpleasant side effects and creating "superbugs"—stronger, drug-resistant bacteria and viruses.

Is Okinawa In Danger Of Losing The Way?

The Okinawa wellness phenomenon results from a fortuitous combination of factors, and we feel privileged to have been able to study it for most of the past quarter-century, especially over the last decade. While we are continuing our research efforts to uncover more about Okinawa's healing foods, plants, exercises, and psychospiritual practices, we've noted that there is definitely trouble in paradise. In the wake of efforts to modernize and westernize, many of the conditions that led to the Okinawans' phenomenal health and longevity are being undone. The land of the immortals seems to be losing its grip on immortality. As the old ways are dying out and being replaced by a lifestyle that is much less wellness-oriented, independent and healthy elders are being increasingly outnumbered by less robust seniors.

Our Vision: The Okinawa Program As A Wellness Model For The World

From 1945 until 1972, the islands were under U.S. control, part of the postwar settlement with Japan. The American influence has left its mark on the eating habits and health care of the Okinawans. Originally it helped to bring about the healthy East-West blend of both eating habits and integrative health care. This was very helpful to the elders, who selectively adopted the best of both worlds. It is a beautiful example of the powerful healing combination that can happen when East meets West in an integrative, mutually beneficial fashion.

However, the pendulum has begun to swing too far toward the Western model. A penchant for processed fast food is sending cholesterol levels soaring and waistlines spreading. The result is seen in Okinawa's youth—indeed, in most anyone born in the postwar generations—who have the highest body-mass index of the Japanese, and higher overall risk factors for heart disease. The young are dying faster and younger than the Okinawan elders. Everything depends on the path they choose in the coming years. This generation of elders is the last reservoir of the wellness message, and when they are gone, so might be the land of everlasting health.

But this potential tragedy can be averted if the old ways are studied, documented, and preserved for future generations. This is beginning to happen as local scientists, scholars, artists, musicians, and other *uchinanchu* (the Okinawan-dialect name for native Okinawans) begin to reclaim their heritage. And this is also what we have been trying to accomplish with our work.

Recently, my brother and I and Dr. Suzuki hosted a joint American-Japanese expedition of scientists and educators in Okinawa. They had come to study the Okinawan longevity phenomenon, and were interested in bringing the wisdom of the elders to a wider audience via the Internet.[6] As the foremost experts on the Okinawan longevity phenomenon, we were recruited as consultants for the project.

One of the project team members was a twenty-something Okinawan woman named Aya Horikawa. Despite having grown up in Okinawa, Ayasan—like most of the younger generation—knew little of the old ways, and was patently unimpressed by them. "I know I don't have the healthiest habits in the world," she confessed one day over a burger and fries and an after-dinner smoke, "but who wants to live to a hundred anyway?" Like other young Okinawans, she was unable to speak the Okinawan dialect and knew little of her culture's deep well of healing potential, or of its ancient spiritual practices.

For one week, Ayasan and our "Island Quest" team (as our group was known) explored shamanistic healing practices among Okinawa's sacred groves, practiced karate and tai chi on the white sandy beaches, dove among rainbow-colored reefs to rediscover traditional fishing methods, and tramped through steamy rain forests looking for healing herbs. All expeditions were led by Okinawa's elder villagers, who happily shared their secrets for a long and healthy life—getting a good night's sleep, said one; eating goya, said another; family harmony, advised another. And so it went. And along the way, the elders also told their life stories.

Each of them had come from a life of hardship. As children they had little to eat, and during the war they had kept alive by hiding in the mountains and eating berries. One of the elders, Setsuko Taira, told how she was captured by an American soldier one day while searching for food, and how she thought she was going to be shot, but was handed biscuits and chocolate instead. "I've been waiting all my life to thank someone for that," she told us, tears streaming down her weathered cheeks. "So now I thank you."

As we traveled together, ate together, laughed together, and listened to the elders' stories, we noticed a gradual change coming over Ayasan. One day, near the end of the trip we found her quietly weeping. When we asked what was the matter, she replied, "For me, this has been a journey of rediscovering my roots, and the wisdom of my own Okinawan culture. I will cherish what I have learned from the elders forever . . . and share it with my friends." We assured her that we would, too.

What the Okinawans have is beautiful—indeed, priceless. Their spirit is a treasure that dwells deep within their hearts and is reflected in their belief that life is sacred. They lived through one of the most horrific battles of the Second World War, yet have arisen from its ashes to enjoy the benefits of spectacular economic development. We pray this development will be sustainable, and won't roll over the old ways as irrevocably as Okinawa was rolled over by Allied tanks during the war.

Human beings have been searching for an elixir of youth and fulfillment throughout recorded time—and the Okinawans have found it. We hope we can do our small part to help them preserve it. And we hope that by sharing their ways with you, we can help you, too, to experience just a little piece of Shangri-la.

12. Recipes for the Okinawa Program[1,2]

BREAKFAST

Mugwort Tea

Soy Smoothie

Banana Smoothie

Flaxseed and Berries Granola

Chinbin Crepes

Okinawan Blueberry Pancakes

Sweet Potato Waffles

Raspberry Pudding

Corn Bread

Carrot and Flax Muffins

Ryukyu Scrambled Eggs

Wild West Omelet

LUNCH

Tofu Tortillas

Picnic Rice Balls with Salmon

Wakame and Soba Noodles with Broth

Somen Chample (Okinawan Fine Noodles)

Cilantro-Scented Tofu Rice Salad

Paradise Burgers

Sweet Potatoes with Orange

Immortal Pâté

Shangri-la Spinach Lasagna

Tofu Chample with Cashews

DINNER

Baked Tofu Mediterranean Style

Stuffed Green Peppers

Stuffed Portobello Mushrooms

East-West Tofu Croquettes

Mexican Herbed Tofu with Chapati Wraps
Baked Tofu with Cheese
Grilled Tofu with Mushrooms
Tofu à la Sesame
Shuri Shrimp Salad
Carrot Leaf Pilaf
Quick Paella
Stir-Fried Rice with Watercress and Tuna
Spinach and Tofu Curry
Beer Crepes
Sunshine Spinach Pasta
Simple Peperoncini Spaghetti
Spicy Tomato Pasta
Zucchini (courgette) Lasagna
Lentil Stroganoff
Tomato Bruschetta
Easy Okinawan Vegetable Chample
Simmered Hechima with Miso Gravy
Tofu, Salmon, and Vegetables with Creamy Miso Sauce
Goya Chample
Okinawan Eggplants with Miso
Kimchee Okinawa Style
Okinawan Sautéed Chicken with Turmeric
Chicken and Vegetables with Mustard Sauce
Chicken Kabobs
Greek Barbecue
Beef Teriyaki with Cabernet Sauce
Simple Simmered Mackerel with Miso
Barbecued Mahi-Mahi with Lime-Soy Sauce
British Columbia Poached Salmon
Italian Baked Fish
Zesty Potatoes Wasabi Style

SALAD AND SOUP
Garden Salad
Tuna Caesar Salad
Warm Mushroom Salad with Garlic Dressing
Tropical Papaya Salad

Indonesian Gado-Gado Salad
Atlantic Caesar Salad
Okinawan White Miso Soup with Vegetables
Simple Wakame and Tofu Miso Soup
Spinach Chicken Soup
Summer Field Gazpacho Soup
Creamy Carrot Soup
Mediterranean Minestrone

DRESSINGS AND SAUCES

Okinawan Tofunaise
Creamy Miso Dressing
Miso-Sesame Barbecue Sauce
Miso-Ginger Mayonnaise

DESSERT

Chocolate-Kahlúa Mousse
Super Vanilla Tofu Cheese Cake
Okinawan Orange Brûlée
Zesty Zucchini Bread
Green Tea Ice Cream
Delectable Strawberry Mousse
Easy Creamed Peach

BREAKFAST

Mugwort Tea
Makes 4 cups

6 cups water
4 tablespoons dried mugwort
3 teaspoons your choice of black tea leaves (best to avoid teas with strong added aroma, such as Earl Grey, apple, peach)

1. Bring the water to a rapid boil.
2. Pour 1 cup of boiling water into a teapot, and divide 1 cup of boiling water into 4 teacups. Swirl the water around in the teapot and cups for a minute or so to warm them.

3. Empty the water from the teapot and cups, place the mugwort and black tea leaves in the teapot, and pour in the remaining hot water. Replace the lid and steep for 4 to 6 minutes.
4. Strain and serve in each cup and enjoy. If it is too strong, add more hot water.

Soy Smoothie
Serves 4

6 ounces silken tofu-lite
1 cup fat-free yogurt (plain or berry flavored)
½ cup fresh or frozen strawberries or raspberries
Combine the tofu, yogurt, and berries in a blender; process until smooth. Pour into four glasses and serve.

Nutrients per Serving
Calories: 55 Protein: 4.9 g (36%) Carbohydrate: 7.2 g (53%)
Fat: 0.6 g (9%) Calcium: 67 mg Fiber: 0.4 g Iron: 0.4 mg Sodium: 65 mg Flavonoids: 7.7 mg
Okinawa Food Pyramid Servings
Grains: 0 Vegetables: 0 Fruits: ¼ Flavonoid Foods: ½ Calcium Foods: ¼
Omega-3 Foods: 0 Condiments: 0 Meat/Eggs: 0 Sweets: 0

Banana Smoothie
Serves 4

2 chopped and frozen bananas
2 tablespoons peanut butter
2 ounces silken tofu-lite
2 tablespoons chocolate syrup
2½ cups skim milk
Combine all the ingredients in a blender. Process until smooth. Pour into four glasses and serve.

Nutrients per Serving
Calories: 196 Protein: 9 g (18%) Carbohydrate: 32.2 g (66%) Fat: 4.9 g (23%)
Calcium: 952 mg Fiber: 2.5 g Iron: 0.8 mg Sodium: 137.6 mg Flavonoids: 12.4 mg
Okinawa Food Pyramid Servings
Grains: 0 Vegetables: 0 Fruits: ½ Flavonoid Foods: 0 Calcium Foods: ½ Omega-3 Foods: 0 Condiments: 0 Meat/Eggs: 0 Sweets: 0

Flaxseed and Berries Granola

Serves 1

1 tablespoon ground flaxseed
6 medium strawberries, cut into halves (about ½ cup)
½ cup low-fat granola
½ cup skim milk

Place the flaxseed, berries, and granola in a small bowl, pour in milk, and serve.

Nutrients per Serving
Calories: 341 Protein: 11.4 g (13%) Carbohydrate: 59.1 g (69%) Fat: 8.1 g (21%)
Calcium: 216.6 mg Fiber: 7 g Iron: 9 mg Sodium: 141 mg Flavonoids: 24 mg
Okinawa Food Pyramid Servings
Grains: 1 Vegetables: 0 Fruits: 1 Flavonoid Foods: 2 Calcium Foods: ½
Omega-3 Foods: 1 Condiments: 0 Meat/Eggs: 0 Sweets: 0

Chinbin Crepes

Makes 8 crepes; serves 4

1 cup all-purpose (plain) unbleached flour
½ cup whole-grain wheat flour
1 teaspoon baking powder
1 cup sugar syrup (beat 1 egg white, add ⅔ cup brown sugar, and whisk; then add ¾ cup water, whisking well)
½ cup calcium-fortified soy milk
¼ cup skim milk
1 cup low-fat plain yogurt
2 kiwi fruit, each cut into 8 slices

1. Sift the two flours and baking powder into a large mixing bowl.
2. Prepare the syrup and add to the flour mixture.
3. Add the milks and mix well.
4. Spray crepe pan with nonstick canola spray and pour in ⅓ cup of batter. Cook over medium-high heat until you see bubbles on the surface. Turn over and cook on other side an additional minute.
5. Remove crepe from pan and place on warmed platter; keep warm. Continue to make crepes with remaining batter.

6. Spoon 2 tablespoons of the yogurt onto each crepe. Top with two slices of kiwi and roll up crepe, tucking in the ends. Serve.

Nutrients per Serving
Calories: 340 Protein: 11.1 g (13%) Carbohydrate: 70.2 g (83%) Fat: 2.3 g (6%)
Calcium: 317.2 mg Fiber: 3.5 g Iron: 2.5 mg Sodium: 172 mg
Okinawa Food Pyramid Servings
Grains: 2 Vegetables: 0 Fruits: 1 Flavonoid Foods: 0 Calcium Foods: 0
Omega-3 Foods: 0 Condiments: 0 Meat/Eggs: 0 Sweets: 0

Okinawan Blueberry Pancakes

Makes 8 pancakes; serves 4

2 eggs (free-range, omega-3)
1½ cups calcium-fortified soy milk
1 teaspoon vanilla extract
2 cups whole-grain wheat flour
3 teaspoons baking powder
3 tablespoons brown sugar
1½ cups fresh blueberries, washed

1. Beat the eggs in a mixing bowl until thick.
2. Slowly add the soy milk to the eggs, stirring constantly. Add the vanilla extract.
3. Sift the flour and baking powder into a separate bowl.
4. Add the sugar and blueberries to the flour and mix well.
5. Add the flour mixture to the egg batter and mix with a wooden spoon.
6. Coat a griddle or skillet with nonstick canola spray. Heat over medium heat.
7. Pour ⅓ cup batter onto griddle or skillet. When the pancake surface is covered with bubbles and the bottom side is browned, about 3 minutes, flip and cook until the other side is set, another minute.
8. Remove the pancake to a warmed platter and keep warm. Make the remaining pancakes with the remaining batter.

Nutrients per Serving
Calories: 333 Protein: 14 g (17%) Carbohydrate: 61 g (73%) Fat: 5.5 g (15%)
Calcium: 547 mg Fiber: 9.9 g Iron: 3.4 mg Sodium: 347 mg Flavonoids: 3.2 mg
Okinawa Food Pyramid Servings
Grains: 2 Vegetables: 0 Fruits: ½ Flavonoid Foods: 0 Calcium Foods: ½
Omega-3 Foods: ½ Condiments: 0 Meat/Eggs: 0 Sweets: 0

Sweet Potato Waffles

Makes 4 waffles; serves 4

¾ cup peeled and cubed sweet potato
1 cup whole-grain wheat flour
½ teaspoon baking powder
1 egg or ¼ cup egg substitute
¼ cup canola oil
1½ cups calcium-fortified soy milk
½ teaspoon ground cinnamon

1. Preheat a waffle iron.
2. Steam the sweet potato until tender, about 10 minutes, then mash with a fork.
3. Sift the flour and baking powder into a mixing bowl.
4. Whisk the egg in another bowl. Add the canola oil, soy milk, cinnamon, flour, and sweet potato. Mix well.
5. Coat the waffle iron with nonstick canola spray, pour in ⅔ cup of batter, and cook until done according to manufacturer's directions. Remove waffle to warmed platter and keep warm while you make remaining waffles.

Note: For optional toppings, consider maple syrup, sliced strawberries, or thawed frozen mixed berries.

Nutrients per Serving
Calories: 297 Protein: 8.6 g (12%) Carbohydrate: 30 g (40%) Fat: 17.2 g (52%)
Calcium: 487 mg Fiber: 5.7 g Iron: 2.1 mg Sodium: 80 mg Flavonoids: 2.1 mg
Okinawa Food Pyramid Servings
Grains: 1 Vegetables: ½ Fruits: ½ Flavonoid Foods: ¼ Calcium Foods: ½
Omega-3 Foods: 0 Condiments: 0 Meat/Eggs: 0 Sweets: 0

Raspberry Pudding

Serves 4

1 cup calcium-fortified soy milk
2 eggs (free-range, omega-3)
3 tablespoons maple syrup
¼ teaspoon ground cinnamon
2 thick slices flaxseed bread
1 cup fresh or frozen raspberries

1. Preheat the oven to 350° F.
2. Combine all the ingredients except the bread and raspberries in a mixing bowl. Whisk vigorously.
3. Coat a 2-quart casserole with nonstick canola spray.
4. Put a slice of bread on the bottom of the casserole. Pour half the liquid on the bread. Top with half of the raspberries.
5. Repeat with other slice of bread, liquid, and the raspberries.
6. Bake in the oven for 50 to 60 minutes, or until lightly browned on top.

Nutrients per Serving
Calories: 146.8 Protein: 7 g (19%) Carbohydrate: 22 g (59%) Fat: 4.1 g (25%)
Calcium: 158 mg Fiber: 5.4 g Iron: 1.5 mg Sodium: 75 mg Flavonoids: 2.4 mg
Okinawa Food Pyramid Servings
Grains: ½ Vegetables: 0 Fruits: ½ Flavonoid Foods: ¼ Calcium Foods: ¼
Omega-3 Foods: ½ Condiments: 0 Meat/Eggs: 0 Sweets: 0

Corn Bread

Serves 8

1½ cups yellow cornmeal
¼ cup ground flaxseed
1 teaspoon baking soda
½ teaspoon sea salt
1½ cups low-fat plain yogurt
1 tablespoon canola oil
¼ cup egg substitute

1. Preheat the oven to 400°F. Coat a 9-inch pie plate with nonstick canola spray.

2. In a mixing bowl, combine the cornmeal, flaxseed, baking soda, and salt.

3. In another mixing bowl, stir together the yogurt, oil, and egg substitute until smoothly blended. Combine the wet with the dry ingredients until just mixed.

4. Pour the batter into the pie plate and bake for 25 to 30 minutes or until golden on top and when a toothpick inserted in the center comes out clean. Set aside on a rack to cool for 10 minutes, then cut into 8 wedges. Serve.

Nutrients per Serving
Calories: 73 Protein: 3.9 g (21%) Carbohydrate: 8.2 g (45%) Fat: 2.8 g (34%)
Calcium: 88.5 mg Fiber: 0.5 g Iron: 0.5 mg Sodium: 348.8 mg Flavonoids: 18 mg
Okinawa Food Pyramid Servings
Grains: 1 Vegetables: 0 Fruits: 0 Flavonoid Foods: 1½ Calcium Foods: 0
Omega-3 Foods: 0 Condiments: 0 Meat/Eggs: 0 Sweets: 0

Carrot and Flax Muffins
Serves 12

¼ cup egg substitute
⅓ cup honey
3 tablespoons canola oil
1⅓ cups skim milk
¾ cup whole-grain wheat flour
½ cup all-purpose (plain) unbleached flour
¾ cup yellow cornmeal
2 tablespoons wheat germ
¼ cup ground flaxseed
2½ teaspoons baking powder
¼ teaspoon sea salt
1¼ cups shredded carrot

1. Preheat the oven to 400°F. Coat twelve 2½-inch muffin cups with non-stick canola spray and set aside.

2. In a mixing bowl, whisk together the egg substitute, honey, and oil. Mix well. Add the skim milk and whisk vigorously.

3. In a large mixing bowl, stir together the flours, cornmeal, wheat germ, flaxseed, baking powder, and salt.

4. Add the milk mixture and the carrot to the dry ingredients and stir just until blended. Do not overmix.
5. Spoon the batter evenly into the prepared muffin cups.
6. Bake the muffins for 18 minutes, or until the muffins turn golden brown and a toothpick inserted in the center comes out clean.

Nutrients per Serving
Calories: 152 Protein: 4 g (10%) Carbohydrate: 25.8 g (65%) Fat: 4.3 g (25%)
Calcium: 13.7 mg Fiber: 6 g Iron: 1.4 mg Sodium: 130 mg Flavonoids: 12 mg
Okinawa Food Pyramid Servings
Grains: 1 Vegetables: 0 Fruits: 0 Flavonoid Foods: 1 Calcium Foods: 0
Omega-3 Foods: 0 Condiments: 0 Meat/Eggs: 0 Sweets: 1

Ryukyu Scrambled Eggs
Serves 4

1 cup egg substitute, such as Egg Beaters
1 3-ounce can water-packed tuna
Pinch of sea salt
Freshly ground pepper
1 6-ounce piece tofu-lite, cut into ½-inch cubes
½ cup chopped celery

1. Beat the egg substitute in a large mixing bowl; add the tuna, salt, and pepper to taste.
2. Heat a wok or a skillet and spray with nonstick canola spray. Cook the tofu until golden, about 2 minutes.
3. Add the celery and cook 2 additional minutes.
4. Pour the egg mixture into the skillet and stir continuously until cooked through.
5. Evenly divide onto four plates and serve.

Nutrients per Serving
Calories: 100 Protein: 15.7 g (64%) Carbohydrate: 1.5 g (6%) Fat: 3.2 g (30%)
Calcium: 64.3 mg Fiber: 0.3 g Iron: 2.1 mg Sodium: 280 mg Flavonoids: 10.5 mg
Okinawa Food Pyramid Servings
Grain: 0 Vegetables: 0 Fruits: 0 Flavonoid Foods: ½ Calcium Foods: 0
Omega-3 Foods: 0 Condiments: 0 Meat/Eggs: ½ Sweets: 0

Wild West Omelet

Makes 2 omelets; serves 4

½ cup cubed potato
½ cup chopped red bell pepper
½ cup chopped green bell pepper
4 slices (½ ounce each) turkey bacon, diced
½ teaspoon dried oregano leaves
2 cups egg substitute

1. Steam the potato for 7 to 10 minutes, or until soft.
2. Coat a skillet with nonstick canola spray and cook the bell peppers and turkey bacon, with the oregano, over medium heat for approximately 6 minutes, or until bell peppers are tender. Add the potato and stir. Remove and set aside.
3. Coat the same skillet with more canola spray and pour in 1 cup egg substitute. Cook over medium heat, lifting the edges to allow uncooked portion to flow underneath, until almost set (approximately 1 minute).
4. Spoon half the vegetables over half of the omelet. Fold the other half of the omelet over the vegetables, then slide omelet onto serving plate.
5. Make another omelet with the remaining egg substitute and vegetable mixture. Serve.

Nutrients per Serving
Calories: 163 Protein: 17.8 g (44%) Carbohydrate: 7.2 g (18%) Fat: 6.8 g (37%)
Calcium: 73.9 mg Fiber: 1.1 g Iron: 3 mg Sodium: 413 mg
Okinawa Food Pyramid Servings
Grains: 0 Vegetables: 1 Fruits: 0 Flavonoid Foods: 0 Calcium Foods: 0
Omega-3 Foods: 0 Condiments: 0 Meat/Eggs: 1 Sweets: 0

LUNCH

Tofu Tortillas
Serves 4

½ cup egg substitute
1 10.5-ounce piece firm tofu-lite
1 cup diced tomato
5 large fresh basil leaves, chopped
¼ teaspoon sea salt
Freshly ground black pepper
4 corn tortillas
¼ cup fat-free cottage cheese
½ cup shredded sharp Cheddar cheese
¼ cup salsa

1. Beat the egg substitute and combine with the tofu, using a fork to mash the tofu.
2. Coat a large skillet with nonstick canola spray and sauté the egg mixture and tomato, stirring, until egg is softly cooked, about 2 minutes. Turn off the heat and add the basil, salt, and pepper to taste. Place in a bowl.
3. Heat the tortillas in a clean skillet. Once tortillas are warmed, set on individual plates.
4. Place one-fourth of the sautéed mixture (approximately 5 tablespoons) inside each tortilla and add 1 tablespoon cottage cheese. Roll up and place in a microwave-safe baking dish.
5. Top each tortilla roll with 2 tablespoons of Cheddar cheese. Put dish in microwave and cook on high, until cheese is melted.
6. Top each tortilla with 1 tablespoon of salsa. Serve.

Nutrients per Serving
Calories: 190 Protein: 16.2 g (33%) Carbohydrate: 16 g (33%) Fat: 7.4 g (34%)
Calcium: 209 mg Fiber: 1.9 g Iron: 2 mg Sodium: 490 mg Flavonoids: 15.5 mg
Okinawa Food Pyramid Servings
Grains: 1 Vegetables: 1 Fruits: 0 Flavonoid Foods: 1 Calcium Foods: ½
Omega-3 Foods: 0 Condiments: 0 Meat/Eggs: 0 Sweets: 0

Picnic Rice Balls with Salmon

Serves 4

Sea salt
2 salmon fillets, about 7 ounces total
6 cups cooked short-grain brown rice, divided into 8 servings, cooled
to lukewarm
4 sheets nori (paper-shaped black and dried seaweed), cut
in half

1. Prepare a grill or broiler.
2. Sprinkle ½ teaspoon of the sea salt over both sides of the
   salmon; let stand for 5 minutes.
3. Grill or broil the salmon 4 minutes on each side, or until
   cooked inside. Slice each fillet into 4 pieces.
4. Sprinkle water on your hands, then a pinch of salt. Hold
   one salmon slice in your palm and add ¾ cup rice. Make a
   ball with your hands, then set it aside. Repeat to make
   eight balls.
5. Cover each ball with half a nori seaweed sheet and
   serve.
6. Note: If you are not planning to eat the balls immediately,
   refrigerate them. These are great for picnics, but remember
   to keep them on ice.

Nutrients per Serving
Calories: 395 Protein: 17.4 g (18%) Carbohydrate: 67.2 g (68%) Fat: 5.8 g (13%)
Calcium: 45 mg Fiber: 5.3 g Iron: 1.6 mg Sodium: 327 mg
Okinawa Food Pyramid Servings
Grains: 3 Vegetables: 0 Fruits: 0 Flavonoid Foods: 0 Calcium Foods: 1
Omega-3 Foods: 0 Condiments: 0 Meat/Eggs: 0 Sweets: 0

Wakame and Soba Noodles with Broth

Serves 4

10 ounces dried soba (buckwheat) noodles (available in health and Asian food stores)
4 large shrimp (king prawns)
4 fresh shiitake mushrooms
5 cups bonito broth (5 cups hot water and 2 teaspoons bonito broth powder)
¼ teaspoon sea salt
1 tablespoon low-sodium soy sauce
¼ cup dried wakame seaweed

1. Cook the noodles as directed on package. Rinse well under cold water to remove surface starch. Set aside.
2. Clean and shell the shrimp, leaving tails attached.
3. Trim the shiitake stems.
4. Bring the bonito broth to a boil in a large pot over medium-high heat. Add the salt and soy sauce and simmer for 3 minutes.
5. Add the shrimp and shiitake to the broth, and bring to a boil over high heat. Reduce the heat to low, and cook for 5 minutes.
6. Add the noodles and wakame to the broth-shrimp mixture, return to a boil, and turn off the heat.
7. Evenly divide the noodles among four serving bowls. Arrange the shrimp, shiitake, and wakame on top of the noodles and pour the broth over the noodles. Serve immediately.

Nutrients per Serving
Calories: 272 Protein: 10.9 g (16%) Carbohydrate: 52.3 g (79%) Fat: 1.4 g (5%)
Calcium: 55.8 mg Fiber: 4 g Iron: 3.7 mg Sodium: 408.9 mg Flavonoids: 1.6 mg
Okinawa Food Pyramid Servings
Grains: 3 Vegetables: 0 Fruits: 0 Flavonoid Foods: 0 Calcium Foods: 3
Omega-3 Foods: 0 Condiments: ½ Meat/Eggs: 0 Sweets: 0

Somen Chample (Okinawan Fine Noodles)

Serves 4

7 ounces dried somen noodles (wheat, white, fine noodles; available at most Asian food stores)
1½ cups julienned green pepper
1⅓ cups julienned carrots
1½ cups shredded cabbage
1 3-ounce can water-packed tuna
Freshly ground black pepper

1. Cook the somen noodles in at least 5 cups of water for 2 minutes, making sure not to overcook them. Rinse under cold water for 3 minutes and drain thoroughly.
2. Coat a large skillet with nonstick canola spray and heat over medium heat. Sauté the vegetables for 4 to 6 minutes, or until tender. Set aside.
3. Spray some more canola oil in the same skillet and heat over medium-high heat. Sauté the somen noodles, stirring continuously.
4. Add the vegetables and tuna to the noodles and cook 1 more minute, stirring.
5. Turn off the heat, add black pepper to taste, and stir.
6. Evenly divide noodles among four plates and serve immediately.

Nutrients per Serving
Calories: 235 Protein: 11.1 g (19%) Carbohydrate: 44.9 g (76%) Fat: 1.3 g (5%)
Calcium: 43.1 mg Fiber: 5 g Iron: 1.5 mg Sodium: 695 mg Flavonoids: 0.1 mg
Okinawa Food Pyramid Servings
Grains: 1½ Vegetables: 2 Fruits: 0 Flavonoid Foods: 0 Calcium Foods: 0
Omega-3 Foods: ¼ Condiments: 0 Meat/Eggs: 0 Sweets: 0

Cilantro-Scented Tofu Rice Salad

Serves 4

1 10.5-ounce container firm tofu-lite
3 cups cooked long-grain brown rice
¼ cup chopped fresh cilantro (coriander)
¼ cup peeled and minced cucumber

Dressing
2 tablespoons canola oil
2 tablespoons apple or cider vinegar
1 garlic clove minced

4 to 8 lettuce leaves
¼ cup minced red onion

1. Cut the tofu into ⅓-inch-thick slices and drain in a colander for 15 minutes. Crumble the tofu into small pieces and place in a mixing bowl. Add the rice, cilantro, and cucumber, tossing evenly.
2. Combine the dressing ingredients in a blender until mixed well.
3. Pour the dressing onto the tofu-rice mixture and toss to coat evenly. Let flavors blend for 20 minutes in the refrigerator.
4. Put the lettuce leaves on four plates; evenly divide the rice and place on top of the lettuce. Scatter the onion over the top of each salad and serve.

Nutrients per Serving
Calories: 261 Protein: 8.5 g (13%) Carbohydrate: 36.3 g (56%) Fat: 9 g (31%)
Calcium: 50.5 mg Fiber: 3.6 g Iron: 1.4 mg Sodium: 70 mg Flavonoids: 15.5 mg
Okinawa Food Pyramid Servings
Grains: 2 Vegetables: ¹/3 Fruits: 0 Flavonoid Foods: 1 Calcium Foods: 0
Omega-3 Foods: 0 Condiments: 1 Meat/Eggs: 0 Sweets: 0

Paradise Burgers

Serves 4

Burgers
2 10.5-ounce pieces firm tofu-lite, excess water squeezed out with a kitchen towel
½ cup minced celery
⅓ cup minced onion
2 garlic cloves, minced
1 3-ounce can water-packed tuna
¼ cup bread crumbs
⅔ teaspoon sea salt
2 teaspoons low-sodium soy sauce
Freshly ground black pepper

4 whole wheat burger buns
2 lettuce leaves, halved
1 tomato, sliced
½ cup sliced onion

1. Preheat the oven to 350°F.
2. Combine the burger ingredients in a large mixing bowl. Knead well until they hold together when compressed. Divide and make four burgers.
3. Spray nonstick canola spray in a baking pan. Place burgers in the pan and bake 8 minutes. Turn burgers over, and bake for 5 minutes more, or until their surfaces are golden.
4. Serve with buns, lettuce, tomato, and onion.

Nutrients per Serving
Calories: 254 Protein: 21.5 g (33%) Carbohydrate: 31.5 g (48%) Fat: 5.5 g (19%)
Calcium: 148.8 mg Fiber: 3.1 g Iron: 4.6 mg Sodium: 980 mg Flavonoids: 47.1 mg)
Okinawa Food Pyramid Servings
Grains: 2 Vegetables: 1 Fruits: 0 Flavonoid Foods: 2 Calcium Foods: 0
Omega-3 Foods: ¼ Condiments: 1 Meat/Eggs: 0 Sweets: 0

Sweet Potatoes with Orange
Serves 4

4 medium sweet potatoes, peeled, cut into ⅓-inch-thick rounds, and soaked in water for 10 minutes, then drained
¼ cup calcium-fortified orange juice with pulp
1 teaspoon chopped lemongrass
1 tablespoon sherry
1 orange, peeled and separated into segments
1 teaspoon brown sugar

1. Place the sweet potatoes in a pot with plenty of water and cook over medium-high heat for 8 to 10 minutes, or until soft. Avoid cooking until they are broken. Drain and set aside.
2. In the same pot, combine the orange juice, lemongrass, and sherry, then bring to a boil. Add the orange segments, brown sugar, and sweet potatoes. Cook until the flavor of the orange is transferred to the sweet potato, about 7 minutes. Serve.

Nutrients per Serving
Calories: 167 Protein: 2.6 g (6%) Carbohydrate: 38.1 g (91%) Fat: 0.5 g (2%)
Calcium: 63.3 mg Fiber: 4.7 g Iron: 0.9 mg Sodium: 17 mg
Okinawa Food Pyramid Servings
Grains: 0 Vegetables: 2 Fruits: ½ Flavonoid Foods: 0 Calcium Foods: 0)
Omega-3 Foods: 0 Condiments: 0 Meat/Eggs: 0 Sweets: 0

Immortal Pâté
Serves 4

1 16-ounce piece firm tofu-lite
½ cup minced fresh mushrooms
1 garlic clove, minced
½ teaspoon fresh lemon juice
1 tablespoon white miso
1 teaspoon prepared mustard
2 tablespoons arrowroot (kudzu) powder
¼ cup minced cucumber

1. Squeeze excess water from the tofu with a clean kitchen towel.
2. Spray a skillet with nonstick canola spray and sauté the mushrooms and garlic over medium heat for 4 minutes. Add the lemon juice and remove from heat.
3. Combine the tofu, miso, mustard, arrowroot powder, cucumber, and mushroom mixture in a mixing bowl. Mash until smooth. Press the mixture into a loaf pan or small cake pan and refrigerate overnight to let the flavors blend.
4. Slice, and serve with whole wheat crackers or whole wheat bread, if you like.

Nutrients per Serving
Calories: 59 Protein: 7.4 g (49%) Carbohydrate: 3.3 g (22%) Fat: 1.7 g (27%)
Calcium: 46.6 mg Fiber: 1.3 g Iron: 1.2 mg Sodium: 171 mg Flavonoids: 25.4 mg
Okinawa Food Pyramid Servings
Grains: 0 Vegetables: 0 Fruits: 0 Flavonoid Foods: 2 Calcium Foods: 0
Omega-3 Foods: 0 Condiments: 0 Meat/Eggs: 0 Sweets: 0

Shangri-La Spinach Lasagna
Serves 4

6 lasagna noodles (sheets)
2 cups chopped spinach
1¼ cups fat-free ricotta cheese
¼ cup grated Parmesan cheese
½ teaspoon dried oregano
½ teaspoon dried basil
Pinch of salt
Freshly ground black pepper
3 cups meatless spaghetti sauce
½ cup shredded reduced-fat soy cheese or part-skim mozzarella cheese

1. Preheat the oven to 350°F.
2. Cook the lasagna noodles per directions on package. Once noodles are cooked and cooled, slice them in half.
3. Coat a large skillet with nonstick canola spray and sauté the spinach for a minute; let cool briefly.

4. In a bowl, mix the spinach, ricotta, Parmesan cheese, oregano, and basil. Adjust the seasoning with salt and pepper to taste.
5. Coat an 8-inch square pan with canola spray.
6. Spread ½ cup spaghetti sauce on the bottom of the pan. Place four noodles over the sauce, and top with half the spinach mixture. Cover with 1 cup spaghetti sauce. Layer with another four noodles and the remaining spinach. Cover with 1 cup of spaghetti sauce. Top with remaining four noodles. Cover with ½ cup spaghetti sauce. Finally top with the soy cheese.
7. Cover the pan with foil and bake for 20 minutes. Uncover and bake 10 more minutes, or until top is lightly browned. Serve.

Nutrients per Serving
Calories: 414 Protein: 23 g (27%) Carbohydrate: 57.9 g (45%) Fat: 9.7 g (29%)
Calcium: 565 mg Fiber: 6.3 g Iron: 3 mg Sodium: 382 mg Flavonoids: 4.4 mg
Okinawa Food Pyramid Servings
Grains: 2 Vegetables: 1 Fruits: 0 Flavonoid Foods: ½ Calcium Foods: ½
Omega-3 Foods: 0 Condiments: 0 Meat/Eggs: 0 Sweets: 0

Tofu Chample with Cashews
Serves 4

2 garlic cloves, thinly sliced
2 10.5-ounce containers regular tofu-lite, wrapped with paper towel and microwaved for 3 minutes, then crumbled into about 16 cubes
½ cup cashew nuts
1 cup quartered button mushrooms
2 teaspoons low-sodium soy sauce
2 tablespoons parsley, minced

1. Coat a large skillet with nonstick canola oil spray, and sauté the garlic over medium heat for 30 seconds. Add the tofu and cashews, and cook over medium-low heat until tofu is golden, 3 to 4 minutes.
2. Add the mushrooms and cook until tender, another 2 minutes.
3. Raise heat to high and add soy sauce. Immediately turn off the heat and add the parsley.
4. Evenly divide mixture among four plates and serve.

Nutrients per Serving
Calories: 170 Protein: 14.2 g (33%) Carbohydrate: 8.9 g (21%) Fat: 10.2 g (54%)
Calcium: 80.7 mg Fiber: 0.8 g Iron: 2.6 mg Sodium: 245 mg Flavonoids: 31 mg
Okinawa Food Pyramid Servings
Grains: 0 Vegetables: ½ Fruits: 0 Flavonoid Foods: 2 Calcium Foods: 0
Omega-3 Foods: 0 Condiments: 0 Meat/Eggs: 0 Sweets: 0

DINNER

Baked Tofu Mediterranean Style
Serves 4

1-pound piece firm or extra-firm tofu-lite
1 tablespoon olive oil
2 cups peeled and crushed tomatoes
½ cup diced mushrooms
¼ teaspoon salt
½ teaspoon dried oregano
1 garlic clove, sliced
5 large basil leaves, chopped

1. Preheat the oven to 350°F.
2. Drain the tofu well in a colander. Cut the tofu into 12 slices, each about ¼ inch thick.
3. In a small saucepan, combine the olive oil, tomatoes, mushrooms, salt, oregano, and garlic. Bring to a boil and cook over medium heat for approximately 5 minutes.
4. Coat a baking dish with nonstick canola spray and add the tofu. Pour the tomato sauce over the tofu and bake for 20 minutes.
5. Divide among four plates and garnish with basil leaves.

Nutrients per Serving
Calories: 91 Protein: 8.9 g (39%) Carbohydrate: 4.2 g (18%) Fat: 5.1 g (50%)
Calcium: 59.3 mg Fiber: 0.7 g Iron: 1.3 mg Sodium: 256 mg Flavonoids: 23.2 mg
Okinawa Food Pyramid Servings
Grains: 0 Vegetables: 1¼ Fruits: 0 Flavonoid Foods: 1 Calcium Foods: 0
Omega-3 Foods: 0 Condiments: 0 Meat/Eggs: 0 Sweets: 0

Stuffed Green Peppers

Serves 4

1 10.5-ounce piece firm tofu-lite, excess water squeezed out with a kitchen towel
½ cup small shrimp, boiled and shelled
4 fresh button mushrooms, minced
1 garlic clove, minced
1 tablespoon arrowroot powder (kudzu)
2 teaspoons curry powder
Pinch of sea salt
Freshly ground black pepper
4 large green peppers, cut into lengthwise halves, seeds removed
1 tablespoon canola oil

1. Preheat the oven to 300°F.
2. Combine the tofu, shrimp, mushrooms, garlic, arrowroot, and seasonings in a bowl. Mix well with your hands until mixture holds together when compressed.
3. Put 2 to 3 tablespoons of the mixture into each green pepper half. Brush canola oil over the stuffing and place peppers in a baking pan sprayed with canola oil.
4. Bake for 10 minutes, then serve.

Nutrients per Serving
Calories: 131 Protein: 10 g (33%) Carbohydrate: 12.9 g (39%) Fat: 5.3 g (37%)
Calcium: 63.1 mg Fiber: 3.4 g Iron: 2.2 mg Sodium: 135 mg Flavonoids: 20.7 mg
Okinawa Food Pyramid Servings
Grains: 0 Vegetables: 2 Fruits: 0 Flavonoid Foods: 1 Calcium Foods: 0
Omega-3 Foods: 0 Condiments: 0 Meat/Eggs: 0 Sweets: 0

Stuffed Portobello Mushrooms

Serves 4

8 large portobello mushrooms
1 10.5-ounce piece firm tofu-lite, excess water squeezed out with a kitchen towel
2 cups chopped fresh spinach
1 garlic clove
½ teaspoon sea salt
½ cup bread crumbs

1. Preheat the oven to 350°F.
2. Remove and clean the mushroom stems; chop well. Clean the mushroom caps.
3. Combine the tofu, spinach, garlic, and salt in a food processor until smooth.
4. Coat a large skillet with canola oil spray, and cook the mushroom stems and tofu puree until the mushroom stems are tender, about 3 minutes.
5. Add the bread crumbs to the tofu mixture. You may need to add additional bread crumbs if the mixture is not dry enough. Add 1 tablespoon at a time; cook until the filling holds together when compressed. Fill each mushroom cap with 4 tablespoons filling.
6. Spray a large baking dish with canola spray. Place the mushroom caps in the dish and bake for about 20 minutes, or until the mushrooms are tender.
7. Serve 2 mushroom caps for each plate.

Nutrients per Serving
Calories: 96 Protein: 11.1 g (46%) Carbohydrate: 10.5 g (43%) Fat: 1 g (10%)
Calcium: 121.1 mg Fiber: 5.5 g Iron: 1.8 mg Sodium: 412 mg Flavonoids: 15.5 mg
Okinawa Food Pyramid Servings
Grains: 0 Vegetables: 3 Fruits: 0 Flavonoid Foods: 1 Calcium Foods: 0
Omega-3 Foods: 0 Condiments: 0 Meat/Eggs: 0 Sweets: 0

East-West Tofu Croquettes

Serves 4

½ cup finely chopped onion
⅓ cup cooked corn kernels
1 3-ounce can water-packed tuna
2 10.5-ounce pieces firm tofu-lite, excess water squeezed out with a
kitchen towel
¼ teaspoon sea salt
Freshly ground pepper
¼ cup whole-grain wheat flour
2 eggs or ½ cup egg substitute, lightly beaten
1 cup bread crumbs
4 bunches watercress

1. Preheat the oven to 350°F.
2. Coat a large skillet with canola oil spray and sauté the onion
   over low heat until soft and transparent, 4 to 5 minutes.
3. Add the corn and tuna and cook over low heat for about 2
   minutes. Set aside and allow to cool.
4. Mash the tofu with a fork in a bowl. Add the onion mixture,
   sea salt, and pepper to taste. Form eight ½-inch-thick patties.
5. Place the flour, eggs, and bread crumbs in three separate
   bowls.
6. Coat each patty with flour, then dip each patty in the eggs
   and dredge in bread crumbs, coating well.
7. Place the tofu patties in a baking pan and bake 7 to 10
   minutes on each side, or until the coating is golden brown.
8. Garnish four plates with watercress and add two
   croquettes. Serve.

Nutrients per Serving
Calories: 183 Protein: 21.8 g (48%) Carbohydrate: 16.2 g (35%) Fat: 4 g (20%)
Calcium: 113 mg Fiber: 1.9 g Iron: 2.8 mg Sodium: 473 mg Flavonoids: 44.6 mg
Okinawa Food Pyramid Servings
Grains: 1 Vegetables: 2 Fruits: 0 Flavonoid Foods: 2 Calcium Foods: 0
Omega-3 Foods: ¼ Condiments: 0 Meat/Eggs: 0* Sweets: 0

* Omega-3 eggs can be counted as an Omega-3 food or as eggs.

Mexican Herbed Tofu with Chapati Wraps

Serves 4

Sauce

1 avocado, peeled and seed removed
½ cup fresh basil leaves
1 teaspoon dried thyme
1 teaspoon fresh dill, minced
2 garlic cloves, minced
1 teaspoon olive oil
¼ teaspoon sea salt
Freshly ground pepper

8 small chapatis, or thin fat-free flour tortilla wraps
1 10.5-ounce container firm tofu-lite, cut into 8 rectangles
1 cup alfalfa sprouts
Salsa (optional)

1. Combine the sauce ingredients in a food processor or blender, processing until smooth.
2. Spread 1 tablespoon of the sauce onto a chapati, top with a slice of tofu, and add 2 tablespoons alfalfa sprouts, then roll up. Repeat for the remaining wraps.
3. Serve with salsa, as desired.

Nutrients per Serving
Calories: 215 Protein: 5.6 g (10%) Carbohydrate: 30.8 g (57%) Fat: 8.8 g (37%)
Calcium: 67.8 mg Fiber: 14.8 g Iron: 1.3 mg Sodium: 546 mg Flavonoids: 16.5 mg
Okinawa Food Pyramid Servings
Grains: 2 Vegetables: 1½ Fruits: 0 Flavonoid Foods: 1 Calcium Foods: 0
Omega-3 Foods: 0 Condiments: 0 Meat/Eggs: 0 Sweets: 0

Baked Tofu with Cheese

Serves 4

2 10.5-ounce piece firm tofu-lite, drained, wrapped with paper towel, and microwaved for 3 minutes, then cut in half horizontally
⅓ cup pesto sauce
⅓ cup crumbled part-skim mozzarella cheese
¼ cup grated Parmesan cheese

1. Preheat the oven to 350°F.
2. Coat the tofu with pesto sauce and refrigerate for 10 minutes.
3. Coat a baking pan with nonstick canola spray. Transfer the tofu to the pan and put the mozzarella cheese on the tofu.
4. Pour the remaining pesto marinade over the tofu, and top with Parmesan cheese.
5. Bake for 6 minutes, then serve on individual plates with whole wheat bread (optional).

Nutrients per Serving
Calories: 204 Protein: 16.8 g (33%) Carbohydrate: 6.2 g (12%) Fat: 12.7 g (55%)
Calcium: 300.7 mg Fiber: 0 g Iron: 1.7 mg Sodium: 496 mg Flavonoids: 31 mg
Okinawa Food Pyramid Servings
Grains: 0 Vegetables: 0 Fruits: 0 Flavonoid Foods: 2 Calcium Foods: ½
Omega-3 Foods: 0 Condiments: 1 Meat/Eggs: 0 Sweets: 0

Grilled Tofu with Mushrooms
Serves 4

4 10.5-ounce pieces firm tofu-lite, drained (see Note)
Sea salt
Freshly ground black pepper
All-purpose (plain) flour, for dusting
8 fresh shiitake mushrooms, stems removed
2 packs enoki mushrooms, hard parts of stems removed, each pack split into 8 pieces
¼ cup minced shallots
2 teaspoons low-sodium soy sauce
1 tablespoon sake

1. Pat a pinch of salt and pepper onto each side of the tofu pieces and coat them lightly with 2 tablespoons of flour.
2. Coat a skillet with canola oil spray. Sauté two tofu pieces in a large skillet over medium heat until golden. Set tofu on the edge of the skillet.
3. Cook half of the shiitakes, enokis, and shallots in the center of the skillet over medium-low heat for about 2 minutes.

4. Remove the skillet from the heat. Pour 1 teaspoon soy sauce and ½ tablespoon sake over the mushrooms and stir. Transfer the tofu to 2 plates and place a portion of the sautéed mushrooms over the tofu.
5. Repeat steps with 2 remaining pieces of tofu and the rest of the mushrooms and shallots. Serve.

Note: To drain tofu's excess water without breaking its shape, wrap one block of firm tofu with two paper towels and put the tofu on a flat cutting board. Put a weight (12–15 oz.) on tofu. (A bag or two of beans is ideal.) Tilt the cutting board very slightly, using a dishcloth under the board. Allow it to sit for 15 to 45 minutes.

Nutrients per Serving
Calories: 151 Protein: 13.6 g (36%) Carbohydrate: 20.2 g (53%) Fat: 2.1 g (13%)
Calcium: 74 mg Fiber: 1.5 g Iron: 2.3 mg Sodium: 394 mg Flavonoids: 61.9 mg
Okinawa Food Pyramid Servings
Grains: 0 Vegetables: 1 Fruits: 0 Flavonoid Foods: 3 Calcium Foods: 0
Omega-3 Foods: 0 Condiments: 0 Meat/Eggs: 0 Sweets: 0

Tofu à la Sesame
Serves 4

2 10.5-ounce pieces extra-firm tofu-lite
¼ cup whole-grain wheat flour

Sauce
3 tablespoons sake rice wine
3 tablespoons low-sodium soy sauce
½ tablespoon roasted sesame oil
1 teaspoon grated ginger

¼ teaspoon minced chili pepper (optional)
½ cup white sesame seed powder (if not available, use whole seeds)
Watercress

1. Drain excess water from tofu by covering it with a paper towel and pressing under a weight (a bag of dried beans or chopped vegetables, ideally 2 pounds) for 10 minutes.
2. Preheat the oven to 450°F.

3. Slice the tofu in half horizontally, making four slices. Coat the tofu with the flour.
4. Mix the sauce ingredients, and soak the tofu slices in this mixture for 5 minutes. Turn them over and soak for 5 additional minutes.
5. Drain the tofu slices and coat with the sesame powder.
6. Coat a baking pan with nonstick canola spray and put slices in. Bake the tofu for 7 to 10 minutes, or until golden.
7. Serve on four plates, garnished with watercress.

Nutrients per Serving
Calories: 176 Protein: 14.1 g (32%) Carbohydrate: 11.2 g (25%) Fat: 8 g (41%)
Calcium: 169.9 mg Fiber: 2.2 g Iron: 3.1 mg Sodium: 595 mg Flavonoids: 31 mg
Okinawa Food Pyramid Servings
Grains: 0 Vegetables: 0 Fruits: 0 Flavonoid Foods: 2 Calcium Foods: 0
Omega-3 Foods: 0 Condiments: 1 Meat/Eggs: 0 Sweets: 0

Shuri Shrimp Salad
Serves 4

1 cup trimmed and chopped asparagus

Dressing
1 garlic clove, minced
¼ cup canola oil
¼ cup apple or cider vinegar
Pinch of sea salt
Freshly ground black pepper

8 ounces medium shrimp (tiger prawns), boiled and cut into ¼-inch pieces
⅔ cup finely diced red onion
3 cups cooked long-grain jasmine rice

1. Steam the asparagus until tender, 4 minutes. Drain well.
2. Combine the garlic and canola oil in a mixing bowl. Slowly add the vinegar, whisking vigorously. Add the salt and black pepper to taste and mix well.

3. Combine the dressing, asparagus, shrimp, and onion. Toss well, coating evenly. Add rice and toss lightly.
4. Serve in a salad bowl.

Nutrients per Serving
Calories: 348 Protein: 15.6 g (18%) Carbohydrate: 37.3 g (43%) Fat: 15 g (39%)
Calcium: 67.7 mg Fiber: 1.6 g Iron: 3.3 mg Sodium: 162 mg Flavonoids: 13.6 mg
Okinawa Food Pyramid Servings
Grains: 1½ Vegetables: ½ Fruits: 0 Flavonoid Foods: 0 Calcium Foods: 0
Omega-3 Foods: 1 Condiments: 1 Meat/Eggs: 0 Sweets: 0

Carrot Leaf Pilaf
Serves 4

1 garlic clove, minced
2 cups chopped carrot leaves
4 cups cooked long-grain brown rice
Pinch of sea salt
Freshly ground pepper

1. Coat a wok or skillet with nonstick canola spray and sauté the garlic over medium heat for 30 seconds. Add the carrot leaves and cook for 1 to 2 minutes, or until soft.
2. Add the rice, stirring continuously for about 3 minutes, or until the rice and carrot leaves are evenly mixed. Season with sea salt and pepper to taste.
3. Evenly divide among four plates and serve.

Nutrients per Serving
Calories: 217 Protein: 5.1 g (9%) Carbohydrate: 45 g (83%) Fat: 1.8 g (7%)
Calcium: 20.9 mg Fiber: 3.5 g Iron: 0.8 mg Sodium: 46 mg Flavonoids: 57.5 mg
Okinawa Food Pyramid Servings
Grains: 2 Vegetables: 1 Fruits: 0 Flavonoid Foods: 0 Calcium Foods: 0
Omega-3 Foods: 0 Condiments: 0 Meat/Eggs: 0 Sweets: 0

Quick Paella

Serves 4

1 cup chopped onion
5 cups water
1¾ cups long-grain white rice
½ cup sliced low-fat turkey sausage
¼ teaspoon saffron threads, crumbled
3 ounces medium shrimp (tiger prawns), shelled, deveined, and halved lengthwise
1½ cups frozen peas
½ teaspoon ground red pepper
8 small clams, scrubbed
12 mussels, scrubbed and beards pulled off

1. Coat a medium saucepan with nonstick canola spray and warm it over medium heat.
2. Add the onion and cook for 2 minutes, stirring continuously.
3. Add the water, rice, turkey sausage, and saffron and bring to a boil, then reduce the heat to low. Cover and simmer for 12 minutes, or until the rice is partially tender and there is still plenty of liquid remaining.
4. Stir in the shrimp, peas, and red pepper and transfer the mixture to a large shallow casserole or baking dish.
5. Preheat the oven to 375°F.
6. Arrange the clams and mussels around the edge of the dish, then cover tightly with foil.
7. Bake the mixture for 30 minutes, or until the clams and mussels open and the rice is tender.
8. Remove and discard any unopened clams and mussels; serve.

Nutrients per Serving
Calories: 474 Protein: 27.8 g (23%) Carbohydrate: 79.4 g (67%) Fat: 4.1 g (8%)
Calcium: 93.8 mg Fiber: 4.3 g Iron: 13.3 mg Sodium: 416 mg Flavonoids: 17.9 mg
Okinawa Food Pyramid Servings
Grains: 2 Vegetables: ½ Fruits: 0 Flavonoid Foods: 1 Calcium Foods: 0
Omega-3 Foods: 1½ Condiments: 0 Meat/Eggs: 0 Sweets: 0

Stir-Fried Rice with Watercress and Tuna

Serves 4

1 garlic clove, minced
1 3-ounce can water-packed tuna
2 cups chopped watercress
4 cups cooked long-grain basmati rice
1 teaspoon Chinese chicken broth powder
Sea salt
Freshly ground black pepper

1. Coat a large skillet with nonstick canola spray and cook the garlic over medium heat for 30 seconds.
2. Add the tuna to the skillet and mix. Add the watercress and cook until the greens wilt, about 2 minutes.
3. Add the rice, reduce the heat, and cook, stirring continuously, until ingredients are mixed well, about 3 minutes.
4. Add the chicken broth powder and salt and pepper to taste.
5. Divide among four bowls and serve.

Nutrients per Serving
Calories: 217 Protein: 9.2 g (17%) Carbohydrate: 41.7 g (77%) Fat: 1.9 g (8%)
Calcium: 49.8 mg Fiber: 2.8 g Iron: 1.2 mg Sodium: 123 mg
Okinawa Food Pyramid Servings
Grains: 2 Vegetables: ½ Fruits: 0 Flavonoid Foods: 0 Calcium Foods: 0
Omega-3 Foods: ¼ Condiments: 0 Meat/Eggs: 0 Sweets: 0

Spinach and Tofu Curry

Serves 4

5 cups finely chopped spinach
1 10.5-ounce piece firm tofu-lite, drained well in a colander
½ large onion, minced (⅔ cup)
2 garlic cloves, minced

Seasoning
1 tablespoon oyster sauce
½ teaspoon sea salt
Freshly ground black pepper
2 tablespoons curry powder
1½ teaspoons cumin powder (optional)

½ cup water
1 tablespoon lemon juice
4 cups long-grain brown rice, cooked

1. Sauté the spinach in a canola-sprayed skillet for 1 minute; set aside.
2. Mash the tofu with a fork or by hand.
3. Heat a wok over medium heat, coating it with canola spray. Place the onion and garlic in the wok, and stir-fry until the onion wilts, about 3 minutes.
4. Combine the seasoning ingredients in a small bowl.
5. Add the tofu to the wok and cook over medium heat about 4 minutes, until the tofu is dry. Add the spinach and seasoning and bring to a boil. Reduce the heat to medium-low, and cook 3 to 4 minutes, until liquid is evaporated.
6. Sprinkle on the lemon juice and mix in. Serve with rice.

Nutrients per Serving
Calories: 283 Protein: 11.5 g (16%) Carbohydrate: 52.5 g (74%) Fat: 3.4 g (11%)
Calcium: 115 mg Fiber: 6.9 g Iron: 3.4 mg Sodium: 478 mg Flavonoids: 29.1 mg
Okinawa Food Pyramid Servings
Grains: 2 Vegetables: 2 Fruits: 0 Flavonoid Foods: 1 Calcium Foods: 0
Omega-3 Foods: 0 Condiments: 1 Meat/Eggs: ½ Sweets: 0

Beer Crepes

Serves 4

Crepes
¾ cup egg substitute
1½ cups skim milk
½ cup beer
1¾ cups all-purpose (plain) flour
Pinch of sea salt
2 tablespoons canola oil

Topping suggestions: Tofunaise, celery, broccoli, squash, carrot, blueberry, shrimp, red beans, rice.

1. Beat the egg substitute well in a large bowl. Add the skim milk and beer, mixing well. Slowly add the flour.
2. Add the sea salt and oil, and whisk vigorously for 5 minutes, until thoroughly combined. Let stand in the refrigerator for 1 hour.
3. Coat a crepe pan or skillet with nonstick canola spray and heat. Pour ⅓ cup batter into the pan and rotate so the batter covers the bottom. Cook for 1 to 2 minutes, or until golden. Flip the crepe and cook on the other side until golden brown. Remove from the pan and keep warm. Make remaining crepes. If the batter gets too thick, add skim milk 1 tablespoon at a time.
4. Top crepes with any vegetable or fruit, and roll. Serve.

Nutrients per Serving (with 1 tablespoon tofunaise, ½ cup chopped celery, and ⅓ cup steamed broccoli)
Calories: 320 Protein: 14 g (18%) Carbohydrate: 44.3 g (55%) Fat: 9 g (25%)
Calcium: 148.3 mg Fiber: 1.4 g Iron: 3.3 mg Sodium: 169 mg Flavonoids: 11.4 mg
Okinawa Food Pyramid Servings
(with 1 tablespoon tofunaise, ½ cup chopped celery, and ⅓ cup steamed broccoli)
Grains: 1 Vegetables: 2 Fruits: 0 Flavonoid Foods: 0 Calcium Foods: ¼
Omega-3 Foods: 0 Condiments: 0 Meat/Eggs: 0 Sweets: 0

Sunshine Spinach Pasta

Serves 4

10 ounces whole wheat spaghetti
2 garlic cloves, minced
½ cup coarsely chopped walnuts
½ cup drained sun-dried tomatoes, cut into ¼-inch-wide strips
Pinch of grated nutmeg
2 cups baby spinach
½ cup feta cheese, crumbled
Pinch of sea salt
Freshly ground black pepper

1. Bring a large pot of water to a boil. Add the pasta and cook until al dente, as instructed on the package.
2. A few minutes before the pasta is done, coat a large skillet with nonstick canola spray and heat over medium heat. Add the garlic and sauté for 1 minute.
3. Add the walnuts and sauté until they darken slightly in color and smell toasted, about 1 minute. Add the tomatoes and sauté about 1 minute, until heated through. Sprinkle in a pinch of nutmeg.
4. Add the spinach to the skillet and stir continuously for 30 seconds, until the leaves begin to wilt.
5. Drain the pasta and toss with the sauce and the crumbled feta cheese. Season to taste with salt and pepper. Evenly divide among four plates and serve immediately.

Nutrients per Serving
Calories: 425 Protein: 16.3 g (16%) Carbohydrate: 60.3 g (58%) Fat: 16.2 g (33%)
Calcium: 156.3 mg Fiber: 8 g Iron: 4.2 mg Sodium: 308 mg
Okinawa Food Pyramid Servings
Grains: 2 Vegetables: 2½ Fruits: 0 Flavonoid Foods: 0 Calcium Foods: ½
Omega-3 Foods: 1 Condiments: 0 Meat/Eggs: 0 Sweets: 0

Simple Peperoncini Spaghetti
Serves 4

10 ounces whole wheat or other spaghetti
1 tablespoon canola oil
5 garlic cloves, minced
1 teaspoon dried red pepper flakes
½ teaspoon sea salt

1. Cook the spaghetti until al dente, as directed on the package.
2. Just before the spaghetti is done, heat the oil in a large skillet over medium heat. Add the garlic and red pepper flakes and cook 30 seconds. Drain the spaghetti.
3. Add the spaghetti to the skillet and give it a stir, then add sea salt, stir, and cook over medium heat for 1 minute. Stir to coat the spaghetti well with the garlic and oil mixture.
4. Evenly divide among four plates and serve immediately.

Nutrients per Serving
Calories: 286 Protein: 10.8 g (13%) Carbohydrate: 55 g (65%) Fat: 8.5 g (22%)
Calcium: 37.1 mg Fiber: 0.3 g Iron: 2.8 mg Sodium: 51 mg
Okinawa Food Pyramid Servings
Grains: 3 Vegetables: 0 Fruits: 0 Flavonoid Foods: 0 Calcium Foods: 0
Omega-3 Foods: 0 Condiments: 0 Meat/Eggs: 0 Sweets: 0

Spicy Tomato Pasta
Serves 4

8 ounces whole wheat spaghetti
1 14.5-ounce can low-sodium stewed tomatoes, undrained
1 green bell pepper (about 5 ounces), cut into thin strips
2 tablespoons low-sodium tomato paste
1 tablespoon chili powder
Pinch of sea salt
¼ teaspoon garlic powder
½ teaspoon dried basil leaves
1 8-ounce can kidney beans, rinsed and drained
2 teaspoons arrowroot (kudzu) powder ¼ cup water

1. Cook the spaghetti according to the package directions, then drain. Cover and keep warm.
2. Meanwhile, in a medium saucepan, combine the tomatoes, bell pepper, tomato paste, chili powder, salt, garlic powder, and basil and cook over medium heat. Bring to a boil, reduce heat to low, cover, and simmer for 3 minutes. Stir in the kidney beans.
3. Blend the arrowroot (kudzu) powder and water and add to the tomato mixture. Cook over low heat, stirring continuously, until thickened and bubbly, about 1 minute. Serve sauce over warm pasta.

Nutrients per Serving
Calories: 438 Protein: 22.8 g (21%) Carbohydrate: 86.9 g (79%) Fat: 1.9 g (4%)
Calcium: 85.6 mg Fiber: 15.9 g Iron: 8 mg Sodium: 95 mg Flavonoids: 6.4 mg
Okinawa Food Pyramid Servings
Grains: 3 Vegetables: 1½ Fruits: 0 Flavonoid Foods: 1 Calcium Foods: 0
Omega-3 Foods: 0 Condiments: 0 Meat/Eggs: 0 Sweets: 0

Zucchini Lasagna
Serves 6

6 lasagna noodles (sheets)
2 medium zucchini (courgettes), sliced lengthwise to make
10 slices
1 cup finely chopped carrots
2 cups finely chopped onions
4 garlic cloves, minced
2 cups prepared marinara sauce
2 tablespoons chopped fresh basil leaves
Freshly ground pepper
1½ cups shredded soy-based mozzarella cheese
½ cup grated Parmesan cheese
½ cup chopped walnuts

1. Preheat the broiler (grill).
2. Cook the lasagna as directed on the package and set aside.

3. Coat a baking sheet with nonstick canola spray and place the zucchini on it in a single layer. Lightly spray with canola oil. Broil the zucchini for 5 minutes, or until crisp-tender, turning once. Let cool.

4. Coat a large saucepan with canola spray and warm over medium heat. Add the carrots, onions, and garlic and cook for 5 minutes, until tender. Stir continuously.

5. Add the marinara sauce, basil, and pepper to taste to the vegetables and bring to a boil, then reduce the heat to low. Cover and simmer for 10 minutes, stirring occasionally.

6. In a small mixing bowl, toss together the mozzarella and Parmesan cheeses, and set aside.

7. Preheat the oven to 375°F.

8. Coat a 2-quart baking dish with nonstick canola spray and lay in two noodles. Spread with one-third of the sauce. Sprinkle with one-third of the walnuts. Top with four slices of zucchini. Sprinkle with one-third of the cheese mixture.

9. Repeat the layering, alternating the direction of three slices of the zucchini in each layer and finishing with the zucchini (reserving remaining cheese mixture).

10. Cover and bake for 20 minutes. Uncover, sprinkle with the cheese mixture, and bake an additional 10 minutes to lightly brown the top. Let stand for 15 minutes before serving for easier cutting.

Nutrients per Serving
Calories: 367 Protein: 17.8 g (21%) Carbohydrate: 37.1 g (29%) Fat: 17 g (53%)
Calcium: 326 mg Fiber: 5.7 g Iron: 2 mg Sodium: 802 mg Flavonoids: 44 mg
Okinawa Food Pyramid Servings
Grains: 2 Vegetables: 2 Fruits: 0 Flavonoid Foods: 2 Calcium Foods: ½
Omega-3 Foods: 1 Condiments: 0 Meat/Eggs: 0 Sweets: 0

Lentil Stroganoff

Serves 4

1½ cups lentils
4½ cups water
Pinch of sea salt
1½ cups sliced button mushrooms
1 cup julienned green bell pepper
½ cup chopped onion
3 tablespoons whole-grain wheat flour
2 teaspoons prepared mustard
Freshly ground black pepper
1 8-ounce container plain low-fat yogurt
3 cups cooked egg noodles
4 tablespoons sliced green onions

1. Combine the lentils, water, and salt in a large saucepan and bring to a boil over high heat. Reduce the heat to medium-low and cover; simmer about 30 minutes, or until the lentils are tender.
2. Drain and save the lentil liquid; add water to make 1½ cups. Set lentils aside and keep warm.
3. Coat a large skillet with nonstick canola spray and warm over medium heat. Add the mushrooms, pepper, and onion, and cook for 5 to 7 minutes, or until the vegetables are tender.
4. In a small mixing bowl, mix the flour, mustard, and black pepper. Stir into the vegetable mixture. Add the reserved lentil liquid to the mixture and stir. Cook over medium heat until mixture is smooth and thickened, about 3 minutes.
5. Add the lentils to the skillet and mix well. Just before serving, stir the yogurt into the lentils.
6. Evenly divide the noodles onto four plates and serve the stroganoff over the noodles. Garnish each serving with 1 tablespoon green onion.

Nutrients per Serving
Calories: 487 Protein: 31.1 g (26%) Carbohydrate: 84.7 g (69%) Fat: 3.8 g (7%)
Calcium: 185.1 mg Fiber: 25.4 g Iron: 9.4 mg Sodium: 174 mg Flavonoids: 11.1 mg
Okinawa Food Pyramid Servings
Grains: 2 Vegetables: 1½ Fruits: 0 Flavonoid Foods: 2 Calcium Foods: ¼
Omega-3 Foods: 0 Condiments: 1 Meat/Eggs: 0 Sweets: 0

Tomato Bruschetta
Serves 4

2 ripe medium tomatoes (about 4 ounces each), cored and sliced in
half across the equator
Sea salt
1 teaspoon cracked black peppercorns
4 baguette slices
1 garlic clove, peeled
2 tablespoons fresh basil leaves, chopped

1. Prepare a grill or broiler.
2. In a bowl, add the tomatoes, a pinch of sea salt, and
   peppercorns. Spray for 2 seconds with nonstick canola
   spray and toss to combine.
3. Place the tomatoes on the grill, cut-side down. Grill for 10
   minutes. Turn tomatoes over and grill on the skin side
   for an additional 5 minutes. Transfer the tomatoes onto a
   sheet tray to cool.
4. When cool, remove and discard tomato skins. Slice the
   tomato halves into two pieces. Season with a pinch of salt
   and pepper.
5. Transfer the bread slices to a serving plate and rub the slices
   with the peeled garlic. Place two tomato pieces on top of
   each bread slice and top with basil. Serve immediately.

Nutrients per Serving
Calories: 83 Protein: 2.8 g (14%) Carbohydrate: 16.3 g (78%) Fat: 1 g (10%)
Calcium: 27.3 mg Fiber: 1.6 g Iron: 1.1 mg Sodium: 194 mg Flavonoids: 0.5 mg
Okinawa Food Pyramid Servings
Grains: 1 Vegetables: ½ Fruits: 0 Flavonoid Foods: 0 Calcium Foods: 0
Omega-3 Foods: 0 Condiments: 0 Meat/Eggs: 0 Sweets: 0

Easy Okinawan Vegetable Chample

Serves 4

6 ounces firm tofu-lite, excess water squeezed out with a paper towel
1½ cups sliced string beans, in 2-inch-long pieces
½ small cabbage, chopped
½ cup soybean sprouts
Sea salt
Freshly ground black pepper

1. Coat a large skillet with nonstick canola spray. Cut the tofu into 1-inch cubes and place in the skillet. Cook over medium heat for 3 to 4 minutes or until golden. Set aside.
2. Coat the same skillet with canola spray and stir-fry the string beans, cabbage, and bean sprouts. Cook over medium heat until tender, 4 to 5 minutes.
3. Return the tofu to the skillet and toss with the vegetables. Season to taste with sea salt and black pepper. Evenly divide among four plates and serve.

Nutrients per Serving
Calories: 47 Protein: 4.3 g (36%) Carbohydrate: 6.7 g (56%) Fat: 0.8 g (16%)
Calcium: 60.2 mg Fiber: 2.9 g Iron: 1.4 mg Sodium: 81 mg Flavonoids: 17.1 mg
Okinawa Food Pyramid Servings
Grains: 0 Vegetables: 2 Fruits: 0 Flavonoid Foods: 1 Calcium Foods: 0
Omega-3 Foods: 0 Condiments: 0 Meat/Eggs: 0 Sweets: 0

Simmered Hechima with Miso Gravy

Serves 4

5 ounces skinless and boneless chicken breast
3 cups sliced hechima, in ½-inch-thick pieces (if hechima is not available, use zucchini [courgette])
½ cup sake
1 teaspoon brown sugar
1½ tablespoons low-sodium miso
4 ounces firm tofu-lite, cut into 1-inch cubes

1. Cover the chicken with plenty of water. Bring to a boil and cook for 5 minutes, or until cooked through. Remove the chicken and reserve 1 cup of the broth.
2. Cut the chicken into 1-inch cubes.
3. Coat a wok with nonstick canola spray. Sauté the hechima and chicken over medium heat, add the reserved broth and the sake, bring to a boil, then reduce the heat to low. Cook until the hechima is tender, 7 to 9 minutes, turning the hechima over several times.
4. Add the sugar and miso and stir to dissolve.
5. Add the tofu and continue cooking until the liquid is evaporated, about 5 minutes.

Nutrients per Serving
Calories: 113 Protein: 11.6 g (41%) Carbohydrate: 6.6 g (23%) Fat: 1 g (8%)
Calcium: 33.1 mg Fiber: 1.2 g Iron: 1 mg Sodium: 145 mg Flavonoids: 7.1 mg
Okinawa Food Pyramid Servings
Grains: 0 Vegetables: 1½ Fruits: 0 Flavonoid Foods: 2 Calcium Foods: 0
Omega-3 Foods: 0 Condiments: 0 Meat/Eggs: ½ Sweets: 0

Tofu, Salmon, and Vegetables with Creamy Miso Sauce
Serves 4

6 ounces firm tofu-lite
2 garlic cloves, minced
15 ounces salmon fillet, cut into ½-inch cubes
1 small head broccoli, cut into small florets (about 3 cups)
1 small carrot, cut into ½-inch cubes (about ½ cup)
2 celery stalks, cut into ½-inch cubes
¼ cup dry white wine
½ cup skim milk
1½ tablespoons low-sodium miso
Freshly ground black pepper

1. Cut the tofu into ½-inch cubes.
2. Coat a large pot with nonstick canola spray and cook the garlic over medium heat. When the garlic is lightly browned, add the salmon and sauté until each side is golden, approximately 3 minutes.

3. Add the broccoli, carrot, celery, tofu, and white wine to the salmon. Bring to a boil over high heat. Pour in the milk, bring to a boil again, then reduce the heat to very low.
4. Add the miso and stir to dissolve. Cook until the liquid is reduced by three-quarters, about 5 minutes.
5. Adjust the seasonings with pepper and serve.

Nutrients per Serving
Calories: 230 Protein: 27.4 g (48%) Carbohydrate: 10.5 g (18%) Fat: 7.7 g (30%
Calcium: 117.8 mg Fiber: 3.3 g Iron: 2.1 mg Sodium: 231 mg Flavonoids: 15.5 mg
Okinawa Food Pyramid Servings
Grains: 0 Vegetables: 4 Fruits: 0 Flavonoid Foods: 6 Calcium Foods: 0
Omega-3 Foods: 1¼ Condiments: 1 Meat/Eggs: 0 Sweets: 0

Goya Chample

Serves 4

1 10.5-ounce piece extra-firm tofu-lite, drained and cut into
1-inch cubes
1 large goya (bitter gourd, available at most Asian food stores), core and
seeds removed, sliced thinly (if not available, use green squash)
2 eggs or ½ cup egg substitute, beaten
Pinch of sea salt
2 teaspoons low-sodium soy sauce

1. Coat a large skillet with nonstick canola spray. Over medium heat, cook the tofu for 2 minutes, or until golden. Set aside.
2. Spray the same skillet with a little more canola spray and cook the goya for about 7 minutes, or until tender. Return the tofu to the skillet, pour in the egg, and cook for 1 minute while stirring. When combined well, add the sea salt and soy sauce. Taste and adjust the seasoning as desired.
3. Evenly divide among four plates and serve.

Nutrients per Serving
Calories: 74 Protein: 9.9 g (54%) Carbohydrate: 4.2 g (23%) Fat: 2 g (24%)
Calcium: 106 mg Fiber: 0.9 g Iron: 7.4 mg Sodium: 279 mg Flavonoids: 15.5 mg)
Okinawa Food Pyramid Servings
Grains: 0 Vegetables: 1½ Fruits: 0 Flavonoid Foods: 1 Calcium Foods: 0)
Omega-3 Foods: ½ Condiments: 0 Meat/Eggs: 0 Sweets: 0

Okinawan Eggplants with Miso
Serves 4

4 large oriental eggplants (aubergines) (about 3 ounces each), cut into ½-inch-thick slices
4 ounces firm tofu-lite, cut into 1-inch cubes
1 3-ounce can water-packed tuna
2 tablespoons sake
⅓ cup water
1 teaspoon brown sugar
1 tablespoon red miso and 1 tablespoon white miso, combined

1. Soak the eggplant slices in cold water for at least 10 minutes to remove their bitter taste. Drain well.
2. Coat a wok with nonstick canola spray and cook the tofu over medium heat for 2 minutes, or until golden. Set aside.
3. Spray the wok again with canola oil and sauté the eggplant slices and tuna over medium heat until eggplants are coated with oil. Add the sake and water, bring to a boil, reduce heat to low, and cook for 4 to 6 minutes, or until eggplants are soft.
4. Add the sugar and miso, and stir to dissolve. Add the tofu, cook until the liquid is reduced by three-fourths, about 3 minutes.
5. Serve on a large plate.

Nutrients per Serving
Calories: 205 Protein: 13 g (25%) Carbohydrate: 36.8 g (72%) Fat: 2.2 g (9%)
Calcium: 57.7 mg Fiber: 13.9 g Iron: 2 mg Sodium: 247 mg Flavonoids: 10.6 mg
Okinawa Food Pyramid Servings
Grains: 0 Vegetables: 2 Fruits: 0 Flavonoid Foods: 2 Calcium Foods: 0
Omega-3 Foods: ¼ Condiments: 0 Meat/Eggs: 0 Sweets: 0

Kimchee Okinawa Style
Serves 4

3 cups small clams
2½ cups fresh spinach
2 cups kimchee (Chinese cabbage Korean style)
2 10.5-ounce pieces regular tofu-lite

Soup

1½ cups water

½ tablespoon Chinese chicken broth powder

2 garlic cloves, minced

1 tablespoon shredded fresh ginger

3 tablespoons kimchee sauce

1 tablespoon low-sodium soy sauce

1 teaspoon roasted sesame oil

½ tablespoon brown sugar

3 cups soybean sprouts

1. Soak the clams in 2 cups salted water for 1 hour to remove sand.
2. Chop the spinach and kimchee. Slice the tofu into 1-inch cubes.
3. Combine the soup ingredients in a large pot. Add the clams and kimchee, and cook over medium heat until clams open. Add the spinach, bean sprouts, and tofu. Cook over medium heat for 5 minutes, or until vegetables are all tender.
4. Evenly divide among four bowls and serve.

Nutrients per Serving
Calories: 276 Protein: 39.1 g (57%) Carbohydrate: 15.8 g (23%) Fat: 7.8 g (25%)
Calcium: 213.4 mg Fiber: 1.2 g Iron: 26.7 mg Sodium: 411 mg Flavonoids: 54.4 mg
Okinawa Food Pyramid Servings
Grains: 0 Vegetables: 4 Fruits: 0 Flavonoid Foods: 5 Calcium Foods: 0
Omega-3 Foods: ½ Condiments: 0 Meat/Eggs: 0 Sweets: 0

Okinawan Sautéed Chicken with Turmeric
Serves 4

12 ounces skinless and boneless chicken thighs

Pinch of sea salt and black pepper

2 eggs or ½ cup egg substitute

2 teaspoons turmeric powder

1 tablespoon sake rice wine

1 tablespoon minced parsley

3 tablespoons all-purpose (plain) flour

1 cup broccoli florets

1 small head romaine lettuce, separated into leaves

8 cherry tomatoes

1. Cut the chicken into 1-inch cubes and sprinkle with salt and pepper. Let stand for 10 minutes.
2. In a mixing bowl, beat the eggs, then add the turmeric, sake, and parsley.
3. Place the flour in a small bowl.
4. Coat the chicken with the flour, then dip the chicken in the egg batter.
5. Coat a large skillet with nonstick canola spray and sauté the chicken over medium-high heat until golden, about 2 minutes, then turn the chicken over, reduce the heat to low, cover, and cook for 5 minutes more, or until done.
6. While the chicken is cooking, steam the broccoli.
7. Line a large platter with the lettuce leaves and place the chicken in the center. Surround it with broccoli and tomatoes. Serve.

Nutrients per Serving
Calories: 175 Protein: 22.6 g (52%) Carbohydrate: 9 g (21%) Fat: 4.8 g (25%)
Calcium: 51.9 mg Fiber: 1.9 g Iron: 3 mg Sodium: 177 mg
Okinawa Food Pyramid Servings
Grains: 0 Vegetables: 2 Fruits: 0 Flavonoid Foods: 0 Calcium Foods: 0
Omega-3 Foods: 0 Condiments: 0 Meat/Eggs: 1 Sweets: 0

Chicken and Vegetables with Mustard Sauce
Serves 4

1½ pounds small red potatoes, cut into quarters
1 large onion (5 ounces), cut into eighths
¼ teaspoon sea salt
¼ teaspoon freshly ground pepper
4 3-ounce skinless and boneless chicken breast halves
1 teaspoon canola oil
2 tablespoons honey mustard

1. Preheat the oven to 450°F.
2. In a large baking pan, add the potatoes, onion, sea salt, and pepper. Spray the ingredients for 1 second with nonstick canola spray, then toss to combine. Bake for 5 to 8 minutes.

3. Meanwhile, place the chicken in a small roasting pan; coat the chicken with canola spray.
4. In a cup, mix the canola oil with honey mustard and set aside.
5. Turn vegetables with a metal or wooden spatula, and return to oven on the lower rack. Place the chicken on the upper rack. Bake for 10 minutes.
6. Remove the chicken and vegetables from the oven and brush with the honey mustard mixture. Return them to the oven and bake for an additional 12 minutes, or until the juices run clear when the thickest part of the chicken is pierced with a knife and the vegetables are golden and tender.
7. Serve the chicken with the vegetables.

Nutrients per Serving
Calories: 240 Protein: 19 g (27%) Carbohydrate: 35.8 g (48%) Fat: 8.2 g (25%)
Calcium: 102.9 mg Fiber: 2.2 g Iron: 1.5 mg Sodium: 291 mg Flavonoids: 15.9 mg
Okinawa Food Pyramid Servings
Grains: 0 Vegetables: 2 Fruits: 0 Flavonoid Foods: 1 Calcium Foods: 0
Omega-3 Foods: 0 Condiments: 0 Meat/Eggs: 1 Sweets: 0

Chicken Kabobs
Serves 4

12 ounces skinless and boneless chicken breasts, cut into large chunks
1 cup calcium-fortified orange juice
1 large onion (5 ounces), chopped into large wedges
12 cherry tomatoes
12 button mushrooms
½ cup (1.5 ounces) green bell peppers, cut into large pieces
½ cup (1.5 ounces) red bell peppers, cut into large pieces
8 taco-size flour tortillas, warmed

1. Prepare a grill or broiler.
2. Marinate the chicken in the orange juice for 10 minutes. Drain.
3. Prepare four skewers, alternating chicken chunks and vegetables. Grill or broil the skewers for 10 to 15 minutes, or until the chicken is cooked through and the vegetables are soft.

4. Place a tortilla in the palm of one hand and put a kabob over the tortilla. Grasp the kabob and pull the skewer, leaving half of the filling inside the tortilla. Repeat with the remaining tortillas and serve warm.

Nutrients per Serving
Calories: 426 Protein: 24.4 g (23%) Carbohydrate: 56.3 g (53%)
Fat: 12.1 g (25%) Calcium: 196.1 mg Fiber: 4.6 g Iron: 4.1 mg Sodium: 378 mg
Flavonoids: 17.1 mg
Okinawa Food Pyramid Servings
Grains: 2 Vegetables: 3 Fruits: 0 Flavonoid Foods: 1 Calcium Foods: ¼
Omega-3 Foods: 0 Condiments: 0 Meat/Eggs: 1 Sweets: 0

Greek Barbecue

Serves 4

8 ounces lean boneless top round (topside)
1 tablespoon prepared mustard
4 cups torn chicory leaves
2 cups sliced green beans
1 red bell pepper, sliced thinly
2 green onions, minced
3 tablespoons red wine vinegar
1 teaspoon olive oil
2 tablespoons fat-free beef-flavored broth
1 teaspoon dried oregano leaves
1 tablespoon crumbled feta cheese
4 whole wheat rolls

1. Prepare a grill or broiler.
2. Rub the beef on both sides with the mustard.
3. Grill or broil the meat about 5 inches from the heat for 7 minutes on each side for medium rare, longer for well done. Let stand for 5 minutes, then slice thinly across the grain.
4. In a large bowl, combine the chicory, beans, pepper, and green onions.
5. In a small bowl, whisk together the vinegar, oil, broth, and oregano. Pour over the greens and toss to combine.

6. Arrange the greens on four serving plates and top with the beef. Sprinkle with the cheese and serve with the rolls.

Nutrients per Serving
Calories: 296 Protein: 21.4 g (28%) Carbohydrate: 34.5 g (45%) Fat: 9.6 g (27%)
Calcium: 261.5 mg Fiber: 10.8 g Iron: 6.7 mg Sodium: 410 mg Flavonoids: 2.7 mg
Okinawa Food Pyramid Servings
Grains: 2 Vegetables: 2½ Fruits: 0 Flavonoid Foods: 0 Calcium Foods: 0
Omega-3 Foods: 0 Condiments: 0 Meat/Eggs: 1 Sweets: 0

Beef Teriyaki with Cabernet Sauce
Serves 4

3 garlic cloves, minced
2 tablespoons lite soy sauce
1 tablespoon brown sugar
1 tablespoon minced fresh ginger
2 tablespoons sake rice wine
1 cup Cabernet Sauvignon or other dry red wine
4 5-ounce lean beef steaks

1. Prepare a grill or broiler.
2. Coat a small saucepan with nonstick canola spray and warm over medium heat. Add the garlic and sauté for 30 seconds.
3. Add the soy sauce, brown sugar, ginger, and wines and bring to a boil. Reduce the heat to low and simmer until the sauce is reduced by half. Set aside.
4. Grill or broil the steaks to desired doneness.
5. Transfer the beef to serving plates and drizzle with sauce, about 2 tablespoons per serving. Serve.

Nutrients per Serving
Calories: 363 Protein: 44.8 g (49%) Carbohydrate: 7.1 g (8%) Fat: 10.2 g (25%)
Calcium: 30.2 mg Fiber: 0.1 g Iron: 5.5 mg Sodium: 353 mg
Okinawa Food Pyramid Servings
Grains: 0 Vegetables: 0 Fruits: 0 Flavonoid Foods: 0 Calcium Foods: 0
Omega-3 Foods: 0 Condiments: 1 Meat/Eggs: 1 Sweets: 0

Simple Simmered Mackerel with Miso

Serves 4

¼ cup sake
4 3.5- to 4-ounce mackerel fillets
1 tablespoon thinly sliced fresh ginger
1 tablespoon low-sodium miso

1. In a flat pan, bring the sake to a boil. Place the mackerel skin-side-down in the pan, sprinkle with ginger, and cook over low heat for 3 minutes, or until the edges start to brown.
2. Turn fish over, add the miso, and stir to dissolve. Cook for 5 minutes on very low heat, then serve.

Note: If fish seems dry, baste with 1 to 2 tablespoons sake.

Nutrients per Serving
Calories: 258 Protein: 21.4 g (33%) Carbohydrate: 2 g (3%) Fat: 15.9 g (55%)
Calcium: 15.8 mg Fiber: 0.1 g Iron: 1.9 mg Sodium: 163 mg Flavonoids: 2.9 mg
Okinawa Food Pyramid Servings
Grains: 0 Vegetables: 0 Fruits: 0 Flavonoid Foods: 1 Calcium Foods: 0
Omega-3 Foods: 1 Condiments: 0 Meat/Eggs: 0 Sweets: 0

Barbecued Mahi-Mahi with Lime-Soy Sauce

Serves 4

Pinch of sea salt
Freshly ground black pepper
1 garlic clove, minced
¼ cup dry white wine
4 4-ounce mahi-mahi fillets

Sauce
¼ cup fresh lime juice
3 tablespoons olive oil
2 tablespoons low-sodium soy sauce

1. Prepare a grill or broiler.
2. Combine the salt, pepper, garlic, and wine in a flat dish, add the mahi-mahi, and marinate for 15 minutes, turning once.

3. Combine the sauce ingredients in a small jar and shake well.
4. Grill or broil the mahi-mahi about 4 minutes on each side, or until cooked through.
5. Place fish on four plates. Drizzle about 2 tablespoons of the sauce over each fillet and serve.

Nutrients per Serving
Calories: 206 Protein: 26.2 g (51%) Carbohydrate: 2.5 g (5%) Fat: 11.1 g (44%)
Calcium: 20 mg Fiber: 0.1 g Iron: 0.5 mg Sodium: 426 mg
Okinawa Food Pyramid Servings
Grains: 0 Vegetables: 0 Fruits: 0 Flavonoid Foods: 0 Calcium Foods: 0
Omega-3 Foods: 1 Condiments: 1 Meat/Eggs: 0 Sweets: 0

British Columbia Poached Salmon
Serves 4

2 garlic cloves, minced
¼ cup dry bread crumbs
2 tablespoons chopped pine nuts
2 tablespoons drained and chopped sun-dried tomatoes
2 tablespoons grated Parmesan cheese
2 tablespoons chopped fresh basil
Pinch of sea salt
Freshly ground pepper
1 tablespoon lemon juice
1 bay leaf
4 3-ounce salmon fillets

1. Coat a large skillet with nonstick canola spray and cook the garlic over low heat for 30 seconds.
2. Stir in the bread crumbs and pine nuts, tossing continuously for 2 minutes, or until lightly toasted. Turn off the heat.
3. Stir in the tomatoes, cheese, and basil. Adjust seasoning to taste with sea salt and pepper. Set aside.
4. Put about 4 cups of hot water, the lemon juice, and bay leaf in a large skillet and bring to a boil.
5. Place the salmon fillets in the boiling water, reduce the heat to medium-low, and simmer for 8 minutes, or until cooked through. (Add water if the fillets are not fully covered.) Drain.

6. Transfer the fillets to four plates and spoon 1½ tablespoons of the bread crumb mixture on top of each serving. Serve.

Nutrients per Serving
Calories: 194 Protein: 20 g (43%) Carbohydrate: 7.2 g (14%) Fat: 9.1 g (42%)
Calcium: 67.5 mg Fiber: 0.6 g Iron: 1.7 mg Sodium: 187 mg
Okinawa Food Pyramid Servings
Grains: 0 Vegetables: 0 Fruits: 0 Flavonoid Foods: 0 Calcium Foods: 0
Omega-3 Foods: 1 Condiments: 0 Meat/Eggs: 0 Sweets: 0

Italian Baked Fish
Serves 4

4 5-ounce orange roughy fillets, or walleye or flounder
⅓ cup pitted ripe olives, drained and coarsely chopped
1 28-ounce can Italian plum tomatoes, drained and chopped (preferably no-salt)
3 tablespoons chopped Italian parsley
2 tablespoons chopped fresh basil
2 tablespoons balsamic vinegar
2 garlic cloves, minced
Freshly ground pepper to taste

1. Preheat the oven to 375°F.
2. Coat a shallow 3-quart baking dish with nonstick canola spray. Place the fillets in a single layer in the dish.
3. In a small mixing bowl, combine the remaining ingredients and spoon over the fillets.
4. Bake for 25 minutes, or until the fish flakes easily when tested with a fork. Serve.

Nutrients per Serving
Calories: 165 Protein: 22.7 g (51%) Carbohydrate: 17.1 g (38%) Fat: 2.2 g (11%)
Calcium: 127.5 mg Fiber: 2.5 g Iron: 5.3 mg Sodium: 190 mg
Okinawa Food Pyramid Servings
Grains: 0 Vegetables: 3 Fruits: 0 Flavonoid Foods: 0 Calcium Foods: 0
Omega-3 Foods: 1½ Condiments: 1 Meat/Eggs: 0 Sweets: 0

Zesty Potatoes Wasabi Style
Serves 6

2 pounds new potatoes, peeled and chunked
Pinch of sea salt
4 garlic cloves, minced
¾ cup coconut milk
2 tablespoons wasabi powder (Japanese horseradish, available at most Asian food stores)
1 teaspoon ground white pepper

1. Bring a large pot of water to a boil. Add the potatoes and boil for 15 minutes, or until tender.
2. Drain the potatoes and return to the pot. Add the sea salt and garlic and mash well.
3. In a small mixing bowl, combine the coconut milk with the wasabi powder and pepper.
4. Add the milk mixture to the potatoes and mash until light and fluffy.

Nutrients per Serving
*Calories: 209 Protein: 3.6 g (7%) Carbohydrate: 34.1 g (65%) Fat: 7.3 g (32%)**
Calcium: 21.6 mg Fiber: 3.5 g Iron: 1.1 mg Sodium: 37 mg
Okinawa Food Pyramid Servings
Grains: 0 Vegetables: 2 Fruits: 0 Flavonoid Foods: 0 Calcium Foods: 0
Omega-3 Foods: 0 Condiments: 0 Meat/Eggs: 0 Sweets: 0

SALAD AND SOUP

Garden Salad
Serves 4

4 cups romaine lettuce leaves, chopped
1 cup chopped cucumber
1 cup chopped tomato

---

* Although this recipe is high in saturated fatty acids, the type of SFA found in coconut milk does not raise cholesterol levels. (So don't worry about it!)

Dressing
Olive oil spray
2 teaspoons balsamic vinegar
Pinch of sea salt

1. Put vegetables in a large salad bowl.
2. Spray the salad with olive oil for 2 seconds and add
   balsamic vinegar and salt.
3. Toss together.

Nutrients per Serving
Calories: 39 Protein: 1 g (12%) Carbohydrate: 4 g (35%) Fat: 2.5 g (53%)
Calcium: 26 mg Fiber: 1.4 g Iron: 0.8 mg Sodium: 4 mg
Okinawa Food Pyramid Servings
Grains: 0 Vegetables: 1½ Fruits: 0 Flavonoid Foods: 0 Calcium Foods: 0
Omega-3 Foods: 0 Condiments: 0 Meat/Eggs: 0 Sweets: 0

Tuna Caesar Salad
Serves 4

4 4-ounce tuna steaks, about 1 inch thick
1 teaspoon fresh ginger, minced
3 tablespoons sake
2 teaspoons low-sodium soy sauce

Dressing
3 tablespoons canola oil
1 garlic clove, minced
2 tablespoons fresh lemon juice
3 tablespoons grated Parmesan cheese
1 tablespoon prepared mustard
Sea salt
Freshly ground black pepper

4 cups chopped romaine lettuce

1. Preheat the broiler or grill.
2. Season both sides of the tuna steaks with ginger, sake, and
   soy sauce. Broil both sides until fork-tender, 4 to 6 minutes.
   When cool enough to handle, cut the tuna into 1-inch
   cubes and set aside.

3. Put the canola oil and garlic in a mixing bowl. Add the lemon juice slowly, whisking constantly. When it is mixed evenly, add the Parmesan cheese, mustard, salt, and black pepper and mix well.
4. Toss the lettuce with the dressing.
5. Evenly divide the lettuce among four plates. Place tuna atop lettuce and serve.

Nutrients per Serving
Calories: 260 Protein: 29.3 g (45%) Carbohydrate: 3.3 g (5%) Fat: 12.7 g (44%)
Calcium: 95.9 mg Fiber: 1 g Iron: 1.6 mg Sodium: 300 mg Flavonoids: 0.7 mg
Okinawa Food Pyramid Servings
Grains: 0 Vegetables: 2 Fruits: 0 Flavonoid Foods: 0 Calcium Foods: 0
Omega-3 Foods: 1 Condiments: 0 Meat/Eggs: 0 Sweets: 0

Warm Mushroom Salad with Garlic Dressing
Serves 4

Dressing
2 tablespoons canola oil
2 tablespoons balsamic vinegar
¼ teaspoon sea salt
4 garlic cloves
½ teaspoon low-sodium soy sauce
Pinch of brown sugar
Freshly ground black pepper

2 large portobello mushrooms, cut into long, thick slices
10 button mushrooms, cut into halves
½ cup wood ears (sometimes called tree ears), prepared as instructed on the package, and chopped (or substitute sliced oyster mushrooms)
1 package enoki mushrooms, hard part of the stems removed, mushrooms split into eight pieces
8 leaves romaine lettuce

1. Combine the dressing ingredients in a food processor or a blender. Set aside.
2. Coat a large skillet with canola oil spray and warm over medium-high heat. Sauté the portobello mushrooms, button mushrooms, and wood ears for 3 minutes.

3. Add the enoki mushrooms and cook for an additional minute.
4. Line four plates with lettuce. Divide the mushrooms among the plates and drizzle 2 tablespoons dressing over each portion. Serve.

Nutrients per Serving
Calories: 107 Protein: 3.4 g (13%) Carbohydrate: 7.9 g (29%) Fat: 7.7 g (65%)
Calcium: 26.2 mg Fiber: 2.1 g Iron: 0.7 mg Sodium: 179 mg
Okinawa Food Pyramid Servings
Grains: 0 Vegetables: 2½ Fruits: 0 Flavonoid Foods: 0 Calcium Foods: 0
Omega-3 Foods: 0 Condiments: 1 Meat/Eggs: 0 Sweets: 0

Tropical Papaya Salad
Serves 4

Juice from 2 limes
1 tablespoon honey
Pinch of sea salt
Freshly ground pepper
2 papayas
2 avocados
4 cups mixed baby lettuce greens

1. Put the lime juice, honey, sea salt, and pepper to taste in a small jar and shake well. Reserve in the refrigerator.
2. Peel the papayas and cut them in half. Using a spoon, remove the seeds and discard. Slice the papaya halves into thin wedges and set aside.
3. Cut the avocados in half and remove the pits. Grasping each avocado half in your hand, slice the flesh into thin strips. Set aside.
4. Arrange the papaya and avocado slices on four salad plates, alternating the slices.
5. Combine the greens and dressing in a bowl and toss well to coat.
6. Mound a portion of the greens in the center of each plate. Drizzle on a ½ tablespoon of dressing.

Calories: 244 Protein: 3.8 g (6%) Carbohydrate: 29.3 g (48%) Fat: 15.3 g (56%)
Calcium: 69.3 mg Fiber: 8.1 g Iron: 1.8 mg Sodium: 56 mg Flavonoids: 1.7 mg
Okinawa Food Pyramid Servings
Grains: 0 Vegetables: 2½ Fruits: 1 Flavonoid Foods: 0 Calcium Foods: 0
Omega-3 Foods: 0 Condiments: 0 Meat/Eggs: 0 Sweets: 0

Indonesian Gado-Gado Salad

Serves 4

Sauce

6 ounces silken tofu
¼ cup smooth natural peanut butter
¼ cup reduced-sodium teriyaki sauce
1 garlic clove, chopped
1 tablespoon minced fresh ginger
½ teaspoon red Thai curry paste, or more to taste
¼ teaspoon ground coriander
1½ teaspoons lime juice

24 baby carrots
4 medium red-skinned potatoes (about 1 pound), cut into 1-inch pieces
3 cups broccoli florets
3 cups cauliflower florets
½ small cabbage, halved and cut crosswise into ¾-inch strips, hard
core discarded
½ medium cucumber, thinly sliced

1. Put about 6 cups of water in a large saucepan and bring to
   a boil over high heat.
2. Combine all the sauce ingredients in a blender or a food
   processor and puree until smooth. Set aside.
3. When water is boiling, add the carrots and potatoes. Cover
   and cook over medium-high heat for 8 minutes.
4. Add the broccoli, cauliflower, and cabbage. Cook over
   medium heat for 4 minutes, or until the vegetables are
   tender but still firm. Drain the vegetables in a colander.
5. Arrange the vegetables on four plates and drizzle a little
   sauce over each plate. Arrange the cucumber slices over
   the vegetables. Serve.

Nutrients per Serving
Calories: 282 Protein: 13.6 g (19%) Carbohydrate: 43.1 g (61%) Fat: 9.5 g (30%)
Calcium: 109.2 mg Fiber: 8.7 g Iron: 2.8 mg Sodium: 293 mg Flavonoids: 15.3 mg
Okinawa Food Pyramid Servings
Grains: 0 Vegetables: 5 Fruits: 0 Flavonoid Foods: ½ Calcium Foods: 0
Omega-3 Foods: 0 Condiments: 1 Meat/Eggs: 0 Sweets: 0

Atlantic Caesar Salad

Serves 4

2 garlic cloves, crushed
⅓ cup fat-free vegetable broth
3 tablespoons low-fat mayonnaise
¼ cup grated Parmesan cheese
½ teaspoon grated lemon peel
2 tablespoons lemon juice
Pinch of salt
13¾-ounce can water-packed sardines, drained
8 cups torn romaine lettuce
2 cups halved cherry tomatoes
1½ cups low-fat croutons

1. Combine the garlic and broth in a small dish. Cover with plastic, and microwave on high for 45 to 60 seconds, or until the garlic is tender when pierced with a knife. Cool.
2. Blend the garlic mixture, mayonnaise, 2 tablespoons of the Parmesan cheese, the lemon peel, lemon juice, and salt in a small food processor until smooth.
3. Trim the sardines and cut in half crosswise.
4. Right before serving, toss together the lettuce, tomatoes, and dressing in a large bowl. Scatter with croutons, sardines, and the remaining 2 tablespoons Parmesan cheese.

Nutrients per Serving
Calories: 220 Protein: 11.3 g (20%) Carbohydrate: 18.2 g (33%) Fat: 12.2 g (50%)
Calcium: 201 mg Fiber: 3.5 g Iron: 2.7 mg Sodium: 488 mg Flavonoids: 2 mg
Okinawa Food Pyramid Servings
Grains: ½ Vegetables: 2 Fruits: 0 Flavonoid Foods: 0 Calcium Foods: 0
Omega-3 Foods: ½ Condiments: 1 Meat/Eggs: 0 Sweets: 0

Okinawan White Miso Soup with Vegetables

Serves 4

5 cups bonito broth (5 cups hot water and 2 teaspoons bonito broth powder)
1½ cups julienned daikon white radish
⅓ cup julienned carrot
½ cup thinly sliced *konnyaku* yam cake (available at Asian food stores)
3 cups chopped fresh spinach
4 shiitake mushrooms, cut into halves
3 ounces regular or silken tofu-lite, cut into ½-inch cubes
1½ ounces white miso
1 tablespoon peanut butter

1. Put the bonito broth in a large pot and bring to a boil.
2. Add the radish, carrot, and *konnyaku,* bring back to a boil over high heat, then reduce heat to medium-low and simmer until radish and carrot are tender, about 7 minutes.
3. Add the spinach, shiitakes, and tofu. Cook 2 to 4 minutes over medium heat.
4. Add the miso and peanut butter and stir to dissolve. Bring to a boil, then turn off the heat.
5. Evenly divide the soup among four soup bowls and serve immediately.

Nutrients per Serving
Calories: 75 Protein: 4.2 g (23%) Carbohydrate: 9.7 g (51%) Fat: 2.8 g (34%)
Calcium: 43.7 mg Fiber: 4.3 g Iron: 2.2 mg Sodium: 250 mg Flavonoids: 16.3 mg
Okinawa Food Pyramid Servings
Grains: 2 Vegetables: 2 Fruits: 0 Flavonoid Foods: 2 Calcium Foods: 0
Omega-3 Foods: 0 Condiments: 0 Meat/Eggs: 0 Sweets: 0

Simple Wakame and Tofu Miso Soup

Serves 4

5 cups bonito broth (5 cups hot water and 2 teaspoons bonito broth powder)
6 ounces silken tofu-lite, diced
3 teaspoons dried wakame seaweed
2 tablespoons low-sodium miso
¼ cup minced chives

1. Put the bonito broth in a pot and bring to a boil.
2. Add the tofu, wakame, and miso. Dissolve miso and bring mixture to a boil, then turn off the heat.
3. Serve in four individual bowls, sprinkled with chives.

Nutrients per Serving
Calories: 30 Protein: 3 g (40%) Carbohydrate: 3 g (38%) Fat: 0.7 g (21%)
Calcium: 22.6 mg Fiber: 0.7 g Iron: 0.5 mg Sodium: 178 mg Flavonoids: 12.9 mg
Okinawa Food Pyramid Servings
Grains: 2 Vegetables: 0 Fruits: 0 Flavonoid Foods: 2 Calcium Foods: ¼
Omega-3 Foods: 0 Condiments: 0 Meat/Eggs: 0 Sweets: 0

Spinach Chicken Soup
Serves 6

5 cups chopped fresh spinach
6 cups canned fat-free, low-sodium chicken broth
¼ cup dry white wine
¾ cup egg substitute
Pinch of sea salt
Freshly ground pepper
3 teaspoons grated Parmesan cheese

1. Steam the spinach for 3 minutes, until cooked.
2. In a large saucepan, heat the broth to simmering over medium-high heat. Add the wine and simmer.
3. In a bowl, beat the egg substitute lightly with a fork. Very slowly, pour the egg substitute into the soup, stirring continuously.
4. Add the spinach to the soup and give a stir. Season to taste with salt and pepper. Serve immediately, topped with a little grated cheese.

Nutrients per Serving
Calories: 83 Protein: 8.9 g (43%) Carbohydrate: 3.2 g (15%) Fat: 3.4 g (37%)
Calcium: 72.7 mg Fiber: 0.7 g Iron: 1.4 mg Sodium: 259 mg
Okinawa Food Pyramid Servings
Grains: 2 Vegetables: 2 Fruits: 0 Flavonoid Foods: 0 Calcium Foods: 0
Omega-3 Foods: 0 Condiments: 0 Meat/Eggs: 0 Sweets: 0

Summer Field Gazpacho Soup

Serves 6

2 cups tomato juice, no added salt
1 20-ounce can diced tomatoes, no added salt
1 cup coarsely chopped zucchini (courgette)
1 cup peeled and coarsely chopped cucumber
1 cup coarsely chopped red pepper
¾ cup coarsely chopped yellow onions
½ cup chopped fresh basil leaves
⅓ cup chopped Italian parsley
⅓ cup chopped fresh cilantro (coriander)
3 garlic cloves, chopped
3 teaspoons red wine vinegar
⅓ cup chicken broth (optional)
Hot pepper sauce
Pinch of sea salt
Freshly ground black pepper

1. Combine all the ingredients except the seasonings in a blender or food processor. Process in short pulses to a coarse puree. If too thick, add chicken broth 2 tablespoons at a time.
2. Add the hot pepper sauce, sea salt, and black pepper to taste. Refrigerate for at least 30 minutes before serving.

Nutrients per Serving
Calories: 60 Protein: 2.8 g (18%) Carbohydrate: 12.3 g (81%) Fat: 0.4 g (6%)
Calcium: 41.6 mg Fiber: 3.2 g Iron: 2.9 mg Sodium: 106 mg Flavonoids: 9.7 mg
Okinawa Food Pyramid Servings
Grains: 2 Vegetables: 3 Fruits: 0 Flavonoid Foods: 1 Calcium Foods: 0
Omega-3 Foods: 0 Condiments: 0 Meat/Eggs: 0 Sweets: 0

Creamy Carrot Soup

Serves 4

1 cup chopped onion (1 large onion)
2 garlic cloves, chopped
½ pound baby carrots
½ cup uncooked instant brown rice
2 14.5-ounce cans fat-free low-sodium chicken broth
1 cup water
½ teaspoon sea salt
2 tablespoons chopped green chili pepper
Juice of 1 lime

1. Coat a large saucepan with nonstick canola spray and warm it over medium heat. Add the onion and sauté for 3 minutes. Add the garlic and sauté 1 minute.
2. Add the carrots, rice, broth, water, and salt and bring to a boil. Reduce the heat to medium-low and simmer, partially covered, for 20 minutes or until the carrots are tender. Stir in the chili pepper and lime juice.
3. Puree the soup in a food processor or blender. Reheat if necessary. Serve warm.

Nutrients per Serving
Calories: 199 Protein: 6.7 g (13%) Carbohydrate: 38.2 g (77%) Fat: 3 g (14%)
Calcium: 69 mg Fiber: 4.7 g Iron: 1.8 mg Sodium: 197 mg Flavonoids: 18.4 mg
Okinawa Food Pyramid Servings
Grains: 2 Vegetables: 3 Fruits: 0 Flavonoid Foods: 1 Calcium Foods: 0
Omega-3 Foods: 0 Condiments: 0 Meat/Eggs: 0 Sweets: 0

Mediterranean Minestrone

Serves 6

Soup
1 cup diced celery
1 cup diced carrot
½ cup finely diced onion
3 cups fat-free, low-sodium chicken broth
2 cups water
2 cups diced peeled baking potatoes
1 cup sliced green beans, in 1-inch lengths
1 28-ounce can Italian plum tomatoes, chopped, undrained
(preferably no-salt)
2 cups cooked macaroni
Freshly ground black pepper

Paste
2 cups fresh basil leaves
¼ cup grated Parmesan cheese
3 tablespoons water
1½ tablespoons olive oil
1 garlic clove

1. Coat a large stockpot with nonstick canola spray and warm over medium-high heat. Add the celery, carrot, and onion and sauté for 4 minutes.
2. Add the chicken broth, water, potatoes, beans, and tomatoes and bring to a boil. Reduce heat to low and simmer 25 minutes.
3. Add the pasta and pepper to taste, and cook 1 minute.
4. Place all the paste ingredients in a food processor or blender and process until smooth. Ladle the soup into six bowls and top with the paste. Serve.

Nutrients per Serving
Calories: 224 Protein: 8.7 g (15%) Carbohydrate: 34.1 g (61%) Fat: 5.9 g (24%)
Calcium: 151.9 mg Fiber: 4.9 g Iron: 4.6 mg Sodium: 176 mg Flavonoids: 11.5 mg
Okinawa Food Pyramid Servings
Grains: 2½ Vegetables: 2 Fruits: 0 Flavonoid Foods: ½ Calcium Foods: 0
Omega-3 Foods: 0 Condiments: 0 Meat/Eggs: 0 Sweets: 0

DRESSINGS AND SAUCES

Okinawan Tofunaise

Makes about 1 cup (1 serving = 1 tablespoon)

5 ounces silken tofu-lite
3 tablespoons canola oil
2 tablespoons apple or cider vinegar
1 teaspoon sea salt
1 tablespoon prepared mustard
Pinch of brown sugar

Drain the tofu well in a colander. Process all the ingredients in a food processor until they are creamy. Keep in the refrigerator until ready to use.

Nutrients per Serving
Calories: 24 Protein: 0.5 g (8%) Carbohydrate: 0.2 g (4%) Fat: 2.3 g (88%)
Calcium: 3.6 mg Fiber: 0.1 g Iron: 0.1 mg Sodium: 146 mg Flavonoids: 1.6 mg
Okinawa Food Pyramid Servings
Grains: 0 Vegetables: 0 Fruits: 0 Flavonoid Foods: 0 Calcium Foods: 0
Omega-3 Foods: 0 Condiments: 1 Meat/Eggs: 0 Sweets: 0

Creamy Miso Dressing

Makes about 2 cups (1 serving = 1 tablespoon)

5 ounces regular tofu-lite
¼ cup calcium-fortified soy milk
2 tablespoons lemon or lime juice
3 tablespoons low-sodium miso
1 tablespoon apple or cider vinegar
Pinch of sea salt
Pinch of brown sugar
1 garlic clove, chopped

Drain the tofu well in a colander. Process all the ingredients in a food processor until creamy. Refrigerate until ready to use.

Nutrients per Serving
Calories: 5 Protein: 0.4 g (31%) Carbohydrate: 0.6 g (51%) Fat: 0.1 g (22%)
Calcium: 5 mg Fiber: 0.1 g Iron: 0 mg Sodium: 30 mg Flavonoids: 2.7 mg
Okinawa Food Pyramid Servings
Grains: 0 Vegetables: 0 Fruits: 0 Flavonoid Foods: 0 Calcium Foods: 0
Omega-3 Foods: 0 Condiments: 1 Meat/Eggs: 0 Sweets: 0

Miso-Sesame Barbecue Sauce

Makes about ¾ cup (1 serving = 1 tablespoon)

½ cup water
3 tablespoons canola oil
3 tablespoons low-sodium miso
2 tablespoons sesame seeds, or 1 tablespoon sesame paste
1 teaspoon brown sugar
2 teaspoons fresh lemon juice
2 garlic cloves, minced
Pinch of sea salt
Pinch of chili powder

Put all the ingredients in a blender and combine until they are creamy.
Refrigerate until ready to use.

Nutrients per Serving
Calories: 28 Protein: 0.2 g (2%) Carbohydrate: 1.2 g (11%) Fat: 2.6 g (90%)
Calcium: 1 mg Fiber: 0 g Iron: 0 mg Sodium: 55 mg Flavonoids: 3 mg
Okinawa Food Pyramid Servings
Grains: 0 Vegetables: 0 Fruits: 0 Flavonoid Foods: 0 Calcium Foods: 0
Omega-3 Foods: 0 Condiments: 1 Meat/Eggs: 0 Sweets: 0

Miso-Ginger Mayonnaise

Makes about ½ cup (1 serving = 1 tablespoon)

2 tablespoons low-sodium miso
1 teaspoon shredded fresh ginger
¼ cup egg substitute
2 tablespoons apple or cider vinegar
2 tablespoons canola oil
Pinch of brown sugar
2 tablespoons water

Process all the ingredients in a food processor until creamy. Refrigerate until ready to use.

Nutrients per Serving
Calories: 31 Protein: 0.8 g (11%) Carbohydrate: 1 g (13%) Fat: 2.7 g (78%)
Calcium: 4.1 mg Fiber: 0.1 g Iron: 0.2 mg Sodium: 54 mg Flavonoids: 2.9 mg
Okinawa Food Pyramid Servings
Grains: 0 Vegetables: 0 Fruits: 0 Flavonoid Foods: 0 Calcium Foods: 0
Omega-3 Foods: 0 Condiments: 1 Meat/Eggs: 0 Sweets: 0

DESSERT

Chocolate-Kahlúa Mousse
Serves 4

1 10.5-ounce piece silken tofu
¼ cup unsweetened cocoa powder
3 tablespoons honey or maple syrup
2 tablespoons Kahlúa liqueur
2 drops vanilla extract

Raspberries, blueberries, sliced orange, or sliced apple, for decoration

Combine all the ingredients except decoration in a blender and process until smooth. Divide among four champagne glasses and refrigerate for 1 hour. When ready to serve, decorate with raspberries, blueberries, sliced orange, or sliced apple.

Nutrients per Serving
Calories: 157 Protein: 5.4 g (17%) Carbohydrate: 24.3 g (61%) Fat: 1.6 g (8%)
Calcium: 30.2 mg Fiber: 1 g Iron: 0.7 mg Sodium: 64 mg Flavonoids: 7.7 mg
Okinawa Food Pyramid Servings
Grains: 0 Vegetables: 0 Fruits: ½ Flavonoid Foods: 1 Calcium Foods: 0
Omega-3 Foods: 0 Condiments: 0 Meat/Eggs: 0 Sweets: 1

Super Vanilla Tofu Cheese Cake

Makes a 9-inch cake; serves 8

6 ounces silken tofu-lite
¾ cup graham cracker (digestive biscuit) crumbs
¼ cup canola oil
1 cup reduced-fat cottage cheese
2½ ounces fat-free soy cream cheese
½ cup fat-free sour cream
¾ cup brown sugar
1 egg (free-range, omega-3)
2 vanilla beans (scoop seeds from pods)
2 tablespoons fresh lemon juice
1 tablespoon all-purpose (plain) flour

1. Preheat the oven to 350°F.
2. Drain excess water from tofu by wrapping with a paper towel and microwaving on high for 3 minutes.
3. Combine the graham cracker crumbs and canola oil. Press into the bottom of a 9-inch round cake pan. Refrigerate the crust.
4. Combine the cottage and cream cheeses, drained tofu, and sour cream in a mixing bowl. Whisk for 7 to 10 minutes by hand or 3 to 5 minutes with an electric mixer, until the mixture is smooth.
5. Add the sugar and mix well. Fold in the egg.
6. Add the vanilla beans, lemon juice, and flour and mix well.
7. Pour batter into the pan and bake until the surface is colored lightly, about 6 minutes. Reduce the heat to 325°F and bake for 60 to 70 minutes, or until a cake tester comes out clean. Let it cool and refrigerate until ready to serve.

Nutrients per Serving
Calories: 211 Protein: 7.6 g (14%) Carbohydrate: 24.8 g (47%) Fat: 8.9 g (38%)
Calcium: 64.7 mg Fiber: 0.5 g Iron: 0.8 mg Sodium: 232 mg Flavonoids: 5.4 mg
Okinawa Food Pyramid Servings
Grains: 0 Vegetables: 0 Fruits: 0 Flavonoid Foods: 1 Calcium Foods: 0
Omega-3 Foods: 0 Condiments: 0 Meat/Eggs: 0 Sweets: 1

Okinawan Orange Brûlée

Serves 12

1½ cups half-and-half (single cream)
¾ cup calcium-fortified soy milk
1 vanilla bean (scoop seeds from pods)
4 egg yolks (free-range, omega-3)
¼ cup brown sugar
Peel of half an orange, finely chopped
Brown sugar, for sprinkling

1. Preheat the oven to 250°F.
2. In a saucepan, combine the half-and-half, soy milk, and vanilla and heat. Turn off the heat just before the liquid reaches the boiling point; do not allow milk to boil.
3. Beat the egg yolks in a mixing bowl, add the sugar, and whisk vigorously until the color is light yellow. Slowly add the hot milk mixture to the egg yolks, stirring well. Add the orange peel, then strain. Chill for 30 to 60 minutes in the refrigerator.
4. Pour the batter into twelve 1-cup ramekins and bake for 20 minutes. Let cool briefly, then refrigerate. When ready to serve, sprinkle tops with brown sugar.

Note: If you have a propane burner (blowtorch), sear the surfaces for a crisp topping.

Nutrients per Serving
Calories: 75 Protein: 2.2 g (12%) Carbohydrate: 4.7 g (25%) Fat: 5.4 g (65%)
Calcium: 61 mg Fiber: 0.2 g Iron: 0.4 mg Sodium: 17 mg Flavonoids: 0.3 mg
Okinawa Food Pyramid Servings
Grains: 0 Vegetables: 0 Fruits: 0 Flavonoid Foods: 0 Calcium Foods: 0
Omega-3 Foods: ¼ Condiments: 0 Meat/Eggs: 0 Sweets: 1

Zesty Zucchini Bread

Makes an 8 × 14-inch loaf; serves 8

2 small zucchini (courgettes)
1 teaspoon fresh lemon juice
2 eggs (free-range, omega-3)
½ cup brown sugar
¼ cup canola oil
1 cup whole-grain wheat flour
¼ cup and 2 tablespoons fat-free soy flour
1 ⅔ teaspoons baking powder
½ teaspoon baking soda
¼ teaspoon sea salt
2 teaspoons ground cinnamon
½ teaspoon ground nutmeg
½ teaspoon ground ginger
¼ teaspoon ground clove
1 vanilla bean (scoop seeds from pods)
Peel of 1 lemon, finely chopped
Juice of 1 lemon
¼ cup and 2 tablespoons roasted and chopped walnuts

1. Preheat the oven to 350°F.
2. Process the zucchini in a food processor until well minced. Sprinkle with the lemon juice and set aside.
3. Combine the eggs, brown sugar, and canola oil in a food processor and process until creamy.
4. Place the flours, baking powder and soda, and seasonings in a large bowl and stir to blend well. Add the zucchini, vanilla, lemon peel and juice, and walnuts and stir well.
5. Spray an 8 × 4-inch loaf pan with canola oil. Pour the batter into the pan and bake for 45 minutes, or until a cake tester comes out clean.

Nutrients per Serving
Calories: 243 Protein: 8.1 g (13%) Carbohydrate: 26.2 g (43%) Fat: 13.2 g (49%)
Calcium: 70.4 mg Fiber: 4.2 g Iron: 2.1 mg Sodium: 178 mg Flavonoids: 10.3 mg
Okinawa Food Pyramid Servings
Grains: ¼ Vegetables: ¼ Fruits: 0 Flavonoid Foods: 0 Calcium Foods: 0
Omega-3 Foods: ½ Condiments: 0 Meat/Eggs: 0 Sweets: 1

Green Tea Ice Cream
Serves 8

2 cups skim milk
½ cup brown sugar
2 tablespoons green tea powder, available at most Asian food stores
4 egg yolks (free-range, omega-3)
½ cup half-and-half (single cream)
1 tablespoon Grand Marnier liqueur
Blackberries (optional)

1. In a saucepan, warm the milk and brown sugar over low heat for 1 to 2 minutes. Mix well so that the sugar is dissolved. Add the green tea powder and stir.
2. Whisk the egg yolks in a small mixing bowl, add the milk mixture, and stir. Pour the mixture back into the saucepan and warm over very low heat for 10 minutes, or until the mixture is thick. Stir continuously with a spatula. Transfer the mixture to a bowl and allow it to cool until lukewarm.
3. Add the half-and-half and stir; add the Grand Marnier and stir again. Pour the mixture into a flat, 3-inch-deep metal container and freeze for 30 to 45 minutes. Remove the container from the freezer and stir well to break up ice crystals. Return to the freezer. Repeat this step three to four times, finally keeping the ice cream in the freezer at least 2 hours.
4. When ready to serve, decorate with blackberries if desired.

Note: When you have no time to make the ice cream from scratch, you can stir together ½ teaspoon green tea powder and 5 tablespoons low-fat vanilla ice cream for 1 serving.

Nutrients per Serving
Calories: 145 Protein: 5.3 g (15%) Carbohydrate: 18.2 g (50%) Fat: 5.9 g (37%)
Calcium: 151 mg Fiber: 0.6 g Iron: 0.7 mg Sodium: 59.6 mg Flavonoids: 0.1 mg
Okinawa Food Pyramid Servings
Grains: 0 Vegetables: 0 Fruits: 0 Flavonoid Foods: 0 Calcium Foods: ¼
Omega-3 Foods: ³/₄ Condiments: 0 Meat/Eggs: 0 Sweets: 1

Delectable Strawberry Mousse

Serves 4

4 3.5-ounce strawberry gelatin (jelly) dessert snacks, at room
temperature
1 cup finely chopped fresh strawberries
1 cup reduced-fat nondairy whipped topping

Whip the gelatin in a mixer briefly. Mash the strawberries in a
blender, then add the strawberry puree to the gelatin and blend
briefly. Mix in the whipped topping just until blended. Spoon into
four serving dishes and store in the refrigerator until ready to serve.

Nutrients per Serving
Calories: 101 Protein: 2.1 g (8%) Carbohydrate: 9.7 g (38%) Fat: 6.1 g (54%)
Calcium: 11.4 mg Fiber: 1 g Iron: 0.2 mg Sodium: 93 mg Flavonoids: 21.7 mg
Okinawa Food Pyramid Servings
Grains: 0 Vegetables: 0 Fruits: ½ Flavonoid Foods: 0 Calcium Foods: 0
Omega-3 Foods: 0 Condiments: 0 Meat/Eggs: 0 Sweets: 1

Easy Creamed Peach

Serves 4

4 peaches, peeled and chopped
2 teaspoons lemon juice
½ cup low-fat whipped cream

1. Prepare the broiler or grill.
2. Place the peaches on a baking sheet. Sprinkle with lemon
   juice and top with whipped cream. Broil for 4 minutes, or
   until lightly browned, then, using a spatula, carefully
   arrange them on four dessert plates.

Nutrients per Serving
Calories: 108 Protein: 1.4 g (15%) Carbohydrate: 20.9 g (71%) Fat: 3.1 g (24%)
Calcium: 10.7 mg Fiber: 3.2 g Iron: 0.2 mg Sodium: 23 mg Flavonoids: 0.8 mg
Okinawa Food Pyramid Servings
Grains: 0 Vegetables: 0 Fruits: 1 Flavonoid Foods: 0 Calcium Foods: 0
Omega-3 Foods: 0 Condiments: 0 Meat/Eggs: 0 Sweets: 1

Appendix A

Additional Information

Important Adult Screening Tests and Procedures

In Your Twenties and Thirties

Women
Blood pressure: Baseline test in your twenties. If normal, then every five years thereafter.
Breast and skin self-exam: Every month.
Cholesterol profile: Baseline in your twenties. If normal, then every five years thereafter.
Clinical breast exam: Every three years.
Complete physical exam: Three times in your thirties.
Dental exam: At least yearly.
Eye exam: Every four to five years.
HIV and hepatitis B and C tests: At least yearly if you engage in risky behavior (e.g., unprotected sex, needle-sharing, etc.).
Pap test: Every year until three normal exams in a row, then every three years thereafter.
Pelvic exam: Every year.
Skin exam: Every three years.

Men
Blood pressure: Baseline test in your twenties. If normal, then every five years thereafter.
Cholesterol profile: Baseline in your twenties. If normal, then every five years thereafter.
Complete physical exam: Three times in your thirties.

Dental exam: At least yearly.

Eye exam: Every four to five years.

HIV and hepatitis B and C tests: At least yearly if you engage in risky behavior (e.g., unprotected sex, needle-sharing, etc.).

Skin exam: Every three years.

Testicular self-exam: Every month.

Immunizations

Diphtheria/tetanus booster: Every ten years.

In Your Forties

Women

Blood pressure: At least every two years.

Bone mineral density test (bone densitometry) if you are perimenopausal.

Breast and skin self-exam: Every month.

Cholesterol profile: Every five years.

Clinical breast exam: Every year.

Complete physical exam: Four times in your forties.

Dental exam: At least yearly.

Eye exam: Every four to five years.

Fasting plasma glucose (diabetes) test: Every three years after age forty-five.

Follicle-stimulating hormone (FSH) test if perimenopausal (confirms if you are going through menopause).

HIV and hepatitis B and C tests: At least yearly if you engage in risky behavior.

Mammogram: Every one to two years.

Pap test: Every three years.

Pelvic exam: Every year.

Skin exam: Every three years.

Men

Blood pressure: At least every two years.

Cholesterol profile: Every five years.

Complete physical exam: Four times in your forties.

Dental exam: At least yearly.

Digital rectal exam if you are African-American or have a strong family history of prostate cancer (first-degree relatives): Every year.

Eye exam: Every four to five years.

Fasting plasma glucose (diabetes) test: Every three years after age forty-five.

HIV and hepatitis B and C tests: At least yearly if you engage in risky behavior.

Prostate specific antigen (PSA) test: Every year at age forty-five in men who are at high risk, including African-Americans or those with a strong family history of prostate cancer.

Skin exam: Every three years.

Testicular self-exam: Every month.

Immunizations

Diphtheria/tetanus booster: Every ten years.

From Your Fifties

Women

Blood pressure: Every year.

Breast self-exam: Every month.

Clinical breast exam: Every year.

Colorectal cancer tests: Fecal occult blood test every year; flexible sigmoidoscopy/barium enema or colonoscopy every three to five years.

Complete physical exam: Five times in your fifties. Annually after sixty.

Dental exam: At least yearly.

Eye exam: Every two to four years; every one to two years if sixty-five or older.

Fasting plasma glucose (diabetes) test: Every three years.

HIV and hepatitis B and C tests: At least yearly if you engage in risky behavior.

Mammogram: Every year.

Perimenopausal: Follicle-stimulating hormone (FSH) test (to check if you are going through menopause).

Pap test: Every three years.

Pelvic exam: Every year.

Skin exam: Every year.

Thyroid-stimulating hormone test: Every five years; every three to five years if sixty or older.

Men

Blood pressure: Every year.

Colorectal cancer tests: Fecal occult blood test every year; flexible sigmoidoscopy/barium enema or colonoscopy every three to five years.

Complete physical exam: Five times in your fifties. Annually after sixty.

Dental exam: At least yearly.

Digital rectal exam (for prostate cancer): Every year.

Eye exam: Every two to four years; every one to two years if sixty-five or older.

Fasting plasma glucose (diabetes) test: Every three years.

HIV and hepatitis B and C tests: At least yearly if you engage in risky behavior.

Prostate specific antigen (PSA) test: Every year.

Skin exam: Every year.

Testicular self-exam: Every month.

Thyroid-stimulating hormone test: Every five years; every three to five years if sixty or older.

Immunizations

Diphtheria/tetanus booster: Every ten years.

Influenza vaccine: Every year if sixty-five or older.

Pneumococcal vaccine: Once every five to ten years after age sixty-five.

Body mass index (BMI) is a rough guide to obesity. It is a good research tool because there are definite risks associated with very high and very low body mass index.

BMI is a good way to estimate the level of body fat, and it's simple to calculate. To find your BMI, take out your calculator and follow these steps:

1. Multiply your weight in pounds by 0.45.
2. Multiply your height in inches by 0.025. Then square this number.
3. Take your answer from step 1 and divide it by your answer from step 2.

This is your BMI.

A quick example: If you weigh 150 pounds and measure 5'6" (66 inches):

1. $150 \times 0.45 = $ **67.5**
2. $66 \times 0.025 = $ **1.65** $1.65 \times 1.65 = $ **2.72**
3. $68 / 2.72 = $ **24.8**

BMI	HEALTH CONSEQUENCES*
17.0–18.4	Probably healthy (excluding cancer, smoking, malnutrition)
18.5–22.9	Definitely healthy
23.0–24.9	Mildly increased health risks
25.0–29.9	Definite increased health risks
30.0 plus	Dangerous[†]

* See Chapter Two, note 71.

† See your physician.

BMI less than 18.5

A BMI of less than 18.5 may contribute to health problems in some people (although current research suggests your BMI may be as low as 17 and you may still be healthy). Some of the health risks you face by being underweight are heart irregularities; depression and other emotional distress; and anemia.

BMI 18.5–22.9

This is a good range for most people. If you fall within this zone and eat sensibly, your weight shouldn't cause any health problems.

BMI 23–24.9

Most experts consider this a healthy range, although there are small increased risks for chronic disease versus the 18.5–22.9 category.

BMI 25–27

A caution zone; watch your weight. A BMI of 25–27 could lead to health problems for some people. Even though it is still considered an "acceptable" range for most people, there are definite increased health risks in this zone.

BMI greater than 27

Research shows that the higher your BMI goes above 27, the more you risk developing high blood pressure, diabetes, coronary heart disease, and certain cancers. Low self-esteem and depression may also result from a high BMI.

Some Big Exceptions

The BMI is designed for adults aged twenty to sixty-five years—those whose body size and composition is fairly stable. It does not apply to babies, children, adolescents, pregnant or nursing women, senior citizens, *very* muscular people, and endurance athletes such as runners.

Cooking Whole Grains
IN A STEAMER

GRAIN (2½ CUPS)	BROTH OR WATER	COOKING TIME
		SHORT
Amaranth	4 cups	30 minutes
Quinoa	4 cups	30 minutes
		MODERATE
Millet	4 cups	40 minutes
		LONGER
Barley	4 cups	75 minutes
Brown rice	4 cups	65–75 minutes
Oat groats	4 cups	75 minutes

GRAIN (2½ CUPS)	BROTH OR WATER	COOKING TIME
Rye	4 cups	75 minutes
Triticale	4 cups	75 minutes
Wheat berries, kamut, spelt	4 cups	75 minutes
Wild rice	4 cups	75 minutes

ON THE STOVETOP

GRAIN (2½ CUPS)	BROTH OR WATER	COOKING TIME
		SHORT
Amaranth	5 cups	20 minutes
Quinoa	5 cups	10–15 minutes
		MODERATE
Brown rice	5 cups	40 minutes
Millet	5 cups	30 minutes
		LONGER
Barley	6 cups	60 minutes
Oat groats	6 cups	60 minutes
Rye	6 cups	60 minutes
Triticale	6 cups	60 minutes
Wheat berries, kamut, spelt	6 cups	60 minutes
Wild rice	6 cups	60 minutes

Adequate and Optimum Vitamin and Mineral Intakes

Here is the best evidence for what intakes you should aim for from our extensive review of more than 2,000 studies, government reports, the WHO database, and our own research.

MINERAL INTAKES

NUTRIENT	GOVERNMENT STANDARD[1]	OPTIMAL INTAKE	SAFE UPPER LIMIT[3]	WHO MAY NOT GET ENOUGH[4]
Calcium	M&F: age 19–50, 1,000 mg M&F: age 51–, 1,200 mg	1,000–1,500 mg	2,500 mg	Very low calorie diets Age >70 Postmenopausal women

NUTRIENT	GOVERNMENT STANDARD[1]	OPTIMAL INTAKE	SAFE UPPER LIMIT[3]	WHO MAY NOT GET ENOUGH[4]
Chromium	50–200 mcg[2]	50–200 mcg	Unknown	Age >70 Very low calorie diets
Copper[5]	1.5–3 mg[2]	Unknown	10 mg[2]	Megadoses of vitamin C or zinc
Iodine	M&F: all age, 150 mcg	Unknown	2 mg[2]	
Iron	M: age 19–, 10 mg F: age 19–50, 15 mg F: age 51–, 10 mg	10–15 mg	30 mg[2]	Heavy menstrual blood losses Very low calorie diets
Magnesium	M: age 19–30, 400 mg M: age 31–, 420 mg F: age 19–30, 310 mg F: age 31–, 320 mg	310–420 mg	350 mg in supplement form	Age >70 Diabetics Very low calorie diets
Manganese	2–5 mg[2]	Unknown	10 mg[2]	Very low calorie diets
Molybdenum	75–250 mcg[2]	Unknown	1 mg[2]	
Phosphorus	M&F: all age, 700 mg	800–1,200 mg	M&F: 19–70, 4,000 mg M&F: 71–, 3,000 mg	Gastric problems
Selenium[6]	M&F: all age, 55 mcg	100–200 mcg	400 mcg	Postmenopausal women
Zinc[7]	M: all age, 15 mg F: all age, 12 mg	12–15 mg	15 mg	Age >70 Vegetarians Diabetics

[1]Dietary reference intakes (DRI); M = male, F = female. Food and Nutrition Board, Institute of Medicine. Wash., D.C.: National Academy Press, 1998.
[2]DRI/safe upper limit not yet determined. Based on the best available evidence.

VITAMIN INTAKES

NUTRIENT	GOVERNMENT STANDARD[1]	OPTIMAL INTAKE	SAFE UPPER LIMIT[3]	WHO MAY NOT GET ENOUGH[4]
WATER-SOLUBLE VITAMINS				
B vitamins Thiamin (B$_1$)	M: all age, 1.2 mg F: all age, 1.1 mg	Unknown	100 mg[2]	Age >70
Riboflavin (B$_2$)	M&F: all age, 1.1 mg	Unknown	100 mg[2]	Too many processed foods Very active adults Low calcium intakes Hyperthyroid
Niacin (B$_3$)	M&F: all age, 14–16 mg	Unknown	35 mg	Age >70 Diabetics Hyperthyroid
Pyridoxine (B$_6$)	M&F: age 19–50, 1.3 mg M: age 51–, 1.7 mg F: age 51–, 1.5 mg	Unknown	100 mg	Oral contraceptive users
Cobalamin (B$_{12}$)	M&F: all age, 2.4 mcg	Unknown	Unknown	Vegans
Biotin	M&F: all age, 30 mcg	Unknown	Unknown	Antibiotic users Smokers Oral contraceptive users

[3]"Safe upper limits" are either US or WHO standards and are not meant to be optimal intakes. They are intakes above which side effects have been reported or insufficient evidence exists to delineate safety. These refer to ages 19–70 only.
[4]Pregnant and breast-feeding women have increased needs for most nutrients.
[5]Copper intake above 10 mg per day can cause free-radical-induced damage and is implicated in some disease processes.
[6]Selenium has a narrow window of toxicity, and we do not advocate supplementing with extra selenium until more evidence supports its use.
[7]Zinc toxicity can be severe with as little as 70 mg per day for extended periods.

NUTRIENT	GOVERNMENT STANDARD[1]	OPTIMAL INTAKE	SAFE UPPER LIMIT[3]	WHO MAY NOT GET ENOUGH[4]
Folate	M&F: all age, 400 mcg	400–800 mcg	1,000 mcg	Age >70 Oral contraceptive users Pregnant women Sickle-cell anemia Heavy alcohol users
Pantothenic acid	M&F: all age, 5 mg	5–12 mg	Unknown	Age >55 Very low calorie diets Smokers
Vitamin C	M: all age, 90 mg F: all age, 75 mg	500–1,000 mg	2,000 mg	Oral contraceptive users Smokers
FAT-SOLUBLE VITAMINS				
Vitamin A	M: all age, 1,000 mcg F: all age, 800 mcg	1,500 mcg	15,000 mcg	Diabetics Toxic chemicals exposure Heavy air pollution
Vitamin D	M&F: age 19–50, 5 mcg M&F: age 51–70, 10 mcg M&F: age 71–, 15 mcg	15–30 mcg	50 mcg	Poor sun exposure Age ›70 Vegetarians Kidney disease
Vitamin E	M&F: all age, 15 mg	50–400 mg	800–1,000 mg	Hyperthyroid Age ›55
Vitamin K	M: age 17–24, 70 mcg M: age 25–, 80 mcg F: age 17–24, 60 mcg F: age 25–, 65 mcg	60–200 mg	Unknown	Very low calorie diets

BURNING FAT

CALORIES BURNED FOR 20 MINUTES OF ACTIVITY

ACTIVITY	125 POUNDS	150 POUNDS	175 POUNDS
Aerobics	125	150	180
Climbing stairs	235	280	335
Cross-country skiing	195	235	270
Cycling	65	80	95
Gardening	60	75	85
Housework, light (dishwashing, cooking)	35	45	50
Housework, heavy (vacuuming, scrubbing floors)	65	80	95
Lawn mowing (push mower)	110	135	160
Running (7 mph)	255	310	360
Swimming (lap)	140	165	190
Tai chi	75	90	105
Walking (3 mph)	85	110	125

Source: Mayo Clinic HealthQuest.

LOW-CALORIE SNACKS
EAT AS MUCH AS YOU WANT

FRUITS	CALORIES	PORTION SIZE
Apple	81	1 medium
Apricot	51	3 medium
Blackberries	84	1 cup
Blueberries	41	½ cup
Cantaloupe	24	⅛ of medium melon
Cherries, Bing	47	10 pieces
Fig	37	1 medium
Grapefruit	38	½ fruit
Grapes	90	1½ cups
Kiwi	46	1 medium
Orange	70	1 medium
Papaya	29	¼ medium
Peach	40	1 medium
Pear	97	1 medium
Pineapple	80	1 cup
Plum	36	1 medium
Raspberries	98	1 cup
Strawberries	36	10 medium
Watermelon	80	2 cups

VEGETABLES AND BEANS	CALORIES	PORTION SIZE
Asparagus	29	1 cup
Baby carrots	45	1 cup
Broccoli	40	1 cup
Cabbage, Savoy	17	1 cup
Cauliflower	28	1 cup
Celery	21	1 cup
Cucumber	38	1 medium
Green soybeans	100	⅔ cup (3 oz.)
Lettuce, romaine	12	1 cup
Mushrooms, button	20	5 medium
Onion	60	1 medium
Radish	24	10
Snap beans	31	1 cup
Spinach	14	1 cup
Sweet potato, baked	117	1 medium
Tofu, lite	35	3 oz.
Tomato	35	1 medium
Turnip	29	1 cup
Watercress	24	1 cup

EAT IN LIMITED AMOUNTS

HEALTHY SNACKS	CALORIES	PORTION SIZE
Burger, veggie, Boca Burger	110	1 burger
Chili, vegetarian, Fat-Free	80	½ cup
Soup, cup, Fantastic, Miso Noodle, Low-Fat	130	1 cup
Soup, cup, Health Valley, Black Bean, Fat-Free	100	1 cup
Soup, cup, Health Valley, Lentil, Fat-Free	130	1 cup
Soup, cup, Health Valley, Pasta Parmesan, Fat-Free	100	1 cup
Soup, can, Health Valley, 14 Garden Vegetable, Fat-Free	80	1 cup
Soup, can, Progresso, Clam Chowder, Manhattan	110	1 cup
Bar, Nature's Choice, Cranberry Filled Cereal Bars	110	1 bar
Bar, Nature's Choice, Granola Bars	80	1 bar
Cookie, Health Valley, Raspberry, Jambo, Fat-Free	80	1 cookie

HEALTHY SNACKS	CALORIES	PORTION SIZE
Corn bread, Arrowhead Mills, Multi-Grain Mix	120	¼ cup
Crackers, Health Valley, Whole Wheat, Low-Fat	60	6 crackers
Crackers, Organic Courtney's, Fine English Water Cracker	60	4 crackers
Crispbread, Wasa, Light Rye, Fat Free	25	1 slice
Gelatin snacks, Jell-O, Sugar-Free, Low-Calorie	7	1 serving
Grissini, Let's Do Organics	60	3 pieces
Ice cream, Cascadian Farm, Organic Sorbet & Cream	110	½ cup
Ice cream, Stonyfield Farm, Nonfat Frozen Yogurt, Raspberry	100	½ cup
Ice cream, Stonyfield Farm, Low-fat Frozen Yogurt, Mocha	130	½ cup
Ice cream, Turtle Mountain, It's Soy Delicious, Vanilla	120	½ cup
Popcorn, microwave, Weight Watchers, Smart Snackers	100	1 package
Yogurt, Whole Soy, Blueberry Yogurt	140	1 container

EAT WITH CARE

OTHER SNACKS	CALORIES	PORTION SIZE
Baked Goods		
Bagel, whole grain	156	1 bagel (3-inch diameter)
Biscuits, low fat, trans-free	63	1 biscuit
Bread, whole-grain wheat	69	1 slice
English muffin, whole wheat	134	1 muffin
Corn bread	173	1 piece (about 2 oz.)
Crackers, whole wheat	71	4 small crackers
Pita bread, whole wheat	74	1 small pita
Pumpernickel bread	65	1 slice
Rye bread, whole grain	82	1 slice
Waffle, ready-to-heat, plain	88	1 waffle
Snacks		
Baked potato (new variety or sweet)	145	1 potato
Chili, vegetarian	227	1 cup
Clam chowder, Manhattan (prepared with water)	78	1 cup

OTHER SNACKS	CALORIES	PORTION SIZE
Corn chips, light, nonhydrogenated oil	126	1 oz.
Rice cakes with brown rice and buckwheat	68	2 cakes
Rice snacks, oriental	110	⅔ cup
Salsa	18	¼ cup
Sushi (salmon)	160	4 small pieces
Dairy Products		
Cream cheese, nonfat	14	1 tbs.
Ice cream, low fat	178	½ cup
Sour cream, nonfat	31	1 tbs.
Yogurt, low-fat	231	1 container (8 oz.)
Yogurt, nonfat	100	1 container (8 oz.)
Desserts, Sweets		
Gelatin dessert, prepared with water	79	½ cup
Ice pops	37	1 bar (1.8 fl. oz.)
Orange marmalade	49	1 tbs.

The Okinawa Program Nutrition Tracker

Nutrition can be a very difficult and complicated subject. It doesn't have to be. We have tried hard to simplify the basic guidelines for eating according to the Okinawa Program. Following these guidelines will bring you the opportunity to reap the same health rewards the Okinawans do, without having to calculate your nutritional intake down to the gram. Nevertheless, for those who would like to further define or gauge their progress, or simply get back on track, we have designed a straightforward method for you to do just that— the Okinawa Program Nutrition Tracker. It provides a step-by-step guide to calculating and tracking the elements that are key to your health.

Step 1. List the Foods You Ate Today

Write down the foods you ate today in the left-hand column of the chart. To fill in the columns on the right side of the chart, go to step 2 and estimate how many servings you had. Calculate your calories and the Glycemic Index of your foods.

THE OKINAWA PROGRAM NUTRITION TRACKER

FOODS YOU HAD TODAY	VEGETABLE SERVINGS	WHOLE-GRAIN SERVINGS	FRUIT SERVINGS	CALCIUM FOOD SERVINGS	FLAVONOID FOOD SERVINGS	OMEGA-3 FOOD SERVINGS	CONDIMENTS/ OILS, OPTIONAL FOODS	CALO-RIES	GLYCE-MIC INDEX*
Totals:									

* Carbohydrates only.

Step 2. Estimate Your Requirements

Find your recommended number of daily food servings and calorie limit based on your age, gender, and activity level and weight loss goals.

Estimating Daily Servings Based On Energy Expenditure

Low Calorie Intake—1,500 calories (approx.) for sedentary women, older adults, and those men and women who are active but seek a healthy approach to weight loss.

Medium Calorie Intake—2,000 calories (approx.) for most children, teenage girls, active women, and sedentary men. Women who are pregnant or breast feeding may need more and should check with their physicians.

High Calorie Intake—2,600 calories (approx.) for teenage boys, active men, and very active women.

	LOW	MED	HIGH
Vegetable servings	7	10	13
Whole-grain servings	7	10	13
Fruit servings	2	3	4
Calcium food servings	2	3	4
Flavonoid food servings	2	3	4
Omega-3 food servings	1	2	3

Convert the foods you listed above into servings, using the Servings Chart below. Then enter this into the appropriate columns of the Okinawa Program Nutrition Tracker.

SERVINGS CHART

VEGETABLES	SERVING	WHOLE GRAINS	SERVING
1 cup raw leafy vegetables	1	½ cup cooked cereal, rice, or pasta	1
½ cup other vegetables, cooked or chopped raw	1	1 ounce ready-to-eat cereal	1
¾ cup vegetable juice	1	1 slice of bread or half whole-grain bagel	1

CALCIUM FOODS (DAIRY)	SERVING	CALCIUM FOODS (VEGETARIAN)	SERVING
1½ oz. low-fat or fat-free cheese	1	3 ounces calcium-fortified tofu	1
1 cup low-fat or fat-free milk	1	⅓ cup prepared seaweed	1
1 cup low-fat or fat-free yogurt	1	½ cup watercress	1

FLAVONOID FOODS	SERVING	FLAVONOID FOODS	SERVING
1 tablespoon ground flaxseed	1	¾ cup miso soup	1
½ cup cooked beans, legumes	1	1 teaspoon miso paste	1
3 ounces regular or firm tofu	1	¾ cup cranberry juice	1
1 teaspoon arrowroot powder	1	¼ cup chopped onion	1
2 tablespoons soy nuts	1	¼ cup soybean sprouts	1

OMEGA-3 FOODS	SERVING	MEAT/POULTRY/ EGGS	SERVING
1 tablespoon ground flaxseed	1	2–3 ounces cooked poultry	1
2 tablespoons chopped walnuts	1	2–3 ounces cooked lean meat	1
3 ounces cooked or raw (sushi or sashimi) fish	1	1 non-omega-3 egg	1
1 omega-3 egg	1		
3 ounces tofu	1		

Step 3. Matching Servings, Calories, and Glycemic Index

Circle the servings that are right for you and write down the servings you had today. Do this for three days. See what your average is over the three days. How well did you do? Are there any areas for improvement? (Don't worry if you go over the recommended servings in these foods. Consider them "free foods," since they are mostly low-calorie and antioxidant-rich.) Then calculate your total calories and your Glycemic Index score. You may use any number of available sources to calculate calories, including recipes, food labels, and the USDA food nutrients database (see Appendix B for the USDA website).

COMPARING RECOMMENDED AND ACTUAL SERVINGS

FOOD GROUP	NUMBER OF SERVINGS			SERVINGS YOU HAD
	LOW	MED	HIGH	
Vegetables	7	10	13	_____
Whole grains	7	10	13	_____
Fruit	2	3	4	_____
Calcium food	2	3	4	_____
Flavonoid food	2	3	4	_____
Omega-3 food	1	2	3	_____

COMPARE GOAL CALORIES WITH ACTUAL CALORIES EATEN

GOAL CALORIES: 1,500   2,000   2,600

CALORIES EATEN _____

CALCULATE THE GI OF FOODS EATEN

AVERAGE GI   _____

Less than 55 = low GI, (excellent job)

55–70 = intermediate GI (good but room for improvement)

More than 70 = high GI (needs major work)

Step 4. Fine-Tuning and Troubleshooting

Look at your eating habits and see where you need to make improvements.

Problem No. 1. Eating too many or too few servings from a food group.

Solution. If you are consistently undereating from specific groups, look for foods that fall within that group that you might enjoy and eat them more often. Stock up on them when you are shopping. If you are consistently overeating from a group, cut your serving sizes in half. You can still eat from that group, but you need to eat smaller portions.

Problem No. 2. Eating too many calories.

Solution. Look for sources of hidden fat in cookies, cakes, vegetable spreads, and dressings. Try fat-free substitutes. Drink more water and tea and less juice.

Problem No. 3. Eating too high on the GI scale.

Solution. Look for specific foods that might be consistent culprits, such as white bread, white rice, and potatoes (try new potatoes). Eat whole grains. Eat more legumes, such as soy, canned beans, or green beans. Add a fiber supplement to your diet and recalculate in a week's time.

Appendix B

Resources

Recommended Reading

Allard, Michel, Victor Lebre, Jean-Marie Robine, and Jeanne Calment. *Jeanne Calment: From Van Gogh's Time to Ours: 122 Extraordinary Years.* New York: W. H. Freeman and Company, 1998.

Bishop, Mark. *Okinawan Karate: Teachers, Styles, and Secret Techniques.* Clarendon, Vt.: Charles E. Tuttle, 1999.

Benson, Herbert, M.D., with Marg Stark. *Timeless Healing: The Power and Biology of Belief.* New York: Fireside, 1997.

Bumgarner, Marlene Anne. *The New Book of Whole Grains.* New York: St. Martin's Press, 1997.

Chesman, Andrea. *366 Delicious Ways to Cook Rice, Beans, and Grains.* New York: Plume, 1998.

Chopra, Deepak, M.D. *Ageless Body, Timeless Mind: The Quantum Alternative to Growing Old.* New York: Three Rivers Press, 1998.

Chopra, Deepak. *How to Know God: The Soul's Journey into the Mystery of Mysteries.* New York: Harmony Books, 2000.

Cohen, Mark Nathan. *Health and the Rise of Civilization.* New Haven: Yale University Press, 1991.

Cousins, Norman. *Anatomy of an Illness As Perceived by the Patient: Reflections on Healing and Regeneration.* New York: W. W. Norton and Company, 1995.

Crose, Royda, Ph.D. *Why Women Live Longer than Men.* San Francisco: Jossey-Bass, 1997.

Dalai Lama and Howard C. Cutler. *The Art of Happiness: A Handbook for Living.* New York: Riverhead Books, 1998.

Dossey, Larry, M.D. *Reinventing Medicine: Beyond Mind-Body to a New Era of Healing.* San Francisco: HarperCollins, 1999.

Hayflick, Leonard, Ph.D. *How and Why We Age.* New York: Ballantine Books, 1996.

Hilton, James. *Lost Horizon.* New York: William Morrow and Company, 1996.

Kerr, George H. *Okinawa: The History of an Island People.* Revised edition. Clarendon, Vt.: Charles E. Tuttle, 2000.

Koenig, Harold G. *Is Religion Good for Your Health?: The Effects of Religion on Physical and Mental Health.* New York: Haworth Press, 1997.

Kübler-Ross, Elisabeth. *On Death and Dying.* New York: Simon and Schuster, 1997.

Kübler-Ross, Elisabeth. *On Life After Death.* Berkeley, Calif.: Celestial Arts, 1991.

Kudaka, Masakazu. *The Forest of Yambaru.* Tokyo, Japan: Toyokan, 2000.

Lee, Richard B. *The Dobe Ju/'Hoansi (Case Studies in Cultural Anthropology).* Fort Worth, Tex.: Harcourt College Publishers, 1993.

Lee, Richard B., and Irven DeVore, editors. *Kalahari Hunter-Gatherers: Studies of the !Kung San and Their Neighbors.* iUniverse.com, 1998.

Love, Susan M. *Dr. Susan Love's Hormone Book.* New York: Random House, 1998.

Martin, William. *The Couple's Tao Te Ching: Ancient Advice for Modern Lovers.* New York: Marlowe and Company, 2000.

Mayo Clinic Health Quest: Guide to Self Care. Rochester, Minn.: Mayo Foundation for Medical Education and Research, 1999.

McCarthy, Patrick. *Ancient Okinawan Martial Arts: Koryu Uchinadi.* Clarendon, Vt.: Charles E. Tuttle, 1999.

Nagamine, Shoshin. *Tales of Okinawa's Great Masters.* Clarendon, Vt.: Charles E. Tuttle, 2000.

Ornish, Dean. *Dr. Dean Ornish's Program for Reversing Heart Disease.* New York: Ivy Books, 1996.

Ornish, Dean. *Love & Survival: 8 Pathways to Intimacy and Health.* New York: HarperCollins, 1999.

Otsuka, Shokyu. *Southern Breeze.* Naha, Japan: Ryukyu Shimpo Press, 2000.

Pelletier, Kenneth R. *The Best Alternative Medicine.* New York: Simon and Schuster, 2000.

Perls, Thomas T., M.D., M.P.H., and Margery Hutter Silver, Ed.D. *Living to 100: Lessons in Living to Your Maximum Potential at Any Age.* New York: Basic Books, 2000.

Rowe, John W., M.D., and Robert L. Kahn, Ph.D. *Successful Aging.* New York: Delacorte Press, 1999.

Saltzman, Joanne. *Amazing Grains: Creating Vegetarian Main Dishes with Whole Grains.* Tiburon, Calif.: H. J. Kramer, 1990.

Sapolsky, Robert M. *Why Zebras Don't Get Ulcers: An Updated Guide to Stress, Stress-Related Diseases, and Coping.* New York: W. H. Freeman and Company, 1998.

Sered, Susan. *Women of the Sacred Groves: Divine Priestesses of Okinawa.* Oxford, England: Oxford University Press, 1999.

Sotile, Wayne, and Mary O. Sotile. *Beat Stress Together.* New York: John Wiley and Sons, 1999.

Walford, Roy, M.D. *Beyond the 120 Year Diet: How to Double Your Vital Years.* New York: Four Walls Eight Windows, 2000.

Wei, Jeanne, M.D., Ph.D., and Sue Levkoff, Sc.D. *Aging Well: The Complete Guide to Physical and Emotional Health.* New York: John Wiley and Sons, 2000.

Weil, Andrew, M.D. *Eating Well for Optimum Health: The Essential Guide to Food, Diet, and Nutrition.* New York: Alfred A. Knopf, 2000.

Weil, Andrew, M.D. *Spontaneous Healing: How to Discover and Enhance Your Body's Natural Ability to Maintain and Heal Itself.* New York: Alfred A. Knopf, 1995.

Wolever, Thomas, M.S., and Jennie Brand-Miller. *The Glucose Revolution: The Authoritative Guide to the Glycemic Index.* New York: Marlowe and Co., 1999.

Websites
Okinawa Centenarian Study: **http://www.okicent.org**

Okinawa Program
See **http://www.okinawaway.com/** for the latest health advice and resources for successful aging.

Okinawan/Japanese Online Stores and Information

Bites of Asia: **http://www.bitesofasia.com**

Gateway Network News: **http://www.gnn.wwma.net**

Japan Update News: **http://www.japanupdate.com**

Japanese Green Tea: **http://www.chikochan.com**

Katagiri: **http://www.katagiri.com**

Let's try Japanese food: **http://www.seagull-ny.com/foods**

Naniwa Food: **http://www.naniwafood.com**

Okinawa Ginza: **http://www.virtualginza.com**

The Oriental Pantry: **http://www.orientalpantry.com**
PacificrimGourmet.com: **http://www.pacificrim-gourmet.com**
SearchOkinawa.com: **http://www.searchokinawa.com**
Virtual Okinawa Interactive Guide: **http://www.virtualokinawa.com**

Health Resources

General

MayoClinic.com: **http://www.mayohealth.org**
National Institutes of Health, NIH Health Information Page: **http://www.nih.gov/health**
University of California at Berkeley National Health Study: **http://www.healthsurvey.org**
US Department of Health and Human Services' Healthfinder: **http://www.healthfinder.org**
Better Health Channel (Aus): **http://www.anzfa.gov.au**
Australian Department of Health and Aged Care: **http://www.health.gov.au**
Ministry of Health (NZ): **http://www.moh.govt.nz/moh.nsf**
Department of Health (UK): **http://www.gov.uk/government/organisations/department-of-health**

Aging

American Association of Retired Persons: **http://www.aarp.org**
American Federation for Aging Research: **http://www.afar.org**
American Geriatrics Society: **http://www.americangeriatrics.org**
Gerontological Society of America: **http://www.geron.org**
National Institute on Aging: **http://www.nih.gov/nia**

Cancer

American Cancer Society: **http://www.cancer.org**
American Institute for Cancer Research: **http://www.aicr.org**
Harvard School of Public Health (find your risk for the twelve most common cancers): **http://www.yourcancerrisk.harvard.edu**
American Academy of Dermatology (provides skin cancer risk estimates): **http://www.aad.org/skinrisk.xhtml**
National Cancer Institute (explains factors in cancer development): **http://www.cancernet.nci.nih.gov**

National Cancer Institute's Breast Cancer Assessment Tool: **http:// cancertrials.nci.nih.gov/forms/CtRiskDisk.xhtml**
The New Zealand Breast Cancer Foundation: **http://www.nzbcf.org.nz**
Cancer Society of New Zealand: **http://www.cancernz.org.nz**
Anti-Cancer Foundation, South Australia: **http://www.cancersa.org. au/i-cms?page=1**
Australian Cancer Society: **http://www.cancer.org.au**
CancerHelp (UK): **http://www.cancerhelp.org.uk**

Centenarian Studies

New England Centenarian Study: **http://www.med.harvard.edu/ programs/necs**
Okinawa Centenarian Study: **http://www.okicent.org**
Heart/Arterial Disease
American Heart Association (information on prevention and control of heart disease): **http://www.americanheart.org**
National Heart, Lung, and Blood Institute (the latest information and research on blood pressure): **http://www.nhlbi.nih.gov**
Heart Foundation of Australia: **http://www.heartfoundation.com.au**
Heart Foundation of New Zealand: **http://www.nhf.org.nz**
British Heart Foundation: **http://www.bhf.org.uk**

Diabetes

American Diabetes Association: **http://www.diabetes.org**
CDC's Diabetes Public Health Resource: **http://www.cdc.gov/diabetes**
Diabetes Australia (Victoria): **http://www.dav.org.au/HomeMain.htm**
Diabetes UK: **http://www.diabetes.org.uk**

Menopause

North American Menopause Society: **http://www.menopause.org**
Australasian Menopause Society: **http://www.menopause.org.au**

Weight Control/Obesity

C. Everett Koop (former U.S. surgeon general's Web site on weight control): **http://www.shapeup.org**
Calorie Control Council (information on diet and fitness): **http://www. caloriecontrol.org**

Automatic Body Mass Index calculation: **http://www.bodymassindex. com**

American Obesity Association: **http://www.obesity.org**

Association for the Study of Obesity (UK): **http://www.aso.org.uk**

Osteoporosis/Arthritis

National Osteoporosis Foundation (new research reports and treatment information): **http://www.nof.org**

Arthritis Foundation (information on nutritional resources): **http:// www.arthritis.org**

Arthritis Society (additional suggestions for coping with arthritis): **http:// www.arthritis.ca/home.xhtml**

Arthritis Queensland (Aus): **http://www.arthritis.org.au**

National Osteoporosis Society (UK): **http://www.nos.org.uk**

Stroke

American Stroke Association: **http://www.strokeassociation.org**

National Stroke Foundation (Aus): **http://www.strokefoundation. com.au**

The Stroke Association (UK): **http://www.stroke.org.uk**

Dementia

Alzheimer's Association (information for patients and caregivers): **http:// www.alz.org**

Alzheimer's Association NSW (Aus): **http://www.alznsw.asn.au**

The Alzheimer's Society (UK): **http://www.alzheimers.org.uk**

Exercise/Physical Activity

Centers for Disease Control (Surgeon General's Report on Physical Activity): **http://www.cdc.gov**

Health Status assessment (calculate your individual calorie requirements): **http://www.healthstatus.com/calorieburn.htm**

National Institute on Aging (an excellent exercise video can be obtained from NIA for $7): **http://www.nih.gov/nia**

National Qigong Association: **http://www.nqa.org**

Change 4 Life (UK): **http://www.nhs.uk/change4life**

Food/Herbs

American Dietetic Association: **http://www.eatright.org**

USDA Food and Nutrition Information Center (includes food nutrients database): **http://www.nal.usda.gov/fnic**

Organic Consumers Association: **http://www.purefood.org**

Vegetarian Resource Group (information on vegetarian nutrition and recipes): **http://www.vrg.org**

Herb Research Foundation (information on herbs): **http://www.herbs.org**

American Botanical Council (information on herbs): **http://www. herbalgram.org**

Australia New Zealand Food Authority: **http://www.anzfa.gov.au**

British Nutrition Foundation: **http://www.nutrition.org.uk**

Others

Biofeedback Association Network: **http://www.biofeedback.net**

Brita water filtration: **http://www.brita.com**

Look for a Book: **http://www.lookforabook.com**

National Self-Help Clearinghouse: **http://www.selfhelpweb.org**

Acknowledgments

To write a book such as ours requires help and support from many different individuals and groups. Written over the span of a year by the three of us working on different continents, crossing oceans and changing academic institutions, we are indebted to many more people than we could possibly mention in a few short words.

Our inspirational team leader Stedman Mays of Clausen, Mays and Tahan Literary Agency was instrumental in finding the right publisher for our book and motivating us to see it through from beginning to end. His thoughtful guidance has been a blessing. Mary Tahan was also there for us whenever we needed it. Our writing was guided every step of the way by Leah Feldon, who helped turn our dry scientific style into intelligible and engaging literature. Her wonderful prose permeates the book. We would also have been lost without our editor, Annetta Hanna, who was a paragon of patience and gave the manuscript the attention it needed throughout the editorial process, as did the whole team at Clarkson Potter. We thank them for their commitment to this project and for believing in us. We also thank our research assistant and nutritional anthropologist Sayaka Mitsuhashi, who created and helped analyze many of the recipes, helped build our nutritional database, and assisted in countless other ways. Without her tireless efforts this book would not have seen the light of day.

There were many researchers who contributed essential information to this project and have helped build the Okinawa Centenarian Study database over the past twenty-five years, only a small part of which we were able to present in this book. These researchers form a part of the Okinawa collaborative network on successful aging and we are greatly indebted to their stellar work. In particular we would like to thank Dr. Hidemi Todoriki, Dr. Masafumi Akisaka, Dr. Ikuya Ashitomi, Dr. Seizo Sakihara, Dr. Hiroshi Ishizu, Dr. Koichi Naka, Dr. Kazuhiko Taira and Professor Liu Asato of the University of the Ryukyus, Faculty of Medicine and School of Health Sciences. We are indebted to our dieticians both in Okinawa and abroad. In particular, to dietician Kristine Kuhnert for her superb nutritional analysis and careful review of the manuscript. We also appreciate the valuable assistance of Drs. Hisashi Tauchi and Yuichiro Gotoh and members of the Tokyo Metropolitan Institute of Gerontology for their help over the years. We thank Dr. Satoshi Sasaki of the Japan National Cancer Center Research Institute for his helpful comments on the manuscript and many fruitful discussions.

Several experts read the manuscript in various stages and contributed valuable suggestions, including the integrative medicine experts Dr. Andrew Weil and Dr. Deepak Chopra. Gifted anthropologists Dr. Matthew Allen and Dr. Janice Turner also provided helpful reviews. Japan National Cancer Center epidemiologist Dr. Yoshihide Kinjo contributed helpful advice regarding statistical analyses and retired Yale University Professor Eitetsu Yamaguchi was an invaluable source of knowledge regarding Okinawan history. We also thank Professors Takashi Tsuha and Seishin Akamine for their deep knowledge and helpful advice regarding traditional Okinawan culture. We thank Rebecca Bell for her helpful review of the manuscript and her untiring commitment to the wellness movement.

Many researchers and academics from the University of Toronto, the alma mater of both Bradley and Craig Willcox, deserve our gratitude and thanks. These include Dr. David Jenkins and Dr. Thomas Wolever of the Department of Nutritional Sciences, Faculty of Medicine whose discovery of the glycemic index and whose groundbreaking research on the health benefits of dietary fiber form the basis of much modern scientific thinking on the dangers of glucose load. Dr. Jenkins also helped support the Willcox brothers to make our first research trip to Okinawa in the early 1990s and for that we will always be grateful. Dr. Cyril Kendall, Dr. Lillian Thompson, Dr. Venket Rao, and the rest of the Toronto nutrition group have been helpful over the years. Dr. Ken Fuchigami was instrumental in analyzing the early nutritional data. Dr. Miriam Rossi and Diana Alli of the Faculty of Medicine at the University of Toronto have been strong supporters. We are grateful to Dr. Shuichi Nagata and Dr. Richard Lee of the Department of Anthropology. Their vast knowledge of anthropology and insight into human behavior is a continuing source of inspiration for our work in medical anthropology. We also thank members of the University of Toronto's Institute for Human Development, Life Course and Aging, who continue to represent the leading edge of research in gerontology and where many long discussions on aging took place.

We thank the Mayo Clinic for permission to reprint several questionnaires and graphs and for assistance in the creation of the Tai Chi images. We appreciate the helpful guidance and strong support over the years of Dr. Donald Hensrud, Dr. Henry Schultz, Dr. Randall Edson, and Dr. Juan Bowen. Dr. Fernando Fervenza, Dr. Marcia Beshara, and Dr. Thomas Lin were constant sources of energy, inspiration and moral support during the long hours of clinical and research work. Many others in the Division of Internal Medicine have helped immensely over the years and we have nothing but the highest praise for the impressive research and clinical work that takes place at the Mayo Clinic. It is a first-class institution.

Our colleagues at Harvard University and Harvard Medical School also deserve our gratitude and praise for their help. Dr. Walter Willet of the Harvard School of Public Health continues to forge a new pathway in the still young field of nutritional epidemiology, Dr. Edward Giovannucci and Dr. Eric Rimm have been a source of inspiration and many helpful discussions. Our colleagues in the Division of Aging represent the cutting edge of research in gerontology and geriatric medicine. We are indebted to Dr. Thomas Perls and Dr. Margery Silver for their help in establishing an international collaboration between Harvard Medical School's New England Centenarian Study and the Okinawa Centenarian Study. We thank Dr. Jean Wei, Dr. Lewis Lipsitz, Dr. Marian Hannan, and many others for their help and support.

Our research has been supported by various foundations and organizations to whom we are very grateful. These include the Japan Ministry of Health and Welfare (Koseisho), the Japan Ministry of Education, Science, Technology and Culture (Monbusho), the Japan Foundation for Aging and Health, the Japan Foundation, the Tokyo Metropolitan Institute of Gerontology, University of Toronto, Mayo Clinic, Harvard University, the Medical Research Council of

Canada, and the Natural Sciences and Engineering Research Council of Canada, among others.

In particular we thank the centenarians, other elders, and their family members, and local government and village officials who participated in our study for so many years as well as the many members of our research team in the Department of Community Medicine at Ryukyu University Hospital and the Okinawa Gerontology Research Center. Without their assistance there would be no Okinawa Centenarian Study.

Most of all, we would like to thank and dedicate this book to our parents, spouses, and other family members for their understanding, patience, support, and helpful advice throughout the writing of this book—they made it all possible.

Notes

Chapter One

1 In standard Japanese, *inkyo* is the most common translation for "retirement". In the Ryukyuan dialect this word does not exist, nor was there a similar *inkyo* system as historically existed in mainland Japan. The Ryukyuan dialect, which was the language of the home until a generation ago in Okinawa, is incomprehensible to other Japanese. However, it does have a number of features in common with mainland Japanese dialects as well as a common origin. The written form is the same as standard Japanese, borrowed from Chinese characters many centuries ago. Ryukyuan dialect also had its regional variations with Shuri dialect, where the government of the Ryukyu Kingdom was located, being the standard for governmental affairs and commerce in Okinawa. After Okinawa reverted to Japanese control in 1972, the use of standard Japanese spread rapidly, and as a result, younger people, born after reversion, are rarely able to speak the local dialect.

2 Calling Okinawa "the real Shangri-la" does not mean that we consider Okinawa to be a paradise such as was portrayed in James Hilton's novel *Lost Horizon*. Obviously, all societies have their problems and Okinawa is no exception. We chose Shangri-la as a metaphor that stands as an evidence-based testament to the power of the Okinawan lifestyle in promoting successful aging and an overall superior state of wellness. Similarly, "everlasting health" is meant to signify a complete state of physical, psychological, social, and spiritual well-being over the life course.

3 The Okinawans are pushing back the frontiers of population life expectancy according to life expectancy data calculated from life tables by the Japanese Ministry of Health. Indeed, the noted gerontologist Dr. S. Olshansky wrote in the highly respected journal *Science* in 1990: "in order for life expectancy at birth to increase to the average (population) biological limit . . . age 85 . . . mortality rates from all

causes of death would need to decline . . . by 55 percent . . . it seems highly unlikely that life expectancy at birth will exceed the age of 85." See Olshansky, S., et al. 1990. In search of Methuselah: Estimating the upper limits to human life expectancy. *Science* 250:634–40. In what came as a shock to most gerontologists, Okinawan women broke that barrier in 1995, and although life-expectancy curves suggest that the pace of gains is slowing, Okinawan life expectancy is still climbing. What may potentially end this meteoric rise is not a biological barrier but the tragic loss of the old ways.

4 World Health Organization. 1996. *1995 World Health Statistics Annual.* Geneva.

5 Japan Ministry of Health and Welfare. 1996. Statistics and Information Division.

6 Ogawa, N. 1982. Japan's limits to growth and welfare. In Kuroda, T., ed., *Population Aging in Japan: Problems and Policy Issues in the 21st Century. International Symposium on an Aging Society: Strategies for 21st Century Japan.* Tokyo: Nihon University, Population Research Institute.

7 The mysterious Eastern Sea Islands held great interest for the early Chinese dynasties. According to the *Shan Hai Ching,* an ancient historical text, the first emperor, Ch'in Shih Huang Ti (221–210 B.C.), sent several missions into the Eastern Sea in the direction of the Ryukyu Islands to search for the secrets of immortality and for a formula that could turn base metals into gold. This journey and others are chronicled in historian George Kerr's book *Okinawa: The History of an Island People* (1958), the most comprehensive English-language historical text on Okinawa. Kerr cites historical documents reporting that these tales of islands of gold and silver that harbored secrets of immortality penetrated Europe from China, spurring a search for the Fountain of Youth, Rica de Oro, and Rica de Plata until the late seventeenth century. See Kerr, G. H. 2000. *Okinawa: History of an Island People.* Revised edition. North Clarendon, Vt.: Tuttle, 29–35. See also C. P. Fitzgerald's book *China: A Short Cultural History* (New York: Praeger, 1954), 226–29, for descriptions of Chinese attempts to find the secrets of immortality in the Eastern Sea Islands.

8. Hilton, J. 1933. *Lost Horizon.* New York: William Morrow and Company.

9. Bennett, G. B., et al. 1983. The centenarian question and old-age mortality in the Soviet Union, 1959–1970. *Demography* 20(4):587–606;

504

Medvedev, Z. A. 1986. Age structure of Soviet populations in the Caucasus: Facts and myths. In A. H. Bittles and K. J. Collins, eds., *The Biology of Human Ageing*. Cambridge, England: Cambridge University Press; Medvedev, Z. A. 1974. Caucasus and Altay longevity: A biological or social problem? *Gerontologist* 13:381–87; Leaf, A. 1982. Long-lived populations: Extreme old age. *J Am Geriatr Soc* 30:485–87.

10. Leaf, A. 1973. Every day is a gift when you are over 100. *National Geographic* 143:93–119; Leaf, A. 1975. *Youth in Old Age*. New York: McGraw-Hill Book Company.

11. Mazess, R. B., et al. 1979. Longevity and age exaggeration in Vilcabamba, Ecuador. *J Gerontol* 34(1):94–98.

12. *Koseki* is a nationwide system of household registry. According to this system, every Japanese household has its registry (*koseki*) which is kept at the government branch in the town, village, or city where the household maintains its permanent address. The *koseki* contains: 1) the permanent address; 2) the name, date of birth, sex, birth order, and names of parents of the household head and all family members. When a person dies, or ceases to be a member of the family (i.e., marries out or sets up independent household), his/her name is crossed out. The household head is required by law to report any household changes. Thus, the *koseki* is not a record of periodic census (which is prone to error) but is a much more accurate registry that is continuously updated. It is one of the oldest and most reliable sources of information on births, deaths and other population statistics in the world. It has been in operation in Okinawa since 1879 and mainland Japan since 1871.

13. Nohara, Y., H. Nozaki, and M. Suzuki. 1997. Independence and nursing care for Okinawan centenarians living at home and in institutions (in Japanese). *Ronen Shakai Kagaku* 18:107–12; Okinawa Centenarian Study database, 2000.

14. It is impossible to know the exact number of centenarians in the United States, since no central birth registration system existed until 1940. Furthermore, there are questions about the accuracy of the U.S. census data for centenarians, with an overestimation of actual centenarian numbers. This results partly from the absence of birth certificates and partly from the U.S. Census Bureau basing its assumptions about actual centenarian mortality rates on those of younger age groups. Actual centenarian mortality in the United States is about 50

percent per year. According to the World Health Organization (2000) and the Japan Ministry of Health and Welfare (2000), Okinawans have about seven more years of disability-free life expectancy than Americans. However, centenarians in the United States experience remarkable health throughout their lives owing to a favorable combination of a healthy lifestyle and genetics, showing that even in the United States good health is possible throughout the life cycle. See Hitt, R., Young-Xu, Y., Silver, M., Perls, T. 1999. Centenarians: The older you get the healthier you have been. *Lancet* 354:652.

15. We present a selection of these findings in Chapter Two. Since the Okinawa Centenarian Study is a cohort study (following a population forward through time) and not an interventional study (experimental versus control group), we cannot say with 100 percent certainty that our findings will apply to a particular individual. Of course, no one can guarantee something with 100 percent certainty in health matters. But based on the best available evidence from our twenty-five years of research, research of top scientists from the U.S. National Institute on Aging and many other prominent scientists, the evidence is highly supportive that the aging process can be slowed. It ranges from cell to human, from biochemical to epidemiological and interventional studies, and we can say with a high degree of confidence that if you follow the Okinawa Program you can significantly cut your risk for coronary heart disease, your risk for hormone dependent cancer and many other cancers, extend your healthy years, and look and feel younger. Interventional studies (the best evidence) in all animal species tested thus far clearly support the validity of our approach. For a review, see Lane, M. A., D.K. Ingram, and G. S. Roth. 1999. Nutritional modulation of aging in non-human primates. *J Nutr Health and Aging* 3:69–76.

16. The low-calorie/high-carbohydrate Okinawan diet has been cited as a less restrictive version and the closest human example of a diet that Dr. Roy Walford of UCLA refers to as the CRON diet (caloric restriction with optimal nutrition). See a review by his colleagues Weindruch, R., and R. Sohal, 1997. Caloric intake and aging. *N Engl J Med* 337:986–94. Dr. Walford is one of the world's foremost researchers on aging and has extensively studied the effects of diet on the aging process. In all animal species tested thus far, caloric restriction (without malnutrition) has been shown in studies of animals to extend

maximum life span by up to 50 percent, corresponding to humans living to 150–160 years old, with reductions in cancers of the breast (almost to zero) and other cancers, markedly reduced diseases of the heart and blood vessels (arterial diseases) and kidneys. Significant decreases in autoimmune diseases, reduced bone loss, and markedly reduced loss of brain function were observed for animals on such a diet. Other biomarkers (biological signs) of aging were remarkably reduced, including blood sugar and blood insulin levels, insulin resistance, and age-associated changes in skeletal muscle function. This diet has also been tested in primates and humans (in the Biosphere 2 experiment) who have undergone the early metabolic changes seen with other animal species, suggesting with a high degree of confidence that the diet will extend the health span and life span of humans. See Walford, R. 2000. *Beyond the 120-year Diet.* New York: Four Walls Eight Windows; and Weyer, C., R. L. Walford, J. T. Harper, et al. 2000. Energy metabolism after 2 years of energy restriction: the Biosphere 2 experiment. *Am J Clin Nutr* 72:946–53.

17. As we have begun publishing our research findings more widely in the English-language scientific literature, the reputation of Okinawa as an area of exceptional health and longevity has become better known in the scientific community. The popular press has now picked up on this, and there have been several diet/aging books published whose authors claim that the Okinawan diet provides evidence for the superiority of their own system. One of these claims is by Barry Sears, the author of the "Zone" series of books. His recent book, *The Soy Zone* (New York: HarperCollins, 2000), claims that the Okinawans eat a diet similar to the Zone Diet, i.e., a high-protein diet (40 percent carbohydrate, 30 percent protein, and 30 percent fat), and quotes two of our nutrition papers to support his claim. If you actually read the papers, you will see that is simply not correct. (See Chan, Y. C., M. Suzuki, and S. Yamamoto. 1997. Nutritional status of centenarians assessed by activity and anthropometric, hematological and biochemical characteristics. *J Nutr Sci Vitaminol* 43:73–81; and Akisaka, M., L. Asato, Y. C. Chan, et al. 1996. Energy and nutrient intakes of Okinawan centenarians. *J Nutr Sci Vitaminol* 42:241–48.) The elders, in fact, eat a 55/20/25 diet, i.e., 55–60% carbohydrate, 15–20% protein, and 25–30% fat. The current balance is about right, and further increases in protein and fat may lead to a further increase in Western

diseases such as coronary heart disease (fat), hormone-dependent cancer (fat), osteoporosis (animal protein), or kidney disease (protein). For a good scientific review of the Zone Diet, see Cheuvront, S. The Zone Diet and athletic performance. 1999. *Sports Medicine* 27(4):213–28. Also see response by Sears and rebuttal by Cheuvront in *Sports Medicine 2000.* 29(4):289–94.

18. Fries, J. F. 1980. Aging, natural death, and the compression of morbidity. *N Engl J Med* 303(3):130–35; Hayflick, L. 1998. How and why we age. *Exp Gerontol* 33(7–8):639–53; Hazzard, W. R. 1997. Ways to make "usual" and "successful" aging synonymous: preventive gerontology. In Successful Aging. *West J Med* 167(4):206–15; Kannisto, V. 1988. On the survival of centenarians and the span of life. *Population Studies* 42: 389–406; Marmot, M. G., and G. D. Smith. 1989. Why are the Japanese living longer? *BMJ* 299(6715):1547–51; Suzuki, M. 1987. The characteristics of centenarians' lifestyles (in Japanese). *Modern Physician* 7:1106–30; Takata, H., M. Suzuki, T. Ishii, et al. 1987. Influence of major histocompatibility complex region genes on human longevity among Okinawan-Japanese centenarians and nonagenarians. *Lancet* 2:824–26; Wetle, T. 1997. Living longer, aging better. Aging research comes of age. Editorial. *JAMA* 278(16):1376–77.

19. See Chapter 2 references 19–21.

Chapter Two

1. The Okinawan prefectural government, recognizing the symbolic importance of the "Shangri-la" bell, moved it to a special hall, the Bridge Between Nations Hall (Bankoku Shinryokan) at Busena, Nago City, for display during the G-8 World Economic Summit, which was held at this hall in July 2000. President Clinton and other world leaders were in attendance.

2. As reported in Kerr, G. 1958. *Okinawa: The History of an Island People.* Clarendon, Vt.: Charles E. Tuttle, 29–30, and Fitzgerald, C. P. 1954. *China: A Short Cultural History.* New York: Praeger, 226–29, one mission sent by the Chinese in the third century B.C. consisted of 3,000 young men and women, numerous artisans, and a cargo of seeds. With these gifts, Emperor Ch'in Shih Huang Ti hoped to win the favor of the "happy immortals" who dwelled on these "islands of

gold and silver." The mission was never heard from again. Historians speculate that they may have landed in the Ryukyu Islands. Chinese coins dating back to the third century B.C. have been unearthed near the city of Naha, providing the earliest tangible evidence that Okinawa might indeed be the "land of the immortals" that was sought after by the Chinese, although there is still much uncertainty regarding the exact location of the mysterious Eastern Sea Islands. By the sixth century A.D. the Chinese had first made "official" mention of the Ryukyu Islands by their current name. See Kerr, G. 1958.

3. Another translation of the term *horai-jima* has been offered in *The Okinawan Arts, vol. 5.* 1989. Naha, Japan: The Okinawan Arts Publishing Committee, where the term was translated as "Isle of Eternal Youth."

4. The heelbone densitometer was courtesy of Dr. J. Vogel of the University of California, Davis, one of the world's leading experts on osteoporosis. Dr. Vogel spent several months with our research group in 1994 investigating the impressive bone health of the Okinawan elders.

5. The Japanese first invaded Okinawa in 1609, when Satsuma, a Japanese warlord from Kagoshima (southwest Japan), could not resist the bountiful treasures of the small island kingdom. Heavy taxes had to be paid to maintain some modicum of independence until full annexation in 1879. Through this shrewd move, Satsuma gained access to the trading riches that the Ryukyu Kingdom had accrued through a tributary relationship with China and trading privileges with other southeast Asian city-states of the period. These included Chosen (Korea), Siam (Thailand), Parenban (Sumatra), Annam (Vietnam), Java (Indonesia), and others. Through this extensive trade network the small Kingdom of the Ryukyus developed as one of East Asia's great merchant city-states. See Kerr, G. 1958, note 2 above.

6. At the time of this writing, Nakajimasan was still alive and, we hope, keeping up his garden.

7. The first scientific publication about the Okinawa longevity phenomenon was Sabe, E., I. Ashitomi, M. Suzuki, et al. 1977. Social and medical survey of centenarians (in Japanese). *Okinawa Public Health J* 9:98–106.

8. For a selection of scientific publications in English from the Okinawa Centenarian Study, see Akisaka, M., M. Suzuki, and H. Inoko. 1997. Molecular genetic studies on DNA polymorphism of the HLA class

II genes associated with human longevity. *Tissue Antigens* 50:489–93; Chan, Y. C., M. Suzuki, and S. Yamamoto. 1997. Nutritional status of centenarians assessed by activity and anthropometric, hematological and biochemical characteristics. *J Nutr Sci Vitaminol* 43:73–81; Takata, H., M. Suzuki, T. Ishii, et al. 1987. Influence of major histocompatibility complex region genes on human longevity among Okinawan-Japanese centenarians and nonagenarians. *Lancet* 2:824–26; Willcox, B. J., M. Suzuki, D. C. Willcox, H. Todoriki, S. Sakihara, and D. D. Hensrud. 2000. Nutrition and human life expectancy. cultural models for successful aging (manuscript in preparation); Akisaka, M., L. Asato, Y. C. Chan, et al. 1996. Energy and nutrient intakes of Okinawan centenarians. *J Nutr Sci Vitaminol* 42:241–48; Naka, K., D. C. Willcox, H. Todoriki, and T. Kageyama. 1998. Suicide in Okinawa from an international perspective: A consideration of socio-cultural factors. *Ryukyu Med J* 18:1–10.

9. Hayflick, L. 1998. How and why we age. *Exp Gerontol* 33(7–8):639–53; Hazzard, W. R. 1997. Ways to make "usual" and "successful" aging synonymous: preventive gerontology. In Successful Aging. *West J Med* 167(4):206–15.

10. For an excellent review of the principles of nutritional epidemiology, see Willet, W. 1998. *Nutritional Epidemiology.* 2nd ed. Oxford, England: Oxford University Press.

11. According to Sackett, D., et al., and the Evidence-Based Medicine Working Groups at McMaster University in Canada and Oxford, England, evidence-based medicine's philosophical origins extend back to mid-nineteenth-century Paris, where Louis, Bichart, and Magendie called for external evidence in the medical treatment of patients. They define it as "the conscientious, explicit and judicious use of the current best evidence in making decisions about the care of individual patients. The practice of evidence-based medicine means integrating individual clinical expertise with the best available external clinical evidence from systematic research." For an excellent review of evidence-based medicine, see Sackett, D. L., W. M. C. Rosenberg, J. A. M. Gray, et al. 1996. Evidence based medicine: what it is and what it isn't. *BMJ* 312:71–72.

12. Blumenthal, M., W. R. Busse, A. Goldberg, et al. 1998. The complete German Commission E monographs: Therapeutic guide to herbal medicines. Austin, Texas: The American Botanical Council.

13. Fontanarosa, P. B., and G. D. Lundberg. 1998. Alternative medicine meets science. Editorial. *JAMA* 280(18):1618–19.

14. Eisenberg, D. M., R. B. Davis, S. L. Ettner, et al. 1998. Trends in alternative medicine use in the United States, 1990–1997. *JAMA* 280(18): 1569–75.

15. "Integrative medicine" is a term that was popularized in large part by Dr. Andrew Weil of the University of Arizona. It refers to the integration of complementary and alternative medical practices into mainstream Western medicine in an evidence-based manner. The goal is to create an approach to wellness that focuses on strengthening the body's own healing system through a healthy lifestyle while maintaining the effective traditional clinical practices of conventional medicine. For a thorough review of Weil's philosophy, see Weil, A. 1998. *Spontaneous Healing: How to Discover and Enhance Your Body's Ability to Maintain and Heal Itself.* New York: Alfred A. Knopf. Further explorations of this concept can be found in Pelletier, K. R. 2000. *The Best Alternative Medicine.* New York: Simon and Schuster.

16. For an excellent review of the arterial health of the Okinawans, see Bonita, R. 1993. Cardiovascular disease in Okinawa. *Lancet* 341:1185. Studies of pulse wave velocity (a measure of the functional health of the aorta, the body's main artery) have shown that Okinawan centenarians have arteries that are equivalent to those of subjects who are twenty to thirty years younger. See Akisaka, M., M. Mukai, M. Suzuki, et al. 1993. The relationship between aortic pulse wave velocity and atherogenic index in centenarians (in Japanese). *Nippon Ronen Igakkai Zasshi* 30:467–73. Arteries with minimal plaque burden are a common finding in autopsy studies of Japanese centenarians (and other centenarian populations), and one of the main reasons for their exceptional longevity. This is explored in more detail in a collection of scientific papers from our group and collaborators at the Tokyo Metropolitan Institute on Gerontology on centenarians in Japan. Tauchi, H., T. Sato, T. Watanabe, eds. 1999. *Japanese Centenarians— Medical Research for the Final Stages of Human Aging.* Aichi, Japan: Aichi Medical University Press.

17. National Center for Health Statistics and the American Heart Association. *Heart and Stroke Statistical Update 1999.*

18. Kinjo, K., Y. Kimura, M. Tomori, et al. 1992. An epidemiological analysis of cardiovascular diseases in Okinawa, Japan. *Hyperten Res*

15(2):111–19; Suzuki, M. 1986. Experience in remote islands—progress in circulatory disease management for the elderly (in Japanese). *Nichijunkankyou Zasshi* 29:333–40; Suzuki, M., T. Asato, and H. Moriku. 1988. Valvular disease of the Okinawan elderly (in Japanese). *Circulatory Medicine* 23:231–39.

19. Curb, J. D., and K. Kodama. 1996. The Ni-Hon-San Study. *J Epidemiol* 6(4 suppl.):S197–201.

20. Yano, K., D. M. Reed, and C. J. MacLean. 1989. Serum cholesterol and hemorrhagic stroke in the Honolulu Heart Program. *Stroke* 20: 1460–65.

21. Mizushima, S., E. Moriguchi, Y. Nakada, et al. 1992. The relationship of dietary factors to cardiovascular diseases among Japanese in Okinawa and Japanese immigrants, originally from Okinawa, in Brazil. *Hyperten Res* 15:45–55.

22. Estimates vary widely (from a high of 17 years to a low of 3 years) and depend on the statistical assumptions about life expectancy, your particular risk factors, and your gender. See Hayflick, L. 1994. *How and Why We Age.* New York: Ballantine Books, p. 99 and Olshansky, S., et al., from Ch. 1 note 3.

23. Boushey, C. J., S. A. A. Beresford, and G. S. Omenn. 1995. A quantitative assessment of plasma homocysteine as a risk factor for vascular disease: Probable benefits of increasing folic acid intakes. *JAMA* 274:1049–57.

24. Refsum, H., P. M. Ueland, O. Nygaard, et al. 1998. Homocysteine and cardiovascular disease. *Annu Rev Med* 49:31–62.

25. Alfthan, G., A. Aro, and K. F. Gey. 1997. Plasma homocysteine and cardiovascular disease mortality. *Lancet* 349:397.

26. Willcox, B. J., M. Suzuki, D. C. Willcox, H. Todoriki, and D. D. Hensrud. Homocysteine levels in Okinawan-Japanese. *J Investigative Med 2000* 48(2):205A.

27. Tonaki, M., N. Fukumine, M. Suzuki, et al. 1977. The elderly in their homes and the elderly in nursing homes: Examination of the circulatory system (in Japanese). *Okinawa Public Health J* 9:83–89; Tonaki, M., N. Fukumine, M. Suzuki, et al. 1977. The elderly in their homes and the elderly in nursing homes: The relationship between blood pressure, serum lipids and blood sugar (in Japanese). *Okinawa Public Health J* 9:90–97; Akisaka, M., M. Mukai, M. Suzuki, et al. 1993. The relationship between aortic pulse wave velocity and atherogenic index in centenarians (in Japanese). *Nippon Ronen Igakkai Zasshi* 30:467–73.

28. Japan Ministry of Health and Welfare. 1995. Center for Health Statistics. Tokyo, Japan.

29. Gordon, T., and W. B. Kannel. 1971. Premature mortality from coronary heart disease. The Framingham Study. *JAMA* 215:1617–25; Castelli, W. P. 1988. Cholesterol and lipids in the risk of coronary heart disease—The Framingham Heart Study. *Can J Cardiol* 4 (suppl. A):5A–10A.

30. National Cholesterol Education Program. 1993. Second report of the expert panel on detection, evaluation, and treatment of high blood cholesterol in adults (adult treatment panel II). National Heart, Lung, and Blood Institute. Publication NIH 93-3095.

31a. van den Hoogen, P. C. W., E. J. M. Feskens, N. J. D. Naglekerke, et al. 2000. The relation between blood pressure and mortality due to coronary heart disease among men in different parts of the world. *N Engl J Med* 342:1–8.

31b. Based on the Sixth Report of the Joint National Committee of Prevention, Detection, Evaluation, and Treatment of High Blood Pressure. National Institutes of Health. Publication No. 98-4080. Nov. 1997.

32. There has also been some concern that low cholesterol levels might increase the risk for cancer or other causes of death, as more cancer deaths were reported among low cholesterol groups in some early studies of coronary heart disease. Several large interventional studies have since negated these fears as lower all-cause mortality has been found in groups with the lowest cholesterol levels. In fact, the longest-lived of the 300,000 plus people in the MRFIT study had very low cholesterol (in the 120–130 range). Martin, M. J., et al. (1986). Serum cholesterol, blood pressure and mortality: implications from a cohort study of 361,662 men. *Lancet* 2:933–36. For a good discussion of this point, also see Miller, M., and R. Vogel. 1996. *The Practice of Coronary Disease Prevention.* Baltimore: Williams & Wilkins, page 42.

33. A recent review of the evidence, including a statistical model of risk-reduction strategies similar to those employed by the Okinawans, strongly suggests that if you follow the recommendations we have made here, you can lower your risk for heart attack by up to 80 percent. See Stampfer, M. J., F. B. Hu, J. E. Manson, et al. 2000. Primary prevention of coronary heart disease in women through diet and lifestyle. *N Engl J Med* 343(1):16–22.

34. To be considered "possible," the majority of observational and case-control studies must support the factor; to be considered "good," observational, case-control, and at least one prospective or interventional study must support the factor; to be considered "excellent," more than one prospective or interventional study and multiple other studies must be supportive. For further review of particular lifestyle factors and arterial health, see Stampfer et al. 2000, note 33 above, and Anderson, J. W. 1995. Meta-analysis of the effects of soy protein intake on serum lipids. *N Engl J Med* 333(5):276–82; Appel, L. J., T. J. Moore, E. Obarzanek, et al. 1997. A clinical trial of the effects of dietary patterns on blood pressure. *N Engl J Med* 336:1117–24; Boushey, C. J., S. A. Beresford, G. S. Omenn, et al. 1995. A quantitative assessment of plasma homocysteine as a risk factor for vascular disease. *JAMA* 274(13):1049–57; Carr, J. J., and G. L. Burke. 2000. Subclinical cardiovascular disease and atherosclerosis are not inevitable consequences of aging. *J Am Geriatr Soc* 48:342–43; Eastern Stroke and Coronary Heart Disease Collaborative Research Group. 1998. Blood pressure, cholesterol, and stroke in eastern Asia. *Lancet* 352:1801–7; Everson, S. A., J. W. Lynch, M. A. Chesney, et al. 1997. Interaction of workplace demands and cardiovascular reactivity in progression of carotid atherosclerosis: Population based study. *BMJ* 314:553–58; Hertog, M.G.L., D. Kromhout, C. Aravanis, et al. 1995. Flavonoid intake and long-term risk of coronary heart disease and cancer in the Seven Countries Study. *Arch Intern Med* 155:381–86; Jha, P., M. Flather, E. Lonn, et al. 1995. The antioxidant vitamins and cardiovascular disease. A critical review of epidemiologic and clinical trial data. *Ann Intern Med* 123(11):860–72; Kagawa, Y., M. Nishizawa, M. Suzuki, et al. 1982. Eicosapolyenoic acids of serum lipids of Japanese Islanders with low incidence of cardiovascular diseases. *J Nutr Sci Vitaminol* 28:441–53; Lichtenstein, A. 1993. Trans fatty acids, blood lipids, and cardiovascular risk: Where do we stand? *Nutr Rev* 51(11):340–43; Morrison, C., M. Woodward, W. Leslie, et al. 1997. Effect of socioeconomic group on incidence of, management of, and survival after myocardial infarction and coronary death: Analysis of community coronary event register. *BMJ* 314:541–46; Ornish, D., S. E. Brown, L. W. Scherwitz, et al. 1990. Can lifestyle changes reverse coronary heart disease? *Lancet* 336:129–33.

35. Anderson, M. W., S. H. Reynolds, M. You, et al. 1992. Role of proto-oncogene activation in carcinogenesis. *Environmental Health Perspective* 98:13–24.

36. Breslow, N., C. W. Chan, G. Dhom, et al. 1977. Latent carcinoma of prostate at autopsy in seven areas. *Int J Cancer* 20:680–88.

37. World Health Organization 1996; Japan Ministry of Health and Welfare 1996; Rose, D. P., A. P. Boyar, and E. L. Wynder. 1986. International comparisons of mortality rates for cancer of the breast, ovary, prostate, and colon, and per capita food consumption. *Cancer* 58: 2363–71 (ovarian cancer data).

38. Weindruch, R., and R. Sohal. 1997. Caloric intake and aging. *N Engl J Med* 337(14):986–94.

39. Baranowski, T., and G. Stables. 2000. Process evaluations of the 5-a-day projects. *Health Educ Behav* 27(2):157–66.

40a. Canola oil and olive oil are compared in note 4, Chapter 3.

40b. For a good review, see la Vecchia, C., E. Negri, S. Franceschi, et al. 1995. Olive oil, other dietary fats, and the risk of breast cancer (Italy). *Cancer Causes Control* 6(6):545–50; Martin-Moreno, J. M., W. C. Willett, L. Gorgojo, et al. 1994. Dietary fat, olive oil intake and breast cancer risk. *Int J Cancer* 58:774–80.

41. Cave, W. T., Jr. 1996. Dietary omega-3 polyunsaturated fats and breast cancer. *Nutr* 12(1):S39–42; Cave, W. T., Jr. 1997. Omega 3 polyunsaturated fatty acids in rodent models of breast cancer. *Breast Cancer Research and Treatment* 46(2–3):239–46; Caygill, C. P., and M. J. Hill. 1995. Fish, n-3 fatty acids and human colorectal and breast cancer mortality. *Eur J Cancer Prev* 4(4):329–32. The Okinawan data are unpublished data from our database.

42. Hankinson, S. E., W. C. Willett, G. A. Colditz, et al. 1998. Circulating concentrations of insulin-like growth factor-I and risk of breast cancer. *Lancet* 351:1393–96; Kaaks, R. 1996. Nutrition, hormones and breast cancer: Is insulin the missing link? *Cancer Causes Control* 6:605–25; Kazer, R. R. 1995. Insulin resistance, insulin-like growth factor I and breast cancer: A hypothesis. *Internatl J Cancer* 62(4):403–6; Chan, J., M. Stampfer, E. Giovannucci. 1998. Plasma insulin-like growth factor I and prostate cancer risk: A prospective study. *Science* 279(5350):563–66; Giovannucci, E. 1995. Insulin and colon cancer. *Cancer Causes Control* 6(2): 164–79.

43. For an excellent review of this topic, see Bruce, W., T. Wolever, and A. Giacca. 2000. Mechanisms linking diet and colorectal cancer: The possible role of insulin resistance. *Nutr Cancer* 37(1): 19–26.

44. Adlercreutz, H., H. Markkanen, and S. Watanabe. 1993. Plasma concentrations of phytoestrogens in Japanese men. *Lancet* 342(8881): 1209–10; Okinawa Centenarian Study Database (unpublished data).

45. Dr. Hidemi Todoriki, personal communication. Japan Public Health Center database.

46. Ingram, D., K. Sanders, M. Kolybaba, et al. 1997. Case-control study of phyto-oestrogens and breast cancer. *Lancet* 350(9083):990–94.

47. World Cancer Research Fund. 1997. *Food, Nutrition and the Prevention of Cancer: A Global Perspective*. Washington, D.C.: American Institute for Cancer Research.

48. Stoll, B. 2000. Adiposity as a risk determinant for postmenopausal breast cancer. *Int J Obes Relat Metab Disord* 24(5):527–33; Huang, Z., W. Willett, G. A. Colditz, et al. 1999. Waist circumference, waist:hip ratio and risk of breast cancer in the Nurse's Health Study. *Am J Epidemiol* 150(12):1316–24.

49. Stoll, B. A. 1998. Western diet, early puberty, and breast cancer risk. *Breast Cancer Research and Treatment* 49(3):187–93.

50. For selected references, see Chlebowski, R. 2000. Reducing the risk of breast cancer. *N Engl J Med* 343(3):191–98; Bartsch, H., J. Nair, R. W. Owen. 1999. Dietary polyunsaturated fatty acids and cancers of the breast and colorectum: Emerging evidence for their role as risk modifiers. *Carcinogenesis* 20(12):2209–18; Wolff, M. S. 1996. Breast cancer and environmental risk factors. *Ann Rev Pharmacol and Toxicol* 36:573–96; Thune, I., T. Brenn, E. Lund, et al. 1997. Physical activity and the risk of breast cancer. *N Engl J Med* 336(18):1269–75; Stoll, B. A. 1992. Breast cancer risk in Japanese women with special reference to the growth hormone–insulin-like growth factor axis. *Jpn J Clin Oncol* 22(1):1–5; Merzenich, H., H. Boeing, and J. Wahrendorf. 1993. Dietary fat and sports activity as determinants for age at menarche. *Am J Epidemiol* 138:217–24; Martin-Moreno, J. M., W. C. Willett, L. Gorgojo, et al. 1994. Dietary fat, olive oil intake and breast cancer risk. *Int J Cancer* 58: 774–80; McTiernan, A. 1997. Exercise and breast cancer—time to get moving? Editorial. *N Engl J Med* 336:1311–12; Lawson, J. S., A. S. Field, S. Champion, et al. 1999. Low oestrogen receptor alpha expression in normal breast tissue underlies low breast cancer

incidence in Japan. *Lancet* 354(9192):1787–88; la Vecchia, C., E. Negri, S. Franceschi, et al. 1995. Olive oil, other dietary fats, and the risk of breast cancer (Italy). *Cancer Causes Control* 6(6):545–50; Krainer, M., S. Silva-Arrieta, M. G. FitzGerald, et al. 1997. Differential contributions of BRCA1 and BRCA2 to early-onset breast cancer. *N Engl J Med* 336:1416–21; Kaaks, R. 1996. Nutrition, hormones and breast cancer: Is insulin the missing link? *Cancer Causes Control* 6:605–25; Ingram, D., K. Sanders, M. Kolybaba, et al. 1997. Case-control study of phyto-oestrogens and breast cancer. *Lancet* 350(9083):990–94; Hankinson, S. E., W. C. Willett, G. A. Colditz, et al. 1998. Circulating concentrations of insulin-like growth factor-I and risk of breast cancer. *Lancet* 351:1393–96; Goldin, B. R., H. Adlercreutz, S. L. Gorbach, et al. 1986. The relationships between estrogen levels and diets of Caucasian, American and Oriental immigrant women. *Am J Clin Nutr* 44:945–53; Cave, W. T., Jr. 1996. Dietary omega-3 polyunsaturated fats and breast cancer. *Nutrition* 12(1):S39–42; Canadian Diet and Breast Cancer Prevention Study Group. (1997). Effects at two years of a low-fat, high-carbohydrate diet on radiologic features of the breast: Results from a randomized trial. *J Natl Cancer Inst* 8:488–96.

51. Suzuki, M. Personal communication.

52. Chan, J., M. Stampfer, and E. Giovannucci. 1998. Plasma insulin-like growth factor I and prostate cancer risk: a prospective study. *Science* 279(5350):563–66.

53. For an excellent review of lycopene's health effects, including the Harvard Study, see Rao, A. V., and S. Agarwal. 2000. Role of antioxidant lycopene in cancer and heart disease. *J Am Coll Nutr* 19(5): 563–69.

54. For selected studies, see M. M. Braun, K. J. Helzlsouer, B. W. Hollis, et al. 1995. Prostate cancer and prediagnostic levels of serum vitamin D metabolites. *Cancer Causes Control* 6:235–39; Fair, W. R., N. E. Fleshner, and W. Heston. 1997. Cancer of the prostate: A nutritional disease? *Urology* 50:840–48; Gann, P. H., C. H. Hennekens, F. M. Sacks, et al. 1994. Prospective study of plasma fatty acids and risk of prostate cancer. *J Nat Cancer Inst* 86:281–86; Giles, G., and P. Ireland. 1997. Diet, nutrition and prostate cancer. *International J Epidemiol* 10(suppl.):13–17; Giovannucci, E., E. B. Rimm, G. A. Colditz, et al. 1993. A prospective study of dietary fat and risk of prostate cancer. *J Nat Cancer Inst* 85:1571–79; Giovannucci, E., A. Ascherio, E. B. Rimm,

et al. 1995. Intake of carotenoids and retinol in relation to risk of prostate cancer. *J Nat Cancer Inst* 87:1767–76; Gronberg, H., L. Damber, and J. E. Damber. 1996. Total food consumption and body mass index in relation to prostate cancer risk: A case-control study in Sweden with prospectively collected exposure data. *J Urol* 155:969–74; Hirayama, T. 1979. Epidemiology of prostate cancer with special reference to the role of diet. *National Cancer Institute Monograph* 53:149–55; Hsing, A. W., and G. W. Comstock. 1993. Serological precursors of cancer: Serum hormones and risk of subsequent prostate cancer. *Cancer Epidemiol Biomarkers Prev* 2:27–32; Liang, T., and S. Liao. 1992. Inhibition of steroid 5-alpha-reductase by specific aliphatic unsaturated fatty acids. *Biochem J* 285:557–62; Moyad, M. A. 1999. Soy, disease prevention and prostate cancer. *Seminars in Urologic Oncology* 17(2): 97–102; Nomura, A. M., G. N. Stemmermann, J. Lee, et al. 1997. Serum micronutrients and prostate cancer in Japanese Americans in Hawaii. *Cancer Epidemiol Biomarkers* 6:487–91; Oesterling, J. E., Y. Kumamoto, T. Tsukamoto, et al. 1995. Serum prostate-specific antigen in a community-based population of healthy Japanese men: Lower values than for similarly aged white men. *British J Urol* 75:347–53; Willcox, B. J., D. J. A. Jenkins, K. Fuchigami, D. C. Willcox, M. Suzuki, H. Todoriki, et al. 1996. Serum fatty acid profiles and PSA in Japanese and Canadian men. *FASEB J* 10(3):A550.

55. For a review, see Archer, S. Y., and R. A. Hodin. 1999. Histone acetylation and cancer. *Curr Opin Genet Dev* 9:171–74.

56. For selected references, see Proportion of colon cancer risk that might be preventable in a cohort of middle-aged US men. 2000. *Cancer Causes Control* 11(7):579–88; Janne, P. A., and R. J. Mayer. 2000. Chemoprevention of colorectal cancer. *N Engl J Med* 342(26):1960–68. Review; Bartsch, H., J. Nair, and R. W. Owen. 1999. Dietary polyunsaturated fatty acids and cancers of the breast and colorectum: Emerging evidence for their role as risk modifiers. *Carcinogenesis* 20(12):2209–18; Giovannucci, E. 1995. Insulin and colon cancer. *Cancer Causes Control* 6(2):164–79; Giovannucci, E., and W. C. Willet. 1994. Dietary factors and risk of colon cancer. *Ann Med* 26:443–52; McKeown-Eyssen, G. E., E. Bright-See, W. R. Bruce, et al. 1994. A randomized trial of a low fat high fibre diet in the recurrence of colorectal polyps. *J Clin Epidemiol* 47:525–36; Goldbohm, R. A., P. A. van den Brandt, P. van't Veer, et al. 1994. A prospective cohort study on

the relation between meat consumption and the risk of colon cancer. *Cancer Research* 54:718–23; Platz, E. A., E. Giovannucci, E. B. Rimm, et al. 1997. Dietary fiber and distal colorectal adenoma in men. *Cancer Epidemiol Biomarkers Prev* 6:661–70.

57. For selected references, see Cannistra, S. A. 1993. Cancer of the ovary. *N Engl J Med* 329:1550–58; Engle, A., J. E. Muscat, and R. E. Harris. 1991. Nutritional risk factors and ovarian cancer. *Nutr Cancer* 15:239–47; Markman, M., ed. 2000. The genetics, screening, and treatment of epithelial ovarian cancer: An update. *Cleveland Clinic J Med* 67(4):294–98; Mori, M., and M. Hirotsugu. 1988. Dietary and other risk factors of ovarian cancer among elderly women. *Jpn J Cancer Res* 79:997–1004.

58. Most of us don't give stomach cancer a second thought because we don't hear much about it—now anyway. It used to be the leading cause of cancer death in the United States. Ask your grandmother how many of her uncles and aunts died from stomach cancer. You might be surprised at the number. There are two important factors that explain why the Japanese suffer from stomach cancer and North Americans and Okinawans don't—salt and refrigeration. At the beginning of the twentieth century, most people preserved food with salt. We salted and cured pork, fish, and vegetables—in the form of pickles—and stored them underground on ice. Later we developed preservatives using nitrates—adding one potential problem to another. Heavily salted foods lead to the breakdown of the mucosal layer of the stomach, which enhances conditions that lead to cancer. Try rubbing salt into a wound and see how it feels. The same thing happens in your stomach. With the advent of refrigeration, we no longer needed salt for preservation. As our salt intake diminished, so did our rates of stomach cancer. More-sanitary refrigerated food storage also diminished many bacteria from our food supply such as *H. pylori*, one of the leading causes of stomach cancer. The Okinawans never developed as strong a taste for salt as the mainland Japanese. Nor did they need to store and preserve food over the winter because fresh food is available year-round.

THE MOST MODIFIABLE PROTECTIVE AND RISK FACTORS FOR STOMACH CANCER

EVIDENCE	PROTECTIVE FACTORS	RISK FACTORS
Excellent	Vegetables and fruits	*Helicobacter pylori*
	Refrigeration	
Good	Vitamin C	Salt
		Salted foods
Possible	Carotenoids	Grilled and barbecued meats
	Garlic, onions, and other allium foods	Cured meats
	Fiber	Nitrosamines
	Selenium	

For selected references, see Coggon, D., D. J. P. Barker, R. B. Cole, et al. 1989. Stomach cancer and food storage. *J Nat Cancer Inst* 81:1178–82; Forman, D. 1991. Helicobacter pylori infection: A novel risk factor in the etiology of gastric cancer. *J Nat Cancer Inst* 83:1702–3; Honjo, S., S. Kono, and M. Yamaguchi. 1994. Salt and geographic variation in stomach cancer mortality in Japan. *Cancer Causes Control* 5:285–86; Howson, C. P., T. Hirayama, and E. L. Wynder. 1986. The decline in gastric cancer: Epidemiology of an unplanned triumph. *Epidemiol Rev* 8:1–27; la Vecchia, C., E. Negri, B. D'Avanzo, et al. 1990. Electric refrigerator use and gastric cancer risk. *British J Cancer* 62:136–37.

Lung Cancer

Lung cancer is the leading cause of cancer death in North America, and is largely a result of cigarette smoking. In fact, cigarettes are responsible for over 80 percent of all lung-cancer deaths. Okinawans don't suffer from lung cancer as much as North Americans do, because smoking didn't catch on there until after the Second World War. Now that more than half of Okinawan men smoke, lung cancer rates are rising—although at a slower pace than might be expected. This may in part be due to the high levels of protective factors found in vegetables and legumes that Okinawans eat in abundance. A recent study at Kyushu University in Japan found that the more one drank green tea (flavonoids), the lower became one's chance of developing lung cancer—more evidence for the protective role diet may play in lung cancer. The most important thing you can do, however, is simply not smoke.

THE MOST MODIFIABLE PROTECTIVE AND RISK FACTORS FOR LUNG CANCER

EVIDENCE	PROTECTIVE FACTORS	RISK FACTORS
Excellent	Vegetables and fruits	Smoking
		Asbestos
		Radon
Possible	Exercise	Total Fat
	Vitamins C, E	Saturated/animal fat
	Selenium	Cholesterol
	Flavonoids	Alcohol

For selected references, see The Alpha-Tocopherol, Beta-Carotene Cancer Prevention Study Group. 1994. The effect of Vitamin E and beta-carotene on the incidence of lung cancer and other cancer in male smokers. *N Engl J Med* 330:1029; Chung, F-L., M. A. Morse, K. I. Eklind, et al. 1993. Inhibition of the tobacco-specific nitrosamine-induced lung tumorigenesis by compounds derived from cruciferous vegetables and green tea. *Ann New York Academy Science* 686:186–201; Wakai, K., Y. Ohno, K. Genka, et al. 1997. Smoking habits, local brand cigarettes and lung cancer risk in Okinawa, Japan. *J Epidemiol* 7: 99–105.

59. Ross, P. D., H. Norimatsu, J. W. Davis, et al. 1991. A comparison of hip fracture incidence among native Japanese, Japanese Americans, and American Caucasians. *Am J Epidemiol* 133:801–9. Part of the difference may lie in a lower frequency of falls in Japanese, which would result in fewer fractures. Some researchers claim a smaller hip angle also reduces the risk, and Japanese have small hip angles. But this does not explain the lower frequency of fractures in Okinawans versus mainland Japanese, since their hip angles are similar.

60. We compared bone mineral density in a group of Okinawans to two groups from mainland Japan and found that similar bone density existed at younger age groups. But by age forty for women and age fifty for men the groups began to diverge. The Japanese began to lose significantly more calcium from their bones than the Okinawans,

suggesting the Okinawans preserve their bone density at healthy levels for longer periods of time than other Japanese. Suzuki, M., I. Ashitomi, M. Akisaka, et al. 1997. Bone density of banks' and flight companies' healthy workers in Okinawa (in Japanese). *Minzoku Eisei* 63(3):166–72.

61. Goldman, E. 1999. Soy estrogens useful but no substitute for HRT. *Intern Med News* 32(21):21 (1 November).

62. Rice, M. 1999. Soy consumption and bone mineral density in older-Japanese-American women in King County, Washington. The Nikkei Bone Density Study. University of Washington. Ph.D. dissertation.

63. In September 2000 researchers at Iowa State University reported the results of their placebo-controlled, double-blind, interventional study. After twenty-four weeks of eating muffins with soy protein isolate (flavonoids 80.4 mg/day), twenty-four perimenopausal women increased their bone mineral density by 6 percent and bone mineral content by 10.3 percent, versus twenty-four women who ate similar soy muffins devoid of flavonoids. Most Okinawans eat at least this level of flavonoids in their usual diets. Alekel, D. L., A. St. Germain, C. T. Peterson, et al. 2000. Isoflavone-rich soy protein isolate attenuates bone loss in the lumbar spine of perimenopausal women. *Am J Clin Nutr* 72:844–52.

64. For selected references, see Abelow, B. J., T. R. Holford, and K. L. Insogna. 1992. Cross-cultural association between dietary animal protein and hip fracture: A hypothesis. *Calcif Tissue Int* 50:14–18; Akisaka, M., and M. Suzuki. 1995. The bone density and activity of daily living in Okinawan centenarians. *Hong Kong J Gerontology: Total Care of the Elderly—A Multidisciplinary Approach.* Hong Kong: Fifth Asia/Oceania Regional Congress of Gerontology; Akisaka, M., L. Asato, M. Suzuki, et al. 1996. Relationship between bone density and nutrient intakes of Okinawan centenarians (in Japanese). *Osteoporosis Jpn* 4(3):503–9; Akisaka, M., and M. Suzuki. 1997. The relationship between bone density and ADLs in the oldest-old (in Japanese). *Medicine and Biology* 135:137–39; Cummings, S. R., J. A. Cauley, L. Palermo, et al. 1994. Racial differences in hip axis lengths might explain racial differences in rates of hip fracture. Study of Osteoporotic Fractures Research Group. *Osteoporosis International* 4:226–29; Dawson-Hughes, B., S. S. Harris, E. A. Krall, et al. 1997. Effect of calcium and vitamin D supplementation on bone density in men and women sixty-five

years of age or older. *N Engl J Med* 337(10):670–76; Erdman, J. W., Jr., R. J. Stillman, and R. A. Boileau. 2000. Provocative relation between soy and bone maintenance. Editorial, *Am J Clin Nutr* 72:679–80; Feskanich, D., W. C. Willet, M. J. Stampfer, et al. 1996. Protein consumption and bone fractures in women. *Am J Epidemiol* 143:472–79; Feskanich, D., W. C. Willet, M. J. Stampfer, et al. 1997. Milk, dietary calcium, and bone fractures in women: a twelve-year prospective study. *Am J Public Health* 87:992–97; Khosla, S., L. J. Melton, III, E. J. Atkinson, et al. 1998. Relationship of serum sex steroid levels and bone turnover markers with bone mineral density in men and women: A key role for bioavailable estrogen. *J Clin Endocrinol Metabolism* 83: 2266–74; Lipsitz, L. A., I. Nakajima, M. Gagnon, et al. 1994. Muscle strength and fall rates among residents of Japanese and American nursing homes: An international cross-cultural study. *J Am Geriatr Soc* 42:953–59; Marcus, R. 1996. Endogenous and nutritional factors affecting bone. *Bone* 18(suppl.):11S–13S; New, S. A., S. P. Robins, M. K. Campbell, et al. 2000. Dietary influences on bone mass and bone metabolism: Further evidence of a positive link between fruit and vegetable consumption and bone health? *Am J Clin Nutr* 71:142–51; Prince, R. L. 1997. Diet and the prevention of osteoporotic fractures. *N Engl J Med* 337(10):701–702.

65. Reynolds, B. A., and S. Weiss. 1993. Central nervous system growth and differentiation factors: Clinical horizons—truth or dare? *Curr Opin Biotechnol* 4(4):734–38.

66. Ogura, C., H. Nakamoto, T. Uema, et al. 1995. Prevalence of senile dementia in Okinawa. *International J Epidemiol* 24:373–80.

67. Jorm, A. F., A. E. Korten, and A. S. Henderson. 1987. The prevalence of dementia: A quantitative integration of the literature. *Acta Psychiatr Scand* 76:465–79; Ogura, C., H. Nakamoto, T. Uema, et al. 1995. Prevalence of senile dementia in Okinawa. *International J Epidemiol* 24:373–80.

68. Graves, A. B., L. Rajaram, J. D. Bowen, et al. 1999. Cognitive decline and Japanese culture in a cohort of older Japanese Americans in King County, WA: The Kame Project. *J Gerontol B Psychol Sci*; White, L., H. Petrovitch, G. W. Ross, et al. 1996. Prevalence of dementia in older Japanese-American men in Hawaii. *JAMA* 276:955–60. More comparative studies are needed to confirm whether these differences are due to genetic and/or environmental factors or to methodological differences.

69. Sano, M., C. Ernesto, R. G. Thomas, et al. 1997. A controlled trial of selegilline, alpha-tocopherol, or both as treatment for Alzheimer's disease: The Alzheimer's Disease Cooperative Study. *N Engl J Med* 17(336):1216–22; Okinawa Centenarian Study database as reported in Suzuki, M., M. Akisaka, and S. Inayama. 1993. Medicobiological studies on centenarians in Okinawa, measuring plasma lipid peroxide, proline, and plasma and intracellular tocopherol. In Beregi, E., I. A. Gergely, and K. Rajczi, eds., *Recent Advances in Aging Science.* Bologna: Monduzzi; and NHANES III database as reported in Ford, E., and A. Sowel. 1999. Serum alpha-tocopherol status database in the United States population: Findings from the Third National Health and Nutrition Examination Survey. *Am J Epidemiol* 150(3):290–300.

70. The graph is based on an average of three studies on the prevalence of dementia in various community populations within the United States and the first study of Japanese dementia rates carried out with a protocol similar enough to that of a U.S. study to allow meaningful comparisons. The Okinawa study was the only published study on the prevalence of senile dementia in Okinawa prefecture. See Kokmen, E., C. Beard, P. O'Brien, et al. 1996. Epidemiology of dementia in Rochester, Minnesota. *Mayo Clinic Proceedings* 71(3):275–82; Evans, D. A., H. H. Funkenstein, M. S. Albert, et al. 1989. Prevalence of dementia in a community population of older persons: Higher than previously reported. *JAMA* 262:2551–56; Pfeffer, R. I., A. A. Afifi, and J. M. Chance. 1987. Prevalence of Alzheimer's disease in a retirement community. *Am J Epidemiol* 125:420–36; Ogura, C., H. Nakamoto, T. Uema, et al. 1995. Prevalence of senile dementia in Okinawa. *Internatl J Epidemiol* 24:373–80; Yamada, M., H. Sasaki, Y. Imori, et al., 1999. Prevalence and risks of dementia in the Japanese population: RERF's Adult Health Study Hiroshima Subjects. *J Am Geriatr Soc* 47:189–195.

71. BMI ranges are consistent with what was reported in the largest cohort studies of BMI and morbidity and mortality. Willett, W. C., W. H. Dietz, and G. A. Colditz. 1999. Primary care: Guidelines for healthy weight. *N Engl J Med* 341(6):427–34; Body fat ranges are based on correlations between BMI and body fat from Gallagher, D., et al. 2000. Healthy percentage body fat ranges: An approach for developing guidelines based on body mass index. *Am J Clin Nutr* 72:694–701.

72. Okinawa Prefectural Government. Department of Health and Welfare. Statistics and Information Division, 2000.

73. Actual testing of Atkins-type diets (e.g., Atkins, Protein Power, etc.) was done by Yang, M. U., and T. B. Van Itallie. 1976. Composition of weight lost during short-term weight reduction. Metabolic responses of obese subjects to starvation and low-calorie ketogenic and non-ketogenic diets. *J Clin Invest* 58(3):722–30.

74. An excellent study of some of the most popular weight-loss regimens is James, W., J. W. Anderson, E. C. Konz, and D.J.A. Jenkins. 2000. Health advantages and disadvantages of weight-reducing diets: A computer analysis and critical review. *J Am Coll Nutr* 19(5):578–90.

75. Most women in the Western world experience menopause between the ages of 45 and 55 (average age 51). Some women experience menopause as early as their 30s and some as late as their 60s. Natural menopause at ages younger than 40 years is called "premature menopause." Menopause at such an early age should be assessed by a physician to rule out possible autoimmune disease or other medical conditions. Premature menopause increases your risk for CHD and osteoporosis.

    A simple blood test that measures your blood level of follicle-stimulating hormone (FSH), the brain hormone that stimulates estrogen release from the ovaries, is helpful to confirm your menopausal status. It typically rises to high levels (30–40 U/L) when menopause occurs. This test, combined with your medical history and exam, can usually confirm your menopausal status.

76. Kolata, G. 2000. Estrogen tied to slight increase in risks to heart, a study hints. *NY Times,* 5 April, 1.

77. Willett, W. C., G. Colditz, and M. Stampfer. 2000. Postmenopausal estrogens—opposed, unopposed, or none of the above. *JAMA* 283(4):534–35.

78. Grodstein, F., M. J. Stampfer, G. A. Colditz, et al. 1997. Postmenopausal hormone therapy and mortality. *N Engl J Med* 336:1769–75.

79. Stephenson, J. 1999. Experts debate drugs for healthy women with breast cancer risk. *JAMA* 282(2):117–18.

80. Chlebowski, R. 2000. Reducing the risk of breast cancer. *N Engl J Med* 343(3):191–98.

81. Willcox, B. J., K. Fuchigami, D. C. Willcox, et al. 1995. Isoflavone intake in Japanese and Japanese-Canadians. Paper presented at the 1995 Meeting of the American Society of Clinical Nutrition.

82. Thompson, L. U. 1994. Antioxidants and hormone-mediated health benefits of whole grains. *Crit Rev Food Sci Nutr* 34:473–97; Thompson,

L. U., P. Robb, M. Serraino, et al. 1991. Mammalian lignan production from various foods. *Nutr Cancer* 16:43–52; Kurzer, M. S., and X. Xu. 1997. Dietary phytoestrogens. *Ann Rev Nutr* 17:353–81; Messina, M. 1999. Legumes and soybeans: Overview of their nutritional profiles and health effects. *Am J Clin Nutr* 70(3 suppl.):439S–50S.

83. Chlebowski, R. T., D. E. Collyar, M. R. Somerfield, et al. 1999. American Society of Clinical Oncology technology assessment on breast cancer risk reduction strategies: Tamoxifen and Raloxifene. *J Clin Oncol* 17:1939–55; Stephenson, J. 1999. Experts debate drugs for healthy women with breast cancer risk. *JAMA* 282(2):117–18.

84. Love, S. 1997. *Dr. Susan Love's Hormone Book.* New York: Random House.

85. Canadian Diet and Breast Cancer Prevention Study Group. 1997. Effects at two years of a low-fat, high-carbohydrate diet on radiologic features of the breast: Results from a randomized trial. *J Natl Cancer Inst* 8:488–96. Interestingly, a Harvard study recently found that denser breasts are associated with higher IGF-I levels, more evidence that the insulin hormones are related to breast cancer. Special digitized mammography may be able to detect this earlier than usual mammography. Byrne, C., G. Colditz, W. Willett, et al. 2000. Plasma insulin-like growth factor I, IGF-binding protein 3 and mammographic density. *Cancer Res* 60(14):3744–48.

86. Maskarinec, G., L. Meng, and K. Shimozuma. 1999. A pilot study of mammographic density patterns among Japanese women. *J Epidemiol* 9(2):73–77.

87. Willett, W. C., G. Colditz, M. Stampfer. 2000. Postmenopausal estrogens—opposed, unopposed, or none of the above. *JAMA* 283(4):534–35.

88. Albertazzi, P., F. Pansini, G. Bonaccorsi, et al. 1998. The effect of dietary soy supplementation on hot flushes. *Obstet Gynecol* 91(1):6–11.

89. Black cohosh is on the German Commission E list as an effective herbal treatment for perimenopausal symptoms. A double-blind interventional study of eighty women found that the group who took black cohosh reported fewer menopausal symptoms than those taking conjugated estrogens (0.625 mg) or a placebo. See Stoll, W. 1987. Phytopharmacon influences atrophic vaginal epithelium. Double-blind study. Cimicifuga versus estrogenic substances. *Therapeuticum* 1:23–31.

90. In a recently published study at Wake Forest University School of Medicine, fifty-one women were assigned to groups that received either a placebo diet or a diet with once- or twice-daily soy (34 mg flavonoids in total). The twice-daily soy group reported a significant improvement in menopausal symptoms (e.g., less severe hot flashes). Moreover, significant declines in total cholesterol (6 percent) and LDL cholesterol (7 percent) were seen in both soy diets. Washburn, S., G. L. Burke, T. Morgan, et al. 1999. Effect of soy protein supplementation on serum lipoproteins, blood pressure, and menopausal symptoms in perimenopausal women. *Menopause* 6:7–13.

91. Willcox, B., D. C. Willcox, M. Suzuki, et al. 2000. Okinawa Centenarian Study Database; Hertog, M., D. Kromhout, C. Aravanis, et al., 1995. Flavonoid intake and long-term risk of coronary heart disease and cancer in the Seven Countries Study. *Arch Intern Med* 155(4):381–386; Lock, M. 1994. Menopause in cultural context. *Experimental Gerontology* 29:307–17; Ross, P. D., H. Norimatsu, J. W. Davis, et al., 1991. A comparison of hip fracture among native Japanese, Japanese Americans, and American Caucasians. *Am J Epidemiol* 133(8):801–9; Japan Ministry of Health, 1996; 1995 World Health Statistics Annual. WHO, 1996. Geneva.

92. Perls, T. T., L. Alpert, and R. C. Fretts. 1997. Middle-aged mothers live longer. *Nature* 389(6647):133.

93. These findings are being further studied with an in-depth analysis of Okinawan hormonal patterns.

94. Suzuki, M., and N. Hirose. 1999. Endocrine function of centenarians. In Tauchi, H., T. Sato, and T. Watanabe, eds. *Japanese Centenarians— Medical Research for the Final Stages of Human Aging.* Aichi: Aichi Medical University; Greendale, G. A., S. Edelstein, and E. Barrett-Connor. 1997. Endogenous sex steroids and bone mineral density in older women and men: The Rancho Bernardo Study. *J Bone Mineral Res* 12:1833–43.

95. Stoll, B. A. 1999. Dietary supplements of DHEA in relation to breast cancer risk. *Eur J Clin Nutr* 53(10):771–75.

96. For a recent review, see Mobbs, C. V. 1998. Dehydroepiandrosterone and aging. In Mobbs, C. V., P. R. Hof, eds. *Functional Endocrinology of Aging.* Basel: Karger, 217–27.

97. Willcox, B. J., D. C. Willcox, M. Suzuki, et al. 2000. Serum estrogen and long term survival in Okinawan-Japanese men and women. *J Am Geriatr Soc* 48(8):S97.

98. Food labeling: Health claims; soy protein and coronary heart disease. Food and Drug Administration, HHS. Final rule. *Fed Regist* 64, no. 206 (26 October 1999):57700–33.

99. For a review, see Hermann, M., and P. Berger. 1999. Hormone replacement in the aging male? *Exp Gerontol* 34(8):923–33.

100. One of our centenarian subjects not only was sexually active over the age of one hundred, but was seeing a woman in her seventies.

101. For a review, see Savine, R., and P. Sonksen. 2000. Growth hormone—hormone replacement for the somatopause? *Hormone Res* 53(suppl. 3): 37–41.

102. Harman, D. 1998. Aging: Phenomena and theories. *Ann NY Acad Sci* 854:1–7.

103. Sohal, R. S., and R. Weindruch. 1996. Oxidative stress, caloric restriction, and aging. *Science* 273:59–63.

104. Weindruch, R., and R. Sohal. 1997. Caloric intake and aging. *N Engl J Med* 337(14):986–94.

105. Suzuki, M., M. Akisaka, and S. Inayama. 1993. Medicobiological studies on centenarians in Okinawa, measuring plasma lipid peroxide, proline, and plasma and intracellular tocopherol. In Beregi, E., I. A. Gergely, and K. Rajczi, eds. *Recent Advances in Aging Science*. Bologna: Monduzzi.

106. Willcox, D. C., H. Todoriki, S. Sakihara, B. J. Willcox, K. Naka, and M. Ariizumi. 2000. Minority Aging in Japan: Subjective Well-Being of Older Okinawans in Cross-Cultural Context. Unpublished manuscript.

107. Naka, K., D. C. Willcox, H. Todoriki, and T. Kageyama. 1998. Suicide in Okinawa from an international perspective: A consideration of socio-cultural factors. *Ryukyu Med J* 18:1–10.

108. The evidence for the positive effects of spirituality on health is impressive and growing. See note 10 for Chapter Seven for key reviews of the scientific literature.

109. See Perls, T. T., and Margery H. Silver. 1999. *Living to 100*. New York: Basic Books, 64–71.

110. See Akisaka, M., et al. 1998. Analysis of Type A behavior pattern associated with longevity (in Japanese). *Jpn J Psychosom Med* 38:415–22.

111. House, J. S., K. R. Landis, and D. Umperson. 1988. Social relationships and health. *Science* 241:540–45.

112. Sakihara, S., and K. Nishi. 1998. Research on Community-Dwelling Elderly Women's Orientation to Independent Living (in Japanese). Unpublished manuscript.

113. Todoriki, H., D. C. Willcox, and K. Naka. 1998. Social support and subjective well-being of Okinawan elderly. *Human Sci* 10:17–23.

114. See Barlett, H. P., and D. R. Phillips. 1995. Aging trends—Hong Kong. *J Cross-Cult Gerontol* 10:257–65; Bennet, C. L., G. K. Pei, and J. E. Ultmann. 1996. Western impressions of the Hong Kong health care system. *Western J Med* 165:37–42.

115. Beach, M. 1999. Role of pharmacies in Chinese world of health care. *Lancet* 354:493.

Chapter Three

1. Pork is a traditional food in Okinawa, but was eaten only a few times per month until living standards rose after the Second World War. Even then it was boiled for hours, with the fatty liquid regularly scooped away, so the result was a very lean meat. Meat consumption is still less than half the current U.S. level, but increasing amounts of processed meats are being eaten by Okinawans with resultant higher cholesterol levels—especially in young Okinawans. The results of these new eating habits have now begun to appear in the form of a higher frequency of heart attacks among young and middle-aged Okinawans.

2. Goldman, E. 1999. Unified dietary guidelines target four key killers. *Intern Med News* 32:14 (1 August). See also Deckelbaum, R. J., et al. 1999. Summary of a scientific conference on preventive nutrition: Pediatrics to geriatrics. *Circulation* 100:450–56.

3. Akisaka, M., L. Asato, B. Willcox, D. C. Willcox, et al. 2001. Dietary habits of Okinawan-Japanese centenarians. (Manuscript submitted for publication.)

4. In Okinawa, canola oil is often blended with soy oil so that a healthy mixture of monounsaturated and omega-3 fatty acids results. Recently, canola oil was compared with olive oil with regard to effects on artery function. Olive oil actually impeded the function of the arteries as much as a fast-food meal (Egg McMuffin, Sausage McMuffin, and two hash-brown patties), unless eaten in the presence of antioxidant-containing

vitamins or vegetables, whereas canola oil had little or no negative effect on the arterial function. See Vogel, R. A. 2000. The Mediterranean diet and endothelial function: Why some dietary fats may be healthy. *Cleve Clin J Med* 67(4):232, 235–36. Also in support of canola oil, the Lyon Diet Heart Study found that eating a canola-oil-rich diet for five years reduced the incidence of heart disease an astonishing 70 percent versus eating a regular diet. The conclusions of this study were to eat more breads (whole grain), vegetables, fruits, beans, and fish, and less meat, and to substitute canola oil for margarine, butter, and cream. This is remarkably similar to what the Okinawans are already eating. See Leaf, A. 1999. Dietary prevention of coronary heart disease. The Lyon Diet Heart Study. Editorial. *Circulation* 99:733–35.

5. Okinawan dietary data from Okinawa Centenarian Study database; U.S. dietary data from the U.S. cohort of the Seven Countries Study from Keys, A. 1980. *Seven Countries: A Commonwealth Fund Book.* Boston: Harvard University Press.

6. Jacobs, D. R., Jr., and M. A. Murtaugh. 2000. It's more than an apple a day: An appropriately processed, plant-centered dietary pattern may be good for your health. *Am J Clin Nutr* 72:899–900.

7. Willett, W. C. 1994. Diet and health: What should we eat? *Science* 264: 532–37.

8. McCay, C. M., M. R. Crowell, and L. A. Maynard. 1935. The effect of retarded growth upon the length of life span and upon the ultimate body size. *J Nutr* 10:63–79.

9. Jenkins, D.J.A., T.M.S. Wolever, V. Vuksan, et al. 1989. Nibbling versus gorging: Metabolic advantages of increased meal frequency. *N Engl J Med* 321:929–34.

10. Much of the carbohydrate phobia is loosely based on a misinterpretation of the carbohydrate research of Dr. David Jenkins and his research group at the University of Toronto, where my brother and I received part of our training in the early 1990s. Dr. Jenkins is well known for developing the Glycemic Index—the tool by which the body's glucose response to carbohydrate is measured, which has implications for insulin levels. Dr. Jenkins' research follows the tradition of a long line of carbohydrate-related research at the University of Toronto and Oxford University. The University of Toronto work on the health effects of carbohydrates began in the 1920s and led to the 1923 Nobel Prize in Physiology/Medicine awarded to Frederick Banting, C. H.

Best, and J. J. R. Macleod for the discovery of insulin, the hormone that packs glucose, the simplest carbohydrate, into the body's cells. Another milestone was reached when a Nobel Prize was awarded to Dr. Jenkins' research supervisor at Oxford University, Sir Hans Krebs, for discovering how carbohydrates are converted into energy during the citric acid cycle. The tradition continued with Dr. Jenkins' and Dr. Tom Wolever's development of the Glycemic Index after an elegant series of experiments that began at Oxford University in the 1960s and continued at the University of Toronto in the 1970s. These experiments were published over the next decade in a landmark collection of scientific papers in *The Lancet* and *Nature*. The classic scientific paper that presented the Glycemic Index to the scientific community was published in the *American Journal of Clinical Nutrition* in 1981. See Jenkins, D. J. A., et al. 1981. Glycemic index of foods: a physiological basis of carbohydrate exchange. *Am J Clin Nutr* 34:362–66.

11. Much of the public is convinced that carbohydrates "make you fat" because they "raise your insulin levels too much." There is no support for this in the scientific literature. Any source of calories (carbohydrate, protein, fat, or alcohol) consumed in excess of the body's total energy requirements will result in storage of that energy as fat. In fact, protein and fat also affect insulin levels. The evidence indicates that it's actually easier for the body to convert dietary fat to body fat than for it to convert carbohydrate into body fat. See Romieu, I., W. C. Willett, M. J. Stampfer, et al. 1988. Energy intake and other determinants of relative weight. *Am J Clin Nutr* 47:406–12.

12. For an excellent treatise on the Glycemic Index for the general public, see *The Glucose Revolution* (New York: Marlowe and Co., 1999) by University of Toronto scientist and Jenkins Research Group member Dr. Tom Wolever and Dr. Jennie Brand-Miller of the University of Sydney and her collaborators. They have published much of the scientific work that has helped to further define the Glycemic Index.

13. United States Department of Agriculture. National Food Review 1987. Washington, D.C.: USDA.

14. Glucose load and diabetes: Salmeron, J., J. Manson, M. Stampfer, et al. 1997. Dietary fiber, glycemic load, and risk of non-insulin-dependent diabetes mellitus in women. *JAMA* 277:472–77. Glucose load and coronary heart disease: Liu, S., W. C. Willett, M. J. Stampfer, et al. 2000. A prospective study of dietary glycemic load, carbohydrate

intake, and risk of coronary heart disease in U.S. women. *Am J Clin Nutr* 71(6):1433–61.

15. For a review of problems associated with too much blood sugar, see Brownlee, M. 2000. Negative consequences of glycation. *Metabolism* 49:9–13.

16. Ludwig, D. S., M. A. Pereira, C. H. Kroenke, et al. 1999. Dietary fiber, weight gain, and cardiovascular disease risk factors in young adults. *JAMA* 282:1539–46.

17. Mathews, D. E. 1999. Protein and amino acids. In Shils, M. E., J. A. Olson, M. Shike, et al. *Modern Nutrition in Health and Disease.* 9th edition. Baltimore: Williams & Wilkins, 11–48.

18. Lappe, F. M. 1992. *Diet for a Small Planet.* New York: Ballantine Books.

19. Hu, F. B., M. J. Stampfer, E. B. Rimm, et al. 1999. A prospective study of eggs and cardiovascular disease in men and women. *JAMA* 281: 1387–94.

20. Lewis, N. M., S. Seburg, and N. L. Flanagan. 2000. Enriched eggs as a source of N-3 polyunsaturated fatty acids for humans. *Poult Sci* 79(7): 971–74.

21. Can walnuts prevent heart disease? 2000. *Harv Health Lett* 10:4; Morgan, W. A., and B. J. Clayshulte. 2000. Pecans lower low-density lipoprotein cholesterol in people with normal lipid levels. *J Am Diet Assoc* 100:312–18.

22. Simopoulos, A. P., A. Leaf, and N. Salem, Jr. 1999. Essentiality of and recommended dietary in-takes for omega-6 and omega-3 fatty acids. *Ann Nutr Metab* 43:127–30.

23. Most foods contain a mixture of different fats and are classified according to the most abundant fat in the food (e.g., olive oil is called monounsaturated, but it also contains saturated and polyunsaturated fat).

24. For a review from one of the world experts, see Katan, M. B. 2000. Trans fatty acids and plasma lipoproteins. *Nutr Rev* 58:188–91.

25. Fat content is required by law to be listed on food labels—except trans fat, which you have to calculate yourself. Fat is usually measured in grams, but sometimes in calories. If the total fat grams are provided on a label, simply subtract the amount of other fat grams from the total of fat grams. The remainder is trans fat. If the fat is listed as calories, do the same subtractions and divide the remainder by nine

(fat = 9 calories per gram). Future legislation will require that trans fat be accounted for in food labels.

26. Source: USDA database, 2000.

27. Bartsch, H., J. Nair, and R. W. Owen. 1999. Dietary polyunsaturated fatty acids and cancers of the breast and colorectum: Emerging evidence for their role as risk modifiers. *Carcinogenesis* 20(12):2209–18; Rose, D. P., and J. M. Connolly. 1999. Omega-3 fatty acids as cancer chemopreventive agents. *Pharmacol Ther* 83(3):217–44; Harbige, L. S. 1998. Dietary n-6 and n-3 fatty acids in immunity and autoimmune disease. *Proc Nutr Soc* 57(4):555–62.

28. Giovannucci, E., E. B. Rimm, G. A. Colditz, et al. 1993. A prospective study of dietary fat and risk of prostate cancer. *J Natl Cancer Inst* 85: 1571–79.

Chapter Four

1. The *nuchi gusui* philosophy has resulted in some interesting health behaviors in Okinawans. One of these is a reluctance to take pharmaceutical preparations (drugs) for medical conditions unless an herb is also present in the pill. To some extent, this philosophy is also present in Japan as a whole and has resulted in many herbal/drug blends and what we perceive as a relatively high frequency of herbal use among the Okinawan population. We are conducting further research to quantify the use of herbal medicines in Okinawa. Some of them have significant antioxidant capacity. For example, the herb that Okinawans call *ucchin (ukon)*, which we know as turmeric, has significant antioxidant capacity, higher than that of vitamin C, and contains a high flavonoid content. See Aniya, Y., M. Shimabukuro, M. Shimoji, et al. 2000. Antioxidant and hepatoprotective actions of the medicinal herb *Artemisia campestris (ukon)* from the Okinawa islands. *Biol Pharm Bull* 23:309–12.

2. Since the beginning of the Okinawa Centenarian Study, our research group has recorded nutritional information about the diets of the Okinawan elders. Despite the fact that there is a yearly National Nutrition Survey in Japan that includes Okinawa, it has been difficult to assess from this survey what the Okinawan elders are eating, since the methodology precludes a precise analysis of nutrient intake by age group. Food is weighed according to what the family eats, and

approximations are made as to who ate what. Furthermore, analyzing the diets of Okinawans has proved challenging because many of their foods are different from mainland Japanese foods and thus are not represented in Japanese food composition tables. We had to construct an entirely new database for Okinawan foods and statistically validate our food-frequency questionnaires against the gold standard (seven-day food records of weighed food consumption) in order to get an accurate idea of what the Okinawans are actually eating. Dr. H. Todoriki, a member of our research network and one of the leading nutritional epidemiologists in Japan, has been instrumental in this effort. Early studies consisted of questions regarding consumption of particular food groups while later studies have included food frequency questionnaires and weighed recording of food intake in elderly and centenarian study subjects, which has given us accurate information about most aspects of the Okinawan diet. See Todoriki, H., M. Ariizumi, I. Ashitomi, M. Suzuki, and B. J. Willcox. 1998. Food frequency methodology in the Kume island study (in Japanese). *Proc Ann Meeting Jap Soc Clin Nutr 102*; Akamatsu, T., K. Komi, M. Suzuki, et al. 1980. Nutritional evaluation of the elderly in Okinawa: Results of geriatric health exams (in Japanese). *Nihon Ronen Igakkai Zasshi* 17:39–48; Chan, Y. C., M. Suzuki, and S. Yamamoto. 1997. Nutritional status of centenarians assessed by activity and anthropometric, hematological and biochemical characteristics. *J Nutr Sci Vitaminol* 43:73–81; Suzuki, M. 1998. Nutrition of centenarians. *JJPEN* 20:699–708; Willcox, B. J., M. Suzuki, D. C. Willcox, H. Todoriki, S. Sakihara, and D. D. Hensrud. 2000. Nutrition and human life expectancy: Cultural models for successful aging (manuscript in preparation); Willcox, B. J., D. J. A. Jenkins, K. Fuchigami, D. C. Willcox, M. Suzuki, H. Todoriki, et al. 1995. Dietary westernization and chronic disease in Japan. *FASEB J* 9(3):A2579.

3. See Chapter Three for further information on how to gauge the number of calories you should be eating. The bottom line is that if you are not staying lean (BMI of 18–23) you need to either eat less or increase your activity level. Excellent advice about caloric intake and health can be found in the publications of Dr. R. Walford and Dr. R. Weindruch, who did much of the pioneering work on caloric restriction, health, and longevity, and who frequently cite the Okinawans as a human example of such a population. See Weindruch, R., and R. Sohal. 1997.

Caloric intake and aging. *N Engl J Med* 337(14):986–94. For the nonscientist, see Walford, R. 2000. *Beyond the 120-year Diet: How to Double Your Vital Years.* New York: Four Walls Eight Windows.

4. It appears that the most important antioxidants may, in fact, be polyphenols, of which flavonoids are among the most prevalent compounds. See Joseph, J., A. Denisova, D. Bielinki, D. Fisher, and B. Shukitt-Hale. 2000. Oxidative stress protection and vulnerability in aging: nutritional implications for intervention. *Mechanisms of Aging and Development* 116(2–3):141–53; and Prior, R., and G. Cao. 2000. Analysis of botanicals and dietary supplements. *J AOAC Int* 83(4): 950–56.

5. Several theories of aging have come and gone over the years, but one that has received consistent support from the scientific literature is the free-radical theory. That is, by-products of normal metabolism called free radicals damage cells, especially cell DNA, so that over the years it becomes less functional and eventually stops working. Many other theories exist, but they can often be reconciled with the free-radical theory. For example, the immunological theory suggests that as we get older, the immune system, which guards against infection and cancer, turns against itself. One could argue that free-radical-induced damage accumulates in cells over the years, such that the immune system begins to recognize these cells as foreign and attacks them. Other theories include the following:

Angioplastic pleotropy: Genes support our bodies in early life and turn against us in later life.

Chaos or loss of complexity theory: Aging is a result of the inability of the body to tolerate complex changes as it ages, and eventually it falls apart.

Disposable soma theory: Evolution preserves the species at the expense of the organism. Therefore, it preserves reproductive performance at the expense of maintenance and repair of the individual.

Glycemic theory: Aging is secondary to glucose-induced damage to proteins and DNA. In the process of glycosylation, glucose makes sugar bonds and "sticks" to other cellular machinery, literally "gumming up the works."

Telomere theory: The telomere (a piece of DNA at the ends of chromosomes) is lost with each cell division, and when it is used up, the cells can no longer reproduce and therefore cannot repair or replace tissue as we age.

6. These foods were chosen since they were among the most frequently consumed foods in our surveys of the Okinawan diet and there is published evidence for health benefits. See Chapter Five for references.

7. Dawson-Hughes, B., S. S. Harris, E. A. Krall, et al. 1997. Effect of calcium and vitamin D supplementation on bone density in men and women sixty-five years of age or older. *N Engl J Med* 337(10):670–76; Pearlstein, T., and M. Steiner. 2000. Non-antidepressant treatment of premenstrual syndrome. *J Clin Psychiatry* 61(suppl. 12):22–27; Janne, P. A., and R. J. Mayer. 2000. Chemo-prevention of colorectal cancer. *N Engl J Med* 342(26):1960–68. Review.

8. Willet, W. C. 1994. Diet and health: What should we eat? *Science* 264: 532–37.

9. Weinsier, R. L., and C. L. Ksumdieck. 2000. Dairy foods and bone health: Examination of the evidence. *Am J Clin Nutr* 72:681–89; Heaney, R. P. 1993. Protein intake and the calcium economy. *J Am Diet Assoc* 93(11):1259–60.

10. Recker, R. R., K. M. Davis, S. M. Hinders, et al. 1992. Bone gain in young adult women. *JAMA* 268:2403–8.

11. Gottlieb, S. 2000. Early exposure to cows' milk increases risk of diabetes in high risk children. *BMJ* 321(7268):1040D; Paronen, J., M. Knip, E. Savilahti, et al. 2000. Effect of cow's milk exposure and maternal type I diabetes on cellular and humoral immunization to dietary insulin in infants at genetic risk for type I diabetes: Finnish trial to reduce IDDM in the genetically at risk study group. *Diabetes* 49(10):1657–65.

12. Mitral, B. K., and S. K. Garg. 1995. Anticarcinogenic, hypocholesterolemic, and antagonistic activities of lactobacillus acidophilus. *Crit Rev Microbiol* 21(3):175–214.

13. Weaver, C. M., and R. P. Heaney, 1999. Calcium. In Shils, M. E., J. A. Olson, M. Shike, et al. *Modern Nutrition in Health and Disease.* 9th ed., Baltimore: Williams & Wilkins, 141–55.

14. Thompson, L. U. 1994. Antioxidants and hormone-mediated health benefits of whole grains. *Crit Rev Food Sci Nutr* 34:473–97; Thompson, L. U., P. Robb, M. Serraino, et al. 1991. Mammalian lignan production from various foods. *Nutr Cancer* 16:43–52; Kurzer, M. S., and

X. Xu. 1997. Dietary phytoestrogens. *Ann Rev Nutr* 17:353–81; Messina, M. 1999. Legumes and soybeans: Overview of their nutritional profiles and health effects. *Am J Clin Nutr* 70(suppl. 3):439S–50S; Peitta, P. G. 2000. Flavonoids as antioxidants. *J Nat Prod* 63(7):1035–42.

15. Accurate measurement of flavonoid intake has been difficult because a comprehensive database does not yet exist for flavonoids. Estimates vary from several milligrams up to one gram a day for total flavonoid intake for individuals depending on intake of particular legumes, vegetables, fruits, and grains and other flavonoid-rich plant foods. Few flavonoids exist in animal foods. See Hom-Ross, P. L., S. Barnes, M. Lee, et al. 2000. Assessing phytoestrogen exposure in epidemiologic studies: Development of a database (United States). *Cancer Causes Control* 11(4):289–98.

16. Hertog, M. G., D. Kromhout, C. Aravanis, et al. 1995. Flavonoid intake and long-term risk of coronary heart disease and cancer in the Seven Countries Study. *Arch Intern Med* 155(4):381–86.

17. Adlercreutz, H., H. Markkanen, S. Watanabe. 1993. Plasma concentrations of phytoestrogens in Japanese men. *Lancet* 342:1209–10.

18. Okinawa Centenarian Study database. 2000; Willcox, B. J., D. C. Willcox, M. Suzuki, et al., 1995. Isoflavone intake in Japanese and Japanese-Canadians. Paper presented at the 1995 Meeting of the American Society for Clinical Nutrition.

19. Setchell, K. D., A. M. Lawson, and F. L. Mitchell. 1980. Lignans in man and animal species. *Nature* 287(5784):740–42.

20. Food labeling: Health claims; soy protein and coronary heart disease. Food and Drug Administration, HHS. Final rule. *Fed Regist* 64, no. 206 (26 October 1999):57700–33.

21. Anderson, J. W. 1995. Meta-analysis of the effects of soy protein intake on serum lipids. *N Engl J Med* 333(5):276–82.

22. Messina, M. 1999. Legumes and soybeans: Overview of their nutritional profiles and health effects. *Am J Clin Nutr* 70(suppl. 3):439S–50S; Barnes, S. 1995. Rationale for the use of genistein containing soy matrices in chemo-prevention trials for breast and prostate cancer. *J Cellular Biochemistry* 22:181–87; Messina, M., and S. Barnes. 1991. The role of soy products in reducing risk of cancer. *J National Cancer Inst* 83:541–46; Messina, M. J., V. Persky, K.D.R. Setchell, et al. 1994. Soy intake and cancer risk: A review of the in vitro and in vivo data. *Nutr Cancer* 21(2): 113–31; Moyad, M. A. 1999. Soy, disease prevention and prostate cancer.

Seminars in Urologic Oncology 17(2): 97–102; Erdman, J. W., Jr., R. J. Still-man, and R. A. Boileau. 2000. Provocative relation between soy and bone maintenance. Editorial. *Am J Clin Nutr* 72:679–80.

23. Scalbert, A., and G. Williamson. 2000. Dietary intake and bioavaila-bility of polyphenols. *J Nutr* 130(suppl. 8S):2073S–85S.

24. Pillow, P. C., C. M. Duphorne, S. Chang, et al. 1999. Development of a database for assessing dietary phytoestrogen intake. *Nutr Cancer* 33:3–19; Mazur, W., et al. 1998. Isoflavonoids and lignans in legumes: Nutritional and health aspects in humans. *J Nutr Biochem* 9:193–200; Herrmann, K., et al. 1976. Flavonols and flavones in food plants: A review. *J Food Technol* 11:433–48; Reinli, K., and G. Block. 1996. Phyto-estrogen content of foods—a compendium of literature values. *Nutr Cancer* 26:123–48; Hertog, M.G.L., et al. 1992. Optimization of a quan-titative HPLC determination of potentially anticarcinogenic flavonoids in vegetables and fruits. *J Agric Food Chem* 40:1591–98; Hertog, M.G.L., et al. 1993. Content of potentially anticarcinogenic flavonoids of tea infusions, wines, and fruit juices. *J Agric Food Chem* 41:1232–46.

25. Hertog, M.G.L., E.J.M. Feskens, P.C.H. Hollman, et al. 1993. Dietary antioxidant flavonoids and risk of coronary heart disease: The Zut-phen Elderly Study. *Lancet* 342:1007–11.

26. Freeman, M. P. 2000. Omega-3 fatty acids in psychiatry: A review. *Ann Clin Psychiat* 2(3):159–65.

27. O'Keefe, J. H., Jr., and W. S. Harris. 2000. From Inuit to implementa-tion: Omega-3 fatty acids come of age. *Mayo Clin Proc* 75(6):607–14.

28. Harbige, L. S. 1998. Dietary n-6 and n-3 fatty acids in immunity and autoimmune disease. *Proc Nutr Soc* 57(4):555–62.

29. Uavy, R., P. Mena, and C. Rojas. 2000. Essential fatty acids in early life: Structural and functional role. *Proc Nutr Soc* 59(1):3–15.

30. Conquer, J. A., and B. J. Holub. 1996. Supplementation with an algae source of docosahexaenoic acid increases (n-3) fatty acid status and alters selected risk factors for heart disease in vegetarian subjects. *J Nutr* 126(12):3032–39.

31. Rose, D. P., and J. M. Connolly. 1999. Omega-3 fatty acids as cancer chemopreventive agents. *Pharmacol Ther* 83(3):217–44.

32. Lopez-Pila, J. M., H. Dizer, and W. Dorau. 1996. Wastewater treat-ment and elimination of pathogens: New prospects for an old problem. *Microbiologia* 12(4):525–36; Addiss, D. G., R. S. Pond, M. Rem-

shak, et al. 1996. Reduction of risk of watery diarrhea with point-of-use water filters during a massive outbreak of waterborne cryptosporidium infection in Milwaukee, Wisconsin, 1993. *Am J Trop Med Hyg* 54(6):549–53; Synder, J. W., Jr., C. N. Mains, R. E. Anderson, et al. 1995. Effect of point-of-use, activated carbon filters on the bacteriological quality of rural groundwater supplies. *Appl Environ Microbiol* 61(12):4291–95; Payment, R., L. Richardson, J. Siemiatycki, et al. 1991. A randomized trial to evaluate the risk of gastrointestinal disease due to consumption of drinking water meeting current microbiological standards. *Am J Public Health* 81(6):703–8.

33. Yang, C. S., and J. M. Landau. 2000. Effects of tea consumption on nutrition and health. *J Nutr* 130(10):2409–12; Diet: Tea and health. 2000. *Harvard Health Lett* 25(12):2–3.

34. Omega-3 eggs can be eaten more liberally (considered an omega-3 food). Studies show that they can actually improve your cholesterol profile. See Lewis, N. M., S. Seburg, and N. L. Flanagan. 2000. Enriched eggs as a source of N-3 polyunsaturated fatty acids for humans. *Poult Sci* 79(7):971–74.

35. There is much controversy over the relative importance of animal and plant foods in the early hominid (humans and their ancestors) diets as well as over the question of whether early hominids obtained meat by hunting or by scavenging. Nothing conclusive can be said as yet about the diets of the earliest hominids, because direct evidence, in the form of food remains, is meager or equivocal at best. Most research relies on inference through dietary studies of other primates; animal bones and stone tools found in archeological sites; hominid skeletal evidence (especially teeth); and analogy with the diets of modern hunter-gatherer societies. Working within these parameters, the majority of anthropologists and other researchers on the "evolutionary diet" agree that plant foods contributed much more to the early hominid diet than did the flesh of animals. By two million years ago, scavenging of animal foods began to increase, and by that point hominids were almost certainly broad-spectrum feeders (diversivores) living in grassland, woodland, and aquatic ecosystems in the tropical and subtropical seasonal environments of Africa. By one million years ago they had spread widely within the Old World tropics. Approximately 100,000 years ago, anatomically modern human beings appeared and spread, as small bands of hunter-gatherers, to all parts of the world.

Although arguments often arise over whether humans are "naturally" more carnivorous or herbivorous, the question has little meaning if the whole human species is considered. Because the nutrients necessary for life occur in so many food resources scattered throughout the world, human beings have evolved enormous adaptive potential, and modern humans *(Homo sapiens)* have come to occupy all habitats ranging from equatorial rain forest to Arctic tundra. As a consequence, the balance between meat-eating and plant-eating varies considerably from population to population (for both environmental and cultural reasons).

Nevertheless, extrapolation from research evidence on modern hunter-gatherer societies shows that meat usually constitutes only a small proportion of the total intake of food, except in high altitudes where plants are scarce and there has been physiological adaptation to diets high in animal fats and proteins. An example of this latter pattern could be seen in the dietary habits of the Inuit of the Canadian Arctic. When edible plants were scarce in winter, Inuit populations obtained nutrients usually associated with vegetables from eating all the tissues, the bone marrow, and the stomach contents of plant-eating animals. Historical records of fifty-eight hunting, gathering, and fishing societies show that hunting was the dominant mode of subsistence only at latitudes greater than 60 degrees. (See Lee, R. B., and I. Devore, eds. 1968. *Man the Hunter.* Chicago: Aldine.) Although hunting was rarely the primary source of food, it did make a consistent and important contribution to the diet of these modern hunter-gatherer societies, and in most cases about a third of total food came from hunting. The most commonly accepted figure from anthropologists and other scientists regarding diet during the Middle Paleolithic (200,000–40,000 years ago), when hunting and gathering gradually became the main subsistence strategy of early humans, was about 65 percent of calories from plant sources (fruits, vegetables, nuts, seeds, grasses, etc.) and 35 percent of calories from animal sources (wild game, reptiles, insects, etc.).

All told, the evidence from looking at human diets in small-scale hunting and gathering societies, diets of other primates, and the modern application of chemical techniques of analysis to ancient bones suggests that plant foods probably always constituted half or more of the human diet among all human populations except those in the arctic regions, throughout human evolutionary history. It is interesting to note that as a rule, meat intake reported for most modern hunter-gatherer groups is comparable to intake by relatively affluent modern Western populations. (It is substantially better than average Third World intake and dramatically better than that of contemporary Third World poor.) However, the important caveat here is that the lean wild meat consumed by modern hunter-gatherer societies and by our ancestors throughout human evolutionary history is vastly different from the meat of domesticated animals, with its high content of saturated fat. See Cohen, M. N. 1989. *Health and the Rise of Civilization*. New Haven: Yale University Press; Whitten, A., and E. M. Widdowson. 1992. *Foraging Strategies and Natural Diet of Monkeys, Apes and Humans*. Oxford: Clarendon Press; Eaton, S. B., and M. Konner. 1985. Paleolithic nutrition: A consideration of its nature and current implications. *N Engl J Med* 312:283–89; Popovich, D. G., D.J.A. Jenkins, C.W.C. Kendall, et al. 1997. The western lowland gorilla diet has implications for humans and other hominoids. *J Nutr* 127:2000–5; Speth, J. D. 1983. *Bison Kills and Bone Counts*. Chicago: University of Chicago Press.

36. Many fad diet books advocating high protein intakes from meat sources have appeared in recent years based on misinterpretations of the amount of protein consumed from animal sources throughout our evolutionary history. With titles such as *Protein Power, Neanderthin,* or *Evolutionary Diet,* they recommend that one should eat "as evolution designed us to eat." The rationale of these high-protein fad diets rests on two false assumptions. The first is that early humans obtained most of their calories from the consumption of meat. The scientific evidence simply does not support this assumption as revealed in the previous reference. The second false assumption is the importance placed on the Stone Age (2.5 million years ago to 10,000 years ago) as an evolutionary period. It is argued that human biology is genetically adapted to the hunter-gatherer lifestyle of the Paleolithic period (Stone Age), and modern humans are viewed as Upper Paleolithic (40,000–10,000 years ago), pre-agricultural, meat-eating hunters. Yet, logically, it would be just as persuasive to argue that the behavior of Upper Paleolithic hunter-gatherers was out of sync with evolution because most of the ancestors of these hunter-gatherers were vegetarians. As any introductory textbook in physical anthropology tells us, *gathering and hunting* only came to gradually predominate over *gathering and scavenging* as a subsistence strategy near the end of the Middle Paleolithic (approximately

60,000 years ago). Moreover, those who view contemporary humans as adapted to the Stone Age assume that human adaptation or evolution ended when the age of agriculture (Neolithic) began, 10,000 years ago. The truth is that the forces of evolution (natural selection, gene flow, mutation, and genetic drift) continue to act on human populations and have demonstrably altered allele frequencies since the origin of agriculture (when human diets came to focus more upon whole grains). The best-documented examples of natural selection in modern human populations are the evolution of malaria resistance and lactose intolerance, which are thought to have originated in the past few thousand years. (See Durham, W. 1991. *Coevolution: Genes, Culture and Human Diversity.* Stanford: Stanford University Press.) In other species natural selection has been observed over just a few generations, reminding us that it is naïve (and plain wrong) to underestimate the importance of microevolution in contemporary human populations. Nonetheless, it is unlikely that a large percentage of the 30,000 or so genes in the human genome are more recent than the Stone Age. Yet, if our genes have changed relatively little over the past 10,000 years, does it logically follow that we have mostly Stone Age genes? The obvious answer is that the 2.5 million years of Stone Age evolution is a blink of an eye compared with the nearly four billion years of evolution behind *Homo sapiens.* In fact, the molecular evidence shows that most of our genes are far older than the Stone Age, and that we continue to share the same genetic code as all other species on Earth, including bacteria. The upshot is that from a genetic standpoint, the Stone Age has no greater significance than any other period of our evolutionary past. For a good paper that puts the Stone Age in its proper evolutionary context, see Strassman, B. I., and R. I. Dunbar. 1999. Human evolution and disease: Putting the Stone Age in perspective. In Stearns, S. C., ed. *Evolution in Health and Disease.* Oxford: Oxford University Press.

37. Eaton, S. B., and M. Konner. 1985. Paleolithic nutrition: A consideration of its nature and current implications. *N Engl J Med* 312:283–89.

38. Perhaps no one is more of an expert on hunter-gatherer societies than University of Toronto anthropologist Dr. Richard Lee. In fact, his book *The !Kung San* (1979) was recently listed by the journal *American Scientist* as among the top 100 most important works of science in the twentieth century. In his widely read works, Dr. Lee shows that women were responsible for supplying the majority of calories in !Kung San

society—and that the calories came mainly from the foraging (gathering) of wild plants—especially nuts, roots and tubers, not hunting meat. Meat was found to be a small but important supplement to the diet, much as it is now in Okinawa. Hunting animals was found to be more important only at higher latitudes, such as in the Arctic region. The effect of this interpretation was to explode the "man as hunter" myth and replace it with the more accurate "man (or woman) as gatherer" reality. See Lee, R. B., and I. Devore, eds. 1968. *Man the Hunter.* Chicago: Aldine.

39. Bingam, S. A. 1999. High meat diets and cancer risk. *Proc Nutr Soc* 58(2):243–48.

40. Norrish, A. E., L. R. Ferguson, M. G. Knize, et al. 1999. Heterocyclicamine content of cooked meat and risk of prostate cancer. *J Natl Cancer Inst* 91(23):2038–44; Commoner, B., A. J. Vithayathil, P. Dolara, et al. 1978. Formation of mutagens in beef and beef extract during cooking. *Science* 201:913–16.

41. MacDonald, K. L., M. J. O'Leary, M. L. Cohen, et al. 1988. Escherichia coli 0157:H7, an emerging gastrointestinal pathogen: Results of a one-year, prospective, population based study. *JAMA* 259:3567–70.

42. Brewer, S., and J. Novakofski. 1996. Mad cow disease. *Food Tech* 50:312.

43. Hu, F. B., M. J. Stampfer, E. B. Rimm, et al. 1999. A prospective study of egg consumption and risk of cardiovascular disease in men and women. *JAMA* 281(15):1387–94.

44. Theobald, H., L. O. Bygren, Carstensen, et al. 2000. A moderate intake of wine is associated with reduced total mortality and reduced mortality from cardiovascular disease. *J Stud Alcohol* 61(5):652–56; Sesso, H. D., M. J. Stampfer, B. Rosner, et al. 2000. Seven-year changes in alcohol consumption and risk of cardiovascular disease in men. *Arch Intern Med* 160(17):2605–12.

45. Das, D. K., M. Sato, P. S. Ray, et al. 1999. Cardioprotection of red wine: Role of polyphenolic antioxidants. *Drugs Exp Clin Res* 25(2–3): 115–20; Kopp, P. 1998. Resveratrol, a phytoestrogen found in red wine: A possible explanation for the conundrum of the French paradox? *Eur J Endocrinol* 138(6):619–20.

46. Kim, Y. I. 1999. Folate and cancer prevention: A new medical application of folate beyond hyperhomocysteinemia and neural tube defects. *Nutr Rev* 57(10):314–21.

47. This finding is controversial. Some studies, such as the Cambridge Heart Study, found non-significant trends toward a larger number

of hemorrhagic strokes in those consuming the highest levels of vitamin E, but others have not found this. A review for the general public can be found in Goldfinger, S. E. 1999. I am undergoing treatment for hypertension, and have been taking 200 mg of vitamin E daily for the past few years. I read that even lower doses might raise my risk of having a hemorrhagic stroke. Is this true? *Harv Health Lett* 24(3):3.

48. This finding is also controversial. For a review, see Cooper, D. A., A. L. Eldridge, and J. C. Peters. 1999. Dietary carotenoids and lung cancer: A review of recent research. *Nutr Rev* 57:133–45.

49. Support is seen in many cohort studies such as Watkins, M. L., J. D. Erickson, M. J. Thun, et al. 2000. Multiple vitamin use and mortality in a large prospective study. *Am J Epidem* 152(2):149–62. Prospective, randomized interventional trials are few. Several such research trials of vitamin intake and primary prevention of several diseases are now under way, and should help resolve this continuing controversy. For a review, see Christen, W. G., J. M. Gaziano, C. H. Hennekens. 2000. Design of Physicians' Health Study II—a randomized trial of beta-carotene, vitamins E and C, and multi-vitamins in prevention of cancer, cardiovascular disease, and eye disease, and review of results of completed trials. *Ann Epidemiol* 10(2):125–34.

50. See calcium and vitamin D sections in Chapter Four.

51. For an excellent review of vitamin C and its relationship to human health, see Jacob, R. A. 1999. Vitamin C. In Shils, M. E., J. A. Olson, M. Shike, et al. *Modern Nutrition in Health and Disease.* 9th ed. Baltimore: Williams & Wilkins, 467–83.

52. Composition of foods: Raw, processed and prepared. Revision of agricultural handbooks no. 8–9 and 8–11. 1984, 1986. U.S. Department of Agriculture, Science and Education Administration.

53. Sinha, R., G. Block, and P. R. Taylor. 1993. Problems with estimating vitamin C intakes. *Am J Clin Nutr* 57:547–50.

54. Maximal tissue stores are seen with regular intake of 250–500 mg per day, but blood levels will continue to rise up to about 1,000 mg per day (80 percent saturation). A daily total of 2,000 mg only brings another 10 percent saturation. So there is little to gain from taking more than that. See Jacob, R. A., C. L. Otradovec, R. M. Russell, et al. 1988. Vitamin C status and nutrient interactions in a healthy elderly population. *Am J Clin Nutr* 48:1436–42.

55. Jariwalla, R. J., and S. Harakeh. 1996. Antiviral and immunomodulatory activities of ascorbic acid. In Harris, J. R., ed. *Subcellular Biochemistry*. Vol. 25, *Ascorbic Acid: Biochemistry and Biomedical Cell Biology*. New York: Plenum Press, 215–31.

56. Block, G., and R. Schwarz. 1994. Ascorbic acid and cancer: Animal and cell culture data. In Frei, B., ed. *Natural Antioxidants in Health and Disease*. San Diego: Academic Press, 129–55; Fontham, E.T.H. 1994. Vitamin C, vitamin C-rich foods and cancer: Epidemiologic studies. In Frei, B., ed. *Natural Antioxidants in Health and Disease*. San Diego: Academic Press, 157–97; and Shklar, G., and J. L. Schwarz. 1996. Ascorbic acid and cancer. In Harris, J. R., ed. *Subcellular Biochemistry*. Vol. 25, *Ascorbic Acid: Biochemistry and Biomedical Cell Biology*. New York: Plenum Press, 233–247.

57. Simon, J. A. 1992. Vitamin C and cardiovascular disease: A review. *J Am Coll Nutr* 11:107–25; Ness, A. R., J. W. Powles, K. T. Khaw. 1996. Vitamin C and cardiovascular risk: A systematic review. *J Cardiovasc Risk* 3(6):113–21.

58. For an excellent review of vitamin D and health, see Holick, M. F. 1999. Vitamin D. In Shils, M. E., J. A. Olson, M. Shike, et al. *Modern Nutrition in Health and Disease*. 9th ed. Baltimore: Williams & Wilkins, 329–45.

59. Matsuoka, L. Y., L. Ide, J. Wortsman, et al. 1987. Sunscreens suppress cutaneous vitamin D_3 synthesis. *J Clin Endocrinol Metab* 65:1165–68.

60. Webb, A. R., L. Kline, and M. F. Holick. 1988. Influence of season and latitude on the cutaneous synthesis of vitamin D_3: Exposure to winter sunlight in Boston and Edmonton will not promote vitamin D_3 synthesis in human skin. *J Clin Endocrinol Metab* 67(2):373–78.

61. Gleup, H., K. Mikkelsen, L. Poulsen, et al. 2000. Commonly recommended daily intake of vitamin D is not sufficient if sunlight exposure is limited. *J Intern Med* 247(2):260–68.

62. Holick, M. F., L. Y. Matsuoka, and J. Wortsman. 1989. Age, vitamin D, and solar ultraviolet. *Lancet* 2:1104–5.

63. Braun, M. M., K. J. Helzlsouer, B. W. Hollis, et al. 1995. Prostate cancer and prediagnostic levels of serum vitamin D metabolites. *Cancer Causes Control* 6:235–39.

64. Platz, E. A., S. E. Hankinson, B. W. Hollis, et al. 2000. Plasma I, 25-dehydroxy- and 25-hydroxy vitamin D and adenomatous polyps of the distal colorectum. *Cancer Epidemiol Biomarkers Prev* 9(10):1059–65.

65. USDA database, 2000.

66. Gesensway, D. 2000. Vitamin D and sunshine. *Ann Intern Med* 133(4): 319–20.

67. Tolerable upper limits have been established at a total daily intake of 1,000 IU (25 mcg) per day for children less than one year old, and 2,000 IU (50 mcg) per day for the rest of us. See Food and Nutrition Board, Institute of Medicine. 1997. Dietary reference intakes for calcium, vitamin D, and fluoride, prepublication copy. Washington, D.C.: National Academy Press.

68. Dawson-Hughes, B., G. E. Dallal, E. A. Krall. 1991. Effect of vitamin D supplementation on winter time and overall bone loss in healthy postmenopausal women. *Ann Intern Med* 115(7):505–12.

69. Matsuoka, L. Y., J. Wortsman, N. Hanifan, et al. 1988. Chronic sunscreen use decreases circulating concentrations of 25-hydroxyvitamin D: A preliminary study. *Arch Dermatol* 124(12):1802–4.

70. Mason, K. E. 1977. The first two decades of vitamin E. *Fed Proc* 36: 1906–10.

71. Thuchiya, M., V. E. Kagan, H. J. Freisleben, et al. 1994. Antioxidant activity of alpha-tocopherol, beta-carotene, and ubiquinol in membranes: Cis-parinaric acid-incorporated liposomes. *Methods Enzymol* 234:371–83.

72. For a review, see Tardif, J. C. 1999. Insights into oxidative stress and atherosclerosis. *Can J Cardiol* 16(suppl. D):2D–4D; and Diaz, M. N., B. Frei, J. A. Vita, et al. 1997. Antioxidants and athero-sclerotic heart disease. *N Engl J Med* 337(6):408–16; Rimm, E. B., and M. J. Stampfer. 2000. Antioxidants for vascular disease. *Med Clin North Am* 84(1): 239–49.

73. Meydani, S. N., M. Hayek, L. Coleman. 1992. Influence of vitamins E and B6 on immune response. *Ann NY Acad Sci* 669:125–39.

74. For a review, see Shklar, G., and S. K. Oh. 2000. Experimental basis for cancer prevention by vitamin E. *Cancer Invest* 18(3):214–22.

75. Tabet, N., J. Birks, E. J. Grimley. 2000. Vitamin E for Alzheimer's disease (Cochrane Review). *Cochrane Database Syst Rev* 4:CD002854; Sano, M., C. Ernesto, R. G. Thomas, et al. 1997. A controlled trial of selegeline, alpha-tocopherol, or both, as treatment for Alzheimer's disease: The Alzheimer's Disease Cooperative Study. *N Engl J Med* 17(336):1216–22.

76. USDA database, 2000.

77. Suzuki, M., M. Akisaka, S. Inayama. 1993. Medicobiological studies on centenarians in Okinawa, measuring plasma lipid peroxide, proline, and plasma and intracellular tocopherol. In Beregi, E., I. A. Gergely, and K. Rajczi, eds. *Recent Advances in Aging Science*. Bologna: Monduzzi; and Ford, E., and A. Sowell. 1999. Serum alpha-tocopherol status in the United States population: Findings from the Third National Health and Nutrition Examination Survey. *Am J Epidemiol* 150:290–300.

78. Ness, A., and G. D. Smith. 1999. Mortality in the CHAOS trial: Cambridge Heart Antioxidant Study. *Lancet* 353(9157):1017–18.

79. Heinonen, O. P., D. Albanes, J. Virtamo, et al. 1998. Prostate cancer and supplementation with alpha-tocopherol and beta-carotene: Incidence and mortality in a controlled trial. *J Natl Cancer Inst* 90(6):440–46.

80. H. K. Mitchell, E. E. Snell, and R. J. Williams. 1941. *J Am Chem Soc* 63: 2284–90.

81. Lucock, M. 2000. Folic acid: Nutritional biochemistry, molecular biology and its role in disease processes. *Mol Genet Metab* 71(1–2):121–38; Loria, C. M., M. J. Klag, and L. E. Caulfield. 2000. Vitamin C status and mortality in U.S. adults. *Am J Clin Nutr* 72(1):139–45.

82. Lawrence, J. M., D. B. Petitti, M. Watkins, et al. 1999. Trends in serum folate after food fortification. *Lancet* 354(9182):915–16.

83. Herbert, V. 1990. Development of human folate deficiency. In Picciano, M. F., E.L.R. Stokstad, J. F. Gregory III, eds. *Folic Acid Metabolism in Health and Disease*. New York: Wiley-Liss, 195–210.

84. Herbert, V. C. 1999. Folic acid. In Shils, M. E., J. A. Olson, M. Shike, et al. *Modern Nutrition in Health and Disease*. 9th ed. Baltimore: Williams & Wilkins, 433–66.

85. USDA database, 2000.

86. Lewis, C. J., N. T. Crane, D. B. Wilson, et al. 1999. Estimated folate intakes: Data updated to reflect food fortification, increased bioavailability, and dietary supplement use. *Am J Clin Nutr* 70(2):198–207.

87. Homocysteine Lowering Trialists' Collaboration. 1998. Lowering blood homocysteine with folic acid supplements—meta-analysis of randomized trials. *BMJ* 316(7135):894–98.

88. Morrison, H. I., D. Shaubel, M. Desmeules, et al. 1996. Serum folate and risk of fatal coronary disease. *JAMA* 275(24):1893–96.

89. Teegarden, D., W. R. Proulx, B. R. Martin, et al. 1995. Peak bone mass in young women. *J Bone Miner Res* 10:71–77.

90. Weaver, C. M., and R. P. Heaney. 1999. Calcium. In Shils, M. E., J. A. Olson, M. Shike, et al. *Modern Nutrition in Health and Disease.* 9th ed. Baltimore: Williams & Wilkins, 141–55.

91. USDA database, 2000.

92. Heineman, D. F. 2000. Osteoporosis: An overview of the National Osteoporosis Foundation clinical practice guide. *Geriatrics* 55(5):31–36.

93. Jackson, R. T., and M. C. Latham. 1979. Lactose malabsorption among Masai children of East Africa. *Am J Clin Nutr* 32:779–82.

94. Meunier, P. J. 1999. Evidence-based medicine and osteoporosis: A comparison of fracture risk data from osteoporosis randomized clinical trials. *Clin Pract* 53(2):122–29.

95. Akisaka, M., L. Asato, Y. C. Chan, et al. 1996. Energy and nutrient intakes of Okinawan centenarians. *J Nutr Sci Vitaminol* 42:241–48.

96. For a review of beta-carotene, see Pryor, W. A., W. Stahl, C. L. Rock. Beta-carotene: From biochemistry to clinical trials. *Nutr Rev* 58(2):39–53.

97. Sempos, C. T., and A. C. Looker. 1999. Iron status and the risk of coronary heart disease. *Nutr Metab Cardiovasc Dis* 9(6):294–303. For the nonscientist, see "My wife and I take a multivitamin that contains iron. I've heard that too much iron can increase my risk of having a heart attack. Should I stop taking the iron?" 2000. *Mayo Clinic Health Letter* 18(9):8.

98. Bender, D. A. 1999. Non-nutritional uses of vitamin B6. *Br J Nutr* 81(1):7–20.

Chapter Five

1. Ota, F., and S. Tawata. 1985. *Okinawa no Yakuso Hyakka.* Naha, Okinawa: Naha Shuppan.

2. Aniya, Y., M. Miyahara, T. Koyama, et al. 2000. Antioxidant action of medicinal herbs from Okinawa Islands. Proceedings of Tenth Biennial Meeting of the International Society for Free Radical Research. Okinawa Satellite Symposium "Aging and Natural Antioxidants," 21–23 October 2000.

3. Terry, C. 2000. Medicine from the rain forest: The ongoing quest for cures. *Rotarian* 176(2): 18–21.

4. Klein, S., and R. S. Rister, trans. 1998. German Commission E monographs: Therapeutic monographs on medicinal plants for human use.

In Blumenthal, M., et al., eds., *The complete German Commission E monographs: Therapeutic guide to herbal medicines.* Austin, Texas: American Botanical Council.

5. Eisenberg, D. M., R. B. Davis, S. L. Ettner, et al. 1998. Trends in alternative medicine use in the United States, 1990–1997. *JAMA* 280(18): 1569–75.

6. McKee, T. C., C. D. Covington, R. W. Fuller, et al. 1998. Pyrano-coumarins from tropical species of the genus Calophyllum: A chemotaxonomic study of extracts in the National Cancer Institute collection. *J Nat Prod* 61(10):1252–56.

7. Newman, R. A., W. Chen, and T. L. Madden. 1998. Pharmaceutical properties of related calanolide compounds with activity against human immunodeficiency virus. *J Pharm Sci* 87(9):1077–80.

8. Izawa, M. 2000. The Galápagos of the East. *Look Japan* 4:32–33.

9. Ernst, E. 1998. Harmless herbs?: A review of the recent literature. *Am J Med* 104(2):170–78.

10. Okinawa Centenarian Study database, 2000.

11. Deodhar, S. D., R. Sethi, R. C. Srimal. 1980. Preliminary study on antirheumatic activity of curcumin. *Indian J Med Res* 71:632–34; Hastak, K., et al. 1997. Effect of turmeric oil and turmeric oleo-resin on cytogenetic damage in patients suffering from oral submucous fibrosis. *Cancer Lett* 116(2):265–69; Kiso, Y., Y. Suzuki, N. Watanabe, et al. 1983. Antihepatotoxic principles of *Curcuma longa* rhizome. *Planta Med* 49(3):185–87; Rafatullah, S., et al. 1990. Evaluation of turmeric *(Curcuma longa)* for gastric and duodenal antiulcer activity in rats. *J Ethnobotany* 29:25–34; Roa, D. S. 1970. Effect of curcumin on serum and liver cholesterol levels in the rat. *J Nutr* 100:1307–16.

12. Deodhar, S. D., R. Sethi, and R. C. Srimal. 1980. Preliminary study on antirheumatic activity of curcumin. *Indian J Med Res* 71:632–34; Chan, M. M., C. T. Ho, and H. I. Huang. 1995. Effects of three dietary phytochemicals from tea, rosemary and turmeric on inflammation-induced nitrite protection. *Cancer Lett* 96(1):23–29; Chuang, S., A. Cheng, J. Lin, et al. 2000. Inhibition by curcumin of diethylnitrosamine-induced hepatic hyperplasia, inflammation, cellular gene products and cen-cycle-related proteins in rats. *Food Chem Toxicol* 38(11):991–95.

13. Ammon, H. P., and M. A. Wahl. 1991. Pharmacology of *Curcuma longa*. *Planta Med* 57(1):1–7; Broadhurst, L. 1997. Curcumin, a powerful bio-

protectant spice, or . . . curry cures! Botanical Medicine Conference. Philadelphia, May 15; Selvam, R., et al. 1995. The anti-oxidant activity of turmeric *(Curcuma longa). J Ethnobotany* 47:59–67; Sreejayan, N., and M. N. Rao. 1996. Free radical scavenging activity of curcuminoids. *Arzneimittelforschung* 46(2):169–71.

14. For a review, see Surh, Y. 1999. Molecular mechanisms of chemo-preventive effects of selected dietary and medicinal phenolic substances. *Mutat Res* 428(1–2):305–27; and Piper, J. T., S. S. Singhal, and M. S. Sala-meh. 1998. Mechanisms of anti-carcinogenic properties of curcumin: The effect of curcumin on glutathione linked detoxification enzymes in the rat liver. *Int J Biochem Cell Biol* 30(4):445–56.

15. Huang, M. T., H. L. Newmark, and K. Frenkel. 1997. Inhibitory effects of curcumin on tumori-genesis in mice. *J Cell Biochem* 27 (suppl.):26–34.

16. Selvam, R., et al. 1995. The anti-oxidant activity of turmeric *(Curcuma longa). J Ethnobotany* 47:59–67.

17. Turmeric. In Fetrow, C. W., and J. R. Avila, eds., 1999. *Professional's Handbook of Complementary and Alternative Medicines,* Springhouse, Pa.: Springhouse Corp, 646–49.

18. Hussain, M. S., and N. Chandrasekhara. 1992. Effect of curcumin on cholesterol gallstone induction in mice. *Ind J Med Res* 96:288–91; Kiso, Y., Y. Suzuki, N. Watanabe, et al. 1983. Antihepatotoxic principles of *Curcuma longa* rhizome. *Planta Med* 49(3):185–87; Roa, D. S. 1970. Effect of curcumin on serum and liver cholesterol levels in the rat. *J Nutr* 100:1307–16.

19. Broadhurst, L. 1997. Curcumin, a powerful bioprotectant spice, or . . . curry cures! Botanical Medicine Conference. Philadelphia, 15 May.

20. Li, C. J., L. J. Zhang, B. J. Dezube, et al. 1993. Three inhibitors of type I human immunodeficiency virus long terminal repeat-directed gene expression and virus replication. *Proc Natl Acad Sci USA* 90(5):1839–42. Several well-conducted studies have been performed since to confirm these effects. For a recent review, see DeClercq, E. 2000. Current lead natural products for the chemotherapy of human immunodeficiency virus (HIV) infection. *Med Res Rev* 20(5): 323–49.

21. Kang, B. Y., Y. J. Song, K. M. Kim, et al. 1999. Curcumin inhibits Th I cytokine profile in CD4+T cells by suppressing interleukin-12 pro-duction in macrophages. *Br J Pharmacol* 128(2):380–84; Churchill, M.,

A. Chadburn, R. T. Bilinski, et al. 2000. Inhibition of intestinal tumors by curcumin is associated with changes in the intestinal immune cell profile. *J Surg Res* 89(2):169–75.

22. Kiso, Y., Y. Suzuki, N. Watanabe, et al. 1983. Antihepatotoxic principles of *Curcuma longa* rhizome. *Planta Med* 49(3):185–87.

23. Rafatullah, S., et al. 1990. Evaluation of turmeric *(Curcuma longa)* for gastric and duodenal antiulcer activity in rats. *J Ethnobotany* 29:25–34.

24. Ravindranath, V., and N. Cjamdraseljara. 1980. Absorption and tissue distribution of curcumin in rats. *Toxicol* 16(3):259–65.

25. Hokama, Y., and K. Matsumoto. 1995. *Okinawa no Aji* (in Japanese). Naha, Okinawa: Nirai-sha.

26. Bitter Melon. (1999). In Bratman, S., and D. Kroll, eds. *Natural Health Bible,* Roseville, CA: Prima Publishing, 137–38.

27. Jilka, C., B. Strifler, G. W. Fortner. 1983. In vivo antitumor activity of the bitter melon *(Momordica charantia)*. *Cancer Res* 43:5151–55; Ng, T. B., W. Y. Chan, H. W. Yeung. 1992. Proteins with abortifacient, ribosome inactivating, immunomodulatory, antitumor and anti-AIDS activities from cucurbitaceae plants. *Gen Pharmacol* 23:575–90.

28. Aslam, M., and I. H. Stockley. 1979. Interaction between curry ingredient (karela) and drug (chlorpropamide). Letter. *Lancet* 1:607; Grover, J. K., and S. R. Gupta. 1990. Hypoglycemic activity of seeds of *Momordica charantia*. *Eur J Pharmacol* 183:1026–27; Leatherdale, B. A., R. K. Panesar, G. Singh, et al. 1981. Improvement in glucose tolerance due to *Momordica charantia* (karela). *BMJ* 282:1823–24; Raman, A., and C. Lau. 1996. Anti-diabetic properties and phytochemistry of *Momordica charantia L.* (Cucurbitaceae). *Phytomedicine* 2:349–62; Srivastava, Y., H. Venkatakrishna-Bhatt, Y. Verma, et al. 1993. Antidiabetic and adaptogenic properties of *Momordica charantia* extract: An experimental and clinical evaluation. *Phytother Res* 7:285–89; Welihinda, J., E. H. Karunanayake, M.H.R. Sheriff, et al. 1986. Effect of *Momordica charantia* on the glucose tolerance in maturity onset diabetes. *J Ethnopharmacol* 17:277–82.

29. Welihinda, J., G. Arvidson, E. Gylfe, et al. 1982. The insulin-releasing activity of the tropical plant *Momordica charantia*. *Acta Biol Med Ger* 41(12):1229–40.

30. Lee-Huang, S., P. L. Huang, H. C. Cheng, et al. 1995. Anti-HIV and anti-tumor activities of recombinant MAP30 from bitter melon. *Gene* 161:151–56; Bourinbaias, A. S., and S. Lee-Huang. 1995. Potentiation

of anti-HIV activity of anti-inflammatory drugs, dexamethasone and indomethacine, by MAP30, the anti viral agent from bitter melon. *Biochem Biophys Res Commun* 208:779–85.

31. Takemoto, D. J., C. Jilka, S. Rockenbach, et al. 1983. Purification and characterization of a cytostatic factor with anti-viral activity from the bitter melon. *Prep Biochem* 13:397–421; Foa-Tomasi, L., G. Campadelli-Fiume, L. Barbieri, et al. 1982. Effect of ribosome-inactivating proteins on virus-infected cells: Inhibition of virus multiplication and of protein synthesis. *Arch Virol* 71:323–32.

32. Bitter Melon. Micromedex® Healthcare Series, vol. 104.

33. Hokama, Y., and K. Matsumoto. 1995. *Okinawa no Aji* (in Japanese). Naha, Okinawa: Nirai-sha.

34. Akisaka, M., L. Asato, Y. C. Chan, et al. 1996. Energy and nutrient intakes of Okinawan centenarians. *J Nutr Sci Vitaminol* 42:241–48.

35. Aslam, M., and I. H. Stockley. 1979. Interaction between curry ingredient (karela) and drug (chlorpropamide). Letter. *Lancet* 1:607.

36. Ng, T. B., W. Y. Chan, and H. W. Yeung. 1992. Proteins with abortifacient, ribosome inactivating, immunomodulatory, antitumor and anti-AIDS activities from cucurbitaceae plants. *Gen Pharmacol* 23:575–90.

37. For a review, see ibid. Since that paper, a third protein has been discovered in hechima called luffin-S. See Gao, W., J. Ling, X. Zhong, et al. 1994. Luffin-S—a small novel ribosome-inactivating protein from *Luffa cylindriea*: Characterization and mechanism studies. *FEBS Lett* 347:257–60.

38. Au, T. K., R. A. Collins, and T. L. Lam. 2000. The plant ribosome inactivating proteins luffin and saporin are potent inhibitors of HIV-I integrase. *FEBS Lett* 471:169–72.

39. Ling, M. H., H. Y. Qi, and C. W. Chi. 1993. Protein, CDNA, and genomic DNA sequences of the towel gourd trypsin inhibitor: A squash family inhibitor. *J Biol Chem* 268:810–14.

40. Garzouli, K., S. Khemouf, S. Amira, et al. 1999. Effects of aqueous extracts from *Quercusilex L.* root bark, *Puni ca granatum L.* fruit peel and *Artemesia heaba-alba asso* leaves on ethanol-induced gastric damage in rats. *Phytother Res* 13:42–45.

41. Tamuki, A., and M. Muratsu. 1994. Clinical trial of SY skin care series containing mugwort extract. *Skin Res* 36:369–78; Tezhuka, T., et al. 1992. The clinical effects of mugwort extract on pruritic skin lesions. *Skin Res* 35:303–11.

42. Davidov, M. I., V. G. Goriunov, and P. G. Kubarikov. 1995. Phytoperfusion of the bladder after adenomectomy (in Russian). *Urol Nephrol* 5: 19–20.

43. Tang, H. Q., H. Hu, L. Yang, et al. 2000. Terpenoids and flavonoids from *Artemisia* species. *Planta Med* 66:391–93.

44. Van Agtmael, M. A., T. A. Eggelte, and C. J. van Boxtel. 1999. Artemisinin drugs in the treatment of malaria—from medicinal herb to registered medication. *Trends Pharmacol Sci* 20:199–205.

45. Willcox, B. J., D. C. Willcox, M. Suzuki, et al. 1995. Isoflavone intake in Japanese and Japanese-Canadians. Paper presented at the 1995 Meeting of the American Society for Clinical Nutrition.

46. The Science and Technology Agency. 1992. *The Japanese Food Composition Tables*. 4th ed. Tokyo: Japanese Ministry of Science and Technology.

47. Reinli, K., and G. Block. 1996. Phytoestrogen content of foods—A compendium of literature values. *Nutr Cancer* 26:123–48.

48. Lissin, L. A., and J. P. Cooke. 2000. Phytoestrogens and cardiovascular health. *J Am Coll Cardiol* 35:1403–10; Messina, M. J., V. Persky, K. D. R. Setchell, et al. 1994. Soy intake and cancer risk: A review of the in vitro and in vivo data. *Nutr Cancer* 21(2):113–31; Food labeling: Health claims; soy protein and coronary heart disease. Food and Drug Administration, HHS. Final rule. *Fed Regist* 64, no. 206 (26 October 1999):57700–33.

49. Lu, L. J., K. E. Anderson, J. J. Grady, et al. 2000. Decreased ovarian hormones during a soya diet: Implications for breast cancer prevention. *Cancer Res* 60:4112–21.

50. Bouker, K. B., and L. Hilakivi-Clarke. 2000. Genestein: Does it prevent or promote breast cancer? *Environ Health Perspect* 108:701–8; Messina, M. 1999. Legumes and soybeans: Overview of their nutritional profiles and health effects. *Am J Clin Nutr* 70(suppl. 3): 439S–50S.

51. Glacken, C. 1955. *The Great Loochoo: A Study of Okinawan Village Life*. Los Angeles: University of California Press.

52. Wild yam. In Fetrow, C. W., and J. R. Avila, eds., 1999. *Professional's Handbook of Complementary and Alternative Medicines*. Springhouse, Pa.: Springhouse Corp, 666–68.

53. Terahara, N., I. Konczak-Islam, M. Nakatani, et al. 2000. Anthocyanins in callus induced from purple storage root of *Ipomoea batatas* L. *Phytochemistry* 54:919–22; USDA database, 2000.

54. Giovannucci, E. 1999. Tomatoes, tomato-based products, lycopene, and cancer: Review of the epidemiologic literature. *J Natl Cancer Inst* 91:317–31.

55. Akisaka, M., L. Asato, B. Willcox, C. Willcox, M. Suzuki, and D. J. Jenkins. 2000. Eating patterns of Japanese-Okinawan centenarians. *J Am Coll Nutr* (submitted).

56. Chan, M. M., D. Forg, C. T. Ho, et al. 1997. Inhibition of inducible nitric oxide synthase gene expression and enzyme activity by epigallocatechin gallate, a natural product from green tea. *Biochem Pharmacol* 54:1281–86.

57. Mazur, W. M., K. Wahala, S. Rasku, et al. 1998. Lignan and isoflavonoid concentrations in tea and coffee. *British J Nutr* 79:37–45.

58. Sho, H. 1988. *Minami no Shima no Eiyougaku (Nutritional Science in the Southern Islands)*. Naha: Okinawa Publishing; Bronner, W. E., and G. R. Beecher. 1998. Method of determining the content of catechins in tea infusions by high-performance liquid chromatography. *J Chromatogr A* 805:137–42.

59. Yang, T. T., and M. W. Koo. 1997. Hypocholesterolemic effects of Chinese tea. *Pharmacol Res* 35:505–12; A. Zhang, Q. Y. Zhu, and Y. S. Luk. 1997. Inhibitory effects of jasmine green tea epicatechin isomers on free-radical-induced lysis of red blood cells. *Life Sci* 61:383–94; Huang, Y., A. Zhang, and C. W. Lau. 1998. Vasorelaxant effects of purified green tea epicatechin derivatives in rat mesenteric artery. *Life Sci* 63:275–83; Chen, J. 1992. The effects of Chinese tea on the occurrence of esophageal tumors induced by N-nitrosomethylbenzylamine in rats. *Prev Med* 21:385–91.

60. Massie, H. R., V. R. Aiello, T. R. Williams. 1993. Inhibition of iron absorption prolongs the life span of drosophila. *Mech Ageing Dev* 67:227–37.

61. Uchida, S., H. Ohta, M. Niwa, et al. 1990. Prolongation of life span in stroke-prone spontaneously hypertensive rats ingesting persimmon tannin. *Chem Pharm Bull* (Tokyo) 38:1049–52.

62. Ono, Y., K. Wakai, K. Genka, et al. 1995. Tea consumption and lung cancer risk: A case-control study in Okinawa, Japan. *Jpn J Cancer Res* 86:1027–34; Liao, S., Y. Umekita, J. Guo, et al. 1995. Growth inhibition and regression of human prostate and breast tumors in athymic mice by tea epigallocatechin gallate. *Cancer Res* 96:239–43; Kinlen, L. J., A. N. Willows, P. Goldblatt, et al. 1988. Tea consumption and

cancer. *British J Cancer* 58:397–401; Imai, K., K. Suga, and K. Nakachi. 1997. Cancer-preventive effects of drinking green tea among a Japanese population. *Prev Med* 26(6):769–75.

63. Wilks, C. 2000. Tea breaks could help calm fluoride debate. *Br Dent J* 188:161.

64. Hertog, M. G. L., P. C. H. Hollman, and B. van de Putte. 1993. Content of potentially anticarcinogenic flavonoids of tea infusions, wines, and fruit juices. *J Agri Food Chem* 41:1242–46.

65. Imai, K., K. Suga, and K. Nakachi. 1997. Cancer-preventive effects of drinking green tea among a Japanese population. *Prev Med* 26(6):769–75; Zheng, W., T. J. Doyle, L. H. Kushi, et al. 1996. Tea consumption and cancer incidence in a prospective cohort study of postmenopausal women. *Am J Epidemiol* 144:175–82; Ono, Y., K. Wakai, K. Genka, et al. 1995. Tea consumption and lung cancer risk: A case-control study in Okinawa, Japan. *Jpn J Cancer Res* 86:1027–34.

66. Ono, Y., K. Wakai, K. Genka, et al. 1995. Tea consumption and lung cancer risk: A case-control study in Okinawa, Japan. *Jpn J Cancer Res* 86:1027–34.

67. Kinlen, L. J., A. N. Willows, P. Goldblatt, et al. 1988. Tea consumption and cancer. *Br J Cancer* 58:397–401.

68. Yang, C. S. 1999. Tea and health. *Nutrition* 15:946–49.

69. Keung, W. M., and B. L. Vallee. 1993. Daidzin and daidzein suppress free choice ethanol intake by Syrian golden hamsters. *Proc Natl Acad Sci* 90(2):10008–12.

70. Shebek, J., and J. P. Rindone. 2000. A pilot study exploring the effect of kudzu root on the drinking habits of patients with chronic alcoholism. *J Altern Complement Med* 6:45–48.

71. Lissin, L. A., and J. P. Cooke. 2000. Phytoestrogens and cardiovascular health. *J Am Coll Cardiol* 35:1403–10.

72. Simons, L. A., S. Gayst, S. Balasubramaniam, et al. 1982. Long-term treatment of hypercholesterolaemia with a new palatable formulation of guar gum. *Atherosclerosis* 45:101–8.

73. Cummings, J. H., W. Branch, D. J. Jenkins, et al. 1978. Colonic response to dietary fibre from carrot, cabbage, apple, bran, and guar gum. *Lancet* 1:5–9; Drenick, E. J. 1975. Bulk producers. *JAMA* 234:271–74; Fujiwara, S., T. Hirota, H. Nakazato, et al. 1991. Effect of konjac mannan on intestinal microbial metabolism in mice bearing human flora and in conventional F344 rats. *Food Chem Toxicol* 29:601.

74. Aro, A., M. Uusitupa, E. Voutilainen, et al. 1981. Improved diabetic control and hypocholesterolaemic effect induced by long-term dietary supplementation with guar gum in type 2 (insulin independent) diabetes. *Diabetologia* 21:29–33; Jenkins, D.J.A. 1979. Dietary fibre, diabetes, and hyperlipidaemia: Progress and prospects. *Lancet* 2:1287–90; Jenkins, D. J. A., A. R. Leeds, B. Slavin, et al. 1979. Dietary fibers and blood lipids: Reduction of serum cholesterol in type II hyperlipidemia by guar gum. *Am J Clin Nutr* 32:16–18; Kiriyama, S., Y. Okazaki, and A. Yoshida. 1969. Hypocholesterolemic effect of polysaccharides and polysaccharide-rich foodstuffs in cholesterol-fed rats. *J Nutr* 97(3): 382–88; Simons, L. A., S. Gayst, S. Balasubramaniam, et al. 1982. Long-term treatment of hypercholesterolaemia with a new palatable formulation of guar gum. *Atherosclerosis* 45:101–8.

75. Luo, D. Y. 1992. Inhibitory effect of refined amorphophallus konjac on MNNG-induced lung cancers in mice (in Chinese). *Zhonghua Zhong Liu Za Zhi* 14:48–50.

76. Aro, A., M. Uusitupa, E. Voutilainen, et al. 1981. Improved diabetic control and hypocholesterolaemic effect induced by long-term dietary supplementation with guar gum in type 2 (insulin independent) diabetes. *Diabetologia* 21:29–33; Doi, K., M. Matsuura, A. Kawara, et al. 1979. Treatment of diabetes with glucomannan (konjac mannan). *Lancet* 1:987–88; Huang, C. Y., M. Y. Zhang, S. S. Peng, et al. 1990. Effect of konjac food on blood glucose level in patients with diabetes. *Biomed Environ Sci* 3(2):123–31; Jenkins, D. J. A., D. V. Goff, A. R. Leeds, et al. 1976. Unabsorbable carbohydrates and diabetes: Decreased post-prandial hyperglycemia. *Lancet* 2:172–74; Jenkins, D. J. A., T. M. S. Wolever, and A. R. Leeds. 1978. Dietary fibres, fibre analogues and glucose tolerance: Importance of viscosity. *BMJ* 1: 1392–94; Jenkins, D. J. A., T. M. S. Wolever, and R. Nineham. 1978. Guar crispbread in the diabetic diet. *BMJ* 2:1744–46; D. J. A. Jenkins. 1979. Dietary fibre, diabetes, and hyperlipidaemia: Progress and prospects. *Lancet* 2:1287–90; Vuksan, V., D. J. A. Jenkins, P. Spadafora, et al. 1999. Konjac-mannan (glucomannan) improves glycemia and other associated risk factors for coronary heart disease in type 2 diabetes: A randomized controlled metabolic trial. *Diabetes Care* 22:913–19; Vuksan, V., J. L. Sievenpiper, R. Owen, et al. 2000. Beneficial effects of viscous dietary fiber from konjac-mannan in subjects with the insulin resistance syndrome. *Diabetes Care* 23:9–14.

77. Drenick, E. J. 1975. Bulk producers. Letter. *JAMA* 234:271–74; Walsh, D. E., V. Yaghoubian, and A. Behforooz. 1984. Effect of glucomannan on obese patients: A clinical study. *Int J Obes* 8:289–93.

78. Canivet, B., G. Creisson, P. Freychet, et al. 1980. Fibre, diabetes, and risk of bezoar. *Lancet* 2:862.

79. Todoriki, H. 1999. Okinawan food culture and kombu (in Japanese). *Aijico News* 195:29.

80. Kagawa, Y., ed. 2000. *Standard Tables of Food Composition in Japan*. 6th edition. Tokyo, Japan: Women's Nutrition University.

81. Teas, J., M. L. Harbison, and R. S. Gelman. 1984. Dietary seaweed (*Laminaria*) and mammary carcinogenesis rates. *Cancer Res* 44:2758–61.

82. Teas, J. 1983. The dietary intake of *Laminaria,* a brown seaweed, and breast cancer prevention. *Nutr Cancer* 4:217–22.

83. Okai, Y., et al. 1993. Identification of heterogeneous antimutagenic activities in the extract of edible brown seaweeds *Laminaria japonicum* (makonbu) and *Undaria pinnatifida* (wakame) by the Umu gene expression system in salmonella typhimurium. *Mutat Res* 303:63–70.

84. Walkin, O., and D. E. Douglas. 1975. Health food supplements prepared from kelp—a source of elevated urinary arsenic. *Clin Toxicol* 8:325–31.

85. Pepper, black. In Fetrow, C. W., and J. R. Avila, eds. 1999. *Professional's Handbook of Complementary and Alternative Medicines*. Springhouse, Pa.: Springhouse Corp., 500–503.

86. Robbins, W. R., et al. 1998. Treatment of intractable pain with topical large-dose capsaicin: Preliminary report. *Anesth Analy* 86:579–83.

87. Klein, S., and R. S. Rister, trans. 1998. German Commission E monographs: therapeutic monographs on medicinal plants for human use. In Blumenthal, M., et al., eds. *The complete German Commission E monographs: Therapeutic guide to herbal medicines*. Austin: American Botanical Council.

88. For a review of cranberries and urinary infections, see Patel, N., and I. R. Daniels. 2000. Botanical perspectives on health of cystitis and cranberries. *J R Soc Health* 120:52–53.

89. For a recent review of echinacea and the common cold, see Giles, J. T., C. T. Palat, S. H. Chien, et al. 2000. Evaluation of echinacea for treatment of the common cold. *Pharmacotherapy* 20:690–97.

90. For a review, see Sato, T., and G. Miyata. 2000. The neutraceutical benefit, part 4: Garlic. *Nutr* 16:787–88.

91. Mowrey, D. B., and D. E. Clayson. 1982. Motion sickness, ginger and psychophysics. *Lancet* 1:655–57.

92. Jariwalla, R. J., and S. Harakeh. 1996. Antiviral and immunomodulatory activities of ascorbic acid. In Harris, J. R., ed. *Subcellular Biochemistry*. Vol. 25, *Ascorbic acid: Biochemistry and Biomedical Cell Biology*. New York: Plenum Press, 215–31.

93. For a review, see Ali, M., M. Thompson, and M. Afzal. 2000. Garlic and onions: Their effect on eicosanoid metabolism and its clinical relevance. *Prostaglandins Leukot Essent Fatty Acids* 62:55–73.

94. Buchanan, R. L. 1998. Toxicity of spices containing methylene dioxybenzene derivatives: A review. *J Food Safety* 1:275–93.

95. Mint. In Fetrow, C. W., and J. R. Avila, eds. 1999. *Professional's Handbook of Complementary and Alternative Medicines*. Springhouse, Pa.: Springhouse Corp., 433–36.

96. USDA database, 2000.

97. Giovannucci, E., A. Ascherio, E. B. Rimm, et al. 1995. Intake of carotenoids and retinol in relation to risk of prostate cancer. *J Natl Cancer Inst* 87:1767–76.

Chapter Six

1. Lai, J. S., C. Lan, M. K. Wong, et al. 1995. Two-year trends in cardiorespiratory function among older Tai Chi Chuan practitioners and sedentary subjects. *J Am Geriatr Soc* 43(11):1222–27; Wolf, S. L., H. X. Barnhart, N. G. Kutner, et al. 1996. Reducing frailty and falls in older persons: An investigation of Tai Chi and computerized balance training. *J Am Geriatr Soc* 44:489–97; Wolfson, L., R. Whipple, C. Derby, et al. 1996. Balance and strength training in older adults: Intervention gains and Tai Chi maintenance. *J Am Geriatr Soc* 44:498–506; Lo, B., M. Inn, R. Amacher, et al. 1979. *The Essence of Tai Chi Ch'uan: The Literary Tradition*. Berkeley, Calif.: North Atlantic Books.

2. Veith, I., trans. 1996. *Huang Ti Nei Ching Su-wen* [*The Yellow Emperor's Classic of Internal Medicine*]. Los Angeles: University of California Press.

3. Nagamine, S. 1976. *The Essence of Okinawan Karate-do*. Trans. K. Shinzato. Tokyo: Charles E. Tuttle Publishing Company; Bishop, M. 1999. *Okinawan Karate*. Clarendon, Vt.: Tuttle Publishing; McCarthy, P. 1987. *Classical Kata of Okinawan Karate*. Burbank: Ohara Publications.

4. Buchner, D. M., S. A. Beresford, E. B. Ladson, et al. 1992. Effects of physical activity on health status in older adults II: Intervention studies. *Ann Rev Pub Health* 13:469–88; Christmas, C., and A. A. Ross. 2000. Exercise and older patients: Guidelines for the clinician. *J Am Geriatr Soc* 48:318–24.

5. Watanabe, S., S. Tsugane, T. Sobue, et al. 1996. *Japan Public Health Center–Based Prospective Study on Cancer and Cardiovascular Diseases* (in Japanese). Tokyo: Japan Public Health Association.

6. We do not mean to pick on weight lifters. From personal experience, most weight lifters that we know have excellent overall physical fitness.

7. Katch, F., and M. MacArdle. 1983. *Nutrition, Weight Control and Exercise*. Philadelphia: Lea & Febiger.

8. U.S. Department of Health and Human Services. 1996. *Physical Activity and Health: A Report of the Surgeon General*. Atlanta, Ga.: U.S. Department of Health and Human Services, Centers for Disease Control and Prevention, National Center for Chronic Disease Prevention and Health Promotion; Wolf, S. L., H. X. Barnhart, N. G. Kutner, et al. 1996. Reducing frailty and falls in older persons: An investigation of Tai Chi and computerized balance training. *J Am Geriatr Soc* 44:489–97.

9. Suzuki, M., M. Akisaka, I. Ashitomi, et al. 1995. Chronological study concerning ADL among Okinawan centenarians (in Japanese). *Jpn J Geriatr* 32:416–23.

10. Fiatarone, M. A., E. C. Marks, N. D. Ryan, et al. 1992. High-intensity strength training in nonagenarians: Effects on skeletal muscle. *JAMA* 253:3029–34.

11. Vik, P. W., K. A. Culbertson, and K. Sellers. 2000. Readiness to change drinking among heavy-drinking college students. *J Stud Alcohol* 61:574–80.

12. Nagamine, S. 1976. *The Essence of Okinawan Karate-do*. Trans. K. Shinzato. Tokyo: Charles E. Tuttle Publishing Company.

13. Lai, J. S., C. Lan, M. K. Wong, et al. 1995. Two-year trends in cardiorespiratory function among older Tai Chi Chuan practitioners and sedentary subjects. *J Am Geriatr Soc* 43:1222–27; Wolfson, L., R. Whipple, C. Derby, et al. 1996. Balance and strength training in older adults: Intervention gains and Tai Chi maintenance. *J Am Geriatr Soc* 44:498–506.

14. For a review, see Kessenich, C. R. 1998. Tai Chi as a method of fall prevention in the elderly. *Orthop Nurs* 17:27–29; Lane, J. M., and

M. Nydick. 1999. Osteoporosis: Current modes of prevention and treatment. *J Am Acad Orthop Surg* 7:19–31.

15. Wolf, S. L., H. X. Barnhart, G. L. Ellison, et al. 1997. The effect of Tai Chi Quan and computerized balance training on postural stability in older subjects. Atlanta FICSIT Group. Frailties and Injuries Cooperative Studies on Intervention Techniques. *Phys Ther* 77:371–81 (discussion 382–84); Wolfson, L., R. Whipple, C. Derby, et al. 1996. Balance and strength training in older adults: Intervention gains and Tai Chi maintenance. *J Am Geriatr Soc* 44:498–506; Wolf, S. L., H. X. Barnhart, N. G. Kutner, et al. 1996. Reducing frailty and falls in older persons: An investigation of Tai Chi and computerized balance training. *J Am Geriatr Soc* 44:489–97.

16. Hong, Y., J. X. Li, P. D. Robinson. 2000. Balance control, flexibility, and cardiorespiratory fitness among older Tai Chi practitioners. *Br J Sports Med* 34:29–34.

17. Lai, J. S., C. Lan, M. K. Wong, et al. 1995. Two-year trends in cardiorespiratory function among older Tai Chi Chuan practitioners and sedentary subjects. *J Am Geriatr Soc* 43:1222–27.

18. Lan, C., J. S. Lai, S. Y. Chen, et al. 1998. 12-month Tai Chi training in the elderly: Its effect on health and fitness. *Med Sci Sports Exerc* 30: 345–51.

19. For a review, see Yocum, D. E., W. L. Castro, M. Corne. 2000. Exercise, education, and behavioral modification as alternative therapy for pain and stress in rheumatic disease. *Rheum Dis Clin North Am* 26: 145–59 x-xi; also see Kirsteins, A. E., F. Dietz, S. M. Hwang. 1981. Evaluating the safety and potential use of a weight-bearing exercise, Tai chi Chuan, for rheumatoid arthritis patients. *Am J Phys Med Rehabil* 70:136–41.

20. Adapted with permission from Mayo Clinic HealthQuest. February 2000.

Chapter Seven

1. Pelletier, K. R. 2000. *The Best Alternative Medicine.* New York: Simon and Schuster.
2. The studies on "distant healing" (i.e., prayer, "distant intentionality," or "nonlocal healing") are fascinating, yet much more research, under

rigorous experimental conditions, is needed in order to draw firm conclusions on its healing efficacy. One example of such a study was carried out by Dr. Elizabeth Targ, director of Psychosocial Oncology Research and clinician at the University of California, San Francisco, School of Medicine, and her colleagues at California Pacific Medical Center in San Francisco. They tested whether praying for patients (distant healing) had a therapeutic effect for AIDS patients. The study used a controlled, randomized clinical trial and the same rigorous scientific standards that are used when a new drug is tested. The study was also double-blind, so that no one involved, including the patients and scientists, knew who was in the group receiving healing prayers. Forty patients with advanced AIDS were included in the study representing various ethnic and cultural groups. All the patients received standard medical care for their illness, but half of the participants received healing prayers in addition. Prayer (distant healing) was carried out by forty volunteers throughout the United States and Canada. Each healer was given a patient's first name and a picture in order to develop a personal connection with the patient. Healers had an average of seventeen years of experience in their respective traditions, and represented eight different faiths, including Christian, Jewish, Buddhist, Native American, and shamanistic practices, and some were graduates of bioenergetic and meditative healing schools. Healers were asked to focus their mental energies on the patient's health and well-being for one hour a day, six days a week, for ten weeks, and each patient was treated by a different healer each week. Patients were assessed by blood tests and psychological testing at the beginning of the study and at the end of the six-month follow-up period. No differences were seen in the CD4 counts (a type of immune cell important for resisting the AIDS virus) between the group that was prayed for and the control group (who received no prayers), but a blind review of their medical charts showed a number of significant differences. The patients who had been prayed for had undergone fewer new AIDS-related illnesses, had less severe illnesses, spent less time in the hospital, required fewer visits to the doctor, and showed significantly improved mood, when compared with controls. Furthermore, psychological tests revealed that the effects of treatment were not affected by the participants' beliefs about which group they were in. See Sicher, et al. 1998. A randomized double-blind study of the effect of distant healing in a population with advanced AIDS: Report of a small-scale study. *West J Med* 169:356–63. For the most celebrated experiment on distant healing, see Byrd, R. 1988. Positive therapeutic effects of intercessory prayer in a coronary care unit population. *South Med J* 81:826–29. For the most detailed treatment in book form of the subject of distant healing, healing through prayer, or distant intentionality (all referred to under the term "nonlocal healing"), see Dossey, L. 1999. *Reinventing Medicine: Beyond Mind-Body to a New Era of Healing.* San Francisco: HarperCollins.

3. Dr. Mitchell Krucoff, associate professor of medicine and cardiology at Duke University Medical Center, and nurse-practitioner Suzanne Crater together coordinate the MANTRA (an acronym for Monitoring and Actualization of Noetic Training) project, a cardio-spiritual program combining high-tech cardiology and intercessory prayer, music, mental imagery, and touch. These interventions were studied on patients undergoing angioplasty (coronary artery dilation). Preliminary results with thirty patients were presented to cardiologists at the American Heart Association's annual meeting in 1998. The outcomes of the group that were prayed for were 50–100 percent better than those of the control group, which did not receive prayer. Although promising, the number of subjects was too few to draw statistically firm conclusions. The study is currently under expansion to include 1,500 patients at five different medical centers throughout America. This particular study gained national attention when *Time* magazine picked up the story. See "A Test of the Healing Power of Prayer" in *Time,* 12 October 1998. Other noteworthy studies of the efficacy of distant healing are taking place at the Mind/Body Medical Institute at Harvard Medical School (headed by Dr. Herbert Benson), where the effects of prayer on 1,200 patients undergoing artery bypass surgery are being investigated, as well as at Mount Sinai School of Medicine, where studies on the ancient Chinese healing art of *qigong* are under way.

4. For an in-depth description of the meetings at Harvard University, see Dossey, L. 1999. *Reinventing Medicine: Beyond Mind-Body to a New Era of Healing.* San Francisco: HarperCollins, 37–49.

5. For systematized research reviews of studies on the efficacy of distant healing, see Schlitz, M., and W. Braud. 1997. Distant intentionality: Assessing the evidence. *Altern Ther* 3:62–73; Targ, E. 1997. Evaluating

distant healing: A research review. *Altern Ther Health Med* 3(6):74–78; Astin, J. A., E. Harkness, and E. Ernst. 2000. The efficacy of "distant healing": A systematic review of randomized trials. *Ann Intern Med* 132: 903–10; Roberts, L., I. Ahmed, and S. Hall. 2000. Intercessory prayer for the alleviation of ill health. *Cochrane Database Syst Rev* (2):CD000368.

6. Clements, W. M., ed. 1989. *Religion, Aging and Health: A Global Perspective* (compiled by the World Health Organization). New York: Haworth.

7. National Institute of Mental Health. 1980. *Religion and Mental Health: A Bibliography*. Washington, D.C.: U.S. Government Printing Office.

8. See National Institutes of Health research programs at www.nih.gov.

9. Research in the area of spirituality, religion, health, and aging has generally been a neglected area until recent years. This situation is quickly reversing itself, however, and many new research programs have been initiated. One such effort comes under the umbrella of the Behavioral and Social Research Program of the National Institute on Aging (NIA). For the past few years, NIA has collaborated with the Fetzer Institute (a private, nonprofit foundation that supports education and scientific research exploring the relationship of the physical, mental, emotional, and spiritual dimensions of life) to further research on aging, health, and religion. As part of this collaborative effort, there has been a major conference as well as smaller work-group meetings on methodological issues. A primary goal of the follow-up work-group activity has been to develop a parsimonious measurement instrument of religiosity/spirituality that could be incorporated into ongoing studies of health and aging. In 1998 the work group developed a measure that was tested in the General Social Survey. The Fetzer Institute, as part of the NIA-funded Studies of Women Across the Nation (SWAN) project, has also provided support to examine how women in midlife view themselves and their aging. Questions about religious affiliation and religious beliefs were included as part of both quantitative and qualitative aspects of the study. Foci of the study include an analysis of how ethnically diverse women view aging and meaning in life; the relationship between religious beliefs, coping styles, and health outcomes; and the development of new measures of daily spiritual experiences. Other research projects focus on the complex interrelationships among religious variables, other mediating psychosocial factors, and health and functioning throughout the life course. Par-

ticular efforts have been focused upon flushing out the biopsychosocial mechanisms by which religion, spirituality, and/or religious affiliations may affect health. See National Institute on Aging research programs at www.nih.gov/nia.

10. The evidence for the positive effects of spirituality on health is impressive. According to key reviews, approximately 400 published empirical studies have investigated the effects of some aspect of spiritual or religious involvement on health or well-being or other similar constructs. Despite methodological limitations and heterogeneity in measures of religious variables, these findings point consistently, though not unanimously, to a positive role for spirituality and religion in health and aging. For general reviews of the research literature and more in-depth analyses of how religion exerts a positive influence on health, see Koenig, H. G. 1997. *Is Religion Good for Your Health? The Effects of Religion on Physical and Mental Health.* New York: Haworth Press; Larson, D. B., and S. S. Larson. 1994. *The Forgotten Factor in Physical and Mental Health: What Does the Research Show?* Rockville, Md.: National Institute for Healthcare Research; Levin, J. S. 1994. *Religion in Aging and Health: Theoretical Foundations and Methodological Frontiers.* Thousand Oaks, Calif.: Sage Publications, Inc.; Jarvis, G. K., and H. C. Northcutt. 1987. Religion and differences in morbidity and mortality. *Soc Sci Med* 25:813–24; Gartner, J., D. Larson, and G. Allen. 1991. Religious commitment and mental health: A review of the empirical literature. *J Psychol Theol* 19:6–25; Levin, J. S. 1996. How prayer heals: A theoretical model. *Altern Ther Health Med* 2:66–73.

11. See Matthews, D. A., and D. B. Larson. 1995. *The Faith Factor: An Annotated Bibliography of Clinical Research on Spiritual Subjects.* Vol. 3. Rockville, Md.: National Institute for Healthcare Research.

12. The National Institute for Healthcare Research (NIHR) is a private nonprofit organization founded in 1991 by Dr. David Larson and based in Rockville, Maryland. NIHR has carried out reviews of medical research that have documented the positive health benefits of spirituality and helped organize several conferences on the subject as well. Reviews from NIHR have found over two dozen studies on religion in peer-reviewed journals in recent years. Of these studies, about half were designed rigorously enough to make firm conclusions (according to principles of evidence-based medicine). In these recent studies, religious participation was found to have protective effects

against heart disease, immune dysfunction, depression, anxiety, and suicide, among others. The effects were seen for both men and women of different ages, ethnicities, and religious preferences. See Matthews, D. A., and D. B. Larson. 1993–96. *The Faith Factor: An Annotated Bibliography of Clinical Research on Spiritual Subjects*. Vols. 1–4. Rockville, Md.: National Institute for Healthcare Research. A few examples follow.

Dr. Thomas Oxman, from Dartmouth Medical School, found that among patients undergoing heart surgery, those who reported themselves to be more religious were three times less likely to die six months after surgery than those who were not religious. See Oxman, T. E., et al. 1995. Lack of social participation or religious strength and comfort as risk factors for death after cardiac surgery in the elderly. *Psychosom Med* 57:5–15.

Dr. Harold Koenig of Duke University Medical Center found, in a study of 1,718 men and women over sixty-five years of age, that those who regularly attended religious services (at least once a week) showed less immune system dysfunction than non-attendees. They were half as likely to have high blood levels of interleukin-6, a protein found in association with inflammatory responses. See Koenig, H. G., et al. 1997. Attendance at religious services, interleukin-6, and other biological parameters of immune function in older adults. *Int J Psychiatry Med* 27:233–50.

An *American Journal of Psychiatry* study reported that religiousness was found to predict more rapid recovery from hip fracture, both in meters walked and in ambulation status at hospital discharge. See Pressman, P., et al. 1990. Religious belief, depression, and ambulation status in elderly women with broken hips. *Am J Psychiatry* 147: 758–60.

13. Strawbridge, W. J., R. D. Cohen, S. J. Shema, and G. A. Kaplan. 1997. Frequent attendance at religious services and mortality over 28 years. *Am J Pub Health* 87:957–61.

14. See Koenig, H. G. 1997. *Is Religion Good for Your Health? The Effects of Religion on Physical and Mental Health*. New York: Haworth Press, 104.

15. Matthews, D. A., and D. B. Larson. 1994. *The Faith Factor: An Annotated Bibliography of Clinical Research on Spiritual Subjects*. Vol. 2. Rockville, Md.: National Institute for Healthcare Research.

16. Ellison, C. G. 1991. Religious involvement and subjective well being. *J Health Soc Behav* 32:80–99.

17. Researchers have reported significant religious denominational variations in incidence of, and mortality from, various types of cancer, particularly those that are linked to lifestyle factors such as excessive alcohol or tobacco consumption. Highly proscriptive groups such as Seventh-Day Adventists, Mormons, or fundamentalist Protestants have generally been found to suffer lower rates. See Cochran, J. K., L. Beeghley, and E. W. Bock. 1998. Religiosity and alcohol behavior: An exploration of reference group theory. *Sociol Forum* 3: 256–76; Jarvis, G. K., and H. C. Northcott. 1987. Religious differences in morbidity and mortality. *Soc Sci Med* 25:813–24; Troyer, H. 1988. Review of cancer among four religious sects: Evidence that life-styles are distinctive sets of risk factors. *Soc Sci Med* 26:1007–17; Dwyer, J. W., L. L. Clarke, and M. K. Miller. 1990. The effect of religious concentration and affiliation on county cancer mortality rates. *J Health Soc Behav* 31:185–202.

18. See Naguib, S. M., P. B. Beiser, and G. W. Comstock. 1968. Response to a program of screening for cervical cancer. *Pub Health Rep* 83:990–98; Umberson, D. 1987. Family status and health behaviors: Social control as a dimension of social integration. *J Health Soc Behav* 28:306–19; Doherty, W. J., H. G. Schrott, and L. Metcalf. 1983. Effect of spousal support and health beliefs on medication adherence. *J Fam Pract* 17:837–41.

19. See Ellison, C. G., and L. K. George. 1994. Religious involvement, social ties and social support in a Southeastern community. *J Sci Study Religion* 33:46–61; Berkman, L. F., and S. L. Syme. 1979. Social networks, host resistance, and mortality: A nine-year follow up study of Alameda County residents. *Am J Epidemiol* 115:684–94.

20. See Seeman, T. E., and B. S. McEwen. 1996. Impact of social environment characteristics on neuroendocrine regulation. *Psychosom Med* 58:459–71; Nelson, P. B. 1989. Ethnic differences in intrinsic/extrinsic religious orientation and depression in the elderly. *Arch Psychiatr Nurs* 3:199–204; Koenig, H. G., et al. 1993. Religion and anxiety disorder: An examination and comparison of associations in young, middle-aged and elderly adults. *J Anxiety Disord* 7:321–42; Stack, S. 1983. The effect of religious commitment on suicide: A cross national analysis. *J Health Soc Behav* 24:362–74; Nisbet, P. A., P. R. Duberstein, Y. Con-

well, and L. Seidlitz. 2000. The effect of participation in religious activities on suicide versus natural death in adults 50 and over. *J Nerv Ment Dis* 188:543–46.

21. Benson, H. 1996. *Timeless Healing: The Power and Biology of Belief.* New York: Simon and Schuster, 195–217.

22. Benson, H., and R. Freidman. 1996. Harnessing the power of the placebo effect and renaming it "remembered wellness." *Ann Rev Med* 47:193–99.

23. Benson, H. 1997. The relaxation response: Therapeutic effect. *Science* 278:1694–95.

24. As mentioned in Dr. Benson's book *Timeless Healing* (see note 21, above), "remembered wellness" has implications for the therapeutic effect of healing rituals observed in aboriginal cultures around the world. We would add that this may very well apply to the benefits we have observed from Okinawan healing rituals.

25. Beecher, H. 1955. The powerful placebo. *JAMA* 159:1602–6.

26. Turner, J. A., R. A. Deyo, J. D. Loeser, et al. 1994. The importance of placebo effects in pain treatment and research. *JAMA* 271:1609–14.

27. Thomas, C. 2000. Dancing with the Dead. Unpublished Ph.D. dissertation. University of Chicago.

28. Sered, S. 1999. *Women of the Sacred Groves: Divine Priestesses of Okinawa.* Oxford, England: Oxford University Press.

29. Although our knowledge of the ancient way is incomplete, we can reconstruct the most important aspects and essential forms of the system, some of which can still be witnessed today. All spiritual traditions start with creation myths, and the ancient Ryukyuans are no exception. The ancients believed that they were the offspring of sibling creator deities and therefore humans were of divine origin. In fact, all natural phenomena are thought to have a core of spiritual essence. The universe is thought to be populated by myriad spiritual beings *(kami)* possessing supernatural powers and capable of appearing before and helping humanity—if proper rituals are performed on their behalf. The *kami* are neither omniscient nor omnipotent, neither good nor bad, but they do have the power to influence human affairs. People also have the responsibility to maintain a reciprocal relationship with the *kami* through the conduct of proper rituals. The main sites for worship are sacred groves *(utaki),* often thought to be sites of first settlement or earliest worship. In daily life, the most important *kami* is that of the hearth or fire *(hi nu kan)*. Most Okinawan homes

still have a small altar in the kitchen devoted to the hearth god, which is maintained by the senior female member of the household. It operates as a kind of link between the household and the highest realms of the *kami,* and important rites are performed on the first and fifteenth of every month of the old lunar calendar. The lunar calendar is quite important for the ritual lives of Okinawans.

Early religious songs contained in the *Omoro Soshi* (an ancient literary collection of Ryukyuan poems and songs) have revealed that women dominated ritual life from the earliest times. This was thought to be due to their innate ability to influence the *kami* as well as to harness spiritual forces. There was a close relationship between the female religious specialist and the male political leader, based on the original mythical relationship between the sibling creator deities. From the time of its unification in the early fifteenth century until its demise in the late nineteenth century, the whole of the Ryukyu Kingdom was organized for religious as well as political ends. An official hierarchy of priestesses existed in the villages, districts, and regions. This hierarchy extended all the way up to the chief priestess, who was usually a close relative of the ruler, and his equal in rank. Priestesses were and still are responsible for the performance of ceremonies related to the health, welfare, and livelihood of the clan, village, and state (when it existed). At the level of the family or household, the hearth god and the ancestors, represented by ancestral tablets *(ihai)* in the altar *(butsudan),* are the focal point of religious activity. Rituals are carried out by the senior female member of the household consistent with cultural ideologies of female sacrality.

Religious affairs are dominated by two main roles, those of priestess and shaman. The priestesses are concerned mostly with keeping in good stead with the *kami* through ritual activity on behalf of the clan and community. The shamans, on the other hand, deal mostly with individual or household problems. Like traditional shamans everywhere, they are believed to possess the psychic ability to commune with the ancients on behalf of their clients. We have met many shamans in the course of our studies in Okinawa. Let us briefly describe the role of shamanism in Okinawan society, for, despite its lack of official organization or agreed-upon doctrine and the often ambiguous status of its practitioners, it is thriving as never before. It is important to realize that although Western medical thinking has infiltrated almost every corner of the earth, people in most societies worldwide continue to rely upon such folk healers either exclusively or in tandem with Western-type health care. This is also the case in Okinawa, where, as mentioned earlier, the expression *isha-hanbun, yuta-hanbun* is commonly used to refer to the need for both the modern physician *(isha)* and the shaman *(yuta)* in order to fully comprehend most afflictions.

The usual reaction of the public official (often male) is to dismiss shamanism as the stuff of "old wives' tales." When explaining shamanism to the outside observer (such as ourselves), he will often quickly dismiss it with an embarrassed chuckle. Yet in the present as in the past, the fact remains that despite its ambiguous status and checkered history, shamanism has been (and continues to be) supported in practice by the majority. The shaman's role in Okinawan society encompasses both that of psychospiritual counselor and family therapist. She uses her powers as a spiritual medium to determine causes of misfortune, direct remedial action, carry out rituals on behalf of her clients, and dispense spiritual counseling. It is primarily women who consult the *yuta*. Consultation takes place either individually or as a group. How does this support our contention that the *yuta* have a broad influence in Okinawan society? Because women in Okinawa manage the household and its affairs, the influence of the shaman extends far beyond the individual housewife and includes the whole household and its members. According to our experience, and corroborated by survey evidence, three-quarters of Okinawan women have had the experience of consulting a shaman. Some, of course, make regular use of them. Some become overdependent on them, and this can cause various problems as well, since shamans charge for their services. Nor are all shamans reliable, although most that we have met have been both sincere and trustworthy. One should still be selective, however. Often the criterion that an effective shaman is judged upon is whether or not she "hits the mark" *(ataru)* with her predictions or insight into the client's problems. For more information on Okinawan traditional religion, see Sered, S. 1999. *Women of the Sacred Groves: Divine Priestesses of Okinawa.* Oxford, England: Oxford University Press; Lebra, W. P. 1966. *Okinawan Religion.* Honolulu: University of Hawaii Press; Mabuchi, T. 1964. Spiritual predominance of the sister. In A. Smith, ed. *Ryukyuan Culture and Society,* Honolulu: University of Hawaii Press, 79–91; Ouwehand, C. 1985. *Hateruma: Socio-Religious Aspects of a South-Ryukyuan Island Culture.* Leiden: E. J. Brill.

30. In Okinawa there exists a folk belief that a long-lived person has a certain supernatural power, and that other people can share in this power by participation in a longevity ritual known as *ayakaru*. Persons who wish to share in the good fortune and longevity of an Okinawan elder say, "I came here to *ayakaru* you," or "Please permit me to *ayakaru* you for your longevity." People then try to touch the elder, or receive a cup of sake from him or her. More than just family rituals, longevity rituals in Okinawa are often community-wide celebrations. In the case of the ninety-seventh-year ritual called *kajimaya*, for example, anyone in the community, even passersby, can participate in the celebration. We participated in one such longevity ritual in 1997. Hundreds had gathered, and a huge banquet hall was rented for the occasion. Speeches and entertainment in the form of dancing or comic skits were then presented. There was much eating, drinking, dancing, and singing. A parade then followed, and the streets were lined with villagers who greeted the elder as she was paraded around in the back of a convertible with the top down. The elder wore red and carried a small pinwheel, which symbolized a return to childhood. Villagers or even passersby tried to shake hands with or be touched by the elder to receive her longevity spirit or power so that they too might live a long and healthy life. We too were fortunate to *ayakaru* the elder on that occasion! We suspect that these longevity rituals have positive benefits for enhancing well-being. See Willcox, D. C., and J. Katata. 2000. Healthy longevity and its relationship to spirituality, belief, and ritual: The case of Okinawa (in Japanese). *Geriatr Med* 38:1357–64.

31. Genetics and biology play important roles in determining health and longevity, and there seems to be little doubt that biological differences between men and women account for a portion of the gender gap in longevity. Yet, as we have been stressing throughout this book, our health behaviors and lifestyle choices, environments, and personality factors are much more important for our own health and longevity in the long run. For example, the reason women outlive men by only one year in India, yet they live twelve years longer than men in Russia, is not determined by differences in biology, but by social and behavioral factors (see article from World Health Organization titled "Press releases 2000: WHO issues new healthy life expectancy rankings" [4 June 2000]). Sex differences in longevity are perhaps best understood by looking at the major causes of death and trying to determine what advantages

women have over men with regard to these risk factors. When we examine the leading causes of death in America today, we can see that men die from all of these causes at greater rates than women, but there are significant sex differences in at least five categories including heart disease (leading cause of death), cancer (second), accidents (fourth), suicide (tenth), and homicide (eleventh). In addition to these leading causes of death, other diseases such as AIDS or lung cancer claim the lives of many more men than women. Of these leading causes of death, at least three are directly related to aggressive or risk-taking behaviors: homicide, suicide, and accidents. The top two causes of death, heart disease and cancer, are also a complex mix of hereditary and lifestyle determinants, as we pointed out in Chapter Two. Along these lines, the World Health Organization points out that in affluent countries such as America, women are generally more health-conscious than men. The research shows that women smoke less, drink less alcohol, eat more healthful foods, and engage in less self-destructive and risk-taking behavior. For more information on gender differences in life expectancy, see Hazzard, W. R. 1994. The sex differences in longevity. In W. R. Hazzard, E. L. Bierman, and J. P. Blass, et al., eds. *Geriatric Medicine and Gerontology*. 3rd ed. New York: McGraw-Hill; Ory, M., and R. Warner, eds. 1990. *Gender, Health and Longevity*. New York: Springer; Perls, T., and M. Silver. 1999. *Living to 100*. New York: Basic Books; Crose, R. 1997. *Why Women Live Longer than Men*. San Francisco: Jossey-Bass.

32. See World Health Organization article "Press releases 2000: WHO issues new healthy life expectancy rankings." (4 June 2000).

33. Crose, R. 1997. *Why Women Live Longer than Men*. San Francisco: Jossey-Bass, 141–42.

34. As pointed out by Dr. Royda Crose, women's traditional roles have, until quite recently, placed them outside of the workforce and shut them out from educational opportunities. Many thus turn to religious activities to give meaning to their lives and to attain personal satisfaction outside of their families. The church then becomes the center of their social activities. This seems to be particularly true for older women who live alone. See Crose, R. 1997. *Why Women Live Longer than Men*. San Francisco: Jossey-Bass, 128–31. See also Levin, J. S., R. J. Taylor, and L. M. Chatters. 1994. Race and gender differences in religiosity among older adults: Findings from four national surveys. *J Gerontol* 49:S137–45.

35. Levin, J. S., R. J. Taylor, and L. M. Chatters. 1994. Race and gender differences in religiosity among older adults: Findings from four national surveys. *J Gerontol* 49:S137–45.

36. Neugarten, B. L., and D. Neugarten, eds. 1996. *The Meanings of Age: Selected Papers of Bernice L. Neugarten.* Chicago: University of Chicago Press.

37. Erikson, E. 1994. *Identity and the Life Cycle.* New York: W. W. Norton and Company.

38. Willcox, D. C., H. Todoriki, S. Sakihara, B. J. Willcox, K. Naka, and M. Ariizumi. 2000. Minority Aging in Japan: Subjective Well-Being of Older Okinawans in Cross-Cultural Context. Unpublished manuscript.

39. Mabuchi, T. 1964. Spiritual predominance of the sister. In A. Smith, ed. *Ryukyuan Culture and Society,* 79–91. Honolulu: University of Hawaii Press.

40. Naka, K., D. C. Willcox, H. Todoriki, and T. Kageyama. 1998. Suicide in Okinawa from an international perspective: A consideration of socio-cultural factors. *Ryukyu Med J* 18:1–10.

41. Spiritual America. 1994. *U.S. News & World Report,* 4 April.

42. Dossey, L. 1999. *Reinventing Medicine: Beyond Mind-Body to a New Era of Healing.* San Francisco: HarperCollins.

43. See Shimai, S. 1992. Emotion and identification of environmental sounds and electroencephalographic activity. *Fukushima J Med Sci* 38: 43–56; Kabuto, M., T. Kageyama, and H. Nitta. 1993. EEG power spectrum changes due to listening to pleasant music and their relation to relaxation effects. *Nippon Eiseigaku Zasshi* 48:807–18 (in Japanese).

44. Moody, R. 1975. *Life After Life.* Covington, Ga.: Mockingbird Books.

45. Suzuki, M. 2000. *Stroke: What Would You Do If It Were You? The Chronicle of a Stroke Victim* (in Japanese). Tokyo, Japan: Taishukan Shoten.

46. Kübler-Ross, E. 1997. *On Death and Dying.* New York: Simon and Schuster.

47. Kübler-Ross, E. 1991. *On Life After Death.* Berkeley, Calif.: Celestial Arts.

48. Letvak, R. 1995. Putting the placebo effect into practice. *Patient Care* 29:93–102.

Chapter Eight

1. Lightman, A. 1998. *Einstein's Dreams.* New York: Pantheon Books.
2. Michaud, E. 2000. When worrying becomes deadly. *Prevention,* February.

3. Our modern use of the term *stress* was actually labeled by the Harvard physiologist Walter Cannon in the 1920s. However, it wasn't until the 1930s that a biochemist named Hans Selye formalized the concept as a young assistant professor at McGill University in Montreal. He did this by adding two ideas: The first is that the body has a surprisingly similar set of responses to a broad array of stressors; Selye called these responses *general adaptation syndrome*. The second is that under certain conditions, stressors can lead to illness. Although Selye formalized the concept of "stress" years ago, there is still no universally accepted definition. Some scientists refer to stress as a stimulus (i.e., being under time pressure), and the response (i.e., stomach ache, migraine) as *strain*. Others prefer the term *stressor* to refer to the stimulus, and the response to it as *stress*. Still others refer to stress as an interaction between stimulus and response. Because of the semantic problems in dealing with the term, many scientists would prefer to drop it altogether. Yet, for lack of a better one, it remains. In keeping with recent research on the importance of attitudes, beliefs, and other factors that mediate the stress experience, we feel that the best description is one that encompasses the subjective experience of the individual. Thus our use of the common terms "good" (eustress) or "bad" (distress) stress is meant to convey the idea that stress can have either positive or negative effects on the body, as defined by the person experiencing it. People experience distress (or bad stress) when they find themselves in situations that have exceeded their ability to cope with them.

4. Sotile, W., and M. O. Sotile. 1999. *Beating Stress Together*. New York: John Wiley and Sons.

5. Eaker, E. D., J. Pinsky, and W. P. Castelli. 1992. Myocardial infarction and coronary death among women: Psychosocial predictors from a 20-year follow-up of women in the Framingham Study. *Am J Epidemiol* 135:854–64.

6. Haines, A. P., J. D. Imeson, and T. W. Meade. Phobic anxiety and ischaemic heart disease. *Br Med J (Clin Res Ed)* 295:297–99.

7. Sapolsky, R. M. 1998. *Why Zebras Don't Get Ulcers*. New York: W. H. Freeman and Company.

8. A variety of immune functions are influenced by stress, as Herbert and Cohen point out in their review of thirty-eight of the best-designed studies in the field. In a meta-analysis of these studies, the conclusion reached was that the evidence strongly supports the con-

tention that stress weakens many different types of immune response. See Herbert, T., and S. Cohen. 1993. Stress and immunity in humans: A meta-analytic review. *Psychosom Med* 55:364–79.

9. An excellent treatment of the complex issue of how prolonged exposure to stress can prematurely age the brain and subsequently affect memory function can be found in Robert Sapolsky's 1992 book, *Stress, the Aging Brain, and the Mechanisms of Neuron Death*. Cambridge, Mass.: MIT Press.

10. Allard, M., V. Lebre, J.-M. Robine, and J. Calment. 1998. *Jeanne Calment: From Van Gogh's Time to Ours: 122 Extraordinary Years*. New York: W. H. Freeman and Company.

11. Perls, T. T., and M. H. Silver. 1999. *Living to 100*. New York: Basic Books.

12. There is a long history of research and theory arguing that certain personalities promote disease or early death, or conversely lead to long and healthy lives. Research designs have generally been weak, and contradictory examples are common. Admittedly, some people who simply vegetate or others who are rigid, unsociable, or negative still live long lives. But positive qualities seem to be far more common in those who live to be one hundred or more. Attempts to discern those qualities have been going on for some time. For example, in 1960, G. Gallup and E. Hill published a book called *The Secret of Long Life* (New York: Bernard Geis), which included the results of interviews with 164 persons ranging in age from 100 to 117. They reported that many of their subjects appeared to be easygoing, cheerful, and self-confident, enjoyed being with other people as well as enjoying their own lives, and, significantly, had a high tolerance for frustration. In 1973, S. Jewett published a paper on longevity in *The Gerontologist*, reporting on the results of interviews with seventy-nine persons between the ages of 87 and 103. He found that long-lived individuals were highly adaptable, active, independent, and creative. (See Jewett, S. 1973. Longevity and longevity syndrome. *The Gerontologist* 13:91–99.) Later, in 1988, D. S. Woodruff-Pak, in *Psychology and Aging* (New Jersey: Prentice-Hall), proposed a personality test on life expectancy. People who were happy, relaxed, satisfied, and calm were purported to live longer, while repressed, dogmatic, stubborn, adventurous, and aggressive people were thought to live shorter-than-average lives.

Recent research on personality and longevity has seen better-designed studies that have included control groups, sophisticated statistical analyses, and better age-verification techniques. These studies provide better quality evidence. For example, in 1999 the Harvard University-sponsored New England Centenarian Study reported that centenarians given the NEO Five Factor Inventory—a personality assessment tool used widely to study the five key personality characteristics of neuroticism, extroversion, openness, agreeability, and conscientiousness—scored similarly to the general population on all dimensions except one. That is, their neuroticism scores were significantly lower. Drs. Margery Silver and Tom Perls point out that "neuroticism" is really a proxy measure for "negative emotionality" or unhealthy feelings such as anger, guilt, fear, and sadness, and includes such emotional facets as depression, anxiety, hostility, self-consciousness, impulsiveness, and vulnerability. Low neuroticism scores indicated that centenarians were calm, collected, and better than average at dealing with stress. Silver and Perls put it this way: "Far from fitting the stereotype of the aimless, despondent, self-indulgent older person, centenarians are emotionally stable, flexible, adaptive and seldom depressed." (See Perls, T. T., and Margery H. Silver. 1999. *Living to 100.* New York: Basic Books, 57–83.)

Other studies on centenarians, such as the Georgia Centenarian Study, have also come up with some interesting findings regarding personality and longevity. Dr. Peter Martin and other researchers compared the personality characteristics of older adults in their sixties, eighties, and hundreds, using the 16PF (personality factor) inventory, and found that centenarians scored higher on dominance and lower on conformity. According to Martin et al., these findings suggest that centenarians can also be assertive and forceful when they need to be. (See Martin, P., et al. 1992. Personality, life events and coping in the oldest-old. *Int J Aging Human Develop* 34:19–30.) Furthermore, psychologist Leonard Poon, who heads the University of Georgia's Centenarian Study, says that centenarians "tend to be independent, score high on optimism and are rarely depressed." (See Poon, L. W., M. H. Bramlett, P. A. Holsberg, M. A. Johnson, and P. Martin. 1997. Who will survive to 105? In *1997 Med Health Annu.* Chicago: Encyclopaedia Britannica.)

Finally, some intriguing research by Dr. H. S. Friedman (1999) and colleagues at University of California–Riverside has shown that "social dependability" or "conscientiousness" in childhood predicts longevity. They analyzed causes of death for 1,528 bright Californian children recruited and followed since 1922. After analyzing mortality patterns, Friedman concluded that, overall, "problems in psychosocial adjustment related to an egocentric impulsivity turned out to be a key general risk factor for all-cause mortality." In other words, such traits as "impulsiveness," "egocentrism," "tough-mindedness (rigidity)," and "undependability" predicted early death. (See Friedman, H. S. 1999. Personality and longevity: Paradoxes. In Robine, J. R., et al., eds. *The Paradoxes of Longevity*. New York: Springer-Verlag, 115–22.)

13. For an explanation of how "positive illusions" can beneficially affect your health, see Taylor, S. E., M. E. Kemeny, G. M. Reed, J. E. Bower, and T. L. Gruenewald. 2000. Psychological resources, positive illusions, and health. *American Psychologist,* January. For a dissenting view, see Colvin, C. R., and J. Block. 1994. Do positive illusions foster mental health?: An examination of the Taylor and Brown formulation. *Psychol Bull* 116:3–20. Taylor and Brown's response to Colvin and Block appears in the same issue of *Psychological Bulletin* on pages 21–27.

14. Although controversial, evidence of the importance of optimism for living longer and healthier lives can be glimpsed from a variety of studies. For example, UCLA psychologist Shelly Taylor and co-researchers studied seventy-eight men with AIDS beginning in the late 1980s. Patients who indicated that they had a "realistic view" of the course of their illness died an average of nine months sooner than those who were more optimistic about living longer. Other competing explanations, such as less severe illness to begin with, were controlled for and therefore ruled out. Dr. Taylor theorizes that an optimistic frame of mind may help boost immune system function. See Taylor, S. E., and J. D. Brown. 1988. Illusion and well-being: A social psychological perspective on mental health. *Psychol Bull* 103: 193–210. The theory has been well received among health psychologists, although researchers still know very little about just how optimism helps the body's defenses.

A thirty-year prospective study by Mayo Clinic researchers also found that optimistic people live longer. In fact, pessimistic patients had a 19 percent increase in their risk of early death. Patients were surveyed between 1962 and 1965 using the Minnesota Multiphasic Personality Inventory (MMPI). The test has an Optimism-Pessimism scale that grades explanatory style of the patient's answer to "how people habitually explain the causes of life's events" and categorizes them as either optimists, pessimists, or mixed. By identifying which patients were still living thirty years later, the researchers were able to study explanatory style as a risk factor for early death. As with the AIDS study, however, this study cannot explain *how* pessimism acts as a risk factor for early death. See Maruta, T., R. C. Colligan, M. Malinchoc, and K. P. Offord. 2000. Optimists vs. pessimists: Survival rate among medical patients over a 30-year period. *Mayo Clin Proc* 75:140–43. Further research on the health-promoting effects of an optimistic attitude has come from research on "self-rated health," which has shown that optimistic appraisals (positive self-ratings) of health are predictive of long-term survival. Borowski et al., for example, in a 1996 article in the *Journal of Gerontology*, reported that "health optimists" were significantly less likely to die in the short term than "poor health realists," despite having a similar state of health to begin with. This finding holds true regardless of a person's objective state of health as assessed by a physician. See Borowski, E. A., J. M. Kinney, and E. Kahana. 1996. The meaning of older adults' health appraisals: Congruence with health status and determinants of mortality. *J Gerontol* 51:S157–70.

How optimism may work to modulate health in a positive way is largely unexplored territory. It may be through better immune response, or it may be that optimists are less likely to develop depression (a known risk factor for early death), learned helplessness, and catastrophic thinking, or to blame themselves for negative life events. Pessimism has been associated with a giving-up response, while optimists have been shown to positively reframe negative situations in some studies. Optimists may also have more positive attitudes toward seeking and receiving medical care. The recent upsurge of interest in the health benefits of positive attitudes and beliefs has made research on optimism a popular field as reflected in the new "positive psychology" advocated by distinguished psychologists such as Martin Seligman, a University of Pennsylvania professor and past president of the American Psychological Association. (See the January 2000 special issue of *American Psychologist*, the flagship journal of the American Psychological Association, for research on the health benefits of optimism.)

As a caveat, we must point out that this view also has its critics, especially if an overly optimistic outlook leads to a false sense of security. Underestimation of risk can result in serious trouble in certain situations. Participants in the Terman study who were rated as "cheerful" in childhood grew up more likely to smoke, drink, and take risks, which helped partly explain an *increased* risk of premature mortality. See Friedman, H. S. 1999. Personality and longevity: Paradoxes. In Robine, J. R., et al., eds. *The Paradoxes of Longevity*. New York: Springer-Verlag, 115–22. The lesson here is that the health relevance of such traits as optimism needs to be more carefully conceptualized. In fact, psychosocial factors might affect many health behaviors besides smoking and drinking, such as dietary habits, exercise patterns, adherence to medical programs, use of prophylactics, exposure to or avoidance of environmental toxins, and more. These behaviors may explain many of the associations between psychological factors (such as optimism) and longevity.

15. See Levy, E., and T. Monte. 1997. Optimism and the immune system. In *The Ten Best Ways to Boost Your Immune System*. New York: Houghton-Mifflin, pp. 151–52.

16. Scheier, M. F., K. A. Matthews, J. F. Owens, et al. 1999. Optimism and rehospitalization after coronary artery bypass graft surgery. *Arch Intern Med* 159:829–35.

17. Peterson, C., S. Maier, and M. Seligman. 1993. *Learned Helplessness: A Theory for the Age of Personal Control*. New York: Oxford University Press.

18. In recent years there has been much debate over which of the Type A personality traits are most associated with cardiovascular disease. A number of studies have tried to break the constellation of Type A personality traits into individual ones, and when doing so, many have found that "hostility" was the most significant predictor of heart disease. For the importance of hostility as a predictor of heart disease by reanalysis of the original Friedman and Rosenman data, see Hecker, M., M. N. Chesney, G. Black, and N. Frautsch. 1988. Coronary-prone behaviors in the Western Collaborative Group Study. *Psychosom Med* 50: 153–64. In fact, many studies have found hostility to be associated with higher death rates from a range of diseases—not only heart disease. For a meta-analytic review of studies on the effects of hostility on health, see Miller, T. Q., T. W. Smith, C. W. Turner, et al. 1996. A meta-analytic review of research on hostility and physical health. *Psychol Bull* 119:322–48. Opposed to this interpretation is the cardiologist Meyer Friedman (who "co-discovered" the Type A pattern) and his colleagues, who suggest that a sense of time pressure is at the core of the hostility seen in Type A behavior. And furthermore, says Friedman, a "sense of insecu-

rity" fuels the time pressure that Type A individuals feel. See Price, V., et al. 1995. Relation between insecurity and Type A behavior. *Am Heart J* 129:488–91. Interestingly, Okinawan elders showed lifelong personality profiles that were neither time-pressured nor insecure. (See Akisaka, M., et al. 1998. Analysis of Type A behavior pattern associated with longevity [in Japanese]. *Jpn J Psychosom Med* 38:415–22.)

19. Personality testing of the Okinawan centenarians was undertaken in 1996 by Dr. Masafumi Akisaka, geriatrician and long-time member of the Okinawan Centenarian Study research team, and published in the *Japanese Journal of Psychosomatic Medicine* in 1998. The survey included ninety-four community-dwelling Okinawan centenarians and a control group of ninety-eight middle-aged controls living in the same areas of Okinawa. A brief questionnaire developed by Maeda and based on the Jenkins Activity Survey was used. This questionnaire was chosen because it is short, easy to administer, and frequently employed for studies of Type A behavioral patterns in Japan. The survey explored the following twelve dimensions of Type A behavior: busyness, sense of time urgency, enthusiasm, absorption, perfectionism, self-confidence, tension, irritability, punctuality, unyieldingness, intensity of temper, and competitiveness. Participants were asked to recall their behavioral patterns in their thirties and forties. When the two groups were compared, no statistically significant differences were found between the centenarians and controls. Both groups scored borderline Type A (seemingly the antithesis of the easygoing Okinawan character type). Upon deeper analysis of the results, however, it was found that the centenarian group and the control group had different test score profiles. Indeed, although both groups had similar distribution peaks in their total scores, which placed them on the border of Type A and non–Type A, the centenarians' score profile revealed low scores in the dimensions of "time urgency" and "tension," but high scores in the dimensions of "self-confidence" and "unyieldingness." What the results seem to suggest is that the first two personality traits may have been helpful in keeping stress levels low and maintaining mental health, while the latter two may have been helpful for maintaining strength of will and resilience of character in the face of adversity for over a century. See Akisaka, M., et al. 1998. Analysis of Type A behavior pattern associated with longevity (in Japanese). *Jpn J Psychosom Med* 38:415–22.

20. Wallace, R. K. (1970). Physiological effects of transcendental meditation. *Science* 167:1751–54.

21. Wallace, R. K., M. Dillbeck, E. Jacobe, and B. Harrington. 1982. The effects of transcendental meditation and TM-Sidhi program on the aging process. *Int J Neurosci* 16:53–58.

22. Martin, W. 2000. *The Couple's Tao Te Ching: A New Interpretation*. New York: Marlowe.

23. Maruta, T., R. C. Colligan, M. Malinchoc, and K. P. Offord. 2000. Optimists vs. pessimists: Survival rate among medical patients over a 30-year period. *Mayo Clin Proc* 75:140–43.

24. Reiman, E. M., et al. 1997. Neuroanatomical correlates of externally and internally generated human emotion. *Am J Psychiatry* 154:918–25.

25. Cousins, N. 1979. *Anatomy of an Illness as Perceived by the Patient*. New York: W. W. Norton.

Chapter Nine

1. Emile Durkheim is considered one of the founders of the discipline of sociology. His prolific research concerned many fundamental social questions, such as the role of religion in society, the division of labor, and sociological theory and methods. His study of suicide was first published in 1897 and is considered a classic. It is particularly revealing in its quantitative (and qualitative) analysis of social isolation (anomie) and its links to suicide. It is required reading in most sociology programs. See Durkheim, E. 1897 (1951). *Suicide*. Trans. J. A. Spaulding and G. Simpson. Glencoe, Ill: Free Press.

2. Cohen, S., W. J. Doyle, D. P. Skoner, et al. 1997. Social ties and susceptibility to the common cold. *JAMA* 277:1940–44.

3. Numerous studies have shown that married people live longer and have lower mortality for almost every major cause of death than those who are single, divorced, separated, or widowed. Those studies show that married people have a lower incidence of disease, a better chance of survival after diagnosis, and a quicker recovery. A number of books do a good job of summarizing these studies. In his original classic, *Broken Heart: The Medical Consequences of Loneliness* (1979. New York: Basic Books), Dr. James J. Lynch helped to pioneer research linking emotional states to physical health. His book reviewed numerous studies to show that the death rate from heart attacks of widows aged twenty-five to thirty-four was five times that of married women of the same age group, and that

divorced people have twice the stroke and lung cancer rates of their married counterparts. Interestingly, divorced white males were shown to be seven times more likely to develop cirrhosis of the liver and ten times more likely to get tuberculosis than married men. In a more recent work, Dr. Lynch claims that loneliness is now a silent epidemic in modern society. (See Lynch, J. J. 2000. *A Cry Unheard: New Insights into the Medical Consequences of Loneliness.* Baltimore: Bancroft Press.)

Another book, by researchers Linda Waite and Maggie Gallagher, also sheds light on why married people are healthier and report greater life satisfaction than unmarried persons. As well, it explores the reasons why men, more often than women, seem to do more poorly when single. As Waite and Gallagher point out, studies show that unmarried men have been found to be more likely to engage in unhealthy behavior, such as excessive drinking, smoking, drug abuse, poor nutritional habits, and lack of exercise. Marriage also provides a key psychological benefit in terms of emotional support. Having someone to talk to when upset or anxious helps to shed stress. Having a spouse appears to be less critical for women in this regard, however, as single, widowed, or divorced women are more likely than men to seek out other members of their own sex for support. See Waite, L., and M. Gallagher. 2000. *The Case for Marriage: Why Married People Are Happier, Healthier and Better Off Financially.* New York: Doubleday.

4. Berkman, L. F., and S. L. Syme. 1979. Social networks, host resistance, and mortality: A nine-year follow-up study of Alameda County residents. *Am J Epidemiol* 109:186–204.

5. Schoenbach, V. J., B. H. Kaplan, L. Friedman, and D. G. Kleinbaum. 1986. Social ties and mortality in Evans County, Georgia. *Am J Epidemiol* 123:577–91.

6. House, J. S., C. Robbins, and H. L. Metzner. 1982. The association of social relationships and activities with mortality: Prospective evidence from the Tecumseh Community Health Study. *Am J Epidemiol* 116:123–40.

7. Seeman, T. L., L. F. Berkman, F. Kohout, et al. 1993. Intercommunity variations in the association between social ties and mortality in the elderly: A comparative analysis of three communities. *Ann Epidemiol* 3:325–35.

8. Orth-Gomer, K., and J. V. Johnson. 1987. Social network interaction and mortality: A six-year follow-up study of a random sample of the Swedish population. *J Chron Dis* 40:949–57.

9. House, Landis, and Umberson summarize and compare the results of five major epidemiological studies including the Alameda County Study, the Evans County Study, and the Swedish Study mentioned above. What the studies showed was that people whose relationships are strong, through family, friends, and organizational memberships, live longer than those whose connections to others are relatively few or weak. In fact, mortality rates, irrespective of age, were found to be two to four times as great for people with poor social relationships. The effect of social support was found to be stronger for men than for women. There is some evidence that the positive effect for social relationships comes mainly from the differences between low and average numbers of persons in one's social support network, and tends to taper off thereafter. See House, J. S., K. R. Landis, and D. Umberson. 1988. Social relationships and health. *Science* 241:540–45.

10. How social support may help mediate the important process of early detection and treatment for diseases like cancer can be seen from a landmark study of over 27,000 cancer patients. Unmarried men and women were found to be more likely be diagnosed at a more advanced stage of cancer, were less likely to be treated, and had a worse rate of survival. It was concluded that the absence of social support delayed both detection and treatment which, in turn, led to earlier death from advanced cancer. See Goodwin, J. S., W. C. Hunt, C. R. Key, and J. M. Samet. 1987. The effect of marital status on stage, treatment and survival of cancer patients. *JAMA* 31:25–30.

11. What experimental studies show is that when persons are exposed to a stressor such as having to perform a mental arithmetic task, having strangers argue with them, or having to give a public speech, with or without a supportive friend present, those with social support suffer lower negative cardiovascular stress reactions. See Lepore, S., K. Allen, and G. Evans. 1993. Social support lowers cardiovascular reactivity to an acute stressor. *Psychosom Med* 55:518–24; Gerin, W., C. Pieper, R. Levy, and T. Pickering. 1992. Social support in social interaction: A moderator of cardiovascular reactivity. *Psychosom Med* 54:324–36; Edens, J., K. Larkin, and J. Abel. 1992. The effect of social support and physical touch on cardiovascular reactions to mental stress. *J Psychosom Res* 36:371–81.

12. Sakihara, S., and K. Nishi. 1998. Research on Community-Dwelling Elderly Women's Orientation to Independent Living (in Japanese).

13. See Mayo Clinic at www.mayohealth.org and type in the search term *social support.*

14. For a look at how volunteering and other altruistic work and attitudes can positively impact your health, see Dr. Kenneth R. Pelletier's book, *Sound Mind, Sound Body: A New Model for Lifelong Health* (1994. New York: Simon and Schuster). Dr. Pelletier, a clinical associate professor of medicine at the Stanford University Center for Research in Disease Prevention, shows how altruistic work seems to be good for both self and others and, further, also seems to be "closely related to the ability to overcome life-threatening crises and disease."

15. Dalai Lama and Howard C. Cutler. 1998. *The Art of Happiness: A Handbook for Living.* New York: Putnam Publishing Group.

Chapter Ten

1. Nutritional analysis of the dietary tracks was based on data from the Science and Technology Agency. 1992. *The Japanese Food Composition Tables.* 4th ed. Tokyo: Japanese Ministry of Science and Technology, Tokyo, Japan, and the USDA on-line Nutrient Database.

Chapter Eleven

1. Weil, A. 1998. *Spontaneous Healing: How to Discover and Enhance Your Body's Ability to Maintain and Heal Itself.* New York: Alfred A. Knopf.

2. Ornish, D. 1990. *Dr. Dean Ornish's Program for Reversing Heart Disease.* New York: Ballantine Books.

3. World Health Organization. 1998. *The World Health Report 1998.* 15 May. Geneva, Switzerland.

4. World Health Organization. 2000. Press releases 2000: WHO issues new healthy life expectancy rankings. 4 June. Washington, D.C.

5. Okinawa Prefectural Government. 1995. *Footprints of Longevity* (in Japanese). Department of Health and Welfare: Naha.

6. For an exploration of *Island Quest,* go to www.classroom.com and click on *The Quest Channel.*

Chapter Twelve

1. The Science and Technology Agency. 1992. *The Japanese Food Composition Tables*. 4th ed. Tokyo: Japanese Ministry of Science and Technology.
2. Lee, R. D., D. C. Nieman, and M. Rainwater. 1995. Comparison of eight microcomputer dietary analysis programs with the USDA nutrient database for standard reference. *J Am Dietetic Assoc* 95:858–67.